MYTHS & LEGENDS
OF THE BRITISH ISLES

MYTHS & LEGENDS OF THE BRITISH ISLES

Edited and introduced by
Richard Barber

The Boydell Press

First published 1999
The Boydell Press, Woodbridge

ISBN 0 85115 748 3

The Boydell Press is an imprint of Boydell & Brewer Ltd
PO Box 9, Woodbridge, Suffolk IP12 3 DF, UK
and of Boydell & Brewer Inc.
PO Box 41026, Rochester, NY 14604–4126, USA

A catalogue record for this book is available
from the British Library

Library of Congress Catalog Card Number: 99–21492

This publication is printed on acid-free paper

Printed in Finland by WSOY

CONTENTS

ILLUSTRATIONS

ACKNOWLEDGEMENTS

All material other than that listed below is © Richard Barber 1999

The author and publishers are grateful to the following writers, publishers and literary representatives for their permission to reprint extracts from copyright material:

'The Story of Hamlet' © Peter Fisher 1979, 1999
from Saxo Grammaticus, *The History of the Danes*
(D. S. Brewer, Cambridge, 1979)

'The Life of Merlin' © Neil Wright 1998
from Geoffrey of Monmouth, *Vita Merlini*
(Boydell & Brewer Ltd, Woodbridge, forthcoming)

'The Story of Arthur' © Neil Wright 1991
from *The Historia Regum Britannie of Geoffrey of Monmouth:*
V. Gesta Regum Britannie (D. S. Brewer, Cambridge, 1991)

'Beowulf' © 1968 Kevin Crossley-Holland
from *The Anglo-Saxon World* (Boydell Press, Woodbridge, 1982)
Reproduced by permission of the author

'Saint Joseph of Arimathea' © David Townsend 1985
from *The Chronicle of Glastonbury Abbey*, edited by James Carley and translated by David Townsend (Boydell Press, Woodbridge, 1985)

'The Empress Helena and the Finding of the True Cross' © M. J. B. Allen 1970 from *Sources and Analogues of Old English Poetry*, edited by M. J. B. Allen and Daniel Calder (D. S. Brewer, Cambridge, 1970)

'Hereward the Wake' © Michael Swanton 1984
from *Lives of the three Last Englishmen*
(Garland Publishing, New York 1984)

INTRODUCTION

And did those feet in ancient time
Walk upon England's mountains green?
And was the Holy Lamb of God
On England's pleasant pastures seen?

WILLIAM BLAKE'S lines from the poem known now as 'Jerusalem' are familiar enough to us, if only from the Last Night of the Proms. But how many who have sung these words, and caught something of the visionary fervour behind them, know where Blake, arch-creator of poetic myths of his own, had found his inspiration? We have lost touch with our legends. Although some of us might think of Glastonbury as the place Blake had in mind, few would be able to identify the story: that when Joseph of Arimathea came to Glastonbury not long after the Crucifixion, he found there a church built by Christ himself, and dedicated to his Mother. This humble hut of wattles undoubtedly existed, whatever its true origin, until it was destroyed in a disastrous fire at the abbey in 1184. But if you go to Glastonbury today, you can still see the famous Glastonbury thorn, a cutting from the original tree which sprang from Joseph of Arimathea's staff when he put it in the ground and it took root. And Glastonbury has been identified with the Avalon of Arthurian legend, which in turn goes back to a yet older myth, the Celtic otherworld, a land of plenty and eternal youth.

For these are tales of gods and heroes and marvels, the antithesis of sober history, reaching back into the beliefs of our distant forebears. The usual distinction between myth and legend is the presence of a supernatural element in the former, and an historical basis in the latter; if we add to this the category of 'wondertale', this gives us the starting point for this book. Myths, as in the case of the Greek or Norse myths, can have a religious background; but we know too little about the religion of the Celts or the elusive paganism of the Anglo-Saxons to begin to compile a volume on the scale of those for Greece or the North. So myth in its proper sense hardly makes an appearance on its own in the following pages; but our stories are shot through with mythical threads, which give the narratives their iridescent sheen of the unreal and the dreamt. The British past, however, is rich in legends – legends originally being the lives of saints, which were to be read (*legenda* in Latin) in books. This became a synonym for stories in general before the sceptical seventeenth century redefined the word as something not deserving of belief, neatly reversing the original meaning. And finally there are the 'wondertales', to use Gwyn Jones's name for them, romances with little historical basis, their adventures almost defiantly unreal.

What I have tried to present is the past of the island of Britain through the eyes of writers of earlier centuries. Allusions to the Bible and to classical literature have grown increasingly remote to us in the last half-century; but our British past and its stories are even further from our present repertory of knowledge. Some episodes will surprise by their unexpected familiarity, others by their utter strangeness; but all are part of our history, and have much to tell us about who we are today.

We begin with a view from outside, that of the classical world peering into the dark edges of the known world and vaguely making out a misty island inhabited by men and spirits alike. From there we move on to the versions of how these islands came to be inhabited. Here there may be dim memories of the great folk-migrations of prehistoric times; a far larger element is the desire of story-tellers to begin at the beginning. Like the Romans, the Irish and Welsh story-tellers discerned at the start of their history an island full of monsters and strange beings, whether they were the giants of Albion, or the Fir Bolg and Tuatha de Danaan of Ireland. All this had to be set in the context of known history, the Bible in the case of the Irish or classical legend for the Anglo-Norman writers who set down versions of the Celtic tales. Historians adrift in a sea of legend needed some safe anchorage for their story, so *The Book of the Takings of Ireland* marries its narrative of the ancient Irish with an abbreviated version of the Old Testament, while the founding fathers of Britain set sail from Homer's Troy. By contrast, we have lost the old tales of the Anglo-Saxon past, and have only a brief genealogy tracing the Saxon kings back to Woden. The Norse myths have contributed very little to Britain's stock of stories in comparison with those of the Celtic world.

These first stories are tales told to fill the spaces in the historian's record, invented history or historical myth. When we come to supposedly historical times, we find legends which contain grains of history or of ancient religious belief. The first of the legends of the early history of Britain, that of Brutus, is probably an older story than that of the giants of Albion, which may have been written as a 'prequel' to it. Brutus, from whom Britain supposedly got its name, was accepted until the Renaissance as the historical founder of Britain, to the extent that many of the Anglo-Norman chronicles of British history are known as 'Bruts' because they begin with his story. The founding of the English kingdoms is the subject of the story of Hengist and Horsa, who are accepted, not without reservations, as historical figures. The Anglo-Saxon historian Bede, writing a little more than two centuries after them, certainly thought that they really existed, and their dealings with Vortigern may well have survived in some lost Welsh poem which formed the basis of the later legend. Here we meet Merlin for the first time, and learn the story of his birth: after Arthur, he is the most familiar figure from all the legends, and we shall come back to him. Two other legends of the early history draw on lost sources, and we cannot tell what lies behind them: King Lear, whose name, but nothing else, may go back to an Irish sea-god, Llyr; while the adventures of Lludd and Llefelys remind us that the Welsh bards remembered their repertoire by grouping it in threes – the headings survive in the so-called *Triads of the Island of Britain*. The theme of the tale is simply that of the Three Plagues of the Island of Britain; but for once we have the full story, and not just the bare remembered outline. On the other hand, *The Dream of Maxen Wledig* centres on a familiar motif of popular tales, the beloved seen in a dream; beneath its fantasy lie historical echoes of the one British general who became emperor.

King Lear is, of course, familiar on the stage, though his original story is much less well known. Even less familiar is the original of the plot of *Hamlet*; it is indeed set in Denmark, but much of the action takes place in Britain, and that, combined with Shakespeare's use of it, certainly qualifies it as part of our mythical heritage. It is a strange story, full of extravagant conceits, reflecting its hero's combination of sophistication and naïvety. Some of its convolutions come from the Germanic love of riddles and similes, others from the elaborate Latin of its author, a twelfth-century Danish cleric.

In these stories the supernatural has faded into the background, but it reappears in the tales of marvels and magic, where relics of the ancient mythology of Ireland and Wales predominate. How far the spellbinding Welsh tales known as the *Mabinogion* represent the old religious beliefs of the Celts will always be a moot point. It seems that the author or authors of the tales collected under this title had no more than scraps of lore handed down in fragmentary and half-forgotten form, from which they wove their own stories. We are in a world where the marvellous is normal, and where the laws of everyday life are suspended; the figures who inhabit this world are shape-shifters, possessors of strange skills, and are certainly the heirs of the ancient gods, if not the gods themselves in involuntary disguise – Manawyddan mab Llyr the sea-god or Bran 'the blessed'. Matthew Arnold, writing of Lady Charlotte Guest's newly published version of the tales which introduced them to a nineteenth-century English audience for the first time, summed it up well:

> The medieval story-teller is pillaging an antiquity of which he does not fully possess the secret; he is like a peasant building his hut on the site of Halicarnassus or Ephesus; he builds, but what he builds is full of materials of which he knows not the history, or knows by a glimmering tradition only.

Welsh historians were aware that they only knew fragments of their own history; and even the historians slip through our fingers. Nennius, author of *The History of the Britons,* is a shadowy figure whose name may have been attached to his work at a later date, but whom recent research has rehabilitated. In the ninth century, he wrote, apropos of his efforts to discover his people's past, 'I have made a heap of all that I can find'; and this is very much the mood in the next work, *Culhwch and Olwen,* a gathering of fragments from a rich but neglected heritage, lovingly listing names of heroes whose deeds have vanished.

And *Culhwch and Olwen* brings us to the greatest of this genus of heroes, Arthur. The legends of Arthur are too extensive to include in their full glory in a volume of this sort, without crowding out less familiar faces. They are also largely a creation of writers outside these islands, and I have chosen here to show Arthur as he was known in Britain rather than sample the international versions of his stories, which were of course avidly read in medieval Britain as elsewhere, but are not British in their tone or content, only in their geography.

We have run on in advance of our theme. There are more marvels and magic of a simpler kind to detain us before we come to the great heroes, beginning with a list of the magical places in the islands of Britain which is part of Nennius's 'heap'. There are stories, too, of the great Welsh bards, Merlin and Taliesin, where shadows of real people once more fall across their imaginary counterparts. Taliesin was very probably a real sixth-century poet, Merlin a contemporary king. The *Life of Merlin* draws not only on the Celtic past, but on medieval lore of all kinds, the stories of beasts and birds from the medieval bestiary, medieval science, the art of prophecy, magic and enchantment. Merlin's history is an exemplary tale of the vanity of human glory; Taliesin's, on the other hand, shows that a bard is more valuable to his patron than gold or lands, an unexpected twist until we look at the reality of Welsh society as reflected in the tenth-century law codes and find that bards were held in the highest esteem.

From the magical we turn to the heroic. In addition to Arthur, the two great heroes of Anglo-Saxon and Celtic myth respectively are Beowulf and Cuchulain; to set them side by side is to see how very different are the two cultures from which they sprang. *Beowulf,* for all the terror of Grendel and her son, and the fury of the dragon robbed of his hoard, belongs to a much sparer, realistic world, where heroes are human and have no more than human powers, and it is the warrior ethos that binds men together, a world where comradeship counts above all else, but where the delights of the mead-hall are tempered by the knowledge that they must be paid for, down to the last drop of blood, in fighting for the lord whose generosity provides them. *Beowulf* is a grave, restrained poem, with little humour or exaggeration: nobility is its keynote.

The world of Cuchulain is much more boisterous and bizarre, and is shot through with the traces of an older social order and its mythology, a tribal community dominated by women like Maeve of Connaught, whose quarrel with her husband as to which of them is richer precipitates the main action, the cattle-raid of Cuailgne. Cuchulain himself learns his skill in arms from a wise woman, who also teaches him spells and becomes his mistress; and he possesses a magic weapon of awesome power, the many-barbed Gae Bolg, which can only be thrown if a particular ritual is observed. It is a world of treachery, adultery, magical prohibitions, and in the original, images bordering on the obscene.* All this takes place in a minutely mapped landscape, the names of places recording the events that took place there. For both in Wales and Ireland, the bards were particularly valued for their skill in the history of names, so that whole stories would be told to explain the meaning of one place-name. But Cuchulain himself dominates the story, with his single-handed defence of Ulster when the men of that province lie sick under a curse. The great feats of arms are his, and there is a vibrant delight in the descriptions of them which heightens the pathos of his eventual death, drawn on inevitably as he is forced to break the magical taboos which bind him.

From heroes we pass on to the saints. Cadog must serve as archetype for the host of Welsh saints, unknown to the authorities in Rome, of the independent Celtic church. The accounts of their lives were designed to aggrandise the monasteries where they were honoured or which they had founded, and to enhance the prestige of the saint himself by showing him as able to overawe the greatest of secular rulers. In *The Life of Saint Cadog* we meet Arthur in unfamiliar guise, being humbled by Cadog as a demonstration of the saint's power, in an episode which takes us back to the world of the *Mabinogion*.

The Roman attitude to saints' lives is very different. Since 1643, the huge volumes of the *Acta Sanctorum,* which list the saints for each day of the year, their story and their miracles, have appeared under the auspices of the order now known as the Bollandists, a group of scholars never more than twenty-four in number, whose enterprise has endured for three and a half centuries of continuous work. Few of their pages, however, relate to British saints, and in recent years St George himself, included in this book as England's patron saint, has been officially disowned. To be fair, his story was denounced as mythical as early as the council of Nicaea in AD 325. The legend of St Joseph of Arimathea in England is equally unofficial, and only that of Helena and the True Cross is included in the constantly revised volumes of the *Acta*.

Ironically, Helena was not British, though she was long believed to be

---

* I have used Lady Gregory's slightly bowdlerised version, because it gives the widest account of Cuchulain's career; Thomas Kinsella's brilliant rendering, *The Tain*, covers only the great cattle-raid.

so. The stories of Helena and St Joseph are both concerned with relics: the True Cross was so popular as a relic that modern cynics have said that there was enough of its wood to build Noah's Ark, and supposed fragments of it were to be found throughout the cathedral treasuries of western Europe. By contrast, Joseph of Arimathea's two vessels containing the blood and sweat of our Lord were only claimed by Glastonbury, though famous examples of the blood with different provenances were to be found elsewhere. The Grail, which is associated with Joseph in romances, is also linked with Glastonbury in modern folklore, but was never part of the vast array of treasures which the monks there claimed to own.

Our last group of legends takes us at first firmly into the realms of history. Stories about the great figures of history have often developed into a kind of legend, particularly when their deeds or their death were dramatic in the extreme. Harold, whose death at Hastings still fascinates laymen and historians alike, was reputed to have lived on as pilgrim and monk, refusing to reclaim his throne, and dying in obscurity on the marches of Wales: he is portrayed as a saint rather than as the skilled but unlucky commander that he really was. Hereward the Wake, on the other hand, lives on in legend in his true colours, as a Saxon rebel defying the entire might of the Norman war-machine. His story was written down fairly shortly after his death, possibly while there were men still alive who remembered him or had even fought alongside him, and his exploits are on the border of legend and history, just on the legendary side of the dividing line between true – or almost true – stories of a real historical figure, embellished in the telling and retelling. On the other side of the line (and hence not included here) lie the stories of William Wallace and Robert the Bruce, for although they are 'legendary' figures in the modern sense of the word, the great poems about them by John Barbour and 'Blind Harry' can be shown to be largely historical.

Richard the Lionheart, on the other hand, leads a dual existence in history and literature: on the one hand we have the dry records of his governance preserved in the Public Record Office, on the other a curious piece about him written in the thirteenth century, in which he becomes a figure of fantasy and a protagonist in a kind of idealised struggle between good and evil, as he fights Saladin in the Holy Land. There is a similar historical basis for the story of Macbeth, whose usurpation of the Scottish throne is recorded in contemporary chronicles; but by the time that Shakespeare came to read about him in Holinshed's *Chronicles* his reputation had been embellished with a tale of strange prophecies and their stranger fulfilment. Our other historic characters have less extravagant adventures: Lady Godiva was a real Saxon noblewoman from the years before the Norman Conquest, whose pious actions – but not her legend – were remembered in the annals of the nunnery she founded.

Much more elusive in historical terms is Robin Hood, for whom it is difficult even to name the century in which he lived. In this he is like Arthur; and it is notable that they both embody a strong streak of the ideal, Arthur as redeemer of his nation and Robin Hood as arbiter of justice between rich and poor. The poems about him were not written down until writing and printing meant that many humbler people were able to read, and he remained a people's hero until his stories were taken up, often by children's writers, in the nineteenth century, and the debate about his historical origins began.

With other heroes, like *King Horn* and *Havelok the Dane,* we are back entirely in the world of the imagination: no one claims to have found the prototypes for either hero in real life, and although *Havelok* reflects the realities of the Danish occupation of Britain, they are both creations of a minstrel's inventive mind, made to delight the audience in the hall of a lord whose grandfather had perhaps come over with William the Conqueror. They are pure story-telling, the common theme of both being the regaining of a lost kingdom by a man generally assumed to be of humble birth. By comparison with Richard the Lionheart's exploits or with those of earlier heroes, they are positively down to earth: there is little magic or fantasy, and the details are largely realistic. They stand at the beginning of the great series of medieval fictions which we call romances, and have a simplicity which their successors rapidly abandoned in favour of a more dramatic and picturesque approach.

The adventures of our last two heroes, Bevis of Hampton and Guy of Warwick, are told in this style. Both poems were probably created to honour great noble families of the twelfth century, and to give them ancestral beginnings of suitable renown. Interestingly, while the main theme of Bevis's history is an elaboration of the theme of *Horn* and *Havelok,* Guy of Warwick is a hero of genuinely humbler birth, the son not even of a lord, but of his steward, who wins the hand of his lord's daughter by deeds alone; nobility is achieved through actions rather than inherited by blood. We are back in the world of the fantastic, with giants and magic rings and mighty deeds against the infidel. This world is similar to that of the French *chansons de geste* (songs of action) which are contemporary with these poems; indeed the original poems were in Norman French and are in effect English examples of an international genre.

Most of the myths and legends retold here are commemorations of the distant or not so distant past by poets who were largely unlettered: in the twelfth century, secular literature was invaded by learned men such as Geoffrey of Monmouth – who, building on sparse writings and spoken tales, created a much more sophisticated form of fiction. Our stories belong to an older world, first created by poets who have become legendary figures themselves: Taliesin in Welsh, Widsith in Anglo-Saxon.

Widsith claimed to have sung before the great kings of past and present – Ermanaric lord of the Goths in fourth-century Italy; Attila, leader of the Huns; Aelfwine, the seventh-century king of the Lombards; Guthere in Burgundy; Hrothgar, the Danish king in *Beowulf*; and Offa, king of the East Saxons. Widsith and Taliesin also allude to heroes and kings whose stories have not come down to us, a reminder of how little we really know of the past: even in the later middle ages there are tales which were clearly very popular which have only survived as names. Ermanaric was the hero of a saga which was known in England and is mentioned in *Beowulf*; Wayland Smith, whose name lingers in the English countryside, survives in the pages of Saxo, author of the story of Hamlet; but Wade and Unwin, Geat and Mechthild, are no more than names, like Ranulf of Chester whom William Langland mentions in the same breath as Robin Hood. But what we have lost is all the more reason for cherishing what survives, and I hope that the present assembly of tales will be a reminder of those riches.

The versions which follow have deliberately been drawn from a variety of sources to give a range of voices to match the variety of the stories themselves. They range from Caxton's version of *The Golden Legend*'s account of St George to a translation from a forthcoming edition of the Latin text of the life of Merlin by one of the best medieval Latin scholars of today. I have tried to modernise and standardise as lightly as possible, to remove only anachronisms of style and spelling which might prove a distraction. I am deeply grateful to Kevin Crossley-Holland for permission to include his powerful version of *Beowulf*; to Neil Wright for his previously unpublished translation of the *Vita Merlini*; to Michael Swanton for permission to adapt his version of *Hereward the Wake* from *Lives of the Last Englishmen*; to Peter Fisher for an updated version of his translation of Saxo's account of Hamlet; to James Carley for his version of the Glastonbury legends; and to Michael J. B. Allen for the translation of the legend of *Helena and the True Cross*. I hope that my own efforts will not seem pedestrian in this distinguished company, particularly since it includes Lady Charlotte Guest's version of the *Mabinogion* and Lady Gregory's *Cuchulain of Muirthemne*.

And now the poets and writers who fashioned these myths and legends ask for your attention: 'Be still and listen!'

A NOTE ON NAMES

The spelling of names, whether in Latin, Welsh, Irish or Middle English, presents considerable problems. There have been at various times different systems for transcribing names from the Celtic languages, and even in Latin and Middle English there are wide discrepancies in the versions of the same character's name. To a modern Celtic scholar, the transcriptions may look antiquated, but rather than attempt to take controversial decisions, I have followed Lady Charlotte Guest's *Mabinogion* for the Welsh and Lady Gregory's *Cuchulain of Muirthemne* for the early Irish. Latin and English names have been standardised wherever possible. This leaves occasional problems of two names for one character, such as Bedwyr in Welsh and Bedivere in English, but no solution can be entirely satisfactory.

PROLOGUE: THE ISLAND AT THE EDGE OF THE WORLD

To the Romans, Britain was a remote island, in the stream of the Ocean which surrounded the known world, a haunted and mysterious place where life and death, human and divine, were interchangeable. To them, the island itself was almost a myth, beyond the ken of the rational Roman mind. Their tales of what lay in the outer seas are a fitting prologue to the legends and myths of the British themselves. First, Procopius, historian of the Byzantine empire, tells us what he knows of the land at the other end of Europe.

LONG ago, in the island of Brittia, the men of that country built a long wall, cutting off a large part of it; and the climate and the soil and everything else is completely different on either side. To the east of the wall the air is healthy, changing with the seasons, moderately warm in summer and cool in winter. And many people dwell there, living much as we do, and the trees abound with fruits which ripen at the right season, and the cornlands flourish as abundantly as any; furthermore, the land seems to display a genuine pride in an abundance of springs of water.

But on the west side everything is the reverse of this, so that it is impossible for a man to survive there for even half an hour. Countless snakes and serpents and every other kind of wild creature occupy this area as their own. And, strangest of all, the inhabitants say that if any man crosses this wall and goes to the other side, he dies straightaway, being quite unable to support the pestilential air of that region. Wild animals which go there are likewise instantly met and taken by death.

It is said that the souls of men who die are always conveyed to Brittia. And I will tell you exactly how this is done, having often heard the people there describe it in all seriousness, though I have come to the conclusion that the tales they tell can probably be attributed to the power of dreams. Along the coast of the ocean which lies opposite the island of Brittia there are numerous villages. These are inhabited by men who fish with nets, or till the soil, or carry on a sea-trade with this island. They are generally subject to the Franks, but never pay them any tribute; for such tribute has been waived from ancient times, reputedly because they perform a certain service, which I will now describe.

The men of this place say that the conducting of souls is a duty which they have to take in turn. The men who must go to do this work on the following night, taking over this service from the others, go back to their own houses and sleep as soon as darkness comes on, while they wait for the man who is to summon them to the enterprise. And late at night they are conscious of a knocking at their doors and hear an indistinct voice calling them together for their task. Without hesitating, they rise from their beds and walk to the shore; they feel compelled to do so, even though they do not know what necessity leads them on. There they see skiffs in readiness with no man in them – these are not their own skiffs, but a different kind. They step into them, and lay hold of the oars. They are aware that the boats are burdened with a large number of passengers; the boats are wet by the waves to the edge of the planks and the rowlocks, leaving hardly a finger's breadth above the water. They themselves, however, see no one, but after rowing for only an hour they put in at Brittia – yet when they make the voyage in their own skiffs, not using sails but rowing, they would be hard-pressed to make this passage in a night and a day. When they reach the island, and have been relieved of their burdens, they depart with all speed, their boats now suddenly light and rising above the waves, sinking no further in the water than the keel itself.

They neither see any man sitting in the boat with them nor disembarking on the other shore, but they say that they hear a kind of voice from the island which appears to make announcement to those who take the souls in charge as the name of each passenger who has come over with them is called – a voice which recites the positions of honour which they once held and calls out their fathers' names as well. And if women also happen to be among those who have been ferried over, they utter the names of the men to whom they were married in life. This, then, is what the men of this country say takes place.

The Roman historian Plutarch, writing a treatise on how oracles have ceased in his own time, heard this story about Britain from one of his informants. Briareus was a hundred-armed giant in classical myth, and Saturn was the Roman god of Time, father of Jupiter, by whom he was overthrown and banished.

Demetrius said that of the islands scattered round Britain, many were deserted and some of them were named after spirits and heroes. He had sailed on the emperor's orders to enquire about and investigate these places, and had reached the nearest of the desert isles, which had but a few inhabitants. These were religious men, held sacred by the Britons. Just after he landed, there was a great tumult in the air, and many meteors and blasts of wind roared past, and whirlwinds descended. When it was calm again, the islanders said that one of the superior powers had just been extinguished. They said that, just as a lamp when burning does no harm, but when it is put out its smoke is noxious to many people, so great souls, when first kindled, are benign and harmless. But often their departure and dissolution, as in the present case, stirs up stormy winds and aerial tumults, infecting the air with pestilential tendencies. In that region also, they said, Saturn was confined in one of the islands by Briareus; his slumber had been artfully produced in order to chain him, and he was cared for and guarded by many attendant spirits.

THE ORIGINS

To begin at the beginning ... When Virgil wanted to write a suitable epic to honour the emperor Augustus, he turned, not to the recent triumphs of Rome, but to its most ancient stories, and described how the Romans were the heirs of Troy, descended from its king, Priam, through his son Aeneas. By so doing, he invested the newly created empire of Rome with a solemn and impressive past. When Rome's power dissolved before the barbarians in the sixth century, the process was repeated, and the individual nations who partitioned the mantle of the Roman emperors each claimed their own distinguished descent, often in order to justify the rule of their king The scholars who composed these stories turned first to the Bible, and added their particular race to the descendants of the sons of Japhet, son of Noah, through whom the earth was repopulated after the Flood. A little later, other writers took up Virgil's theme, and sought classical origins for the subject of their fictions, so that a Trojan past became just as desirable as a Biblical one. These stories, at first relatively simple, were elaborated, and in particular came to be used to explain the names of different lands and peoples: we shall meet Albina, foundress of Albion, Scota, the ancestor of the Scots, and Brutus, the conqueror of Britain. The tales are often confused in their attempts to reconcile Biblical and Trojan chronology, or have been overlaid by other stories, but in this confusion lies the root of all our legends.

1. THE GIANTS OF THE ISLAND OF ALBION

The origin of the name Albion is obscure; it has been suggested that it came from the white cliffs of Dover, albus *in Latin, but this is far from certain. It was current as an alternative poetic name for* **Britain** *by the mid-thirteenth century, when this story seems to have been written. It draws on the common tradition that the earth was inhabited by giants, that 'there were giants in those days', but it may also have had political overtones, because Edward I was trying to establish his claim as overlord of Scotland, and this story shows the island as a single political unit: Edward, as Albina's successor, could lay claim to the whole island. The story also provides a 'prequel' to Geoffrey of Monmouth's famous* **History of the Kings of Britain,** *in that it explains the presence of the giants whom, according to Geoffrey, Brutus found in Britain when he first landed there. It has come down to us as an Anglo-Norman poem, but the earliest version was probably written in Latin.*

HERE you may learn how the great giants first came to this island, their number and origins; they were the first to occupy England, which was first known as Albion. Now listen carefully and I will tell you in brief the whole story of the giants, just as I heard it from a wise man, who was well versed in writings about the adventures of former times.

Three thousand nine hundred and seventy years after the creation of the world there was a powerful king in Greece, who was so brave and noble and proud that he held sway over all kings. He had a beautiful, well-bred queen, by whom he had thirty daughters; everyone thought them very beautiful, and they were all brought up together. The father and mother were tall, and the children grew up like their parents. I cannot tell you their names, except that of the eldest, who was a very tall and beautiful girl called Albina. And when they were all of age, the king and queen gave all the daughters in marriage to kings of high rank.

But though each of them wedded a king, and was queen in her own right, through pride and temper they plotted a great crime. They did not think that anything could go amiss with their plans, but gathered together and took secret counsel. And they agreed among themselves that none of them should be subject to the authority of anyone else, whether it was their lord, their neighbour, their brother, their cousin or any other lord. 'But our husbands keep us in subjection all the time, and rule over us just as they please.' They were the daughters of the great king, and had never submitted to anyone; nor did they wish to, nor did they wish to have any master, nor be forced to do anything. Rather they wanted to rule over their lords and all they possessed. The idea that no one should command them was pleasing to them all; and as they did not want to do as their lords wished, obeying them and performing all their desires, they made a pact and swore an oath that each of them would kill their lord on the same day when he came to her privately and embraced her and looked for solace. They set a day to accomplish this, and all agreed, save the youngest, who did not want to harm her lord, as she loved him dearly.

When their counsel was over, they all returned to their various countries. The plot did not please the youngest at all, for she loved her lord and had given herself to him. She in no way wished to see her lord harmed, but while she was at the meeting she dared not contradict her sisters, because if she had said anything against them they would have murdered her on the spot. As soon as she came home and saw her lord, her grief increased; and when he saw that she was sad, he asked her what the reason was. The gentle lady fell at her lord's feet and begged him for mercy. She asked pardon for her sin, and told him of the treachery which her sisters had plotted, and how they had sworn to kill him against her will. Her lord took her in his arms and kissed her, and solaced her more than he had ever done before. 'Lady,' he said, 'be at ease, and forget your sorrow.'

The next day at dawn, he dressed to go to her father to speak with him, and he told his wife to get ready to go with him. They did not delay a moment, but both made their way to her father, the king of Greece. The king made them very welcome, and they told him exactly what his daughters had been up to. He was so dismayed by what his youngest daughter told him, that he sent out a summons to them all commanding them to come to him at once.

When they were all present the king accused them of treason, and of maliciously plotting the death of their lords, to their great dishonour. The ladies were dismayed by the accusation and by the treason which they had been prevented from committing, but of which they would always be guilty. Each tried to clear herself on oath; but they could not contradict the charges. Their husbands were so furious that they wanted them all put to death. Their father, who was equally angry, cross-examined them so that nothing remained hidden, and everything that they had decided at their council was revealed. He convicted them all of this enormity and wickedness, save for the youngest, who had told everything to her lord and was greatly honoured by him thereafter.

When all the sisters had been convicted of that grievous crime, they were seized by their father and their husbands and shut up in a dungeon for their iniquities and evil. They suffered greatly there as they waited for judgement as was ordained. But the judges were wise: because the accused were of noble birth, the judges did not wish to dishonour the family of their mother and father, who held such wide domains, nor the families of the lords of rich lands who had married them. Therefore they did not condemn them to death, but ordered instead that they should all be exiled from the country of their birth forever, without hope of returning. Nor was there any appeal from this judgement, whether they liked it or not. They were led in sorrow, without anyone to help them, to a sea-port which was nearby.

All that I can tell you is that they were taken and put in a large, well-found ship, without a rudder and without provisions. They wept bitterly, but no one took pity on them, because the crime that they had plotted was so terrible. The ship was pushed out to sea; the waves tossed it hither and thither, and it was in great peril as it drifted away from the land. The sisters were all in great sorrow, exiled from the country where they had been queens and lived in luxury: now they were poorer than nuns. They did not know what would become of them, whether they would live or die.

These women suffered much; the ship was driven by chance, buffeted by great winds and menaced by the waves. But none of this was as bad as the hunger that gnawed at them, for they had nothing to eat; yet the danger made them lament pitifully and forget their hunger. They were tormented on all sides, and were ready to die, for a gale got up and the sea rose to a storm, with huge waves which lifted the ship up and then brought it down again, turning it round so much that the women fell on the deck and lay there for three whole days and nights without moving, as if in a trance. Meanwhile the storm carried them onwards until they were near the shore.

When the storm ceased, the weather became clear and calm, and the ship had been driven so far west that it came to the land which is now called England – though in those days it had no name because no one dwelt there. When the tide went out, the ship lay on the shore. At this the women woke up, and lifted their heads. They were overjoyed to find themselves so near land, and at once left the ship where they had suffered so much.

But the eldest sister hastened to be the first to leave and take possession of the land: she was called Albina. The others came out of the ship, weak from the pain and fasting they had undergone at sea. They all sat down, and the great hunger which they had forgotten came back. They were hungry beyond measure and thought of nothing else, even though they did not know where to find anything to eat. In the end they ate raw herbs, which they found in great plenty, and fruit which was on the trees. Acorns, chestnuts and sorb-apples kept them alive; they found plums and bullaces, pears and apples, and this was all the food they ate. They were all very anxious, for they did not know where they had landed, what the country was called, or whether it was at peace or war. They had to stay there, for there was nowhere else they could go.

When they had recovered their strength, they explored the country to see what kind of people lived there and what sort of life they led. Although they searched everywhere, they found no human beings either in the woodland, the plains, the valleys or the hills. There was neither man nor woman, and this astonished them; nor could they find any sign that men had been there. But they found fine forests and woods and many wild beasts, plenty of fowl on land, and rivers full of fish, bordered by delightful flower-filled meadows. And the wild birds sang loudly in the woods which gave them comfort.

But when they realised that they could never return home and that the land which they had found had never been inhabited by man born of woman – for it was open and deserted – Albina, the eldest sister, said: 'We have been exiled from the land where we were born: we know we have deserved our punishment and that we will never return. Such is our fate; but fortune has given us this land. I should be acknowledged as its ruler, for I was the first to take possession of it when we left the ship. If anyone has anything to say against this, let them do so now.' They all agreed that the land should be hers.

Then Albina said: 'We do not know the name of this land, or if it has ever had a lord. As I am now its ruler it should be named after me. Albina is my name, so it shall be called Albion, and our shame shall always be remembered here. We shall have to remain here, nor should we want to go elsewhere, because the land is full of good things, even though we lack meat.'

They were very eager to have meat – it was their hearts' desire. They saw plenty of wild animals and birds to tempt them, and would gladly have eaten them if they could have laid hands on them. They all tried to think how they could catch a wild beast or bird, of which there was no shortage. They knew how to hunt from the days when they were queens, and they knew the lie of the land; but they had neither bow nor arrow, falcon nor hound, with which to catch their prey. But they were cunning and clever, and after much thought they built more than a hundred traps. They made ropes from creepers, and caught deer with them; they made traps from twigs to catch fowl. And they made other such devices which deceived both beast and bird, and caught many of them. When they had caught what they wanted, they skinned the deer and lit a fire by striking stones together; there was no shortage of firewood. They cooked the beasts in their skins and roasted them over the fire, both the deer and fowl which they had caught. They ate them gladly, drinking clear water from the fountain.

This way of life sustained them so well that they regained their strength, recovered completely from their adventures and grew fat on their new diet. The heat of nature overcame them, and in their lechery they longed for men to make love to them – a common enough temptation. The evil beings called incubi saw this. They are spirits which have the power to take on human form, and they mingle with women and give them such delight that they lie with them and make them pregnant, and then disappear. So it happened with Albina and her sisters: when desire overcame them, the evil spirits were ready to fulfil their wishes and all of them coupled with the incubi. They gave birth to children who became giants, and held the land after them. But when the incubi had gone, the women could find no one to play the man's part with them, so when their sons came of age, they wickedly begot sons and daughters on their mothers. Sisters bore children by their brothers, and all of them grew to great stature: they were exceptionally large and tall. The huge bones which can be found in many places throughout the world are evidence for this; men dig them up in both the country and the city – teeth, legs and ribs, and thighbones four feet long, shoulder-blades as large as a shield. Many people are perplexed by this and wonder if there can ever have been men with such huge skeletons. The giants were hideous to look at because evil spirits had begotten them; their fathers were devils, and their mothers were tall and well-built. They were just the children you would expect from such a union.

This fairy race multiplied greatly and spread through the land, making caves in the ground and raising huge walls and ditches. They preferred to live on the mountains. In many places you can still see the great walls which they built, though many of them have been battered down by storms. This race held the land until the Britons came, which happened eleven hundred and thirty-six years before our Lord was born; I am sure of this.

From the time when the women came who first held the land until the arrival of Brutus, who took the land by force and changed its name from Albion to Britain, two hundred and sixty years elapsed according to the chronicle. All this time the giants held the land. But as their race multiplied, they each took a different part of the land and made it their stronghold; they lived each for himself, so proudly and wickedly that every one of them tried to overcome the others, trusting to his own strength and despising the rest. They all strove to conquer the whole land and become lord and master; and in the civil wars which resulted they slew each other until only twenty-four remained, and it was they who came to fight Brutus when he first landed. But Brutus soon overthrew them, all except for their leader, Gogmagog, whose life he spared. For he was amazed by his height – he was twenty feet tall – and wanted to find out how his race had come to the land, and what his lineage was. He told Brutus the whole story of how his ancestors had arrived, and what had happened, and how long they had held the land, just as it had been passed down and as he had heard it from his elders. And Brutus made a record of it, so that others might know of it afterwards and make a story of it to tell at high feasts, so that the marvellous story would be remembered.

Now you have heard the true story about those who first came to England and held it, and what the island's name was, and who bestowed it, and how long they held it before the Britons came and changed its original name and called it Britain. It will never hurt to know the tales and writings of ancient adventures. May God bless him who sets them down in writing.

2. THE ORIGINS OF THE SCOTTISH NATION

This version of the origin of Scotland is taken from John of Fordun's Scoti-chronicon, *a fifteenth-century history of the Scottish nation, and it is the fullest telling of the story. By the time John of Fordun was writing, historians had begun to collect different accounts of the origin story and had realised that it was not always possible to reconcile them with each other. There is a curious feature about the Scottish legend, in that the land is named neither after a hero descended from Noah, nor one of the Trojans, but after the daughter of the pharoah who had driven Moses out of Egypt. The political subtext here is to emphasise the independence of Scotland in ancient days, and hence to resist the English claims to overlordship. The marble throne of Simon Brecc is presumably a reference to that talisman of Scottish liberty, the Stone of Scone.*

IN the days of Moses there was a king in Greece called Neolus, and he had a son called Gaythelos, who was handsome but of uncertain temper. Because of this, he was not given any position of authority in the kingdom, which aroused his anger: he and a large company of young men inflicted many injuries on his father's realm, with horrific cruelty, much to the outrage of his father and his subjects, who were offended by his violent behaviour. He was therefore expelled from Greece, and, after fighting in different places and enduring many hardships, made his way to Egypt with his followers. Pharoah, king of Egypt, welcomed him as a brave and daring soldier, and enlisted his help in oppressing the Israelites. He married Scota, the only daughter of the Egyptian ruler, and was expected to succeed to the throne. When Pharoah was drowned in the Red Sea, pursuing the Israelites as they fled from his tyranny, Gaythelos was at Heliopolis. Some say that when he claimed the throne the Egyptians refused to accept him; others relate that he left before the advent of plagues which God inflicted on Egypt, having foreseen their coming. At all events, he and his followers went into exile again. He was unable to return to Greece, so he sailed westward in search of new lands to conquer, hoping to find either a territory which he could seize from the inhabitants, or preferably uninhabited lands which he and his men could occupy.

At first they travelled through North Africa, and, like the children of Israel, their wanderings there lasted for forty years, after which they set sail again, through the straits of Gibraltar, and landed on the Atlantic coast of Spain, where they hoped to find provisions and rest. But the inhabitants attacked them and Gaythelos and his men had to fight fiercely to overcome them. In the end he defeated them, and plundered much of their territory, before pitching camp and fortifying his position.

Later he built a strongly walled city called Brigantia, which is now called La Coruña, and in it he set up a very high tower with a deep moat which can be seen there today. But the war with the native Spanish continued, and although Gaythelos was victorious, he lost men in each encounter and had nowhere to find reinforcements. He foresaw that his army would eventually be overwhelmed by sheer numbers, and could see no hope of eventual peace. So he turned to his original plan, which had been to find lands where no one dwelled and where there would be no opposition to a settlement. In this way he would not offend the gods, who had assigned Spain to other peoples, but would regain their favour. So with the agreement of his companions he sent out ships to search for such lands; and his scouts found an island far out in the ocean, which had a good harbour and proved to be very beautiful. When they reported their discovery to Gaythelos, he urged his sons to go and settle there, but he himself died suddenly before he could leave Brigantia.

It was therefore under the leadership of Gaythelos's son Hiber that his people made their way to the island. Hiber found it completely uninhabited, and left his brother Hymec there with his family, while he himself returned to Spain. The names of Gaythelos, Scota and Hiber are all to be found in the modern names of these places: the Gaels are called after Gaythelos, Scotland after Scota, and Hibernia, which is now Ireland, after Hiber. But those of Gaythelos's followers who stayed behind in Spain led a wretched existence, driven back by the other inhabitants of Spain into the desolate wastes of the Pyrenees, where they eked out their existence by preying on others, robbing and stealing: they themselves possessed almost nothing, and dressed in rags and animal skins.

Yet they would never submit to a strange ruler, but guarded their freedom jealously even though it meant extreme poverty. Once again, a new leader named Partholomus, a descendant of Gaythelos, saw that the only hope for his people was to find a new home, and to escape from the oppression of their neighbours. So he gathered them together with their few possessions, and managed to assemble a fleet: they sailed across the bay of Biscay to the west of the British Isles.

They were off the Orkneys when they met Gurgunt Bartrud, king of the Britons, who asked who they were and where they had come from. Partholomus told him that they came in peace, but were searching for a land empty of inhabitants where they might settle; they had already travelled for a year and a half without finding anywhere that was suitable. Gurgunt sent them to Ireland, which was almost empty of inhabitants: those who were living there were of course also descendants of Gaythelos, and Partholomus was welcomed by them as their new leader.

There were, however, other peoples who cast envious eyes on Ireland. Among them were the Picts, but the Scots, as they were now called, refused to let them settle there and sent them on to the north of Albion.

After this, a third invasion of the descendants of Gaythelos from Spain took place under the leadership of Simon Brecc. His father, king Milo, had other sons, and Simon Brecc was not his heir; but his father loved him best, so he sent him to conquer Ireland.

Milo gave his son a marble throne, made by great craftsmen long ago, which had been the throne of the Scottish kings of Spain. This throne was set up at Tara, which became the site of the royal palace, and the centre of the kingdom. A different version of the story says that Simon Brecc anchored in a storm off the Irish coast and only raised his anchors with great effort. When he at last hauled them up, he found a block of marble carved in the shape of a chair entangled in them. There was a prophecy about this throne which said that if it was ever forcibly removed from the Scots and kept elsewhere, their descendants would rule in that place.

In the meantime the Picts who had settled in Albion asked the Scots to send over their daughters so that they could marry them, for they had no women of their own. The Scots agreed to this, on condition that the kingship of the Picts should descend through the female line; and this custom was always observed as long as the Picts had kings of their own. Because Albion was much more fertile and welcoming than Ireland, however, many of the Scots crossed the sea to join the Scottish women who were already there; and any Scot who fell foul of the law escaped punishment by going over to the Pictish lands. In due course, the attractions of Albion came to the attention of Fergus, son of Feradach, who gathered a great company of Scots and invaded Albion; he joined up with the other Scots who were already there, and established himself as king in the western part of the land. When the Romans came to Britain, one of their historians, Solinus, described them as follows:

> The Scottish nation were always rough, and ready to fight, and their customs were inhuman. When boys were born, their fathers were accustomed to offering them their first food on the point of a spear, so that they would wish for no other death than to be slain in battle fighting for their liberty. And when they grew up and became skilled in battle, they celebrated their victories by first drinking the blood of the fallen, and then smearing it on their faces. They are a free-spirited people, eating sparingly, fierce and forbidding in appearance, roughly spoken; but they are courteous and welcoming to their fellow-countrymen, preferring games and hunting to work.

The later history of the Scots can be found in the histories of Julius Caesar and other Roman writers, but this completes the story of the origins of the Scottish nation, drawn from several chroniclers. They often contradict one another, as Walter Bower points out in his *Scotichronicon*, or history of the Scots, and it is not easy to settle on the true story.

3. THE BOOK OF THE TAKINGS OF IRELAND

The Irish account of the settlement of Ireland exists in very late manuscripts, written down in the sixteenth century. It had been handed down by bards and story-tellers, and the result is considerable confusion – as the writers themselves admit, despite their confident opening offering 'a clear statement of the matter'. The founders of Ireland are said to be descended from Noah, and the whole narrative is embedded in a vernacular version of the Bible, to give it the authority of scripture. The complicated chronology is a result of trying to reconcile Biblical and classical events, since both play their part. But the third element is Irish mythology, with the account of the Fir Bolg and the Tuatha de Danaan, and is genuine tradition, much more powerful than the painstaking inventions of learned writers which precede it. As so often with the mythology of a lost religion, however, many of the details are not merely obscure but quite impenetrable, and read to us today as a kind of incantation rather than as proper narrative.

THIS is an explanation of the Takings of Ireland, and of her history, and of her royal roll, with a clear statement of the matter before us.

The island of Ireland is situated in the west: as the Paradise of Adam is situated on the southern coast of the east side of the world, so Ireland is in the northern portion, towards the west side of the world. Those lands are as similar in nature as in their positions on the earth; for as Paradise has no noxious beasts in it, so learned men tell us that Ireland has no serpent, lion, toad, injurious rat, dragon, scorpion, nor any hurtful beast, save only the wolf. And so Ireland is called 'the island of the west', Hibernia. It is next to the island of Britannia, and in extent of territory it is narrower, but its soil is more fertile. It is also known as Scotia, because it is inhabited by the nations of the Scots. Within it are no serpents, rare birds nor bees; indeed, if anyone were to scatter dust or gravel carried from Ireland amongst beehives anywhere else in the world, the swarms would desert the honeycombs.

The Scoti are named after Scota, daughter of the pharaoh of Egypt, who was wife of Nel. They are called Fenians after Feinius Farsaid. The Scots are the same as the Picts, so called from their painted bodies, inasmuch as they mark themselves with a variety of devices by means of iron needles and ink. The country is also called Heriu after its heroes.

Let him whom reads, sweat!

The peoples who came to Ireland before the Gaedil were born of the progeny of Magog, son of Japhet: namely, Partholon, son of Sera, son of Sru, son of Esru, son of Bimbend, son of Aithech, son of Magog, son of

Japhet; and Nemed, son of Agnomain, son of Pamp, son of Tat, son of Sera, son of Sru; and the progeny of Nemed, the Gaileoin, Fir Domnann, Fir Bolg and Tuatha de Danaan.

Noah divided the world into three parts among his three sons. As for Ham, he settled in Africa and on the southern side of Asia. Shem occupied the middle of Asia, from the river Euphrates to the eastern border of the world. Japhet took the north side of Asia, and the people of all Europe are descended from him. We, the Gaedil, are of his progeny.

Gaidel Glas, our ancestor, was son of Nel, son of Feinius Farsaid, son of Eogan, son of Glunfhind, son of Lamfhind, son of Etheor, son of Thoe, son of Bodb, son of Shem, son of Mar, son of Aurthacht, son of Aboth, son of Ara, son of Iara, son of Sru, son of Esru, son of Baath, son of Rifath Scot, from whom the Scots are descended.

Now it was Rifath Scot who brought the Scotic language from the Tower of Babel, for he was one of the six principal chieftains who were at the building of the Tower of Babel. And after the confounding of the Tower of Babel they were given seventy-two languages, and at the end of ten years Feinius Farsaid extracted the speech of the Gaedil out of the seventy-two languages, and set it forth to his fosterling, Gaedil, the son of Agnomain.

So Nel, son of Feinius Farsaid, dwelt in the south of Egypt, and it fell out that the sons of Israel, as they fled from captivity, came to the estate where Nel lived with his son Gaidel Glas. And Aaron came to him, and told him all that had befallen them, and Nel gave wine and wheat to the people of God as provisions. Aaron told Moses of this, who sent his thanks to Nel. Now that same night Gaidel Glas, Nel's only son, was stung by a serpent; and the lad was carried to Moses, who made fervent prayer before God, and put the sacred rod on the place where the serpent had stung him, so that he was cured. And Moses commanded, in God's name, that no serpent should harm the boy or his descendants for ever after, nor should any serpent dwell in the homeland where his descendants settled. 'There shall be', he said, 'kings and lords, saints and righteous men, of the seed of this boy and their dwelling place shall be in the northern island of the world.' This, then, is the reason why there are no serpents in Ireland.

Although Nel himself suffered no harm from befriending the children of Israel, because Pharoah and his hosts were swallowed up in the Red Sea, his descendants were attacked by the Egyptians because they had helped the Israelites. In the end they were driven from their estates, and they set out, twenty-four married couples in each ship, and sailed to Ceylon, and then north and west until they reached Scythia. And the children of Nel and his brother Nenual fought between themselves for the princedom of Scythia for nine hundred and twelve years, until Mil, son of Bile, killed Refloir, son of Noemius, for which he was sent into exile.

Mil set out with four ships, and fifteen married couples and a servant in each ship, and returned by way of Ceylon to Egypt, which Alexander the Great conquered soon afterwards. And Mil and his followers lived in Egypt for eight years. They learnt craftsmanship and the art of the druids, the law and the art of warfare. Here Mil married the daughter of Nectanebus, who was then pharoah: she was known as Scota, because her husband was a Scot. And at the end of eight years they set sail again, from the Red Sea to Ceylon and thence to Scythia, where they were enchanted for three weeks by the sirens, until the druid Caicher freed them by melting wax in their ears so that they could not hear the sirens' song. Then they rowed until they reached the Libyan Sea, by way of the Black Sea; and Caicher prophesied that they would have no rest until they reached the noble island of Ireland.

They rowed for a whole year on the Western Ocean, past Germany and Thrace, until they reached Dacia; then they went from the Aegean to the island of Tenedos, and thence to Crete, Sicily and the land of the Belgi and Burgundy, to the columns of Hercules and to Gibraltar, at the southern corner of Spain. Fifty-four battles they won against the Frisians and the Lombards, and they took Spain by force. In Spain Breogan, son of Brath, founded a city named Braganza, with a tower to protect it. And it was from that tower, on a winter's evening, that Ith, son of Breogan, saw Ireland.

Let us leave the stories of the Gaedil, and tell of the seven peoples who took possession of Ireland before them; these were the seven Takings of Ireland.

Cessair, daughter of Bith, son of Noah, took Ireland forty days before the Flood. For Noah had said to her 'Rise and go to the western edge of the world; perhaps the Flood will not reach it.' So she set forth from the river Nile in Egypt; and she was in Egypt for ten years. She sailed across the Caspian Sea to the Cimmerian Sea and the Torrian Sea until she came, twenty days later, to the Alps; and in another nine days she reached Spain. It took as long again for her to sail to Ireland, and when the ships reached Ireland they were wrecked. Only Cessair and the crew of her ship escaped, but the Flood overwhelmed them.

Partholon, son of Sera, took Ireland three hundred years after the Flood. Nemed, son of Agnomain of the Greeks of Scythia, took Ireland thirty years after Partholon. The Fir Bolg took Ireland thereafter, and after them the Fir Domnann and the Gaileoin along with them, and lastly the Tuatha de Danaan, before the sons of Mil.

But who was the first to take possession of Ireland after the creation of the world? The Book of Druim Snechta says that it was a woman called Banba, who came with thrice fifty maidens and three men. Ladra was one of the men, and he was the first man to die in Ireland. They lived in the island for forty years until a plague struck them, so that they all died in one week.

For two hundred years no one lived in Ireland: after this came the Flood, and Ireland lay under it for a year and forty days. At the end of three hundred years, Partholon took Ireland, and lived there for five hundred and fifty years until the Cynocephali drove him out, and not one of his children escaped alive. For thirty years after that the land was uninhabited.

Before the Flood, Capa and Luasad and Luaigne came into Ireland, but they are not counted among the Takers of Ireland because they were blown thither as they fished off Spain. They went back to Spain to fetch their wives, but when they returned, the Flood overtook them, and they were drowned at Tuad Inbir.

As for Partholon, he came to Ireland from Sicily, with three men and four women and his servant Ith, because he had slain his mother and father so that his brother should become king. And he was accursed thereafter for murdering his kin.

Three years after Partholon arrived, the first battle in Ireland was fought against the Fomorians who had but one leg and one arm apiece, for they were demons in human shape. They fought against Partholon, and their ranks broke under his onslaught. They fought that battle for a week, but no one was killed there, for it was a magic battle. But Partholon died from the venom of the wounds that he suffered.

And in Partholon's time oxen were first used to plough; and the eldest of Partholon's chieftains set up the first inn in Ireland, and cooked flesh in a cauldron; and the same man introduced duelling into the country. It was Partholon's companion, Samaile the Grey, who first made beer and ale, and first stood surety for his neighbour. Building, and the grinding of grain in a quern, and the making of butter in a churn, were all first done in Ireland under the Taking of Partholon.

His four sons divided Ireland into four parts, and that was known as the first division of Ireland. But this division lasted only until the plague came upon them, on the Monday before midsummer, the feast of Beltane. Nine thousand died of that plague before the next Monday, and but one man escaped – Tuan, son of Starn, the son of Partholon's great-nephew. And God fashioned him in different forms at different times, so that he alone survived from the days of Partholon to the days of Colum Cille. He related to them the Takings of Ireland from the time of Cessair down to their own time.

Now after Partholon's death, Ireland was waste for a space of thirty years, until Nemed, son of Agnomain of the Greeks of Scythia, came there with his four sons, his chieftains, Starn and Iarbonel the Soothsayer, Annind and Fergus Red-Side. Forty-four ships had he on the Caspian Sea for a year and a half, but only his ship reached Ireland. It was Nemed who won the battle of Ros Fraechain against Gand and Sengand, two kings of the Fomorians, and both of them were slain there. Two royal forts were dug by Nemed in Ireland, Raith Chimbaith in Semne and Raith Cindeich in Ui Niallain. The four sons of Matan Munremar dug Raith Cindeich in one day; they were slain before the morrow by Nemed, lest they should dig another and better fort. He won three battles against the Fomorians, and afterwards died of the plague.

After his days in Ireland, his children were under great oppression at the hands of More, son of Dela, and Conand, son of Febar. After Conand is the Tower of Conand named, and in it was the great fleet of the Fomorians. Two thirds of Nemed's progeny, and of the wheat and the milk of the people of Ireland, had to be brought every Samhain to Mag Cetne; because of the burden of the tax wrath and sadness seized on the men of Ireland. They all went to fight against the Fomorians, and three of the sons of Nemed were their champions. Thirty thousand of them went by sea and thirty thousand by land to attack the Tower of Conand; and Conand and his progeny fell. But More, son of Dela, came upon them with the crews of threescore ships after the tower was taken, and they slaughtered one another. The sea came up over them, but, so savage was the fighting, none fled, save one ship containing thirty warriors.

After the battle, the progeny of Nemed departed from Ireland. Semeon went into the lands of the Greeks, and his progeny multiplied there until they were numbered in thousands: there the Greeks enslaved them, and made them carry clay upon the rough mountains until they became plains filled with flowers. But they wearied of slavery, and five thousand fled, making ships of their bags. They came again into Ireland, the land of their fathers, two hundred and thirty years after Nemed. And the Fir Bolg and Fir Domnann are of the progeny of Semeon. And the children of Bethach, who was son of Iarbonel the Soothsayer, went into the northern islands of the world to learn druidry and heathenism and devilish knowledge, so that they were expert in every art; and they too returned to Ireland, and became the Tuatha de Danaan.

But as for Fergus Red-Side and his son Britain Mael, from whom all the Britons in the world are descended, they filled the great island of Britain with their offspring, until Hengist and Horsa, the two sons of Guietglis, the king of the Old Saxons, came and conquered them.

And the Fir Bolg gave battle to the Tuatha de Danaan on the plain called Mag Tuired: they were a long time fighting that battle. At last the Fir Bolg broke, and as the slaughter pressed northward, a hundred thousand of them were slain westward between there and the shore at Eochaill. There king Eochu was overtaken, and he fell at the hands of the three sons of Nemed. Yet the Tuatha de Danaan suffered great loss in the battle, and they left their king on the field with his arm cut from him; the leeches were seven years healing him. All but a few of the Fir Bolg fell in that battle, and they fled from the Tuatha de Danaan, leaving Ireland to go to the islands, where they remained until the Cruithne drove them out. They came to the domains of Cairbre nia Fer and he gave them lands, but they were unable to remain because he taxed them so heavily. So they fled from him and sought the protection of Maeve and Ailell, who gave them lands.

For the Tuatha de Danaan, as we have said, were the children of the grandson of Nemed, who went to the northern islands of the world, learning druidry and knowledge and prophecy and magic, until they were expert in the arts of pagan cunning. There were four cities where they studied: Failias, Goirias, Findias, Muirias. From Failias was brought the Lia Fail which is in Temair, and which used to utter a cry under every king that conquered Ireland. From Goirias was brought the spear which Lug had; battle would never go against the man who wielded it. From Findias was brought the sword of Nuadu; there was no escaping it, and when it was drawn from its battle-scabbard, there was no resisting it. From Muirias was brought the cauldron of the Dagda; no company would leave it without being satisfied.

They came into Ireland in this wise: without vessels or barks, in dark clouds over the air and by the might of druidry, and they landed on the mountains in Connaught. Thereafter they wrought a darkness over the sun for the space of three days and three nights. It was then that the first battle of Mag Tuired was fought, for the Tuatha de Danaan had demanded the sovereignty over the Fir Bolg.

Nuadu of the Silver Hand was king over the Tuatha de Danann for seven years before their coming into Ireland, till his arm was cut from him at the battle of Mag Tuired. An arm of silver was made for him, with the full activity of a man's arm in each finger and each joint; Dian Cecht the leech fitted it for him, with the help of Creidne the silversmith. And Dian Cecht's grandson was Lug, who became king after Nuadu was slain in the last battle of Mag Tuired. Then Nuadu was killed by Balar the Strong Smiter, the other grandfather of Lug; but Lug killed Balar with a stone from his sling. And the tally of men that fell in the battle was seven men, seven score, seven hundred, seven fifties.

Lug's father Cian was killed when he took the form of a lapdog and went to visit Lug; and as blood-price Lug demanded of his father's killers seven things, namely:

— the two horses of the king of the island of Sicily: Gaine and Rea were their names, and wounds, waves or lightning could not harm them;

— the spear of Assal, ridged in red gold: if it sheds a man's blood, that man cannot live; and no cast goes astray if the thrower cries 'Yew', but if the thrower cries 'Reyew', it will turn back at once;

— the skin of the pig of Duis: everyone who lay on it was healed of his wound and of his sickness, and it was as large as the hides of four oxen;

— the six pigs of Essach, which were slaughtered every night, and if their bones were kept without breaking or gnawing, they would come to life each morning;

— the whelp of the royal smith of Ioruath, a hound by night and a sheep by day: if water was cast upon it, it became wine;

— the revealing of the island of Caire Cendfinne, which is hidden between Ireland and Scotland;

— and the harvest of apples that are under the sea near that island.

And Lug was slain forty years after the battle; the Dagda succeeded him, and ruled for eighty years, and after him his sons and grandsons. But his grandsons had no children, and then the Gaedil, of whom we have already spoken, took Ireland after them.

4. THE DESCENT OF THE ANGLO-SAXON KINGS FROM WODEN

If there were ancient legends from the Anglo-Saxon past about their origins, they have totally disappeared; what has survived is the ancient genealogy of the Saxon kings, showing their descent from Woden, greatest of the old gods. The genealogy, although pagan, is recorded by the Christian scribes who wrote the **Anglo-Saxon Chronicle.**

626 AD Penda reigned for thirty winters, and he was fifty winters old when he began to reign. Penda was the son of Pybba, son of Cryda, son of Cynewold, son of Cnebba, son of Icel, son of Eomaer, son of Angeltheow, son of Offa, son of Waermund, son of Wihtlaeg, son of Woden.

755 AD And this year Offa began to reign, and he ruled for thirty-eight winters. And Offa was the son of Thingcferth, son of Enawulf, son of Osmod, son of Eawa, son of Pybba, son of Cryda, son of Cynewold, son of Cnebba, son of Icel, son of Eomaer, son of Angeltheow, son of Offa, son of Waermund, son of Wihtlaeg, son of Woden.

THE EARLY HISTORY OF BRITAIN

5. BRUTUS CONQUERS BRITAIN

In the twelfth century, Norman historians in the English monasteries began to record their versions of the past of the newly-conquered land, drawing on Anglo-Saxon sources. This interest in the island's history extended into Wales, where the Normans gained a foothold in the late eleventh century: thirty years later, Geoffrey of Monmouth, whose name proclaims his Welsh connections, wrote his famous History of the Kings of Britain, which aimed to provide the Welsh with a suitably classical account of their predecessors. Unlike the Norman historians in England, Geoffrey did not have an ordered set of written chronicles on which to draw; our problem today is to know how much was due to his imagination, and how much to old traditions handed down by bards, highly trained in the art of memory, but also skilled in rhetoric and poetry. The answer is probably that there are fragments of history embedded in a work which owes more to imagination than to the material Geoffrey was able to collect. He claimed to have used a 'very ancient book' given to him by Walter, archdeacon of Oxford; but, even if the book was not in itself a legend, it is unlikely to have contained anything resembling the text that Geoffrey produced.

In the passage which follows, Geoffrey provides the Britains with a Trojan ancestry of the kind we have discussed in the section on Origins. He makes it clear that Brutus was not the first inhabitant of the island, and we have seen the antecedents of his story of the giants whom Brutus conquered in the story of Albina. Brutus, however, was much more famous than Albina. The popular success of Geoffrey's History was such that copies of it are commoner than almost any other medieval secular text; and it is of course in Geoffrey's pages that Arthur's history is told in detail for the first time. The section on Brutus displays Geoffrey's classical learning rather than his expertise in Welsh lore.

AFTER the Trojan War, Aeneas, fleeing from the desolation of Troy, came by ship to Italy with Ascanius. When Aeneas was worshipfully received by king Latinus, Turnus, king of the Rutulians saw it, and, growing envious, made war against him. They met in battle, and Aeneas had the upper hand. After Turnus was slain, he gained the kingdom of Italy and the hand of Lavinia, the daughter of Latinus.

Aeneas was succeeded after his death by his son Ascanius, who founded Alba on Tiber and had a son whose name was Silvius. Silvius, unknown to his father, had fallen in love with and secretly married a certain niece of Lavinia, who was now about to become a mother. When this came to the knowledge of Ascanius, he commanded his wise men to discover whether Silvius's wife should be brought to bed of a boy or a girl. When they had made sure of the matter by magic, they told him that the child would be a boy; that he would slay his father and his mother; and that after travelling through many lands, he would be exiled but would nonetheless attain the highest honours.

Nor were the wise men proved wrong; when the day came that she should be delivered of a child, the mother bore a son, but died in child-birth. The child was named Brutus and was given to a nurse. When he was fifteen, the lad, out hunting with his father, killed him by striking him unwittingly with an arrow. For when the huntsmen drove the deer in front of them, Brutus, thinking to take aim at them, struck his own father under the breast. His relations, angered by this dreadful deed, drove him out of Italy. Exiled, he went to Greece, where he fell in with the descendants of Helenus, the son of Priam, who at that time were held in bondage under the power of Pandrasus, king of the Greeks. For after the overthrow of Troy, Pyrrhus, the son of Achilles, had led away Helenus and a great number of others besides in fetters, and had ordered them to be held in slavery in revenge for his father's death.

When Brutus understood that they were also descended from the Trojans, he made his home among them, and became so renowned for his knighthood and prowess that he was beloved by kings and dukes above all the other youths of the country. He was as wise among the wise as he was valiant among warriors; if he won gold or silver or ornaments, he gave it all in largess to his comrades in battle. His fame was wide-spread at home and abroad, and the Trojans came to him from all parts, beseeching him that he should be their king and deliver them from the slavery of the Greeks. They said that this might easily be done, because they had now so multiplied in the land that without counting the women and children there were already seven thousand of them.

There was, moreover, a young nobleman in Greece, called Assaracus, who was no less favourable to their cause. He was born of a Trojan mother, and he was certain that, with their help, he would be able to resist the harassment and persecution of the Greeks. Assaracus's mother had been a concubine; his brother, on the other hand, was Greek on both his father's and mother's side, and though Assaracus had been granted three castles by his father on his deathbed, his brother was laying claim to them, and had rallied the king and the rest of the Greeks to the support of his cause. Brutus, seeing how great was the number of Trojan fighting men, and how strong the castles of Assaracus were in which he could take refuge, granted their request without misgiving.

When Brutus was chosen as leader, he summoned the Trojans from every quarter and garrisoned the strongholds of Assaracus. Assaracus himself, with the rest of the men and women, occupied the forests and hills. Then Brutus sent a letter addressed to the king in these words:

To Pandrasus, king of the Greeks, Brutus, leader of the remainder of the Trojans, sends greeting. Our nation is of the illustrious race of Dardanus, and should not have been treated in thy kingdom other than as their noble descent deserved. So they have withdrawn into the depths of the forests, holding it better to live like the wild beasts on flesh and herbs, but in freedom, rather than enjoy every kind of luxury and remain any longer in slavery under your rule. If this offends your power and dignity, pardon rather than blame them, for all that are in captivity desire to recover their former liberty. Show mercy towards them, and deign to give them back their lost freedom, allowing them to inhabit the forest clearings that they have occupied, so that they can cease to be slaves. But if you cannot grant this, at least allow them to depart and find a home elsewhere in peace and goodwill.

When Pandrasus learned the contents of this letter, he was astonished that his former slaves should be so bold as to address such a message to him. He summoned a council of his nobles, and ordered that an army should be raised in order to hunt the Trojans down. But while he was searching the wildernesses where he supposed them to be, Brutus sallied out of the stronghold of Sparatinum with three thousand men, and suddenly attacked him when the king was expecting nothing of the kind. Hearing of the king's arrival, Brutus had occupied the stronghold the night before, so that he might make a sudden attack on them when they were unarmed and not in marching order. The Trojans charged the royal troops and attacked them stoutly; the Greeks, taken by surprise, scattered in all directions and retreated in disorder, the king at their head, to get safely across the nearby river Akalon. But in fording it they encountered strong currents: Brutus caught up with them and massacred them, some in the river and others on the banks. Those he did not kill were drowned.

When Antigonus, the brother of Pandrasus, saw this, he was in despair, and as soon as he could regroup his straggling comrades, he returned and charged the Trojans. For he preferred to die fighting rather than take to his heels, only to be drowned in the muddy whirlpools of the river. With his men in a solid battalion, he urged his comrades to resist like men and hurl back the deadly weapons with all their might. But it did him little good, for the Trojans were fully armed, while they lacked protection. This advantage made the Trojans attack all the more boldly, inflicting heavy losses on the Greeks, until they had killed almost all of them, and Antigonus and his comrade Anacletus had been taken captive.

When Brutus had won this victory, he garrisoned the stronghold with six hundred men and then sought out the recesses of the forest where the Trojan people were expecting his protection. But Pandrasus, much

troubled by his own flight and the capture of his brother, spent the night
in getting his scattered forces together again, and when the next morning
dawned, he marched with his reassembled people to besiege the stronghold. For he thought that Brutus was back in the fortress together with
Antigonus and the other prisoners. When he arrived in front of the walls,
he examined the situation of the castle, and distributed his army in companies, and placed them in various positions around it. Some men were
detailed to prevent any of the occupants from getting out; others were
sent to divert the course of the rivers, and others again were ordered to
shatter the fabric of the walls with a multitude of battering-rams and
other engines .

They all obeyed his orders to the best of their endeavours, trying different ways of harassing the besieged. At nightfall they chose the boldest
of their number to keep guard over the camp and tents against any
stealthy attack of the enemy, while the rest, worn out with labour and
fatigue, refreshed themselves with uninterrupted sleep.

The besieged, on the other hand, standing on the top of the walls,
tried with all their strength to beat back the enemy onslaughts. They
mounted a spirited defence, flinging down missiles and torches of
flaming brimstone among them. When the wall was undermined by
sappers working under shelter of a siege machine called a 'tortoise', they
compelled the enemy to retreat by pouring Greek fire and boiling water
on them. But they suffered from a lack of food and the arduous work of
defending the city; so they sent a messenger to Brutus, begging him to
hasten to their assistance, for they feared that they might be forced to
surrender the fortress.

Brutus, although he was anxious to come to their aid, knew that he
did not have enough men to risk a pitched battle. He cleverly resolved to
attack the enemy's camp by night, to surprise the enemy by deceiving the
sentinels, and kill them as they slept. He knew this could only be done
with the assistance and assent of a Greek; so he summoned Anacletus,
Antigonus' comrade, and, unsheathing his sword, said to him:

'Noble youth, your own life and that of Antigonus are already at an
end, unless you faithfully agree to carry out my orders. Tonight I
intend to attack the Greek camp, take them by surprise and kill
them. But I am afraid that their sentinels will discover my secret
plot, and that the plan will fail. So, since we shall have to attack the
watch first of all, I want you to decoy them, so that I have a clear
passage for attacking the others. You will go, as warily as possible,
to the guard, at the second hour of the night, and allay their suspicions by saying that you have helped Antigonus to escape from my
dungeons, and that he is hidden in a valley in the forest, where he is
unable to get any further because you will say that he is still in

chains. Then you are to guide them to the edge of the forest as if to set him free; I will be there with a company of armed men ready to kill them.'

Anacletus, terrified all this time by the sight of the sword, which Brutus was holding ready to kill him as he spoke, promised on oath that he would execute this command as long as both he and Antigonus were spared. So the plot was agreed, and as it was already almost the second hour of the night, Anacletus set out towards the guard as he had been commanded. When at length he arrived near the camp, the sentinels on lookout duty ran up and asked him why he had come, and whether he was intending to betray the army? He pretended to be overjoyed, and replied: 'Truly, I do not come as a traitor to my own people; I have escaped from the prison of the Trojans and fled here; I beg you to come with me to help Antigonus, who I have rescued from the chains of Brutus. He is hindered by the weight of his shackles, and I have told him to lie hidden in the undergrowth on the edge of the forest until I can find someone who I can take to him to set him free.'

While they were still arguing as to whether he was telling the truth, an old acquaintance of his came up; he greeted him and told his comrades who he was. At this they hesitated no longer, but summoned the rest of the company who were a little way off to come as quickly as they could. They all followed him as far as the wood, where he had said that Antigonus was hiding. As they were making their way through the undergrowth, Brutus and his armed companies came out and charged them: his men soon inflicted a terrible slaughter on the panic-stricken guard. Then he marched on to the camp, dividing his comrades into three companies, and commanding that each should carefully and silently approach the enemy at a different point. Once they had gained entrance into the camp, they should refrain from killing anyone until such time as he and his bodyguard had taken possession of the king's pavilion, when he would blow his own horn as a signal for them.

So they quietly made their way into the camp, and, having carried out their orders, they awaited the promised signal. This was not long in coming, for Brutus gave it as soon as he was outside the tent of Pandrasus, which was the one he most wished to attack. When the signal was given, his men swiftly unsheathed their swords and rushed into the tents where the enemy was sleeping and laid about them with death-dealing blows.

In this way they went through the whole camp. The rest were woken at the groans of the dying, and were so dismayed by the sight of the killers that, like sheep suddenly attacked by wolves, they could do nothing. They could not protect themselves, since they did not even have enough time either to lay hands on their arms or to take flight. They could only run, unarmed as they were, to and fro amidst the enemy, who cut them to pieces. Anyone who escaped half-alive and hastened to take flight was thrown to the ground among the rocks and trees and brambles, and gave up the ghost in a pool of his own blood. Even those who had a shield or other protection, dropped down through fear of death among the same rocks, or fled through the darkness of the night, only to fall and break a leg or an arm. Anyone who escaped either of these disasters, not knowing which way to go, was drowned in the rushing waters of the neighbouring rivers, so that hardly a single one got away unharmed. The men within the fortress, when they knew of the arrival of Brutus and his men, made a sally and played their part in the slaughter.

When Brutus seized the royal tent, he was careful to bind the king and to keep him safe. For he knew that he could attain his object more readily by sparing the king's life than by his death. But his companions did not cease from the slaughter until they had cleared the camp and extermi-nated everyone in it. When dawn revealed how great a loss had been inflicted on Pandrasus's men, Brutus was overjoyed and gave permission to his comrades to deal as they pleased with the spoils of the slain. Then he entered the fortress with the king, and distributed the treasure. When that had been done, he put a new garrison in the castle and gave orders for the burial of the dead.

Then the valiant duke reassembled his troops and returned to the forest rejoicing in his victory. He summoned the elders and asked what they thought they should demand of Pandrasus. Now that he was in their power, he would grant anything they asked, provided he were allowed to go free. Some at once proposed one thing, and some another; one group exhorted him to ask for part of the kingdom as their own land; others said he should obtain leave to go elsewhere and make the king provide whatever might be of use to them on the journey. Seeing that after a long while they still hesitated, a man called Mempricius stood up and asked for silence; then he addressed them as follows:

'Why do you all hesitate about the best course of action? There is only one thing we should ask for, if you want you and your children to have lasting peace, and that is leave to depart. For if you grant Pandrasus his life in return for part of Greece, and live in the midst of the Danai, you will never enjoy an enduring peace so long as the brothers and sons and grandsons of the men who you killed yester-day live among you or are your next-door neighbours. As long as they remember the killing of their kinsmen they will always hate you, and will use the least excuse to get revenge. Because there are fewer of you, you will not be strong enough to resist their attacks, for if it comes to war, their numbers will increase and yours will dwindle. So ask Pandrasus for his eldest daughter Ignoge as a wife for our duke, and, along with her, gold and silver, ships and corn, and whatever else may be needed for our voyage. If he will grant this, we will then with his leave depart to seek out other lands.'

When he finished his speech, the whole assembly applauded him. It was agreed that Pandrasus should be brought before them, and that, if he did not grant their request, he should be condemned to the cruellest possible death. They did not delay but went to fetch him and tied him to a chair on a scaffold. He was told what tortures he would suffer if he refused to accede to their demands, to which he replied:

'Since the gods are against me, and have delivered me and my brother Antigonus into your hands, I must grant your petition. If I refuse you will kill me. Every man treasures his life, so it is no wonder that I should be willing to ransom it at the price of my goods and possessions. Reluctantly, therefore, I will obey your orders. It is some comfort that I will be giving my daughter to a young man of such prowess, whose nobility and fame make him a worthy scion of the house of Priam and Anchises. Only he could have delivered the exiles of Troy, enslaved by such mighty princes, from their chains; only he could have urged them to successful resistance against the nation of the Greeks; only he would have challenged such a host of armed warriors with so few men, and at the first attack have led away their king in fetters. But since this noble youth has conquered me, I give him my daughter Ignoge, together with gold and silver, ships, corn, wine and oil, and whatever is needed for your journey. And if you should change your mind, and decide to live here with the Greeks, I will give you one third of my kingdom as your own land. To assure you that this will be carried out, I will remain hostage until I have done everything I have pledged to do.'

Once this was agreed, messengers were sent to gather ships together from all the shores of Greece; three hundred and twenty-four, laden with provision of all sorts, formed the fleet which was presented to Brutus. The king's daughter was married to Brutus, and each man, according to his rank, was presented with gold and silver. When all his promises were fulfilled, the king was set free from prison; and at the same time the Trojans departed from his lands with a favourable wind. But Ignoge, standing on the lofty poop of the ship, fell fainting again and again into the arms of Brutus, sobbing and weeping as she left her family and her country; she would not look away from the shore for as long as it was in sight. Brutus soothed her with gentle words, taking her in his arms, or softly kissing her; nor did he stop trying to comfort her until, weary with weeping, at last she fell asleep.

The ships sailed on for two days and a night, running before a following wind, until at length they came to a certain island called Leogecia, which had been uninhabited ever since it was laid waste by pirates many years before. Brutus, not knowing this, sent three hundred men inland to discover if there were any inhabitants. His men, finding not a soul, killed the deer that they found in the meadows and the forests. They came to a deserted city, and there they found a temple of Diana, in which was an image of the goddess, and an inscription which said that the statue responded to questions which the worshippers asked of it. At last they returned to their ships, laden with the venison they had found, and told their comrades the lie of the land and the situation of the city. They suggested to the duke that he should go to the temple and, after making offerings to propitiate the goddess, should ask her what land she would grant them as a permanent home. It was agreed that Brutus should take Gerion the augur and twelve of the elders with him, and should go to the temple, taking everything necessary for making sacrifice. When they arrived they put on garlands and, according to immemorial custom, set up three altars before the holy place, to the three Gods, Jove and Mercury and Diana, making a special libation to each deity. Brutus himself, holding in his right hand a vessel full of sacrificial wine and the blood of a white hind before the altar of the goddess, looked up at her image, and spoke as follows:

> 'Goddess and forest queen, the wild boar's terror,
> Thou who the maze of heaven or nether mansions
> Walketh at will, vouchsafe thy speech to earth-bound men!
> Say in what lands thou willest us to dwell?
> What sure abode? Lo, there to thee for ever
> Temples I vow, and chant of holy maidens!'

After he had repeated this nine times, he walked four times round the altar, poured wine on the hearth of offering, and lay down upon the skin of a hind that he had stretched in front of the altar, where he fell asleep. At the third hour of the night, when men are visited by the sweetest sleep, it seemed that the goddess stood there before him, and spoke to him, saying:

> 'Brutus – past the realms of Gaul, beneath the sunset
> There lies an island, surrounded by the sea,
> Guarded by ocean – once the haunt of giants,
> Desert of late and fit for this thy people.
> Seek it ! For there is your abode for ever.
> There by your sons again shall Troy be builded;
> There of your blood shall kings be born hereafter
> Sovereign in every land the wide world over.'

On awakening from this vision, the duke was not sure whether it was a dream that he had seen, or whether it was the living goddess herself who had prophesied to him about the land he should seek. At last he called his companions and told them everything that had happened to him in his sleep. They were exceedingly joyful at this news, and advised that they should return to their ships at once, and, while the wind was still blowing fair, should get under way as quickly as possible, setting full sail for the west in search of the land which the goddess had promised.

So they rejoined their comrades and launched out into the deep, and after ploughing the waves for a run of thirty days, made the coast of Africa, still not knowing in which direction to steer their ships. They came to the altars of the Phileni, near the saltpans, and steered from there between Ruscicada and the Azarae mountains, where they were attacked by pirates. But they won the battle, and went on their way enriched by the spoil and plunder they had taken. They passed the mouth of the river Malva, and arrived in Mauritania, where lack of food and drink compelled them to disembark. Dividing themselves into companies, they ravaged the whole region from end to end.

When they had revictualled their ships, they set sail for the Pillars of Hercules, where they saw many of the monsters of the deep known as sirens, which surrounded the ships and almost overwhelmed them. But they managed to escape, and came to the Tyrrhenian sea, where they found near the shore four generations born of the exiles from Troy, who had accompanied Antenor when he fled from the city. Their duke was called Corineus, a sober-minded man, excellent in counsel, mighty in body, valour and endurance; if he had to deal with a giant in single combat he would throw him at once as if he were wrestling with a boy. When they discovered from whom he was descended, they took him into their company, as well as the people of whom he was chieftain. They became known as Cornishmen, after the name of their duke. He was more help to Brutus in the battles that followed than any of the others.

So they came to Aquitaine and sailed into the mouth of the Loire, where they cast anchor; and there they stayed for seven days and explored the lie of the land. Goffarius Pictus was king of Aquitaine at that time, and, when he heard rumours of a foreign people who had come with a great fleet and had landed within his domains, he sent messengers to ask whether they came as friends or enemies. While the messengers were on their way to the fleet, they met Corineus who had just landed with two hundred men to hunt for venison in the forest. They stopped him and asked him by whose leave he was trespassing in the king's forest to slay his deer. Corineus replied that he needed neither leave nor license, at which one of them, Imbert by name, rushed forward, and, drawing his bow, aimed an arrow at him. Corineus avoided the arrow, rushed at Imbert as fast as he could, and with the bow that he carried broke his skull. Thereupon the rest fled, only just managing to escape from Corineus, and reported Imbert's death to Goffarius. The king took this as a great insult, and at once assembled a great army to take vengeance on them for the death of his messenger.

Brutus, hearing news of his coming, set guards on his ships, and told the women and children to remain on board, while he himself and his whole army marched to meet the enemy. When the engagement at last began the fighting was fierce on both sides; but after most of the day had been spent in battle, the Trojans had still not gained the upper hand, and the men of Aquitaine held their ground stoutly. Corineus thought this a shame and, calling his own men to form up to one side on the right of the battle, he charged the enemy. When, with his men in close order, he had broken the front ranks, he did not cease to strike down the enemy till he had cut his way right through the battalion and forced them all to flee. He had lost his sword, but had luckily picked up a battle-axe, with which he cut in two any of the enemy that came near him, from the crown of their head down to the waist. Both Brutus and his comrades were amazed at the boldness and courage of the man, who, brandishing his battle-axe among the enemy army as they fled, terrified them by shouting, 'Where are you running away to, cowards? Turn round and fight Corineus! Shame on you! Thousands of you are running away from me alone? Run away, then; if it is any comfort, you are escaping from a man who has often put the Tyrrhene giants to flight, and has hurled them to hell three or four at a time!'

At these words, an earl named Subardus turned round with three hundred men and charged him. But Corineus raised his shield to ward off their blows, and lifting his battle-axe above his head, he struck the earl on the top of his helmet and cut him completely in two. After this, he rushed into the throng, whirling his axe and slaughtering the enemy in his rage. Rushing to and fro, he struck down the enemy on all sides without receiving a single blow himself. He cut off one man's hand and arm; the next had his shoulders cut from his body; another's head he struck off at a single blow, another's legs were severed at the thigh.

Brutus saw all this and hurried forward with a company to help him. Both armies shouted their war-cries, and the fighting was redoubled, with many casualties on both sides. But it did not last long. The Trojans won the day, and drove king Goffarius and the Poitevins in flight before them. Goffarius, escaping by the skin of his teeth, retreated to Gaul to seek help from his kinsfolk and friends. At that time there were twelve kings in Gaul, each of equal rank, who ruled the whole country. They all received him kindly, and with one accord promised to drive out this foreign race that had arrived on the frontiers of Aquitaine.

Brutus, overjoyed by his victory, enriched his comrades with the spoils of the slain. Then he formed up the army in marching order, and led his host inland with the intention of sacking the whole country and loading his ships with countless treasure. He burnt cities in all directions, fire after fire, and ransacked their hidden hoards. Even the fields were laid waste, and townsmen and countrymen alike were slaughtered, his aim being to exterminate the unhappy race to the last man. But after he had made his bloodthirsty way across almost the whole of Aquitaine, he came to the place where the city of Tours now stands. He examined the lie of the land carefully, and, as the place offered good protection, he decided to pitch his camp there, in case he needed to retreat to a safe place. He was very concerned by the arrival of Goffarius, who had marched into the neighbourhood along with the kings and princes of Gaul and a huge army, in the hope of challenging him to a battle. When his encampment was completed, he waited there for Goffarius for two days, confident alike in his own tactics and in the courage of the young men whom he led.

Now, when Goffarius heard where the Trojans were, he advanced by forced marches day and night until he was in sight of Brutus's camp. He looked on it with a grim smile, and exclaimed: 'Fate has dealt us a grievous blow, by sending these brutal exiles to pitch their camp in my lands. To arms, men, to arms, and charge through their ranks! We will soon take these brutes like sheep, and keep them in our kingdom as slaves!'

At once, all the men who had come with him armed themselves, and marched upon their enemies in twelve battalions. But Brutus was a match for them; he carefully instructed his troops as to what they were to do, how to advance, and in what order to hold their ground; then he gave the word to charge. At the first onset, the Trojans for a time had the upper hand and made a fearful slaughter of the enemy: nearly two thousand of them fell, and the rest were so daunted at the sight that they almost turned to flee. But victory is often on the side of the greater number. In this case, because there were three times as many of them, the Gauls, despite being beaten back at first, were able to form up again and charge the Trojans from every side. In the end, after much bloodshed, they compelled the Trojans to take refuge in their camp. After this victory, they besieged them in the camp, expecting them either to surrender, or suffer a cruel and lingering death from the pangs of hunger.

But the next night Corineus and Brutus took counsel, and Corineus suggested that he should leave the camp that same night by secret paths, and should hide in the neighbouring forest until daybreak. Brutus was to make a foray just before dawn and engage the enemy in battle, while Corineus and his companions were to attack them in the rear, and put them to the sword. Brutus approved this plan and Corineus cautiously left the camp, as he had proposed, with three thousand men, making his way into the depths of the forest. So at daybreak the next morning Brutus drew up his men in companies, and, opening the gates of the camp, marched into battle. The Gauls at once drew up their men to resist him, and soon came to close quarters with him. Many thousands of men were at once cut down on both sides, and many were the wounds given and received, for not a man spared his adversary.

A certain Trojan happened to be present, a nephew of Brutus named Turnus. No one was braver than him, except Corineus himself; his sword alone killed no less than six hundred men. Unhappily he himself was killed before his time by a surprise attack by the Gauls; and the city of Tours was so called because he was buried there. While the troops on both sides were in the heat of battle, Corineus suddenly charged the enemy at the double in the rear. The rest of the Trojans renewed the attack more fiercely against the enemy front, and did their utmost to complete the slaughter.

The Gauls were in dismay as soon as they heard the war-cry of Corineus's men as they charged in on the rear, and, thinking that there were more of them than there really were, fled hot-foot from the field. The Trojans followed on their heels, cutting them down as they fled, and pursuing them until the victory was theirs. Brutus, although glad of such a victory, was nevertheless very anxious on one account: he saw that, while his army grew less and less each day, that of the Gauls was increasing. So, seeing it was doubtful whether he could hold out against them any longer, he preferred to retreat to his ships while the greater part of his army was still intact and the glory of the victory was still fresh. He decided to set sail in quest of the island which the oracle of Diana had prophesied should be his own. Nor was there any delay; with the assent of his men, he returned to his fleet, and, after loading his ships with all the treasures he had acquired, he re-embarked. The wind was favourable, and he reached at last the promised island, where he landed in safety at Totnes.

At that time the island was called Albion, and was only inhabited by a few giants. The pleasant aspect of the land, the abundance of fish in its rivers and deer in its forests filled Brutus and his companions with the desire to settle there. So, after exploring part of the land, they drove the giants they found there to take refuge in mountain caves, and divided the country among them by casting lots. They began to till the fields and build houses, so that in a little while you might have thought it had been inhabited from time immemorial. Then Brutus called the island Britain, and his companions Britons, after his own name, in order to perpetuate his memory. Thus the language of the country, which used to be called Trojan or crooked Greek, was later called British.

But, following Brutus's example, Corineus named that share of the kingdom which had fallen to him by lot, Cornwall, from his own name, and the people Cornishmen. For although he might have had the first choice of any province, he preferred to have that part of the land which is now called Cornwall either because it is the *cornu* or horn of Britain, or from a corruption of the name Corineus. For nothing gave him greater pleasure than to wrestle with the giants, and there were more of them in Cornwall than in any of the provinces that had been shared amongst his comrades.

Among the giants was a certain hateful one, by name Gogmagog, twelve cubits in height, whose strength was such that he would wield an oak tree that he had torn up by the roots as lightly as if it were a hazel twig. One day when Brutus was holding a festival in honour of the gods in the port where he had first landed, this one, along with a score of other giants, fell on his men and killed many of them. But the British regrouped and summoned reinforcements, so that they won the day, killing them all, except Gogmagog. Brutus had commanded him to be kept alive, because he wanted to see a wrestling bout between the giant and Corineus, who was extremely keen to match himself against such monsters.

Corineus, overjoyed at the prospect, prepared himself for the encounter, and taking off his armour, challenged him to wrestle. At the start, Corineus and the giant each hugged the other tight in an armlock, making the air quake with their breathless gasping. It was not long before Gogmagog, clasping Corineus with all his strength, broke three of his ribs, two on the right side and one on the left. This infuriated Corineus, who gathered up all his strength, heaved the giant up on his shoulders and ran with his burden as fast as he could, considering the weight, to the nearest shore. He climbed to the top of a high cliff and, disengaging himself, hurled the deadly monster into the sea, where, falling on the sharp rocks, he was broken in pieces and dyed the waves with his blood: that place has ever since been known as Lamgogmagog, that is, Gogmagog's Leap.

When he had surveyed his kingdom, Brutus decided to build a capital city, and went round the whole of the land in search of a fitting site. When he came to the river Thames, he walked along the banks till he found the place best suited to his purpose. Here he founded his city and called it New Troy; and it was known by this name for many centuries thereafter, until at last, by corruption of the word, it came to be called Trinovantium. But afterwards, Lud, the brother of Cassibelaunus, who fought with Julius Caesar, seized the kingdom and surrounded the city with noble walls and cunningly built towers, commanding that it should be called Caerlud, that is, the City of Lud, after his own name. For this reason a quarrel arose between him and his brother Nennius, who did not like the idea that he should do away with the name of Troy in his own country.

6. KING LEAR

The story of Lear is first told in Geoffrey of Monmouth's History of the Kings of Britain, *and has been called Geoffrey's most original contribution to British legends. There is now no trace of a Welsh original, and the motif of the ungrateful and grateful daughters is a well-established one in the world of folktales. The only identifiable Welsh connection is with Llyr, the father of Branwen in Welsh stories, whose name may mean 'seafarer'; but Geoffrey may have had in mind another character, Leir, the supposed founder of Leicester, who is equally shadowy.*

THEN Bladud succeeded to the throne, and the kingdom remained in his hands for twenty years. He built the city of Caerbadon, now called Bath, and made the hot baths there which he placed under the guardianship of the goddess Minerva. He set fires in her temple that could not be quenched and never turned into ashes, but as they began to fail became like round balls of stone. Bladud was a cunning craftsman, and taught the magic arts throughout the realm of Britain. Nor did he cease his spells until he tried to mount up in the air on wings which he had fashioned: he fell on to the temple of Apollo in the city of Trinovantium, and was dashed to pieces.

After Bladud had thus met his fate, his son Lear became king and ruled the country with a firm hand for sixty years. He built the city on the river Soar, called Caerleir by the Britons; though the Saxons know it as Leicester. He had no sons, his only children being three daughters named Goneril, Regan and Cordelia. He loved them all greatly, but he was most fond of the youngest, Cordelia. When he was growing old, he wanted to divide his kingdom among them, and marry them to husbands who were worthy of them and fit to rule their share of the kingdom. But in order to decide which of them deserved the largest share, he needed to discover which of them loved him most.

When he asked Goneril how much she loved him, she swore by all the gods of heaven that her father was dearer to her than her own soul. At this, her father replied: 'Because you have set me, in my old age, before your own life, my dearest daughter, I will marry you to whoever you choose, and will give you one third of Britain.'

Then he turned to his second daughter, Regan. She, eager to follow her sister's example and to persuade her father to treat her as kindly, replied to his question by swearing that she loved him better than any one else in the world. Her father believed her, and made the same promise to her as he had done to her elder sister.

But the last, Cordelia, when she saw how her father had been deceived by the flatteries of her sisters, decided to see if she could bring him to his senses. So her reply to his question was this: 'Father, is there a daughter anywhere who would presume to love her father more than as a father? Unless they were speaking in jest, I do not believe there is anyone who would pretend otherwise. As far as I am concerned, I have always loved you as a father, and will always do so. You want me to say more, but listen to the true measure of my love. This is my answer: just as you are worth whatever you possess, so I love you for what you are.'

Her father, thinking that she really meant exactly what she said, was very angry with her and at once declared: 'Since you despise me in my old age, and do not begin to love me as your sisters love me, I shall reward you accordingly: you shall never share the kingdom with your sisters. But since you are my daughter, the least I can do is to find you a stranger from some other country who will marry you – if such a man exists. But be assured I shall not trouble to marry you in the same honourable style as your sisters. Until now I have loved you better than the others; but it seems that you love me less than they do.' So, taking the advice of his nobles, Lear married the two elder sisters to the dukes of Cornwall and Albany, and gave them half the kingdom between them during his lifetime, and the whole of it after his death.

Now it so happened that about this time Aganippus, king of the Franks, hearing of Cordelia's beauty, sent ambassadors to the king, to ask for her hand in marriage. Her father was still angry with her and replied that he would be prepared to grant his request, but that he would not give her any dowry, since he had shared his kingdom along with all his possessions between Cordelia's sisters, Goneril and Regan. Aganippus was so in love with the girl that when this reply was brought to him, he sent a message back to Lear saying that, as ruler of a third of Gaul, he had possessions enough, and that he would be happy to marry her without a dowry; their sons would inherit his lands. Thus the bargain was struck, and Cordelia was sent to Gaul to be married to Aganippus.

A long while after this, as Lear grew old, the two dukes who had married his daughters and with whom he had divided Britain, rebelled against him and stripped him of crown and kingdom, bringing his glorious reign to an inglorious close. In the end a truce was reached, and one of his sons-in-law, Maglaunus, duke of Albany, agreed to maintain him with a household of sixty knights, so that he could live in reasonable state. But after he had lived with his son-in-law for two years, his daughter Goneril grew angry at the number of his knights, who taunted her servants because she did not give them adequate food. So she talked to her husband, and ordered her father to be content with thirty knights in his service: he was to dismiss the other thirty.

At this, the king was furious, and, leaving Maglaunus, he turned to Henvin, duke of Cornwall, who had married his other daughter. At first he was received with honour, but within the year disagreements had arisen between the men of the king's household and those of the duke's; and Regan angrily ordered her father to dismiss all his companions except for five knights. Her father could not bear this insult and returned to his eldest daughter, hoping that she would take pity on him and support him and his retinue. But she was just as angry and determined as she had been before he left, and swore by all the gods of heaven that she would never take him in unless he contented himself with the service of a single knight and dismissed all the rest. Moreover she berated the old man, saying that if he had nothing he could call his own, he should not expect to go about with such a retinue.

Lear realised that she would not give way to his wishes in any way whatsoever; so he was forced to obey, and was left with one knight only, dismissing the rest. But when he remembered how he used to be honoured, and compared that with the miserable state in which he now found himself, he began to think of going overseas, to the court of his youngest daughter. He was not at all sure that she would do anything for him, seeing that he had treated her so dishonourably over her marriage; nevertheless, rather than live so mean an existence any longer, he set out across the Channel to Gaul. But when he found that two other princes were making the passage at the same time, and that he was treated as their inferior, he broke down and wept, exclaiming:

'O implacable Fates, why did you ever raise me to such fleeting happiness? The memory of my past happiness is more painful than my present suffering. Those were the days, when I led thousands of warriors and went to throw down the walls of cities and to lay waste the provinces of my enemies. The memory of them hurts me more than the disasters that have overtaken me now, and my present humiliation. Even those who once grovelled at my feet have deserted me in my feebleness. O angry fortune! Will the day ever come when I can requite the evil turn that has driven me out in poverty at the end of my days? Cordelia, my daughter, how true was your answer when I asked you how much you loved me! You said that, just as you are worth whatever you possess, so I love you for what you are. As long as I had wealth to dispose of, I seemed worthy of honour to those who loved, not me, but my gifts. They loved me at times, but they loved the presents I gave them more. And now that there are no more presents, they too have vanished. But, dearest of my children, how shall I dare to appear before you – I who, angry with you for telling the truth, wanted to marry you less honourably than your sisters, who, after all the kindnesses I have done them, have allowed me to become an outcast and a beggar?'

Filled with these thoughts, he landed at last, and came to Karitia where his daughter lived. He did not enter the city, but waited outside and asked a messenger to tell her how he had fallen into poverty, and to beg for his daughter's compassion, since he had neither food nor clothing. On hearing the news, Cordelia was much moved and wept bitterly. When she asked how many knights he had with him, the messenger told her that he had no one except for a single knight, who was waiting with him outside the city. So she took as much gold and silver as was necessary and gave it to the messenger, telling him to take her father to another city and see that he was bathed, clothed and fed – pretending that he was a sick man. She also ordered that he should have a retinue of forty knights, well appointed and armed, and that when he was recovered, he should duly announce his arrival to Aganippus and herself. The messenger accompanied king Lear into another city, and kept him there in secret until he had carried out everything that Cordelia had commissioned him to do.

As soon as he had been dressed in his royal robes and provided with a train of retainers, he sent word to Aganippus and his daughter that he had been driven out of the realm of Britain by his sons-in-law, and had come to them to seek their help in recovering his kingdom. They and their great counsellors and nobles came out to receive him with all honour, and made him regent of the whole of Gaul until such time as they had restored him to his kingdom.

In the meanwhile, Aganippus sent messengers throughout the whole of Gaul to summon every knight who could bear arms to help him to recover the kingdom of Britain for his father-in-law, king Lear. When everything was ready, Lear, together with Aganippus and his daughter, led the assembled army into Britain, where he fought a battle with his sons-in-law and defeated them. He took all their lands under his own rule. Three years later, both he and Aganippus died. Cordelia, now queen of Britain, buried her father in a certain underground chamber which she had had made under the river Soar at Leicester. This underground chamber was founded in honour of Janus, the two-faced god of the end and beginning of the year; when the annual festival came round, all the workmen of the city began on that day whatever project was to occupy them for the rest of the year.

Now, when Cordelia had governed the kingdom in peace for five years, Margan, son of Maglaunus, and Cunedag, son of Henvin, two sons of her sisters, began to harass her; they were both of them ambitious and able young men, who had succeeded to their fathers' dukedoms when Maglaunus and Henvin died. They took it ill that Britain should be subject to the rule of a woman, so they assembled an army and rebelled against the queen. This outrage continued until they had laid waste a number of provinces, and had defeated her in several battles. At last they captured her and put her in prison: there, overwhelmed with grief for the loss of her kingdom, she killed herself.

7. LLUDD AND LLEFELYS

This story of the three great plagues of the island of Britain is one of the rare surviving examples of a complete tale of the kind memorised by Welsh bards in the so-called triads – collections of headings by which they remembered and linked their stories. A typical triad reads:

Three Harmful Blows of the Island of Britain:

The first of them Matholwch the Irishman struck upon Branwen, daughter of Llyr;

The second Gwenhwyfach struck upon Gwenhwyfar; and for that cause there took place afterwards the Action of the Battle of Camlan;

And the third Golydan the Poet struck upon Cadwalladr the Blessed.

This aide-memoire may have acted as a prologue, and could lead to a recital of one, or all three, of the stories. In the present case, the motif of the three plagues is contained within a single tale: the episode of the dragons is reminiscent of the story of Vortigern's tower in Geoffrey of Monmouth's **History of the Kings of Britain,** *(see page 60), where Merlin shows that the reason a tower cannot be built is that there are two dragons asleep under the foundations.*

BELI the Great, the son of Manogan, had three sons, Lludd, and Caswallawn, and Nynyaw; and according to the story he had a fourth son called Llefelys. And after the death of Beli, the kingdom of the island of Britain fell into the hands of Lludd his eldest son; and Lludd ruled prosperously. He rebuilt the walls of London, and surrounded it with countless towers; he ordered the citizens to build houses in it, such as no houses in the kingdom could equal. Moreover he was a mighty warrior, and generous and liberal in giving meat and drink to all who asked. Though he had many castles and cities, he loved this city more than any other. And he lived there for most of the year; so it was called Caer Lludd, and at last Caer Lundein. And after the stranger-race came and took it, it was called Lundein, or Lwndrys.

Lludd loved Llefelys best out of all his brothers, because he was a wise and discreet man. Having heard that the king of France had died leaving no heir except a daughter, and that he had left all his possessions in her hands, Llefelys came to Lludd to ask for his counsel and aid, suggesting that he might go to France to woo the girl for his wife, not so much for his own welfare, as to seek to add to the glory and honour and dignity of his family. His brother discussed it with him and the plan pleased him.

So Llefelys prepared ships, filled them with armed knights and set out for France. As soon as they had landed they sent messengers to inform the nobles of France of the reason for the embassy, and by the joint counsel of the nobles of France and of the princes, the girl was given to Llefelys, and the crown of the kingdom with her. And from that day until the day he died, he ruled the land discreetly, and wisely, and happily.

After a time, three plagues fell on the island of Britain, the like of which no one had ever seen. The first of these plagues was a certain people who arrived called the Coranians: so great was their knowledge, that there was no conversation on the island, however low it might be spoken, which, if the wind met it, was not known to them. And because of this they could not be harmed.

The second plague was a shriek which was heard on every May eve over every hearth in the island of Britain. And this fell on people's hearts and so terrified them that the men lost their colour and their strength, and the women their children, and the young men and the girls lost their senses, and all the animals and trees and the earth and the waters were left barren.

The third plague was that however much food and provisions might be prepared in the king's courts, even if it was as much as a year's provision of meat and drink, none of it could ever be found except what was eaten on the first night. And because no one could perceive the cause of two of these plagues, it seemed that there was better hope of being freed from the first than from the second and third.

At this king Lludd felt great sorrow and care, because he did not know how these plagues might be brought to an end. He called all the nobles of his kingdom to him and asked their advice as to what should be done against these afflictions. And by the common counsel of the nobles, Lludd, the son of Beli, went to Llefelys, his brother, king of France, to seek his advice, for he was a man of great wisdom.

They prepared a fleet, in secret and in silence, lest the Coranians should know the cause of their errand – or indeed anyone besides the king and his counsellors. And when they were ready, Lludd and his chosen companions went aboard their ships, and they began to sail towards France. When this news came to Llefelys, he set out from the other shore to meet him, with a vast fleet, since he did not know the cause of his brother's sailing. Lludd, seeing this, left all his ships at sea except for one in which he went to meet his brother. Llefelys likewise came to meet him with a single ship, and when they met, each put his arms about the other's neck, and they welcomed each other with brotherly love.

After Lludd had explained to his brother the cause of his errand, Llefelys said that he already knew why he had come to those lands. And they discussed how they might talk together in some other way, lest the wind were to catch their words and the Coranians discover what they had said. Then Llefelys had a long horn made out of brass, and they talked through this horn. But whatever words they spoke through this horn, neither could hear anything but harsh and hostile words. And when Llefelys saw this, he realised that there was a demon thwarting and disturbing them in this horn, so he had wine poured in to wash it out; and through the virtue of the wine the demon was driven out of the horn.

When they could talk without hindrance, Llefelys told his brother that he would give him some insects. Some he was to keep to breed, in case the same affliction came a second time. And the rest of these insects he should take and crush in water. This water, said Llefelys, would have power to destroy the race of the Coranians: when Lludd came home to his kingdom he should call together all the people both of his own race and of the race of the Coranians for a conference, as if he intended to make peace between them; and when they were all together, he should take this magic water and cast it over all alike. And he assured him that the water would poison the race of the Coranians but that it would not kill or harm those of his own race.

'As for the second plague in your lands,' he said, 'it is a dragon: another dragon of a foreign race is fighting with it, and trying to overcome it. And so your dragon makes a fearful outcry. You can prove this in the following way. After you have returned home, see that the island be measured, its length and breadth, and in the place where you find the exact central point, have a pit dug there, and have a cauldron full of the best mead that can be made put in the pit, with a covering of satin over the mouth of the cauldron. You yourself must keep watch there, and you will see the dragons fighting in the form of monstrous animals. At length they will take the form of dragons in the air. And in the end, worn out with fierce and furious fighting, they will fall in the form of two pigs on the silk covering, and they will sink in, and the covering with them, and they will draw it down to the very bottom of the cauldron. They will drink up all the mead, and after that they will sleep. You must at once fold the covering around them, and bury them in a stone coffin in the strongest place you have in your kingdom, and hide them in the earth. And as long as they stay in that strong place no plague shall come to the island of Britain from elsewhere.'

'The cause of the third plague', he said, 'is a mighty man of magic, who takes your meat and your drink and your provisions. And he puts everyone to sleep through illusions and charms. So you yourself must keep watch over your food and your provisions. And in case he should overcome you with sleep, have a cauldron of cold water by your side, and when you are oppressed with sleep, plunge into the cauldron.'

Then Lludd returned to his land. And he at once summoned the whole of his own race and of the Coranians. And as Llefelys had instructed him, he bruised the insects in water and cast the water over all

who were gathered there; and it destroyed the whole tribe of the Coranians, without harming any of the Britons. Then Lludd had the island
measured, both its length and its breadth. And in Oxford he found the
central point, and there he had a pit dug in the earth, and set in that pit a
cauldron full of the best mead that could be made, with a covering of
satin over the face of it. And he himself kept watch that night, and saw
the dragons fighting. And when they were weary they fell, and came
down upon the top of the satin, and drew it with them to the bottom of
the cauldron. And when they had drunk the mead they slept. And in
their sleep, Lludd folded the covering around them, and in the securest
place he had in Snowdon, he hid them in a stone coffin: after that this
spot was called Dinas Emreis, but before it, Dinas Ffaraon. And so the
fierce outcry ceased in his lands.

When this was accomplished, king Lludd had an huge banquet
prepared. And when it was ready he placed a vessel of cold water by his
side, and he himself kept watch. And as he sat there in his armour, some
time after midnight, he heard many voices and music, and various songs,
which made him drowsy and urged him to sleep. In case he should be
prevented from doing what he intended because he had fallen asleep, he
went several times into the water; and at last, a man of vast size, clad in
strong, heavy armour, came in, bearing a hamper. And, as was his
custom, he put all the food and provisions of meat and drink into the
hamper, and was about to leave, taking it with him. And nothing amazed
Lludd more than the amount which the hamper held.

And king Lludd went after him and called: 'Stop, stop, though you
have robbed me in the past and done me much harm, you shall not do so
any more, unless your skill in arms and your prowess are greater than
mine.' Then the man instantly put down the hamper on the floor and
awaited his attack. And a fierce battle between them followed; glittering
sparks flew from their armour. At last Lludd grappled with him, and as
fate would have it, Lludd was victorious, throwing his oppressor and
holding him to the ground. Since the king had overcome him by strength
and might, the man begged for his mercy.

'How can I grant you mercy', said the king, 'after all the many injuries
and wrongs that you have done me?'

'All the losses that I have ever caused you', he said, 'I will make good,
to the amount that I have taken. And I will never do such deeds from
now on, but will be your faithful vassal.' And the king accepted this.

And so Lludd freed the island of Britain from the three plagues. From
then until the end of his life, Lludd, the son of Beli, ruled the island of
Britain in prosperous peace.

This tale is called the Story of Lludd and Llefelys; and this is its ending.

8. THE DREAM OF MAXEN WLEDIG

With this tale, probably written in Wales in the early twelfth century, we come across our first definitely historical character, the emperor Maximus, a Spaniard who was commander of the garrison in Britain, and who in AD 383 killed his predecessor Gratian. He ruled Gaul, Spain and Britain for some years, but failed in his attempt to conquer Italy and take Rome itself. Theodosius defeated him in 388. He lived on in British memory as the one emperor who had started his career in these islands. The city at the entrance of a river and the towers of various colours are said to be an echo of the walls of Byzantium, with their distinctive striped appearance. When Edward I came to build Caernarfon Castle, his architect imitated the pattern of the imperial walls. The theme of the story, the beloved seen in a dream, is a familiar one from folklore and literature. Helen of the Hosts was believed to be responsible for the building of the great Roman roads in Britain.

MAXEN Wledig was emperor of Rome, and he was more handsome, and a better and wiser ruler than any emperor before him. One day he held a council of kings, and he said to his friends, 'Tomorrow I wish to go hunting.' And on the morning of the next day he set out with his retinue, and came to the valley of the river that flowed towards Rome. And he hunted through the valley until midday. With him there were thirty-two crowned kings, who were his vassals, and the emperor did not go hunting for the pleasure of it, but so that he could meet the kings on equal terms.

The sun was high in the sky over their heads and the heat was great, and sleep overcame Maxen Wledig. His attendants stood around him and set up their shields upon the shafts of their spears to protect him from the sun: they placed a gold enamelled shield under his head, and so he slept.

And he had a dream. And this was his dream. He was journeying along the valley of the river towards its source; and he came to the highest mountain in the world, which seemed as high as the sky. When he came over the mountain it seemed to him that he went through the fairest and most level regions that man ever yet beheld. And he saw large and mighty rivers descending from the mountain to the sea; and he went towards the mouths of the rivers, until he came to the mouth of the largest river ever seen. There he beheld a great city, and a vast castle in the city, and he saw many high towers of various colours in the castle. He saw a fleet at the mouth of the river, the largest ever seen. And he saw one ship among the fleet, larger and fairer than all the others. What could be seen of the ship above the water had one plank gilded and the other silvered over. He saw a bridge made of the bone of a whale from the ship to the land, and he thought he went over the bridge and came into the ship. A sail was hoisted on the ship, and it was carried along the sea and out into the ocean.

Then it seemed that he came to the fairest island in the whole world, and he crossed the island from sea to sea, to its furthest shore. He saw valleys and cliffs and rocks of wondrous height, and rugged precipices, such as he had never seen before. And from that shore he beheld an island in the sea, facing this rugged land. Between him and this island was a country in which the plain was as large as the sea, the mountain as vast as the wood. From the mountain he saw a river that flowed through the land and fell into the sea. At the mouth of the river he beheld a castle, the fairest that man ever saw, and the gate of the castle was open, and he went in. In the castle he saw a fair hall, of which the roof seemed to be all gold; the walls of the hall seemed to be entirely of glittering precious gems, the doors seemed all to be of gold. Golden seats he saw in the hall, and silver tables. And on a seat opposite him he beheld two auburn-haired youths playing a board game, with a silver board, and golden pieces thereon. The youths were dressed in jet-black satin, and chaplets of red gold bound their hair, on which were sparkling jewels of great price – rubies, and gems, alternately with imperial stones. They had buskins of new Cordovan leather on their feet, fastened by slides of red gold.

And beside a pillar in the hall he saw a hoary-headed man, sitting in a chair of ivory, with the figures of two eagles in red gold thereon. Bracelets of gold were upon his arms, and many rings on his hands, and a golden torque about his neck; and his hair was bound with a golden diadem. He was of powerful aspect. A board of gold was before him, and a rod of gold, and a steel file in his hand. And he was carving out pieces for the game.

And he saw a girl sitting before him in a chair of red gold. Such was her beauty that it was as easy to gaze upon the sun at its brightest as to look upon her. She wore a vest of white silk, with clasps of red gold at the breast, and a surcoat of gold tissue, and a coronet of red gold upon her head, and rubies and gems were in the coronet, alternating with pearls and imperial stones. And her girdle was of red gold. She was the fairest sight that ever man beheld.

The girl rose from her chair before him, and he threw his arms about the neck of the girl, and they both sat down together in the chair of gold: and there was as much room in the chair for them both as for the girl alone. And as he had his arms about the girl's neck, and his cheek by her cheek, behold, through the chafing of the hounds at their leashes, and the clashing of the shields as they struck against each other, and the beating together of the shafts of the spears, and the neighing of the horses and their prancing, the emperor awoke.

And when he awoke, there was no life or spirit left in him, because of the girl whom he had seen in his sleep, for love of her pervaded his whole frame. His attendants said to him, 'Lord, is it not past the time for you to eat?' The emperor mounted his palfrey, the saddest man that mortal ever saw, and went on his way towards Rome.

And so he remained for the whole of the next week. When his household went to drink wine and mead out of golden vessels, he would not go with them. When they went to listen to songs and tales, he would not go there; nor could he be persuaded to do anything but sleep. And whenever he slept, he beheld in his dreams the girl he loved best; but he saw nothing of her except when he slept, for he had no idea where in the world she was.

One day the page of the chamber spoke to him; although he was page of the chamber, he was king of the Romans. 'Lord,' said he, 'all the people revile you.' 'Why do they revile me?' asked the emperor. 'Because they can get neither message nor answer from you, such as men should have from their lord. This is the reason why they speak evil of you.' 'Youth,' said the emperor, 'bring to me the wise men of Rome, and I will tell them why I am sorrowful.'

Then the wise men of Rome were brought to the emperor, and he addressed them. 'Sages of Rome,' he said, 'I have dreamt a dream. And in the dream I saw a girl, and because of the girl there is no life, nor spirit, nor existence within me.' 'Lord,' they answered, 'since you judge us worthy to counsel you, we will give you counsel. And this is our counsel; that you send messengers for three years to the three parts of the world to seek for your dream. And as you do not know what day or what night good news may come to you, the hope of it will support you.'

So the messengers journeyed for the space of a year, wandering about the world, and seeking news concerning his dream. But, when they came back at the end of the year, they were not one word wiser about it than on the day they set out. And then the emperor was exceedingly sorrowful, for he thought that he should never have word of her whom he loved best.

Then the king of the Romans said to the emperor: 'Lord,' said he, 'go forth to hunt by the way you seemed to go in your dream, whether it was to the east, or to the west.' So the emperor went hunting, and he came to the bank of the river: 'Look,' he said, 'this is where I was when I saw the dream, and I went westward towards the source of the river.'

And thereupon thirteen of the emperor's messengers set out, and before them they saw a high mountain, which seemed to them to touch the sky. And the messengers were dressed for their journey like this: one sleeve was on the cap of each of them in front, as a sign that they were messengers, so that no harm would be done them whatever hostile land they might pass through. And when they had come over this mountain they saw vast plains, and large rivers flowing through them. 'Look,' they said, 'the land which our master saw.'

And they went along the mouths of the rivers, until they came to the mighty river which they saw flowing to the sea, and the vast city, and the many-coloured high towers in the castle. In the harbour of the river, they saw the largest fleet in the world, and one ship that was larger than any of the others.

'Look, once more,' they said, 'the dream that our master saw.'

And in the great ship they crossed the sea, and came to the island of Britain. They crossed the island until they came to Snowdon.

'Look,' they said, 'the rugged land that our master saw.' They went on until they saw Anglesey before them, and Arfon as well.

'Look,' they said, 'the land our master saw in his sleep.'

And they saw Aber Sain, and a castle at the mouth of the river. They saw that the portal of the castle was open; into the castle they went, and they saw a hall in the castle.

Then they said, 'Look, the hall which he saw in his sleep.'

They went into the hall, and they saw two youths playing chess on the golden bench. And they saw the hoary-headed man beside the pillar in the ivory chair, carving chessmen. And they saw the girl sitting on a chair of red gold.

The messengers knelt before her. 'Empress of Rome, all hail!' 'Whoever you are,' said the girl, 'you look to me like honourable men, and bear the badge of envoys, so what mockery is this you do to me?' 'We do not mock you, lady; the emperor of Rome has seen you in his sleep, and he has neither life nor spirit left because of you. You shall have the choice, lady: you can come with us and be made empress of Rome, or the emperor can come here and take you for his wife.' 'Lords,' said the girl, 'I will not deny what you say, nor will I really believe it. If the emperor loves me, let him come here to seek me.'

So by day and by night the messengers hastened back; when their horses failed, they bought others which were fresh. When they came to Rome, they saluted the emperor, and asked for their reward, which was given to them, exactly as they requested. 'We will be your guides, lord,' they said, 'over sea and over land, to the place where you will find the woman whom you love best, for we know her name, and her family, and her race.'

Immediately the emperor set forth with his army, and these men were his guides. They went across the sea and the ocean towards the island of Britain. He conquered the island from Beli the son of Manogan, and his sons, and drove them to the sea, and advanced as far as Arfon. The emperor recognised the land when he saw it. And when he saw the castle of Aber Sain, 'Look there,' he said, 'that is the castle where I saw the girl whom I best love.' And he went forward into the castle and into the hall, and there he saw Kynan, the son of Eudav, and Adeon, the son of Eudav, playing a board game. And he saw Eudav, the son of Caradawc, sitting on a chair of ivory carving pieces for the game. And he saw the girl whom he had looked on in his sleep, sitting on a chair of gold. 'Empress of Rome,' he said, 'all hail!' And the emperor threw his arms about her neck; and that night she became his bride.

And the next day, in the morning, the girl asked for her bride portion. And he told her to name what she would. And for her father, she asked to have the island of Britain, from the Channel to the Irish Sea, together with the three adjacent islands, to hold under the empress of Rome; and to have three chief castles made for her, in whatever places she might choose in the island of Britain. And she chose to have the highest castle made at Arfon. And they brought thither earth from Rome that it might be more healthful for the emperor to sleep, and sit, and walk upon. After that the two other castles were made for her, which were Caerleon and Carmarthen.

And one day the emperor went to hunt at Carmarthen, and he came so far as the top of Y Frenni Fawr, and there the emperor pitched his tent. And that encampment is called Cadeir Maxen, Maxen's Camp, even to this day. And because he built the castle with a myriad men, he called it Caerfyrddin, the castle of thousands. Then Helen decided to make high roads from one castle to another throughout the island of Britain, and so it was done. This is why they are called the roads of Helen of the Hosts, because she was the daughter of a native of this island, and the men of the island of Britain would not have made these great roads for any save for her.

The emperor passed seven years in this island. Now, at that time, the men of Rome had a custom that if an emperor should remain in other lands more than seven years, he must stay there and should never return to Rome again.

So they made a new emperor. And this one wrote a threatening letter to Maxen. There was nothing in the letter but this: 'If you come, and if you ever come to Rome.' And this letter reached Maxen at Caerleon, with news of the new emperor. At this he sent a letter to the man who styled himself emperor in Rome. There was nothing in that letter either, but only: 'If I come to Rome, and if I come.'

At once Maxen set out towards Rome with his army, and vanquished France and Burgundy and all the lands on the way, and encamped before the city of Rome. The emperor spent a year before the city, and he was no nearer taking it than on the first day. And the brothers of Helen of the Hosts followed him from the island of Britain, and a small army with them, and the warriors in that small army were better than twice as many Romans. And the emperor was told that a host had been seen, which had halted close to his army and encamped; and no man ever saw a fairer or better appointed host for its size, nor more handsome standards.

And Helen went to see the hosts, and she knew the standards of her brothers. Then Kynan, the son of Eudav, and Adeon, the son of Eudav, came to meet the emperor. And the emperor was glad to see them, and embraced them. Then they looked at the Romans as they attacked the city.

Kynan said to his brother, 'We will try to attack the city more expertly than this.'

So they measured the height of the wall by night, and they set their carpenters to work, and a ladder was made for every four men of their number. Now when these were ready, every day at midday the emperors went to meat, and they ceased fighting on both sides till all had finished eating. And in the morning the men of Britain took their food and they drank until they were invigorated. And while the two emperors were at their midday meal, the Britons came to the city, and placed their ladders against it, and came straight into the city. The new emperor had no time to arm himself before they fell upon him, and slew him and many others with him. And it took them three nights and three days to subdue the men in the city and take the castle. Meanwhile some of them held the city, lest any of Maxen's army should enter before they had subjected all to their will.

Then Maxen said to Helen of the Hosts: 'I marvel, lady, that your brothers have not conquered this city for me.' 'Lord, emperor,' she answered, 'my brothers are the wisest youths in the world. Go and ask them for the city, and if they have it in their possession you shall have it gladly.' So the emperor and Helen went and asked for the city. And they told the emperor that no one had taken the city, and that no one could give it him, apart from the men of the island of Britain. Then the gates of the city of Rome were opened, and the emperor sat on the throne, and all the men of Rome submitted themselves to him.

Then the emperor said to Kynan and Adeon, 'Lords, I have now regained possession of the whole of my empire. I give you this host to vanquish whatever region you may desire in the world.' So they set forth and conquered lands, and castles, and cities. And they killed all the men, but the women they kept alive. And so they continued until the young men who had come with them were grown greyheaded, because they had been on their conquests for so long.

Then Kynan said to Adeon his brother, 'Would you rather stay in this land, or go back to the land from which you started?' Now Adeon chose to go back to his own land, and many with him. But Kynan stayed there with the others and lived there. And they took counsel and cut out the tongues of the women, lest they should corrupt their speech. And because the women were silenced, and the men spoke on, the men of

Llydaw or Brittany are called Britons. From that time there came frequently, and still come, men who speak that language to the island of Britain.

And this tale is called the Dream of Maxen Wledig, emperor of Rome. And here it ends.

9. HENGIST AND HORSA

Hengist and Horsa, the first leaders of the Saxon invaders, together with the British king Vortigern, first appear in the pages of Bede's History of the English Church and People *in the early eighth century, and again in the* Anglo-Saxon Chronicle, *where they figure as the founders of the Saxon kingdom of Kent. They may well have been historical figures; Bede, who had many friends in Kent, records that Horsa's monument was still visible in the east of Kent. The conquered Britons remembered them too, and in* The History of the Britons, *there are the beginnings of a legend, perhaps based on ancient tales, which recorded how Vortigern had invited them to help him in his wars with neighbouring kings, and how they had treacherously taken his kingdom. The love of Vortigern for the Saxon princess Rowena also appears in these pages, and the whole story has been described as 'good entertainment for Welshmen [which] helped to reconcile them to their defeat and provide a national scapegoat'. Geoffrey of Monmouth elaborates on it in his* History of the Kings of Britain, *and it is this version which follows.*

WHEN Constans became king, he entrusted Vortigern with the management of the kingdom, and took his advice in everything he did. Nothing was done unless Vortigern ordered it. Constans did this because he was completely at a loss, having learnt nothing at all about ruling a kingdom while he had been shut up in a monastery. Once Vortigern realised this, he began to think how he might become king instead of Constans. He had long harboured this ambition, and now he saw an opportunity for achieving his wish without too much difficulty for the whole kingdom was at his command, and Constans, although he was called king, was the merest shadow of a prince. He had no strength of purpose, nor the will to do justice. No one feared him, neither at home nor abroad. His brothers, Uther Pendragon and Aurelius Ambrosius, were not yet out of the cradle, and incapable of ruling the kingdom. Furthermore, as ill luck would have it, all the elder barons of the realm were dead, and Vortigern, politic and prudent, seemed the only counsellor of any weight. The rest were almost all mere youths, who had inherited their lands and titles when their fathers and uncles had been killed in the recent battles.

So Vortigern saw that fortune favoured him, and he plotted the easiest and most devious way of deposing Constans the monk and stepping into his shoes, while maintaining his good reputation. First, he decided to delay his plans until he had firmly established his power in the various parts of the kingdom and accustomed everyone to his rule. He began by demanding that the royal treasure should be put in his custody, and that he should have command of the cities and their garrisons, on the pretext

51

that there was talk of an imminent attack by the men of the Outer Isles. When this demand was granted, he put his own men in command of the cities, to hold them as his allies.

His next step in plotting his treason was to go to Constans and tell him that he needed to increase the number of his own household, to secure himself against the enemies that might invade.

Constans replied: 'Everything is at your command, as I have ordered. Do whatever you like, as long as your men swear allegiance to me.'

Vortigern answered: 'I have been informed that the Picts are planning to lead the Danes and Norwegians against us, to try to overwhelm us. So I propose, since it seems to me the safest course, that you should retain some of the Picts in your court who can act as go-betweens to bring us news from their fellow-countrymen outside. If it is true that they have already begun to rebel, they will keep us informed about any plots the Picts may hatch, so you can escape them.'

But Vortigern himself was the secret enemy and traitor; he gave Constans this advice not for his safety, but because he knew the Picts to be without conscience and easily lured into crime. When they were drunk or enraged, they could easily be encouraged to see the king as their enemy, and so murder him out of hand. If something of the kind should happen, the way to the throne, which he so much desired, would be open to him. So he sent messengers into Scotland, and invited a hundred Pictish soldiers to join the king's retinue.

Once they had arrived, he treated them as his favourites, showering gifts on them and feasting them to excess, so that they regarded him as their ruler. They would attend him in the streets singing songs in his praise, the gist of which was that Vortigern was worthy to rule over Britain, while Constans was not. Vortigern gave them more and more gifts to ensure their support, and when he had won the hearts of them all, he made them drunk, and told them that he was thinking of leaving Britain to seek his fortune, because his scanty allowance from the king was nothing like enough to keep fifty soldiers in his pay. Then, pretending that he was saddened by this, he made his way home without being noticed, and left them drinking in the hall.

When they saw this, the Picts, who believed what he had said, were furious, and began to say to each other: 'Why do we let this monk live? Why don't we kill Constans, so that Vortigern may succeed to the throne? No one else deserves to inherit the crown, and he is the best possible choice as king, because he is so liberal with his gifts to us!'

With this in mind, they burst into the king's sleeping-chamber and attacked Constans, cutting off his head, which they took to Vortigern. But Vortigern, when he saw it, burst into tears as if he was overcome with sorrow, though in fact he was secretly overjoyed. Calling together the citizens of London, where all this had happened, he ordered the Picts to be imprisoned in chains as traitors, and then had them beheaded for such a heinous crime. Some people thought that Vortigern was behind the treason, because the Picts would not have done such a deed except with his knowledge and consent, while others had no hesitation in declaring him innocent. But since the matter remained unresolved, the guardians of the two brothers, Aurelius Ambrosius and Uther Pendragon, escaped with them into Brittany, fearing that Vortigern would kill them. There king Budec gave them shelter and brought them up in his household with the honour due to their rank.

Now Vortigern, seeing that there was no one in the kingdom who could claim to be his equal, had himself crowned king, and seized precedence over all his fellow-princes. But in the end his part in Constans's death came to light, and the people of the Outer Isles, whom the Picts had taken with them to Britain, rebelled against him. For the Picts were angry that their comrades-in-arms had been put to death for the murder of Constans, and wanted their revenge. Vortigern was not only much disturbed by this, but lost many of his soldiers in the battles that ensued. Most of all, however, he was in terror of Aurelius Ambrosius and his brother Uther Pendragon, who had fled to Brittany. For they were now grown men, and day after day there were rumours that they had built a huge fleet in order to reclaim the kingdom which was rightfully their own.

In the meanwhile three brigantines, which we call 'long-boats', arrived on the coasts of Kent full of armed warriors. Their captains were two brothers, Hengist and Horsa. Vortigern was then at Dorobernia, which is now called Canterbury, a city which he often visited. When messengers told him that unknown men, taller than was usual, had arrived, he gave the messengers letters of protection and told them to bring the strangers to him.

When the newcomers arrived, his attention was caught by the two brothers, who stood out from the others both in dignity and in appearance. When he had inspected the rest of the company, he asked where they had been born, and why they had come to Britain. Hengist, as the eldest and wisest of them, answered for all of them:

'Most noble of all kings, we were born in Saxony, one of the countries of Germany, and we have come to offer our services to you or to some other prince. We have been banished from our country, but only because of the custom there. When the population grows too great, the princes of the various provinces meet and summon the young men of the whole kingdom. Then they cast lots and choose the likeliest and strongest to go to seek their livelihood in other lands, so that their native country may be relieved of men it cannot support. Because there are too many people in our own land, the princes selected us, and ordered us to obey the ancient custom. They appointed myself, Hengist, and my brother Horsa as captains, since we were born of a princely family. So, in obedience to the decrees made in past days, we have put to sea, and guided by Mercury have reached your kingdom.'

At the name of Mercury the king looked up and asked what their religion might be.

Hengist replied: 'We worship our native gods, Saturn, Jove and the rest of the governors of this world, but most of all Mercury, whom we call Woden: our forefathers dedicated the fourth day of the week to him, and we still call it Wednesday. After him we worship the most powerful of goddesses, Freia, to whom the sixth day is dedicated, which we call Friday.'

Vortigern said: 'I am grieved to hear of your belief, or rather your unbelief; yet nonetheless I am glad of your coming, for either my God or perhaps your God has brought you here to help me in my hour of need. My enemies are pressing me on every side, and if you will fight for me in my battles, I will retain you in my service with honour, and give you rich lands and fees.'

The barbarians at once agreed, and after the contract had been confirmed they remained at Vortigern's court. Soon after, the Picts came out of Scotland with a huge army and began to ravage the northern parts of the island. As soon as Vortigern had intelligence of this, he called his men together and marched to meet the Picts north of the Humber. When the British came to close quarters with the enemy, both sides fought fiercely; but the Britons hardly needed to fight, for the Saxons engaged the Picts so fiercely that the latter, who were accustomed to having the upper hand, were immediately put to flight.

Vortigern, having won the victory with their help, increased his gifts to them and gave their leader Hengist many lands in Lincolnshire with which to maintain himself and his fellow-soldiers. Hengist was a cunning and crafty man, and when he found that the king acted in such a friendly fashion, he said to him:

'My lord, your enemies persecute you on all sides, and few of your own people bear you any love. They all threaten you and say that they will bring your brother Aurelius Ambrosius from the shores of Brittany; and when they have deposed you, they will make him king. Allow us to send messengers to our own country, and invite warriors from those parts to increase the number of our fighting men. And there is one other thing I would ask of you, if I were not afraid you would refuse it.'

Vortigern replied: 'Send men to Germany and invite whoever you want; and ask of me whatever you wish, and I will not refuse you.'

Hengist bowed and thanked him, saying: 'You have given me houses and lands, but, seeing that my fathers were leaders in their own lands, have not given me the honour appropriate to a leader; you might have given me some city or castle, and the lords of your kingdom would have thought more of me for it. Equally, you could have made me an earl, like my ancestors at home.'

Vortigern answered: 'I am forbidden to grant anything of this kind to you as foreigners and heathen, and I do not know how to make you the equals of my own men according to your own customs; nor could I make such a grant if the barons of the realm were against it.'

Hengist said: 'Grant me as much land as can be encircled by a single strip cut from one hide, within the land you have already granted me, so that I can build a fortress in which I can take refuge. I will be loyal to you, and will swear an oath of fealty to you.'

So the king, moved by his words, granted his request, and told him to send his envoys into Germany at once, so that the warriors he invited could hasten at once to his aid. As soon as he had despatched messengers to Germany, Hengist took a bull's hide, and cut it into a continuous single thong. He marked out with his thong a rocky place which he had carefully chosen: in this area he began to build the castle that was later called Kaercorrei in British, but in Saxon, Thongceaster.

Meanwhile the envoys returned from Germany, bringing with them eighteen ships full of chosen warriors. They had also fetched Hengist's daughter, Rowena by name, whose beauty was unparalleled. When they arrived, Hengist invited Vortigern to his castle to look at the new building and the newly arrived warriors. The king came privately soon after, and not only praised the work which had been so swiftly carried out, but received the soldiers who had been invited into his retinue. When the royal banquet in his honour had ended, Rowena came out of her chamber bearing a golden cup filled with wine, and approached the king, kneeling before him and saying in Saxon: 'Lauerd king, wacht heil!'

When Vortigern saw her, he was amazed at her beauty and at once lost his heart to her. Then he asked his interpreter what the girl had said, and he replied: 'She called you "Lord King", and greeted you by wishing you health. You should reply "Drinc heil".'

At this Vortigern said 'Drinc heil!' and commanded the damsel to drink. Then he took the cup from her hand and kissed her, and drank; and from that day to this it has been the custom in Britain that he who drinks at a feast says to his neighbour, 'Wacht heil!' and he who receives the cup after him answers 'Drinc heil!'

Vortigern, drunk with the different kinds of liquor, fell in love with the damsel, and asked her father for her hand. Satan had entered his heart, I say, if he, a Christian, wanted to take a heathen woman as his bride. Hengist feared that this was just a whim of the king's, and at once took the advice of his brother Horsa and the rest of the senior men of his company as to what they should do in answer to the king's request. They all agreed that the girl should be given to the king, and that they should demand the county of Kent in return for her. So the matter was quickly settled. The girl was given to Vortigern, and the province of Kent was presented to Hengist without the knowledge of earl Gorangon who was rightful lord of it. That same night the king was married to this heathen woman, and he doted on her from then on. But by doing so he had made enemies of both the lords of the kingdom and his own children – the three sons born to him by a previous marriage, who were called Vortimer, Katigern and Pascentius.

At this time St Germanus, bishop of Auxerre, and Lupus, bishop of Troyes, came to preach the word of God to the Britons. For their Christianity had been corrupted, not only because the king had brought a heathen people to live in their midst, but also because of the heresy of Pelagius, a poison which had long infected them. The preaching of these blessed men restored the religion of the true faith among them, and through them God performed many miracles, as Gildas tells us in his little book.

Now, when the girl was given to the king, Hengist said to him: 'I am now your father-in-law and should be your chief adviser; and if you do as I suggest, you will overcome all your enemies through the courage of my people. Let us invite my sons Octa and Ebissa, who are excellent fighters, and give them the lands that lie in the northern parts of Britain next to the wall between Deira and Scotland. There they will bear the brunt of the barbarians' assaults and you will be able to live in peace south of the Humber.'

Vortigern obeyed, and told them to invite anyone who might bring him valuable support. Messengers were sent once more, and Octa, Ebissa and Cerdic came with three hundred ships filled with armed men. Vortigern received them all kindly, and gave them lavish gifts. He conquered all his enemies by theft, and won every battle with the help of the Saxons.

Hengist gradually invited more and more ships and increased the numbers of the Saxons each day. When the Britons saw what he was doing, they began to fear treason and begged the king to banish them from the kingdom, saying that pagans should not communicate with Christians nor be thrust into the midst of them, because it was forbidden by Christian law. Besides, so many had already arrived that the ordinary British people were terrified, and no one could tell which were the pagans and which Christians, for the former had wedded the latter's daughters and kinswomen. For these reasons they urged the king to dismiss them from his retinue, lest they should suddenly betray him and overrun the country.

But Vortigern refused to listen to them, because he favoured the Saxons above all other peoples on account of his wife. When the Britons realised this, they deserted Vortigern and agreed unanimously to make Vortimer, his son, their king. He took their advice and at once began to drive out the barbarians, making war on them and continually harassing them with fresh incursions. He fought four pitched battles against them; the first on the river Derwent, the second at Episford, where Horsa and Katigern, another son of Vortigern, met in hand to hand combat and killed each other. The third battle was on the coast, when the Saxons fled like women to their ships and took refuge in the isle of Thanet. But Vortimer besieged them there and harassed them day after day by attacking them from his ships. When they could no longer resist the British forays, they sent Vortigern, who had been with them in all their battles, to his son Vortimer to beg that he would allow them to depart in safety for Germany. And while the negotiations were in progress, the Saxons took the occasion to embark, and returned into Germany leaving their women and children behind them.

Vortimer, once he had conquered the Saxons, began to restore their possessions to the British and to treat them with affection and honour. He repaired the churches at the bidding of St Germanus. But the devil, envious of his goodness, entered into the heart of his stepmother Rowena, who plotted to murder him. Using her knowledge of witchcraft, she bribed one of his household servants to give him poison in his drink. No sooner had Vortimer drunk it than he was struck down with a sudden illness, so serious that there was no hope that he would survive. He at once summoned all his soldiers, and, telling them that death was already upon him, distributed amongst them his gold and silver and all the treasure that his forefathers had gathered. He tried to comfort them as they wept by reminding them that his fate was no other than the way of all flesh. He urged his brave young companions in battle to fight for their country and to defend it against all their enemies. And yielding to pride, he ordered that a brazen pyramid should be made and set in the harbour where the Saxons usually landed. After his death his body was to be buried on the top of it, so that when the barbarians saw his image on it, they would turn back to their home in Germany. He boasted that none of them would dare to approach if they as much as saw his image. But this proud ambition, to terrify his enemies even after his death, came to nothing, for the Britons ignored his wishes and buried his corpse in the city of Trinovantium.

After the death of his son, Vortigern was restored to his kingdom, and at the urging of his wife sent his messengers to Hengist in Germany, telling him to come back again to Britain, but to do so in secret and with only a few men – if he came openly, a quarrel might arise between the barbarians and the Britons. But Hengist, hearing of Vortimer's death, raised an army of three hundred thousand men, and, fitting out a fleet, returned to Britain.

As soon as the arrival of this huge force was reported to Vortigern and his barons, they were deeply troubled, and decided to defend the kingdom and drive out the invaders. News of their decision was at once sent to Hengist by messengers from his daughter, and he began to plan a way of gaining his objective without an encounter in the field. In the end he decided to deceive the Britons by approaching them under a show of peace. So he sent messengers to the king, explaining that he had not brought his army with him in order to conquer the country or to harm its inhabitants, but because he believed Vortimer to be still alive, and needed to be prepared in case Vortimer attacked him. Now he knew that Vortimer was dead, he would submit to Vortigern's wishes as to how many of his men should stay, and how many should return to Germany forthwith. If Vortigern was willing to accept these terms, he begged him to name a day and place for them to meet, so that they could then settle everything in accordance with his wishes.

When this message was brought to Vortigern, he was very pleased because he did not want Hengist to leave again. So he fixed the time and place of the meeting at Amesbury abbey, at the beginning of May, a few days later. Now Hengist had devised a new kind of treason: he ordered all his comrades to have a long knife hidden in the sole of the boot, and when the Britons were discussing the business of the meeting, he himself would say, 'Nemet oure saxes', at which each of them was to draw his knife to cut his throat as swiftly as might be and cut the throat of the Briton standing next to them. So the meeting took place as arranged and both sides began to discuss the terms of peace. When Hengist decided that the moment had come to carry out his treachery, he shouted out, 'Nemet oure saxes!' and seized Vortigern and held him by his royal robe.

The moment the Saxons heard the signal they drew their long knives and attacked the barons, who were completely unsuspecting. They cut the throats of about four hundred and sixty of them, whose bodies were afterwards given Christian burial by the blessed Eldad, in the churchyard of the monastery founded by Abbot Ambrus not far from Kaercaradoc, that is now called Salisbury. The Britons had come unarmed, thinking that they were safe at such a peace conference, and the Saxons were able to kill them easily; but they did not escape without injury, for the Britons seized stones and sticks to defend themselves, and killed many of the murderers in the act.

Among others who were present was Eldol, duke of Gloucester, who, seeing this treachery, took up a stake that he had found by chance and defended himself. Whoever he could reach, he either broke their heads, arms, shoulders or legs or despatched them altogether; he did not leave the place until he had killed seventy men with his stake. But when he could no longer resist so many men, he managed to escape and return to his own city.

The Saxon treachery was successful, and the Britons were defeated; but even so they did not want to kill Vortigern, but bound him and threatened him with death, and demanded his cities and fortresses as ransom for his life. He agreed to all this as long as his life was spared, and confirmed it by oath. So they freed him from his fetters, and then marched to London, which they took, followed by York and Lincoln as well as Winchester, ravaging the country at will, killing the inhabitants as wolves kill sheep left without a shepherd. When Vortigern saw the terrible devastation, he went secretly into Wales, not knowing what to do to get rid of this accursed people.

At last he took the advice of his wizards, who told him that he ought to build an exceedingly strong tower, since he had lost all his other castles. He searched everywhere to find a suitable place, and at last came to Snowdon. Here he assembled a great gang of masons from various countries, and ordered them to build the tower. The stonemasons began to lay the foundations, but whatever they did one day was swallowed up by the earth the next, so they did not know where their work had disappeared to. Vortigern, when he heard about this, once more asked his wizards to tell him the reason for this. They said that he must search for a boy who had never had a father; and when he had found him, he should kill him and sprinkle his blood over the mortar and the stones. This, they said, would make the foundation of the tower hold firm.

Messengers were sent everywhere to look for such a boy. When they came to Carmarthen, they saw some lads playing before the gate: they sat down, weary with travel, and looked round them in the hope of finding what they sought. Towards evening, a couple of youths whose names were Merlin and Dalbutius suddenly quarrelled; and as they argued, Dalbutius said to Merlin: 'What a fool you are to think you are a match for me! I come from royal blood on both my mother's and father's side, but no one knows who you are, because you never had a father!' At this the messengers pricked up their ears, and asked the bystanders who this Merlin might be. They told them that no one knew his father, but that his mother was daughter of the king of Dyfed, and that she lived with the nuns in St Peter's Church in that same city.

The messengers hurried off to the reeve of the city, and ordered him in the king's name to have Merlin and his mother sent to the king. When he learnt of their errand, the reeve at once sent Merlin and his mother to Vortigern for him to do whatever he wanted with them. And when they were brought into his presence, the king received the mother with due respect knowing that she was of noble birth. Then he asked her who the father of her son might be.

She replied: 'On my soul, my lord king, I know of no man who was his father. All I can tell you is that once, when I and my attendants were in our chambers, someone appeared to me in the shape of a handsome young man, who embraced me and kissed me and stayed with me for some time. Then he suddenly vanished and I never saw him again: he often spoke to me when I was alone, though I never saw him. When he had haunted me in this way for a long time I conceived and bore a child. This is the truth, my lord king, whatever you may make of it; I know of no one who is the father of this boy.'

Amazed by her words, the king asked for Maugantius to be brought; and when the latter had heard the story from first to last, he said to Vortigern: 'In books and histories written by wise men I have found that many men have been born in this way. Apuleius says that there are certain spirits between the moon and the earth, which we call incubi. Their nature is partly human, partly angelic, and they take on the shape of men at will and associate with mortal women. Perhaps one of these appeared to this lady and is the father of the youth.'

When Merlin heard all this, he came to the king and said: 'Why have my mother and I been summoned here?'

Vortigern answered: 'My wizards have declared that I should seek out a boy who never had a father, because when I have sprinkled his blood upon the foundation of the tower I am building it will stand firm.'

Merlin said: 'Summon your wizards and I will show that they are lying.'

The king, amazed at his words, summoned his wizards so that Merlin could confront them. Merlin said to them: 'Don't you know what is preventing the foundation of this tower from being laid? You have advised that it should be built with mortar mixed with my blood, to make it stand securely. But ask yourselves what is hidden under the foundation, which prevents it from standing?' The wizards were frightened and said nothing.

Then Merlin (who was also called Ambrosius) said: 'My lord king, call your workmen and get them to dig, and you will find a pool under the tower that prevents it from standing.'

They did this, and a pool was indeed discovered.

Then Merlin Ambrosius again questioned the wizards: 'Tell me now, you liars and flatterers, what is under the pool?' But they were all dumb and said not a word. He said to the king: 'Order that the pool is to be drained; in the bottom you will find two dragons asleep.' The king did so, since Merlin had been proved right about the pool; and once more, to his astonishment, he found that it was as Merlin said. And after that, Merlin prophesied the future history of Britain, to the amazement and bafflement of his hearers.

When Vortigern had listened to him, he wanted to learn what his own fate would be; and Merlin's answer was as follows:

'Escape from the fire of the sons of Constantine, if you can! At this very moment they are fitting out their ships; at this very moment they are leaving the coast of Brittany and sailing out into the open sea towards Britain, which they will invade. They will defeat the accursed Saxons, but before that they will besiege you in a tower and set fire to it. It was your actions that brought this fate upon you when you betrayed their father and invited the Saxons into Britain as your bodyguard; they will come over as your executioners. Two deaths await you, and I cannot tell which of them you will escape. The Saxons will lay waste your kingdom and will try to kill you. And Aurelius and Uther Pendragon will invade your lands seeking revenge for their father's death. So take refuge if you can. Tomorrow they will land at Totnes. The Saxons will suffer bloody injuries: Hengist will be killed, and Aurelius Ambrosius will be crowned king. He will reign in peace and will restore the churches, but he will die of poison. His brother Uther Pendragon will succeed him, but his reign will also be cut short by poison. Your descendants will be there when this happens, and Uther's son Arthur will revenge his father!'

At dawn the next day Aurelius Ambrosius and his brother landed with ten thousand men; and when the news of their coming spread through the country, the Britons, who had been scattered with such slaughter, regrouped: encouraged by the arrival of their fellow-countrymen their morale was restored. They called the clergy together, who anointed Aurelius as king, and everyone did homage to him according to custom. But when they advised him to attack the Saxons, the king dissuaded them: he wanted first to hunt down Vortigern, because he still grieved for the death of his father through Vortigern's treason. So he led his army into Wales, and made his way to the castle of Genoreu where Vortigern had taken refuge.

When Ambrosius reached the castle, he remembered the treachery which his father and brother had suffered, and said to Eldol, duke of Gloucester:

'Look at the walls of this city! Will they be strong enough to protect Vortigern, and to prevent me from plunging my sword into his bowels? He deserves to die a violent death for he betrayed my father Constantine, who had delivered him and his country from the ravages of the Picts; then he raised Constans, my brother, to be king, only to destroy him. Then, when he was a marked man because of these treacheries, he brought in the heathen to exterminate everyone who had remained loyal to me. Yet by God's grace he has fallen into his own trap: the Saxons threw him out of the kingdom for his misdeeds, to no one's regret. But I am troubled that this cursed people, invited here by this cursed man, have slaughtered my loyal freemen, have laid waste my fruitful country, have destroyed its holy churches and almost rooted out Christianity from sea to sea. So, my fellow-countrymen, acquit yourselves like men, and avenge yourselves first of all upon the man who has brought all these evils upon you! Then let us turn our arms against the enemies who surround us, and save the country from being swallowed up in their insatiable maw!'

They at once brought up their siege-engines and did their best to breach the walls; but when all else failed, they set the place on fire, and the fire blazed up till it had burned down the tower and Vortigern in it.

When Hengist and his Saxons heard this, they were very much frightened, because they feared the prowess of Aurelius. He was so bold and brave that when he was in Gaul no one there would meet him in single combat. For when he met anyone in mounted combat, he would either thrust his enemy from his horse or shatter his spear in pieces. He was generous with his gifts, diligent in matters of religion, moderate in all things, and hated liars. He was redoubtable on foot; yet more so on horseback, and he was an expert general. His reputation so terrified the Saxons that they retreated to the far side of the Humber and garrisoned the cities and castles there, because that country had always served them as a refuge. Because it bordered on Scotland, and the Scots were always seeking an occasion to harm the people of the country, this inhospitable tract of land, empty of inhabitants, had always offered safe refuge to strangers: the Picts and Scots, Danes and Norwegians had all landed there when they planned to lay waste the island. Knowing that they would be safe from their neighbours in that part of the country, they fled there.

When Aurelius was told of this, he took heart and hoped for a victory. So he called the men of the country together as quickly as he could to reinforce his own army, and started on his march north. As he passed through the various counties he was sad to see how desolate they were, particularly because all the churches had been razed to the ground: he vowed to restore them if he was victorious.

When Hengist learnt of his arrival, however, he took courage again, and encouraged those of his soldiers who most needed it, telling them to stand firm, and not to fear Aurelius who only had a few Bretons with him, perhaps ten thousand men in all. As for the Britons themselves, they were no danger, because he had often defeated them in battle. So he promised his men victory because of their greater numbers, for the Saxon army consisted of some two hundred thousand men.

He advanced towards Aurelius as far as a place called Maesbeli, through which Aurelius would have to pass: here he hoped to ambush the Britons and surprise them. But Aurelius got wind of the plan: so far from hesitating for that reason, he marched on more rapidly, and when he came in sight of the enemy he drew up his troops in order. He detailed three thousand Bretons to fight alongside the knights, and the rest he set in the line of battle, interspersing them among the Britons. The men of Dyfed he stationed on the hills, the men of Gwynedd in the forest nearby, so that if the Saxons fled that way, they would meet with resistance.

Meanwhile Eldol, duke of Gloucester, said to the king: 'I only want to see out this day and then die if God will allow me to fight Hengist in single combat: one of us would surely die before the fight was over. I well remember the day when we met to make peace, and he betrayed everyone who was there, stabbing them all to death. I alone escaped, but four hundred and sixty unarmed barons and earls died there. It was only because God provided me with a stake with which to defend myself that I got away.'

When Eldol had reminded them of this, Aurelius exhorted all his comrades to set their hopes only on the Son of God, and to attack the enemy boldly and fight with one mind for their country. On the other side, Hengist set his troops in fighting order, and gave them orders as to their duty in the battle, walking to and fro between the battalions and encouraging his men. When all the companies on both sides were drawn up in battle-order, the front ranks engaged, dealing blow for blow and shedding not a little blood. Both Britons and Saxons fell mortally wounded: Aurelius urged on the Christians, and Hengist encouraged the heathens.

As the battle raged, Eldol sought an opportunity to get to grips with Hengist, but he did not succeed, because Hengist, when he saw his own men fall back before the British onslaught, at once fled to the castle of Kaerconan, now called Knaresborough. Aurelius went in hot pursuit, killing or capturing any Saxons he found on the way. Hengist, seeing that Aurelius was intent on hunting him down, decided against entering the castle, and ordered his troops to draw up in battle array, for he knew that the castle would not resist a siege by Aurelius, and that his only defence lay in his own sword. When Aurelius caught up with him, the Britons regrouped and charged fiercely against the Saxons, who held their ground. The struggle was fierce and bloody, and the Saxons would have prevailed had it not been for a company of Breton knights whom Aurelius had stationed to one side, as he had done in the first battle. When they charged the Saxons, the latter were forced to give ground, and once their line was broken, they were unable to form in rank again. The Britons pressed home the attack, encouraged by Aurelius; while Eldol, hurrying to and fro across the battlefield, killing many of the enemy as he went, still sought the moment when he could engage Hengist man to man.

At last, in the confusion of battle, the two met on equal terms, and a furious duel began, each matching the other's blows stroke for stroke until the sparks flew from their swords like lightning. The outcome was in doubt for a long while: now Eldol had the upper hand, and now Hengist regained it. While this battle was going on, Gorlois, duke of Cornwall arrived with his battalion and began to harass the enemy. At this, Eldol took heart and renewed his efforts. He seized Hengist by the nose-piece of his helmet, and dragged him into the midst of the British troops, taking him prisoner.

Eldol shouted to his men: 'God granted my wish! Destroy the rest of the Saxons, because now Hengist is in our hands, the rest are defeated!'

So the Britons charged the Saxon lines repeatedly, until at last the Saxons fled: some sought refuge in the cities, others in the forests and mountains, others in their ships. But Hengist's son Octa, with the greater part of those who survived, made his way to York, while Fosa, his kinsman, made for the city of Alclud, and garrisoned it with a host of armed men.

When Aurelius had won this victory, he took Knaresborough, and stayed there for three days. He ordered that the dead should be buried, the wounded should be cared for and the weary given rest. Then he called together his dukes and asked them to say what should be done with Hengist. Eldad, bishop of Gloucester and brother of Eldol, was present, a man of the highest wisdom and piety. When he saw Hengist standing before the king, he ordered the rest to be silent, and made this speech: 'If everyone here were to try to set this man free, I myself would still cut him to pieces, like Samuel, who, when he had Agag, king of the Amalekites, in his power killed him, saying, "As thy sword hath made mothers childless, so shall thy mother be childless among women." So do the same to Hengist, for he is another Agag.'

At this Eldol took his sword, led Hengist outside the city and cut off his head, sending his soul to hell. But Aurelius, who was always restrained in such matters, ordered that he should be decently buried, and a mound of earth heaped above his body as was the Saxon custom.

10. THE STORY OF HAMLET

Amleth, or Hamlet as we usually know him, appears for the first time in The History of the Danes *by the twelfth-century writer Saxo Grammaticus. His story, that of revenge on a wicked stepfather, is a classic topic of folktales: what gives Saxo's version its interest is the detailed account of Hamlet's skilful intrigues. Hamlet may have been known as an expert in riddles, and riddles play a large part in Saxo's story; while the theme of the prince who pretends to be an idiot in order to escape the unwelcome notice of his enemies is another folktale motif. Much of the story is set in Britain. This is, of course, the source for Shakespeare's* Hamlet, *and some critics believe that Shakespeare may have worked directly from Saxo's original Latin, though he may have first encountered it in a popular version by a French author. The story is a strange but vivid mixture of themes, and is carefully constructed: minor episodes, such as Hamlet's making of hooks in his madness, prove to have important consequences later in the story.*

ORVENDIL and Fengi, sons of the Jutish governor Gervendil, were both appointed by king Rørik to rule Jutland. Now Orvendil, after controlling the province for three years, had devoted himself to piracy and reaped such high renown that Koller, the king of Norway, wishing to rival his deeds and widespread reputation, judged it would suit him very well if he could transcend him in warfare and cast a shadow over the brilliance of this world-famed sea-rover. He cruised about, combing various parts of the seas, until he lit upon Orvendil's fleet. In the midst of the ocean there was an island held by each of the pirates, who had moored their ships on different sides. The leaders were attracted by the delightful prospect of the beaches; the beautiful vista from off-shore encouraged them to view the woods of the interior in spring and wander among the glades and remote expanses of forest. Their chance steps led Koller and Orvendil to an unwitnessed meeting.

Orvendil took the initiative and asked his opponent how he wanted to fight, stressing that the most superior method was one which exercised the sinews of the fewest men. He thought that single combat was more effective than any other type of contest for securing the honours of bravery, since a person must rely on his own valour and refuse any other man's aid.

Each gave his word of honour on this point and they fell to battle. They were not deterred from assailing each other with their blades by the novelty of their meeting or the springtime charm of that spot, for they took no heed of these things. Orvendil's emotional fervour made him more eager to set upon his foe than defend himself; consequently he disregarded the protection of his shield and laid both hands to his sword.

This daring had its results. His rain of blows deprived Koller of his shield by cutting it to pieces; finally he carved off the other's foot and made him fall lifeless. He honoured their agreement by giving him a regal funeral, constructing an ornate tomb and providing a ceremony of great magnificence. After this he hounded down and slew Koller's sister Sela, a warring amazon and accomplished pirate herself.

Three years were passed in gallant military enterprises, in which he marked the choicest of the plunder for Rørik, to bring himself into closer intimacy with the king. On the strength of their friendship Orvendil wooed and obtained Rørik's daughter Gerutha for his wife. She bore him a son, Amleth.

Fengi was inflamed with jealousy at his successes and determined to set a trap for his brother. A man of true worth is not even safe from his near relatives. Once given an opportunity to despatch him, Fengi dyed his hand in blood in order to satisfy his black desires. Besides butchering his brother he added incest to fratricide by taking possession of his wife.

When a man commits one crime, he soon finds himself sliding downhill towards the next; the first speeds on the second. Fengi covered up this foul deed with such presumptuous cunning that he manufactured an excuse of kindheartedness for his crime, and gave the murder a colouring of scrupulous conduct. He made out that Gerutha, though she was too mild to do anyone the slightest harm, was so violently loathed by her husband that he had removed him only to preserve her: it seemed a disgrace that such a gentle creature without bitterness should endure the overbearing arrogance of this man. This persuasive argument did not fail. If buffoons are sometimes favoured and slanderers honoured, people will certainly believe the lies of princes. The villain showed no hesitation in turning his murderous hands to unlawful embraces, pursuing both these sacrileges with the same viciousness.

Hamlet observed this and, to avoid stirring his uncle's suspicions by behaving intelligently, pretended to be an imbecile, acting as if his wits had gone quite astray. This piece of artfulness, besides concealing his true wisdom, safeguarded his life. Every day he would stay near his mother's hearth, completely listless and unwashed, and would roll on the ground to give his person a repulsive coating of filth. His grimy complexion and the refuse smeared over his face grotesquely illustrated his lunacy. Everything he said was the raving of an idiot, everything he did smacked of a deep lethargy. Need I go on? You would not have called him a man so much as a ridiculous freak created by Fate in a madcap mood. He often sat by the fire, scraping the embers with his fingers and making wooden hooks which he would harden in the flames; he turned back the ends to form prongs, so that they would hold with a tighter grip. When they asked why he did it, he replied that he was getting these stings sharp to avenge his father. The answer brought delighted guffaws; everyone sneered at his pointless labours, though later these were to assist his scheme.

However, it was this very skill which aroused in spectators of the wiser sort the first suspicions of his cleverness. His diligence in this humble technique suggested the craftsman's hidden ingenuity: anyone with the brains to execute articles of such finished workmanship could hardly be thought witless. Lastly he would keep a most careful watch over his pile of charred stakes. Some men averred that his intelligence was lively enough and he was concealing deep designs under a cloak of feeble-mindedness; the best way to reveal his trickery, they said, was to bring him to some shady nook where a supremely attractive woman could lure his heart into sexual entanglement. Men's characters are so naturally inclined towards love that no subtlety may keep its existence secret. His cunning could not obstruct so violent an emotion and so, even if he simulated indifference, once the opportunity presented itself he would succumb to the powers of pleasure there and then. So fellows were found who would conduct the young man on horseback to a distant part of the forest and expose him to a temptation of this sort.

Among these there chanced to be a foster-brother of Hamlet who still cherished a regard for him due to their mutual upbringing. Setting the memory of their past association before his present orders, he accompanied Hamlet and his allotted companions with no intention of leading him into a trap, but rather to bring him warning. He had no doubt that if Hamlet gave even a half indication of his true sanity he would come to grief – above all if he were openly to perform the act of love. Hamlet was well aware of this. When he was told to mount his horse he sat on purpose with his back to the creature's mane facing the tail. This he began to encircle with the bridle, just as though he could restrain his steed at that end while it was at full gallop. By this thoughtful move he foiled the device and overcame his uncle's stratagem. It was quite ludicrous to see a rider without reins gallop forward guiding the horse by its tail.

Further on, Hamlet came across a wolf in the undergrowth and, when his companions told him that he had encountered a young colt, he added that there were very few of that breed serving in Fengi's stable, a moderate but witty criticism which hit at his uncle's affluence. When they observed that he had given a clever reply, he admitted that his speech was considered; nowhere in his words did he wish to appear a liar. Hamlet wanted to be held a stranger to falsehood and mingled artfulness with plain speaking, so that he adhered to the truth without letting it show through to betray his acute mind.

They were going along the shore when his attendants discovered the rudder of a wrecked ship and said to Hamlet that they had found an amazingly large knife.

'All the better to cut an outsize ham with,' he answered, obviously referring to the sea, since its vastness suited the dimensions of the rudder.

As they passed the sand-dunes they told him to look at this flour, at which he remarked that it had been ground by the foaming billows when it was stormy. The company congratulated him on this response, which he again agreed was a wise pronouncement.

They intentionally went on ahead of him to give him a great opportunity to satisfy his lust. After he had met the woman in a sheltered spot, apparently by chance but really because she had been sent by his uncle, he would have had his pleasure with her if his foster-brother had not, by a silent warning, given him an inkling of the plot.

This friend was debating with himself how he could suitably convey a secret hint and stop the young man from dangerously indulging his sensuality, so he picked up a straw from the ground, inserted it beneath the tail of a horse-fly and then let it glide on. He drove it towards the particular locality where he knew Hamlet was and thereby did him a special service when he was off guard. The signal was recognised with the same astuteness with which it was delivered, for Hamlet, spying the horse-fly and at the same time the straw beneath its tail, examined it closely and concluded that it was a secret caution against some treachery he must avoid. Alarmed at the scent of an ambush, he caught the woman in his arms and, in order to satisfy his desires in comparative safety, brought her to a remote and trackless fen. After having intercourse with her he earnestly begged her not to disclose the incident to anyone. Her silence was promised as readily as it was sought: because they had once grown up together and shared the same guardians in childhood, Hamlet enjoyed the girl's deep affection.

When he returned home they all asked him by way of a joke whether he had had his fill of lovemaking, and he admitted that he had slept with the girl. Then they asked where he had performed the act and on what sort of pillow. He answered that he had rested on a colt's foot, a cock's comb and a piece of roof; indeed when he set out on his test he had gathered specimens of all these to avoid having to lie. His reply was received with loud laughter from the bystanders, though he had not departed a jot from the truth in his jest. The girl, questioned on this matter, retorted that he had done no such thing. Her denial gained easier credence when it was ascertained that her retinue had not witnessed the event.

Then the man who had fixed the notice to the horse-fly, to show that Hamlet's escape had been based on his ruse, told the prince he had recently been exceptionally devoted to him. The prince answered pertinently: to indicate that he was grateful for the loyal prompting, he reported that he had seen something gliding quickly towards him, wearing a straw mattress in its buttocks. While everyone else rocked with laughter at this quip, it delighted his supporter by its sagacity.

Hamlet outdid them all, so that none could find the key to disclose the young man's secret purposes. Then one of Fengi's friends, who had more self-assurance than cunning, said it was impossible to expose the intricate nature of his intelligence by the usual old tricks. He felt Hamlet was too obstinate for them to make headway with trifling attempts and they should not therefore test his many-sided vigilance straightforwardly. By his own deeper perspicacity he claimed to have hit on a more subtle method, practical to put into operation and highly expedient for the present investigation. Fengi, on the plea of important business, would proclaim his departure; and then Hamlet must be shut up alone with his mother in her bedroom after a person had been planted, without either of them knowing, somewhere in a dark corner to listen carefully to their conversation. If her son were in his right mind he would trust his mother and be ready to speak openly in her hearing. The courtier eagerly offered his services for this detective work, no less anxious to be the executant than the inventor of the plot. Fengi was delighted with the scheme and, letting it be known that he had to go on a long journey, left the palace.

The courtier who had concocted the plan went silently to the room where Hamlet was in private conference with his mother and crawled under some straw for concealment. But Hamlet turned the tables on this spy: he was apprehensive in case any hidden ears might be eavesdropping, so he first ran through his usual tomfoolery, crowing like a noisy cock and clapping his arms together like beating wings. Then he climbed on to the straw and began to jump up and down to find out if anything was lurking there. When he felt a lump beneath his feet, he prodded the place with his sword, transfixed the man underneath, dragged him from his hiding-place and butchered him. Afterwards he sliced the body into chunks, cooked it in boiling water and threw the sorry limbs into the mouth of an open sewer where, smirched with putrid filth, they could be gobbled up by the pigs.

Now he had dodged the snare he returned to the bedroom. When his mother's violent shrieks had subsided and she was weeping instead over his fuddled wits, the son confronted her with these words:

'You low woman, why do you try to gloss over your gross infamy with false laments? Like a lewd harlot you fly to a damnable, loathsome bed, clasp your husband's murderer to your incestuous bosom, and fawn with the most disgusting endearments and caresses on the man who destroyed the father of your son. This is the way mares copulate with the stallions which have overmastered their mates! Only brute beasts rush promiscuously into a variety of marriages; your conduct makes it clear that your late husband's memory has grown stale. I wear this motley appearance for my own benefit, as I've no doubt whatever that a ruffian who can kill his brother is also likely to savage his other kinsmen with equal ferocity. That's why I prefer to adopt the behaviour of an imbecile instead of a purposeful sanity, and ensure my safety by looking like an out-and-out maniac.

'Yet in my heart there is this persistent yearning to avenge my father and I'm on the watch for opportunities, always waiting for the right moment. There are different times for different under-takings. Against a secretive and pitiless mind deeper machinations have to be employed. Consider how needless it is to mourn over my foolishness, when you ought really to be weeping for your own dis-honour. You shouldn't be shedding tears over another's imperfec-tions, but your own. As to the rest, be silent.'

His mother, rent by this reproof, was recalled to the practice of virtue, and Hamlet showed her how to set the flame of her previous love before her present bewitchment.

Fengi returned to discover that his spy was nowhere to be found, not even by unremitting investigation, nor had anyone caught a glimpse of him. Hamlet too was asked in jest whether he had detected any trace of him: he replied that the man had gone into the drain, tumbled down to the bottom and, buried under a heap of sewage, had been devoured by the pigs which frequented the place. This story, though it revealed the truth, seemed crazy to his audience and caused merriment.

Although Fengi was determined to do away with his stepson, of whose counterfeiting he had no doubts, he did not dare put this into exe-cution owing to the disfavour he would incur from his wife and her father, Rorik. He therefore determined that the king of Britain should do him the favour of killing Hamlet. The deed would be performed by proxy, as it were, and he would preserve an air of innocence. In the desire to keep his barbarity hidden he preferred to contaminate a friend than harm his own reputation.

On his departure Hamlet secretly asked his mother to adorn the palace with tapestries and to conduct a pretended funeral for him after a year had elapsed; at which time, he promised, he would return. Two of Fengi's parasites set out with him bearing a letter engraved on wood (at one time this was a familiar kind of writing material), in which the British king was enjoined to slay the young man sent over to him. Hamlet combed through their baggage while they were sleeping and purloined the letter. Having read over the commission, he scratched away all that was inscribed there and substituted new characters to alter the gist of the command and turn his sentence on the heads of his com-panions. Not satisfied with removing his death warrant and transferring the peril to others, he added a request, below Fengi's forged signature, that the British king should bequeath his daughter in matrimony to this highly intelligent young ambassador.

When they arrived in Britain the two envoys came to the king and presented him with the letter giving instructions for their own death, believing it made provision for another man's doom. The king kept the contents to himself and entertained them kindly and hospitably. But Hamlet spurned the state banquet in its entirety as though it were coarse fare, drew back from the lavish feast with a peculiar restraint and touched neither food nor drink. Everyone was amazed that this youthful foreigner turned his nose up before the exquisite delicacies and luxurious dishes on the royal table as if at some peasant's fodder. Once the entertainment was over and his friends sent to their rest, the king secretly despatched a servant to their bedroom to overhear his guests' conversation that night.

Hamlet, asked by his fellows why during the evening he had shunned the feast as if it were poison, replied that the bread was tainted with blood, the drink had the flavour of iron and the banquet meat was smothered in the odour of a corpse, as though it had been polluted by proximity to the stench of death. Aiming the real brunt of his criticism not so much at the dinner as its providers, he added that the king had the eyes of a slave and that his queen had displayed three mannerisms of a maidservant. It was not long before his companions began to reprove that old weakness in his brains and to mock him with various taunts because he found fault with things perfectly proper and acceptable. This was aggressive and disrespectful talk about a famous king and a queen of impeccable decorum, quite disgraceful aspersions on a pair who deserved nothing but praise.

When the king learnt this from his henchman, he declared the author of these pronouncements must be possessed with superhuman genius or stupidity – thus gauging the full depth of Hamlet's activities in one short phrase. He then summoned his steward and enquired where he had obtained the bread. The man swore that it had been prepared by the king's own baker, and was then asked in what place the corn which supplied the flour had been grown, and whether there was any sign of it being the scene of slaughter. The other answered that there was a field close by which still bore evident traces of a massacre long ago, strewn as it was with the ancient bones of men slain; in spring he had sown it with grain himself, thinking it promised high fertility and a more abundant crop than the rest. Could the bread possibly have picked up a suspicious taste from the gore?

On hearing this the king guessed that Hamlet had spoken the truth and was anxious to know too where the pork had come from. The steward revealed that his pigs had escaped from their sty through negligence and had fed on the decaying carcase of a robber; thus, quite by chance, their meat had gathered a tang similar to that of rotting flesh. As the monarch discovered that Hamlet was right in this too, he demanded to know with what liquid the drink had been mixed. When he discovered that it had been diluted with honey and water, he proceeded to dig to the root of the spring which had been pointed out to him, and found several swords eaten away by rust which it was believed must have infected the water. Others relate that Hamlet disparaged the drink because in sipping he had detected an unpleasant edge to it; this had previously been passed through to the honeycomb by bees which had bred in the belly of a corpse.

The king saw that the reasons for Hamlet's disapproval of the flavour were convincing, and, since he realised that the same man's accusation of an ignoble look about his eyes pointed to some strain of impurity, he met the queen mother in private and questioned her about his paternity. She denied having submitted herself to anyone besides her royal husband, but when he threatened to check the matter by torture, the mystery of his birth, which Hamlet had stigmatised, was cleared up. He wrung from her the confession that he was the son of a slave. Impressed by the young man's penetration as much as he was mortified by his low pedigree, the king asked Hamlet why he had sullied the queen by charging her with servile habits. But even while he deplored the scepticism about his wife's courtliness which the visitor had shown in his late-night talk, he was told that she was indeed the daughter of a female slave. Hamlet said he had observed three shortcomings in her, denoting a serf's demeanour: first, she covered her head with her mantle like a maidservant; secondly, she tucked up her robe when she walked, and thirdly, she picked out with a spill the morsels of food sticking between the crevices of her teeth and then chewed them. He reminded the king that her mother had been captured and reduced to slavery, since he wished to ascribe this behaviour to her birth rather than her own manners.

The king worshipped his powers like some God-given talent and gave him his daughter in marriage, taking to heart his declarations as though they were heavenly oracles. But the two companions he hanged the next day to fulfil his friend Fengi's instructions. Following this service Hamlet pretended to be disgruntled as if an affront had been given, and as compensation accepted gold from the king, which he secretly melted down afterwards and had poured into hollow rods.

After staying in Britain for a year he begged leave to depart, and returned to his homeland, though he took nothing of the panoply of regal wealth with him save the rods full of gold. When he reached Jutland he altered his present way of life to the old one, and the habits he had cultivated to his credit were intentionally changed back to clownishness. Daubed with muck, he entered the banqueting hall where his obsequies were being conducted and gave them all a tremendous shock, because the false report of his death was widely current. Eventually fright gave way to laughter, with the guests light-heartedly chiding each other for having held a funeral for a supposedly dead man, who was there with them in person. Asked about his fellow-travellers, he pointed to the staffs he was holding: 'Here's one and that's the other,' he answered. You could not tell whether it was uttered seriously or for a joke. Though most people took it as moonshine, his statement was nothing but the truth, for it referred to the compensation for the executed pair.

Next, to afford the banqueters greater amusement, he joined the troop of cupbearers and scrupulously carried out the duty of pouring refreshment. So that the looser uniform should not impede his step, he bound a sword to his side, which he would often purposely unsheath, pricking his fingers with the point. The bystanders therefore had the sword and scabbard riveted through with an iron pin.

To make safer preparation for his ambush, Hamlet circulated with goblets among the nobles, plying them with drink after drink: he so deluged them with wine that they became too intoxicated to stand up and went to sleep there in the palace, making the scene of the feast their bed-chamber. As soon as he saw them in fit condition for his plot and the time ripe, he took from his bosom the wooden hooks, prepared long ago, and entered the hall in which the courtiers, their bodies splayed everywhere over the floor, were belching away in alcoholic slumber. There, spread over the interior walls, he found the tapestry which his mother had woven, cut it away from its fastenings and tore it down. Then he threw it over the snorers, and, using the crooked sticks, he tied it with such Gordian knots that none of those lying beneath, however vigorously they strained, could manage to get to their feet. After this he started a fire, whose flames grew to a widespread conflagration and enveloped the entire building. The palace was destroyed and its inhabitants cremated, whether they were enjoying deep sleep or vainly struggling to rise.

Hamlet next sought Fengi's chamber, in the pavilion to which the king's friends had conducted him, and, snatching up a sword hanging next to the bed, substituted his own for it. He then woke his uncle and informed him that his noblemen had been burnt to death, and that through the aid of his old bent hooks he, Hamlet, was at his side, eager to inflict the punishment now due for his father's murder. At these words Fengi leapt from the bed, but, deprived of his own sword and unable with all his efforts to draw the other, was struck down.

What a brave man this Hamlet was, worthy of everlasting fame! He had wisely fortified himself by an incredible performance of stupidity, submerging under it a brilliant reason transcending mortal faculties; and thus his wits had provided him with a safe-conduct and kept him alive until the moment arrived for avenging his father. Considering the skill with which he had preserved himself, and the energy with which he exacted atonement, one can hardly decide which to extol more, his courage or his wisdom.

After he had destroyed his stepfather, Hamlet was afraid to expose the deed to the unpredictable judgement of his countrymen, and decided to go into hiding till he had found out which way the mob of common people leaned. The men of the neighbourhood, who during the night had viewed the holocaust, next morning inspected the ashes of the wrecked palace to discover its cause. Though they examined the still-warm ruins, they were unable to perceive anything but the shapeless remains of charred bodies. The hungry flames had so completely devoured everything that there was not a single clue to the origin of this vast devastation. The body of Fengi, run through with a sword, could also be made out among his bloodstained clothing. Some were gripped with open anger, others with grief, yet others by secret joy. The onlookers received the king's death with divided feelings, as one section mourned the passing away of its leader and another gave thanks that this fratricide's despotic rule had been laid to rest.

When the populace continued calm, Hamlet gathered confidence to come out of his retreat and called to the assembly those men in whose minds he knew a more vivid recollection of his father was still rooted. Then he addressed them with this speech:

'If the death of poor Orvendil still moves you, do not be stirred, my lords, by the sight of the disaster here. I repeat, do not be stirred if you still feel loyalty to a king and duty towards a parent. You are gazing at the end of a murderer, not a monarch. When you saw your king sadly mauled by a vile cut-throat (I cannot call him brother), that was a sorrier spectacle. You yourselves looked with eyes full of compassion on the mangled limbs of Orvendil, his body consumed with many a gash. Who can doubt that that barbarous scoundrel stole his life so that he could strip your fatherland of its liberty? The same hand condemned him to death and you to slavery. Is anyone so insane that he could prefer Fengi's sadism to Orvendil's affection? Remember with what kindness the latter fostered you, with what equity he tended you, with what humanity he loved you. Remember too how this gentle ruler and just father of his people was snatched away to be replaced by a tyrant and kin-slayer; you were robbed of your rights, all things were polluted, your country was stained with crimes, a yoke was planted on your necks and any power of freedom removed.

'All this is now ended, for you can discern how the miscreant has been overwhelmed by his own evil deeds, the assassin taken to account for his wickedness. What moderately sensible observer will not feel that he has been benefited, not wronged? What sane person could grieve because the villainy has recoiled on its perpetrator? Who could weep for the overthrow of this bloody executioner? Who could bewail the fitness of this cruel autocrat's downfall? Here stands the man responsible for the event you witness. Certainly I confess that I set out to avenge my father and my country. It was I who executed the task, but that task was equally your duty. Though you and I had an obligation to accomplish it together, I carried it out alone. Let me emphasise that nobody was my associate, no comrade lent his hand to the act. Even so, I am quite aware you would have devoted your energies to this business if I had asked you, for you have undoubtedly retained your love and allegiance towards your true sovereign. Nevertheless it seemed better for me to punish the scoundrels without endangering you. For I thought other men's shoulders should not be made to prop a burden I believed could be adequately sustained by my own.

'I have burnt the others and left your hands to incinerate Fengi's corpse; on him at least you can sate your longing for a proper revenge. Run quickly, build a pyre, commit the ungodly carcase to the flames, roast his wicked parts, sprinkle the guilty dust, cast away his pitiless ashes; no urn, no burial mound shall enclose the accursed relics of his bones. Nothing must survive to remind us of that murder, let no sanctuary be in our land for these corrupt limbs, no region catch the plague from his presence; neither sea nor earth shall be contaminated by harbouring his execrable body. I have done the rest; only this pious duty remains for you, to celebrate such funeral rites for a tyrant and fratricide. When a man has plucked the liberty from his country, it is not fitting for his country to cover his remains.

'Apart from this, why should I rehearse my sorrows, number my misfortunes, weave my miseries anew? You know them better than I. My stepfather aimed at my death, my mother despised me, my friends spat on me, and I passed my years in weeping, my days in grief, all the time unsettled by constant perils and fear. In short, I have spent every part of my life depressed by utmost adversity. You often groaned quietly to each other over my bereaved wits; he could be no avenger, you said, on his father's slayer. This brought me unspoken proof of your affection, seeing that the memory of the royal murder had not as yet faded from your minds. Who could have so hard a heart, such craggy inflexibility, that he would not soften and bend with compassion at my afflictions? Condole with your young prince, be moved by my hardships, you whose hands are innocent of Orvendil's death. Commiserate too with my distressed mother and, as she was once your queen, rejoice that her disgrace is expunged; embracing as she did the brother-in-law who killed her husband, she was forced to submit her woman's body to a double weight of shame.

'Therefore, to hide my motives of revenge, I kept my brains in shadow and put on a lassitude feigned rather than actual. Pretending imbecility, I contrived to mislead people about my intelligence, but whether that was effective and achieved its full purpose is for you to judge. I am happy for you to make this important judgement. Stamp now on those murderous ashes, spurn the remnants of one who butchered his brother, corrupted and shamefully defiled his brother's queen, struck down his lord, treasonably attacked royalty, inflicted galling tyranny on you, abolished your freedom and crowned homicide with incest.

'Since I was an agent of righteous revenge striving to fulfil my responsibility, support me with your noble spirits, give me the respect that is due, revive me with your warm regard. I myself have wiped out our country's infamy, obliterated my mother's dishonour, thrust off the sway of a tyrant, crushed an assassin, countered the moves and baffled the treacherous hand of my uncle, whose crimes, had he lived, would have redoubled daily. Grieving at the violence to my father and fatherland, I wiped out the wretch who fiercely forded it over you in a way no men should have to bear. Acknowledge my service, do honour to my abilities and grant me the kingdom if I have earned it. You see here the dispenser of this favour, no killer nor degenerate heir to his father's power, but the lawful inheritor of the realm and dutiful avenger of fratricide. To me you owe the restoration of liberty, the abolition of the tormentor's rule, the removal of the oppressor's yoke, the murderer's authority shaken off and the tyrant's sceptre trampled underfoot. It is I who have stripped you of slavery and dressed you in freedom, set you back on the heights, repaired your renown, evicted the despot, triumphed over a hangman. The prize is in your hands. Since you know my merits, I ask you, out of your goodness, to bestow the reward.'

The young man's speech had swayed every heart; some were moved to pity, some even reduced to tears. But as soon as their sadness had abated, he was appointed king by prompt and general acclamation. Everyone put the greatest trust in his abilities, for he had contrived the sum total of his actions with deepest cunning and worked everything to an astounding conclusion. Many, you could tell, were staggered that he could have put this precise plan into operation over such a long stretch of time.

After his exploits in Denmark, Hamlet fitted out three ships at great expense and paid another visit to Britain to see his wife and father-in-law. Under his patronage he had also enrolled youths outstanding in arms and clad in great splendour. Whereas he had long gone about in contemptible garments, he now had all his accoutrements lavishly prepared, and all that had once borne the marks of poverty was converted to a costly luxury. He had ordered a shield to be designed for him, representing in finely-executed pictures the entire series of his exploits from early manhood onwards. In carrying this spokesman, as it were, of his prowess, he ensured the spread of his fame.

On the shield you could see Fengi cutting Orvendil's throat and then his incest, the criminal uncle and his nephew's antics, the hooked sticks, the stepfather's suspicions and the covering-up by his stepson, Hamlet's dealing with different tests, the woman brought to trap him, the open-jawed wolf, the discovery of the rudder, passing the sand-dune, entering the wood, the straw inserted in the horse-fly and Hamlet's recognition of the signal, how he foiled the companions and in seclusion had his way with the girl. You could have observed the palace portrayed, the queen and her son together, the spy cut to pieces, then cooked and thrown into the sewer for the pigs, his limbs plastered with filth and left for the animals to devour. You would have seen also how Hamlet detected the secret of his sleeping comrades, how he effaced the shape of the letters and substituted others, how he spurned the food and drink at the feast, how he criticised the king's looks and censured ignoble traits in the queen. You might have remarked the hanging of the emissaries, the depiction of Hamlet's marriage, the return voyage to Denmark, his funeral celebrated by a banquet, the rods shown to the enquirers in lieu of his companions, the young man carrying out a butler's duties and hacking his fingers intentionally with the drawn sword which was after-wards riveted, the increasing hubbub among the guests and their wilder and wilder dancing, the tapestry thrown over the sleepers, held fast by the clasping hooks and wrapped firmly round them, the brand flung into the building and the revellers burnt alive, the palace consumed by the fire and collapsing in ruins, the visit to Fengi's bedroom, the stolen sword and the useless one set in its place, and finally the king slain at his step-son's hand with the point of his own blade. The assiduous artist had painted all these events on Hamlet's war-shield with consummate skill, creating lifelike shapes to catch an exact image of his deeds. His retinue, to parade themselves in greater magnificence, covered their shields in a layer of pure gold.

The British king received them graciously and waited on them with royal and lavish dispensation. In the midst of their feasting he asked eagerly whether Fengi were alive and prospering, and learnt from his son-in-law that any enquiry about his welfare was vain, for he had perished by the sword. The king pressed to ascertain the murderer's identity with repeated questioning, till he found that the announcer of Fengi's death was also its cause. At this discovery he was inwardly aghast, for he realised at once that he was honour bound to avenge him. On one occasion Fengi and he had decided by mutual agreement that one of them should avenge the other's killing. Devotion to his daughter and affection for his son-in-law pulled him one way, but he was tugged in the other direction by loyalty to his friend and reverence for his binding oath, a two-way contract which it was heinous to desecrate. In the end, despising family ties, he allowed his sworn word to weigh more and, subordinating kinship to plighted faith, bent his thoughts to vengeance. Since he believed it was a sin to violate the sacred laws of hospitality, however, he chose to execute the role of avenger by another's hand and cloak his villainy with pretended innocence.

He therefore devised his plot under cover of kindnesses and hid his malignant purpose under busy courtesies. As his wife had recently succumbed to an illness, he asked Hamlet if he would act as delegate in arranging his second marriage, claiming to be delighted by the Dane's remarkable capabilities. He told Hamlet that there was a Scottish queen whose hand he passionately desired, although he really knew that she was not merely a spinster through modesty, but also cruelly arrogant inflicting the ultimate punishment on her suitors with unremitting hatred; of her many wooers none had yet escaped with his head.

Hamlet, then, complied with his instructions and set out, whatever the dangers of the imposed mission, relying partly on his own, partly on the king's servants. He entered Scotland, and not far from the queen's palace came to a meadow adjoining the roadside where he could refresh his horses. The pleasant babbling of a stream induced drowsiness so that, charmed by the scenery, he thought he would take a rest there after stationing sentinels a little way off. When the queen received report of this she sent out ten young men to investigate the newly-arrived strangers and their equipment. One of the livelier-witted of these dodged the guards, crept determinedly up to Hamlet and removed the shield (on which, as it happened, he had pillowed his head) with such stealth that he disturbed the sleep neither of its owner nor any of his numerous company, for the man wished to inform his mistress not just by word of mouth but with an actual exhibit. The letter entrusted to Hamlet he filched with equal dexterity from the wallet where it was being kept.

These were conveyed to the queen, who, by gazing attentively at the shield, worked out the whole story from the explanatory inscriptions: she gathered that the man nearby had followed the most precise, clever calculations to punish his uncle for his father's murder. After scanning also the letter which contained the request for her hand, she erased all the writing, since she was quite repelled by the idea of wedlock with elderly men and aimed at being linked with someone younger. She went on to pen a commission, supposedly despatched to her by the British king and subscribed like the other with his name and title; in it she forged a request for her consent to marry the messenger. Further, she made sure that the adventures she had learned about from his shield were referred to in the script, in such a way that you would have thought that the shield and the letter confirmed each other. She then ordered the same scouts as before to return the shield and letter to their rightful places in a bid to imitate Hamlet's method of deception when he made dupes of his two companions.

Meanwhile Hamlet realised his shield had been guilefully withdrawn from beneath his head and kept his eyes shut on purpose, so that by astute pretence of unconsciousness he might regain what he had lost when he was actually asleep. He thought that if a single attempt had gone smoothly the trickster would more readily try to repeat his game. Nor was he mistaken. When the spy stole up, wishing to restore the shield and paper to their former places, Hamlet jumped forward, grabbed the fellow and clamped him in fetters. Then, rousing his attendants, he proceeded to the queen's abode. Here he tendered his father-in-law's salutations and offered her the letter signed in the king's handwriting.

As soon as Herminthrud (that was the queen's name) had taken it and read it through, she warmly commended his skilful labours and pronounced that Fengi had been punished legitimately. Hamlet himself, with his unfathomable intelligence, had achieved wonders surpassing human estimation: through his deep perspicacity he had devised recompense for Fengi's extinction of his father and bedding of his mother, and his remarkable principles had led him to seize the kingdom from the man who had frequently tried to ensnare him.

For this reason, she said, she was puzzled that such an accomplished individual could already have stumbled into a misguided marriage. Though his splendour almost outstripped mortal capacity, he appeared nevertheless to have slipped into a dim, undignified union. His wife's parents were slaves, even though good luck had tricked them out with royal preferment. In seeking a partner, a wise man should make his evaluation not by dazzling looks but by her family. If he therefore desired a proper alliance he must consider her lineage and not be captivated by beauty, a provocative enticement which, with a cheap smear of rouge, had stripped many a man of his integrity.

There was a lady he could take, however, of equal rank with himself. Possessed of adequate means and noble blood she herself would be the ideal partner for his embraces, since he did not surpass her in regal wealth nor did his brilliant ancestry excel hers. She was a queen, indeed could be counted a king if her sex were disregarded; more to the point, whichever man she honoured with her bed would actually be king, and receive a realm and her caresses together. Her sceptre and her hand were complementary. It was no paltry kindness to be offering her favours like this, seeing that she was wont to signal her refusal of others by execution. She urged him to turn his charm in her direction, transfer his marriage vows to her and learn to set birth before a fair shape. With these words she ran to clasp him tightly in her arms.

Entranced by the girl's affable speech, he hastened to return her kisses and hugged her hard, declaring that her desires were his own. Next a banquet was held, friends invited, the chieftains collected and the marriage ceremony performed. When all was completed he returned to Britain with his bride, having ordered a stout force of Scotsmen, whose aid he could enlist against various hostile stratagems, to follow immediately behind.

As he was journeying back, his first wife, the British king's daughter, met him. Although she complained that she felt wounded at being superseded by this concubine, she maintained that it was beneath her dignity to set disgust at her husband's adultery before her love for him. She would not, therefore, turn her back on him to the extent of keeping quiet about the sinister schemes which she knew were directed at him. Regard for her son, a token of their union, should at best prompt her to marital affection.

'He can hate his mother's rival,' she said; 'I shall love her. No setback shall lull my passion for you, nor spite prevent me revealing any evil machinations against you that I have unearthed. Be sure to watch my father, since you reaped a happy outcome from your embassy and, by obstinately seizing the initiative, have transferred the whole profit of the venture to yourself and sidestepped the wishes of the man who sent you.' Her words revealed that she was more devoted to her husband than to her father.

While she was addressing Hamlet, the British king appeared, embraced his son-in-law firmly but without warmth, and conducted him in to a feast, bent on hiding his dishonest intentions by a show of generosity. Hamlet, recognising his duplicity, disguised his fears, put on a protective shirt of mail and took with him to the feast a train of two hundred knights. He humoured his host and preferred the danger of complying with the king's hypocrisy rather than churlishly opposing him. A code of honour, to his mind, must be observed in everything. As he was riding up to the king, the king attacked him beneath the archway at the double gates and would have transfixed him with his javelin if his sturdy undergarment had not resisted the steel. Hamlet had received merely a light wound and so he sped to the place where he had bidden the Scottish warriors wait on guard. He then sent back to the king his new wife's spy, whom he had captured, to report how he had secretly extracted from the wallet the letter meant for his mistress, thereby intending to throw the blame back on Herminthrud and acquit himself of a charge of treachery by a genuine excuse.

The king lost no time in pressing hotly on his trail and beggared him of most of his troops, so that when the following day Hamlet was on the point of contesting for his life, he altogether despaired of having the strength to resist. In order to make his army appear larger than it was, he took the lifeless bodies of his comrades and propped some up on staves, secured others to nearby rocks, sat some on horseback as if they were alive, and disposed them all with their complete military equipment in lines and formations as though they were about to join combat. The wing of corpses was just as densely packed as his company of live soldiers. Anyone must have been stunned at the sight of dead men being whirled into battle and carcasses mustered to decide the issue. It was no idle scheme, for the forms of the deceased warriors, as they were struck by the sun's rays, appeared like a mighty host. Those senseless figures made his army seem as large as it had been on the previous day, and you would have thought that the carnage of the day before had not thinned his band in the slightest. Terrified at the sight, the Britons fled before the battle, conquered by the corpses of those they had overcome when living. I cannot judge whether this victory owed more to cunning or luck. The king was rather slow taking to flight and the Danes, hard behind, annihilated him. When the conquering Hamlet had snatched a heavy share of British booty, he made for his own country with his wives.

Meanwhile, on the death of Rorik, Viglek had assumed the Danish kingship. After harassing Hamlet's mother with every kind of insolence he had deprived her of her royal wealth and gone on to complain that her son had seized control of Jutland and cheated the king of Leire, for it was his prerogative to confer and remove the duties of high office. Hamlet bore this charge with such equanimity that when he bestowed the finest spoils of his victory on Viglek, he seemed to be repaying slander with bounty. Later, however, he saw a chance to exact revenge: he challenged and defeated the other in warfare and came out into the open as his enemy. He forced into exile the governor of Scania, Fialler, who, so the story goes, withdrew to a place called Undensakre, which is unknown to our people.

After this, Viglek, whose fortunes were resuscitated by the soldiery of Scania and Sjeelland, sent ambassadors to invite him to battle. Hamlet's alert brain perceived that he was balanced between one decision involving disgrace, another spelling danger. He knew that if he took up the challenge he was imperilling his life, and if he shrank from it military dishonour loomed. The desire to preserve his integrity weighed more in a mind which dwelt on gallantry, and a keen thirst for fame blunted his fear of defeat. This prevented the true blaze of his glory from being dimmed by a timid cowering from his fate. He observed too that there is just about the same gulf between an undistinguished life and a magnificent death as men are agreed there is between disdain and honour. He was bound to Herminthrud by such great affection that he was more anxious about her future widowhood than he was over his own death; consequently he paid keen attention to securing a second marriage for her before he went into battle. At this she protested a masculine confidence and swore that she would not abandon her husband even in the front line: she loathed the woman who was frightened to join her husband at his end. Nevertheless she did not stick very closely to this rare promise, for after Viglek had killed Hamlet when they fought in Jutland, she voluntarily yielded herself as a trophy to become the victor's bride.

Every female vow is stolen away by changes of fortune or evaporates with shifting seasons: a woman's steadfastness stands on slippery soles and is weakened by chance accidents. Her faith is glibly pledged but executed slowly, hampered by the various allurements of pleasure: always eager to seek out new interests and forget the old, it leaps away breathlessly towards its desire.

Such was Hamlet's departure. If fate had tended him as kindly as nature, he would have shone as brightly as the gods and his courage would have allowed him to surpass the labours of Hercules. There is a plain in Jutland famous as his burial place and named after him.

MARVELS AND MAGIC

11. ON THE MARVELS OF BRITAIN

In the early ninth century an unknown Welsh writer collected materials for a history of his people. It survives in widely differing versions, one of which is ascribed to a certain Nennius, under whose name it is often quoted. As the editor of one of these versions says in his preface, 'I have heaped together everything I could find', and the History of the Britons *contains everything from scraps of genuine history to purest legend. It also contains the following splendid collection of folklore about different places in Britain. Some of these stories are recognisable natural phenomena, like the account of the Severn Bore; while others also have a foundation in reality, but, because they are based on hearsay reports, have been transformed into something strange and magical. The third kind of story is pure invention, arising from imaginative interpretations of place-names, rather than any that could actually be found there. As we shall see, the Welsh and Irish bards were fascinated by place-names, and topographical lore in general, and this chapter reflects that poetic interest, transmuted into rather less extravagant language, which makes the marvels described all the more unexpected.*

THE first marvel is the lake of Lumonoy [Loch Lomond]. In it there are sixty islands and men dwell on them; and sixty rocks surround it, and there is an eagle's nest on each one. And sixty rivers flow into it, and not one goes from it to the sea, save one river, which is called Lemn [Leven].

The second marvel is at the estuary of the river Trehannon [?Trent], for one wave like a mountain covers it at once, but the water recedes as on other shores.

The third marvel is a hot pool, which is in the country of the Hwicce [near Worcester] and is surrounded by a wall made of bricks and stone. Men go into it to bathe at all times, and the temperature changes for each of them as they wish: if one man wants a cold bath, it will be cold, and if another wants a hot bath, it will be hot.

The fourth marvel is a number of salt wells, from which salt is extracted – various foods are salted with it. Yet the wells are not close to the sea, but spring from the earth.

There is another marvel called 'the two kings of the Severn'; when the tide rushes in at the mouth of the Severn, two heaps of foam gather separately and fight each other like battering-rams, hurling themselves on each other and colliding, then withdrawing and rushing together again. And this they have done from the beginning of the world until this very day.

There is another marvel called Aber Llyn Llywan. The mouth of that river flows into the Severn, and when the tide floods into the Severn, it floods into that river as well, and goes into the lake at the mouth like a whirlpool, but the water level does not rise. The bank by that river is not touched by water even when the Severn is in flood. When the sea and the Severn ebb, then the lake of Llywan regurgitates all the water it has swallowed up, and the water touches the bank, and bursts out like a mountainous breaking wave. And if all the troops of that country were lined up facing the wave, it would draw them in, horses and all, wetting their clothes. But if the army had their backs towards it, it would not harm them. When the tide ebbs, the whole bank where the wave has passed is stripped bare, and the sea draws back from it.

There is another marvel in the region between Wye and Severn – a well called Finnaun Gurur Helic. No stream flows out of it or into it. Men go to fish in this well: some go to the eastern side and catch fish on that side; others go to the north, south and west, and all of them catch fish. But each side yields a different kind of fish. It is a marvel that fish should be found in a well into which no river flows and out of which no river flows, and that four kinds of fish should be there. It is neither very large nor very deep; indeed, it is only knee-deep, and twenty feet in length and breadth, with steep banks on every side.

Near the river Wye, apples are found on an ash-tree in the woodland which slopes down towards the mouth of the river.

There is another marvel in Gwent, a pit out of which the wind blows all the time, without interruption; when the air is still in summer, it continues to blow from this pit, and no one can stand in front of the mouth of the pit. It is a great marvel that wind should blow out of the earth.

There is another marvel in Gower, at Oystermouth – an altar which is held up by the will of God. The story of the altar is this. While St Illtud was praying in a cave near the seashore which faced the sea, he saw a ship sailing towards him with two men sailing it. And they had the body of a holy man with them; and above the holy man's face hovered an altar-stone, supported by God's will. The saint went towards them, and the altar-stone remained stationary above the body of the holy man, and could not be separated from it. And the sailors said to St Illtud: 'This man of God entrusted the altar to us, and told us to bring it to you, so that he should be buried with you. You must not reveal his name to any man, lest men use his name in their oaths.' They buried him, and when this was done, the two men returned to their ship and sailed away. And St Illtud founded a church around the body of the holy man, and around the altar, and it remains supported by the will of God to this day. A certain princeling came to test the truth of this, and he tried it with a rod in his hand, he bent it round the altar, and held the rod in place with his two hands, and pulled it towards him, proving the truth of the matter; but he did not survive until the next month. Another man looked under the altar, and lost his sight; he too did not survive until the next month.

There is another marvel in the aforementioned region of Gwent. There is a well there near the walls of Pwyll Meurig, in the midst of which there is a log. Men come and stand on the log and wash their hands and faces in the well, as I have seen for myself. When the tide floods, the Severn spreads out over the whole seashore, and reaches as far as the well and fills it; and it draws the log with it into the open sea, and for three days it is tossed in the sea; but on the fourth day it can be found back in the well. A countryman who stole it and buried it died before the end of the month.

There is another miracle in the region called Buellt. There is a heap of stones there, with one stone on top of the heap, bearing the footprint of a dog. When Arthur the soldier hunted the boar Troynt, his dog Cabal left his footprint in the stone, and Arthur later gathered the heap of stones and placed it on top, and called it Carn Cabal. Men come and take up the stone in their hands for a day and a night, and the next day it is to be found again on top of the cairn.

There is another marvel in the region which is called Archenfield. There is a grave there by a fountain, which is called Licat Anir, for the name of the man who is buried there was Anir. He was the son of Arthur the soldier, and the latter killed him there and buried him. Men come to measure the tomb, and it is sometimes six feet long, sometimes nine feet, sometimes twelve, sometimes fifteen. Whatever it measures on one occasion, it will be different on the next, as I have discovered myself.

There is another marvel in the region called Cardigan. There is a hill there called Cruc Maur, and a tomb on the summit of it. Every man who comes to that tomb and lies down beside it will find that the tomb is the same length as he is. If he is short and small, the tomb will be short, according to his stature. If he is tall and large, so the tomb will be large to match his stature, even if he is more than six feet tall. The tomb will match the size of any man. And if a wanderer in his weariness shall bow down three times beside it, there shall fall no shadow of weariness on him until the day of his death, nor will he be weighed down with weariness even if he travel alone to the ends of the world.

THE MARVELS OF THE ISLE OF ANGLESEY

The first marvel is a beach without a sea.

The second marvel is a hill that turns round three times in a year.

The third marvel is a ford there, which floods whenever the tide floods, and when the tide ebbs, it ebbs as well.

The fourth marvel is a stone which walks at nighttime above the valley of Citheinn: long ago it was thrown into the whirlpool of Pwyll Ceris in the midst of the Menai Straits, and the next day the very same stone was found on the bank of the aforesaid valley.

SOME MARVELS OF IRELAND

There is a bog called Loch Lein, which is bounded by four circles. The bog is surrounded by a circle of tin, then a circle of lead, then a circle of iron, and finally a circle of bronze. And many pearls are found in the swamp, which kings wear in their ears.

There is another bog which makes wood as hard as stone. Men shape wood, and having done so throw it into the swamp. It is left there until the end of the year, and at the year's end it is found to be stone. And it is called Loch Echach.

12. CULHWCH AND OLWEN

This tale was probably written in Wales in the early twelfth century, just before Geoffrey of Monmouth had made Arthur famous in his History of the Kings of Britain. *It is as if the writer had wanted to gather as many as possible of the traditional stories about the heroes and places of Wales into one book; but the compiling of great lists was a feature of early Welsh literature, and there may well have been other tales in this vein which have been lost. The roll-call of Arthur's men, and of the tasks which Culhwch must undertake, are a kind of incantation of impossible skills and equally impossible feats, which are matched as Culhwch gradually acquires the objects required for Olwen's bridal. The hunting of the Twrch Trwyth is an almost self-contained episode, which takes us on a breathless journey through the heartlands of Arthurian legend. The story of the winning of the giant's daughter is a familiar folktale, but it rarely appears in such heroic guise.*

KILYDD, the son of prince Kelyddon, desired a wife as a helpmeet, and the wife that he chose was Goleuddydd, the daughter of prince Anlawdd. And after their union, the people prayed that they might have an heir. These prayers were answered, and they had a son. While she was pregnant Goleuddydd became wild, and wandered about, shunning the houses of men; but when her delivery was at hand, her reason came back to her. Then she went to a mountain where there lived a swineherd, keeping a herd of pigs. And through fear of the pigs the queen was delivered of her child. And the swineherd took the boy, and brought him to the palace; and he was christened Culhwch, because he had been found in a pig-run. Despite his name, the boy was from a noble family, and cousin to Arthur; and they put him out to nurse.

After this the boy's mother fell sick. Then she called her husband to her, and said to him: 'Of this sickness I shall die, and you will take another wife. Now wives are gifts of God, but you must not wrong your son. Therefore I charge you that you do not take a wife until you see a briar with two blossoms upon my grave.' And this he promised her. Then she besought him to dress her grave every year, that nothing might grow on it. So the queen died, and at first the king sent an attendant every morning to see if anything were growing upon the grave. And at the end of the seventh year the king neglected his promise to the queen.

One day the king went to hunt, and he rode to his wife's grave to find out if it were time for him to take a wife; and the king saw the briar with two blossoms. And when he saw it, the king took counsel where he should find a wife. One of his counsellors said: 'I know a wife that will suit you well: she is the wife of king Doged.' And they resolved to go to seek her; and they killed the king, and stole his wife and one daughter that she had along with her. And they conquered the king's lands.

One day, as the lady went walking, she came to the house of an old crone who lived in the town, who had no tooth in her head. And the queen said to her, 'Old woman, tell me that which I shall ask you for the love of heaven. Where are the children of the man who has carried me away by force?' The crone said, 'He has no children.' 'Woe is me, that I should have come to one who is childless!' Then the hag said, 'You need not lament on account of that, for it is foretold that he shall have an heir by you and by none other. Moreover, be not sorrowful, for he already has one son.'

The lady went joyfully back home and asked her husband, 'Why have you hidden your child from me?' The king said, 'I will do so no longer.' And he sent messengers for his son, and he was brought to the court.

His stepmother said to him, 'It would be well for you to have a wife, and I have a daughter who is sought of every man of renown in the world.' 'I am not yet of an age to wed,' answered the youth.

Then she said to him, 'I declare to you, that it is your destiny not to be wedded to a wife until you obtain Olwen, the daughter of Ysbaddaden, the Chief of Giants.' At that the youth blushed, and love of the girl took hold of him, body and soul, although he had never seen her. And his father asked him, 'What has come over you, my son, and what is wrong with you?' 'My stepmother has declared to me that I shall never have a wife until I obtain Olwen, the daughter of Ysbaddaden, the Chief of Giants.' 'That will be easy for you,' answered his father. 'Arthur is your cousin. Go to Arthur, to have your hair cut, and ask this of him as a gift.'

So the youth set out on a four-year-old horse with a head dappled grey, firm of limb, his hooves like shells, a bridle of linked gold and a saddle of costly gold. And in the youth's hand were two spears of silver, sharp, well-tempered, headed with steel and ten feet in length. They had an edge on them to wound the wind, and would cause blood to flow swifter than the fall of the dewdrop from the blade of reedgrass upon the earth when the dew of June is at the heaviest. At his side he wore a gold-hilted sword, the blade of which was of gold, bearing a cross of inlaid gold of the hue of the lightning of heaven: his war-horn was of ivory. Before him were two brindled, white-breasted greyhounds, with strong collars of rubies round their necks, reaching from the shoulder to the ear. The one that was on the left side bounded across to the right side, and the one on the right to the left, and like two sea-swallows they played around him. And his courser cast up four sods with his four hoofs, like four swallows in the air, about his head, now above, now below. His cloak was a four-cornered cloth of purple, and an apple of gold was at each corner, and every one of the apples was worth a hundred head of cattle. And there was precious gold of the value of three hundred cattle on his shoes and on his stirrups, from his knee to the tip of his toe. The blades of grass did not even bend beneath him, so light was his courser's tread as he journeyed towards the gate of Arthur's palace.

The youth called, 'Is there a porter?'

'There is; and if you do not hold your peace, small will be your welcome. I am Arthur's porter every first day of January. And during every other part of the year, the office is filled by Huandaw, and Gogigwr, and Llaesgymyn, and Penpingyon, who goes upon his head to save his feet, neither towards the sky nor towards the earth, but like a rolling stone upon the floor of the court.'

'Open the gates.'

'I will not open them.'

'Why not?'

'The knife is in the meat, and the drink is in the horn, and there is revelry in Arthur's hall, and no one may enter but the son of a king of a privileged country, or a craftsman bringing his craft. But there will be refreshment for your dogs, and for your horses; and for you there will be meat cooked and peppered, and luscious wine and mirthful songs, and food for fifty men shall be brought to you in the guest chamber, where the strangers and the sons of other countries eat, who do not come into the precincts of the palace of Arthur. You will fare no worse there than you would with Arthur in the court. A lady will smooth your couch, and will lull you with songs; and early tomorrow morning, when the gate is open for the crowds that come here each day, it will be opened first for you, and you may sit in any place that you choose in Arthur's hall, from the upper end to the lower.'

The youth said, 'I will do none of these things. If you open the gate, all will be well. If you do not open it, I will bring disgrace on your lord, and give you a bad name. And I will shout three shouts at this very gate, the deadliest that ever man heard, from the top of Pengwaed in Cornwall to the bottom of Dinsol in the north, and to Esgair Oerfel in Ireland. And all the women in this palace that are pregnant shall lose their offspring; and those who are not pregnant shall have their hearts turned by illness, so that they shall never bear children from this day forward.'

'Whatever noise you may make,' said Glewlwyd Gafaelfawr, 'you will not enter contrary to the laws of Arthur's palace until I first go and speak with Arthur.'

Then Glewlwyd went into the hall. And Arthur said to him, 'Have you news from the gate?'

'Half of my life is past, and half of thine. I was heretofore in Caer Se and Asse, in Sach and Salach, in Lotor and Fotor; and I have been heretofore in India the Great and India the Lesser; and I was in the battle of Dau Ynyr, when the twelve hostages were brought from Llychlyn. And I have also been in Europe, and in Africa, and in the islands of Corsica, and in Caer Brythwch, and Brythach, and Ferthach; and I was there when in other days you killed the family of Clis, the son of Merin, and when you killed Mil Du, the son of Ducum, and when you conquered Greece in the east. And I have been in Caer Oeth and Anoeth, and in Caer Nefenhyr, where we saw nine kings in their own right, handsome men; but never did I behold a man of equal dignity with him who is now at the outer gate.'

Then Arthur said, 'If you came from the gate walking, return there running. And everyone who sees the light, and everyone who opens and shuts their eyes, show him respect, and serve him, some with gold-mounted drinking-horns, others with meat cooked and peppered, until food and drink can be prepared for him. It is not fitting to keep such a man as you say he is, in the wind and the rain.'

But Kai said, 'By the hand of my friend, if you followed my advice, you would not break the laws of the court because of him.'

'Not so, blessed Kai. It is an honour to us that such men come here, and the greater our courtesy the greater will be our renown, and our fame, and our glory.'

So Glewlwyd came to the gate, and opened the gate before him; and although everyone else dismounted upon the horseblock at the gate, Culhwch did not dismount, but rode in upon his charger. Then he spoke: 'Greetings to you, sovereign ruler of this island; and this greeting is no less for the lowest as for the highest, and it is equally for your guests, and your warriors, and your chieftains – let all share in it as completely as yourself. And may your favour, and your fame, and your glory, throughout all this island be complete.'

'Greetings to you also,' said Arthur. 'Sit between two of my warriors, and you shall have minstrels before you, and you shall enjoy the privileges of a king born to a throne as long as you remain here. And when I dispense my presents to the visitors and strangers in this court, you shall be the first to receive them.'

The young man said 'I did not come here to consume meat and drink; but if I obtain the boon that I seek, I will repay you for it, and speak well of you; and if I do not get it, I will carry your dispraise to the four quarters of the world, as far as your renown has extended.'

Then said Arthur, 'Since you will not remain here, chieftain, you shall receive whatever gift your tongue may name, as far as the wind dries, and the rain moistens, and the sun revolves, and the sea encircles, and the earth extends; save only my ship; my mantle; Caledfwlch, my sword; Rhongomyant, my lance; Wynebgwrthucher, my shield; Carnwennan, my dagger; Gwenhwyfar, my wife. By the truth of heaven, you shall have it cheerfully, name what you will.'

'I want you to trim my hair.'

'That I will grant you.'

And Arthur took a golden comb, and scissors, whose loops were of
silver, and he trimmed his hair. And Arthur asked him who he was. 'For
my heart warms to you, and I know that you are of my blood. Tell me,
therefore, who you are.'

'I will tell you,' said the youth. 'I am Culhwch, the son of Kilydd, the
son of prince Kelyddon, by Goleuddydd my mother, the daughter of
prince Anlawdd.'

'That is true,' said Arthur; 'you are my cousin. Whatever you may ask,
you shall receive it, whatever your tongue shall name.'

'Pledge the truth of heaven and the faith of your kingdom on it.'

'I pledge it to you, gladly.'

'I beg of you then, that you obtain for me Olwen, the daughter of
Ysbaddaden, the Chief of Giants; and this I likewise seek as a gift at the
hands of your warriors. I seek it from Kai, and Bedwyr, and Greidawl
Galldonyd, and Gwythyr the son of Greidawl, and Greid the son of Eri,
and Kynddelig Kyfarwydd, and Tathal Twyll Goleu, and Maelwys the
son of Baeddan, and Crychwr the son of Nes, and Cubert the son of
Daere, and Percos the son of Poch, and Lluber Beuthach, and Corfil
Berfach, and Gwynn the son of Nudd, and Edeyrn the son of Nudd, and
Gadwy the son of Geraint, and prince Fflewddur Fflam, and Ruawn
Pebyr the son of Dorath, and Bradwen the son of Moren Mynawc, and
Moren Mynawc himself, and Dalldaf the son of Cimin Cof, and the son
of Alun Dyfed, and the son of Saidi, and the son of Gwryon, and
Uchtryd Ardywad Kad, and Kynwas Curfagyl, and Gwrhyr Gwartheg-
fras, and Isperyr Ewingath, and Gallcoyt Gofynynat, and Duach and
Grathach and Nerthach, the sons of Gwawrddur Kyrfach (these men
came from the confines of hell), and Kilydd Canhastyr, and Canhastyr
Canllaw, and Cors Cant-Ewin, and Esgair Gulhwch Gofynkawn, and
Drustwrn Hayarn, and Glewlwyd Gafaelfawr, and Lloch Llawwynnyawc,
and Aunwas Adeiniawc, and Sumoch the son of Seithfed, and Gwenn-
wynwyn the son of Naw, and Bedyw the son of Seithfed, and Gobrwy
the son of Echel Forddwyttwll, and Echel Forddwyttwll himself, and
Mael the son of Roycol, and Dadweir Dallpenn, and Garwyli the son of
Gwythawc Gwyr, and Gwythawc Gwyr himself, and Gormant the son of
Ricca, and Menw the son of Teirgwaedd, and Digon the son of Alar, and
Selyf the son of Smoit, and Gusg the son of Atheu, and Nerth the son of
Kedarn, and Drudwas the son of Tryffin, and Twrch the son of Perif, and
Twrch the son of Anowas, and Iona king of France, and Sel the son of
Selgi, and Teregud the son of Iaen, and Sulyoun the son of Iaen, and
Bradwen the son of Iaen, and Moren the son of Iaen, and Siawn the son
of Iaen, and Cradawc the son of Iaen. (They were men of Caerdathal, of
Arthur's family on his father's side.)

'Dirmyg the son of Kaw, and Justic the son of Kaw, and Etmic the
son of Kaw, and Anghawd the son of Kaw, and Ofan the son of Kaw,

and Kelin the son of Kaw, and Connyn the son of Kaw, and Mabsant the son of Kaw, and Gwyngad the son of Kaw, and Lkvybyr the son of Kaw, and Coth the son of Kaw, and Meilic the son of Kaw, and Kynwas the son of Kaw, and Ardwyad the son of Kaw, and Ergyryad the son of Kaw, and Neb the son of Kaw, and Gilda the son of Kaw, and Calcas the son of Kaw, and Hueil the son of Kaw (he never yet asked anything of any lord).

'And Samson Finsych, and Taliesin the chief of the bards, and Manawyddan the son of Llyr, and Llary the son of prince Kasnar, and Ysperni the son of Fflergant king of Armorica, and Saranhon the son of Glythwyr, and Llawr Eilerw, and Annyanniawc the son of Menw the son of Teirgwaedd, and Gwynn the son of Nwyfre, and Fflam the son of Nwyfre, and Geraint the son of Erbin, and Ermid the son of Erbin, and Dyfel the son of Erbin, and Gwynn the son of Ermid, and Kyndrwyn the son of Ermid, and Hyfeidd Unllenn, and Eiddon Fawr Frydic, and Reidwn Arwy, and Gormant the son of Ricca (Arthur's brother by his mother's side; the chief elder of Cornwall was his father), and Llawnrodded Farfawc, and Nodawl Faryf Twrch, and Berth the son of Kado, and Rheidwn the son of Beli, and Iscofan Hael, and Iscawin the son of Panon, and Morfran the son of Tegid (no one struck him in the battle of Camlan because of his ugliness; all thought he was a devil who was taking part in the fight. He had hair on him like the hair of a stag). And Sandde Bryd Angel (no one touched him with a spear in the battle of Camlan because of his beauty; all thought he was a ministering angel). And Kynwyl Sant (the third man that escaped from the battle of Camlan, and he was the last who parted from Arthur on Hengroen his horse).

'And Uchtryd the son of Erim, and Eus the son of Erim, and Henwas Adeinawg the son of Erim, and Henbedestyr the son of Erim, and Sgilti Yscawndroed the son of Erim. (These three men possessed these three qualities: there was no one who could keep pace with Henbedestyr, either on horseback or on foot; no four-footed beast could run the distance of an acre with Henwas Adeinawg, much less go beyond it; and as to Sgilti Yscawndroed, when he intended to go upon a message for his lord, he never sought a path, but knowing where he was to go, if his way lay through a wood he went along the tops of the trees. During his whole life, no blade of reedgrass ever bent, much less broke, beneath his feet, so lightly did he tread.) Teithi Hen the son of Gwynhan (his lands were swallowed up by the sea, and he himself hardly escaped, and he came to Arthur; and his knife had this peculiarity, that from the time that he came there no heft would ever remain on it, and owing to this a sickness came over him, and he pined away during the remainder of his life, and died of the sickness).

'And Carneddyr the son of Gofynyon Hen, and Gwenwynwyn the son of Naf Gyssefin, Arthur's champion, and Llysgadrudd Emys, and Gwrbothu Hen (they were Arthur's uncles, his mother's brothers).

Kulvanawyd the son of Goryon, and Llenlleawg Wyddel from the headland of Ganion, and Dyfynwal Moel, and Dunard king of the North, Teirnon Twryf Bliant, and Tegfan Gloff, and Tegyr Talgellawg, Gwrdinal the son of Ebrei, and Morgant Hael, Gwystyl the son of Rhun the son of Nwython, and Llwyddeu the son of Nwython, and Gwydre the son of Llwyddeu (Gwenabwy the daughter of [Kaw] was his mother, Hueil his uncle stabbed him, and there was hatred between Hueil and Arthur because of the wound).

'Dream the son of Dremidyd (when the gnat arose in the morning with the sun, he could see it from Kelli Wic in Cornwall, as far off as Pen Blathaon in north Britain). And Eidyol the son of Ner, and Glwyddyn Saer (who constructed Ehangwen, Arthur's hall). Kynyr Keinfarfewc (when he was told he had a son born he said to his wife, 'Girl, if your son be mine, his heart will be always cold, and there will be no warmth in his hands; and he will have another peculiarity, if he is my son he will always be stubborn; and he will have another peculiarity, when he carries a burden, whether it be large or small, no one will be able to see it, either before him or at his back; and he will have another peculiarity, no one will be able to resist fire and water so well as he will; and he will have another peculiarity, there will never be a servant or an officer equal to him'). Henwas, and Henwyneb (an old companion to Arthur). Gwall-goyc (when he came to a town, though there were three hundred houses in it, if he wanted anything, he would not let sleep come to the eyes of anyone while he remained there). Berwyn the son of Gerenhir, and Paris king of France, and Osla Big-Knife (who bore a short broad dagger. When Arthur and his hosts came before a torrent, they would seek for a narrow place where they might pass the water, and would lay the sheathed dagger across the torrent, and it would form a bridge sufficient for the armies of the three islands of Britain, and of the three islands adjacent, with their spoil).

'Gwyddawg the son of Menestyr (who killed Kai, and whom Arthur killed, together with his brothers, to revenge Kai). Garanwyn the son of Kai, and Amren the son of Bedwyr, and Ely Amyr, and Rheu Rhwyd Dyrys and Rhun Rhudwern, and Eli, and Trachmyr (Arthur's chief huntsmen). And Llwyddeu the son of Kelcoed and Hunabwy the son of Gwryon, and Gwynn Godyfron and Gweir Dathanfenniddawg, and Gweir the son of Cadell the son of Talaryant, and Gweir Gwrhyd Ennwir and Gweir Paladyr Hir (the uncles of Arthur, the brothers of his mother). The sons of Llwch Llawwynnyawg (from beyond the raging sea). Llenlleawg Wyddel, and Ardderchawg Prydain. Cas the son of Saidi, Gwrfan Gwallt Afwyn, and Gwilenhin the king of France, and Gwittart the son of Oedd king of Ireland, Garselit Wyddel, Panawr Pen Bagad, and Ffleudor the son of Naf, Gwynnhyfar mayor of Cornwall and Devon (the ninth man who rallied the army at the battle of Camlan).

'Keli and Kueli, and Gilla Coes Hydd (he would clear three hundred acres at one bound: he was the chief leaper of Ireland). Sol, and Gwadyn Ossol, and Gwadyn Odyeith. (Sol could stand all day on one foot. If Gwadyn Ossol stood upon the top of the highest mountain in the world it would become a level plain under his feet. As for Gwadyn Odyeith, the soles of his feet emitted sparks of fire when they struck upon things hard, like the heated mass when drawn out of the forge. He cleared the way for Arthur when he came to any obstruction.) Hirerwm and Hiratrwm. (The day they went on a visit three cantrefs provided for their entertainment, and they feasted until noon and drank until night, when they went to sleep. And then they devoured the heads of the vermin through hunger as if they had never eaten anything. When they made a visit they left neither the fat nor the lean, neither the hot nor the cold, the sour nor the sweet, the fresh nor the salt, the boiled nor the raw.) Huarwar the son of Halawn (who asked Arthur for a gift which would satisfy him. When he received it, it was the third great plague of Cornwall. None could get a smile from him except when he was satisfied).

'Guare Gwallt Euryn. The two cubs of Gast Rhymhi, Gwyddrud and Gwyddneu Astrus. Sugyn the son of Sugnedydd (who would suck up the sea on which were three hundred ships so as to leave nothing but a dry shore. He was broad-chested). Cacamwri, the attendant of Arthur (any barn he was shown, even if it held the produce of thirty plough-lands within it, he would strike it with an iron flail until the rafters, the beams, and the boards were no better than the small oats in the chaff upon the floor of the barn). Dygyflwng and Anoeth Feidawg. And Hir Eiddyl, and Hir Amreu (they were two attendants of Arthur). And Gwefyl the son of Gwestad (on the day that he was sad, he would let one of his lips drop below his waist, while he turned up the other like a cap upon his head). Uchtryd Faryf Draws (who spread his red untrimmed beard over the forty-eight rafters in Arthur's hall). Elidyr Gyfarwydd. Yskyrdav and Yscudydd (they were two attendants of Gwenhwyfar. Their feet were swift as their thoughts when bearing a message). Brys the son of Bryssethach (from the hill of the Black Fernbrake in north Britain).

'And Grudlwyn Gorr. Bwlch, and Kyfwlch, and Sefwlch, the sons of Cleddyf Kyfwlch, the grandsons of Cleddyf Difwlch. (Their three shields were three gleaming glitterers; their three spears were three pointed piercers; their three swords were three grinding gashers), Glas, Glessic, and Gleisad. Their three dogs, Call, Cuall, and Cafall. Their three horses, Hwyrdyddwg, and Drwgdyddwg, and Llwyrdyddwg. Their three wives, Och, and Garam, and Diaspad. Their three grandchildren, Lluched, and Nefed, and Eissiwed. Their three daughters, Drwg, and Gwaeth, and Gwaethaf Oll. Their three handmaids, Eheubryd the daughter of Kyfwlch, Gorasgwrn the daughter of Nerth, Gwaedan the daughter of Kynfelyn Keudawd Pwyll the half-man.

'Dwnn Diessic Unbenn, Eiladyr the son of Pen Llarcau, Kynedyr Wyllt the son of Hettwn Talaryant, Sawyl Ben Uchel, Gwalchmai the son of Gwyar, Gwalhafed the son of Gwyar, Gwrhyr Gwastawt Ieithoedd (to whom all languages were known), and Kethcrwm the Priest. Clust the son of Clustfeinad (though he were buried forty feet beneath the earth, he would hear the ant fifty miles off rise from her nest in the morning). Medyr the son of Methredydd (from Celli Wig he could, in a twinkling, shoot a wren through the two legs upon Esgair Oerfel in Ireland). Gwiawn Llygad Cat (who could cut a haw from the eye of the gnat without hurting him). Ol the son of Olwydd (seven years before he was born his father's pigs were carried off, and when he grew to be a man he tracked the pigs, and brought them back in seven herds). Bedwini the bishop, who blessed Arthur's meat and drink.

'The golden-chained daughters of this island: Gwenhwyfar its chief lady, and Gwennhwyach her sister, and Rathtyen the only daughter of Clemenhill, and Rhelemon the daughter of Kai, and Tannwen the daughter of Gweir Datharweniddawg. Gwenn Alarch the daughter of Kynwyl Canbwch. Eurneid the daughter of Clydno Eiddin. Eneuawc the daughter of Bedwyr. Enrydreg the daughter of Tudvathar. Gwennwledyr the daughter of Gwaledyr Kyrfach. Erddudnid the daughter of Tryffin. Eurolwen the daughter of Gwdolwyn Gorr. Teleri the daughter of Peul. Indeg the daughter of Garwy Hir. Morfudd the daughter of Urien Rheged. Gwenllian Deg the majestic girl. Creiddylad the daughter of Lludd Llaw Ereint. (Creiddylad was the most splendid girl in the three islands of the mighty, and in the three neighbouring islands, and for her Gwythyr the son of Greidawl and Gwynn the son of Nudd fight every first of May until Doomsday.) Ellylw the daughter of Neol Kynn-Crog (she lived three ages). Essyllt Finwen and Essyllt Fingul.'

And all these Culhwch, the son of Kilydd, named and bound to help him to obtain his gift.

Then Arthur said, 'Oh chieftain, I have never heard of the girl of whom you speak, nor of her family, but I will gladly send messengers in search of her. Give me time to seek her.'

And the young man said, 'I will willingly grant you from tonight until New Year's Eve to do so.'

Then Arthur sent messengers to every land within his dominions to seek for the girl; and at the end of the year Arthur's messengers returned without having gained any more knowledge or intelligence concerning Olwen than they had on the first day. Then Culhwch said, 'Everyone has received his gift, but I still lack mine. I will depart and take your honour with me.'

Then said Kai, 'Rash chieftain, do you reproach Arthur? Go with us, and we will not part until you either confess that the girl does not exist in this world, or until we get her for you.' With this he stood up. Kai had this peculiarity, that his breath lasted nine nights and nine days underwater, and he could exist nine nights and nine days without sleep. No physician could heal a wound from Kai's sword. Kai was a shape-shifter: when he so wished, he could make himself as tall as the highest tree in the forest. And he had another peculiarity: so great was the heat of his nature, that, when it rained hardest, whatever he carried remained dry for a hand's breadth above and below his hand; and when his companions were coldest, it was to them as fuel with which to light the fire.

And Arthur called Bedwyr, who never shrank from any enterprise upon which Kai was bound. None was equal to him in swiftness throughout this island except Arthur and Drych Ail Kibddar. And although he was one-handed, three warriors could not shed blood faster than he on the field of battle. Another property he had; his lance would produce a wound equal to those of nine opposing lances.

And Arthur called to Kynddelig the Guide: 'Go on this expedition with Culhwch.' For he was as good a guide in a land which he had never seen as he was in his own. He called Gwrhyr Gwalstawt Ieithoedd, because he knew every language that existed.

And Arthur called Gwalchmai, the son of Gwyar, because he never returned home without achieving the adventure of which he went in quest. He was the best of footsoldiers, and the best of knights. He was nephew to Arthur, the son of his sister, and his cousin. And Arthur called Menw, the son of Teirgwaedd so that if they went into a savage country, he might cast a spell of illusion over them, so that none might see them, while they could see everyone.

So Culhwch and his companions journeyed until they came to a vast open plain, on which they saw a great castle, the fairest castle in the world. And they journeyed that day until the evening, and when they thought they were near the castle, they were no nearer to it than they had been in the morning. And the second and the third day they journeyed, and even then they only reached it with difficulty. When they reached the castle, they saw a vast flock of sheep, which was boundless and endless. On the top of a mound there was a herdsman, keeping the sheep. He had a rug made of skins on him; and by his side was a shaggy mastiff, larger than a horse nine winters old. This herdsman had never lost even a lamb from his flock, much less a grown sheep. He let no occasion ever pass without doing some hurt and harm. All the dead trees and bushes in the plain he burnt to the ground with his breath.

Then Kai said, 'Gwrhyr Gwalstawt Ieithoedd, go and greet that man.'

'Kai,' he replied, 'I did not promise to go further than you yourself.'

'Let us go together then,' answered Kai. Menw the son of Teirgwaedd said, 'Do not be afraid to go there, for I will cast a spell upon the dog, so that he shall injure no one.'

So they went up to the mound where the herdsman was, and they said to him, 'Is all well with you, herdsman?' 'May it be as well with you as it is with me.' 'Are you indeed the lord of this land?' 'No one except myself can harm me.' 'Whose are the sheep that you keep, and to whom does that castle belong?' 'You must be fools! The whole world knows that this is the castle of Ysbaddaden, the Chief of Giants.' 'And who are you?' 'I am called Custennin the son of Dyfnedig, and my brother Ysbaddaden the Chief of Giants oppressed me because of my possessions. And likewise, who are you?' 'We are ambassadors from Arthur, come to seek Olwen, the daughter of Ysbaddaden the Chief of Giants.' 'The mercy of Heaven be upon you! Do not do that for all the world. No one who ever came here on that mission has returned alive.'

The herdsman stood up, and, as he arose, Culhwch gave him a ring of gold. And he tried to put on the ring, but it was too small for him, so he put it in the finger of his glove. And he went home, and gave the glove to his wife to keep. And she took the ring from the glove when he gave it to her, and she said, 'Where did this ring come from? You are not usually so fortunate.'

'I went', he said, 'to the sea to seek for fish, and I saw a corpse borne by the waves, the fairest I ever saw, and from its finger did I take this ring.' 'Since when does the sea permit its dead to wear jewels? Show me this body.' 'Wife, you will see him to whom this ring belonged here, in the evening.' 'And who is he?' asked the woman. 'Culhwch, the son of Kilydd, the son of prince Kelyddon, by Goleuddydd, his mother, the daughter of prince Anlawdd, who has come to seek Olwen as his wife.'

And when she heard that, her feelings were divided between her joy at the arrival of her nephew, the son of her sister, and sorrow because she had never known anyone return alive who had come on that mission.

And Culhwch and his company came to the gate of the house of Custennin the herdsman. And when she heard their footsteps, she ran out with joy to meet them. Kai snatched a log of wood out of the pile, and when she met them she sought to throw her arms about their necks, but Kai placed the log between her two hands, and she squeezed it so that it became a twisted coil.

'Woman,' said Kai, 'if you had squeezed me like that, no one could ever again have had any affection for me. That would have been but evil love.'

They entered the house, and were given food; and soon after they all went out to amuse themselves. Then the woman opened a stone chest in the chimney corner, and out of it rose a youth with yellow curling hair. Gwrhyr said, 'It is a pity to keep this youth hidden. I am sure he is not punished because he has committed a crime.'

'This is all that is left to me,' said the woman. 'Ysbaddaden, the Chief of Giants, has killed twenty-three of my sons, and I have no more hope of this one than of the others.'

Then Kai said, 'Let him come and be a companion with me, and he shall not be killed unless I am also killed with him.' So they ate.

And the woman asked them, 'What errand brings you here?' 'We come to seek Olwen for this youth.' Then the woman said, 'In the name of heaven, since no one from the castle has seen you yet, go back where you came from.' 'Heaven is our witness, that we will not return until we have seen the girl.'

Kai said, 'Does she ever come here so that we can see her?' 'She comes here every Saturday to wash her head, and in the vessel where she washes, she leaves all her rings, and she never either comes herself or sends any messengers to fetch them.' 'Will she come here if she is sent for?' 'Heaven knows that I will not destroy my soul, nor will I betray those that trust me; unless you will pledge me your faith that you will not harm her, I will not send for her.' 'We pledge it,' they said.

So a message was sent, and she came.

The girl was clothed in a robe of flame-coloured silk; round her neck was a collar of red gold, on which were precious emeralds and rubies. Her hair was more yellow than the flower of the broom, and her skin was whiter than the foam of the wave, and her hands and fingers were fairer than the blossoms of the wood anemone in the spray of the meadow fountain. Her glance was brighter than the eye of the trained hawk, or that of the thrice-mewed falcon. Her breast was more snowy than the breast of the white swan, her cheek was redder than the reddest roses. Whoever saw her was filled with love for her. Four white trefoils sprang up wherever she trod; and for this reason she was called Olwen. She came into the house, and sat beside Culhwch on the nearest bench; and as soon as he saw her he knew her.

Culhwch said to her, 'Ah! girl, you are she who I have loved; come away with me, lest they speak evil of you and of me. I have loved you for a long time.'

'I cannot do this, for I have promised father not to go without his counsel, for his life will last only until the time of my marriage. Whatever is, must be. But I will give you advice if you will take it. Go and ask my father for my hand, and agree to do whatever he shall require of you, and you will get me; but if you refuse anything, you will not get me, and you will do well to escape with your life.'

'I promise all this, if I have the chance to do it,' said he.

She returned to her chamber, and they all rose up and followed her to the castle. And they killed the nine porters that were at the nine gates in silence. And they killed the nine watchdogs without one of them barking. And they went on into the hall.

'The greeting of heaven and of man to you, Ysbaddaden, the Chief of

Giants,' they said. 'And why have you come?' 'We come to ask for the hand of your daughter Olwen, for Culhwch, the son of Kilydd, the son of prince Kelyddon.'

'Where are my pages and my servants? Raise up the forks beneath my two eyebrows which have fallen over my eyes, so that I can see what kind of man my son-in-law is.'

And they did so.

'Come here tomorrow, and you shall have an answer.'

They rose to go, and Ysbaddaden, Chief of Giants, seized one of the three poisoned darts that lay beside him, and threw it after them. And Bedwyr caught it, and flung it, and pierced Ysbaddaden, Chief of Giants, with it through the knee, wounding him grievously. Then he said, 'A cursed ungentle son-in-law, truly. I shall always walk the worse for his rudeness, and shall never be cured. This poisoned iron pains me like the bite of a gadfly. Cursed be the smith who forged it, and the anvil on which it was wrought, it is so sharp!'

That night they stayed in the house of Custennin the herdsman. The next day at dawn they dressed in haste and went to the castle; and when they entered the hall, they said, 'Ysbaddaden, Chief of Giants, give us your daughter in consideration of her dower and her marriage fee, which we will pay to you and also to her two kinswomen. And unless you will do so, you shall meet with your death on her account.'

Then he answered, 'Her four great-grandmothers, and her four great-grandsires are still alive; I must ask their advice.'

'So be it,' they answered, 'we will go and eat.'

As they stood up, he took the second dart that lay beside him, and threw it after them. And Menw, the son of Gwaedd, caught it, and flung it back at him, striking him in the middle of his breast, so that it came out at the small of his back.

'A cursed ungentle son-in-law, truly,' he said, 'the hard iron pains me like the bite of a horse-leech. Cursed be the hearth on which it was heated, and the smith who formed it, it is so sharp. From now on, whenever I go up a hill, I shall be short of breath, and have a pain in my chest, and I shall often loathe my food.' And they went to eat.

And on the third day they returned to the palace. And Ysbaddaden, Chief of Giants, said to them, 'Do not shoot at me again unless you seek to meet your death. Where are my attendants? Lift up the forks of my eyebrows which have fallen over my eyeballs, so that I can see what kind of man my son-in-law is.' Then they stood up, and, as they did so, Ysbaddaden, Chief of Giants, took the third poisoned dart and cast it at them. And Culhwch caught it and threw it vigorously and wounded him through the eyeball, so that the dart came out at the back of his head.

'A cursed ungentle son-in-law, truly! As long as I live, my eyesight will be the worse. Whenever I go against the wind, my eyes will water, and perhaps my head will burn, and I shall feel giddy every new moon. Cursed be the fire in which it was forged. The wound of this poisoned iron is like the bite of a mad dog.' And they went to eat.

And the next day they came again to the palace, and they said, 'Do not throw more darts at us, unless you want the kind of hurt and harm and torment that you already have, only worse.' And Culhwch added, 'Give me your daughter, and if you will not give her, you shall go to your death because of her.'

'Where is he that seeks my daughter? Come here where I may see you.' And they put a chair for him face to face with Ysbadadden.

Ysbaddaden, Chief of Giants, asked, 'Is it you who seek my daughter?'

'It is I,' answered Culhwch.

'I must have your pledge that you will do no injustice to me; when I have got whatever I shall name, you shall have my daughter.'

'I promise you that willingly,' said Culhwch, 'name whatever you want.'

'I will do so,' he said. 'Do you see that huge hill?'

'I do.'

'I require it to be rooted up, and that the grubbings be burned for manure to put on the land; and it is to be ploughed and sown in one day, and the grain must ripen in one day. From that wheat I intend to make food and drink fit for the wedding of you and my daughter. And all this is to be done in the space of a day.'

'That is easily done, though you may not think so.'

'This may be easy for you, but there is something else which will not be so. No farmer can till or prepare this land, so wild is it, except Amaethon, the son of Don, and he will not come with you by his own free will, and you will not be able to compel him.'

'That is easily done, though you may not think so.'

'Even if you get this, there is something you will not get. Gofannon, the son of Don, must come to the headland to set the iron for the plough; he will do no work of his own goodwill except for a lawful king, and you will not be able to compel him.'

'It will be easy for me to accomplish this.'

'Even if you get this, there is something you will not get: the two dun oxen of Gwlwlyd, both yoked together, to plough the wild land over there stoutly. He will not give them of his own free will, and you will not be able to compel him.'

'It will be easy for me to accomplish this.'

'Even if you get this, there is something you will not get: I need the yellow bull and the brindled bull yoked together.'

'It will be easy for me to accomplish this.'

'Even if you get this, there is something you will not get: the two horned oxen, one of which is the far side of the mountain peak, and the other which is this side of the mountain, yoked together in the same plough. And these are Nynniaw and Peibaw, whom God turned into oxen on account of their sins.'

'It will be easy for me to accomplish this.'

'Even if you get this, there is something you will not get. Do you see the red ploughed field over there? When first I met the mother of this girl, nine measures of flax were sown there, and none has yet sprung up, neither white nor black; and I have the measure by me still. I need to have the flax to sow in the new land over here, so that when it grows up it may make a white veil for my daughter's head, on the day of your wedding.'

'That is easily done, though you may not think so.'

'Even if you get this, there is something you will not get: honey that is nine times sweeter than the honey of the virgin swarm, without scum and bees. I need this to make mead for the feast.'

'That is easily done, though you may not think so.'

'The vessel of Llwyr, the son of Llwyryon, which is of the utmost value. There is no other vessel in the world that can hold this drink. You will not get it of his free will, and you cannot compel him.'

'That is easily done, though you may not think so.'

'Even if you get this, there is something you will not get. The basket of Gwyddneu Garanhir: if the whole world should come together, thrice nine men at a time, the meat that each of them desired would be found within it. I require to eat from it on the night that my daughter becomes your bride. He will give it to no one of his own free will, and you cannot compel him.'

'That is easily done, though you may not think so.'

'Even if you get this, there is something you will not get. The horn of Gwlgawd Gododin to serve us with liquor that night. He will not give it of his own free will, and you will not be able to compel him.'

'That is easily done, though you may not think so.'

'Even if you get this, there is something you will not get. The harp of Teirtu to play to us that night. When a man desires that it should play, it does so of itself, and when he desires that it should cease, it ceases. And this he will not give of his own free will, and you will not be able to compel him.'

'That is easily done, though you may not think so.'

'Even if you get this, there is something you will not get. The cauldron of Diwrnach Wyddel, the steward of Odgar, the son of Aedd, king of Ireland, to boil the meat for your marriage feast.'

'That is easily done, though you may not think so.'

'Even if you get this, there is something you will not get. I need to wash my head, and shave my beard, and I require the tusk of Yskithyrwyn Penbaedd to shave myself, neither shall I profit by its use if it is not plucked alive out of his ear.'

'That is easily done, though you may not think so.'

'Even if you get this, there is something you will not get. There is no one in the world that can pluck it out of his head except Odgar, the son of Aedd, king of Ireland.'

'It will be easy for me to accomplish this.'

'Even if you get this, there is something you will not get. I will not trust anyone to keep the tusk except Gado of north Britain. Now the threescore cantrefs of north Britain are under his sway; of his own free will he will not come out of his kingdom, and you will not be able to compel him.'

'That is easily done, though you may not think so.'

'Even if you get this, there is something you will not get. I must spread out my hair in order to shave it, and it will never be spread out unless I have the blood of the jet-black sorceress, the daughter of the pure white sorceress, from the head of the valley of grief on the confines of hell.'

'That is easily done, though you may not think so.'

'Even if you get this, there is something you will not get. I will not have the blood unless I have it warm, and no vessels will keep warm the liquid that is put in them except the bottles of Gwyddolwyd Gorr, which preserve the heat of the liquor that is put into them in the east until they arrive at the west. And he will not give them of his own free will, and you will not be able to compel him.'

'That is easily done, though you may not think so.'

'Even if you get this, there is something you will not get. Some will desire fresh milk, and it will not be possible to have fresh milk for all unless we have the bottles of Rhinnon Rhin Barnawd, in which no liquor ever turns sour. And he will not give them of his own free will and you will not be able to compel him.'

'That is easily done, though you may not think so.'

'Even if you get this, there is something you will not get. Throughout the world there is not a comb or scissors with which I can arrange my hair, on account of its rankness, except the comb and scissors that are between the two ears of Twrch Trwyth, the son of prince Tared. He will not give them of his own free will, and you will not be able to compel him.'

'That is easily done, though you may not think so.'

'Even if you get this, there is something you will not get. It will not be possible to hunt Twrch Trwyth without Drudwyn, the whelp of Greid the son of Eri.'

'That is easily done, though you may not think so.'

'Even if you get this, there is something you will not get. Throughout the world there is not a leash that can hold him, except the leash of Cwrs Cant Ewin.'

'That is easily done, though you may not think so.'

'Even if you get this, there is something you will not get. Throughout the world there is no collar that will hold the leash except the collar of Canhastyr Canllaw.'

'That is easily done, though you may not think so.'

'Even if you get this, there is something you will not get. The chain of Kilydd Canhastyr to fasten the collar to the leash.'

'That is easily done, though you may not think so.'

'Even if you get this, there is something you will not get. Throughout the world there is not a huntsman who can hunt with this dog, except Mabon, the son of Modron. He was taken from his mother when three nights old, and it is not known where he now is, nor whether he is living or dead.'

'That is easily done, though you may not think so.'

'Even if you get this, there is something you will not get. Gwynn Mygdwn, the horse of Gweddw, that is as swift as the wave, to carry Mabon, the son of Modron to hunt the boar Trwyth. He will not give him of his own free will, and you will not be able to compel him.'

'That is easily done, though you may not think so.'

'Even if you get this, there is something you will not get. You will not get Mabon, for it is not known where he is, unless you find Eidoel, his kinsman in blood, the son of Aer. For otherwise it would be useless to seek for him. He is his cousin.'

'That is easily done, though you may not think so.'

'Even if you get this, there is something you will not get. Garselit the Gwyddelian is the chief huntsman of Ireland; the Twrch Trwyth can never be hunted without him.'

'That is easily done, though you may not think so.'

'Even if you get this, there is something you will not get. A leash made from the beard of Dillus Farfawc, for that is the only one that can hold those two cubs. And the leash will be of no use unless it be plucked from his beard while he is alive, and twitched out with wooden tweezers. While he lives he will not suffer this to be done to him, and the leash will be of no use should he be dead, because it will be brittle.'

'That is easily done, though you may not think so.'

'Even if you get this, there is something you will not get. Throughout the world there is no huntsman that can hold those two whelps except Kynedyr Wyllt, the son of Hettwn Glafyrawc; he is nine times more wild than the wildest beast upon the mountains. You will never get him, nor will you ever get my daughter.'

'That is easily done, though you may not think so.'

'Even if you get this, there is something you will not get. It is not possible to hunt the boar Trwyth without Gwynn, the son of Nudd, whom God has placed over the brood of devils in Annwfn, lest they should destroy the present race. He will never be allowed to leave that place.'

'That is easily done, though you may not think so.'

'Even if you get this, there is something you will not get. There is not a horse in the world that can carry Gwynn to hunt the Twrch Trwyth, except Du, the horse of Mor of Oerveddawg.'

'That is easily done, though you may not think so.'

'Even if you get this, there is something you will not get. Until Gwilenhin the king of France shall come, the Twrch Trwyth cannot be hunted. It will be not be proper for him to leave his kingdom for your sake, and he will never come here.'

'That is easily done, though you may not think so.'

'Even if you get this, there is something you will not get. The Twrch Trwyth can never be hunted without the son of Alun Dyfed; he is skilful in letting loose the dogs.'

'That is easily done, though you may not think so.'

'Even if you get this, there is something you will not get. The Twrch Trwyth cannot be hunted unless you get Aned and Aethlem. They are as swift as a gale of wind, and they were never let loose upon a beast that they did not kill.'

'That is easily done, though you may not think so.'

'Even if you get this, there is something you will not get; Arthur and his companions to hunt the Twrch Trwyth. He is a mighty man, and he will not come for you, neither will you be able to compel him.'

'That is easily done, though you may not think so.'

'Even if you get this, there is something you will not get. The Twrch Trwyth cannot be hunted unless you get Bwlch, and Kyfwlch (and Sefwlch), the grandsons of Cleddyf Difwlch. Their three shields are three gleaming glitterers. Their three spears are three pointed piercers. Their three swords are three grinding gashers, Glas, Glessic, and Gleisad. Their three dogs, Call, Cuall, and Cafall. Their three horses, Hwyrdyddwg, and Drwgdyddwg, and Llwyrdyddwg. Their three wives, Och, and Garam, and Diaspad. Their three grandchildren, Lluched, and Nefed, and Eissiwed. Their three daughters, Drwg, and Gwaeth, and Gwaethaf Oll. Their three handmaids (Eheubryd, the daughter of Kyfwlch; Gorasgwrn, the daughter of Nerth; and Gwaedan, the daughter of Kynfelyn). These three men shall sound the horn, and all the others shall shout, so that all will think that the sky is falling to the earth.'

'That is easily done, though you may not think so.'

'Even if you get this, there is something you will not get. The sword of Gwrnach the Giant; he will never be killed except with that sword. He will not give it of his own free will, either for a price or as a gift, and you will never be able to compel him.'

'That is easily done, though you may not think so.'

'Even if you get this, there is something you will not get. You will meet with difficulties, and nights without sleep, in seeking this, and if you do not obtain it, you will not get my daughter.'

'Horses shall I have, and chivalry; and my lord and kinsman Arthur will obtain for me all these things. And I shall gain your daughter, and you shall lose your life.'

'Go on your way. And you shall not bear the cost of food or clothing for my daughter while you are seeking these things; and when you have accomplished all these marvels, you shall have my daughter for your wife.'

All that day they journeyed, until the evening, and then they saw a vast castle, which was the largest in the world. And a black man, bigger than three of the men of this world, came out from the castle.

They asked him, 'Where have you come from, man?' 'From the castle which you see over there.' 'Whose castle is that?' they asked. 'You are truly stupid. Everyone in the world knows to whom this castle belongs. It is the castle of Gwrnach the Giant.' 'What treatment is there for guests and strangers that arrive in that castle?' 'Lord, heaven protect you. No guest ever came back alive from there, and no one may enter it unless he brings with him his craft.'

So they went to the gate. Gwrhyr Gwalstawt Ieithoedd said, 'Is there a porter?' 'There is. And you, if you have a tongue in your head, why do you call him?' 'Open the gate.' 'I will not open it.' 'Why do you refuse?' 'The knife is in the meat, and the drink is in the horn, and there is revelry in the hall of Gwrnach the Giant, and except for a craftsman who brings his craft, the gate will not be opened tonight.'

'Truly, porter,' said Kai, 'I bring a craft with me.' 'What is your craft?' 'I am the best burnisher of swords in the world.' 'I will go and tell Gwrnach the Giant, and I will bring you an answer.'

So the porter went in, and Gwrnach said to him, 'Have you any news from the gate?' 'I have. There is a party at the door of the gate who desire to come in.' 'Did you enquire of them if they possessed any art?' 'I did,' he said, 'and one of them told me that he was skilled in the burnishing of swords.'

'We need him then. For some time I have searched for someone to polish my sword, and could find no one. Let this man enter, since he brings with him his craft.'

At this the porter returned and opened the gate. And Kai went in by himself, and he greeted Gwrnach the Giant. And a chair was placed for him opposite Gwrnach. And Gwrnach said to him, 'Is it true what is reported of you, that you know how to burnish swords?' 'I know very well how to do so,' answered Kai.

Then the sword of Gwrnach was brought to him. And Kai took a blue whetstone from under his arm, and asked him whether he would have it burnished white or blue. 'Do what seems best to you, as if it were your own sword.'

Then Kai polished one half of the blade and put it in his hand. 'Will this please you?' he asked. 'I would give everything in my lands to have all of it like this. It is a marvel to me that such a man as you should be without a companion.' 'Sir, I have a companion, though he is not skilled in this art.' 'Who may he be?' 'Send the porter out, and I will tell him how to recognise him. The head of his lance will leave its shaft, and draw blood from the wind, and will return to its shaft again.'

Then the gate was opened, and Bedwyr entered. And Kai said, 'Bedwyr is very skilful, although he does not know this art.'

And there was much discussion among those who were still outside the gate, because Kai and Bedwyr had gone in. And a young man who was with them, the only son of Custennin the herdsman, also got in. And he caused all his companions to keep close to him as he passed the three sentry posts, and until he came into the midst of the castle. And his companions said unto the son of Custennin, 'You are the best of all men for doing this.' And from then on he was called Goreu, the son of Custennin. Then they dispersed to the lodgings, that they might slay those who lodged there, unknown to the giant.

The sword was now polished, and Kai gave it to Gwrnach the Giant, to see if he were pleased with his work. And the giant said, 'The work is good; I am content with it.' Kai said, 'It is your scabbard that has rusted your sword; give it to me that I may take out the wooden sides and put in new ones.'

And he took the scabbard from him, and the sword in the other hand. He came and stood by the giant, as if he was about to put the sword into the scabbard; and with it he struck at the head of the giant, and cut off his head at one blow. Then they sacked the castle, and took from it what goods and jewels they would. And on the same day that they had set out, at the beginning of the year, they came to Arthur's court, bringing with them the sword of Gwrnach the Giant.

Now, when they told Arthur of their adventures, Arthur said, 'Which of these marvels will it be best for us to seek first?' 'It will be best to seek Mabon, the son of Modron; and he will not be found unless we first find Eidoel, the son of Aer, his kinsman.'

Then Arthur set out, and the warriors of the islands of Britain with him, to seek for Eidoel; and they travelled until they came before the castle of Glini, where Eidoel was imprisoned. Glini stood on the summit of his castle, and he said, 'Arthur, what do you require of me, since I have nothing left in this fortress, and I have neither joy nor pleasure in it; neither wheat nor oats? Do not try to harm me.'

Arthur answered, 'I did not come to injure you, but to seek for the prisoner who is with you.' 'I will give you my prisoner, though I had not thought that I would give him up to anyone; and I will assist you from now on.'

Arthur's followers said to him, 'Lord, return home, you cannot proceed with your host in quest of such small adventures as these.' Then Arthur said, 'Gwrhyr Gwalstawt Ieithoedd, you should go on this quest, for you know all languages, and are familiar with those of the birds and the beasts. You, Eidoel, ought likewise to go with my men in search of your cousin. And as for you, Kai and Bedwyr, I expect that you will achieve any adventure that you undertake, so achieve this adventure for me.'

They travelled on until they came to the Ousel of Cilgwri. And Gwrhyr adjured her for the sake of heaven, saying, 'Tell me if you know anything of Mabon, the son of Modron, who was taken when three nights old from between his mother and the wall.'

And the Ousel answered, 'When I first came here, there was a smith's anvil in this place, and I was then a young bird, and from that time no work has been done upon it, save the pecking of my beak every evening, and now what remains is not even the size of a nut, yet may heaven take vengeance on me, if during all that time I have ever heard of the man about whom you ask. Nevertheless I will do what I should, since you come as ambassadors from Arthur. There is a race of animals who were formed before me, and I will be your guide to them.'

So they proceeded to the place where the Stag of Redynfre lived. 'Stag of Redynfre, we have come to you as ambassadors from Arthur, for we have not heard of any animal older than you. Tell us, do you know anything of Mabon the son of Modron, who was taken from his mother when three nights old?'

The Stag said, 'When I first came here, there was a plain all around me, without any trees save one oak sapling, which grew up to be an oak with a hundred branches. And that oak has since perished, so that now nothing remains of it but the withered stump; and from that day to this I have been here, yet have I never heard of the man about whom you ask. Nevertheless, as you are ambassadors from Arthur, I will be your guide to the place where there is an animal which was formed before I was.'

So they proceeded to the place where the Owl of Cwm Cawlwyd was. 'Owl of Cwm Cawlwyd, here are ambassadors from Arthur; do you know anything of Mabon, the son of Modron, who was taken after three nights from his mother?'

'If I knew I would tell you. When I first came here, the wide valley you see was a wooded glen. And a race of men came and rooted it up. And there grew there a second wood, and this wood is the third. Look at my wings; they are withered stumps; yet all this time, until today, I have never heard of the man about whom you ask. Nevertheless, I will be the guide of Arthur's ambassadors until you come to the place where the oldest animal in this world lives, and the one that has travelled most, the Eagle of Gwern Abwy.'

Gwrhyr said, 'Eagle of Gwern Abwy, we have come to you as ambassadors from Arthur, to ask you if you know anything of Mabon, the son of Modron, who was taken from his mother when he was three nights old.'

The Eagle said, 'I have been here for a great space of time; when I first came here there was a rock from the top of which I pecked at the stars every evening and now it is not so much as a foot high. From that day to this I have been here, and I have never heard of the man about whom you ask, except once when I went in search of food as far as Llyn Llyw. And when I came there, I struck my talons into a salmon, thinking he would serve me as food for a long time. But he dragged me under, and I was scarcely able to escape from him. After that I went with my whole family to attack him, and to try to destroy him, but he sent messengers and made peace with me; and came and begged me to take fifty fish spears out of his back. If he does not know something of the man you seek, I do not know who will. However I will guide you to the place where he is.'

So they went there; and the Eagle said 'Salmon of Llyn Llyw, I have come to you with ambassadors from Arthur, to ask you if you know anything about Mabon the son of Modron, who was taken away at three nights old from his mother.'

'As much as I know I will tell you. With every tide I go up river, until I come near to the walls of Gloucester, and there have I found such wrong as I never found elsewhere; so that you will believe me, let two of you go there, one on each of my two shoulders.' So Kai and Gwrhyr Gwalstawt Ieithoedd went upon the two shoulders of the salmon, until they came unto the wall of the prison, and they heard a great wailing and lamenting from the dungeon. Gwrhyr asked, 'Who is it that laments in this house of stone?'

'Alas, there is reason enough for whoever is here to lament. It is Mabon, the son of Modron, who is imprisoned here; and no imprisonment was ever so harsh as mine, not even the imprisonment of Llud Llaw Ereint or that of Greid, the son of Eri.'

'Do you hope to be released for gold or for silver, or for any rich gifts, or must it be through battle and fighting?'

'It is only by fighting that anything can be gained for me.'

Then they left Gloucester, and returned to Arthur, and they told him where Mabon, the son of Modron, was imprisoned. And Arthur summoned the warriors of the island, and they travelled as far as Gloucester, to the place where Mabon was in prison. Kai and Bedwyr went on the shoulders of the fish, while the warriors of Arthur attacked the castle.

And Kai broke through the wall into the dungeon, and brought out the prisoner upon his back, while the warriors were fighting. So Arthur returned home, and Mabon with him at liberty.

Arthur said, 'Which of the marvels will it be best for us to seek next?' 'It will be best to seek for the two cubs of Gast Rhymhi.' 'Does anyone know', asked Arthur, 'where she is?' 'She is in Aber Deu Cleddyf,' said one.

Then Arthur went to the house of Tringad, in Aber Cleddyf, and he asked him whether he had heard of her there. 'In what form is she?' 'She is in the form of a she-wolf,' he said; 'and with her there are two cubs; she has often slain my herds, and she is there below in a cave in Aber Cleddyf.'

So Arthur went in his ship Prydwen by sea, and the others went by land, to hunt her. And they surrounded her and her two cubs, and God changed them again into their own form for Arthur. And the host of Arthur dispersed themselves into parties of one and two.

One day, as Gwythyr, the son of Greidawl was walking over a mountain, he heard a wailing and a grievous cry. And when he heard it, he ran forward, and went towards it. And when he came there, he drew his sword and smote off an ant-hill close to the earth, whereby it escaped being burned in the fire. And the ants said to him, 'Receive from us the blessing of heaven; we will give you something which no man can give you.' Then they fetched the nine bushels of flax-seed which Ysbaddaden, Chief of Giants, had required of Culhwch, and they brought the full measure without lacking any, except one flax-seed; and that the lame ant brought in before nightfall.

As Kai and Bedwyr sat on a beacon cairn on the summit of Plinlimmon, in the highest wind in the world, they looked around them, and saw a great smoke towards the south, afar off, which did not bend with the wind. Then said Kai, 'By the hand of my friend, look, over there is the fire of a warrior!' Then they hastened towards the smoke, and they came so near to it, that they could see Dillus Farfawc scorching a wild boar; and he was the greatest warrior that ever fled from Arthur. Bedwyr said to Kai, 'Do you know him?' 'I know him,' answered Kai, 'he is Dillus Farfawc, and no leash in the world will be able to hold Drudwyn, the cub of Greid the son of Eri, except a leash made from the beard of that man over there. And even that will be useless, unless his beard is plucked while he is alive with wooden tweezers; for if he is dead, it will be brittle.'

'What do you think we should do about this?' said Bedwyr. 'Let us allow him', said Kai, 'to eat as much as he wants of the meat, and after that he will fall asleep.' And during that time they employed themselves in making the wooden tweezers. And when Kai was sure that he was asleep, he made a pit under his feet, the largest in the world, and he struck him a violent blow, and squeezed him into the pit. And there they twitched out his beard completely with the wooden tweezers; and after that they killed him stone dead.

And from there they both went to Kelli Wic, in Cornwall, and took the leash made of Dillus Farfawc's beard with them, and they gave it to Arthur. Then Arthur composed this englyn*:

> Kai made a leash
> Of Dillus', son of Eurus, beard.
> Were he alive, your death he'd be.

And thereupon Kai was so angry that the warriors of the island could scarcely make peace between Kai and Arthur. And after that Kai would never come to Arthur's aid, whatever trouble he was in, and whether his men were being killed or not.

Arthur said, 'Which of the marvels is it best for us now to seek?' 'It is best for us to seek Drudwyn, the cub of Greid the son of Eri.'

A little while before this, Creiddylad, the daughter of Lludd Llaw Ereint, and Gwythyr, the son of Greidawl, were betrothed. And before she had become his bride, Gwynn son of Nudd came and carried her away by force; and Gwythyr, the son of Greidawl, gathered his host together, and went to fight with Gwynn son of Nudd. But Gwyn overcame him, and captured Greid, the son of Eri, and Glinneu, the son of Taran, and Gwrgwst Iedlwm, and Dynfarth, his son. And he captured Penn, the son of Nethawg, and Nwython, and Kynedyr Wyllt, his son. And they slew Nwython, and took out his heart, and constrained Kynedyr to eat the heart of his father. And this drove Kynedyr mad. When Arthur heard of this, he went to the north, and summoned Gwynn son of Nudd before him, and set free the nobles whom he had put in prison, and made peace between Gwynn son of Nudd and Gwythyr, the son of Griedawl. And these were the peace terms that were made: the girl was to remain in her father's house, without advantage to either of them, and Gwynn son of Nudd and Gwythyr, the son of Greidawl, should fight for her every first of May, from then until the day of doom, and that whichever of them should then be conqueror should have the girl.

And when Arthur had reconciled these lords, he obtained Mygdwn, Gweddw's horse, and the leash of Cwrs Cant Ewin. And after that Arthur went into Brittany, and with him Mabon, the son of Mellt, and Gware Gwallt Euryn, to seek the two dogs of Glythmyr Ledewic. And when he had got them, he went to the west of Ireland, in search of Gwrgi Seferi; and Odgar, the son of Aedd, king of Ireland, went with him. And from there Arthur went into the north, and captured Kynedyr

---

* *Englyn*: a generic name (like 'sonnet') for the earliest Welsh poetic form, usually stanzas of three lines.

Wyllt; and he went after Yskithyrwyn Chief Boar. And Mabon, the son
of Mellt, came with the two dogs of Glythmyr Ledewic in his hand, and
Drudwyn, the cub of Greid the son of Eri. And Arthur went hunting
himself, leading his own dog Cafall. And Kaw, of north Britain,
mounted Arthur's mare Llamrei, and was first in the attack. Then Kaw of
north Britain, armed with a mighty axe, boldly and courageously came
up to the boar, and smote his head in two. And Kaw took away the tusk.
Now the boar was not slain by the dogs that Ysbaddaden had mentioned,
but by Cafall, Arthur's own dog.

And after Yskithyrwyn Chief Boar was killed, Arthur and his army left
for Kelli Wic in Cornwall. And from there he sent Menw, the son of
Teirgwaedd, to see if the jewels were between the two ears of Twrch
Trwyth, since it would have been useless to hunt him if they were not
there. However it was certain where he was, for he had laid waste the
third part of Ireland. And Menw went to seek him, and he found him in
Ireland, in Esgair Oerfel. And Menw took the form of a bird and settled
on the top of his lair, and tried to snatch one of the jewels from him, but
he carried away nothing but one of his bristles. And the boar rose up
angrily and shook himself so that some of his venom fell upon Menw,
and he was never well from that day onwards.

After this Arthur sent an embassy to Odgar, the son of Aedd, king of
Ireland, to ask for the cauldron of Diwrnach Wyddel, his steward. And
Odgar commanded him to give it. But Diwrnach said, 'As heaven is my
witness, if it would help him at all even to look at it, I would not let him
do so.' And Arthur's ambassadors returned from Ireland with this refusal.
And Arthur set out with a small retinue, and boarded Prydwen, his ship,
and crossed to Ireland. And they went to the house of Diwrnach Wyddel.
And the hosts of Odgar saw their strength. When they had eaten and
drunk as much as they wished, Arthur demanded the cauldron. And he
answered, 'If I would have given it to anyone, I would have given it at
the word of Odgar, king of Ireland.'

When he had denied their request, Bedwyr arose and seized hold of
the cauldron, and placed it upon the back of Hygwyd, Arthur's servant,
who was brother, by the mother's side, to Arthur's servant, Cacamwri.
His office was always to carry Arthur's cauldron, and to place fire under
it. And Llenlleawg Wyddel seized Caledfwlch, and brandished it. And
they slew Diwrnach Wyddel and his company. Then the Irish came and
fought with them. And when he had put them to flight, Arthur and his
men went to the ship, carrying with them the cauldron full of Irish
money. And he disembarked at the house of Llwydden, the son of
Kelcoed, at Porth Kerddin in Dyfed.

Then Arthur summoned all the warriors that were in the three islands
of Britain, and in the three islands adjacent, and all that were in France
and in Brittany, in Normandy and in the Summer Country, and the best

dogs and horsemen that he could find. And with all these he went to Ireland; and there was great fear and terror at his coming. When Arthur had landed in the country, the saints of Ireland came to him and sought his protection. And he granted his protection to them, and they gave him their blessing. Then the men of Ireland came to Arthur, and brought him provisions. Arthur went as far as Esgair Oerfel in Ireland, to the place where the boar Trwyth was with his seven young pigs. And the dogs were let loose upon him from all sides. That day until evening the Irish fought with him, but he still laid waste the fifth part of Ireland. And on the day following the household of Arthur fought with him, and they were worsted by him, and gained no advantage. And the third day Arthur himself encountered him; he fought with him nine nights and nine days and all he achieved was to kill one little pig. The warriors asked Arthur what was the origin of the boar; and he told them that he was once a king, and that God had transformed him into a boar for his sins.

Then Arthur sent Gwrhyr Gwalstawt Ieithoedd, to endeavour to speak with him. And Gwrhyr assumed the form of a bird, and alighted upon the top of the lair, where he was with the seven young pigs. And Gwrhyr Gwalstawt Ieithoedd asked him, 'By him who turned you into this form, if you can speak, let some one of you, I beseech you, come and talk with Arthur.'

Grugyn Gwrych Ereint made answer to him. (Now his bristles were like silver wire, and whether he went through the wood or through the plain, he was to be traced by the glittering of his bristles.) And this was Grugyn's answer: 'By him who turned us into this form, we will not do so, and we will not speak with Arthur. That we have been transformed thus is enough for us to suffer, without your coming here to fight with us.'

'I will tell you. Arthur comes but to fight for the comb, and the razor, and the scissors which are between the two ears of Twrch Trwyth.'

Grugyn said, 'Except he first take his life, he will never have those precious things. And tomorrow morning we will leave here, and we will go into Arthur's country, and there will we do all the mischief that we can.'

So they went into the sea and crossed towards Wales. And Arthur and his hosts, and his horses and his dogs, boarded Prydwen, so as to meet them as soon as possible. Twrch Trwyth landed in Porth Cleis in Dyfed, and Arthur came to Mynyw. The next day Arthur was told that they had gone by, and he overtook them as they were killing the cattle of Kynnwas Kwrr y Fagyl, having slain all that were at Aber Gleddyf, both man and beast, before the arrival of Arthur.

Now when Arthur approached, Twrch Trwyth went on as far as Preseleu, and Arthur and his hosts followed him thither, and Arthur sent men to hunt him: Eli and Trachmyr, leading Drudwyn, the whelp of

Greid the son of Eri, and Gwarthegyd, the son of Kaw, in another quarter, with the two dogs of Glythmyr Ledewic, and Bedwyr leading Cafall, Arthur's own dog. And all the warriors ranged themselves around the Nyfer. And there came there the three sons of Cleddyf Difwlch, men who had gained much fame at the slaying of Yskithyrwyn Penbaedd; and they went on from Glyn Nyfer, and came to Cwm Kerwyn.

And there Twrch Trwyth made a stand, and killed four of Arthur's champions, Gwarthegyd, the son of Kaw, and Tarawc of Allt Clwyd, and Rheidwn, the son of Eli Atfer, and Iscofan Hael. And after he had killed these men, he made a second stand in the same place. And there he killed Gwydre, the son of Arthur, and Garselit Wyddel, and Glew, the son of Ysgawd, and Iscawyn, the son of Panon; and there he himself was wounded.

And the next morning before it was day, some of the men came up with him. And he slew Huandaw, and Gogigwr, and Penpingyon, the three attendants of Glewlwyd Gafaelfawr, so that heaven knows he had not a single attendant left excepting for Llaesgymyn, a man who never did anyone any good. And as well as these he killed many of the men of that country, and Gwlydyn Saer, Arthur's chief builder.

Then Arthur overtook him at Pelumyawc, and there he killed Madawc, the son of Teithyon, and Gwyn, the son of Tringad, the son of Nefed, and Eiryawn Penllorau. Thence he went to Aberteifi, where he made another stand, and where he killed Kyflas, the son of Kynan, and Gwilenhin, king of France. Then he went as far as Glyn Ystu, where the men and the dogs lost him.

Then Arthur summoned Gwynn son of Nudd, and asked him if he knew anything of Twrch Trwyth. And he said that he did not. And all the huntsmen went to hunt the pigs as far as Dyffryn Llychwr. And Grugyn Gwallt Ereint and Llwydawg Gofynnyad closed with them and killed all the huntsmen, so that only one man escaped. Arthur and his army came to the place where Grugyn and Llwydawg were, and he let loose all the dogs on them. At the shouting and the barking that arose, Twrch Trwyth came to their assistance.

And from the time that they came across the Irish sea, Arthur had never got sight of him until then. So he set men and dogs upon him, and the boar started off and went to Mynydd Amanw. And there one of his young pigs was killed. Then they set upon him life for life, and Twrch Llawin was slain, and then there was slain another of the pigs, called Gwys. After that he went on to Dyffryn Amanw, and there Banw and Bennwig were killed. Only Grugyn Gwallt Ereint and Llwydawg Govynnyad of all his pigs went alive with him from that place.

He went on to Llwch Ewin, and Arthur caught up with him there, and he made a stand. And there he killed Echel Forddwytwll, and Garwyli, the son of Gwyddawg Gwyr, and many men and dogs likewise.

And thence they went to Llwch Tawy. Grugyn Gwrych Ereint parted from them there, and went to Din Tywi. And Twrch Trwyth moved on to Cardigan; Eli and Trachmyr followed him with a multitude of others. Then he came to Garth Gregyn, and there Llwydawg Gofynnyad fought in the midst of them, and killed Rhudfyw Rhys and many others with him. Llwydawg went to Ystrad Yw, where the men of Brittany met him, and there he killed Hirpeissawg the king of Brittany, and Llygatrudd Emys, and Gwrbothu, Arthur's uncles, his mother's brothers, and there Llwydawg was himself killed.

Twrch Trwyth went from there to between Tawy and Euyas, and Arthur summoned all Cornwall and Devon unto him, to the estuary of the Severn, and he said to the warriors of this island: 'Twrch Trwyth has slain many of my men, but, by the courage of my warriors, while I live he shall not go into Cornwall. And I will not follow him any longer, but I will fight with him life for life. Do as it pleases you.'

And he decided that he would send a body of knights, with the dogs of the island, as far as Euyas, who should return from there to the Severn, and that tried warriors should traverse the island, and force him into the Severn. And Mabon, the son of Modron, caught up with him at the Severn, on Gwynn Mygdwn, the horse of Gweddw, and with him were Goreu, the son of Custennin, and Menw, the son of Teirgwaedd; this was between Llyn Lliwan and Aber Gwy. And Arthur attacked him with all the champions of Britain. And Osla Big-Knife got near him with Manawyddan, the son of Llyr, and Cacamwri, the servant of Arthur, and Gwyngelli, and they seized hold of him, catching him first by his feet, and plunged him in the Severn, so that it overwhelmed him. On the one side, Mabon, the son of Modron, spurred his horse and snatched his razor from him, and Kynedyr Wyllt came up with him on the other side, on another horse, in the Severn, and took the scissors from him. But before they could obtain the comb, he found his footing in the water, and from the moment that he reached the shore, neither dog, nor man, nor horse could overtake him until he came to Cornwall. If they had had trouble in getting the jewels from him, they had much more in trying to save the two men from being drowned: as they pulled Cacamwri out, he was dragged by two millstones into the deep. And as Osla Big-Knife was running after the boar, his knife dropped out of the sheath, and he lost it; after that, the sheath became full of water, and its weight dragged him down into the water, as they were pulling him out.

Then Arthur and his army went on until they overtook the boar in Cornwall, and the trouble which they had met with before was mere play to what they encountered in seeking the comb. But despite one difficulty and another, the comb was at length obtained. And then he was hunted from Cornwall, and driven straight into the ocean. And no one ever knew where he went after that; and Aned and Aethlem went with him.

Then Arthur went to Kelli Wic, in Cornwall, to bathe and to recover from his weariness.

Arthur said, 'Is there any of the marvels which has not yet been obtained?'

One of his men said, 'There is: the blood of the black sorceress, the daughter of the white sorceress, from the head of the valley of grief, on the confines of hell.' Arthur set out towards the north, and came to the witch's cave. And Gwynn son of Nudd, and Gwythyr, the son of Greidawl, counselled him to send Cacamwri, and his brother Hygwyd, to fight the witch. And as they entered the cave, the witch seized them, and she caught Hygwyd by the hair of his head, and threw him on the floor beneath her. And Cacamwri caught her by the hair of her head, and dragged her to the earth from off Hygwyd, but she turned on them both, and drove them both out with kicks and with cuffs.

And Arthur was angry at seeing his two attendants almost killed, and he wanted to enter the cave; but Gwynn and Gwythyr said unto him, 'It would not be fitting or seemly for us to see you squabbling with a hag. Let Hiramreu and Hireidil go to the cave.' So they went. But if the first two found themselves in great trouble, the second pair found much worse. Heaven knows that not one of the four could move from the spot, until they were all put on Llamrei, Arthur's mare. And then Arthur rushed to the door of the cave, and at the door he struck at the witch, with Carnwennan, his dagger, and cut her in two, so that she fell in two parts. And Kaw of north Britain took the blood of the witch and kept it.

Then Culhwch set out, with Goreu, the son of Custennin, with him, and all who had a quarrel with Ysbaddaden, Chief of Giants. And they took the marvels with them to his court. And Kaw of north Britain came and shaved his beard, skin, and flesh clean off to the very bone from ear to ear.

'Are you shaved, man?' said Culhwch.

'I am shaved,' he answered.

'Is your daughter mine now?'

'She is yours,' said he, 'but do not thank me, but Arthur who has accomplished this for you. If it had been my choice, you would never have had her, for with her I lose my life.'

Then Goreu, the son of Custennin, seized him by the hair of his head, and dragged him to the keep, and cut off his head and placed it on a stake on the citadel. Then they took possession of his castle, and of his treasures.

And that night Olwen became Culhwch's bride, and she continued to be his wife as long as she lived. And the armies of Arthur dispersed themselves, each man to his own country. And thus did Culhwch obtain Olwen, the daughter of Ysbaddaden Chief of Giants.

13. THE LIFE OF MERLIN

We have already seen how Geoffrey of Monmouth used Welsh stories to construct his largely imaginary history of the Britons; in The Life of Merlin, *he uses the same kind of material as the basis for a Latin poem, drawing on classical imagery and diction to recast the Celtic stories in a strange hybrid between the two cultures. He displays his learning in wide-ranging quotations, from sources such as the Bestiary (the medieval book of beasts) and the Welsh poems attributed to Taliesin; he also includes material from his earlier* Prophecies of Merlin, *and retells much of the story of the* History of the Kings of Britain, *as well as inserting nature poetry in the classical style and prophecies reflecting contemporary politics.*

The tale of Merlin's madness was an old one; there are references to Myrddin Wyllt in the early Welsh poems, and many of the other characters in the poem come from these poems as well. The tradition of the wild-man of the woods goes back to Nebuchadnezzar in the Bible *and extends to the medieval 'wodewoses' and 'green man' images: this particular story, told of a certain Lailoken who lived on the Scottish border, recurs in the* Life of St Kentigern, *and Merlin is indeed called Llallogan in some Welsh sources.*

Merlin Silvestris (Myrddin Wyllt) and Merlin Ambrosius, whom we have met in the story of Hengist and Horsa, seem to have been two distinct characters in Welsh myth, and the composite figure of Merlin the magician, to whom Arthur is entrusted by his father Uther, is a later invention of the writers of romances.

I PREPARE to sing of Merlin's madness and the jesting muse of a prophetic bard. Robert, glorious bishop, guide my pen and correct my poem. Philosophy has, I know, bathed you with holy nectar and made you the master of every discipline, so that you may demonstrate your skills as a leader and teacher throughout the world. Look favourably on my enterprise; and offer your poet the protection of better auspices than did your immediate predecessor. Your promotion to a well-deserved honour was demanded by your character, your distinguished life and nobility, the advantages of your appointment, and also by the clergy and people; as a result, Lincoln is now raised jubilantly to the stars. For this reason, I should like to embrace you in worthy verse, but I cannot, not even if my mouth were to sing with the combined poetic talents of Orpheus, Camerinus, Macer, Marius and Rabirius with all his eloquence. Sound the lyre, then, you Muses who are accustomed to sing with me; let us undertake the task we have in hand.

Having lived his life under many kings, Merlin the Briton enjoyed fame in the eyes of the world. A king and bard, he dispensed justice to the proud people of Demetia, and used to predict the future to their rulers.

Meanwhile several of the kingdom's nobles happened to be at war against each other, and cruel fighting had ravaged the innocent people in their cities. Peredurus, duke of the Venedoti, was fighting Guennolous, ruler of the kingdom of Scotland. Once the appointed day for war had arrived, the leaders met on the field and their forces engaged, both sides enduring pitiful slaughter. Merlin and Rodarchus, king of the Cumbri, had come to fight for Peredurus, a fierce pair whose hateful swords slew the enemy before them. The leader's three brothers, who had followed him to war, hacked at the opposing formations, killing without respite. Amid this slaughter, they rushed fiercely through the enemy ranks, only to be suddenly cut down.

Merlin was grieved to see this. He spread sad lamentation throughout the army, crying out: 'Has unlucky chance wrought so much harm as to snatch away from me these mighty companions, whom so many kings and remote kingdoms feared? Man's life is uncertain; death is close by, ever at hand to smite men with its hidden sting and drive the wretched life from their bodies! Alas, for their glorious youth! Who now will stand at my side in battle, and with me drive back the attacking companies, whose leaders are bent on my ruin? Rash young men, your boldness has deprived you of the sweet years of your youth! A moment ago you rushed through the battlelines in arms, cutting down those who opposed you on every side; now you drum the ground, soaked in red gore.' So Merlin, bathed in tears, lamented amid the ranks and mourned for the warriors, as the terrible struggle raged on. The armies were locked together to destroy the enemy; blood was flowing everywhere and men were falling on both sides. Finally the Britons rallied their companies. They massed together in a body and rushed amidst the weapons to attack the Scots. They dealt out wounds and overpowered the enemy troops, not ceasing until they had turned tail and scattered along wasteland paths. Merlin recalled his companions from the fight and ordered them to bury the brothers in different chapels. He lamented for them and wept incessantly. He scattered dust in his hair and tore his clothes; he threw himself to the ground, tossing this way and that. Peredurus and the nobles and leaders consoled him, but he would neither be comforted nor endure their words of entreaty.

For three days Merlin wept and refused food – so great was the grief that fired him. Then, after he had filled the air with all his lamentation, a strange madness seized him and he stealthily slipped away. He fled to the woods, unwilling to be observed in his flight, and entered the forest. It pleased him to hide among the mountain-ashes, and in the glades he wondered at the wild animals, as they fed on the grass; some of them he pursued, others he outstripped as he ran. He lived on the roots of herbs, on grass, on the fruit of trees and on bramble-berries. He became a wildman, as though he had been born in the woods. For the whole summer, oblivious of himself and his family, he hid undiscovered in the woods, concealed like a wild beast. Then winter came, depriving him of herbs and the fruit of trees. Since he had nothing to eat, in a wretched voice he poured out these complaints:

'Lord Christ of heaven, what am I to do? Where on earth shall I be able to live, now that I can see nothing to eat, neither grass on the ground nor acorns on the trees? Here there stood a full nineteen apple-trees, loaded with fruit: now they are gone. Who has stolen them from me? Where have they suddenly disappeared? I could see them before, now I cannot: by first allowing me to see them and then preventing it, fate is at one moment my ally and at another my foe. Now I have no apples, nor anything else. The forest stands without leaves or fruit: I feel the loss of both keenly, since I have neither leaves to cover me nor fruit to eat. Winter and showers of rain, brought on by the south wind, have taken everything. If I happen to find food deep beneath the earth, then greedy sows and ravenous boars rush up and snatch the food from me as I pluck it from the turf. You, wolf, are my dear companion, accustomed to wander the pathless glades of the forest with me. You can scarcely cross the fields; relentless hunger has made both of us languish. You inhabited these woods before me, and age has turned you grey; yet you can get no mouthful, nor know how to. This amazes me, since the glades are full of goats and other animals which you could catch. Perhaps your own hateful old age has sapped your strength and prevents you from running. All you can do is fill the air with your howling and let your wasted limbs fall, supine, on the ground.'

As Merlin repeated these words among the bushes and hazel-thickets, the sound of his voice reached the ears of a passer-by. The man made his way to the spot where the words had been uttered and found the speaker there. On seeing him, Merlin fled. The traveller followed, but was unable to restrain him in his flight. He therefore set off again in the direction he had been travelling and continued his journey, musing on the fate of the man who had run off. Suddenly he was met by another traveller, who came from the court of Rodarchus, king of the Cumbri. Rodarchus had married Merlin's sister, Ganieda, and rejoiced at having so beautiful a wife. Ganieda was grieving over her brother's fate and had sent servants to the woods and distant fields to bring him back. It was one of these men that came upon the traveller and was likewise met by him. Immediately they fell in with one another and struck up a conversation. The servant who had been sent to seek Merlin asked if the other man had seen him in the woods or glades. The latter replied that he had seen such a man amid the thorny thickets of the forest of Calidon; and that, when he wished to speak and sit with him, the man had run off swiftly through the trees. Such was the tale he told.

The servant departed and entered the woods. Traversing low-lying valleys and crossing high mountains, he penetrated their shady depths and searched for Merlin everywhere. At the very top of a mountain there was a spring, surrounded on all sides by hazel thickets and dense shrubs. Merlin had climbed there, and was gazing from this vantage point at all the woods and at the running and gambolling of the wild beasts. The envoy climbed the mountain, scaling its heights with silent steps, as he searched for his man. At last he saw the spring and Merlin, who was sitting on the grass behind it, giving voice to these laments:

'What does this mean, Ruler of the World? Why is it that the seasons have been divided into four, and are not identical? Spring duly provides flowers and foliage; summer produces crops; autumn, sweet apples; then icy winter follows, to devour and lay waste all things through the return of rain and snow. Its harmful storms bring everything to a halt and prevent the earth from putting forth its various flowers, the trees their acorns, and the pear-trees their pears. If only there were no winter and no hoar-frost. If only it were spring or summer, to bring back the cuckoo and its melody; and the swift, which comforts sad hearts with its pious song; and the turtle-dove, which observes a chaste marriage; among the green leaves, the other birds would lift up their voices in harmony, to soothe me with their song; the fresh earth would breathe forth the scent of flowers, newborn amid the green grass; springs would babble gently as they flowed; and beside them, doves would murmur peacefully from the foliage, to lull me to sleep.'

When he heard Merlin, the envoy interrupted the bard's lamentations by playing a lyre, which he had deliberately brought with him to outwit the madman and soothe him. Hidden behind Merlin, he plucked its strings in a mournful sequence and sang in hushed tones:

'The terrible groaning of Guendoloena as she grieves, alas! The sad tears of Guendoloena as she weeps! How I pity Guendoloena as she dies wretchedly! There was no woman in Wales more beautiful than her. Her whiteness surpassed goddesses and outdid the foliage of white privet, roses in springtime and the fragrant lilies of the meadow. The glory of spring used to shine out in that one woman. Her two eyes had the beauty of a star, and her fine hair shone with the gleam of gold. All this is no more; she has completely lost her beauty, her colour, her looks and the glory of her snowy skin. Because of her many troubles she is no longer what she was. She does not know where her lord has gone, whether he is alive or dead. So she languishes in misery and is utterly undone, worn out by long sorrow. Ganieda, who grieves inconsolably for her lost brother, weeps with her and shares her complaints. One weeps for a brother, the other for a husband, and together both women give themselves up to tears and spend their time in sadness. By night they wander through the thickets, consoled by neither food nor sleep, both of which are precluded by their great grief. So Dido lamented the sailing of Aeneas's fleet as he hurried to depart; so Phyllis groaned and wept most bitterly when Demophoon did not return after the agreed time: so Briseis shed tears for the absent Achilles. So sister and wife weep in unison and, in their continual grief, are quite consumed by inner pain.'

The envoy sang this to the accompaniment of his mournful lyre. The music charmed Merlin's ears and, as it soothed him, he shared the singer's pleasure. He swiftly arose and addressed the man playfully, begging him to pluck the strings again with his fingers and repeat the elegy. The other applied his fingers to the instrument and played the song again, as he had been requested: his playing slowly made the bard recover from his madness under the lyre's sweet influence. As he regained his wits, Merlin remembered who he was, and was amazed and appalled by his madness. His old faculties and awareness returned, and, once his rational mind was restored, he groaned. Overcome by family feeling at the mention of his sister and wife, he asked to be taken to king Rodarchus's court. The envoy obeyed. They gladly left the woods together and arrived at the king's city. The queen rejoiced to have her brother back, and his wife was cheered by her husband's return. They vied to shower him with kisses and were so moved that they threw their arms around his neck. The king too and all the members of his household treated the returning bard with due honour. The nobles in the city celebrated.

Yet when Merlin saw the crowds of people, they were more than he could bear. Madness seized him for a second time and again filled him with frenzy. He longed to return to the forest and tried stealthily to depart. Rodarchus ordered that he be kept under guard and his madness soothed with the lyre. In his grief, the king stood beside Merlin and entreated him to recover his senses and stay with him; he begged him not to desire to enter the woods and live like a wild beast, when he could rule a kingdom and exercise power over his fierce people. Then he promised him lavish gifts, and ordered them to bring clothes, birds, dogs, swift horses, gold, sparkling gems and goblets made by Wayland in the city of Sigenum. All these Rodarchus displayed and offered to the bard, urging him to stay at his side and forsake the woods.

Merlin spurned the gifts and replied: 'Let such things be the possessions of rulers, who are blinded by their need; their desires are excessive, since they cannot be satisfied with a little. In place of these gifts I prefer the spreading oaks in the forest of Calidon, with its lofty mountains and the green meadows beneath them. That is what pleases me, not your gifts. Keep them for yourself, Rodarchus: my home shall be among the nut-bearing woods of Calidon, which I prize above all things.'

Finally, after none of his gifts had been able to detain the unhappy bard, the king ordered him to be bound with strong chains and deprived of the freedom of escaping to the uninhabited woods. When he felt the chains around him, which prevented him from departing for the forest of Calidon, Merlin was immediately downcast; he remained sad and silent, with all mirth banished from his face, and he would neither speak nor laugh. Meanwhile the queen came into the court to visit her lord. The king applauded her arrival, as was fitting; he took her hand and told her to sit, embracing her and pressing his lips to hers. As he turned his face towards her, he saw a leaf clinging in her hair. He stretched out his fingers to remove it and threw it aside, joking gaily with his love. The bard cast a glance at this and let out a laugh, which made the bystanders turn to look at him in amazement, since he had refused to smile. The king too was amazed. He asked the madman to explain his sudden laughter and added to his words the promise of many gifts. Merlin was silent and refused to account for his mirth. This made Rodarchus redouble his efforts to persuade him by means of gifts and entreaties. The bard was angered by these offers and finally said to him: 'Greedy men love gifts and eagerly strive for them. By giving them a bribe, their minds can easily be directed wherever you wish, since what they have is not sufficient for them. The acorns of beautiful Calidon are enough for me, and the sparkling springs that flow through its fragrant meadows. I cannot be ensnared by gifts, so give them to the greedy. Unless you grant me the freedom to return to the fertile valleys of the forest, I shall refuse to explain my laughter.'

No gift was able to persuade Merlin, nor could Rodarchus understand why he had laughed. So he immediately ordered his bonds to be loosed and permitted him to set off for the deserted woods, provided he would reveal the reason for his laughter, as the king desired. Merlin was happy at being allowed to go and said:

'This was the cause of my laughter, Rodarchus, just now, when you removed the leaf which the queen unwittingly had in her hair, your action could be both praised and blamed. For you were more faithful to her than she was to you when she went into the bushes: her lover met her there and made love to her; and while she lay on her back, there happened to catch in her loose hair the leaf which you brushed off in your ignorance.'

This accusation immediately dismayed Rodarchus. He turned his face from his wife and cursed the day that he had married her. Ganieda was unmoved, and hid her shame beneath a smiling face. She said to her husband: 'Why are you so sad, my love? You have no cause to be angry and condemn me unfairly. Do you believe a madman whose mind confuses truth with falsehood? Those who trust madmen are often made more foolish than them. Listen. Lest I am mistaken, I shall prove that he is mad and has not told the truth.'

Among the many courtiers was one boy in particular. As she gazed at him, the cunning queen quickly devised a novel stratagem to discredit her brother. She summoned the boy and asked her brother to foretell the manner of his death.

He replied: 'Dearest sister, this man will die by falling from a high cliff.'

Smiling at this, she told the boy to go and take off the clothes which he was wearing, to put on others and to cut his long hair, so that no one would recognise him on his return. The boy obeyed and came back wearing different clothes, as he had been commanded. Then the queen again asked her brother: 'Tell your sister how this boy will die, my dear.'

Merlin replied: 'When he grows up, he will meet a terrible death in a tree, while his wits are wandering.'

At this, Ganieda said to her husband: 'Has this false prophet been able to mislead you into thinking that I committed such a crime? If you consider what he has just said about the boy, you will realise that he made up his story about me, in order to be able to depart for the woods. I would never do such a thing. I shall keep our bed unsullied and always be chaste, as long as there is breath in my body. I have exposed him by asking about the boy, now I shall expose him again; you weigh it carefully.'

With these words Ganieda quietly ordered the boy to withdraw and then return after putting on women's clothes. The boy departed at once to do as he was told, and returned in female attire. When he stood before Merlin in this disguise, the queen said jokingly: 'Come, brother, tell me how this virgin will die.'

'Whether virgin or not, "she" will die in a river,' replied her brother.

This assertion made king Rodarchus laugh, because Merlin had foretold three deaths, when asked about a single boy. And so the king thought that Merlin had lied about his queen. He no longer trusted him, and was saddened and disgusted that, through believing him, he had condemned his love. Seeing this, the queen forgave him and gladdened his heart with her kisses and blandishments.

Meanwhile Merlin turned his thoughts to departing for the forest. He left the palace and ordered that the gates be opened. His sister blocked his path, and tearfully begged him to stay with her longer and cease his raving. He insisted that the gates be unbolted and struggled to leave; he raged and fought, and cowed the servants with his fury. Finally, when no one could restrain his desire to leave, the queen swiftly commanded the presence of Guendoloena, who was bemoaning his departure. She came and humbly begged her husband to stay. But he ignored these entreaties and would neither remain nor grant her a joyful look, as he used to. She lamented, pouring forth tears, tearing her hair, scratching her cheeks with her nails, and rolling on the ground as if she were dying.

Seeing this, the queen said to him: 'What is your Guendoloena to do, who is dying like this on your account? Is she to be married to a husband, or do you want her to remain a widow, or to accompany you wherever you journey? As long as she can keep you as her lover, she will gladly go with you to live in the woods and green glades of the forest.'

Merlin replied: 'Sister, I have no desire for a cow which pours a spring of water from its gaping crack, like the Virgin's urn in summer. Nor shall I change my inclinations, as Orpheus once did when he entrusted his pen to the possession of boys, after Eurydice crossed over the sandy banks of the Styx. Unsullied by either act, I shall remain untainted by physical love. Let her therefore be granted the right to marry freely and take by her own choice whomsoever she wishes. Yet whoever marries her should take good care never to meet with or approach me, but should keep away, lest he feel the blow of my sword, if I have the chance to get near him. When the day for celebrating her nuptial rites comes and lavish food is laid before the banqueters, I shall be present myself, armed with honourable gifts, to enrich Guendoloena handsomely when she is given in marriage.'

With this, he said farewell to both of them, and set off unhindered towards the woods for which he longed. Guendoloena and the queen stood watching sadly at the threshold. They were moved by their friend's fate, and astonished that in his madness he knew nature's secrets and had been aware of his sister's infidelity.

All the same, they thought that he had lied about the boy's death, since he had foretold three deaths instead of one. Merlin's prophecy seemed false for many years, until the boy reached manhood: then it was finally made clear and gained general approval. When the boy was hunting with his dogs, he roused a stag that was lurking in a leafy wood. He unleashed his hounds, which, on catching sight of the stag, rushed off the track and filled the air with their baying. The boy himself spurred on his horse to follow. He blew his horn and shouted, to urge on his hunting-attendants and make them advance more quickly. There was in that place a high mountain, surrounded on every side by rocks, with a river flowing through the level ground below. As it fled, the stag crossed the mountain until it came to the river, then followed the usual path to its lair. The youth passed directly over the mountain in pursuit, looking for the animal in the low-lying rocks. Meanwhile, as it galloped, his horse happened to slip over a high cliff and, by chance, the man fell down the steep mountain into the river, yet in such a way that his foot caught in a tree, whilst the rest of his body was under water. So he fell, was drowned, and hung from a tree; and these three perils proved the prophet right.

Merlin had entered the forest and was living like a wild beast. He endured the icy cold, chilled by snow, rain and the harsh blasts of the wind: yet this pleased him more than holding sway over his cities and taming fierce peoples. He spent his life in this way amid the woodland animals as time passed.

Then, some years later, Guendoloena was given in lawful marriage to a new husband. It was night: a crescent moon shone brightly, and all the stars blazed under the dome of heaven. The air was clearer than usual; a cold wind from the north had dispersed the dark clouds and calmed the sky, as its arid breath swept away their vapours. The bard was observing the movements of the stars from a high peak beneath the open sky. Quietly he said to himself: 'What does the brightness of Mars portend? Perhaps its recent brilliance signals the death of one king and the accession of another? So it seems. For Constantine has died and his nephew Conan has assumed the crown, after wickedly murdering his uncle to secure the succession. You, mighty Venus, travel in company with the sun, as your fixed path passes through the zodiac; but why are your rays divided as they cut the air? Does this division foretell the end of my love? For such a beam denotes the separation of lovers. Perhaps Guendoloena has abandoned me in my absence and rejoices to be held tight by another man. So I am conquered, so another enjoys her, so my rights are snatched from me while I tarry. It must be so: for a tardy lover is no match for one who is energetic and at hand to press his suit. Yet I am not jealous: let her marriage enjoy good omens; let her have a new husband with my full consent. When tomorrow dawns, I shall go, and take with me the gift which I promised her on my departure.'

So saying, Merlin traversed all the woods and glades, where he collected in a single body herds of stags, does and she-goats. He mounted a stag and drove the herd before him, hurrying off at daybreak to Guendoloena's wedding. When he arrived, he made the stags stand obediently before the doors, and shouted 'Come, Guendoloena, come: these gifts are for you.'

She quickly came, smiling and surprised to see her husband mounted on a stag; she was amazed that the beast obeyed him, and that he could gather and drive so many animals, like a shepherd who is accustomed to take sheep to pasture. The bridegroom stood watching from a high window and laughed in amazement at the strange rider. The bard saw him and realised who he was. Immediately he tore the antlers from the stag on which he was riding and brandished them. He hurled them at the bridegroom and utterly smashed his head, killing him and scattering his life to the breezes. Then he swiftly set the stag in motion with a kick of his heels and made ready to return to the woods. At this, servants rushed out on all sides and ran swiftly through the fields in pursuit of the bard. His speed put him so far ahead that he would have reached the forest safely if a river had not blocked his path. As the stag jumped across the stream, Merlin slipped offend fell into the swift-flowing water. The servants surrounded the banks and captured the bard as he swam, then brought him back and presented him to his sister in chains. Once captured, the bard again became morose. He longed to escape to the woods and struggled to break his bonds. He would not laugh, eat or drink, and his sadness distressed his sister.

When Rodarchus saw that Merlin had renounced all joy and would not taste the dishes prepared for him, he took pity on him. In the hope that going to see the new merchandise on sale in the market would make Merlin happier, he ordered him to be taken out into the city among the people. So he was led out and, as he left the court, he saw before the doors a servant guarding them; the man was poorly dressed and, with trembling lips, was begging passers-by for a gift with which to buy new clothes. The bard immediately stopped and laughed in amazement at the beggar. After he set off again, he saw a young man holding new shoes, for which he was buying patches. Again Merlin laughed, and then refused to walk through the market any longer, in full view of the people he was observing. He often turned his eyes longingly to the forest and, though restrained, struggled to direct his steps there. The servants went home and reported that he had laughed twice, but now wanted to return to the woods. Rodarchus immediately wished to know what Merlin's laughter had meant. He quickly ordered his bonds to be loosed, and gave him permission to return to his beloved woods, if he explained his mirth.

The bard was cheered and replied: 'A doorman was sitting at the gates in shabby dress, asking passers-by for money to buy clothes, as though he was poor. Yet all the time the man had piles of coins concealed beneath him, but was unaware of his riches. That made me laugh. Dig up the ground underneath him and you will find the money that has long been hidden there. Then, when I was led on towards the market, I saw someone buying shoes and also patches, so that, when they were split and holed by wear, he could repair the shoes and restore them to their former state. Again I laughed, for the poor wretch will have no use for the patches he means to apply, seeing that he has already been drowned in a stream. He is floating by the bank: go to look, and you will see him.'

Rodarchus wished to put Merlin's words to the test. He ordered his servants quickly to search the river and report back immediately if they found such a man drowned on the nearby banks. The servants carried out their master's orders. Combing the river, they found the drowned man on a deserted sandbank. They then returned home and told the king. He meanwhile had removed the doorkeeper and, when he had dug up the earth and found the treasure buried beneath it, he gladly acknowledged Merlin's prophetic power. After this, Merlin was eager to return home to the woods, since he loathed the people in the city. Queen Ganieda tried to persuade him to stay and to curb his longing for the forest until after the winter, whose cold snows were then imminent; once summer returned, he would be able to eat the ripe fruit, until the season was no longer sunny.

But Merlin's desire to depart outweighed the cold. He refused and replied: 'Why do you try to detain me, dear sister? Winter storms cannot frighten me nor the icy north wind, whose cruel blasts rage and lash the flocks of sheep with unexpected hail. The south wind may disturb the streams with squalls of rain, but that will not stop me from entering the green glades in the empty woods. Even if everything there is in the grip of hoar-frost, I shall be able to endure it, content with a little. In summer it will be pleasant to lie there beneath the leafy trees, amid the scent of flowers in the grass. To prevent me starving in wintertime, however, build huts in the forest; and send servants to do my bidding and prepare food for me, when the earth is devoid of grass and the trees of fruit. In front of these huts build another at a distance, with seventy portals and windows, from which I shall be able to see the fiery sun when I come: and at night I shall observe the movements of the stars in heaven, and so discover what is to befall the people of this kingdom. Let there also be seventy scribes to write down what I say and record my prophecies carefully on writing-tablets. You too, dear sister, come often; then you will be able to satisfy my hunger with food and drink.'

With these words he hurried off into the forest. His sister obeyed him; she built the hall and the other huts, as he had instructed, and did everything which he had demanded of her. While the apples lasted and the sun climbed high among the stars, Merlin remained under the trees and wandered through the forest in delight, as the zephyrs ruffled the mountain-ashes. Then wild winter's icy storms arrived and stripped the woods and earth of all their produce. When his food was exhausted and rain was falling, Merlin would visit the hall, sad and hungry. Often the queen was there, glad to bring her brother food and drink. After he had refreshed himself with various dishes, he would then rise and rejoice with his sister. Next he would walk through the hall to observe the stars, and make these predictions of what he knew the future to hold.

'The madness of the Britons! They take more pride in their continual and abundant riches than they ought! They will not enjoy peace, but are goaded on by a Fury to engage in civil war and family feuds. They allow the churches of the Lord to be ruined and exile holy bishops to far kingdoms. The descendants of the Boar of Cornwall are throwing everything into confusion. They set ambushes to kill each other with their wicked swords; they will not wait to take power legitimately, but seize the crown of our kingdom. The fourth will be crueller and harsher than his predecessors. A sea-wolf will attack him, beat him, and drive him into the barbarian realms beyond the Severn. Then the wolf will besiege Cirencester and will cast down its houses and walls with the help of sparrows. His ships will attack the Gauls, but he will fall by a king's spear. Rodarchus is dying, and after his death protracted strife will long afflict the Scots and Cumbri, until Cumbria is presented to the growing tooth. The Cumbri will make war on the Gewissi, and the Gewissi on the Cornish: no law will tame them. Cumbria will always delight in spilling blood: why do you take pleasure in bloodshed, you race hateful to God? Cumbria will force brothers to join in battle and condemn their progeny to a wicked death. Parties of Scots will frequently cross the Humber and pitilessly slaughter those who resist them; but not without retribution, for their leader will be cut down and killed. His foe will be named after a horse, and his heir will depart from our shores in exile. Sheathe your naked swords quickly, Scots! Your might will be no match for our fierce people. The city of Alclud will fall, and no king will ever rebuild it until the Scots are subjected to a little boar. Carlisle will lose its bishop and remain vacant until the rod of the Lion restores its staff. The city of Sigenum will lament with its towers and great palaces in ruins, until the Kambri return to their old farms. Porchester will see the walls of its port breached until a wealthy man rebuilds it with a fox's tooth. Richborough will lie in ruins on the shore; but a Ruthenian with a helmeted ship will rebuild it. The fifth after him will repair the walls of St David's, and return the archbishop's pallium of which it has been deprived for many years. Caerleon will fall into the Severn's bosom and lack inhabitants for a long time. They will return when a bear comes in the form of a lamb. The Saxon kings will drive out our countrymen and occupy our cities, fields and homes for many years. Nine dragons from among them will wear the crown. Two hundred monks will be slain at Leicester, and a Saxon will empty its walls, having driven off its leader. The first of the English to bear the crown of Brutus will restore the city which has been emptied by slaughter. The barbarian people will prevent the rite of unction in our land and place pagan idols in God's houses. Then Rome will bring God back with the help of a monk's hood. A holy priest will sprinkle His houses with sacred drops, and renew them by again establishing shepherds within. Many of them will observe the commandments of divine law and win a place in heaven. The wicked race, full of poison, will disrupt this once more and confound right and wrong with their violence. They will attract the wrath of the Thunderer by selling their sons and relatives in lands far across the sea. Unspeakable crime! To sell and lead off, bound like oxen, beings whom the Maker of the world created to be free and to deserve the honour of heaven! You will succumb, wretched dragon, you who long ago betrayed your master when first you entered this kingdom. The Danes will come in their ships and conquer your people. They will reign for a short time, before retiring after being driven off. Two men will rule them, before being wounded by a blow from the tail of a serpent, which forgets a treaty in its desire for royal power.

'Then the Normans, with faces both in front and behind, will be carried across the waves by wood. With iron tunics and sharp swords they will fiercely attack the English, slaughter them and take their land. They will conquer many realms and will, for a time, overcome foreign peoples, until a Fury flies everywhere, scattering her poison over them. Then peace, faith, and all goodness will depart. Our citizens will join battle throughout our lands; men will betray their neighbours, and no friend will be found. Husbands will spurn their wives and visit whores; wives will spurn their husbands and marry whom they like. No one will honour the Church, order will perish. Then bishops will bear arms and go on campaign; they will build towers and walls on hallowed ground, and give to their troops the money owed to the needy. Blinded by riches, they will pant for worldly things, and snatch from God what is forbidden by their holy mitres. Three men will wear the crown. After them, a fourth, favoured by new men, will hold the sceptre. He will be harmed by a show of piety, until he dons the mantle of his father; having been girded with the Boar's teeth, he will surpass the shadow of the helmeted one. Four who seek high power will be anointed out of order; and there will succeed two who set the crown spinning, so that they incite the Gauls to make fierce war upon them. The sixth will overthrow the Irish and their walls, and restore our people and cities through his piety and wisdom. I once foretold these things more fully to Vortigern, as we sat on the bank of a drained pool and I explained for him the mysterious battle of two dragons. You, dear sister, go home to see the dying king, and tell Taliesin to come: there are many things I wish to say to him. He has recently returned from the region of Armorica, where he has studied the sweet teachings of Gildas the Wise.'

Ganieda went home to find that Taliesin had returned, and that Rodarchus's servants were grieving for their lord's death. Overcome by tears, Ganieda collapsed among her friends. She tore her hair and declared:

'Lament Rodarchus's death with me, women. Weep for a man whose like, to the best of our knowledge, the world has not yet seen. He loved peace, and the laws he dispensed to his fierce people ensured that no one inflicted violence on another. He treated the holy clergy with justice and moderation, and allowed both high and

low to be ruled according to the rights due to them. In his generosity he gave much and kept little. He was all things to all men, and
did what befitted each. Rodarchus, you were once, alas! the flower
of knighthood, an ornament among kings, and the pillar of your
kingdom: now you have gone to feed the worms before your time,
while your body rots in an urn. Is this the bed now readied for you
after silken couches? Will the white flesh of your royal limbs be
buried beneath a cold stone? Will you be nothing but dust and
bones? Yes, for man's wretched fate has always decreed that he can
never recapture his former glory. There is nothing to be had from
the pomp of this insubstantial world, which comes and goes, to
deceive the mighty and undo them. The bee smears with honey
those whom it later stings: just so the treacherous glory of the world
tricks those whom it seduces and crushes them with a flick of its
ungrateful tail. Its gifts are short-lived, it offers nothing lasting, its
favours trickle away like flowing water. Roses may be red, lilies may
be white in springtime, men, horses and other things may be beautiful. Yet they are not the work of this world, but of its Creator.
Happy are those whose hearts stand firm in piety, who obey God
and renounce the world. They will enjoy eternal honour through
Christ, who created everything and rules forever. Therefore I
abandon you nobles, you lofty walls and houses, and you sweet
children, and everything which belongs to the world; I shall live in
the woods with my brother, and serve God happily beneath a black
robe.'

So saying, she conducted the last rites for her husband and set the following verses over his grave: 'Here in a small urn rests a mighty man,
Rodarchus the Open-handed, who was more generous than any in the
world.'

Meanwhile Taliesin had arrived to visit the prophet Merlin. He had
been sent by Merlin to discover the nature of wind and clouds, since both
were then threatening and together forming storm clouds. Taliesin gave
the following account, displaying his sharp wit:

'Out of nothing the world's Creator produced four elements, upon
which all creation depends, taking them as its basis, once they have
been harmoniously and peacefully united. The sky, which stands at
the summit and encloses everything like a nutshell, He painted with
stars. Then He made the air, the medium which allows us to speak,
and through which the sun and moon give us day and night. He
also made the sea, which surrounds the land; its tides flow in four
directions and strike the air to produce winds, of which, they say,
there are four. The earth He placed below, fixed by its own mass
rather than floating lightly, and divided into five zones. The central

zone is uninhabitable because of the heat, whilst the outer two are deserted because of the cold. The remaining two zones He permitted to be temperate, and these are inhabited by men, birds, and throngs of animals. He put clouds in the sky to provide unexpected showers, and, by their gentle watering, to grow produce on the trees and in the earth. By His hidden laws, these clouds are, with the sun's help, filled up from rivers, like waterskins. Then, climbing high into the air, they are driven along by strong winds and pour out the water which they have absorbed. This is the cause of rain, and also of snow and round hailstones, depending on whether a cold or warm wind blows, since the effect of each, as it penetrates the clouds, is to produce water of the same kind; the character of each wind is determined by the zone nearest to which it has its origin.

'Beneath the firmament, where He fixed the shining stars, the Creator placed the ethereal heaven. This He gave as a home to the angelic hosts, who are sustained for ever by their worthy contemplation of God's wonderful sweetness. It too He decorated with the planets and the bright sun, so as to display the orderly way in which each travels a fixed path through the part of the sky assigned to it. Beneath, where the massy moon shines, He placed the airy heaven. Its lofty regions are filled with hosts of spirits, which suffer or rejoice with us, depending on the mood we feel. It is their custom to carry men's prayers through the breezes. They seek God's favour for them and report His will in dreams, verbally or by other signs, to pass on knowledge to mankind. Below the moon, the air teems with evil spirits, skilled in trickery, who deceive and tempt us; they often shape bodies for themselves from air, and frequently appear to us to tell us many things. Moreover, they have intercourse with women and make them pregnant, leaving them to give birth in this blasphemous manner. In this way God caused the heavens to be inhabited by three orders of spirit, to nurture all things and to renew the world through their regeneration.

'The sea too He subdivided, so that it could create things of itself and give birth continually. Part of the sea is hot, part cold, and the third part, which provides us with food, is tempered by the other two. The hot sea surrounds hell and its black inhabitants: it separates their foul world from the other waters, feeding the flames with its fiery tides. Thither descend those who break the law and ignore God, they follow the prompting of their wicked will and are eager for the sins which they have been forbidden. A grim judge stands there, giving each his just reward and meting out fit punishment. In the waves of the cold sea are tossed precious sands, which that sea first generates through the neighbouring warmth of Venus' star, as its beams mingle with the water. The Arabs claim that this planet produces sparkling jewels whenever it passes through Pisces, and directs its flames at the sea. These jewels have the power to help those who wear them: they restore many to health or prevent illness. Gems, like everything else, were divided by their Maker into different types, so that by their shape and colour we can clearly tell of what sort they are and what powers they have. The third class of sea, that which surrounds our world, confers many gifts upon us by its proximity. It nourishes fish, produces salt from its waves, and carries merchant ships back and forth, so that a poor man may suddenly become rich through his profits. It enriches the neighbouring land and feeds birds, which they say took their origin there, like fish.

'Birds, however, are governed by nature's law in a different way, since fire plays a greater part in their constitution than in that of the fish. Thus the birds are light enough to soar on high and fly through the air, whereas fish are nourished by the water, which keeps them under the waves and prevents their survival when they are exposed to light on dry land. The Maker of the fish divided them too into various types, giving each one particular qualities, to create eternal wonder and to cure the sick. They say that the mullet extinguishes the fires of lust, but that it also blinds the eater's eyes. The timallus, which obtained its name because it smells like the flower of thyme, causes anyone who eats it frequently to smell like this river fish. They say that lampreys are all female with no sperm; yet they mate, reproduce and increase their stock by breeding with another species: for snakes frequently assemble beside the shores where they live, and, by making welcome hissing noises, are accustomed to lure out the lampreys and mate with them. Another marvel is the echinus: if it fixes itself to a ship, it can, though scarcely half a foot long, hold it on the open sea, as if the vessel were moored to the shore; nor will the ship be released until the echinus itself departs with all its fearsome power. Sailors are always fearful lest their vessel be approached by the swordfish, so called because of its sharp and deadly beak. If it gets underneath, the fish immediately pierces the hull, holes it, and sinks the ship with a sudden flood. Another danger is the saw-fish, which attacks with its crest when it swims beneath boats, holing them and sinking them beneath the waves; its crest is as deadly as any sword. The water-dragon, which is said to have poison under its fins, is a menace to those who catch it: to be scratched is dangerous because it exudes venom. The stingray is considered to be deadly in another way: if someone touches it while it is still alive, then their hands, feet and other limbs are numbed, and become dead and useless; such is the danger of the charge in its body. God enriched the sea with these and other fish.

'Amid its waves He also placed many islands, which are inhabited because of the abundance men find there, thanks to the earth's fertile soil. They say that the first and best of the islands is Britain, whose richness produces all things. It contains crops – which every year provide the noble gift of grain for man's use – as well as woods and glades, dripping with honey, airy mountains, wide green fields, springs, rivers, fish, animals domesticated and wild, fruit-bearing trees, gems, precious metals and everything which is usually afforded by inventive Nature. Moreover it furnishes springs of hot water that can cure and tend the sick, and alluring baths, from which people depart in good health, their illnesses suddenly banished. Bladud established these baths when he ruled the kingdom, and gave them the name of his queen, Alaron. Their waters provide medicine useful against many complaints, particularly those of women, as has often been shown.

'Near Britain lies Thanet with its bountiful produce. There are no serpents on the island, and its soil, if drunk mixed with wine, provides an antidote to their poison. Our shores also divide us from the Orkneys. These consist of thirty-three islands separated by the sea, of which twenty are deserted, and the rest inhabited. The furthest island is Thule. This gets its name from the sun, which makes its summer solstice there, turning aside its rays to limit and suppress daylight; as a result, the air is always darkened by continual night and freezes the sea with its cold, making it sluggish and impassable to ships. Ireland is said to outdo all islands except our own with its pleasant fruitfulness. There is also something more: it produces only a very few bees and birds, and has no snakes at all. Thus its soil, or a stone brought from there, drives off serpents and bees, if placed upon them. Near Hercules's Cadiz is the island of Gades, where there grows a tree from whose bark drips gum, which produces jewels when smeared on pieces of glass. The islands of the Hesperides are said to contain an unsleeping dragon, which, so they claim, guards golden apples on a tree. The Gorgades are inhabited by women with hairy bodies, whose speed is said to outstrip hares. The islands of Argire and Chrysse are thought to produce gold and silver, just as Corinth does common stones. Taprobana is welcoming with its green and fertile turf. It yields two crops every year, with two summers, two springs, two grape- and other harvests: and it is graced by shining gems. On Tiles eternal springtime produces fresh flowers and lush fruits at every season.

'The isle of Apples, which is called the Blessed, has gained this name from its nature, since it produces all things spontaneously. It needs no farmers to till its soil: its only cultivation is that provided by nature. Untended, it bears rich crops, grapes and, in its woods, apples born of precious seed. Its soil freely produces everything like grass. The people on it live for a hundred years or more. Nine sisters rule there by right of birth over those who come to them from our lands. Their leader is more skilled in healing and more beautiful than her sisters. She is called Morgan, and has learned the properties each plant has to cure sick bodies. She also has the power of changing her shape, and of flying through the air on strange wings, like Daedalus. She can be at Brest, Chartres or Pavia whenever she wishes, or glide from the sky onto our shores. She is also said to be learned in mathematics according to her sisters, Moronoe, Moroe, Gliorn, Glitonea, Gliten, Tythonoe, Tython and Tithen, famed above all for playing the lyre.

'After the battle of Camlan we took the wounded Arthur to their island, led by Barinthus who was familiar with the sea and stars. With our ship under his direction, we arrived there with our leader and Morgan received us with due honour. She placed the king on golden coverlets in her bedchamber and herself exposed his wound with her noble hand. After examining it for a long while, she said that he might eventually recover his health, if he remained with her for a long time and was willing to submit to her care. So we joyfully entrusted the king to her and returned with a following wind in our sails.'

At this, Merlin said, 'My dear companion, what troubles our kingdom has endured since then through the breaking of treaties! It is no longer what it was! An evil fate has seduced our leaders, who have turned on each other and thrown everything into confusion. As a result, abundant riches have left our country, all goodness has departed, and the towns have been abandoned by their forsaken inhabitants. Moreover the Saxons have subjected us to wicked warfare; they are again mercilessly destroying us and our cities, and will desecrate God's law and churches. Assuredly God has allowed these disasters to come upon us because of our sins, in order to punish our foolishness.'

Before he had finished, Taliesin replied: 'Our people should, then, send someone to the king and, if he has recovered, bid him return on a swift ship to ward off our enemies with his customary might and re-establish the peace which our citizens have lost.'

Merlin answered: 'That race will not yield so easily once it has fixed its claws in our fields. First it will conquer our kingdom, peoples and cities, and rule over them by force for many years. Three among us will resist them with great bravery, will kill many and master them in the end. But it will do no good, because it is the will of the Highest Judge that, through their weakness, the Britons shall lose their noble kingdom for many ages, until Conan comes from his Breton chariot, accompanied by

Cadwalladr, venerable duke of the Cumbri. Together they will unite the Scots, Cumbri, Bretons and Cornishmen in a lasting alliance, drive out the foe, and return the lost crown to their people; they will renew the age of Brutus, and give sacred laws to their cities. Once again they will begin to conquer foreign kings and subjugate their realms in mighty battles.'

Taliesin replied: 'None of us alive today will survive to see that. I think that none of our countrymen has seen so many fierce battles as you.'

'Just so,' said Merlin, 'for I have lived long and seen much, caused both by our citizens fighting amongst themselves and by the barbarians spreading confusion everywhere. I remember the crime by which king Constans was betrayed, and which sent his infant brothers, Uther and Ambrosius, overseas in flight. Our leaderless kingdom was immediately racked by war. Vortigern, count of the Gewissi, led his armies into every province to establish his power, subjecting the innocent people to dreadful slaughter. Eventually by a sudden stroke he seized the crown, having killed many nobles, and took complete control of the country. But the blood-relatives of the two brothers would not endure this, and began to burn all their ill-starred leader's cities: they and their cruel soldiers harassed his kingdom and would not allow him to hold it in peace. In his anxiety at not being able to resist the rebel forces, Vortigern was prepared to invite foreigners to participate in his wars, so that he could face his enemies. Mercenary bands thereupon assembled from different parts of the world, and were received with honour.

'The Saxons too entered his service, helmeted warriors borne on curved ships. They were led by two bold-spirited brothers, Hengist and Horsa, who afterwards with vile treachery harried Vortigern's people and destroyed their cities. For, when they had bound Vortigern to them by their ready obedience, they saw that they could easily take over the kingdom, since his countrymen were in the grip of local quarrels: accordingly they turned their weapons on his fierce subjects and went back on their word. By preparing a trap, they murdered nearly six hundred nobles, who had been called together to arrange a peace-treaty with the Saxons; and they drove our leader over craggy Snowdon, where I began to predict the future for him. Then they roamed our country, putting homes to the torch in order to establish total mastery.

'Yet, after his father had been expelled from Brutus's hall, Vortimer perceived the great danger which the kingdom faced. With the people's agreement he assumed the crown, and attacked the fierce race that was massacring his countrymen. After many engagements, he compelled them to retreat to Thanet, where the fleet lay which had brought them. During this rout, the warrior Horsa and many others fell, killed by our men. The king followed and immediately surrounded Thanet, conducting a siege by land and sea, but without success. The Saxons unexpectedly manned their ships and forced a way through; when they reached the high seas, they rowed for all they were worth towards their homeland. Vortimer, now a leader respected throughout the world, ruled this kingdom with justice and restraint. But Hengist's sister Rowena was angry at his success. With stealthy deceit she mixed poison; and, playing the wicked stepmother for her brother's sake, she gave it to Vortimer to drink and so brought about the drinker's death. She immediately sent a message overseas to her brother, telling him to sail back with as many troops as it would take to conquer our warlike people. So he did, and fell upon our armies with such might that he seized all their estates in battle and put places to the torch throughout the country.

'During this time, Ambrosius and Uther had been in Brittany with king Budicus. Now, girded with swords of knighthood and tried in battle, they gathered together from all sides various forces, in order to invade their homeland and drive off the barbarians who sought to destroy their native country. They committed their ships to wind and wave, and landed to protect their countrymen. They pursued Vortigern through the kingdoms of Wales, shut him up in his tower and burned both together. Then they turned their swords afresh against the English; they met them in battle, sometimes defeating them and sometimes themselves defeated. Finally, our troops mustered all their strength in a pitched battle and inflicted heavy losses on the enemy; they killed Hengist and, with Christ's aid, triumphed.

'After this, at the wish of the clergy and the people, the crown was conferred on Ambrosius, who ruled the kingdom justly in all affairs. Twenty years passed, until he was betrayed by a doctor and perished through drinking poison. His younger brother Uther then succeeded, but was at first unable to maintain peace in the kingdom. For the wicked English, accustomed of old to return, had arrived with their usual forces and were laying waste to everything. Uther engaged them in terrible battles and sent them rowing back across the sea in defeat. Then he laid down his arms and re-established peace. He fathered a son, who afterwards proved himself second to none.

'This son was called Arthur, who ruled our kingdom for many years after his father died. Uther's death too came as a sad blow, a trial marked by the slaughter of many warriors in many engagements. While he was ill, the treacherous barbarians had come from Angle and ravaged the whole country beyond the Humber with fire and sword. Moreover, Arthur was still a boy, not yet old enough to overcome such forces. Therefore he was advised by the clergy and his subjects to request that Hoel, king of Brittany, should sail swiftly with a fleet to support him; for ties of family and affection bound each of them to come to the aid of the other. Hoel immediately readied for battle formidable warriors from all quarters and came to us with many thousands of men. He joined Arthur and crushed the enemy in a series of engagements, inflicting terrible slaughter. With Hoel as his ally, Arthur felt safe, and, strengthened by all his troops, he marched against the enemy. Eventually Arthur defeated them, and, after forcing them to return home, he settled his kingdom under the rule of law.

'Immediately after this struggle, Arthur also vanquished the Scots. Then, turning his arms on the fierce Irish, he landed his forces, and conquered their whole country. With a hostile fleet he attacked the Norse and Danes, far off over the wide sea, and overwhelmed them. He subjugated the people of Gaul and killed Frollo, into whose care the country had been entrusted by the might of Rome. When the Romans attacked his kingdom, he met and defeated them, slaying the procurator Lucius Hiberus, who was at that time the colleague of the Emperor Leo and had come to Gaul on the senate's orders to take it from Arthur.

'Meanwhile Mordred, the guardian of our kingdom, had treacherously begun to seize power and was carrying on a foolish affair with the queen. For they say that Arthur had entrusted his queen to Mordred along with his realm, when he wished to cross over to engage his foes. When this monstrous tale reached Arthur's ears, he postponed his plans for the Roman war. Returning home, he landed with many thousands of men, attacked his nephew, and sent him fleeing across the sea. There Mordred, full of treachery, gathered Saxons from all sides, and set about joining battle with our leader again; but he fell, betrayed by the wicked people whom he had trusted in undertaking such an enterprise. Alas! the slaughter of warriors, the grief of mothers whose sons were killed in that battle! The king too was mortally wounded there. He relinquished his crown and went to the court of the nymphs, sailing with you over the sea, as you have said.

'Then Mordred's two sons, each wishing to win the kingdom for himself, began to make war on their relatives and inflict mutual slaughter on them. The king's nephew, Constantine, attacked them savagely, ravaging their people and cities. Once both had died a cruel death, he assumed the crown and ruled our people. But still there was no peace, because his relative Conan began a terrible war. He threw everything into confusion by killing the king and snatching his territory, which he now rules weakly and without good sense.'

While Merlin was saying this, his servants suddenly arrived to tell him that a spring had newly appeared in those mountains. From it was flowing fresh water which traversed the hollows of a long valley, babbling as it meandered and wound its way through the glades. Both men immediately rose to see the new spring. After viewing it, Merlin sat on the grass and praised the spot, amazed at the way the flowing water burst from the turf. Seized by thirst, he bent down to the stream, drank his fill, and bathed his temples. Once the moist liquid had reached deep within his belly and stomach and had cooled the heat inside his body, he instantly regained his wits and self-awareness, and all his madness departed. His mind, which had wandered for so long, cleared again; all his faculties were restored, and remained as sound and healthy as they had ever been.

To praise God, Merlin lifted his face to the stars and pronounced words full of devotion: 'The starry workings of heaven depend on Your power, my king; through You, the sea and land produce and nurture their offspring, rich and fertile, and often aid mankind with this lavish bounty. Through You, my mind has cleared and my madness vanished. I had lost all self-awareness, and, like some spirit, knew the doings of people long dead; I could foretell the future and understand the mysteries of nature, the night of birds, the paths of the planets, and the swimming of fishes. It used to torture me and completely deny me the peace of mind natural to man. Now I have come to myself and seem to feel again the strength with which my spirit formerly imbued my limbs. Therefore, since I am so much in Your debt, Almighty Father, I shall express due praise with a right heart, ever glad to worship You joyfully. By providing the gift of this new spring in the green turf, Your generous hand has worked twice to my sole benefit: for now I have the water which I lacked before; and by drinking it I have regained my sanity. But, Taliesin, my dear companion, what power is responsible for the flow of this new spring, which has restored my mind, when before I was distracted and raving?'

Taliesin replied: 'The bountiful Ruler of Nature has divided rivers into various classes, and freely given each of them particular qualities, which frequently aid the sick. Throughout the world there are springs, rivers and lakes which often have the power to cure many people. In Rome there runs the swift and salubrious stream of the Albula, which is said to provide a sure remedy for wounds. In Italy flows another spring, named after Cicero, which can cure any wound to the eyes. The Ethiopians are said to possess a lake which makes one's face shine as if it has been bathed with oil. In Africa there is a spring commonly known as Zama, which can make the drinker's voice suddenly tuneful. Lake Clitorius in Italy can make people give up wine. Those who drink from the spring of Chios are said to become simple. The land of Boeotia is said to have two springs; one makes drinkers forget, the other makes them remember. It also contains the terrible menace of a lake so deadly that it makes people mad or fires them with uncontrollable lust. The spring of Syticus protects against love and the desire for intercourse. It is claimed that in the region of Campania there flow rivers which, when drunk, can make barren women fertile; they are also said to cure men's madness. In the land of the Ethiopians is a spring which flows red; those who drink from it return mad. The spring of Leinus prevents all abortion. Sicily has two springs, one of which makes girls barren, while the other makes them fertile, to give birth in due course. Thessaly contains two very powerful rivers: if a sheep drinks at one, it turns black, if at the other, white; but if it drinks from both, then its fleece becomes spotted. The lake of Clitumnus in the land of Umbria is said sometimes to produce huge oxen. Whenever horses cross the sands of lake Reate, their hooves immediately harden. In Judaea bodies cannot sink in the lake of Asphalt, as long as there is breath in them: whereas nothing floats in lake Siden in India, but sinks immediately to the bottom. In lake Alce nothing sinks: everything floats, even leaden stones. The spring of Marsida also makes stones float.

'The river Styx flows from a cliff and kills those who drink it, deaths to which the land of Achaea bears witness. The Idumean spring is said miraculously to turn four colours, changing as the days go by: it goes from dusty to green, next becomes bloody, then a fine, clear stream. They say that it regularly remains each of these colours for three months of the year. Then there is lake Rogotis with its flowing waters; three times a day it is salty, three times fresh and drinkable. At the spring of Epirus, extinguished torches are said to be kindled and afterwards to go out again. The spring of the Garamantes is said to be ice cold during the day and, conversely, to boil at night, so that no one can enter it, because of the alternating cold and warmth. There are also hot springs which boil with the great heat they absorb when they pass through alum or sulphur, and which posses fiery properties, useful to medicine. God endowed streams with these and similar qualities so that the sick might have the relief of an unexpected cure: and also to demonstrate the Creator's complete mastery over Nature, as He works through it in this manner. I think that the waters of this spring too are beneficial according to the Almighty's plan: and it is for that reason that their fresh-flowing water has been able to effect your sudden cure. Previously they used to run through cavities hidden under the ground, just as many other streams are said to flow beneath us. I think that their mouth has perhaps been blocked by an obstructing rock or mass of fallen earth, so that they have turned back and gradually seeped through the soil to form a spring. One can observe many streams which flow like this before going underground again, to flow through their caverns once more.'

Meanwhile the story spread that a new spring had appeared in the woods of Calidon, and that drinking from it had cured a man who had been out of his mind and had for a long time lived in those woods, like a wild beast. Soon leaders and nobles came to see and to congratulate the bard on his cure at the spring. They gave him a full account of his country, begging him to resume his position as king and guide the people with his customary power.

Merlin replied: 'That would be contrary to the dictates of my years, young men; old age is upon me and so grips my limbs that I can scarcely muster the strength to cross the fields. I have gloried long enough in times of happiness, when overflowing wealth and great riches smiled bountifully on me. There stands in this wood an old and mighty oak, so eaten by all-consuming age that its sap has dried up and it is completely rotten. I saw when it first began to grow. I saw the acorn which gave it birth; it happened to fall when a woodpecker perched above it and shook the branch. I know the spot where it has grown, for I was sitting a little way back, watching everything – that was in the days when I used to hunt in these glades – and I have noted the place in my memory. Therefore I have lived a long time. Old age has long weighed me down; I refuse to rule again. To stay beneath the green leaves amid the riches of Calidon delights me more than the jewels which India bears; more than the gold which is said to lie on the banks of the Tagus; more than the crops of Sicily or the sweet grapes of Methys; more than lofty towers, cities girt with walls, or clothes blazing with Tyrian dye. I take no pleasure in anything which might separate me from my own Calidon, always delightful in my eyes. I shall stay here as long as I live. Happy with fruit and herbs, I shall purify my flesh through holy fasting, so as to enjoy eternal life without end.'

As Merlin said this, the nobles saw long columns of cranes in the sky. Their flight wheeled through the void in formation, so that, in the limpid air high above, a letter could clearly be perceived in the flock. In amazement, they asked Merlin to explain the reason why the birds flew in this way.

Merlin immediately answered: 'The Creator of the world gave birds, like everything else, their own natural characteristics, as I have learned by living so long in the woods. The property of cranes is that, if many of them gather together while crossing the heavens, we can often make out various shapes as they fly. One crane warns the rest to maintain the order of their flight by its call, so that their formation is neither confused nor loses its customary shape. When the leading bird grows hoarse and tired, another takes its place. At night they set guards; and, when the lookouts want to ward off sleep, they hold a stone in their claws: if they see anyone, they wake the birds with a sudden cry. The feathers of all cranes go black when they grow old.

'Eagles take their name from the sharpness of their sight; their vision is said to be so superior to other birds' that they can stare directly into the sun. They expose their chicks to its rays, to find out if any show themselves unworthy by avoiding them. They hover high above water with their wings motionless, and spot their prey deep beneath the surface; then they drop through the air in a swift dive and catch the fish while they swim, as their nature demands. The vulture, surprising to relate, often conceives and gives birth without intercourse, not needing a male's sperm. Soaring like an eagle, the vulture lifts its beak to smell out a body far off over the water and, though it flies slowly, has no compunction in approaching to take its fill of the desired prey. It lives and thrives for a hundred years.

'The stork heralds spring by clashing its beak. It is said to be so attentive a nurse to its young that it will strip the feathers from its own breast. It is also said to avoid storms at the onset of winter by making for the territory of Asia, led by a crow. In its decrepit old age, the stork is fed by its chick for as many days as the parent bird had performed the same duty. The swan, a bird beloved by sailors, excels all others by the sweetness of its song when it is dying. In the realms of Hyperborea, they say that it will be attracted by the sound of a lyre which happens to be played on the shore. The ostrich abandons its eggs, leaving them buried under the dust, to be incubated there even though it neglects them: and so its chicks are hatched by the sun's rays instead of in their mother's nest. The heron, which hates rain and storms, flies up into the clouds to avoid such hazards. For this reason, sailors say that sudden rainstorms are imminent whenever they see herons high in the sky.

'In the lands of the Arabs is found the phoenix, a single, immortal bird, which God permits to be resurrected with its body restored. When it grows old, the phoenix visits regions which are more parched by the sun's heat, and heaps up spices in great piles to build a pyre: this it lights by vigorously flapping its wings, then climbs on and is completely consumed. The ashes of its body produce another bird, and so by this immutable law the phoenix is eternally reborn. The cinnomolgus* gathers cinnamon when it wants to make a nest, which it builds in a high tree. Men who are accustomed to sell the cinnamon have discovered how to dislodge the pile with feathered darts. The kingfisher frequents sea pools and builds its nest during stormy weather. While it is incubating, the sea is calm for seven days; the winds fall and storms abate, duly providing the bird with a quiet spell. The sound of an unseen parrot can easily be mistaken for a human voice, since it playfully intermixes the words "ave" and "chaire". The pelican habitually kills its young, only to be overcome by grief and lament for three days. Eventually it lowers its beak to tear at its own body and opens its veins so that the blood flows, restoring the chicks to life with its drops. When the Diomedeae voice their tearful song of lamentation, they are said to foretell the sudden death of kings or great danger for a kingdom. Whenever these birds see anyone, they can immediately tell whether they are Greek or barbarian: if Greek, they beat their wings and approach in a friendly manner with cries of happiness; if not, they circle, borne on hostile wings, and attack them like enemies with a terrible sound. Every five years, the Memnonides are said to make the long return flight to Memnon's tomb and weep for that chief slain in the Trojan War. The bright hercynea* has an amazing feather, which at dead of night shines like a lamp and which shows the way if carried

---

* *Cinnomolgus* and *hercynea*: this passage is taken from a medieval bestiary. There are no satisfactory modern equivalents for these birds. *Ed.*

ahead. When the woodpecker is nesting, it extracts nails and wedges that no one could dislodge from trees, and the whole neighbourhood resounds to its blows.'

When Merlin finished speaking, a madman suddenly approached them, who arrived as if by chance. He filled the woodland breezes with terrible cries, foaming at the mouth like a savage boar when it threatens to attack. They swiftly captured him and made him sit with them, in the hope that his talk might make them smile and laugh. Then the bard looked at him more closely and remembered who the man was. He groaned with all his heart and said:

'This man's appearance was quite different long ago when we were in the flower of youth. Then he was a handsome, brave knight, a noble descendant from the line of kings. He, along with many others, was one of my retinue when I was rich. People thought me fortunate to have so many good companions, and I was. While we were hunting in the high mountains of Argustli, we happened to arrive at an oak-tree whose branches spread high into the air. Amid the green grass there flowed a spring, its water good for men to drink. Seized by thirst, we all sat down there and eagerly tasted the spring's clear water. Then we suddenly saw on its bank fragrant apples lying in the soft grass. This madman, who was sitting nearest, immediately collected them and offered them to me, smiling over the unexpected gift. I took the apples and gave them to my companions, leaving myself out because there were not enough to go round. The others, on receiving the fruit, laughed and called me generous. They filled their mouths and ate greedily, lamenting that the apples were too few. Instantly a dreadful madness seized them all, including this man; they lost their wits and tore at themselves, biting each other like dogs. They hissed and foamed at the mouth, rolling madly on the ground. Finally they fled and filled the empty breezes with their wretched howling, like wolves. The apples were, I think, intended for me, not them, as I later learned. At that time there was in that region a woman who had loved me once, and who had taken her pleasure with me for many years. After I had rejected her and refused to make love to her, she was seized by a sinister desire to injure me. When her other schemes proved futile, she smeared these gifts with poison and placed them by the spring where I would return: she hoped thereby to do me harm, if I ate the apples when I happened to find them in the grass. But I was more fortunate, and was saved from them, as I have just told you. Please, make this man drink the medicinal water of the new spring: if he is lucky enough to regain his health and come to his senses again, he can labour for the Lord with me in these woods for the rest of his life.'

The leaders obeyed. Once the newly-arrived madman had drunk the water, he recovered and was immediately cured, recognising his friends.

Then Merlin said to him: 'You must now strive constantly for the Lord, who, as you bear witness, has restored your senses to you, after so many years of living in the wilderness and wandering without purpose like a brute beast. Now that you have regained your sanity, do not leave these green glades and thickets. Stay with me and serve the Lord, to compensate for the days which your overwhelming madness stole from you; from now on, your service will in all ways be linked with mine, for as long as we both live.'

Maeldin – for this was the madman's name – replied: 'I accept, venerable father. I am happy to live with you in the woods; and, as long as there is breath in these trembling limbs, I shall serve God with all my heart, which you shall teach me to purify.'

Taliesin interjected: 'I shall do the same and join you as a third in despising the ways of the world. I have spent too long in idle living: now is the moment for me to find myself again, under your guidance. Leaders, you should depart to defend your cities. It is not fitting that your voices disturb our solitude any longer. You have congratulated your friend enough.'

The nobles departed, leaving behind the three men and Merlin's sister Ganieda: she had finally embraced the bard's way of life and was living in chastity after the death of king Rodarchus. Her word had been law to the many subjects over whom she had formerly ruled, but now nothing was sweeter to her than to stay in the woods with her brother. Sometimes Ganieda's spirit carried her too up to the heights and she often predicted the future of the kingdom. One day she stood in her brother's hall and saw it lit up by the sun. With her wits dazed, she uttered the following ambiguous pronouncements from a window:

'I see the city of Oxford full of people wearing helmets, and holy men with holy mitres thrown into chains through the plotting of youths. A shepherd will wonder on high at a lofty tower, and be forced to open an earthenware vessel to his cost. I see Lincoln surrounded by fierce soldiers and two men trapped within; but one of them will be plucked out. He will return to the ramparts, accompanied by a savage people and their leader, and defeat the fierce band by capturing the king. What a crime it is, alas, for the stars, which glide beneath, to take the sun prisoner, though they are driven to it by neither force nor war! I see twin moons in the sky near Winchester and two lions, buoyed up by the greatest ferocity. One gazes in wonder at two men; and the other at another two, as they prepare for battle and stand at close quarters. The first three men charge and fiercely attack the fourth with savage arms but without prevailing.

He stands his ground, parrying with his shield and resisting with his weapons: then he triumphs and swiftly crushes his three opponents, forcing two to flee through Bootes's cold kingdom, whilst granting the third's request for pardon. At this, the stars flee everywhere throughout the whole plain. The boar of Brittany, protected by his ancestral oak, will carry off the moon, wielding his sword behind him. I see two stars join battle against wild beasts at the foot of Urien's hill, where the Deiri and Gewissi have come together under the leadership of great Coel. Men will be drenched with sweat and the ground soaked in blood, whilst wounds are dealt to foreign peoples! Star will clash with star, to be eclipsed in darkness and hide their rays when the sun's light returns. How terrible a famine strikes, alas, to hollow out bellies and deprive the people's limbs of their strength! It begins among the Kambri, but stalks the highest in the kingdom and forces the wretched population to cross the sea. Scotland's cattle perish in this terrible disaster: and their calves, which are accustomed to live on the milk, are scattered. Begone, Normans! Prevent your violent soldiers from bearing their weapons through our noble kingdom any longer. There is nothing left to satisfy your appetite: you have consumed everything which Mother Nature in her plentiful bounty once produced here. Help your people, Christ; tame these lions, and grant our kingdom the respite of peace and an end to war.'

With that, Ganieda fell silent, to the amazement of her companions and her brother. Merlin immediately went to her and offered words of friendly congratulation: 'Has the spirit moved you, sister, to foretell the future, thus closing both my mouth and my book? The task is now yours: take joy in it, and pronounce everything devoutly with my blessing.'

I have brought my poem to its close. Britons, award a crown of laurel to Geoffrey of Monmouth; he is one of you. Once he sang of the battles you and your leaders waged, and wrote a book famous throughout the world, which they now call 'The Deeds of the Britons'.

14. TALIESIN

This telling of the story of Taliesin was put together in the nineteenth century by Lady Charlotte Guest in her version of the Mabinogion. *It is a skilful compilation from a number of sources, ranging from the earliest Welsh poems to late medieval lives of the Welsh poets, of whom Taliesin was, of course, the first.*

Behind the romantic story there perhaps lies a real historical figure, author of a dozen or so of the oldest Welsh poems, in praise of the kings of sixth-century Britain, particularly the lords of north-west Britain and southern Scotland. Two collections of poems, the Book of Taliesin, *and the* Ystoria Taliesin, *as well as a group of ninth-century political poems, are all attached to his name; the legend which follows is largely drawn from the Ystoria.*

IN the past there lived in Penllyn a man of good family, named Tegid Foel, and his house was in the midst of the lake Tegid, and his wife was called Caridwen. And his wife bore him a son named Morfran son of Tegid, and a daughter named Creirwy, the fairest girl in the world; and they had a brother, the ugliest man in the world, Afagddu.

Now Caridwen, his mother, thought that, by reason of his ugliness, he was not likely to be admitted among men of noble birth unless he had outstanding merits or knowledge. For it was in the beginning of Arthur's time and of the Round Table. So she resolved, according to the arts of the books of the Fferyllt, to boil a cauldron of inspiration and knowledge for her son, so that he would be respected because of his knowledge of the mysteries of the future state of the world. Then she began to boil the cauldron, which from the beginning of its boiling could not be allowed to cease to boil for a year and a day, until the three blessed drops of the grace of inspiration were produced. And she put Gwion Bach, the son of Gwreang of Llanfair in Caereinion in Powys, to stir the cauldron, and a blind man named Morda to kindle the fire beneath it, and she ordered them to see that it did not cease boiling for the space of a year and a day. And she herself gathered charm-bearing herbs each day, according to the books of the astronomers, and in planetary hours.

And one day, towards the end of the year, as Caridwen was culling plants and making incantations, it chanced that three drops of the magic liquor flew out of the cauldron and fell upon the finger of Gwion Bach. And because they were very hot, he put his finger to his mouth, and the instant he put those marvel-working drops into his mouth, he foresaw everything that was to come, and realised that his chief care must be to guard against the wiles of Caridwen, for she was very skilled in the magic arts. And he fled towards his own country, in very great fear, while the cauldron burst in two, because all the liquor within it except the three charm-bearing drops was poisonous, so that the horses of Gwyddno Garanhir were poisoned by the water of the stream into which the liquor of the cauldron ran, and the confluence of that stream was called the Poison of the Horses of Gwyddno from that time forth.

And Caridwen came in and saw that her year's labour had been lost. And she seized a log of wood and struck the blind Morda on the head until one of his eyes fell out down his cheek.

And he said, 'You do wrong to disfigure me like this, for I am innocent. Your loss was not because of me.'

'You are telling the truth,' said Caridwen, 'it was Gwion Bach who robbed me.' And she ran after him. And he saw her, and changed himself into a hare and fled. But she changed herself into a greyhound and turned him. And he ran towards a river and became a fish. And she chased him in the form of a she-otter under the water, until he turned himself into a bird of the air. She, as a hawk, followed him and gave him no rest in the sky. And just as she was about to stoop upon him, and he was in fear of death, he espied a heap of winnowed wheat on the floor of a barn; and he dropped among the wheat, and turned himself into one of the grains. Then she transformed herself into a high-crested black hen, and went to the wheat and scratched it with her feet, and found him out and swallowed him. And, as the story says, she bore him nine months, and when she was delivered of him, she could not find it in her heart to kill him, by reason of his beauty. So she wrapped him in a leather bag, and cast him into the sea to the mercy of God, on the 29th day of April.

And at that time the weir of Gwyddno was on the strand between Dyfi and Aberystwyth, near to his own castle, and fish to the value of a hundred pounds was taken in that weir every May eve. And in those days Gwyddno had an only son named Elphin, the most unfortunate of youths, and the most needy. And his father was grieved for him, for he thought that he was born in an evil hour. And by the advice of his council, his father had granted him the drawing of the weir that year, to see if good luck would ever befall him, and to give him something with which to make his way in the world.

And the next day when Elphin went to look, there was nothing in the weir. But as he turned back he perceived the leather bag upon a pole of the weir. Then one of those who looked after the weir said to Elphin, 'You were never unlucky until tonight, and now you have destroyed the virtues of the weir, which always yielded the value of a hundred pounds every May eve. Tonight there is nothing but this leather skin within it.'

'Well,' said Elphin, 'there may be the value of a hundred pounds in it.'

So they took up the leather bag, and the man who opened it saw the forehead of the boy, and said to Elphin, 'Look, a noble brow!'

'Let him be called Taliesin,' said Elphin. And he lifted the boy in his arms, and, lamenting his mischance, he placed him sadly behind him. And he made his horse go at a gentle walk, which had been trotting before, and he carried him as softly as if he had been sitting in the easiest chair in the world. And presently the boy made a poem of consolation and praise to Elphin, and foretold that honour would come to him. And this was the first poem that Taliesin ever sang, to console Elphin in his grief at losing the revenue from the weir, and, what was worse, that all the world would consider that it was through his fault and ill-luck. And then Gwyddno Garanhir asked him what he was, man or spirit; and he answered in another song, which told the story of his birth.

So Elphin came to the house of Gwyddno, his father, and Taliesin with him. And Gwyddno asked him if he had had a good haul at the weir, and he told him that he had got something better than fish.

'What was that?' said Gwyddno.

'A bard,' answered Elphin.

And Gwyddno said, 'Alas, what good will he be to you?' Taliesin himself replied and said, 'He will profit him more than the weir ever profited you.'

Gwyddno asked, 'Can you speak then, even though you are so little?'

Taliesin answered him, 'I am better at speaking than you are at questioning me.'

'Let me hear what you can say,' said Gwyddno.

Then Taliesin sang a song telling of his wisdom and knowledge of the future, and praising the Creator for all His works. Elphin gave his haul to his wife, and she nursed him tenderly and lovingly. From that day onwards Elphin increased in riches more and more, day after day; and he grew in the love and favour of the king. Taliesin lived there until he was thirteen years old, when Elphin, son of Gwyddno, was invited for Christmas to his uncle, Maelgwn Gwynedd, who some time after this held open court at Christmastide in the castle of Dyganwy, for all his lords, both spiritual and temporal, with a vast throng of knights and squires.

And they talked among themselves and said, 'Is there in the whole world a king so great as Maelgwn, or one on whom heaven has bestowed so many spiritual gifts as upon him? He is handsome, meek and strong, and has all the spiritual virtues!' And besides this they said that heaven had given one gift that exceeded all the others, which was the beauty, and comeliness, and grace, and wisdom, and modesty of his queen; whose virtues surpassed those of all the ladies and noble girls throughout the whole kingdom. And they asked each other whether anyone had braver men, fairer or swifter horses or greyhounds, more skilful or wiser bards than Maelgwn?

Now at that time the bards were in great favour with the great men of the kingdom; and no one performed the office of those who are now called heralds, unless they were learned men, not only expert in the service of kings and princes, but studious and well versed in the lineage, and arms, and exploits of princes and kings, and in discussions concerning foreign kingdoms, and the ancient things of this kingdom, and chiefly in the history of the foremost nobles. And they were always ready with their answers in various languages, Latin, French, Welsh and English. And together with this they were great chroniclers, and recorders, and skilful in framing verses, and ready in making poems in every one of those languages.

Now there were twenty-four bards at that feast within the palace of Maelgwn, the chief of them being called Heinin Bardd. When they had finished praising the king and his gifts, Elphin happened to say, 'Truly, only a king can compare himself with a king; but if he was not a king, I would say that my wife was as virtuous as any lady in the kingdom, and also that I have a bard who is more skilful than all the king's bards.' In a short space some of his companions told the king of Elphin's boast; and the king ordered him to be thrown into a strong prison, until he could discover the truth as to the virtues of his wife, and the wisdom of his bard.

Now when Elphin had been put in a tower of the castle, with a thick chain about his feet (it is said that it was a silver chain, because he was of royal blood), the king, as the story relates, sent his son Rhun to enquire into the demeanour of Elphin's wife. Now Rhun was the most graceless man in the world, and he never talked with a wife or a girl without speaking ill of her afterwards. While Rhun went in haste towards Elphin's dwelling, determined to bring disgrace on his wife, Taliesin told his mistress how the king had thrown his master into prison, and how Rhun was coming in haste to try to bring disgrace upon her. So he got his mistress to dress one of her kitchenmaids in her clothes, which the noble lady was glad to do; and she put on the girl's hands the best rings that she and her husband possessed. Taliesin got his mistress to put the girl, in disguise, to sit at the table in her place at supper, and he made her seem like the mistress, and the mistress seemed like the maid. And when at suppertime they were sitting at table in this fashion, Rhun suddenly arrived at Elphin's dwelling, and was received with joy, for all the servants knew him well; and they brought him quickly to the room of their mistress; and the kitchenmaid in her disguise rose up from supper and welcomed him gladly. And afterwards she sat down to supper again the second time, and Rhun with her. Then Rhun began to joke with the maid, still disguised as her mistress. And the story goes that the girl became so intoxicated, that she fell asleep; and according to the tale, Rhun put a powder into the drink that made her sleep so soundly that she never felt it when he cut off her little finger, on which was the signet ring of Elphin, which he had sent to his wife as a token a short time before. And Rhun returned to the king with the finger and the ring as a proof, to show that he had cut it from off her hand, without awakening her from her drunken slumber.

The king was delighted by this news, and sent for his councillors, to whom he told the whole story from the beginning. And he had Elphin to be brought out of his prison, and he reprimanded him because of his boast, saying, 'Elphin, there is no doubt that it is foolish for a man to trust in the virtues of his wife further than he can see her; as proof of her fickleness, here is her finger, with your signet ring on it, which was cut from her hand last night, while she slept a drunken sleep.'

Then Elphin answered, 'With your leave, mighty king, I cannot deny that it is my ring, for it is widely known; but I deny that the finger around which it is, was ever attached to the hand of my wife – for there are three truly remarkable things about it, none of which ever applied to any of my wife's fingers. The first of the three is that it is certain, by your grace's leave, that wherever my wife is at this moment, whether sitting, or standing, or lying down, this ring would be too loose to stay on her thumb, where you can plainly see that it would be hard to draw it over the joint of the little finger of the hand from which this was cut; the second thing is, that my wife has never failed, since I have known her, to go to bed without cutting her nails on a Saturday, and you can see that the nail of this little finger has not been cut for a month. The third is that the hand from which this finger came was kneading rye dough within three days before the finger was cut off and I can assure you that my wife has never kneaded rye dough.'

Then the king was exceedingly angry with Elphin for opposing him so stoutly and defending his wife's reputation; so he ordered him to his prison a second time, saying that he was not to be released until he had proved the truth of his boast about the wisdom of his bard, just as he had proved that about the virtues of his wife.

In the meantime his wife and Taliesin remained peacefully at Elphin's house. And Taliesin told his mistress that Elphin was in prison because of them, but he told her not to be sad, for he was going to Maelgwn's court to free his master. So he took leave of his mistress, and came at last to the court of Maelgwn, who was about to take his seat in his hall and dine in royal state, as was the custom in those days for kings and princes at every chief feast. And as soon as Taliesin entered the hall, he placed himself in a quiet corner, near the place where the bards and the minstrels used to come and do their duty to the king, as was the custom at the high festivals when gifts were given.

And so, when the bards and the heralds came for the giving of gifts, and to proclaim the power of the king and his strength, as they passed by the corner wherein he was crouching, Taliesin pouted out his lips after them, and played 'Blerwm, blerwm', with his finger upon his lips. They did not take much notice of him as they went by but went and stood before the king, to whom they bowed, as was customary; but they did not speak a single word. Instead, they pouted out their lips, and making faces at the king, played 'Blerwm, blerwm', on their lips with their fingers, as they had just seen the boy do.

This astonished the king, who presumed that they had all drunk too much. So he ordered one of the lords who was serving at table to go to them and tell them to come to their senses, and to consider where they were and how they should behave in his presence. The lord did so, but they did not stop their foolish behaviour. So the king repeated his order, and repeated it again, telling them to leave the hall. In the end the king ordered one of his squires to strike the chief bard, Heinin Bardd; and the squire took a broom and struck him on the head, so that he fell back in his seat. Then he stood up, and went on his knees, begging the king to be merciful, and saying that he could show that their behaviour was not through stupidity or drunkenness, but by the influence of some spirit who was in the hall. And he told the king that it was a spirit that sat in the corner in the form of a child.

The king at once commanded the squire to fetch him; and he went to the corner where Taliesin sat, and brought him before the king, who asked him what he was, and where he came from. And he answered the king in verse, saying that he was chief bard to Elphin, and that his country was the land of the summer stars; and he told of the wonders he had seen, and how he had been with God at the fall of Lucifer, and had borne a banner in Alexander's army. He had helped to build the Tower of Babel and had witnessed the Crucifixion, and had had many other adventures, for he would be on the face of the earth until Doomsday.

When the king and his nobles heard the song, they were amazed, because they had never heard anything like it from a boy so young as he. And when the king knew that he was the bard of Elphin, he ordered Heinin, his first and wisest bard, to answer Taliesin and to compete with him in verse. But when he came, he could do nothing except play 'Blerwm' on his lips; and when he sent for the other twenty-four bards they all did the same, and could do nothing else. Maelgwn asked the boy Taliesin what was his errand, and he answered him in song, saying that he had come to defeat the king's bards and set Elphin free. And the end of his song was a spell to summon the wind; as he was singing his verse near the door there arose a mighty storm of wind, so that the king and all his nobles thought that the castle would fall on their heads. The king made them fetch Elphin in haste from his dungeon, and placed him before Taliesin; who at once sang a verse, so that the chains on his feet opened.

Taliesin, now that he had set his master free from prison, and had protected the innocence of his wife, and silenced the bards, so that not one of them dared to say a word, now brought Elphin's wife before them, and showed that she did not lack a little finger. And both Elphin and Taliesin were joyful.

Then Taliesin told Elphin to make a bet with the king, that he had a horse both better and swifter than the king's horses. And this Elphin did, and the day and time and place for the contest were fixed; and the king went there with all his people, and twenty-four of the swiftest horses he possessed. And after much preparation the course was marked, and the horses were brought to the start. Taliesin came up with twenty-four holly twigs, which he had burnt black, and he made the youth who was to ride his master's horse place them in his belt. He ordered him to let all the king's horses get before him, and as he overtook one horse after the other, to take one of the twigs and strike the horse with it over the crupper, and then let that twig fall; and after that to take another twig, and do the same to every one of the horses as he overtook them. He gave him strict instructions to watch when his own horse stumbled, and to throw down his cap on the spot. All these things the youth did, giving a blow to each of the king's horses, and throwing down his cap on the spot where his horse stumbled. Taliesin brought his master to this spot after his horse had won the race. And he got Elphin to bring workmen to dig a hole there; and when they had dug the ground deep enough, they found a large cauldron full of gold. And Taliesin said, 'Elphin, here is a reward for you, for having taken me out of the weir, and for having brought me up from that time until now.'

15. THE WILD HUNT

Herla and his companions appear in Courtiers' Trifles *written by Walter Map in the late twelfth century. Map was a member of the court of Henry II, and his literary reputation was such that the standard version of the Arthurian romances, the so-called 'Vulgate' cycle, was attributed to him in the fourteenth century. Map's amusing collection of stories centres round his complaints about court life, one of which is that the king is always on his travels; and Henry was indeed a restless and swift traveller. The Wild Hunt, for Map, is a good image of what life was like at Henry's heels, and it is in this context that he tells the story.*

THE old stories tell us that Herla, the king of the very ancient Britons, entered into a pact with another king, who was like a pygmy he was so low in stature, being no taller than an ape. As the story has it, this dwarf first approached him sitting on a huge goat: he looked just like those portrayals of Pan, with glowing face, enormous head, a red beard so long that it touched his breast (which was brightly adorned with a dappled fawn skin), a hairy belly, and thighs which degenerated into cloven hooves.

Herla took him aside and spoke to him privately.

The pygmy said: 'I am king of many kings and chiefs, and of a people numerous beyond all counting. They have sent me to you and I come willingly; for though I am unknown to you, yet I glory in the fame which has raised you high above other kings, since you are the best and nearest to me in rank and blood. Moreover, you are worthy that I should grace – as a guest of high honour – your wedding, on the day that the king of the French gives his daughter to you – an arrangement concluded without your knowledge; for his messengers come this very day. Let there be an abiding compact between us, that I shall attend your wedding, and you mine a year later to the day.'

With these words he turned his back with more than a tiger's swiftness and vanished from the king's sight. Then the king, returning in amazement, received the ambassadors and accepted their terms. As he was sitting in high state at the wedding feast, the pygmy entered before the first course with so great a multitude of his fellows that the tables were filled, and more had to find places without than within, in the pygmy's own pavilions which were pitched in a moment. From these tents, servants sprang forth with vases made of precious stones, perfect in form and fashioned with inimitable art, and they filled the palace and pavilions with gold and crystal vessels, nor did they serve any food or drink in silver or in wood. They were present wherever they were wanted, and offered nothing from the royal or other stores, only a bountiful entertainment from their own, and thus, from the supplies brought with them, they outstripped the desires and requests of everyone. Everything which Herla had prepared was left untouched. His servants sat in idleness, for they were not called upon and hence rendered no service. The pygmies were everywhere, winning everybody's thanks, aflame with the glory of their garments and gems, like the sun and moon before other stars, a burden to no one in word or deed, never in the way and never out of the way.

Their king, in the midst of the ministrations of his servants, thus addressed king Herla: 'O best of kings, the Lord is my witness that I am present at your wedding, according to our compact. If you crave anything besides what you see here, you have only to ask and I shall willingly supply it: but if not, you must not put off your requital of this high honour when I shall ask for it.'

Without pausing for an answer to these words he suddenly returned to his pavilion and departed with his men about the time of cock-crow. But just a year later he suddenly appeared to Herla; and sought from him the discharge of his compact. Herla assented, and having provided himself with the wherewithal for the discharge of his debt, followed where he was led.

He and his guide entered a cavern in a very lofty cliff, and after a space of darkness they passed into light, not the light of sun nor of moon but of many lamps – to the home of the pygmies – a mansion glorious in every way, like the palace of the sun in Ovid's description. Having celebrated there the marriage, and having discharged fittingly his debt to the pygmy, Herla, with the sanction of his host, withdrew laden with gifts and with presents of horses, dogs, hawks and all things befitting venery and falconry. The pygmy conducted his guests to the edge of the darkness and, at parting, gave to them a small bloodhound, instructing that it was to be carried, and strictly forbidding any one of Herla's whole company to dismount until the dog should leap forward out of his bearer's arms. Then, having said farewell, he returned to his country.

When, in a short time, Herla was restored to sunlight and to his kingdom, he accosted an old shepherd and asked for news of his queen by name. Then the shepherd, regarding him with wonder, thus replied:

'My lord, I scarcely understand your language, since I am a Saxon and you are a Briton. But I have never heard of the name of that queen, except in stories; for there was a queen of the very ancient Britons of that name, wife of king Herla, who, legend says, disappeared with a pygmy into this cliff. He was never seen on earth again. The Saxons, having driven out the natives, have possessed this kingdom for full two hundred years.'

The king, who thought that his stay had lasted only three days, could scarcely sit on his horse for wonder. Some of his fellows, indeed, heedless of the pygmy's warnings, dismounted before the dog jumped down, and were immediately changed to dust. But the king, understanding the reason for this change, prohibited anyone to touch the earth before the dog, under pain of the same kind of death. But the dog never jumped down, so the story has it that king Herla, trapped in endless wandering, makes mad marches with his army without stopping or resting. Gatherings of those troops of night-wanderers, whom men call followers of Herla (Herlethingi), were very famous in England up to the time of Henry II, our present king; it was an army of infinite wandering, of the maddest meanderings, of insensate silence, in which many who were known to be dead appeared alive. This band of Herlethingi was last seen on the borders of Wales and Hereford in the first year of king Henry II at high noon, in the same guise in which the royal court wanders abroad, with chariots and beasts of burthen, with pack-saddles and bread-baskets, with birds and dogs, with men and women running side by side.

Those who first saw them roused the whole neighbourhood against them with shouts and trumpets. As is the custom in Wales, where they are always on the lookout, many groups fully equipped with arms came at once, and because they were unable to extort a word from the strange troop in reply to their words, they prepared to exact a reply with their spears. But the visitors, rising into the air, suddenly disappeared. From that day, this troop has nowhere been seen.

HEROES AND SAINTS

16. THE STORY OF ARTHUR

Arthur is the overarching figure of British myth and legend. It would require more than a whole book to do him justice, and the literature on him, both creative and critical, is truly immense. He commands as much attention from today's novelists as from scholars of the Middle Ages. To set such a gigantic figure in the context of the other legends in the book within the space of a brief introduction and a few thousand words of text is obviously impossible, since, as William Blake put it, 'The acts of Arthur are the deeds of the giant Albion.'

What follows is a thirteenth-century account of his career. Although the whole topic of Arthur's place in history is still hotly debated, he seems to have been a heroic figure, probably remembered for a briefly successful resistance to the invading Saxons, in the late fifth or early sixth century. His name, rather than any account of his deeds, survived, and became the magnet for other stories, originally unrelated to him. When Geoffrey of Monmouth came to write his History of the Britons *in the twelfth century, Arthur was an established if elusive figure in Welsh stories, and he became the great hero of Geoffrey's work, his overseas empire perhaps a memory of the exploits of Maximus or a reflection of the ambitions of contemporary Norman kings. The huge popularity of Geoffrey's work meant that it had many imitators, among them a Breton author who put it into Latin verse. It is this version that is given below, a succinct account, clothed in classical style, of what were believed to be the historical exploits of Arthur: we begin in the sixth book of the poem, which has already recounted the deeds of Brutus and his successors.*

AT Uther's command his dukes, clergy and the other nobles come to London duly to observe the festival of Easter. There too comes duke Gorlosius of Cornwall with the partner of his bed, who outshines other girls as Cynthia does the stars and Phoebus the moon. When he sees the eyes and face of the duchess, the king burns with love for her. Nowhere does he turn his eyes from her; he sighs, his mind is racked, and, forgetting his position, he wishes to become Gorlosius.

Gorlosius notices the king's fault, and secretly retires to his homeland with his wife. Her lover is touched within by bitter pain. With fire and sword he lays Cornwall waste. But the duke possesses two heavily defended towns: Tintagel, completely surrounded by sea, where Igerna lies hidden, and Dimilioc, which the duke occupies. There Uther besieges him. But when the king's mind recalls the beauty and face of the duchess, swift flames creep into his heart. Since he cannot long hide his love, he reveals the pain it makes him suffer to Ulphinus, who approaches Merlin and asks his aid for the sorrowing king. By repeating a spell, Merlin transforms the king into the likeness of the duke, gives Ulphinus the shape of Jordanus of Tintagel, and himself takes that of Britel, the duke's servant. They go to Tintagel, where the gate-keeper admits them. The king enters the bedchamber for which he longs and, gaining his desires, remains there for three days and nights, while all believe he is Gorlosius. One night was not enough for the generation of so great a man as was conceived then: as long as the four corners of the world remain, Arthur's name will be immortal.

Meanwhile the besieged learn of the king's absence. Duke Gorlosius therefore sallies out from the open gates with three thousand men and attacks the enemy, carving a path with his sword. He falls, killed at the head of his men. A messenger reports the fate of the duke to his wife, but the king's pretended form gives him the lie. The king abandons his false shape and resumes his true appearance. The woman whom he has taken as an adulterer he now takes as a husband, and conceives a child by her; so are born noble Arthur and his sister Anna. Then for a long time the island enjoys the pleasures of peace.

But because it often happens that joy is mixed with sorrow, the mirth of the whole kingdom is turned to grief. Eosa and Octa together escape from the king's prison and harry him and his kingdom with war. The king is too ill to oppose them, but entrusts the reins of power to a distinguished man, Loth, who takes the king's place as far as he is able. He leads the Britons against the enemy forces and is sometimes defeated, sometimes victorious.

The king, who is accustomed always to triumph, complains at being beaten by his foes and has himself carried against the German army in a litter. When the Saxons see him brought in the litter, they refuse to employ their weapons against a king who is already half dead. But he launches his troops against them. The dukes Octa and Eosa fall with the majority of their men, the rest fleeing. The paeans and cheers of victory make the king forget the pain of his illness.

After such celebrations, however, the symptoms of his affliction affect him more seriously and badly weaken him. Near the king's court flows a spring clearer than silver, where he is accustomed to bathe his limbs and relieve his thirst. This spring is poisoned during the night; the king drinks the poison from it and dies.

In the seventh book Arthur is ennobled with the king's crown. Colgrinus attacks Arthur, who besieges his enemies; he retreats on the arrival of Cheldricus, but, when Hoel of Brittany comes to his aid, scatters them. He defeats the Irish and turns back the Scoti. He observes a festival and gives three kingdoms to three men. He takes a wife. He conquers the neighbouring kingdoms, subdues the ocean, and overcomes the realms of Gaul by force; he gives various rewards to his troops. He returns to York and there holds a celebration with his subjects. After the feast they indulge in games.

Bright Calliope, come from Helicon in the company of your band of sisters and moisten my hollow, thirsty breast from your sacred spring; for I do not presume to describe Arthur's deeds in verse without you, lest I seem to demean them. Without your blessing, Homer, Ovid, Virgil, and Cicero himself would fail in this task, since Arthur's glory exceeds that of Achilles by as much as Achilles's glory outstrips that of Thersites. The author of the *Aeneid* would have preferred Arthur's praises, which are worthy of the poetry of the Maeonian bard, to the story of old Anchises; weighty Lucan would have passed over Caesar's doings, and ancient Thebes would have lacked eternal fame, if only Arthur's deeds had preceded these poets. But, lest so great a hero perish without due recognition, I shall try to raise a paean to the invincible prince. It is obvious that my service is unworthy of his merits; yet the pauper finds a ready welcome at the altar, nor does the Deity judge his gift by its cost in money, but by the sincerity of the sacrificer. The calf slaughtered by Croesus is no more welcome an offering than the lamb killed by a poor man.

On the king's death, the British assemble and judge Arthur worthy of his father's crown. He is recommended by his steady mind, grace in Christ, generous hand, unconquerable valour, learned tongue, handsome face, clear judgement, and strong right hand. To the cheers of the British people, archbishop Dubricius in the company of the bishops of the realm crowns the fifteen-year-old boy with the diadem of king. The new king is not corrupted by his new-found honour, but reveres Christ as he always has. He lavishly scatters his wealth among all the British and wins their love with the gifts he bestows; he protects the kingdom with well-armed soldiers.

Germany had meanwhile heard of the sudden death of Uther, and sent thither strong men under the leadership of Colgrinus. They plunder the kingdom, raging against the people and their homes with fire and sword. Everywhere perish young men and old; babies at the breast and the mothers giving them suck, innocent and guilty, all die the same death. They make the churches into foul pagan temples; there is no respect for the order of the clergy and the name of Christ is destroyed; paganism triumphs over Christianity from the Humber to the sea off Caithness.

The king groans on hearing of the dreadful carnage among his people. He therefore gathers his forces and sets off against the enemy. The martial hero attacks the Saxons just as a hungry lion with jaws thirsty for blood pounces on the herd. Marching to York, where the Saxons are reported to be, he encounters them with his people. The river Doulasius flows in a swift, straight course; there they clash, pagan on one side, Christian on the other. Their blows show how great is the desire to rule which touches either side equally; both similarly wish and long to win the kingdom at the cost of their blood. Both lose some of their men, either drowned in the river or falling to the pitiless blade. After slaughter on both sides, the pagans flee; Arthur pursues, dealing blows as they retreat. They enter the city of York, where he blockades them; arrows fly through the void this way and that.

Soon Baldulphus, Colgrinus's brother, marches to the besieged city, intending to attack the unsuspecting Britons by night with his forces. Learning of this stratagem, Arthur carefully prepares to repulse it by another: that night he sends six hundred knights and three thousand foot under the duke of Cornwall to counter him. As Baldulphus and his army pass, the well-armed Britons ambush the unarmed troops. An unequal struggle is joined, for the armed force slaughters unequipped men who cannot strike back; the German company turns tail in flight. Since Baldulphus cannot parley safely with his besieged brother, he has his beard and hair shaved off contrary to his people's custom; laying aside his pagan guise, he takes a harp and, pretending to be a harper, enters the Christian camp. Fearfully he approaches the city walls. He is recognised by his brother, who throws down a rope and drags him up; so brother rejoices to find brother.

At length, when the besieged are giving up hope, when Arthur scents victory, when the walls begin to give way, there suddenly arrive almost six hundred ships filled with men, which Germany had despatched there under the command of Cheldricus. On hearing of their arrival, the king abandons the siege lest he suffer a reverse and takes his army with all speed to London. Hoel, king of Armorica, brings fifteen thousand men to the king's aid. Trusting in their numbers, he attacks the enemy, who are holding Lincoln under siege. The treacherous pagans obstinately resist the Christians, drawing their swords to exchange mighty blows. Protected by the shield of Christ, the army of the faithful kills six thousand unbelievers. When they realise that their idols are no help to them, the savage pagans quit the field and give rein to flight.

The forest of Calidon stands thick with leafy boughs. In it the fierce pagans recover themselves and, taking a stand there with renewed courage, resist the British attack by hurling spears and stones. The Britons see that their own missiles are useless because the wood wards off their blows. They cut down trees to trap the Saxons. When they realise that their means of escape has been cut off, to avoid death by starvation the Saxons ask the king for their lives alone, and swear that Germany will pay an annual tribute as servant to the Christian British; all the bronze and gold they have they surrender to the king. On hearing these terms, the king agrees; he frees his enemies and, after taking hostages, sends them home. They board their ships and spread their canvas to the winds.

Once they reach mid-ocean and the shore of their native land is in sight, they regret their return, since they recognise that they come without glory; they think it more noble to die fighting than to live a base

1. Brutus invades Britain: fifteenth century tapestry from Saragossa Cathedral

(Institut Amatller diArt Hispanic)

2. The Deeds of Merlin

Illumination from a fourteenth century manuscript of the *Brut* chronicle

(British Library MS Egerton 3028, f. 25)

3. *Kilhwych the King's Son* by Arthur Gaskin
(*Birmingham Museums and Art Gallery*)

4. Arthur fights a Roman general
(Bibliothèque Nationale de France, MS Arsenal 5077, f. 298)

5. *Hamlet and Ophelia* by Dante Gabriel Rossetti

(© The British Museum)

6. *Riders of the Sidhe* by John Duncan

7. *The Wedding of St George and Princess Sabra* by Dante Gabriel Rossetti
(© Tate Gallery, London 1998)

8. Richard Coeur de Lion rides against Saladin
Thirteenth century tile from Chertsey Abbey

(© The British Museum)

9. The winner in a tournament receives a garland
from a lady

(Universitätsbibliothek, Heidelberg, MS Cod.pal.Germ 848, f. 52)

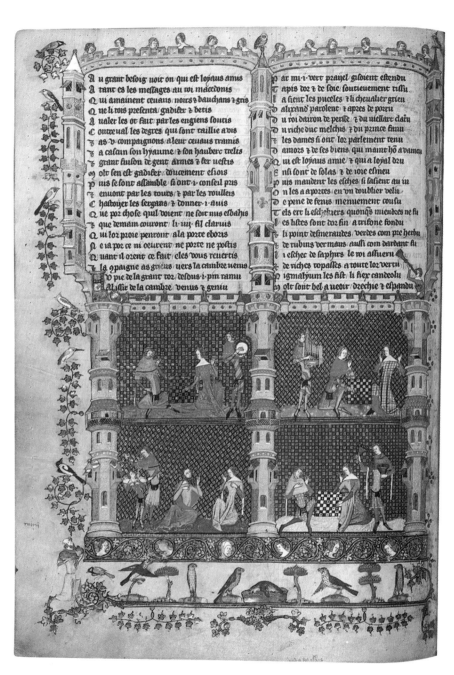

10. Scenes from courtly life

(The Bodleian Library, University of Oxford, MS Bodl. 264, f. 127v)

11. *'Stay you imperfect speakers, tell me more'*: scene from Macbeth, by John Martin
(*National Gallery of Scotland*)

12. *Lady Godiva preparing to ride through Coventry*
by George Jones
(© Tate Gallery, London 1998)

life in such dishonour. Turning back their ships, they sail for the shore of Totnes. When they have landed, they roam indiscriminately over the fields. Fire rages against houses, the sword against farmers. In a short time everything from that shore to the Bristol Channel has been laid waste. They come to the city of Bath, which they try to subjugate by siege.

After news of these events comes to the ears of the king, he executes the hostages and marches on the besieged city. His heart is troubled because king Hoel lies sick. When he views their siege-lines in the distance, he says with indignation: 'Comrades, by your valour – if only I live – the whole world, conquered from the setting to the rising of the sun, will serve me with head bowed. Lo, this evil band, hostile to the faith in which we believe, in despite of their sworn undertaking are ravaging our realm with fire and sword. Attack these perjurers, lay the liars low with your strong hands. Perjury ought to bring ruin on those who practise it. Let the soldier whose intention is to conquer imitate the deeds of Arthur in this battle. If anyone sees Arthur retreating, and not fighting in the front rank – which will never be – let him fly as I do and match my cowardice with his own.'

Bishop Dubricius stands on a knoll and, expounding the content of the Holy Scripture, proclaims: 'The sacred text teaches that Christ laid down His soul at His enemy's feet for our sake: lay down your souls for Christ's limbs, which are being torn by the insanely motivated tyranny of the Saxon people. Defend your motherland and the churches of God, which are being destroyed by hostile fire. The span of life on earth is short; but the life to come is without death. To the just man death brings glory, to the sinner eternal punishment, where he is preserved amid the pains of death. The good man's death destroys the body, while the sinner's kills the soul. The former death is caused by nature, the latter by a man's previous deeds. The former death perishes with the body, while death of the soul lasts for ever. For such sinners the danger is to be unable to perish; their inability to die is a death more harsh than any other. Those who suffer this stay of death curse it. When the Just Judge examines mens' deeds, he will starkly pass the final sentence, from which there is no appeal, saying to the wicked "Depart" and to the good "Come". Then after the sundering of their first marriage, the flesh will again be wedded to the soul under eternal law; together they will enjoy life or death – life for the blessed, death for the damned. Our merits in the field that is this world decide who will either eternally rejoice in the one, or forever lament the other: he who has spent his time in wicked deeds will lament; he who has lived well will rejoice. He who has fought the good fight will be given a crown in recompense. So, brothers, fight for the safety of your brothers. If it happens that you die in battle, you will receive the Eternal Kingdom in return for one that is transient. The purple of martyrdom, precious beyond all price, is foremost in heaven, excelling all honours: reverence is owed to martyrs along with Christ, Himself a martyr, to whom be glory, power and honour for all time.'

The prelate has hardly finished, when the whole army snatches its weapons and eagerly demands to enter the fray. Arthur dons a hauberk worthy of a prince; he puts on a helmet, on whose crest shines a dragon bright with gold; on his shoulder he bears a shield named Pridwen, on which the image of the Mother of Christ blazes forth; he wears a sword, whose name is Excalibur; in his right hand he carries a spear called Ron, an apt instrument of slaughter. When the armies are drawn up opposite each other, the Britons attack the Saxons. The German ranks fight back face to face throughout the whole day, but when the sun disappears in the west, they occupy the peak of a high hill, thinking that they will be safely defended by it. However, when the following day's sun eclipses the stars, the unconquerable Britons hasten to mount the hill more swiftly than birds. Scarcely have they reached its crest, when they rush on the Saxons with their swords, who resist with theirs.

But when a great part of the day has passed without result and neither side has gained victory, tireless Arthur is moved by anger to assault the resisting enemy. As a lion, driven by the hunger in its empty belly, leaps on sheep to overpower and tear them, and does not wish to slake its hunger on the fallen, but rather to pull down those it sees still standing, so the martial hero attacks, slaughters and destroys the foe, single-handedly sending five hundred men to hell. Cheldricus and his army abandon the field, while the king wins glorious praise.

Then Cador, duke of Cornwall, pursues the retreating Saxons; by a forced march he reaches their ships before them, and deprives them of the hope of returning home. The king, having heard that the Scoti and Picts are besieging his nephew, who is stricken by a serious illness, is marching thither lest he be captured by the savage enemy. Once he has captured the ships, Cador leads his troops against the foe. Here fight the Saxons, there the Britons. It is difficult to give the exact total of men who fall by the sword. At last the perjured pagans turn their backs in shameful rout, seeking out as they flee caverns in the earth and hiding-places in the woods. Thanet lies far off, an island of the great ocean; there the remnants of the German foe retreat. Cador, who is stronger than the enemy, pursues them there. Cheldricus dies by Cador's hand, and at his death the remainder are forced to surrender.

Then Cador follows after Arthur, who has reversed the situation and is blockading the trapped Picts and Scoti around Loch Lomond. This loch contains several islands, where nest eagles which foretell disasters to the region with their piercing screams. There Arthur besieges his enemies for fifteen days. Weakened by hunger the Scoti are dying in thousands, but Gillominus prepares a fleet, leaves the shore of Ireland, and leads the best

warriors of his kingdom against Arthur. The king abandons the siege
and, turning his sword against the Irish, forces them to sail back with
many casualties. Then he returns to attack the Scoti, but a crowd of
Christian bishops and clerics, dressed in their sacred robes, barefoot, and
carrying the relics of their saints in reliquaries of pure gold, openly and
meekly meet him in his anger and address him with bended knee and
flowing tears:

> 'Bravest of youths, greatest of kings, you are made good by your
> unconquerable valour, merciful by your grace in Christ, pleasing by
> your appearance, wise by your speech: hear the groans and lamenta-
> tions of the servants of Christ when they beg you. We ask you to
> have mercy on these wretches. The guilty have suffered the penalty
> which they deserved; the instigators of deceit have undergone their
> punishment. Vengeance should not be allowed to go beyond the
> extent of the sin. We submit ourselves to you; let this province be
> yours. Let your mercy overcome you, who conquer all else.'

Moved by their tears, he weeps himself and is persuaded by the pious
prayers of the pious men to agree to their wishes.

The king's nephew, Hoel, king of Armorica, stares in amazement at
the rocks, eagles' nests, islands, and rivers of Loch Lomond. But Arthur
says to him:

> 'There is a more amazing lake not far from here, whose formation is
> astounding. It is square, and its length is no greater than its width,
> both being twenty feet; but its depth is no more than five feet.
> There are fish of four types in the lake, each type remaining in the
> part apportioned to it; nor does one kind exceed its bounds in envy
> of another, but, content with the lot given to it by the eternal law of
> Mother Nature, abides within it. There is another pool, more mar-
> vellous than these, near the mouth of the Severn. When the tide
> flows into it, it swallows the seawater like a bottomless whirlpool;
> but when the sea ebbs, it pours forth the water like a mountain. If
> anyone turns his face to look at the water of the pool while it rushes
> out in this manner and it splashes the clothes of the bystander with a
> light spray, then the current of the water carries him off as he
> stands, so that he can only escape the force of the wave with diffi-
> culty, if at all; but if the onlooker turns his back, the water does not
> harm him.'

Then, having pardoned the Scoti, the king comes to York in glorious
triumph. When he sees its ruined walls and churches, with pain in his
heart he sympathises with the inhabitants of the oppressed and emptied
city, and shares the grief of the diocese, which has lost its prelate. For St
Samson had been driven from the see in flight before the swords of the

enemy, and was now by his example and his word instructing the people of Dol as their bishop. The king therefore provides the widowed city with a pastor, Piramon, of noted merit and shining virtue. Now the day is near on which Christ once wished to be born of a virgin as a man. In order to celebrate the holy festival of this day, Arthur summons the clergy and nobles to York and wears the crown as was his custom. After holding the holy service of Mass and a feast of dishes of various kinds, he gives generous gifts to his troops and, repairing the churches destroyed by the enemy, bestows perennial endowments on them.

He gives three kingdoms to three brothers of royal lineage: Scotia is the lot of Auguselus, Muresia of Urianus, Lodonesia of Loth. To Loth is married Arthur's sister Anna; by her he becomes the father of two illustrious youths, each of marvellous worth, whom he calls Mordred and Gawain. Then Arthur marries Guinevere, who is of Roman descent; the bright stars marvel at her beauty and the sun's rays yield before her.

Once these matters are set in order, Arthur energetically sails for Ireland and subdues the king and his kingdom. Then he proceeds to the realm of Iceland, conquers it, and brings it under British control. The spreading fame of the king alarms the neighbouring kingdoms, which voluntarily promise to pay him tribute to avoid being subjugated by force. When the western regions have, either through coercion or willingly, submitted to British rule, the king returns home, where the people acclaim his triumph, and he allows the kingdom to enjoy complete peace for almost twelve years.

During that time the youthful sons of noble families come to him from the remotest parts; gladly the king honours them and makes them his young warriors, ennobling them with horses and armour and enriching them with gifts. His court is open to all, without question of whence or with what motive they come. There is no private property, all possessions are shared: Arthur retains for himself only the use of the title of king.

The spread of Arthur's renown strikes fear into distant kingdoms: Germany is alarmed, Gaul fortifies its walls, Rome trembles, Spain is not safe. As soon as Arthur realises that kings fear him, he conceives great ambitions. Refurbishing his fleet with strong, well-armed men, he leads it to the shores of Norway, which had been left to Loth in the will of king Sichelis, his uncle. But the nobles of the region take as their leader Riculphus, who, with the Norwegians, resists Arthur with a bold front; but he falls with many of his men. Loth, of noted valour, takes the crown and rules the Norwegians and Danes as sub-king under Arthur.

Assembling his forces, the warlike hero sails for the shores of the Gauls. The province of Gaul is subject to Rome, being ruled by the Roman tribune Frollo. He prepares his Gallic subjects for battle and leads them against Arthur. Neither side will yield: each attacks the other with weapons like thunderbolts; each engages the other with spears of

ash; each hacks the other with deadly swords; each dyes the plain red
with torrents of blood. Both sides suffer casualties, but Arthur's are
lighter than those of the tribune. Frollo, seeing that his men can do no
more, turns tail before the British, retreats to Paris, and fortifies the city
with walls. Arthur surrounds the fortifications with many troops; he
attacks the walls, which the Gauls defend.

After almost a month, Frollo, seeing that the Gauls are dying of
hunger, writes the following to Arthur: 'Illustrious king, paeans in whose
praise are sung from the sun's rising to its setting: lest both our peoples
perish, in single combat engage in a duel with Frollo man to man, and let
the victor take the kingdom of the vanquished without strife.'

Arthur consents, and a binding agreement is made. They take their
weapons and are mounted on their horses. Which of them is the greater,
which the lesser, which of unequal strength is uncertain. Near the city
wall there lies a pleasant island surrounded by the river Seine; thither go
both warriors. When they are a certain distance apart, they spur on their
chargers, approach each other swiftly with lances levelled, and deal heavy
blows. The king's spear proves the more effective, throwing Frollo from
his saddle. He, fiercer than an angry lion, attacks the king with spear held
before him and overthrows him. On seeing the king fall to the ground,
the Britons, in contravention of the prior agreement, are hurrying to aid
their sprawling lord, when suddenly they observe the king rising with his
weapons. Now both are on foot grasping their shields and swords and
hacking the one to pieces with the other. For a short while each is bent
on the other's execution; their blows bear witness to how much they care
for victory. They smite each other frequently. Using all his might, Frollo
pierces the king's helmet and strikes his forehead. At the sight of his
blood red on his armour, the heroic son of Uther blazes with anger, and
subjects the author of his wound to a terrific onslaught; he grasps the
naked Excalibur, and, his whole body poised to summon his strength, he
splits his opponent's helmet and his head. Frollo falls, the king departs
the victor, the Britons cheer, and the citizens throw open their gates to
do him honour.

Then the king divides his forces into two equal parts, entrusting one
to great-spirited Hoel, and retaining the other himself. With it he
conquers the neighbouring regions. Hoel defeats the men of Poitou and
their leader Guitardus. He forces the Vascones, who are accustomed to
thirst for human blood, to abandon their savagery and submit their necks
to the British yoke: once they are subdued, he gives them laws, intro-
duces new customs, and teaches them for the first time to eat the same
food as other men. The sun has eleven times completed the course of the
long year when the king returns to Paris with great praise for his
triumph. Fittingly he gives generous gifts to his troops according to their
merit: the lot of Bedivere, his butler, is the whole of Normandy; Anjou

he gives to Kay; to many others he grants more cities, towns, villages and riches. He institutes his own laws and customs, protecting peace and faith. At the beginning of spring he spreads his sails to the zephyrs, crosses the water of the ocean, and re-enters his kingdom amid its cheers.

And now the day is at hand on which fire from heaven once consoled and encouraged the sad hearts of the disciples. King Arthur wishes to summon his subject kings and dukes duly to celebrate a solemn feast on that day, so that, if any dispute has arisen, it can justly and peaceably be resolved. The invited band of kings, clergy and dukes assembles before the king. Were I to set down all their names in verse, I would be considered too verbose. York, a noble and pleasantly situated city watered by the flowing Osca, seems suitable to house all these people. Thither to greet the king come a hundred bishops, a thousand priests, sixteen kings, and twenty consuls, in addition to counts, dukes and nobles whose number is difficult to tell, and much more so that of the lesser nobility.

Wearing the crown of the kingdom, the king approaches the threshold of the cathedral church, which is thronged by a venerable band of bishops and crowds of kings and dukes. He is preceded by four kings, who bear before him four shining swords, blazing with pure gold. In front of the rest, a procession of clergy praises the King of Kings and sings sweet hymns. Arthur's royal wife, wearing the regalia of queen and surrounded by holy bishops and throngs of matrons, goes to the church dedicated to St Julius. Before her walk four kings carrying, according to custom, white doves in their hands; they are preceded by choirs of virgins singing with delicate voices and moving all by the sweetness of their song. The queen attends the service of Holy Mass in that church, Arthur in the other; here girls sing with soft voices, there boys to the harmonious organ.

Although all this takes up a great part of the day, yet it seems short to those who are present. Then they go off to banquet. The men feast with the king, the women with the queen, according to the ancient custom of the Trojan people. Kay and a thousand nobles, an illustrious troop clad in ermine, serve diverse dishes; Bedivere with as many servants, all dressed in vair, pour out nectar and wine. Having had their fill of wine and food, the joyous knights engage in various sports: some prefer athletics, some war training, others dice; some participate in wrestling bouts, others strive to win races. The king bestows large rewards on the victors. A crowd of women crowns the topmost walls. Each has there a favourite whom she supports, for whom she fears, and for whose love she languishes; but no girl permits herself to be the beloved of anyone unless he has shown himself triumphant in war three times.

In the eighth book Lucius, emperor of Rome, sends envoys. Taking the advice of his nobles, the king gives his response. Lucius is angered and orders the kings of the east to prepare for war. Arthur assembles the kings of the ocean. Each side hastens to the Aube. Gawain kills Quintilianus, flees, and is pursued by a thousand men. Ydernus meets them, captures some, and hands them over to the king in chains: they are sent to Paris. Lucius sends warriors to intercept them, but they are captured. Caesar makes off in retreat; the king anticipates him.

It pleases them to celebrate the holy festival for three whole days. But serious matters interrupt their pleasurable sport and distract their minds from gladness. Twelve old men arrive with measured steps, who stand before the king and make the following speech: 'Lucius Augustus, master of the whole world, marvels at the audacity with which you have dared to exceed your limits and, having broken the terms of law, to usurp our rights for yourself. Why do you apply your sickle to the crops of others? You reap where you have sown no seed; but where you sow, another will gather the ears of corn. What business of yours are the Gauls, whom Julius once made subject to our empire? Why does Britain, which our men have conquered, disdain to pay its tribute to us? You ought, king Arthur, to be content with the possessions you hold by ancestral right; surrender to Rome her legal dues. Descendant of Brutus, take pity on yourself, take pity on your subjects, lest perhaps your rash boldness bring ruin on them. The Roman emperor commands you to come before the senate, in his own presence, at a certain prescribed date, so that retribution may teach you how dangerous, how serious it is to have offended the Roman senate. If you prevaricate, punishment awaits your crime: you will be scourged by dreadful slaughter and deprived of your own kingdom; if after the loss of all your possessions your life is spared, then the emperor in his mercy will have been less harsh than you deserve.'

They have scarcely managed to finish when the king summons his chosen nobles to the Giants' Tower to ask their view of what should be done in this situation. While they are climbing the steps of the tower, duke Cador, breaking into a smile at the joy in his heart, says to his comrades as they all proceed: 'My one fear was that continual peace would make the Britons cowardly, and that, if we sluggishly enjoyed peace for too long, inactivity would destroy our reputation as soldiers, by which we are considered superior in arms to all peoples. Five years have passed since we last waged war: and through this lack of action we have now become soft. But lest our reputation for glory fade, see, God in His goodness has stirred up the Romans against us.'

Surrounded by a circle of kings and nobles, Arthur says: 'Your minds are known to me by experience in war and peace: tell me what is to be done, what answer to be made. Rome rashly demands tribute from us on the pretext of the premeditated but specious argument that Julius Caesar once imposed tribute on our people by force. But this does not give any rights to the house of Caesar; indeed, it is a shameful argument to press the unjust claim of its instigator in this way, because under no law does violence make a master, nor does this prescription avail him. If we may press this case without legal basis further, then, seeing that a violent free-booter gains tribute for Rome, she is by the same reasoning subject to us: did not Belinus and Brennius, both Britons, conquer Rome and hold the office of emperor? And Constantine, the most famous son of Helena, and Maximianus too, ruled the empire; I am their successor, no unworthy heir. If you agree, comrades, and think it to my advantage, I shall command Rome to restore to me the rights of my predecessors, since she is depriving me of my honour.'

The king's voice is still completing this speech, when Hoel, king of Armorica, replies: 'I am overwhelmed by joy, most noble of kings, at seeing you to be of great spirit and with such powers of judgement. By claiming what is rightfully yours, Rome gives you the right to claim what is rightfully hers: use the right she has granted you. Lo, in you will be fulfilled the prophecy of the Sibyl, which predicts that a king will come from British regions to conquer Rome by sword, flame, and famine. Seize the rights bestowed on you by fate, take the imperial sceptre which Rome has given you the right to wield. With ten thousand men ready for war I shall do my duty to you; my one particular wish is to be among your soldiers when you conquer Rome.'

After Hoel finishes his speech with these words, king Auguselus says: 'Greatest of kings, no tongue can tell the extent of the joy I felt when I heard you give a reply worthy of a prince, and that your firm resolve was not changed or shaken by any fear of threats. Haughty Rome grows proud, refuses to recognise an equal, and assumes she may do anything, right or wrong: she believes that whatever she commands or enacts has the power of holy law, thinking that everything is the property of the Roman treasury and that distant regions owe her servitude. In these assumptions does she not fear to transgress the laws of Nature, to whom property and servitude are reprehensible and hateful? Has she not justly deserved to endure herself the law which she has promulgated? She declares that might should be employed instead of law, and, in Rome's opinion, he who holds a possession, no matter by what means, is thought to have the better claim in law. Let the senatorial order, then, experience the laws which it has laid down; and let the emperor, who arrogantly demands servile tribute from you, lament it, when he is beaten by the selfsame whip and himself suffers the sentence which he has passed. If it happens – as I desire with all my heart – that we meet the Romans on the same field of battle, with my sword as witness I shall prove how much I love liberty, and how sad it is to bear the yoke of slavery. Let us attack them before they attack us. Take, with me, two thousand cavalry and the same number of foot soldiers to participate in your campaign.'

When Auguselus finishes, the remaining crowd of kings and the band of dukes encourage Uther's son, with words and wishes, to wage war to protect their freedom. Each one undertakes to bring with him in the king's service as many horse and foot as he can muster: Gaul pledges twelve legions of cavalry; the total of infantry promised exceeds all numbers. Rejoicing that so many warriors are ready to obey him, Arthur thanks the kings and dukes and sends them to their own lands; he commands them to come swiftly with the agreed numbers of troops to Barfleur, and as the day for the assembly of the army fixes that on which the chains once fell from Peter's hands.

At his words the nobles quickly descend from the Giants' Tower and return to their homes, while the king replies thus to the twelve old men despatched by the emperor: 'Tell the Romans who sent you that according to no law are the Britons subject to Roman power; let them know that we are fierce in war, but tranquil in peace. I shall come to Rome equipped not with money but with arms, either to receive tribute as the victor or to pay it as the vanquished.' Then the old men return to Rome and repeat the king's reply to the Romans; at the news, Rome is angered.

On hearing the king's reply, Lucius summons kings and crowds of nobles from the east. Egypt, Libya, Babylon, Greece and Crete lament the departure of their kings and nobility. Teuther, king of Phrygia, Boccus of Media, Echion of the Persians, Evander of Syria, Xerses of the Yturei, and the dukes of their kingdoms bring to Rome twelve legions of cavalry. The might of Rome arms itself in preparation for the campaign; the Roman citizens weep to behold Rome, which they will never see again; the bridegroom, himself in tears, leaves his betrothed weeping; the faithful wife clings to her husband's embrace. Hanging from his father's neck by his little arms, a son cries out: 'Where are you rushing, father? For whom are you deserting your wife? For whom are you abandoning myself and my brothers? We brothers are left as orphans even though our father lives.'

Lo, a virgin, believed to be the most beautiful of girls, but who is nurturing concealed love for a handsome warrior, leaves her chambers and, urged on by the mad passion of desire, discloses the fires which she had hidden. As a maenad driven by the frenzy of Bacchus is excited into fury, her hair loose at her back, so she, out of her senses and her passion plain upon her face, throws herself into the crowd, grasps the young man's reins, and cries: 'You are mine, mine! Where are you rushing? What have you to do with wars, which always bring death? What have you to do with the Normans, the savage Britons, the Scoti, the Picts, and the Venedoti? I am frightened of Arthur, who engaged the tribune Frollo in single combat and killed him. Loth, Cador, Auguselus, Kay, Gawain, Hoel – the mere sound of these names terrifies me.' There is weeping in every home, lamentation in every street. The wailing voices of women strike the sky; the reverberating echo repeats the pitiful uproar; the distraught wife pays the last rites to her husband, though he yet lives.

Meanwhile the waves of the ocean are ploughed by the fleets in which the kings and nobles of the west are carried to Barfleur with the pre-arranged forces. The king entrusts his queen and kingdom to the care of Mordred and makes for the port called Southampton. They swiftly embark on the ships and spread their sails to the wind. At about the middle of the night, the king has a dream: it seems to him that a bear comes from the regions of Spain and a terrible dragon rises from the south; a mighty battle is fought between them, the terrible dragon at length overcoming the bear. When he awakes, he still remembers the dream and reveals what he saw to his augurs. Gerio, the most learned of them, says: 'The dragon signifies you, good king, and the bear a giant whom you will trample, having severed his head with your sword.' The next day dawns. The entire fleet reaches the shore of the port they long for; they disembark from the ships and pitch their camp.

Arthur hears news that a giant has made off with Helena, the niece of king Hoel, and is occupying the summit of a nearby mountain: this becomes an island when the sea-tide rises; but when it ebbs, it is easily accessible on foot. The king duly journeys there, content with two companions, Kay and Bedivere. They see two mountains, one of which is smaller, and great fires blazing on both. They cannot tell on which the girl and her abductor may be found. Bedivere, the butler, sails alone in a small skiff to discover which mount is the home of the monster. Chance brings him to the smaller mount, and, as he climbs it, he hears a woman's voice. Approaching the fire, he sees a grave with an old woman weeping beside it, beating her weak breast, and saying with sighs following her words: 'Pitiless God, why do You permit me to go on living after the death of my dear charge – if a fate which is worse than dying and crueller than any punishment may rightly be called life? O maiden, how pitiful was the manner of your death. Yet I take this solace in your death, that you lie buried without the loss of your chastity.'

She is still speaking when she raises her eyes and sees the man. She says: 'What madness has brought you to this mountain? You will die a miserable death at the hands of an unspeakable foe this very night. Retreat while you can. The giant, an ugly monster who thirsts for human gore, will soon come with bloody jaws, mangle you horribly, and bury you in his empty belly. Hoel's niece, whom I nourished with my own milk, ended her life in his embrace, terrified by the monster's appearance, but not violated; I buried her corpse in this grave, which I guard with these lamentations. But after the giant was prevented by Helena's death from corrupting her with his foul lust, he turned the fury of his passion on me and had intercourse with me. I call to witness heaven and its laws that he forced me against my will. Poor wretch, flee from here; he is coming even now to enjoy his accustomed intercourse. If he finds us together, his fierce anger will be doubled by hunger and jealousy.'

Moved by her words, Bedivere says: 'Cease your laments, lay aside your fears; an avenger of Hoel's outraged niece is coming, who will free you from the giant's captivity.' Then he returns and reports what he has seen to the king. Arthur is indignant at the virgin's death and begs his companions to allow him to fight the giant man to man and not to aid him unless they see him being beaten and unable to stand up to the monster. Then they make for the summit of the larger mount. There he is, an object of shame to his mother, a disgrace to Nature, a terror and an insult to men; his mouth is stained by the blood of pigs, his beard matted with foul gore; his nose is twisted, his teeth awry and crooked; his jaws gape like hell, his eyes squint, and his head is a wonder to behold; he sits over the blazing fire, wearing no other clothes than the bristles growing all over his body.

As soon as he sees the king and his comrades, he seizes in his hand his club, which two youths could hardly lift. The king draws Excalibur and, behind the protection of his shield, attacks the giant, who wields his triple-knotted club and smites the shield, the sound of the blow filling the whole shore. The king assaults the giant with his sword and strikes him on the forehead. Blood gushes from his brow and its copious flow blinds the monster's eyes. But the wound is not mortal, as his club had checked the sword and lessened the blow. Maddened by the wound, he attacks the foe who dealt it, grasps him round the middle, and, grappling with him, forces him to bend his knees to the ground. But the martial hero summons his strength, rises, and strikes the savage three or four times with his sword, burying it in the giant's brain. He cries and falls; his mother earth groans and trembles; surrounding regions feared an earthquake.

At the sight of the dead body sprawling, the king laughs, saying to his astounded comrades: 'With my sword I have defeated among the giants none more fierce than this monster – with the exception of Rito who had barbarically made a cloak out of the beards of the kings whom he had killed. He commanded me to rip out my beard, promising as a concession to my honour that, when he sewed it in place with the beards of the others, he would reverently put it at the top. When I refused to give what he requested, we fought a duel together on mount Aravius. I overcame and killed him.'

He severs the head of the giant and takes it back with him to the tents of his camp. The desire to see brings the troops to the cursed head; and they extol the king as worthy of a paean of praise for defeating so marvellous a monster and freeing his citizens from its depredations. But the Armorican king, grieved at his niece's fate, founds a church at the spot where the virgin Helena lies buried; and he orders that the whole mountain be called Tumba Helenes, which is its name up to the present.

Then Arthur swiftly moves his camp, leading forces without number to the river Aube, where he pitches his tents. For rumour has it that the Roman citizens have made their camp nearby. Untroubled, the king sends to them three nobles, named Boso, Gerinus and Gawain, his nephew. They make the following speech: 'Whoever contravenes Arthur's orders condemns himself by that very action: Arthur commands you, illustrious Lucius, to retreat from this region while there is still time.'

To them Quintilianus replies at the prompting of his anger: 'The Britons are fools in name and deed: their warfare is threats, their bravery boastfulness. His imperial majesty has come not to flee, but to put to flight. Let the Britons retreat, and, content with the realm of Britain, pay us our tribute without dispute.'

As he is about to continue, Gawain, giving him a fierce glance, says: 'I shall make you the witness to prove that the Britons are not only good at talking but also at fighting.' So saying, he draws his sword and strikes off his head. Then the envoys ride off, urging their horses with their spurs, and retreat towards their army. The Roman youths pursue them, eager to take revenge for the killing of their fellow-citizen. Boso reins in and, charging the Romans, shakes his spear and pierces a distinguished young man belonging to the family of the Fabii. When the consul of Carnotum sees this, he is jealous of Boso's deeds and, wheeling round, rushes on the foe; he strikes Titius, who is his nearest opponent, and dashes him from the saddle with a mortal wound.

Mucius gains on Gawain from behind, but Gawain kills him by severing his head and helmet from his body, adding: 'When you join Quintilianus in hell, be a witness that the Britons excel with tongue and hand; be too a proof that the Italians are remiss.' He encourages his two comrades with these words: 'Unconquerable nobles, hasten with me to slaughter the effeminate Romans!'

They hasten and quickly cut down those nearest to them; then they retreat as victors. There lies a dark valley, thick with wooded forest: here are concealed six thousand Britons, awaiting the arrival of their companions. As their comrades flee there, they unite with them and make a joint assault on the enemy. In the first clash a thousand Roman citizens fall and a thousand are captured. The remainder flee until they are aided by Petreius, with ten thousand men, and many others. They force the Britons to turn back their horses and to retreat at the gallop to the wood from which they had issued. There the Britons close the entrances to the forest with a tight ring of steel, resist the oncoming attack, and aggressively slay their foes.

The son of Ennutus, Ydernus of marvellous repute, brings five thousand cavalry to aid his comrades as they retreat before the enemy. Their boldness grows, those who were showing their backs now facing the foe. Both sides inflict wounds and equal carnage. But the Romans attack or retire more skilfully, being instructed by their leader now to turn their backs in flight, now to fight back strongly. Whereas the Britons charge without order, their concern being not so much with victory as to prove the extent of their courage: hence they everywhere suffer the greater slaughter.

When Boso realises this, he assembles and separates a band of brave men, whom he knows to be bold and eager for war, and says the following to them: 'High-spirited youths, we have begun this struggle without our king's permission. If – heaven forbid – we happen to be beaten in this engagement, Arthur will accuse us of dishonour in defeat, and so will experience damage to his cause; moreover, the Italian army will grow more bold if part of our forces are vanquished. There is no way for us to enjoy the smile of victory except to capture or kill the consul Petreius. Let us break through the Roman companies to capture him; then all of them will turn their backs and run.'

They obey, rush on Petreius, and capture him; and, once captured, Boso leads him away through the ranks of his comrades. Then the Roman citizens run to his aid, and the Britons close their formation to meet them. Shouting, confusion, slaughter and uproar ensue. There it is abundantly clear on both sides who fights well with the spear, who with the sword.

At length the Romans, leaderless after the capture of their commander, quit the field. The Britons hack at their fleeing backs, cut them down, and strip them. Some they capture and present in chains to the king. Hardly restraining the happiness in his rejoicing heart, he grants the victors rich gifts. Afterwards at the king's orders the captives are taken to Paris by Cador, Bedivere, Borellus and Richerius, and innumerable others under the command of these four.

Pondering this, Lucius chooses fifteen thousand men, putting them under the command of the kings of Libya and Syria and two men honoured by the consular fasces, and sends them to intercept the forces despatched by the king. Beneath the dark cloak of night they hide in a valley to await the enemy. The Britons arrive, bringing the Roman captives. The foe emerge from the dark valley which had concealed them. The force sent by the king is striker by sudden terror, and can scarcely grasp its weapons firmly or draw up its companies in order. However, it parts and divides into two companies, one to fight, the other to guard the captives: that which guards is commanded by Richerius and Bedivere; that which fights by Cador, duke of Cornwall, and the consul Borellus. The enraged mass of Romans charges in disorder and cuts down the British as they form in their divisions. The king's forces despair and are almost retreating, when Guitardus, duke of Aquitaine, learns of the ambush and brings with him against the enemy three thousand men ready for the fray. Reinforced by them, the Britons drive back the

Roman ranks. But in the first clash they lose many of their men; Borellus dies, slain by the king of the Syrians. The Roman youths turn in rout and retreat in flight to their tents, enduring wounds on their backs. Vulteius and Evander, the Syrian king, are cut down and killed. Those whom flight does not save are slaughtered or captured. Victory smiles on the Britons. They send the captives of the first battle to Paris, but return those of the second to the king; the fact that so many have been conquered by so few gives Arthur hope of defeating the Romans.

Amazed by the news of his men's rout, Lucius is unsure what to do: should he fight or retreat before the Britons? He chooses to fall back while it is still possible for the emperor Leo to help him. He therefore strikes camp on the following night. Looking for a place of refuge, he enters Langres. When Arthur realises that the Romans have retired, he anticipates their flight.

He draws up his troops in formation and encourages them with the following speech: 'Partners of such of my labours as are worthy of song, by whose advice and bravery I have conquered so many territories of the world, and whom the whole world will serve, lo, the day we long for is at hand, the day on which Rome will expose her neck to our axe. She will regret demanding tribute when she is forced to pay it. The reward sought by our swords is eternal liberty. Let anyone whose hand grows tired of striking become an unworthy slave. Whoever is not intimidated by the enemy's numbers is a dutiful man, and he who rages against the foe to avoid slavery is free from reproach. Lucius and the Romans have placed their only hope of return in a shameful flight. In fear of our weapons they have entered Langres in order to flee at first light and retire to the Alps. We have pre-empted them. When they arrive here at dawn, we with our weapons will catch them unarmed and butcher them with the sword. The imminent battle will not be like our previous deeds. We have effected nothing covertly or by stealth. We have seen fit to do everything openly in broad daylight, and nothing by night: it is the Italians who have always been experienced in engineering stratagems and traps. In my view there is nothing reprehensible in deceiving the deceitful and countering trickery with trickery. Let us defeat an enemy who is already beaten. Our triumph may win scant praise, but its rewards are great: this contest will place the whole world from east to west in my power, and in your power too. My desire is to have only the name of victor; cities, castles, houses, villages, riches and other rewards I make over to you.'

He has scarcely finished, when the whole assembly eagerly takes up arms, chafes at the delay, and demands the encounter with voice and prayer; although battle is not over nor even begun, they already see themselves as the victors.

When Lucius discovers this ambush, believing that flight is useless to him, he calls together his men, and speaks these words of exhortation:

'Nobles, to whose care the power of Rome is entrusted, I beg you to remember your ancestors: in order to avoid the fall of the Roman empire to savage foes, they were by no means unwilling to shed their blood, and valued Rome above themselves, bequeathing a fine model of excellence to their descendants. Accustomed more often to conquer than be conquered, they extended our dominion; by their counsel the republic always grew, by their bravery the four corners of the earth were subjected to the Roman empire in servitude. Therefore I admonish you, I entreat you to defend the rights of Roman power, which were increased by the blood of your parents; attack with avenging sword the stiff-necked Britons, who, alone of all the peoples in the world, strive to confound our state.'

He has hardly finished his speech, when the body of senators and kings, the mass of dukes and the crowds of nobles swear that, in protecting the ancient rights of the city of Romulus, which rules the whole world, they will not fear to lose their lives and undergo death. Yet in the faces both of the emperor as he issues these commands and of the nobles as they make their firm undertakings it is easy to read that they are the beaten side in the war. All swiftly arm themselves and leave the city. They march to the valley where the king resolutely awaits their retreat. The two sides come into view of each other.

Brave men, what madness drives you to sacrifice the Eternal Kingdom for a transient realm? You will lose both by exceeding the bounds. Britain ought to be content with her own territory; Rome need not have demanded the tribute which she seeks unjustly. But the enemy of the human race, to whom justice, rectitude and loyalty are known to be anathema, and who is enraged by times of peace, prepares both sides' weapons and promises triumph to each. Yet he cares not which is gladdened by victory; for he is prince, fount and instigator of evil, sowing treachery, breeding hatred, stirring up anger, subverting laws, untying the knots of love; to observe men's acts of virtue and successes is torture to him, and in his envy he thwarts good deeds. Although the wretch can never return to the place which he once lost, still he hates and harries all those whom he sees aspiring to occupy that same seat. Nature's promptings have taught him what trickery can most quickly deceive the heart. There are some who avoid the corruption of forbidden love; but he makes them like foolish virgins. Others are not men of violence, do not steal, nor bear false witness; but they are tainted with the fault of greed, which is tantamount to idolatry. Another generously distributes very many gifts to the poor; but this only draws the attention of human praise upon him, and he loses both his possessions and his reward. Others are distinguished by eloquence, a learned tongue, a lavish hand, a handsome face, a strong right arm, and other virtues; but all these are obliterated by pride. It is pride alone which has sent the Romans against the Britons.

In the ninth book battle is waged. With Caesar slain, the victory goes to Arthur. A fresh rumour reports that Mordred has defiled Arthur's marriage. He therefore returns home, while the adulterer blocks his path; this causes both their deaths. They are succeeded by Constantine.

On the preceding night a comet revealed its shining head to mortal gaze, a sinister omen for so many kings. Owls and nocturnal birds sang out the imminent slaughter of a great many nobles. The howling of fighting wolves, the baying of dogs, and an echo which reverberated to them all stuck terror into every man. Fleeing her senile husband, Dawn gives sure warning of the impending disaster by blushing with ruddy face, appearing with muted rays and bedewed with tears, The sun rises from the eastern shores more slowly than is usual; pale and sad at the sight of the lines of battle ready for war, he languishes with grim light, and, hiding his head behind the clouds, diminishes his beams to avoid witnessing the fate of so many dukes, the death of so many kings.

When the Romans are drawn up opposite the Britons, Bellona comes between them, ministering swords and spears to the soldiers. Though their spirit is the same, their numbers are unequal. The Roman army is more numerous than the British, but the Britons are more courageous. Lo, both sides' battlelines charge. Tumult and the crash of arms; shouting, fanfares and their echo; all confusedly resound together as if the last day has arrived; one would think that the elements are slipping into the ancient abyss, the fabric of the world having been shattered. Auguselus and brave Cador, duke of Cornwall, are at the head of the force entrusted to them. The consul Catellus opposes them with the legion which he commands, directing his Romans with him. The Britons resist the enemy, both sides inflicting wounds; flames leap from the meeting of swords.

Then Gerinus and Boso arrive with the legion under their orders. They charge and penetrate the struggling companies, making for the king of the Parthians, who is attacking Achilles, king of Denmark. There rages the Danish axe, there the sword rampages; no hand is idle. Each side strives for the other's destruction. Each kills and is killed, but the Britons suffer the greater slaughter. The butler Bedivere is slain and falls, as does Kay, wounded by a deadly blow. For, while fighting with the king of the Medes, Bedivere is cut down by his enemy's sword: and when Kay wishes to avenge his sad death, he receives a mortal wound in the chest. Yet he breaks through the king of Libya's ranks and, even though he will not survive Bedivere long, he brings the dead body to Arthur's presence. Groaning, sorrow and cries ensue in the camp, but the pressing hour of battle does not allow them to lament for long.

Brave Hyrelglas, Bedivere's doughty nephew, wild with grief at his uncle's death, picks out three hundred youths ferocious in war and, leading them into battle, makes for the standard of the king of Media. He attacks the king with his sword, overwhelms and kills him, and, bringing his corpse to his uncle's body, completely dismembers it. Then he admonishes his men to attack the enemy bravely; they assault and cut them down, but are also cut down themselves. On the Roman side the kings of Spain and Babylon, two senators and a huge crowd of soldiers fall. Among the British, two kings and three dukes are felled.

Their divisions turn their backs in flight on the death of their leaders and join with the command of king Hoel and duke Gawain. The leaderless troops unite with the Armoricans, fighting beside them and attacking with them. The mass of Romans which had put them to flight now turns to flee, and those of the Britons who were not retreating rout the Romans and decimate their ranks. Hewing a path with their swords, the men make with all their might for the company among whom Lucius Caesar stands. As soon as he sees the massacre of his comrades, he is greatly angered and hurls himself into the midst of the enemy. Then follows a shout and a pitiful engagement. A thousand Britons fall, a thousand Romans are slain.

The praiseworthy Hoel, king of Armorica, and duke Gawain lead their battalions, hacking at the enemy with their swords; it is not easy to tell which of them is the mightier in arms, which the greater. They break into Caesar's division, fearless of any superiority in numbers. At their hands die a thousand men; a stream of blood spreads wide through the fields. Then Gawain, as swift as a fast-flowing river, meets Caesar's attack, which he desires more ardently than anything, and assaults him with drawn sword. Lucius is overjoyed to be able to join combat with so brave and so mettlesome a warrior. They fight each other: both are of equal age and distinguished by the same nobility, both have equal strength and the same proud spirit. They are dealing frequent sword strokes, each eager to end the other's life, when a company of Romans intervenes and forces the Armoricans to retreat swiftly to Arthur.

He supports them, saying: 'Trusty and bold comrades, hasten with me; overthrow the womanish Romans and add them to the list of our conquests.'

They obey, and show which of them has a mind to win glory. They prefer to go before the king to meet death, than to follow him in victory. Drawing Excalibur, the king rushes on the Romans, and overthrows and slaughters them, making a path with his sword; whomever he strikes once, he sends straight to hell; he cuts down horses and riders together. As Jupiter's eagle scatters birds, as a lion of noble anger, prompted by the cravings of hunger and driven by the pangs in his empty belly, fiercely and bloodthirstily hurls himself on bulls, seizing some and tearing others to pieces: just so the martial hero rages against the Romans. Lo, two kings are snatched away by an evil fate, both felled by Arthur's sword;

whoever is wounded by his spear or sword pours out his life with his blood. Arthur exhorts the Britons to fight well, and Caesar the Romans. In the struggle, the Romans sometimes have the upper hand over the Britons, sometimes the Britons over them.

While it is thus uncertain which side the die of war will favour, the consul of Gloucester, Morindus, charges the enemy with his legion, breaking Caesar's unsuspecting troops by attacking them from the rear. Lucius's reign is ended when he is struck beneath the chest by a blow from Morindus's deadly spear. The Romans despair and after Caesar's death do not cease to yield before the slaughterers until victory falls to the descendants of Brutus and the victors win all the spoils of the vanquished.

Then the British king separates from the Romans those of his nobles who died in the battle, and commands that they be buried with full honours; he also orders the Roman corpses to be interred in mounds as was their custom; and he has Caesar's body carried to the senators in the city of Romulus as a substitute for the tribute they demanded. The sun has weighed the length of night and day with perfect balance in the scales of Libra, when the victor marches on the cities of the Allobroges and subdues them. There he waits for winter to end and for Aries to make good the loss of daylight by shortening the hours of night, so that, when the snow melts and the first swallow flies, he may cross the range of the Alps with a great army, subjugate Italy and Rome to the senate's dismay, and exercise control over the conquered empire.

But the power of God thwarts these lofty aspirations. News arrives that Mordred, completely without justice or loyalty to those entrusted to him, has defiled the king's bed and assumed the crown, usurping the kingdom of Britain. Worried by this report, Arthur hands over responsibility for the Gauls to Hoel and sails back across the sea to his realm with the kings of the islands of the ocean. The false king, a rash instigator of wrong-doing, makes a treaty with the Saxons, granting to them that part of the kingdom which stretches from the river Humber to the people of Scotland, and those lands which Hengist and Horsa held under Vortigern. Duke Cheldricus brings to Mordred's aid eight hundred ships driven by the east wind, full of armed pagans. Mordred assembles all the neighbouring peoples and those whom Arthur considers his foes, and, his army swelled by pagans and Christians, comes to Richborough.

Arthur meets and attacks them. A thousand men fall on either side; among them are the famous Gawain and the Scottish king Auguselus, who is succeeded by the son of his brother Urianus, Yvenus, a mighty heir for a brave man. At last Arthur gains the shore with a great effort and forces Mordred and his troops to turn tail, enduring deadly slaughter at their backs. Then the traitor flees, and that night makes for Winchester. The queen enters a venerable church, where she joins a band of nuns and assumes a life of widowhood; yet, though she pretends to be a widow, she remains married to two living men, illegitimately to the second of them.

But king Arthur, troubled and sad that so many of his men have fallen, buries their corpses. Following his enemies more swiftly than an eagle, he marches on Winchester, and besieges it and king Mordred. Mordred quickly leaves the city to attack Arthur. It is no brief task to set down how many brave men each side loses in the engagement. Eventually the treacherous party quits the field. They retire defeated to Cornwall, where they regroup their scattered forces and await Arthur and his nobles as they follow them. The sandy Cambula flows in a straight course.

There on both sides they assemble and threaten each other with civil war: breaking the bond of brotherhood, brother wishes to cut brother's throat; against paternal feeling, son pants against father, and fathers threaten their sons with death. All Nature's laws lie shattered: while they wish to conquer with the sword, both right and wrong seem equally legitimate. A man who wields savage weapons cares not what is honourable. Yet what is clearly more damaging than any error and worse than death itself is that it is to the sword of pagans that so much freedom is given to tear the limbs of Christ. This is your doing, Mordred, and an eternal disgrace to the British people. Miserable wretch, take pity on yourself and on your nation. Let there be no treaty between you and the Saxons. For the Saxons derive both their character and their name from stones, than which they are more rough and more unforgiving. Drive out the wicked enemy, and reconcile yourself to your king, your realm, and your people. You have sinned: repent! King Arthur will be a kinder foe to you than the Saxons: he toils at waging a just war for the freedom of your citizens; they strive and wish with all their hearts to submit you to the yoke of slavery. Do you not know what Hengist once did to his son-in-law? That wicked father-in-law deprived him of his kingdom. All who belong to the Saxon race retain the same desire. His treacherous descendants are plotting to betray you: resist them while you still can. But because you are infected with so great a longing to rule, you are forbidden to yield to the king by the angel of ambition, who, mindful of his own fall and the cause of his ruin, traps you with the same offence and raises you up in order to cast you down and make you fall in worse ruin. Lo, the swift and mighty avenger of your crime comes bravely to crush in battle the Saxons, whom he has so often defeated and driven from this land. The four corners of the earth fear his courage: Wales serves him; Ireland is beaten into submission; Scotland is subdued; Iceland obeys him meekly; Norway rises before him and Denmark bows; France yields to him. With Caesar slain, Rome has almost become a province; from the far east to the icy Alps, the world, deprived of its kings, willingly promises to give tribute; the people who live beneath the pole-star now have two reasons to tremble; and those whom torrid Spain burns shiver for fear of Arthur. Whoever contradicts him through pride craves peace and begs for pardon; and condemns himself and proves himself to be a guilty criminal, unworthy to live. Wretch soon to die, what error leads you to think that with a few foes you can overcome him whom the whole world fears, of whom all the people of the Antipodes are frightened, and to whom according to Merlin – if we are to believe him – the road to death is closed?

Since no one is allowed to contravene the laws of destiny, however, both leaders set out to the battle which has already been decreed by fate. Both arrange their forces. Mordred draws up three divisions, placing a legion in each; he holds in reserve six legions as his guards. Raised up, he exhorts his companions with clear voice as follows: 'Young and brave warriors, conquer with me these few, exhausted old men, who are worn out by the long succession of their sufferings. The cities, castles, and homes which your enemies possess, I grant to you.'

Arthur disposes nine divisions, under the same number of commanders, and addresses them in this manner: 'Exalted band of nobles, to whom I owe the fact that the world has come to fear me, and by whose counsel in war and peace I have conquered so many parts of the earth, lo, in its search for places to which it can retreat the rebel army has reached Cornwall; and here it remains because it can go no further. They have given up hope and are leaving everything in the lap of fate. Let us gain praise and eternal renown by overcoming so many when we are so few: nor will it be a difficult task. Moreover, they are bearing arms in defiance of right and duty, and do not fear to break their faith and the laws of their ancestors. We are inspired by the righteous cause of defending our motherland. Does anyone think that the Saxon mercenaries, who entered camp for money, will be reliable in battle or loyal to their master? When the air is rent by the sounding of trumpets, shouting, the neighing of horses, the clash of arms, uproar, and cries magnified by a resounding echo, the contemptible hirelings will turn tail and abandon the field.'

Without further ado, the battlelines meet and the sky shakes with such a roar as would be heard if heaven, earth and sea were slipping back into the ancient abyss. In the first clash of arms, a thousand are felled by arrows, a thousand by javelins. Severed human limbs lie deep, harvested by the sword. A stream of blood spreads wide and flows into the river. The Cambula is amazed that its water is transformed. The swollen, bloody torrent bursts its banks and carries the bodies of the dead to the sea; many whose lives have not yet drained away can be observed swimming and calling for help. While it is still uncertain which side will gain the glory of praise, lo, Arthur, with a legion he had placed under his own command, rushes where he sees Mordred stand. As he carves a way through the foe, his sword before him, to his right and left fall more men than can easily be numbered. Mordred, the instigator and fount of the betrayal, is cut down.

Yet the traitor's army does not retreat on its leader's death, but fights bravely, slaying the Britons and being slain by them. Almost the whole of the armies and all the kings and dukes are killed, although king Arthur, to whom the door of death is believed to be closed, still lives. Yet even he stands with a mortal wound in his chest. He gives the crown of Britain to Constantine, son of Cador.

The ocean surrounds a remarkable island, which lacks no blessing: no thief, no robber, no foe sets traps there; there is no snow, no mist, nor is summer intemperately hot. There is unending peace and harmony; it is spring – eternally warm – and flowers, lilies, roses and violets are not lacking; the apple-tree bears beneath its foliage both blossom and fruit together. There youths ever live with girls without the loss of their chastity. There is no old age, illness has no power, there is no sorrow. All is full of joy. There are no possessions there, everything is held in common. The island and its benefits are ruled over by a regal woman: a most beautiful nymph surrounded by comely virgins, she has a pleasing face, is born of noble parents, is wise in counsel, and renowned for her skill in medicine. As soon as Arthur relinquishes the crown of his realm and creates a king in his place, he crosses to the island: it is the five hundred and forty-second year after the Word was made flesh without a father's seed. Badly wounded, he goes to the court of the king of Avalon, where the regal woman examines his wound and keeps his cured limbs for herself. They live on together, if we are to believe it.

17. BEOWULF

Beowulf has only come down to us by the greatest of good fortune. In 1731, the superb collection of manuscripts formed by Sir Robert Cotton in the early seventeenth century, and which had been made a public library by act of parliament in 1701, was the scene of a disastrous fire which burned some two hundred of them. The volume containing the unique copy of Beowulf *was slightly damaged, but survived. Without this manuscript, our knowledge of Anglo-Saxon poetry would be limited to tantalising scraps and fragments. As it is, we have here a poem which may have been written for the royal court of the Wuffings in East Anglia, whose palace was at Rendlesham and whose royal cemetery was at Sutton Hoo. Some years ago, this translation was read on the mounds at Sutton Hoo at dusk of a stormy October evening, lit by braziers: an unforgettable occasion, reuniting poem and place, and demonstrating the living power of the ancient legends.*

Although Beowulf *is an Anglo-Saxon poem, it harks back to the origins of the Anglo-Saxon invaders, and tells of men and events in the land of the Geats, the south of Sweden, and in Denmark, where king Hrothgar rules; if there is a historical basis for the story, it belongs to the sixth century or earlier. The monster Grendel and the dragon which is the cause of Beowulf's death are creatures from Germanic legend, however, and there are a number of digressions which deal with other episodes concerning Germanic heroes such as Sigemund. It reflects the roots of the Anglo-Saxon conquerors rather than their exploits in Britain itself; but it also tells an English audience about their forefathers and the past history of their race.*

Listen!
      The fame of Danish kings
in days gone by, the daring feats
worked by those heroes are well known to us.
   Scyld Scefing often deprived his enemies,
many tribes of men, of their mead-benches.
He terrified his foes; yet he, as a boy,
had been found a waif; fate made amends for that.
He prospered under heaven, won praise and honour,
until the men of every neighbouring tribe,
across the whale's way, were obliged to obey him
and pay him tribute. He was a noble king!
Then a son was born to him, a child
in the court, sent by God to comfort
the Danes; for He had seen their dire distress,
that once they suffered hardship for a long while,

lacking a lord; and the Lord of Life,
King of Heaven, granted this boy glory;
Beow was renowned – the name of Scyld's son
became known throughout the Norse lands.
By his own mettle, likewise by generous gifts
while he still enjoys his father's protection,
a young man must ensure that in later years
his companions will support him, serve
their prince in battle; a man who wins renown
will always prosper among any people.
　　Then Scyld departed at the destined hour,
that powerful man sought the Lord's protection.
His own close companions carried him
down to the sea, as he, lord of the Danes,
had asked while he could still speak.
That well-loved man had ruled his land for many years.
There in harbour stood the ring-prowed ship,
the prince's vessel, icy, eager to sail;
and then they laid their dear lord,
the giver of rings, deep within the ship
by the mast in majesty; many treasures
and adornments from far and wide were gathered there.
I have never heard of a ship equipped
more handsomely with weapons and war-gear,
swords and corslets; on his breast
lay countless treasures that were to travel far
with him into the waves' domain.
They gave him great ornaments, gifts
no less magnificent than those men had given him
who long before had sent him alone,
child as he was, across the stretch of the seas.
Then high above his head they placed
a golden banner and let the waves bear him,
bequeathed him to the sea; their hearts were grieving,
their minds mourning. Mighty men
beneath the heavens, rulers in the hall,
cannot say who received that cargo.
　　When his royal father had travelled from the earth,
Beow of Denmark, a beloved king,
ruled long in the stronghold, famed
amongst men; in time Healfdene the brave
was born to him; who, so long as he lived,
grey-haired and redoubtable, ruled the noble Danes.
Beow's son Healfdene, leader of men,

was favoured by fortune with four children:
Heorogar and Hrothgar and Halga the good;
Yrse, the fourth, was Onela's queen,
the dear wife of that warlike Swedish king.

   Hrothgar won honour in war,
glory in battle, and so ensured
his followers' support – young men
whose number multiplied into a mighty troop.
And he resolved to build a hall,
a large and noble feasting-hall
of whose splendours men would always speak,
and there to distribute as gifts to old and young
all the things that God had given him –
but not men's lives or the public land.
Then I heard that tribes without number, even
to the ends of the earth, were given orders
to decorate the hall. And in due course
(before very long) this greatest of halls
was completed. Hrothgar, whose very word was counted
far and wide as a command, called it Heorot.
He kept his promise, gave presents of rings
and treasure at the feasting. The hall towered high,
lofty and wide-gabled – fierce tongues of loathsome fire
had not yet attacked it, nor was the time yet near
when a mortal feud should flare between father-
and son-in-law, sparked off by deeds of deadly enmity.

   Then the brutish demon who lived in darkness
impatiently endured a time of frustration:
day after day he heard the din of merry-making
inside the hall, and the sound of the harp
and the bard's clear song. He who could tell
of the origin of men from far-off times lifted his voice,
sang that the Almighty made the earth,
this radiant plain encompassed by oceans:
and that God, all powerful, ordained
sun and moon to shine for mankind,
adorned all regions of the world
with trees and leaves; and sang that He gave life
to every kind of creature that walks about earth.
So those warrior Danes lived joyful lives,
in complete harmony, until the hellish fiend
began to perpetrate base crimes.
This gruesome creature was called Grendel,
notorious prowler of the borderland, ranger of the moors,

the fen and the fastness; this cursed creature
lived in a monster's lair for a time
after the Creator had condemned him
as one of the seed of Cain – the Everlasting Lord
avenged Abel's murder. Cain had
no satisfaction from that feud, but the Creator
sent him into exile, far from mankind,
because of his crime. He could no longer
approach the throne of grace, that precious place
in God's presence, nor did he feel God's love.
In him all evil-doers find their origin,
monsters and elves and spiteful spirits of the dead,
also the giants who grappled with God
for a long while; the Lord gave them their deserts.
    Then, under cover of night, Grendel came
to Hrothgar's lofty hall to see how the Ring-Danes
were disposed after drinking ale all evening;
and he found there a band of brave warriors,
well-feasted, fast asleep, dead to worldly sorrow,
man's sad destiny. At once that hellish monster,
grim and greedy, brutally cruel,
started forward and seized thirty thanes
even as they slept; and then, gloating
over his plunder, he hurried from the hall,
made for his lair with all those slain warriors.
Then at dawn, as day first broke,
Grendel's power was at once revealed;
a great lament was lifted, after the feast
an anguished cry at that daylight discovery.
The famous prince, best of all men, sat apart in mourning;
when he saw Grendel's gruesome footprints,
that great man grieved for his retainers.
This enmity was utterly one-sided, too repulsive,
too long-lasting. Nor were the Danes allowed respite,
but the very next day Grendel committed
violent assault, murders more atrocious than before,
and he had no qualms about it. He was caught up in his crimes.
Then it was not difficult to find the man
who preferred a more distant resting-place,
a bed in the outbuildings, for the hatred
of the hall-warden was quite unmistakable.
He who had escaped the clutches of the fiend
kept further off, at a safe distance.
    Thus Grendel ruled, resisted justice,

one against all, until the best of halls
stood deserted. And so it remained:
for twelve long winters the lord of the Danes
was sorely afflicted with sorrows and cares;
then men were reminded in mournful songs
that the monster Grendel fought with Hrothgar
for a long time, fought with fierce hatred
committing crime and atrocity day after day
in continual strife. He had no wish for peace
with any of the Danes, would not desist
from his deadly malice or pay *wergild* –
No! None of the counsellors could hold out hope
of handsome compensation at that slayer's hands.
But the cruel monster constantly terrified
young and old, the dark death-shadow
lurked in ambush; he prowled the misty moors
at the dead of night; men do not know
where such hell-whisperers shrithe in their wanderings.
Such were the many and outrageous injuries
that the fearful solitary, foe of all men,
endlessly inflicted; he occupied Heorot,
that hall adorned with treasures, on cloudless nights.
This caused the lord of the Danes deep,
heart-breaking grief. Strong men often sat
in consultation, trying in vain to devise
a good plan as to how best valiant men
could safeguard themselves against sudden attack.
At times they offered sacrifices to the idols
in their pagan tabernacles, and prayed aloud
to the soul-slayer that he would assist them
in their dire distress. Such was the custom
and comfort of the heathen; they brooded in their hearts
on hellish things – for the Creator, Almighty God,
the judge of all actions, was neglected by them;
truly they did not know how to praise the Protector of Heaven,
the glorious Ruler. Woe to the man who,
in his wickedness, commits his soul to the fire's embrace;
he must expect neither comfort nor change.
He will be damned for ever. Joy shall be his
who, when he dies, may stand before the Lord,
seek peace in the embrace of our Father.
　　Thus Healfdene's son endlessly brooded
over the afflictions of this time; that wise warrior
was altogether helpless, for the hardship upon them –

violent visitations, evil events in the night –
was too overwhelming, loathsome, and long-lasting.
    One of Hygelac's thanes, Beowulf by name,
renowned among the Geats for his great bravery,
heard in his own country of Grendel's crimes;
he was the strongest man alive,
princely and powerful. He gave orders
that a good ship should be prepared, said he would sail
over the sea to assist the famous leader,
the warrior king, since he needed hardy men.
Wise men admired his spirit of adventure.
Dear to them though he was, they encouraged
the warrior and consulted the omens.
Beowulf searched out the bravest of the Geats,
asked them to go with him; that seasoned sailor
led fourteen thanes to the ship at the shore.
    Days went by; the boat was on the water,
moored under the cliff. The warriors, all prepared,
stepped onto the prow – the water streams eddied,
stirred up sand; the men stowed
gleaming armour, noble war-gear deep
within the ship; then those warriors launched
the well-built boat and so began their journey.
Foaming at the prow and most like a sea-bird,
the boat sped over the waves, urged on by the wind;
until next day, at about the expected time,
so far had the curved prow come
that the travellers sighted land,
shining cliffs, steep hills,
broad headlands. So did they cross the sea;
their journey was at its end. Then the Geats
disembarked, lost no time in tying up
the boat – their corslets clanked;
the warriors gave thanks to God
for their safe passage over the sea.
    Then, on the cliff-top, the Danish watchman
(whose duty it was to stand guard by the shore)
saw that the Geats carried flashing shields
and gleaming war-gear down the gangway,
and his mind was riddled with curiosity.
Then Hrothgar's thane leaped onto his horse
and, brandishing a spear, galloped
down to the shore; there, he asked at once:
'Warriors! Who are you, in your coats of mail,

who have steered your tall ship over the sea-lanes
to these shores? I've been a coastguard here
for many years, kept watch by the sea,
so that no enemy band should encroach
upon this Danish land and do us injury.
Never have warriors, carrying their shields,
come to this country in a more open manner.
Nor were you assured of my leaders' approval,
my kinsmen's consent. I've never set eyes
on a more noble man, a warrior in armour,
than one among your band; he's no mere retainer,
so ennobled by his weapons. May his looks never belie him,
and his lordly bearing. But now, before you step
one foot further on Danish land like faithless spies,
I must know your lineage. Bold seafarers,
strangers from afar, mark my words
carefully: you would be best advised
quickly to tell me the cause of your coming.'
   The man of highest standing, leader of that troop,
unlocked his hoard of words, answered him:
'We are all Geats, hearth-companions of Hygelac;
my father was famed far and wide,
a noble lord, Ecgtheow by name –
he endured many winters before he,
in great old age, went on his way; every wise man
in this world readily recalls him.
We have sailed across the sea to seek your lord.
Healfdene's son, protector of the people,
with most honourable intentions; give us your guidance!
We have come on an errand of importance
to the great Danish prince; nor, I imagine, will the cause
of our coming long remain secret. You will know
whether it is true – as we have heard tell –
that here among the Danes a certain evil-doer,
a fearful solitary, on dark nights commits deeds
of unspeakable malice – damage
and slaughter. In good conscience
I can counsel Hrothgar, that wise and good man,
how he shall overcome the fiend,
and how his anguish shall be assuaged –
if indeed his fate ordains that these foul deeds
should ever end, and be avenged;
he will suffer endless hardship otherwise,
dire distress, as long as Heorot, best of dwellings,

stands unshaken in its lofty place.'
   Still mounted, the coastguard,
a courageous thane, gave him this reply:
'The discriminating warrior – one whose mind is keen –
must perceive the difference between words and deeds.
But I see you are a company well disposed
towards the Danish prince. Proceed, and bring
your weapons and armour! I shall direct you.
And I will command my companions, moreover,
to guard your ship with honour
against any foe – your beached vessel,
caulked so recently – until the day that timbered craft
with its curved prow shall carry back
the beloved man across the sea currents
to the shores of the storm-loving Geats:
he who dares deeds with such audacity and valour
shall be granted safety in the squall of battle.'
   Then they hurried on. The ship lay still;
securely anchored, the spacious vessel
rode on its hawser. The boar crest, brightly gleaming,
stood over their helmets: superbly tempered,
plated with glowing gold, it guarded the lives
of those grim warriors. The thanes made haste,
marched along together until they could discern
the glorious, timbered hall, adorned with gold;
they saw there the best-known building
under heaven. The ruler lived in it;
its brilliance carried across countless lands.
Then the fearless watchman pointed out the path
leading to Heorot, bright home of brave men,
so that they should not miss the way;
that bold warrior turned his horse, then said:
'I must leave you here. May the Almighty Father,
of His grace, guard you in your enterprise.
I will go back to the sea again,
and there stand watch against marauding bands.'
   The road was paved; it showed those warriors
the way. Their corslets were gleaming,
the strong links of shining chain-mail
clinked together. When the sea-stained travellers
had reached the hall itself in their fearsome armour,
they placed their broad shields
(worked so skilfully) against Heorot's wall.
Then they sat on a bench; the brave men's

armour sang. The seafarers' gear
stood all together, a grey-tipped forest
of ash spears; that armed troop was well equipped
with weapons.
                    Then Wulfgar, a proud warrior,
asked the Geats about their ancestry:
'Where have you come from with these gold-plated shields,
these grey coats of mail, these visored helmets,
and this pile of spears? I am Hrothgar's
messenger, his herald. I have never seen
so large a band of strangers of such bold bearing.
You must have come to Hrothgar's court
not as exiles, but from audacity and high ambition.'
Then he who feared no man, the proud leader
of the Geats, stern-faced beneath his helmet,
gave him this reply: 'We are Hygelac's
companions at the bench: my name is Beowulf.
I wish to explain to Healfdene's son,
the famous prince, your lord,
why we have come if he, in his goodness,
will give us leave to speak with him.'
Wulfgar replied – a prince of the Vandals,
his mettle, his wisdom and prowess in battle
were widely recognized: 'I will ask
the lord of the Danes, ruler of the Scyldings,
renowned prince and ring-giver,
just as you request, regarding your journey,
and bring back to you at once whatever answer
that gracious man thinks fit to give me.'
   Then Wulfgar hurried to the place where Hrothgar sat,
grizzled and old, surrounded by his thanes;
the brave man moved forward until he stood
immediately before the Danish lord;
he well knew the customs of warriors.
Wulfgar addressed his friend and leader:
'Geatish men have travelled to this land,
come from far, across the stretch of the seas.
These warriors call their leader Beowulf;
they ask, my lord, that they should be allowed
to speak with you. Gracious Hrothgar,
do not give them *no* for answer.
They, in their armour, seem altogether worthy
of the highest esteem. I have no doubt of their leader's
might, he who has brought these brave men to Heorot.'

Hrothgar, defender of the Danes, answered:
'I knew him when he was a boy;
his illustrious father was called Ecgtheow;
Hrethel the Geat gave him his only daughter
in marriage; now his son, with daring spirit,
has voyaged here to visit a loyal friend.
And moreover, I have heard seafarers say –
men who have carried rich gifts to the Geats
as a mark of my esteem – that in the grasp
of his hand that man renowned in battle
has the might of thirty men. I am convinced
that Holy God, of His great mercy,
has directed him to us West-Danes
and that he means to come to grips with Grendel.
I will reward this brave man with treasures.
Hurry! Tell them to come in and meet
our band of kinsmen; and make it clear, too,
that they are most welcome to the Danes!'
Then Wulfgar went to the hall door with Hrothgar's reply:
'My conquering lord, the leader of the East-Danes
commands me to tell you that he knows your lineage
and that you, so bold in mind, are welcome
to these shores from over the rolling sea.
You may see Hrothgar in your armour,
under your helmets, just as you are;
but leave your shields out here, and your deadly ashen spears,
let them await the outcome of your words.'
    Then noble Beowulf rose from the bench,
flanked by his fearless followers; some stayed behind
at the brave man's bidding, to stand guard over their armour.
Guided by Wulfgar, the rest hurried into Heorot
together; there went that hardy man, stern-faced
beneath his helmet, until he was standing under Heorot's roof.
Beowulf spoke – his corslet, cunningly linked
by the smith, was shining: 'Greetings, Hrothgar!
I am Hygelac's kinsman and retainer. In my youth
I achieved many daring exploits. Word of Grendel's deeds
has come to me in my own country;
seafarers say that this hall Heorot,
best of all buildings, stands empty and useless
as soon as the evening light is hidden under the sky.
So, Lord Hrothgar, men known by my people
to be noble and wise advised me to visit you
because they knew of my great strength:

they saw me themselves when, stained by my enemies' blood,
I returned from the fight when I destroyed five,
a family of giants, and by night slew monsters
on the waves; I suffered great hardship,
avenged the affliction of the Storm-Geats and crushed
their fierce foes – they were asking for trouble.
And now, I shall crush the giant Grendel
in single combat. Lord of the mighty Danes,
guardian of the Scyldings, I ask one favour:
protector of warriors, lord beloved of your people,
now that I have sailed here from so far,
do not refuse my request – that I alone, with my band
of brave retainers, may cleanse Heorot.
I have also heard men say this monster
is so reckless he spurns the use of weapons.
Therefore (so that Hygelac, my lord,
may rest content over my conduct) I deny myself
the use of a sword and a broad yellow shield
in battle; but I shall grapple with this fiend
hand to hand; we shall fight for our lives,
foe against foe; and he whom death takes off
must resign himself to the judgement of God.
I know that Grendel, should he overcome me,
will without dread devour many Geats,
matchless warriors, in the battle-hall,
as he has often devoured Danes before. If death claims me
you will not have to cover my head,
for he already will have done so –
with a sheet of shining blood; he will carry off
the blood-stained corpse, meaning to savour it;
the solitary one will eat without sorrow
and stain his lair; no longer then
will you have to worry about burying my body.
But if battle should claim me, send this most excellent
coat of mail to Hygelac, this best of corslets
that protects my breast; it once belonged to Hrethel,
the work of Weland. Fate goes ever as it must!'
    Hrothgar, protector of the Scyldings, replied:
'Beowulf, my friend! So you have come here,
because of past favours, to fight on our behalf!
Your father Ecgtheow, by striking a blow,
began the greatest of feuds. He slew Heatholaf of the Wylfings
with his own hand; after that, the Geats
dared not harbour him for fear of war.

So he sailed here, over the rolling waves,
to this land of the South-Danes, the honoured Scyldings;
I was young then, had just begun to reign
over the Danes in this glorious kingdom,
this treasure-stronghold of heroes; my elder brother,
Heorogar, Healfdene's son, had died
not long before; he was a better man than I!
I settled your father's feud by payment;
I sent ancient treasures to the Wylfings
over the water's back; and Ecgtheow swore oaths to me.
It fills me with anguish to admit to all the evil
that Grendel, goaded on by his hatred,
has wreaked in Heorot with his sudden attacks
and infliction of injuries; my hall-troop is depleted,
my band of warriors; fate has swept them
into Grendel's ghastly clutches. Yet God can easily
prevent this reckless ravager from committing such crimes.
After quaffing beer, brave warriors of mine
have often boasted over the ale-cup
that they would wait in Heorot
and fight against Grendel with their fearsome swords.
Then, the next morning, when day dawned,
men could see that this great mead-hall was stained
by blood, that the floor by the benches
was spattered with gore; I had fewer followers,
dear warriors, for death had taken them off.
But first, sit down at our feast, and in due course,
as your inclination takes you, tell how warriors
have achieved greatness.'
                          Then, in the feasting-hall,
a bench was cleared for the Geats all together,
and there those brave men went and sat,
delighting in their strength; a thane did his duty –
held between his hands the adorned ale-cup,
poured out gleaming liquor; now and then
the poet raised his voice, resonant in Heorot; the warriors caroused,
no small company of Scyldings and Geats.
Ecglaf's son, Unferth, who sat at the feet
of the lord of the Scyldings, unlocked his thoughts
with these unfriendly words – for the journey of Beowulf,
the brave seafarer, much displeased him
in that he was unwilling for any man
in this wide world to gain more glory than himself:
'Are you the Beowulf who competed with Breca,

vied with him at swimming in the open sea
when, swollen with vanity, you both braved
the waves, risked your lives on deep waters
because of a foolish boast? No one,
neither friend nor foe, could keep you
from your sad journey, when you swam out to sea,
clasped in your arms the water-streams,
passed over the sea-paths, swiftly moved your hands
and sped over the ocean. The sea heaved,
the winter flood; for seven nights
you both toiled in the water; but Breca outstayed you,
he was the stronger; and then, on the eighth morning,
the sea washed him up on the shores of the Heathoreams.
From there he sought his own country,
the land of the Brondings who loved him well;
he went to his fair stronghold where he had a hall
and followers and treasures. In truth, Beanstan's son
fulfilled his boast that he could swim better than you.
So I am sure you will pay a heavy price –
although you have survived countless battle storms,
savage sword-play – if you dare
ambush Grendel in the watches of the night.'
Beowulf, the son of Ecgtheow, replied:
'Truly, Unferth my friend, all this beer
has made you talkative: you have told us much
about Breca and his exploits. But I maintain
I showed the greater stamina, endured
hardship without equal in the heaving water.
Some years ago when we were young men,
still in our youth, Breca and I made a boast,
a solemn vow, to venture our lives
on the open sea; and we kept our word.
When we swam through the water, we each held
a naked sword with which to ward off
whales; by no means could Breca
swim faster than I, pull away from me
through the press of the waves –
I had no wish to be separated from him.
So for five nights we stayed together in the sea,
until the tides tore us apart,
the foaming water, the freezing cold,
day darkening into night – until the north wind,
that savage warrior, rounded against us.
Rough were the waves; fishes in the sea

were roused to great anger. Then my coat of mail,
hard and hand-linked, guarded me against my enemies;
the woven war-garment, adorned with gold,
covered my breast. A cruel ravager
dragged me down to the sea-bed, a fierce monster
held me tightly in its grasp; but it was given to me
to bury my sword, my battle weapon,
in its breast; the mighty sea-beast
was slain by my blow in the storm of battle.
In this manner, and many times, loathsome monsters
harassed me fiercely; with my fine sword
I served them fittingly.
I did not allow those evil destroyers to enjoy
a feast, to eat me limb by limb
seated at a banquet on the sea-bottom;
but the next morning they lay in the sand
along the shore, wounded by sword strokes,
slain by battle-blades, and from that day on
they could not hinder seafarers from sailing
over deep waters. Light came from the east,
God's bright beacon; the swell subsided,
and I saw then great headlands,
cliffs swept by the wind. Fate will often spare
an undoomed man, if his courage is good.
As it was I slew nine sea-beasts
with my sword. I have never heard
of a fiercer fight by night under heaven's vault
nor of a man who endured more on the ocean streams.
But I escaped with my life from the enemies' clutches,
worn out by my venture. Then the swift current,
the surging water, carried me
to the land of the Lapps. I have not heard tell
that you have taken part in any such contests,
in the peril of sword-play. Neither you nor Breca
have yet dared such a deed with shining sword
in battle – I do not boast because of this –
though of course it is true you slew your own brothers,
your own close kinsmen. For that deed, however clever
you may be, you will suffer damnation in hell.
I tell you truly, son of Ecglaf,
that if you were in fact as unflinching
as you claim, the fearsome monster Grendel
would never have committed so many crimes
against your lord, nor created such havoc in Heorot;

but he has found he need not fear unduly
your people's enmity, fearsome assault
with swords by the victorious Scyldings.
So he spares none but takes his toll
of the Danish people, does as he will,
kills and destroys, expects no fight
from the Spear-Danes. But soon, quite soon,
I shall show him the strength, the spirit and skill
of the Geats. And thereafter, when day dawns,
when the radiant sun shines from the south
over the sons of men, he who so wishes
may enter the mead-hall without terror.'
    Then the grizzled warrior, giver of gold,
was filled with joy; the lord of the Danes,
shepherd of his people, listened to Beowulf's
brave resolution and relied on his help.
The warriors laughed, there was a hum
of contentment. Wealhtheow came forward,
mindful of ceremonial – she was Hrothgar's queen;
adorned with gold, that proud woman
greeted the men in the hall, then offered the cup
to the Danish king first of all.
She begged him, beloved of his people,
to enjoy the feast; the king, famed
for victory, ate and drank in happiness.
Then the lady of the Helmings walked about the hall,
offering the precious, ornamented cup
to old and young alike, until at last
the queen, excellent in mind, adorned with rings,
moved with the mead-cup towards Beowulf.
She welcomed the Geatish prince and with wise words
thanked God that her wish was granted
that she might depend on some warrior for help
against such attacks. The courageous man
took the cup from Wealtheow's hands
and, eager for battle, made a speech:
Beowulf, the son of Ecgtheow, said:
'When I put to sea, sailed
through the breakers with my band of men,
I resolved to fulfil the desire
of your people, or suffer the pangs of death,
caught fast in Grendel's clutches.
Here, in Heorot, I shall either work a deed
of great daring, or lay down my life.'

Beowulf's brave boast delighted Wealhtheow:
adorned with gold, the noble Danish queen
went to sit beside her lord.
      Then again, as of old, fine words were spoken
in the hall, the company rejoiced,
a conquering people, until in due course
the son of Healfdene wanted to retire
and take his rest. He realized the monster
meant to attack Heorot after the blue hour,
when black night has settled over all –
when shadowy shapes come shrithing
dark beneath the clouds. All the company rose.
Then the heroes Hrothgar and Beowulf saluted
one another; Hrothgar wished him luck
and control of Heorot, and confessed:
'Never since I could lift hand and shield,
have I entrusted this glorious Danish hall
to any man as I do now to you.
Take and guard this greatest of halls.
Make known your strength, remember your might,
stand watch against your enemy. You shall have
all you desire if you survive this enterprise.'
      Then Hrothgar, defender of the Danes,
withdrew from the hall with his band of warriors.
The warlike leader wanted to sleep with Wealhtheow,
his queen. It was said the mighty king
had appointed a hall-guard – a man who undertook
a dangerous duty for the Danish king,
elected to stand watch against the monster.
Truly, the leader of the Geats fervently trusted
in his own great strength and in God's grace.
Then he took off his helmet and his corslet
of iron, and gave them to his servant,
with his superb, adorned sword,
telling him to guard them carefully.
And then, before he went to his bed,
the brave Geat, Beowulf, made his boast:
'I count myself no less active in battle,
no less brave than Grendel himself:
thus, I will not send him to sleep with my sword,
so deprive him of life, though certainly I could.
Despite his fame for deadly deeds,
he is ignorant of these noble arts, that he might strike
at me, and hew my shield; but we, this night,

shall forego the use of weapons, if he dares fight
without them; and then may wise God,
the holy Lord, give glory in battle
to whichever of us He should think fitting.'
Then the brave prince leaned back, put his head
on the pillow while, around him,
many a proud seafarer lay back on his bed.
Not one of them believed he would see
day dawn, or ever return to his family
and friends, and the place where he was born;
they well knew that in recent days
far too many Danish men had come to bloody ends
in that hall. But the Lord wove the webs of destiny,
gave the Geats success in their struggle,
help and support, in such a way
that all were enabled to overcome their enemy
through the strength of one man. We cannot doubt
that mighty God has always ruled
over mankind.
                Then the night prowler
came shrithing through the shadows. All the Geats
guarding Heorot had fallen asleep –
all except one. Men well knew that the evil enemy
could not drag them down into the shadows
when it was against the Creator's wishes,
but Beowulf, watching grimly for his adversary Grendel,
awaited the ordeal with increasing anger.
Then, under night's shroud, Grendel walked down
from the moors; he shouldered God's anger.
The evil plunderer intended to ensnare
one of the race of men in the high hall.
He strode under the skies, until he stood
before the feasting-hall, in front of the gift-building
gleaming with gold. And this night was not the first
on which he had so honoured Hrothgar's home.
But never in his life did he find hall-wardens
more greatly to his detriment. Then the joyless warrior
journeyed to Heorot. The outer door, bolted
with iron bands, burst open at a touch from his hands:
with evil in his mind, and overriding anger,
Grendel swung open the hall's mouth itself. At once,
seething with fury, the fiend stepped onto
the tessellated floor; a horrible light,
like a lurid flame, flickered in his eyes.

He saw many men, a group of warriors,
a knot of kinsmen, sleeping in the hall.
His spirits leapt, his heart laughed;
the savage monster planned to sever,
before daybreak, the life of every warrior
from his body – he fully expected to eat
his fill at the feast. But after that night
fate decreed that he should no longer feed off
human flesh. Hygelac's kinsman,
the mighty man, watched the wicked ravager
to see how he would make his sudden attacks.
The monster was not disposed to delay;
but, for a start, he hungrily seized
a sleeping warrior, greedily wrenched him,
bit into his body, drank the blood
from his veins, devoured huge pieces;
until, in no time, he had swallowed the whole man,
even his feet and hands. Now Grendel stepped forward,
nearer and nearer, made to grasp the valiant Geat
stretched out on his bed – the fiend reached towards him
with his open hand; at once Beowulf perceived
his evil plan, sat up and stayed Grendel's outstretched arm.
Instantly that monster, hardened by crime,
realized that never had he met any man
in the regions of earth, in the whole world,
with so strong a grip. He was seized with terror.
But, for all that, he was unable to break away.
He was eager to escape to his lair, seek the company
of devils, but he was restrained as never before.
Then Hygelac's brave kinsman bore in mind
his boast: he rose from the bed and gripped
Grendel fiercely. The fiend tried to break free,
his fingers were bursting. Beowulf kept with him.
The evil giant was desperate to escape,
if indeed he could, and head for his lair
in the fens; he could feel his fingers cracking
in his adversary's grip; that was a bitter journey
that Grendel made to the ring-hall Heorot.
The great room boomed; all the proud warriors –
each and every Dane living in the stronghold –
were stricken with panic. The two hall-wardens
were enraged. The building rang with their blows.
It was a wonder the wine-hall withstood
two so fierce in battle, that the fair building

did not fall to earth; but it stood firm,
braced inside and out with hammered
iron bands. I have heard tell that there,
where they fought, many a mead-bench,
studded with gold, started from the floor.
Until that time, elders of the Scyldings
were of the opinion that no man could wreck
the great hall Heorot, adorned with horns,
nor by any means destroy it unless it were gutted
by greedy tongues of flame. Again and again
clang and clatter shattered the night's silence;
dread numbed the North-Danes, seized all
who heard the shrieking from the wall,
the enemy of God's grisly lay of terror,
his song of defeat, heard hell's captive
keening over his wound. Beowulf held him fast,
he who was the strongest of all men
ever to have seen the light of life on earth.
By no means did the defender of thanes
allow the murderous caller to escape with his life;
he reckoned that the rest of Grendel's days
were useless to anyone. Then, time and again,
Beowulf's band brandished their ancestral swords;
they longed to save the life, if they
so could, of their lord, the mighty leader.
When they did battle on Beowulf's behalf,
struck at the monster from every side,
eager for his end, those courageous warriors
were unaware that no war-sword,
not even the finest iron on earth,
could wound their evil enemy,
for he had woven a secret spell
against every kind of weapon, every battle blade.
Grendel's death, his departure from this world,
was destined to be wretched, his migrating spirit
was fated to travel far into the power of fiends.
Then he who for years had committed crimes
against mankind, murderous in mind,
and had wared with God, discovered
that the strength of his body could not save him,
that Hygelac's brave kinsman held his hand
in a vice-like grip; each was a mortal enemy
to the other. The horrible monster
suffered grievous pain; a gaping wound

opened on his shoulder; the sinews sprang apart,
the muscles were bursting. Glory in battle
was given to Beowulf; fatally wounded,
Grendel was obliged to make for the marshes,
head for his joyless lair. He was
well aware that his life's days were done,
come to an end. After that deadly encounter
the desire of every Dane was at last accomplished.

In this way did the wise and fearless man
who had travelled from far cleanse Hrothgar's hall,
release it from affliction. He rejoiced in his night's work,
his glorious achievement. The leader of the Geats
made good his boast to the East-Danes;
he had removed the cause of their distress,
put an end to the sorrow every Dane had shared,
the bitter grief that they had been constrained
to suffer. When Beowulf, brave in battle,
placed hand, arm and shoulder – Grendel's
entire grasp – under Heorot's spacious roof,
that was evidence enough of victory.

Then I have heard that next morning
many warriors gathered round the gift-hall;
leaders of men came from every region,
from remote parts, to look on the wonder,
the tracks of the monster. Grendel's death
seemed no grievous loss to any of the men
who set eyes on the spoor of the defeated one,
saw how he, weary in spirit, overcome in combat,
fated and put to flight, had made for the lake
of water-demons – leaving tracks of life-blood.

There the water boiled because of the blood;
the fearful swirling waves reared up,
mingled with hot blood, battle gore;
fated, he hid himself, then joyless
laid aside his life, his heathen spirit,
in the fen lair; hell received him there.

After this, the old retainers left the lake
and so did the company of young men too;
brave warriors rode back on their gleaming horses
from this joyful journey. Then Beowulf's exploit
was acclaimed; many a man asserted
time and again that there was no better
shield-bearer in the whole world, to north or south
between the two seas, under the sky's expanse,

no man more worthy of his own kingdom.
Yet they found no fault at all with their friendly lord,
gracious Hrothgar – he was a great king.
   At times the brave warriors spurred their bays,
horses renowned for their speed and stamina,
and raced each other where the track was suitable.
And now and then one of Hrothgar's thanes
who brimmed with poetry, and remembered lays,
a man acquainted with ancient traditions
of every kind, composed a new song
in correct metre. Most skilfully that man
began to sing of Beowulf's feat,
to weave words together, and fluently
to tell a fitting tale.
                    He recounted all he knew of
Sigemund, the son of Wæls; many a strange story
about his exploits, his endurance, and his journeys
to earth's ends; many an episode
unknown or half-known to the sons of men, songs
of feud and treachery. Only Fitela knew of these things,
had heard them from Sigemund who liked to talk
of this and that, for he and his nephew
had been companions in countless battles –
they slew many monsters with their swords.
After his death, no little fame attached to Sigemund's name,
when the courageous man had killed the dragon,
guardian of the hoard. Under the grey rock
the son of the prince braved that dangerous deed
alone; Fitela was not with him;
for all that, as fate had it, he impaled
the wondrous serpent, pinned it to the rock face
with his patterned sword; the dragon was slain.
Through his own bravery, that warrior ensured
that he could enjoy the treasure hoard
at will; the son of Wæls loaded it all
onto a boat, stowed the shining treasure
into the ship; the serpent burned in its own flames.
Because of all his exploits, Sigemund,
guardian of strong men, was the best known
warrior in the world – so greatly had he prospered –
after Heremod's prowess, strength and daring
had been brought to an end, when, battling with giants,
he fell into the power of fiends, and was at once
done to death. He had long endured

surging sorrows, had become a source
of grief to his people, and to all his retainers.
And indeed, in those times now almost forgotten,
many wise men often mourned that great warrior,
for they had looked to him to remedy their miseries;
they thought that the prince's son would prosper
and attain his father's rank, would protect his people,
their heirlooms and their citadel, the heroes' kingdom,
land of the Scyldings. Beowulf, Hygelac's kinsman,
was much loved by all who knew him, by his friends;
but Heremod was stained by sin.
   Now and then the brave men raced their horses,
ate up the sandy tracks – and they were so absorbed
that the hours passed easily. Stout-hearted warriors
without number travelled to the high hall
to inspect that wonder; the king himself, too,
glorious Hrothgar, guardian of ring-hoards,
came from his quarters with a great company, escorted
his queen and her retinue of maidens into the mead-hall.
Hrothgar spoke – he approached Heorot,
stood on the steps, stared at the high roof
adorned with gold, and at Grendel's hand:
'Let us give thanks at once to God Almighty
for this sight. I have undergone many afflictions,
grievous outrages at Grendel's hands; but God,
Guardian of heaven, can work wonder upon wonder.
Until now, I had been resigned,
had no longer believed that my afflictions
would ever end: this finest of buildings
stood stained with battle blood,
a source of sorrow to my counsellors;
they all despaired of regaining this hall
for many years to come, of guarding it from foes,
from devils and demons. Yet now one warrior
alone, through the Almighty's power, has succeeded
where we failed for all our fine plans.
Indeed, if she is still alive,
that woman (whoever she was) who gave birth
to such a son, to be one of humankind,
may claim that the Creator was gracious to her
in her child-bearing. Now, Beowulf,
best of men, I will love you in my heart
like a son; keep to our new kinship
from this day on. You shall lack

no earthly riches I can offer you.
Most often I have honoured a man for less,
given treasure to a poorer warrior,
more sluggish in the fight. Through your deeds
you have ensured that your glorious name
will endure for ever. May the Almighty grant you
good fortune, as He has always done before !'
   Beowulf, the son of Ecgtheow, answered:
'We performed that dangerous deed
with good will; at peril we pitted ourselves
against the unknown. I wish so much
that you could have seen him for yourself,
that fiend in his trappings, in the throes of death.
I meant to throttle him on that bed of slaughter
as swiftly as possible, with savage grips,
to hear death rattle in his throat
because of my grasp, unless he should escape me.
But I could not detain him, the Lord
did not ordain it – I did not hold my deadly enemy
firm enough for that; the fiend jerked free
with immense power. Yet, so as to save
his life, he left behind his hand,
his arm and shoulder; but the wretched monster
has bought himself scant respite;
the evil marauder, tortured by his sins,
will not live the longer, but agony
embraces him in its deadly bonds,
squeezes life out of his lungs; and now this creature,
stained with crime, must await the day of judgement
and his just deserts from the glorious Creator.'
   After this, the son of Ecglaf boasted less
about his prowess in battle – when all the warriors,
through Beowulf's might, had been enabled
to examine that hand, the fiend's fingers,
nailed up on the gables. Seen from in front,
each nail, each claw of that warlike,
heathen monster looked like steel –
a terrifying spike. Everyone said
that no weapon whatsoever, no proven sword
could possibly harm it, could damage
that battle-hardened, blood-stained hand.
   Then orders were quickly given for the inside of Heorot
to be decorated; many servants, both men and women,
bustled about that wine-hall, adorned that building

of retainers. Tapestries, worked in gold,
glittered on the walls, many a fine sight
for those who have eyes to see such things.
That beautiful building, braced within
by iron bands, was badly damaged;
the door's hinges were wrenched; when the monster,
damned by all his crimes, turned in flight,
despairing of his life, the hall roof only
remained untouched. Death is not easy
to escape, let him who will attempt it.
Man must go to the grave that awaits him –
fate has ordained this for all who have souls,
children of men, earth's inhabitants –
and his body, rigid on its clay bed,
will sleep there after the banquet.
                                    Then it was time
for Healfdene's son to proceed to the hall,
the king himself was eager to attend the feast.
I have never heard of a greater band of kinsmen
gathered with such dignity around their ring-giver.
Then the glorious warriors sat on the benches,
rejoicing in the feast. Courteously
their kinsmen, Hrothgar and Hrothulf,
quaffed many a mead-cup, confident warriors
in the high hall. Heorot was packed
with feasters who were friends; the time was not yet come
when the Scyldings practised wrongful deeds.
Then Hrothgar gave Beowulf Healfdene's sword,
and a battle banner, woven with gold,
and a helmet and a corslet, as rewards for victory;
many men watched while the priceless, renowned sword
was presented to the hero. Beowulf emptied
the ale-cup in the hall; he had no cause
to be ashamed at those precious gifts.
There are few men, as far as I have heard,
who have given four such treasures, gleaming with gold,
to another on the mead-bench with equal generosity.
A jutting ridge, wound about with metal wires,
ran over the helmet's crown, protecting the skull,
so that well-ground swords, proven in battle,
could not injure the well-shielded warrior
when he advanced against his foes.
Then the guardian of thanes ordered
that eight horses with gold-plated bridles

be led into the courtyard; onto one was strapped
a saddle, inlaid with jewels, skilfully made.
That was the war-seat of the great king,
Healfdene's son, whenever he wanted
to join in the sword-play. That famous man
never lacked bravery at the front in battle,
when men about him were cut down like corn.
Then the king of the Danes, Ing's descendants,
presented the horses and weapons to Beowulf,
bade him use them well and enjoy them.
Thus the renowned prince, the retainers' gold-warden,
rewarded those fierce sallies in full measure,
with horses and treasure, so that no man
would ever find reason to reproach him fairly.
Furthermore, the guardian of warriors gave
a treasure, an heirloom at the mead-bench,
to each of those men who had crossed the sea
with Beowulf; and he ordered that gold
be paid for that warrior Grendel slew
so wickedly – as he would have slain many another,
had not foreseeing God and the warrior's courage
together forestalled him. The Creator ruled over
all humankind, even as He does today.
Wherefore a wise man will value forethought
and understanding. Whoever lives long
on earth, endures the unrest of these times,
will be involved in much good and much evil.

    Then Hrothgar, leader in battle, was entertained
with music – harp and voice in harmony.
The strings were plucked, many a song rehearsed,
when it was the turn of Hrothgar's poet
to please men at the mead-bench, perform in the hall.
He sang of Finn's troop, victims of surprise attack,
and of how that Danish hero, Hnæf of the Scyldings,
was destined to die among the Frisian slain.

    Hildeburh, indeed, could hardly recommend
the honour of the Jutes; that innocent woman
lost her loved ones, son and brother,
in the shield-play; they fell, as fate ordained,
stricken by spears; and she was stricken with grief.
Not without cause did Hoc's daughter
mourn the shaft of fate, for in the light of morning
she saw that her kin lay slain under the sky,
the men who had been her endless pride

and joy. That encounter laid claim
to all but a few of Finn's thanes,
and he was unable to finish that fight
with Hnæf's retainer, with Hengest in the hall,
unable to dislodge the miserable survivors;
indeed, terms for a truce were agreed:
that Finn should give up to them another hall,
with its high seat, in its entirety,
which the Danes should own in common with the Jutes;
and that at the treasure-giving the son of Folcwalda
should honour the Danes day by day,
should distribute rings and gold-adorned gifts
to Hengest's band and his own people in equal measure.
Both sides pledged themselves to this peaceful
settlement. Finn swore Hengest solemn oaths
that he would respect the sad survivors
as his counsellors ordained, and that no man there
must violate the covenant with word or deed,
or complain about it, although they
would be serving the slayer of their lord
(as fate had forced those lordless men to do);
and he warned the Frisians that if, in provocation,
they should mention the murderous feud,
the sword's edge should settle things.
The funeral fire was prepared, glorious gold
was brought up from the hoard: the best of Scyldings,
that race of warriors, lay ready on the pyre.
Blood-stained corslets, and images of boars
(cast in iron and covered in gold)
were plentiful on that pyre, and likewise the bodies
of many retainers, ravaged by wounds;
renowned men fell in that slaughter.
Then Hildeburh asked that her own son
be committed to the flames at her brother's funeral,
that his body be consumed on Hnæf's pyre.
That grief-stricken woman keened over his corpse,
sang doleful dirges. The warriors' voices
soared towards heaven. And so did the smoke
from the great funeral fire that roared
before the barrow; heads sizzled,
wounds split open, blood burst out
from battle scars. The ravenous flames
swallowed those men whole, made no distinction
between Frisians and Danes; the finest men departed.

Then those warriors, their friends lost to them,
went to view their homes, revisit the stronghold
and survey the Frisian land. But Hengest stayed
with Finn, in utter dejection, all through
that blood-stained winter. And he dreamed
of his own country, but he was unable to steer
his ship homeward, for the storm-beaten sea
wrestled with the wind; winter sheathed the waves
in ice until once again spring made its sign
(as still it does) among the houses of men:
clear days, warm weather, in accordance as always
with the law of the seasons. Then winter was over,
the face of the earth was fair; the exile
was anxious to leave that foreign people
and the Frisian land. And yet he brooded
more about vengeance than about a voyage,
and wondered whether he could bring about a clash
so as to repay the sons of the Jutes.
Thus Hengest did not shrink from the duty of vengeance
after Hunlafing had placed the flashing sword,
finest of all weapons, on his lap;
this sword's edges had scarred many Jutes.
And so it was that cruel death by the sword later
cut down the brave warrior Finn in his own hall,
after Guthlaf and Oslaf, arrived from a sea-journey,
had fiercely complained of that first attack,
condemned the Frisians on many scores:
the Scyldings' restless spirits could no longer be restrained.
Then the hall ran red with the blood
of the enemy – Finn himself was slain,
the king with his troop, and Hildeburh was taken.
The Scylding warriors carried that king's
heirlooms down to their ship,
all the jewels and necklaces they discovered
at Finn's hall. They sailed over the sea-paths,
brought that noble lady back to Denmark
and her own people.
                              Thus was the lay sung,
the song of the poet. The hall echoed with joy,
waves of noise broke out along the benches;
cup-bearers carried wine in glorious vessels.
Then Wealhtheow, wearing her golden collar, walked
to where Hrothgar and Hrothulf were sitting side by side,
uncle and nephew, still friends together, true to one another.

And the spokesman Unferth sat at the feet
of the Danish lord; all men admired
his spirit and audacity, although he had deceived
his own kinsmen in a feud. Then the lady of the Scyldings
spoke these words: 'Accept this cup, my loved lord,
treasure-giver; O gold-friend of men,
learn the meaning of joy again, and speak words
of gratitude to the Geats, for so one ought to do.
And be generous to them too, mindful of gifts
which you have now amassed from far and wide.
I am told you intend to adopt this warrior,
take him for your son. This resplendent ring-hall,
Heorot, has been cleansed; give many rewards
while you may, but leave this land and the Danish people
to your own descendants when the day comes
for you to die. I am convinced
that gracious Hrothulf will guard our children
justly, should he outlive you, lord of the Scyldings,
in this world; I believe he will repay our sons
most generously if he remembers all we did
for his benefit and enjoyment when he was a boy.'
Then Wealhtheow walked to the bench where her sons,
Hrethric and Hrothmund, sat with the sons of thanes,
fledgling warriors; where also that brave man,
Beowulf of the Geats, sat beside the brothers.
To him she carried the cup, and asked in gracious words
if he would care to drink; and to him she presented
twisted gold with courtly ceremonial –
two armlets, a corslet and many rings,
and the most handsome collar in the world.
I have never heard that any hero had a jewel
to equal that, not since Hama made off
for his fortress with the Brosings' necklace; that pendant
in its precious setting; he fled from the enmity
of underhand Ermenaric, he chose long-lasting gain.
Hygelac the Geat, grandson of Swerting,
wore that necklace on his last raid
when he fought beneath his banner to defend his treasure,
his battle spoils; fate claimed him then,
when he, foolhardy, courted disaster,
a feud with the Frisians. On that occasion the famous prince
had carried the treasure, the priceless stones,
over the cup of the waves; he crumpled under his shield.
Then the king's body fell into the hands of Franks,

his coat of mail and the collar also;
after that battle, weaker warriors picked at
and plundered the slain; many a Geat lay dead, guarding
that place of corpses.
                            Applause echoed in the hall.
Wealhtheow spoke these words before the company:
'May you, Beowulf, beloved youth, enjoy
with all good fortune this necklace and corslet,
treasures of the people; may you always prosper;
win renown through courage, and be kind in your counsel
to these boys; for that, I will reward you further.
You have ensured that men will always sing
your praises, even to the ends of the world,
as far as oceans still surround cliffs,
home of the winds. May you thrive, O prince,
all your life. I hope you will amass
a shining hoard of treasure. O happy Beowulf,
be gracious in your dealing with my sons.
Here, each warrior is true to the others,
gentle of mind, loyal to his lord;
the thanes are as one, the people all alert,
the warriors have drunk well. They will do as I ask.'
    Then Wealhtheow retired to her seat
beside her lord. That was the best of banquets,
men drank their fill of wine; they had not tasted
bitter destiny, the fate that had come and claimed
many of the heroes at the end of dark evenings,
when Hrothgar the warrior had withdrawn
to take his rest. Countless retainers
defended Heorot as they had often done before;
benches were pushed back; the floor was padded
with beds and pillows. But one of the feasters
lying on his bed was doomed, and soon to die.
They set their bright battle-shields
at their heads. Placed on the bench
above each retainer, his crested helmet,
his linked corslet and sturdy spear-shaft,
were plainly to be seen. It was their habit,
both at home and in the field,
to be prepared for battle always,
for any occasion their lord might need
assistance; that was a loyal band of retainers.
    And so they slept. One man paid a heavy price
for his night's rest, as often happened

after Grendel first held the gold-hall
and worked his evil in it, until he met his doom,
death for his crimes. For afterwards it became clear,
and well known to the Scyldings, that some avenger
had survived the evil-doer, still lived after
that grievous, mortal combat.
                                 Grendel's mother
was a monster of a woman; she mourned her fate –
she who had to live in the terrible lake,
the cold water streams, after Cain slew
his own brother, his father's son,
with a sword; he was outlawed after that;
a branded man, he abandoned human joys,
wandered in the wilderness. Many spirits, sent
by fate, issued from his seed; one of them, Grendel,
that hateful outcast, was surprised in the hall
by a vigilant warrior spoiling for a fight.
Grendel gripped and grabbed him there,
but the Geat remembered his vast strength,
that glorious gift given him of God,
and put his trust for support and assistance
in the grace of the Lord; thus he overcame
the envoy of hell, humbled his evil adversary.
So the joyless enemy of mankind journeyed
to the house of the dead. And then Grendel's mother,
mournful and ravenous, resolved to go
on a grievous journey to avenge her son's death.

   Thus she reached Heorot; Ring-Danes, snoring,
were sprawled about the floor. The thanes suffered
a serious reverse as soon as Grendel's mother
entered the hall. The terror she caused,
compared to her son, equalled the terror
an Amazon inspires as opposed to a man,
when the ornamented sword, forged on the anvil,
the razor-sharp blade stained with blood,
shears through the boar-crested helmets of the enemy.
Then swords were snatched from benches, blades
drawn from scabbards, many a broad shield
was held firmly in the hall; none could don helmet
or spacious corslet – that horror caught them by surprise.
The monster wanted to make off for the moors,
fly for her life, as soon as she was found out.
Firmly she grasped one of the thanes
and made for the fens as fast as she could.

That man whom she murdered even as he slept
was a brave shield-warrior, a well-known thane,
most beloved by Hrothgar of all his hall retainers
between the two seas. Beowulf was not there;
the noble Geat had been allotted another lodging
after the giving of treasure earlier that evening.
Heorot was in uproar; she seized her son's
blood-crusted hand; anguish once again
had returned to the hall. What kind of bargain
was that, in which both sides forfeited the
lives of friends?
                            Then the old king,
the grizzled warrior, was convulsed with grief
when he heard of the death of his dearest retainer.
    Immediately Beowulf, that man blessed with victory,
was called to the chamber of the king. At dawn
the noble warrior and his friends, his followers,
hurried to the room where the wise man was waiting,
waiting and wondering whether the Almighty
would ever allow an end to their adversity.
Then Beowulf, brave in battle, crossed
the floor with his band – the timbers thundered –
and greeted the wise king, overlord of Ing's
descendants; he asked if the night had passed off
peacefully, since his summons was so urgent.
    Hrothgar, guardian of the Scyldings, said:
'Do not speak of peace; grief once again
afflicts the Danish people. Yrmenlaf's
elder brother, Æschere, is dead,
my closest counsellor and my comrade,
my shoulder-companion when we shielded
our heads in the fight, when soldiers clashed on foot,
slashed at boar-crests. Æschere was all
that a noble man, a warrior should be.
The wandering, murderous monster slew him
in Heorot; and I do not know where that ghoul,
drooling at her feast of flesh and blood,
made off afterwards. She has avenged her son
whom you savaged yesterday with vice-like holds
because he had impoverished and killed my people
for many long years. He fell in mortal combat,
forfeit of his life; and now another mighty
evil ravager has come to avenge her kinsman;
and many a thane, mournful in his mind

for his treasure-giver, may feel she has avenged
that feud already, indeed more than amply;
now that hand lies still which once sustained you.
   I have heard my people say,
men of this country, counsellors in the hall,
that they have seen *two* such beings,
equally monstrous, rangers of the fell-country,
rulers of the moors; and these men assert
that so far as they can see one bears
a likeness to a woman; grotesque though he was,
the other who trod the paths of exile looked like a man,
though greater in height and build than a Goliath;
he was christened *Grendel* by my people
many years ago; men do not know if he
had a father, a fiend once begotten
by mysterious spirits. These two live
in a little-known country, wolf-slopes, windswept headlands,
perilous paths across the boggy moors, where a mountain stream
plunges under the mist-covered cliffs,
rushes through a fissure. It is not far from here,
if measured in miles, that the lake stands
shadowed by trees stiff with hoar-frost.
A wood, firmly-rooted, frowns over the water.
There, night after night, a fearful wonder may be seen –
fire on the water; no man alive
is so wise as to know the nature of its depths.
Although the moor-stalker, the stag with strong horns,
when harried by hounds will make for the wood,
pursued from afar, he will succumb
to the hounds on the brink, rather than plunge in
and save his head. That is not a pleasant place.
When the wind arouses the wrath of the storm,
whipped waves rear up black from the lake,
reach for the skies, until the air becomes misty,
the heavens weep. Now, once again, help may be had
from you alone. As yet, you have not seen the haunt,
the perilous place where you may meet this most evil monster
face to face. Do you dare set eyes on it?
If you return unscathed, I will reward you
for your audacity, as I did before,
with ancient treasures and twisted gold.'
   Beowulf, the son of Ecgtheow answered:
'Do not grieve, wise Hrothgar! Better each man
should avenge his friend than deeply mourn.

The days on earth for every one of us are
numbered; he who may should win renown
before his death; that is a warrior's
best memorial when he has departed from this world.
Come, O guardian of the kingdom, let us lose
no time but track down Grendel's kinswoman.
I promise you that wherever she turns –
to honeycomb caves, to mountain woods,
to the bottom of the lake – she shall find no refuge.
Shoulder your sorrows with patience
this day; this is what I expect of you.'
    Then the old king leaped up, poured out his gratitude
to God Almighty for the Geat's words.
Hrothgar's horse, his stallion with plaited mane,
was saddled and bridled; the wise ruler
set out in full array; his troop of shield-bearers
fell into step. They followed the tracks
along forest paths and over open hill-country
for mile after mile; the monster had made
for the dark moors directly, carrying the corpse
of the foremost thane of all those
who, with Hrothgar, had guarded the hall.
Then the man of noble lineage left Heorot far behind,
followed narrow tracks, string-thin paths
over steep, rocky slopes – remote parts
with beetling crags and many lakes
where water-demons lived. He went ahead
with a handful of scouts to explore the place;
all at once he came upon a dismal wood,
mountain trees standing on the edge
of a grey precipice; the lake lay beneath,
blood-stained and turbulent. The Danish retainers
were utterly appalled when they came upon
the severed head of their comrade Æschere
on the steep slope leading down to the lake;
all the thanes were deeply distressed.
    The water boiled with blood, with hot gore;
the warriors gaped at it. At times the horn sang
an eager battle-song. The brave men all sat down;
then they saw many serpents in the water,
strange sea-dragons swimming in the lake,
and also water-demons, lying on cliff-ledges,
monsters and serpents of the same kind
as often, in the morning, molest ships

on the sail-road. They plunged to the lake bottom,
bitter and resentful, rather than listen
to the song of the horn. The leader of the Geats
picked off one with his bow and arrow,
ended its life; the metal tip
stuck in its vitals; it swam more sluggishly
after that, as the life-blood ebbed from its body;
in no time this strange sea-dragon
bristled with barbed boar-spears, was subdued
and drawn up onto the cliff; men examined
that disgusting enemy.
                                    Beowulf donned
his coat of mail, did not fear for his own life.
His massive corslet, linked by hand
and skilfully adorned, was to essay the lake –
it knew how to guard the body, the bone-chamber,
so that his foe's grasp, in its malicious fury,
could not crush his chest, squeeze out his life;
and his head was guarded by the gleaming helmet
which was to explore the churning waters,
stir their very depths; gold decorated it,
and it was hung with chain-mail as the weapon-smith
had wrought it long before, wondrously shaped it
and beset it with boar-images, so that
afterwards no battle-blade could do it damage.
Not least amongst his mighty aids was Hrunting,
the long-hilted sword Unferth lent him in his need;
it was one of the finest of heirlooms; the iron blade
was engraved with deadly, twig-like patterning,
tempered with battle blood. It had not failed
any of those men who had held it in their hands,
risked themselves on hazardous exploits,
pitted themselves against foes. That was not
the first time it had to do a hard day's work.
Truly, when Ecglaf's son, himself so strong,
lent that weapon to his better as a swordsman,
he had forgotten all those taunts he flung
when tipsy with wine; he dared not chance
his own arm under the breakers, dared not
risk his life; at the lake he lost
his renown for bravery. It was not so with Beowulf
once he had armed himself for battle.
    The Geat, son of Ecgtheow, spoke:
'Great son of Healfdene, gracious ruler,

gold-friend of men, remember now –
for I am now ready to go –
what we agreed if I, fighting on your behalf,
should fail to return: that you would always
be like a father to me after I had gone.
Guard my followers, my dear friends,
if I die in battle; and, beloved Hrothgar,
send to Hygelac the treasures you gave me.
When the lord of the Geats, Hrethel's son,
sees those gifts of gold, he will know
that I found a noble giver of rings
and enjoyed his favour for as long as I lived.
And, O Hrothgar, let renowned Unferth
have the ancient treasure, the razor sharp
ornamented sword; and I will make my name
with Hrunting, or death will destroy me.'
    After these words the leader of the Geats
dived bravely from the bank, did not even
wait for an answer; the seething water
received the warrior. A full day elapsed
before he could discern the bottom of the lake.
    She who had guarded its length and breadth
for fifty years, vindictive, fiercely ravenous for blood,
soon realized that one of the race of men
was looking down into the monsters' lair.
Then she grasped him, clutched the Geat
in her ghastly claws; and yet she did not
so much as scratch his skin; his coat of mail
protected him; she could not penetrate
the linked metal rings with her loathsome fingers.
Then the sea-wolf dived to the bottom-most depths,
swept the prince to the place where she lived,
so that he, for all his courage, could not
wield a weapon; too many wondrous creatures
harassed him as he swam; many sea-serpents
with savage tusks tried to bore through his corslet,
the monsters molested him. Then the hero saw
that he had entered some loathsome hall
in which there was no water to impede him,
a vaulted chamber where the floodrush
could not touch him. A light caught his eye,
a lurid flame flickering brightly.
    Then the brave man saw the sea-monster,
fearsome, infernal; he whirled his blade,

swung his arm with all his strength,
and the ring-hilted sword sang a greedy war-song
on the monster's head. Then that guest realized
that his gleaming blade could not bite into her flesh,
break open her bone-chamber; its edge failed Beowulf
when he needed it; yet it had endured
many a combat, sheared often through the helmet,
split the corslet of a fated man; for the first time
that precious sword failed to live up to its name.

 Then, resolute, Hygelac's kinsman took his courage
in both hands, trusted in his own strength.
Angrily the warrior hurled Hrunting away,
the damascened sword with serpent patterns on its hilt;
tempered and steel-edged, it lay useless on the earth.
Beowulf trusted in his own strength,
the might of his hand. So must any man
who hopes to gain long-lasting fame
in battle; he must risk his life, regardless.
Then the prince of the Geats seized the shoulder
of Grendel's mother – he did not mourn their feud;
when they grappled, that brave man in his fury
flung his mortal foe to the ground.
Quickly she came back at him, locked him
in clinches and clutched at him fearsomely.
Then the greatest of warriors stumbled and fell.
She dropped on her hall-guest, drew her dagger,
broad and gleaming; she wanted to avenge her son,
her only offspring. The woven corslet
that covered his shoulders saved Beowulf's life,
denied access to both point and edge.
Then the leader of the Geats, Ecgtheow's son,
would have died far under the wide earth
had not his corslet, his mighty chain-mail,
guarded him, and had not holy God
granted him victory; the wise Lord,
Ruler of the Heavens, settled the issue
easily after the hero had scrambled to his feet.

 Then Beowulf saw among weapons an invincible sword
wrought by the giants, massive and double-edged,
the joy of many warriors; that sword was matchless,
well-tempered and adorned, forged in a finer age,
only it was so huge that no man but Beowulf
could hope to handle it in the quick of combat.
Ferocious in battle, the defender of the Scyldings

grasped the ringed hilt, swung the ornamented sword
despairing of his life – he struck such a savage blow
that the sharp blade slashed through her neck,
smashed the vertebrae; it severed her head
from the fated body; she fell at his feet.
The sword was bloodstained; Beowulf rejoiced.

A light gleamed; the chamber was illumined
as if the sky's bright candle were shining
from heaven. Hygelac's thane inspected
the vaulted room, then walked round the walls,
fierce and resolute, holding the weapon firmly
by the hilt. The sword was not too large
for the hero's grasp, but he was eager to avenge
at once all Grendel's atrocities,
all the many visits the monster had inflicted
on the West-Danes – which began with the time
he slew Hrothgar's sleeping hearth-companions,
devoured fifteen of the Danish warriors
even as they slept, and carried off as many more,
a monstrous prize. But the resolute warrior
had already repaid him to such a degree
that he now saw Grendel lying on his death-bed,
his life's-blood drained because of the wound
he sustained in battle at Heorot. Then Grendel's corpse
received a savage blow at the hero's hands,
his body burst open: Beowulf lopped off his head.

At once the wise men, anxiously gazing at
the lake with Hrothgar, saw that the water
had begun to chop and churn, that the waves
were stained with blood. The grey-haired Scyldings
discussed that bold man's fate, agreed
there was no hope of seeing that brave thane again –
no chance that he would come, rejoicing in victory,
before their renowned king; it seemed certain
to all but a few that the sea-wolf had destroyed him.

Then the ninth hour came. The noble Scyldings
left the headland; the gold-friend of men
returned to Heorot; the Geats, sick at heart,
sat down and stared at the lake.
Hopeless, they yet hoped to set eyes
on their dear lord.
                    Then the battle-sword
began to melt like a gory icicle
because of the monster's blood. Indeed,

it was a miracle to see it thaw entirely,
as does ice when the Father (He who ordains
all times and seasons) breaks the bonds of frost,
unwinds the flood fetters; He is the true Lord.
The leader of the Geats took none of the treasures
away from the chamber – though he saw many there –
except the monster's head and the gold-adorned
sword-hilt; the blade itself had melted,
the patterned sword had burnt, so hot was that blood,
so poisonous the monster who had died in the cave.
He who had survived the onslaught of his enemies
was soon on his way, swimming up through the water;
when the evil monster ended his days on earth,
left this transitory life, the troubled water
and all the lake's expanse was purged of its impurity.

    Then the fearless leader of the seafarers
swam to the shore, exulting in his plunder,
the heavy burdens he had brought with him.
The intrepid band of thanes hurried towards him,
giving thanks to God, rejoicing
to see their lord safe and sound of limb.
The brave man was quickly relieved of his helmet
and corslet.
               The angry water under the clouds,
the lake stained with battle-blood, at last became calm.

    Then they left the lake with songs on their lips,
retraced their steps along the winding paths
and narrow tracks; it was no easy matter
for those courageous men, bold as kings,
to carry the head away from the cliff
overlooking the lake. With utmost difficulty
four of the thanes bore Grendel's head
to the gold-hall on a battle-pole;
thus the fourteen Geats, unbroken
in spirit and eager in battle, very soon
drew near to Heorot; with them, that bravest
of brave men crossed the plain towards the mead-hall.
Then the fearless leader of the thanes,
covered with glory, matchless in battle,
once more entered Heorot to greet Hrothgar.
Grendel's head was carried by the hair
onto the floor where the warriors were drinking,
a ghastly thing paraded before the heroes and the queen.
Men stared at that wondrous spectacle.

Beowulf, the son of Ecgtheow, said:
'So, son of Healfdene, lord of the Scyldings,
we proudly lay before you plunder from the lake;
this head you look at proves our success.
I barely escaped with my life from that combat
under the water, the risk was enormous;
our encounter would have ended at once if God
had not guarded me. Mighty though it is,
Hrunting was no use at all in the battle;
but the Ruler of men – how often He guides
the friendless one – granted that I
should see a huge ancestral sword hanging,
shining, on the wall; I unsheathed it.
Then, at the time destiny decreed, I slew
the warden of the hall. And when the blood,
the boiling battle-blood burst from her body,
that sword burnt, the damascened blade
was destroyed. I deprived my enemies
of that hilt; I repaid them as they deserved
for their outrages, murderous slaughter of the Danes.
I promise, then, O prince of the Scyldings,
that you can sleep in Heorot without anxiety,
rest with your retainers, with all the thanes
among your people – experienced warriors
and striplings together – without further fear
of death's shadow skulking near the hall.'
Then the golden hilt, age-old work of giants,
was given to Hrothgar, the grizzled warrior,
the warlike lord; wrought by master-smiths,
it passed into the hands of the Danish prince
once the demons died; for that embittered fiend,
enemy of God, guilty of murder
had abandoned this world – and so had his mother.
Thus the hilt was possessed by the best
of earthly kings between the two seas,
the best of those who bestowed gold on Norse men.
Hrothgar spoke, first examining the hilt,
the ancient heirloom. On it was engraved
the origins of strife in time immemorial,
when the tide of rising water drowned
the race of giants; their end was horrible;
they were opposed to the Eternal Lord,
and their reward was the downpour and the flood.
Also, on the sword-guards of pure gold,

it was recorded in runic letters, as is the custom,
for whom that sword, finest of blades,
with twisted hilt and serpentine patterning
had first been made.
                              Then Healfdene's wise son
lifted his voice – everyone listened:
'This land's grizzled guardian, who promotes truth
and justice amongst his people, and forgets nothing
though the years pass, can say for certain that this man
is much favoured by fate! Beowulf my friend,
your name is echoed in every country to earth's end.
You wear your enormous might
with wisdom and with dignity. I shall keep
my promise made when last we spoke. You will
beyond doubt be the shield of the Geats
for days without number, and a source
of strength to warriors.
                              Heremod was hardly that
to Ecgwala's sons, the glorious Scyldings;
he grew to spread slaughter and destruction
rather than happiness amongst the Danish people.
In mad rage he murdered his table-companions,
his most loyal followers; it came about
that the great prince cut himself off
from all earthly pleasures, though God had endowed him
with strength and power above all other men,
and had sustained him. For all that, his heart
was filled with savage blood-lust. He never gave
gifts to the Danes, to gain glory. He lived joyless,
agony racked him; he was long an affliction
to his people. Be warned, Beowulf,
learn the nature of nobility. I who tell you
this story am many winters old.
                              It is a miracle
how the mighty Lord in his generosity
gives wisdom and land and high estate
to people on earth; all things are in His power.
At times he allows a noble man's mind to experience
happiness, grants he should rule over a pleasant,
prosperous country, a stronghold of men,
makes subject to him regions of earth,
a wide kingdom, until in his stupidity
there is no end to his ambition.
His life is unruffled – neither old age

nor illness afflict him, no unhappiness
gnaws at his heart, in his land no hatred
flares up in mortal feuds, but all the world
bends to his will. He suffers no setbacks
until the seed of arrogance is sown and grows
within him, while still the watchman slumbers;
how deeply the soul's guardian sleeps
when a man is enmeshed in matters of this world;
the evil archer stands close with his drawn bow,
his bristling quiver. Then the poisoned shaft
pierces his mind under his helmet
and he does not know how to resist
the devil's insidious, secret temptations.
What had long contented him now seems insufficient;
he becomes embittered, begins to hoard
his treasures, never parts with gold rings
in ceremonial splendour; he soon forgets
his destiny and disregards the honours
given him of God, the Ruler of Glory.
In time his transient body wizens and withers,
and dies as fate decrees; then another man
succeeds to his throne who gives treasures and heirlooms
with great generosity; *he* is not obsessed with suspicions.
Arm yourself, dear Beowulf, best of men,
against such diseased thinking; always swallow pride;
remember, renowned warrior, what is more worthwhile –
gain everlasting. Today and tomorrow
you will be in your prime; but soon you will die,
in battle or in bed; either fire or water,
the fearsome elements, will embrace you,
or you will succumb to the sword's flashing edge,
or the arrow's flight, or terrible old age;
then your eyes, once bright, will be clouded over;
all too soon, O warrior, death will destroy you.
    I have ruled the Ring-Danes under the skies
for fifty years, shielded them in war
from many tribes of men in this world,
from swords and from ash-spears, and the time had come
when I thought I had no enemies left on earth.
All was changed utterly, gladness
became grief, after Grendel,
my deadly adversary, invaded Heorot.
His visitations caused me continual pain.
Thus I thank the Creator, the Eternal Lord,

that after our afflictions I have lived to see,
to see with my own eyes this blood-stained head.
Now, Beowulf, brave in battle,
go to your seat and enjoy the feast;
tomorrow we shall share many treasures.'
   The Geat, full of joy, straightway went
to find his seat as Hrothgar had suggested.
Then, once again, as so often before,
a great feast was prepared for the brave warriors
sitting in the hall.
                        The shadows of night
settled over the retainers. The company arose;
the grey-haired man, the old Scylding,
wanted to retire. And the Geat, the shield-warrior,
was utterly exhausted, his bones ached for sleep.
At once the chamberlain – he who courteously
saw to all such needs as a thane,
a travelling warrior, had in those days –
showed him, so limb-weary, to his lodging.
   Then Beowulf rested; the building soared,
spacious and adorned with gold; the guest
slept within until the black raven gaily
proclaimed sunrise. Bright light
chased away the shadows of night.
                          Then the warriors
hastened, the thanes were eager to return
to their own people; the brave seafarer
longed to see his ship, so far from that place.
Then the bold Geat ordered that Hrunting,
that sword beyond price, be brought before Unferth;
he begged him to take it back and thanked him
for the loan of it; he spoke of it as an ally
in battle, and assured Unferth he did not
underrate it: what a brave man he was!
After this the warriors, wearing their chain-mail,
were eager to be off; their leader,
so dear to the Danes, walked to the dais
where Hrothgar was sitting, and greeted him.
   Beowulf, the son of Ecgtheow, spoke:
'Now we seafarers, who have sailed here from far,
beg to tell you we are eager
to return to Hygelac. We have been happy here,
hospitably entertained; you have treated us kindly.
If I can in any way win more of your affection,

O ruler of men, than I have done already,
I will come at once, eager for combat.
If news reaches me over the seas
that you are threatened by those around you
(just as before enemies endangered you)
I will bring thousands of thanes,
all heroes, to help you. I know that Hygelac,
lord of the Geats, guardian of his people,
will advance me in word and deed
although he is young, so that I can back
these promises with spear-shafts, and serve you
with all my strength where you need men.
Should Hrethric, Hrothgar's son, wish
to visit the court of the Geatish king,
he will be warmly welcomed. Strong men
should seek fame in far-off lands.'

    Hrothgar replied: 'The wise Lord put these words
into your mind; I have never heard a warrior
speak more sagely while still so young.
You are very strong and very shrewd,
you speak with discerning. If your leader,
Hrethel's son, guardian of the people,
were to lose his life by illness or by iron,
by spear or grim swordplay, and if you survived him,
it seems to me that the Geats could not choose
a better man for king, should you wish to rule
the land of your kinsmen. Beloved Beowulf,
the longer I know you, the greater my regard for you.
Because of your exploit, your act of friendship,
there will be an end to the gross outrages,
the old enmity between Geats and Danes;
they will learn to live in peace.
For as long as I rule this spacious land,
heirlooms will be exchanged; many men
will greet their friends with gifts, send them
over the seas where gannets swoop and rise;
the ring-prowed ship will take tokens of esteem,
treasures across the waters. I know the Geats
are honourable to friend and foe alike,
always faithful to their ancient code.'

    Then Healfdene's son, guardian of thanes,
gave him twelve treasures in the hall,
told him to go safely with those gifts
to his own dear kinsmen, and to come back soon.

That king, descendant of kings,
leader of the Scyldings, kissed and embraced
the best of thanes; tears streamed down
the old man's face. The more that warrior thought,
wise and old, the more it seemed
improbable that they would meet again,
brave men in council. He so loved Beowulf
that he could not conceal his sense of loss;
but in his heart and in his head,
in his very blood, a deep love burned
for that dear man.
                      Then Beowulf the warrior,
proudly adorned with gold, crossed the plain,
exulting in his treasure. The ship
rode at anchor, waiting for its owner.
Then, as they walked, they often praised
Hrothgar's generosity. He was an altogether
faultless king, until old age deprived him
of his strength, as it does most men.
    Then that troop of brave young retainers
came to the water's edge; they wore ring-mail,
woven corslets. And the same watchman
who had seen them arrive saw them now returning.
He did not insult them, ask for explanations,
but galloped from the cliff-top to greet the guests;
he said that those warriors in gleaming armour,
so eager to embark, would be welcomed home.
Then the spacious ship, with its curved prow,
standing ready on the shore, was laden with armour,
with horses and treasure. The mast towered
over Hrothgar's precious heirlooms.
    Beowulf gave a sword bound round with gold
to the ship's watchman – a man who thereafter
was honoured on the mead-bench that much the more
on account of this heirloom.
                      The ship surged forward,
butted the waves in deep waters;
it drew away from the shores of the Scyldings.
Then a sail, a great sea-garment, was fastened
with guys to the mast; the timbers groaned;
the boat was not blown off its course
by the stiff sea-breezes. The ship swept
over the waves; foaming at the bows,
the boat with its well-wrought prow sped

over the waters, until at last the Geats
set eyes on the cliffs of their own country,
the familiar headlands; the vessel pressed forward,
pursued by the wind – it ran up onto dry land.

   The harbour guardian hurried down to the shore;
for many days he had scanned the horizon,
anxious to see those dear warriors once more.
He tethered the spacious sea-steed with ropes
(it rode on its painter restlessly)
so that the rolling waves could not wrench it away.
Then Beowulf commanded that the peerless treasures,
the jewels and plated gold, be carried up from the shore.
He had not to go far to find the treasure-giver,
Hygelac, son of Hrethel, for his house and the hall
for his companions stood quite close to the sea-wall.
That high hall was a handsome building;
it became the valiant king.

                    Hygd, his queen,
Hæreth's daughter, was very young; but she
was discerning, and versed in courtly customs,
though she had lived a short time only
in that citadel; and she was not too thrifty,
not ungenerous with gifts of precious treasures
to the Geatish thanes.

                  Queen Thryth was proud
and perverse, pernicious to her people.
No hero but her husband, however bold,
dared by day so much as turn his head
in her direction – that was far too dangerous;
but, if he did, he could bargain on being cruelly
bound with hand-plaited ropes; soon
after his seizure, the blade was brought into play,
the damascened sword to settle the issue,
to inflict death. It is not right for a queen,
compelling though her beauty, to behave like this,
for a peace-weaver to deprive a dear man of his life
because she fancies she has been insulted.
But Offa, Hemming's kinsman, put an end to that.
Ale-drinking men in the hall have said
that she was no longer perfidious to her people,
and committed no crimes, once she had been given,
adorned with gold, to that young warrior
of noble descent – once she had sailed,
at her father's command, to Offa's court

beyond the pale gold sea. After that,
reformed, she turned her life to good account;
renowned for virtue, she reigned with vision;
and she loved the lord of warriors in the high way
of love – he who was, as I have heard,
the best of all men, the mighty human race,
between the two seas. Offa the brave
was widely esteemed both for his gifts
and his skill in battle; he ruled his land
wisely. He fathered Eomer, guardian
of thanes, who was Hemming's kinsman,
grandson of Garmund, a Goliath in battle.

    Then Beowulf and his warrior band walked
across the sand, tramped over
the wide foreshore; the world's candle shone,
the sun hastening from the south. The men hurried too
when they were told that the guardian of thanes,
Ongentheow's slayer, the excellent young king,
held court in the hall, distributing rings.
Hygelac was informed at once of Beowulf's arrival –
had come back alive to the fortified enclosure,
was heading for the hall unscathed after combat.
Space on the benches for Beowulf and his band
was hastily arranged, as Hygelac ordered.

    The guardian of thanes formally greeted
that loyal man; then they sat down –
the unfated hero opposite the king,
kinsman facing kinsman. Hæreth's daughter
carried mead-cups round the hall,
spoke kindly to the warriors, handed the stoups
of wine to the thanes. Hygelac began
to ask his companion courteous questions
in the high hall; he was anxious to hear
all that had happened to the seafaring Geats:
'Beloved Beowulf, tell me what became of you
after the day you so hurriedly decided
to do battle far from here over the salt waters,
to fight at Heorot. And were you able
to assuage the grief, the well-known sorrow
of glorious Hrothgar? Your undertaking
deeply troubled me; I despaired, dear Beowulf,
of your return. I pleaded with you
not on any account to provoke that monster,
but to let the South-Danes settle their feud

with Grendel themselves. God be praised
that I am permitted to see you safe and home.'

Then Beowulf, the son of Ecgtheow, said:
'Half the world, lord Hygelac, has heard
of my encounter, my great combat
hand to hand with Grendel in that hall
where he had harrowed and long humiliated
the glorious Scyldings. I avenged it all;
none of Grendel's brood, however long
the last of that hateful race survives,
steeped in crime, has any cause to boast
about that dawn combat.
                                        First of all,
I went to the ring-hall to greet Hrothgar;
once Healfdene's great son knew of my intentions,
he assigned me a seat beside his own sons.
Then there was revelry; never in my life,
under heaven's vault, have I seen men
happier in the mead-hall. From time to time
the famous queen, the peace-weaver, walked across the floor,
exhorting the young warriors; often she gave
some man a twisted ring before returning to her seat.
At times Hrothgar's daughter, whom I heard
men call Freawaru, carried the ale-horn
right round the hall in front of that brave company,
offered that vessel adorned with precious metals
to the thirsty warriors.
                                        Young, and decorated
with gold ornaments, she is promised to Froda's noble son,
Ingeld of the Heathobards; that match was arranged
by the lord of the Scyldings, guardian of the kingdom;
he believes that it is an excellent plan
to use her as a peace-weaver to bury old antagonisms,
mortal feuds. But the deadly spear rarely sleeps
for long after a prince lies dead in the dust,
however exceptional the bride may be!

For Ingeld, leader of the Heathobards, and all
his retainers will later be displeased when he
and Freawaru walk on the floor – man and wife –
and when Danish warriors are being entertained.
For the guests will gleam with Heathobard heirlooms,
iron-hard, adorned with rings,
precious possessions that had belonged
to their hosts' fathers for as long as they

could wield their weapons, until in the shield-play
they and their dear friends forfeited their lives.
Then, while men are drinking, an old
warrior will speak; a sword he has seen,
marvellously adorned, stirs his memory
of how Heathobards were slain by spears;
he seethes with fury; sad in his heart,
he begins to taunt a young Heathobard,
incites him to action with these words:
    "Do you not recognize that sword, my friend,
the sword your father, fully armed, bore into battle
that last time, when he was slain by Danes,
killed by brave Scyldings who carried the field
when Withergyld fell and many warriors beside him?
See how the son of one of those
who slew him struts about the hall;
he sports the sword; he crows about that slaughter,
and carries that heirloom which is yours by right!'
In this way, with acid words, he will endlessly
provoke him and rake up the past,
until the time will come when a Danish warrior,
Freawaru's thane, sleeps blood-stained,
slashed by the sword, punished by death
for the deeds of his father; and the Heathobard
will escape, well-acquainted with the country.
Then both sides will break the solemn oath
sworn by their leaders; and Ingeld will come
to hate the Scyldings, and his love for his wife
will no longer be the same after such anguish and grief.
Thus I have little faith in friendship with Heathobards;
they will fail to keep their side of the promise,
friendship with the Danes.
                          I have digressed;
Grendel is my subject. Now you must hear,
O treasure-giver, what the outcome was
of that hand-to-hand encounter. When the jewel of heaven
had journeyed over the earth, the angry one,
the terrible night-prowler paid us a visit –
unscathed warriors watching over Heorot.
A fight awaited Hondscio, a horrible end
for that fated man; he was the first to fall;
Grendel tore that famous young retainer to bits
between his teeth, and swallowed the whole body
of that dear man, that girded warrior.

And even then that murderer, mindful of evil,
his mouth caked with blood, was not content
to leave the gold-hall empty-handed
but, famed for his strength, he tackled me,
gripped me with his outstretched hand.
A huge unearthly glove swung at his side,
firmly secured with subtle straps;
it had been made with great ingenuity,
with devils' craft and dragons' skins.
Innocent as I was, the demon monster
meant to shove me in it, and many another
innocent besides; that was beyond him
after I leapt up, filled with fury.
It would take too long to tell you how I repaid
that enemy of men for all his outrages;
but there, my prince, I ennobled your people
with my deeds. Grendel escaped,
and lived a little longer; but he left
behind at Heorot his right hand; and, in utter
wretchedness, sank to the bottom of the lake.

The sun rose; we sat down together to feast,
then the leader of the Scyldings
paid a good price for the bloody battle
gave me many a gold-plated treasure.
There was talk and song; the grey-haired Scylding
opened his immense hoard of memories;
now and then a happy warrior touched
the wooden harp, reciting some story,
mournful and true; at times the generous king
recalled in proper detail some strange incident;
and as the shadows lengthened, an aged thane,
cramped and rheumatic, raised his voice
time and again, lamenting his lost youth,
his prowess in battle; worn with winters,
his heart quickened to the call of the past.

In these ways we relaxed agreeably
throughout the long day until darkness closed in,
another night for men. Then, in her grief,
bent on vengeance, Grendel's mother
hastened to the hall where death had lain
in wait for her son – the battle-hatred
of the Geats. The horrible harridan avenged
her offspring, slew a warrior brazenly.
Æschere, the wise old counsellor, lost

his life. And when morning came,
the Danes were unable to cremate him,
to place the body of that dear man
on the funeral pyre; for Grendel's mother
had carried it off in her gruesome grasp,
taken it under the mountain lake.
Of all the grievous sorrows Hrothgar
long sustained, none was more terrible.
Then the king in his anger called upon your name
and entreated me to risk my life,
to accomplish deeds of utmost daring
in the tumult of waves; he promised me rewards.
And so, as men now know all over the earth,
I found the grim guardian of the lake-bottom.
For a while we grappled; the water boiled
with blood; then in that battle-hall,
I lopped off Grendel's mother's head
with the mighty sword. I barely escaped
with my life; but I was not fated.

And afterwards the guardian of thanes,
Healfdene's son, gave me many treasures.
Thus the king observed excellent tradition:
in no wise did I feel unrewarded
for all my efforts, but Healfdene's son
offered me gifts of my own choosing;
gifts, O noble king, I wish now
to give to you in friendship. I still depend
entirely on your favours; I have few
close kinsmen but you, O Hygelac!'

Then Beowulf caused to be brought in
a standard bearing the image of a boar,
together with a helmet towering in battle,
a grey corslet, and a noble sword; he said:
'Hrothgar, the wise king, gave me
these trappings and purposely asked me
to tell you their history: he said that Heorogar,
lord of the Scyldings, long owned them.
Yet he has not endowed his own brave son,
Heoroweard, with this armour, much as
he loves him. Make good use of everything!'

I heard that four bays, apple-brown,
were brought into the hall after the armour
– swift as the wind, identical. Beowulf gave them
as he gave the treasures. So should a kinsman do,

and never weave nets with underhand subtlety
to ensnare others, never have designs
on a close comrade's life. His nephew,
brave in battle, was loyal to Hygelac;
each man was mindful of the other's pleasure.

    I heard that he gave Hygd the collar,
the wondrous ornament with which Wealhtheow,
daughter of the prince, had presented him,
and gave her three horses also, graceful creatures
with brightly-coloured saddles; Hygd
wore that collar, her breast was adorned.

    Thus Ecgtheow's son, feared in combat,
confirmed his courage with noble deeds;
he lived a life of honour, he never slew
companions at the feast; savagery
was alien to him, but he, so brave in battle,
made the best use of those ample talents
with which God endowed him.

                     He had been despised
for a long while, for the Geats saw no spark
of bravery in him, nor did their king deem him
worthy of much attention on the mead-bench;
people thought that he was a sluggard,
a feeble princeling. How fate changed,
changed completely for that glorious man!

    Then the guardian of thanes, the famous king,
ordered that Hrethel's gold-adorned heirloom
be brought in; no sword was so treasured
in all Geatland; he laid it in Beowulf's lap,
and gave him seven thousand hides of land,
a hall and princely throne. Both men
had inherited land and possessions
in that country; but the more spacious kingdom
had fallen to Hygelac, who was of higher rank.

    In later days, after much turmoil,
things happened in this way when Hygelac lay dead
and murderous battle-blades had beaten down
the shield of his son Heardred,
and when the warlike Swedes, savage warriors,
had hunted him down amongst his glorious people,
attacked Hereric's nephew with hatred,
the great kingdom of the Geats passed
into Beowulf's hands. He had ruled it well

for fifty winters – he was a wise king,
a grizzled guardian of the land – when, on dark nights,
a dragon began to terrify the Geats:
he lived on a cliff, kept watch over a hoard
in a high stone barrow; below, there was
a secret path; a man strayed
into this barrow by chance, seized
some of the pagan treasures, stole drinking vessels.
At first the sleeping dragon was deceived
by the thief's skill, but afterwards he avenged
this theft of gleaming gold; people far and wide,
bands of retainers, became aware of his wrath.
    That man did not intrude upon the hoard
deliberately, he who robbed the dragon;
but it was some slave, a wanderer in distress
escaping from men's anger who entered there,
seeking refuge. He stood guilty of some sin.
As soon as he peered in, the outsider
stiffened with horror. Unhappy as he was,
he stole the vessel, the precious cup.
There were countless heirlooms in that earth-cave,
the enormous legacy of a noble people,
ancient treasures which some man or other
had cautiously concealed there many years
before. Death laid claim to all that people
in days long past, and then that retainer
who outlived the rest, a gold-guardian
mourning his friends, expected the same fate –
thought he would enjoy those assembled heirlooms
a little while only. A newly-built barrow
stood ready on a headland which overlooked
the sea, protected by the hazards of access.
To this barrow the protector of rings brought the heirlooms,
the plated gold, all that part of the precious treasure
worthy of hoarding; then he spoke a few words:
'Hold now, O earth, since heroes could not,
these treasures owned by nobles! Indeed, strong men
first quarried them from you. Death in battle,
ghastly carnage, has claimed all my people –
men who once made merry in the hall
have laid down their lives; I have no one
to carry the sword, to polish the plated vessel,
this precious drinking-cup; all the retainers
have hurried elsewhere. The iron helmet

adorned with gold shall lose its ornaments;
men who should polish battle-masks are sleeping;
the coat of mail, too, that once withstood
the bite of swords in battle, after shields were shattered,
decays like the warriors; the linked mail may no longer
range far and wide with the warrior,
stand side by side with heroes. Gone is the pleasure
of plucking the harp, no fierce hawk
swoops about the hall, nor does the swift stallion
strike sparks in the courtyard. Cruel death
has claimed hundreds of this human race.'
    Thus the last survivor mourned time passing,
and roamed about by day and night,
sad and aimless, until death's lightning struck
at his heart.
                The aged dragon of darkness
discovered that glorious hoard unguarded,
he who sought out barrows, smooth-scaled
and evil, and flew by night, breathing
fire; the Geats feared him greatly.
He was destined to find the hoard
in that cave and, old in winters, guard
the heathen gold; much good it did him!
    Thus the huge serpent who harassed men
guarded that great stronghold under the earth
for three hundred winters, until
a man enraged him; the wanderer carried
the inlaid vessel to his lord, and begged him
for a bond of peace. Then the hoard was raided
and plundered, and that unhappy man
was granted his prayer. His lord examined
the ancient work of smiths for the first time.
    There was conflict once more after the dragon
awoke; intrepid, he slid swiftly
along by the rock, and found the footprints
of the intruder; that man had skilfully
picked his way right past the dragon's head.
Thus he who is undoomed will easily survive
anguish and exile provided he enjoys
the grace of God. The warden of the hoard
prowled up and down, anxious to find
the man who had pillaged it while he slept.
Breathing fire and filled with fury,
he circled the outside of the earth mound

again and again; but there was no one
in that barren place; yet he exulted at the thought
of battle, bloody conflict; at times he wheeled back
into the barrow, hunting for the priceless heirloom.
He realized at once that one of the race of men
had discovered the gold, the glorious treasure.
Restlessly the dragon waited for darkness;
the guardian of the hoard was bursting with rage,
he meant to avenge the vessel's theft
with fire.
           Then daylight failed
as the dragon desired; he could no longer
confine himself to the cave but flew in a ball
of flame, burning for vengeance. The Geats
were filled with dread as he began his flight;
it swiftly ended in disaster for their lord.
   Then the dragon began to breathe forth fire,
to burn fine buildings; flame tongues flickered,
terrifying men; the loathsome winged creature
meant to leave the whole place lifeless.
Everywhere the violence of the dragon, the venom
of that hostile one, was clearly to be seen –
how he had wrought havoc, hated and humiliated
the Geatish people. Then, before dawn, he rushed back
to his hidden lair and the treasure hoard.
He had girdled the Geats with fire, with ravening flames;
he relied on his own strength,
and on the barrow and the cliff; his trust played him false.
Then news of that terror was quickly brought
to Beowulf, that flames enveloped
his own hall, best of buildings,
and the gift-throne of the Geats. That good man
was choked with intolerable grief.
Wise that he was, he imagined
he must have angered God, the Lord Eternal,
by ignoring some ancient law; he was seldom
dispirited, but now his heart surged with dark fears.
   The fire dragon had destroyed the fortified hall,
the people's stronghold, and laid waste with flames
the land by the sea. The warlike king,
prince of the Geats, planned to avenge this.
The protector of warriors, leader of men,
instructed the smith to forge a curious shield
made entirely of iron; he well knew

that a linden shield would not last long
against the flames. The eminent prince
was doomed to reach the end of his days on earth,
his life in this world. So too was the dragon,
though he had guarded the hoard for generations.
    Then the giver of gold disdained
to track the dragon with a troop
of warlike men; he did not shrink
from single combat, nor did he set much store
by the fearless dragon's power, for had he not before
experienced danger, again and again
survived the storm of battle, beginning with that time
when, blessed with success, he cleansed
Hrothgar's hall, and crushed in battle
the monster and his vile mother?
                          That grim combat
in which Hygelac was slain – Hrethel's son,
leader of the Geats, dear lord of his people,
struck down by swords in the bloodbath
in Frisia – was far from the least
of his encounters. Beowulf escaped
because of his skill and stamina at swimming;
he waded into the water, bearing no fewer
than thirty corslets, a deadweight on his arms.
But the Frankish warriors who shouldered
their shields against him had no cause to boast
about that combat; a handful only
eluded that hero and returned home
Then the son of Ecgtheow, saddened and alone,
rode with the white horses to his own people.
Hygd offered him heirlooms there, and even
the kingdom, the ancestral throne itself; for she feared
that her son would be unable to defend it
from foreign invaders now that Hygelac was gone.
But the Geats, for all their anguish, failed
to prevail upon the prince – he declined
absolutely to become Heardred's lord,
or to taste the pleasures of royal power.
But he stood at his right hand,
ready with advice, always friendly,
and respectful, until the boy came of age
and could rule the Geats himself.
                            Two exiles,
Ohthere's sons, sailed to Heardred's court;

they had rebelled against the ruler of the Swedes,
a renowned man, the best of sea-kings,
gold-givers in Sweden. By receiving them,
Heardred rationed the days of his life;
in return for his hospitality, Hygelac's son
was mortally wounded, slashed by swords.
Once Heardred lay lifeless in the dust,
Onela, son of Ongentheow, sailed home again;
he allowed Beowulf to inherit the throne
and rule the Geats; he was a noble king!
But Beowulf did not fail with help
after the death of the prince, although years passed;
he befriended unhappy Eadgils, Ohthere's son,
and supplied him with weapons and warriors
beyond the wide seas. Eadgils afterwards
avenged Eanmund, he ravaged and savaged
the Swedes, and killed the king, Onela himself.

    Thus the son of Ecgtheow had survived
these feuds, these fearful battles, these acts
of single combat, up to that day
when he was destined to fight against the dragon.
Then in fury the leader of the Geats set out
with eleven to search for the winged serpent.
By then Beowulf knew the cause of the feud,
bane of men; the famous cup
had come to him through the hands of its finder.
The unfortunate slave who first brought about
such strife made the thirteenth man
in that company – cowed and disconsolate,
he had to be their guide. Much against his will,
he conducted them to the entrance of the cave,
an earth-hall full of filigree work
and fine adornments close by the sea,
the fretting waters. The vile guardian,
the serpent who had long lived under the earth,
watched over the gold, alert; he who hoped
to gain it bargained with his own life.

    Then the brave king sat on the headland,
the gold-friend of the Geats wished success
to his retainers. His mind was most mournful,
angry, eager for slaughter; fate hovered
over him, so soon to fall on that old man,
to seek out his hidden spirit, to split
life and body; flesh was to confine

the soul of the king only a little longer.
Beowulf, the son of Ecgtheow, spoke:
'Often and often in my youth I plunged
into the battle maelstrom; how well I remember it.
I was seven winters old when the treasure guardian,
ruler of men, received me from my father.
King Hrethel took me into his ward, reared me,
fed me, gave me gold, mindful of our kinship;
for as long as he lived, he loved me no less
than his own three sons, warriors with me
in the citadel, Herebeald, Hæthcyn, and my dear Hygelac.
A death-bed for the firstborn was unrolled
most undeservedly by the action of his kinsman –
Hæthcyn drew his horn-tipped bow
and killed his lord-to-be; he missed his mark,
his arrow was stained with his brother's blood.
That deed was a dark sin, sickening
to think of, not to be settled by payment of *wergild;*
yet Herebeald's death could not be requited.

   Thus the old king, Hrethel, is agonized
to see his son, so young, swing
from the gallows. He sings a dirge, a song
dark with sorrow, while his son hangs,
raven's carrion, and he cannot help him
in any way, wise and old as he is.
He wakes each dawn to the ache
of his son's death; he has no desire
for a second son, to be his heir
in the stronghold, now that his firstborn
has finished his days and deeds on earth.
Grieving, he wanders through his son's dwelling,
sees the wine-hall now deserted, joyless,
home of the winds; the riders, the warriors,
sleep in their graves. No longer is the harp
plucked, no longer is there happiness in that place.
Then Hrethel takes to his bed, and intones
dirges for his dead son, Herebeald;
his house and his lands seem empty now,
and far too large. Thus the lord of the Geats
endured in his heart the ebb and flow
of sorrow for his firstborn; but he could not
avenge that feud on the slayer – his own son;
although Hrethel had no love for Hæthcyn,
he could no more readily requite death

with death. Such was his sorrow that he lost
all joy in life, chose the light of God;
he bequeathed to his sons, as a wealthy man does,
his citadel and land, when he left this life.
      Then there was strife, savage conflict
between Swedes and Geats; after Hrethel's death
the feud we shared, the fierce hatred
flared up across the wide water.
The sons of Ongentheow, Onela and Ohthere,
were brave and battle-hungry; they had no wish
for peace over the sea but several times,
and wantonly, butchered the people of the Geats
on the slopes of Slaughter Hill. As is well known,
my kinsmen requited that hatred, those crimes;
but one of them paid with his own life –
a bitter bargain; that fight was fatal
to Hæthcyn, ruler of the Geats.
Then I heard that in the morning
one kinsman avenged another, repaid
Hæthcyn's slayer with the battle-blade,
when Ongentheow attacked the Geat Eofor;
the helmet split, the old Swede fell,
pale in death; Eofor remembered
that feud well enough, his hand and sword
spared nothing in their death-swing.
      I repaid Hygelac for his gifts of heirlooms
with my gleaming blade, repaid him in battle,
as was granted to me; he gave me land
and property, a happy home. He had
no need to hunt out and hire mercenaries –
inferior warriors from the Gepidae,
from the Spear-Danes or from tribes in Sweden:
but I was always at the head of his host,
alone in the van; and I shall still fight
for as long as I live and this sword lasts,
that has often served me early and late
since I became the daring slayer
of Daeghrefn, champion of the Franks.
He was unable to bring adornments,
breast-decorations to the Frisian king,
but fell in the fight bearing the standard,
a brave warrior; it was my battle-grip,
not the sharp blade, that shattered his bones,
silenced his heartbeat. Now the shining edge,

hand and tempered sword, shall engage in battle
for the treasure hoard. I fought many battles
when I was young; yet I will fight again,
the old guardian of my people, and achieve
a mighty exploit if the evil dragon dares
confront me, dares come out of the earth-cave!'
   Then he addressed each of the warriors,
the brave heroes, his dear companions,
a last time: 'I would not wield a sword
against the dragon if I could grasp this hideous being
with my hands (and thus make good my boast),
as once I grasped the monster Grendel;
but I anticipate blistering battle-fire,
venomous breath; therefore I have with me
my shield and corslet. I will not give an inch
to the guardian of the mound, but at that barrow
it will befall us both as fate ordains,
every man's master. My spirit is bold,
I will not boast further against the fierce flier.
Watch from the barrow, warriors in armour,
guarded by corslets, which of us will better
weather his wounds after the combat.
This is not your undertaking, nor is it
possible for any man but me alone
to pit his strength against the gruesome one,
and perform great deeds. I will gain the gold
by daring, or else battle, dread destroyer
of life, will lay claim to your lord.'
   Then the bold warrior, stern-faced beneath his helmet,
stood up with his shield; sure of his own strength,
he walked in his corslet towards the cliff;
the way of the coward is not thus!
Then that man endowed with noble qualities,
he who had braved countless battles, weathered
the thunder when warrior troops clashed together,
saw a stone arch set in the cliff
through which a stream spurted; steam rose
from the boiling water; he could not stay long
in the hollow near the hoard for fear
of being scorched by the dragon's flames.
Then, such was his fury, the leader of the Geats
threw out his chest and gave a great roar,
the brave man bellowed; his voice, renowned
in battle, hammered the grey rock's anvil.

The guardian of the hoard knew the voice for human,
violent hatred stirred within him. Now no time
remained to entreat for peace. At once
the monster's breath, burning battle-vapour,
issued from the barrow; the earth itself snarled.
The lord of the Geats, standing under the cliff,
raised his shield against the fearsome stranger;
then that sinuous creature spoiled
for the fight. The brave and warlike king
had already drawn his keen-edged sword,
(it was an ancient heirloom); a terror of each other
lurked in the hearts of the two antagonists.
While the winged creature coiled himself up,
the friend and lord of men stood unflinching
by his shield; Beowulf waited ready armed.
   Then, fiery and twisted, the dragon swiftly
shrithed towards its fate. The shield protected
the life and body of the famous prince
for far less time than he had looked for.
It was the first occasion in all his life
that fate did not decree triumph for him
in battle. The lord of the Geats raised
his arm, and struck the mottled monster
with his vast ancestral sword; but the bright blade's
edge was blunted by the bone, bit
less keenly than the desperate king required.
The defender of the barrow bristled with anger
at the blow, spouted murderous fire, so that flames
leaped through the air. The gold-friend of the Geats
did not boast of famous victories; his proven sword,
the blade bared in battle, had failed him
as it ought not to have done. That great Ecgtheow's
greater son had to journey on from this world
was no pleasant matter; much against his will,
he was obliged to make his dwelling
elsewhere – sooner or later every man must leave
this transitory life. It was not long
before the fearsome ones closed again.
The guardian of the hoard was filled with fresh hope,
his breast was heaving; he who had ruled a nation
suffered agony, surrounded by flame.
And Beowulf's companions, sons of nobles –
so far from protecting him in a troop together,
unflinching in the fight – shrank back into the forest

scared for their own lives. One man alone
obeyed his conscience. The claims of kinship
can never be ignored by a right-minded man.
    His name was Wiglaf, a noble warrior,
Weohstan's son, kinsman of Ælfhere,
a leader of the Swedes; he saw that his lord,
helmeted, was tormented by the intense heat.
Then he recalled the honours Beowulf had bestowed
on him – the wealthy citadel of the Wægmundings,
the rights to land his father owned before him.
He could not hold back then; he grasped the round,
yellow shield; he drew his ancient sword,
reputed to be the legacy of Eanmund,
Ohthere's son.
               Weohstan had slain him
in a skirmish while Eanmund was a wanderer,
a friendless man, and then had carried off
to his own kinsmen the gleaming helmet,
the linked corslet, the ancient sword
forged by giants. It was Onela,
Eanmund's uncle, who gave him that armour,
ready for use; but Onela did not refer to the feud,
though Weohstan had slain his brother's son.
For many years Weohstan owned that war-gear,
sword and corslet, until his son was old enough
to achieve great feats as he himself had done.
Then, when Weohstan journeyed on from the earth,
an old man, he left Wiglaf – who was
with the Geats – a great legacy of armour
of every kind.
              This was the first time
the young warrior had weathered the battle-storm,
standing at the shoulder of his lord.
His courage did not melt, nor did his kinsman's sword
fail him in the fight. The dragon found that out
when they met in mortal combat.
    Wiglaf spoke, constantly reminding
his companions of their duty – he was mournful.
'I think of that evening we emptied the mead-cup
in the feasting-hall, partook and pledged our lord,
who presented us with rings, that we would repay him
for his gifts of armour, helmets and hard swords,
if ever the need, need such as this, arose.
For this very reason he asked us

to join with him in this journey, deemed us
worthy of renown, and gave me these treasures;
he looked on us as loyal warriors,
brave in battle; even so, our lord,
guardian of the Geats, intended to perform
this feat alone, because of all men
he had achieved the greatest exploits,
daring deeds. Now the day has come
when our lord needs support, the might
of strong men; let us hurry forward
and help our leader as long as fire remains,
fearsome, searing flames. God knows
I would rather that fire embraced my body
beside the charred body of my gold-giver;
it seems wrong to me that we should shoulder
our shields, carry them home afterwards,
unless we can first kill the venomous foe,
guard the prince of the Geats. I know
in my heart his feats of old were such
that he should not now be the only Geat to suffer
and fall in combat; in common we shall share
sword, helmet, corslet, the trappings of war.'
    Then that man fought his way through the fumes,
went helmeted to help his lord. He shouted out:
'Brave Beowulf, may success attend you –
for in the days when you were young, you swore
that so long as you lived you would never allow
your fame to decay; now, O resolute king,
renowned for your exploits, you must guard your life
with all your skill. I shall assist you.'
    At this the seething dragon attacked a second time;
shimmering with fire the venomous visitor fell on his foes,
the men he loathed. With waves of flame, he burnt
the shield right up to its boss; Wiglaf's
corslet afforded him no protection whatsoever.
But the young warrior still fought bravely, sheltered
behind his kinsman's shield after his own
was consumed by flames. Still the battle-king
set his mind on deeds of glory; with prodigious strength
he struck a blow so violent that his sword stuck
in the dragon's skull. But Nægling snapped!
Beowulf's old grey-hued sword
failed him in the fight. Fate did not ordain
that the iron edge should assist him

in that struggle; Beowulf's hand was too strong.
Indeed I have been told that he overtaxed
each and every weapon, hardened by blood, that he bore
into battle; his own great strength betrayed him.

    Then the dangerous dragon, scourge of the Geats,
was intent a third time upon attack; he rushed
at the renowned man when he saw an opening:
fiery, battle-grim, he gripped the hero's neck
between his sharp teeth; Beowulf was bathed
in blood; it spurted out in streams.
Then, I have heard, the loyal thane
alongside the Geatish king displayed great courage,
strength and daring, as was his nature.
To assist his kinsman, that man in mail
aimed not for the head but lunged at the belly
of their vile enemy (in so doing his hand
was badly burnt); his sword, gleaming and adorned,
sank in up to the hilt and at once the flames
began to abate. The king still had control then
over his senses; he drew the deadly knife,
keen-edged in battle, that he wore on his corslet;
then the lord of the Geats dispatched the dragon.
Thus they had killed their enemy – their courage
enabled them – the brave kinsmen together
had destroyed him. Such should a man,
a thane, be in time of necessity!

                                That was the last
of all the king's achievements, his last
exploit in the world. Then the wound
the earth-dragon had inflicted with his teeth
began to burn and swell; very soon he
was suffering intolerable pain as the poison
boiled within him. Then the wise leader
tottered forward and slumped on a seat
by the barrow; he gazed at the work of giants,
saw how the ancient earthwork contained
stone arches supported by columns.
Then, with his own hands, the best of thanes
refreshed the renowned prince with water,
washed his friend and lord, blood-stained
and battle-weary, and unfastened his helmet.

    Beowulf began to speak, he defied
his mortal injury; he was well aware
that his life's course, with all its delights,

had come to an end; his days on earth
were exhausted, death drew very close:
'It would have made me happy, at this time,
to pass on war-gear to my son, had I
been granted an heir to succeed me,
sprung of my seed. I have ruled the Geats
for fifty winters; no king of any
neighbouring tribe has dared to attack me
with swords, or sought to cow and subdue me.
But in my own home I have awaited
my destiny, cared well for my dependents,
and I have not sought trouble, or sworn
any oaths unjustly. Because of all these things
I can rejoice, drained now by death-wounds;
for the Ruler of Men will have no cause to blame me
after I have died on the count that I deprived
other kinsmen of their lives. Now hurry,
dear Wiglaf; rummage the hoard
under the grey rock, for the dragon sleeps,
riddled with wounds, robbed of his treasure.
Be as quick as you can so that I may see
the age-old store of gold, and examine
all the priceless, shimmering stones; once I
have set eyes on such a store, it will be
more easy for me to die, to abandon
the life and land that have so long been mine.'
    Then, I have been told, as soon as he heard
the words of his lord, wounded in battle,
Wiglaf hastened into the earth-cavern,
still wearing his corslet, his woven coat of mail.
After the fierce warrior, flushed with victory,
had walked past a daïs, he came upon
the hoard – a hillock of precious stones,
and gold treasure glowing on the ground;
he saw wondrous wall-hangings; the lair
of the serpent, the aged twilight-flier;
and the stoups and vessels of a people
long dead, now lacking a polisher,
deprived of adornments. There were many old,
rusty helmets, and many an armlet
cunningly wrought. A treasure hoard,
gold in the ground, will survive its owner
easily, whosoever hides it!
And he saw also hanging high over

the hoard a standard fashioned with gold strands,
a miracle of handiwork; a light shone from it,
by which he was able to distinguish the earth
and look at the adornments. There was no sign
of the serpent, the sword had savaged and slain him.
Then I heard that Wiglaf rifled the hoard
in the barrow, the antique work of giants –
he chose and carried off as many cups and salvers
as he could; and he also took the standard,
the incomparable banner; Beowulf's sword,
iron-edged, had injured
the guardian of the hoard, he who had held it
through the ages and fought to defend it
with flames – terrifying, blistering,
ravening at midnight – until he was slain.
Wiglaf hurried on his errand, eager to return,
spurred on by the treasures; in his heart he was troubled
whether he would find the prince of the Geats,
so grievously wounded, still alive
in the place where he had left him.
Then at last he came, carrying the treasures,
to the renowned king; his lord's life-blood
was ebbing; once more he splashed him
with water, until Beowulf revived a little,
began to frame his thoughts.
       Gazing at the gold,
the warrior, the sorrowing king, said:
'With these words I thank
the King of Glory, the Eternal Lord,
the Ruler, for all the treasures here before me,
that in my lifetime I have been able
to gain them for the Geats.
And now that I have bartered my old life
for this treasure hoard, you must serve
and inspire our people. I will not long be with you.
Command the battle-warriors, after the funeral fire,
to build a fine barrow overlooking the sea;
let it tower high on Whaleness
as a reminder to my people.
And let it be known as *Beowulf's barrow*
to all seafarers, to men who steer their ships
from far over the swell and the saltspray.'
 Then the prince, bold of mind, detached
his golden collar and gave it to Wiglaf,

the young spear-warrior, and also his helmet
adorned with gold, his ring and his corslet,
and enjoined him to use them well;
'You are the last survivor of our family,
the Wægmundings; fate has swept
all my kinsmen, those courageous warriors,
to their doom. I must follow them.'
   Those were the warrior's last words
before he succumbed to the raging flames
on the pyre; his soul migrated from his breast
to meet the judgement of righteous men.
   Then it was harrowing for the young hero
that he should have to see that beloved man
lying on the earth at his life's end,
wracked by pain. His slayer lay
there too, himself slain, the terrible
cave-dragon. That serpent, coiled evilly,
could no longer guard the gold-hoard,
but blades of iron, beaten and tempered
by smiths, notched in battle, had taken him off;
his wings were clipped now, he lay
mortally wounded, motionless on the earth
at the mound's entrance. No more did he fly
through the night sky, or spread his wings,
proud of his possessions; but he lay prostrate
because of the power of Beowulf, their leader.
Truly, I have heard that no hero of the Geats,
no fire-eater, however daring, could quell
the scorching blast of that venomous one
and lay his hands on the hoard in the lair,
should he find its sentinel waiting there,
watching over the barrow. Beowulf paid
the price of death for that mighty hoard;
both he and the dragon had travelled to the end
of this transitory life.
              Not long after that
the lily-livered ones slunk out of the wood;
ten cowardly oath-breakers, who had lacked
the courage to let fly with their spears
as their lord so needed, came forward together;
overcome with shame, they carried their shields
and weapons to where their leader lay;
they gazed at Wiglaf. That warrior, bone-weary,
knelt beside the shoulders of his lord; he tried

to rouse him with water; it was all in vain.
For all his efforts, his longing, he could not
detain the life of his leader on earth,
or alter anything the Ruler ordained.
God in His wisdom governed the deeds
of all men, as He does now.
    Then the young warrior was not at a loss
for well-earned, angry words for those cowards.
Wiglaf, Weohstan's son, sick at heart,
eyed those faithless men and said:
'He who does not wish to disguise the truth
can indeed say that – when it was a question
not of words but war – our lord completely wasted
the treasures he gave you, the same war-gear
you stand in over there, helmets and corslets
the prince presented often to his thanes on the ale-bench
in the feasting-hall, the very finest weapons
he could secure from far and wide.
The king of the Geats had no need to bother
with boasts about his battle-companions;
yet God, Giver of victories, granted
that he should avenge himself with his sword
single-handed, when all his courage was called for.
I could hardly begin to guard his life
in the fight; but all the same I attempted
to help my kinsman beyond my power.
Each time I slashed at that deadly enemy,
he was a little weaker, the flames leaped
less fiercely from his jaws. Too few defenders
rallied round our prince when he was most pressed.
Now you and your dependents can no longer delight
in gifts of swords, or take pleasure in property,
a happy home; but, after thanes from far and wide
have heard of your flight, your shameful cowardice,
each of your male kinsmen will be condemned
to become a wanderer, an exile deprived
of the land he owns. For every warrior
death is better than dark days of disgrace.'
    Then Wiglaf ordered that Beowulf's great feat
be proclaimed in the stronghold, up along the cliff-edge,
where a troop of shield-warriors had waited all morning,
wondering sadly if their dear lord was dead,
or if he would return.
                              The man who galloped

to the headland gave them the news at once;
he kept back nothing but called out:
'The lord of the Geats, he who gave joy
to all our people, lies rigid on his death-bed;
slaughtered by the dragon, he now sleeps;
and his deadly enemy, slashed by the knife,
sleeps beside him; he was quite unable
to wound the serpent with a sword. Wiglaf,
son of Weohstan, sits by Beowulf,
the quick and the dead – both brave men –
side by side; weary in his heart
he watches over friend and foe alike.
     Now the Geats must make ready for a time
of war, for the Franks and the Frisians,
in far-off regions, will hear soon
of the king's death. Our feud with the Franks
grew worse when Hygelac sailed with his fleet
to the shores of Frisia. Frankish warriors
attacked him there, and outfought him,
bravely forced the king in his corslet
to give ground; he fell, surrounded
by his retainers; that prince presented
not one ornament to his followers. Since then,
the king of the Franks has been no friend of ours.
     Nor would I in the least rely on peace
or honesty from the Swedish people; everyone
remembers how Ongentheow slew Hæthcyn,
Hrethel's son, in battle near Ravenswood
when, rashly, the Geats first attacked the Swedes.
At once Ongentheow, Ohthere's father,
old but formidable, retaliated; he killed
Hæthcyn, and released his wife from captivity,
set free the mother of Onela and Ohthere,
an aged woman bereft of all her ornaments;
and then he pursued his mortal enemies
until, lordless, with utmost difficulty,
they reached and found refuge in Ravenswood.
Then Ongentheow, with a huge army, penned in
those warriors, exhausted by wounds,
who had escaped the sword; all night long
he shouted fearsome threats at those shivering thanes,
swore that in the morning he and his men would let
their blood in streams with sharp-edged swords,
and string some up on gallows-trees

as sport for birds. Just as day dawned
those despairing men were afforded relief;
they heard the joyful song of Hygelac's
horn and trumpet as that hero came,
hurrying to their rescue with a band of retainers.
After that savage, running battle, the soil
was blood-stained, scuffled – a sign of how
the Swedes and the Geats fomented their feud.
Then Ongentheow, old and heavy-hearted,
headed for his stronghold with his retainers,
that resolute man retreated; he realized
how spirit and skill combined in the person
of proud Hygelac; he had no confidence
about the outcome of an open fight with the seafarers,
the Geatish warriors, in defence of his hoard,
his wife and children; the old man thus withdrew
behind an earth-wall. Then the Swedes were pursued,
Hygelac's banner was hoisted over that earth-work
after the Geats, sons of Hrethel, had stormed
the stronghold. Then grey-haired Ongentheow
was cornered by swords, the king of the Swedes
was constrained to face and suffer his fate
as Eofor willed it. Wulf, the son
of Wonred, slashed angrily at Ongentheow
with his sword, so that blood spurted
from the veins under his hair. The old Swede,
king of his people, was not afraid
but as soon as he had regained his balance
repaid that murderous blow with interest.
Then Wonred's daring son could no longer
lift his hand against the aged warrior
but, with that stroke, Ongentheow had sheared
right through his helmet so that Wulf, blood-stained,
was thrown to the ground; he was not yet doomed to die
but later recovered from that grievous wound.
When Wulf collapsed, his brother Eofor,
Hygelac's brave thane, swung his broad sword,
made by giants, shattered the massive helmet
above the raised shield; Ongentheow fell,
the guardian of the people was fatally wounded.
Then many warriors quickly rescued Wulf,
and bandaged his wounds, once they had won control
(as fate decreed) of that field of corpses.
Meanwhile Eofor stripped Ongentheow's body

of its iron corslet, wrenched the helmet
from his head, the mighty sword from his hands;
he carried the old man's armour to Hygelac.
He received those battle-adornments, honourably
promised to reward Eofor above other men;
he kept his word; the king of the Geats,
Hrethel's son, repaid Eofor and Wulf
for all they had accomplished with outstanding gifts
when he had returned home; he gave each of them
land and interlocked rings to the value
of a hundred thousand pence – no man on earth
had cause to blame the brothers for accepting
such wealth, they had earned it by sheer audacity.
Then, as a pledge of friendship, Hygelac gave
Eofor his only daughter to grace his home.

   That is the history of hatred and feud
and deadly enmity; and because of it,
I expect the Swedes to attack us
as soon as they hear our lord is lifeless –
he who in earlier days defended a land
and its treasure against two monstrous enemies
after the death of its heroes, daring Scyldings,
he who protected the people, and achieved feats
all but impossible.
                        Let us lose no time now
but go and gaze there upon our king
and carry him, who gave us rings,
to the funeral pyre. And let us not grudge gold
to melt with that bold man, for we have a mighty hoard,
a mint of precious metal, bought with pain;
and now, from this last exploit, a harvest
he paid for with his own life; these the fire
shall devour, the ravening flames embrace.
No thane shall wear or carry these treasures
in his memory, no fair maiden shall hang
an ornament of interlinked rings at her throat,
but often and again, desolate, deprived of gold,
they must tread the paths of exile,
now that their lord has laid aside laughter,
festivity, happiness. Henceforth, fingers must grasp,
hands must hold, many a spear
chill with the cold of morning; no sound of the harp
shall rouse the warriors but, craving for carrion,
the dark raven shall have its say

and tell the eagle how it fared at the feast
when, competing with the wolf, it laid bare the bones of corpses.'
    Thus the brave messenger told of and foretold
harrowing times; and he was not far wrong.
Those events were fated. Every man in the troop
stood up, stained with tears, and set out
for Eagleness to see that strange spectacle.
There they found him lifeless on the sand,
the soft bed where he slept, who often before
had given them rings; that good man's days
on earth were ended; the warrior-king,
lord of the Geats, had died a wondrous death.
But first they saw a strange creature
there, a loathsome serpent lying
nearby; the fire-dragon, fierce
and mottled, was scorched by its own flames.
It measured fifty paces from head to tail;
sometimes it had soared at night
through the cool air, then dived
to its dark lair; now it lay rigid in death,
no longer to haunt caverns under the earth.
Goblets and vessels stood by it,
salvers and valuable swords, eaten through
by rust, as if they had lain
for a thousand winters in the earth's embrace.
That mighty legacy, gold of men long dead,
lay under a curse; it was enchanted
so that no human might enter
the cavern save him to whom God,
the true Giver of Victories, Guardian of Men,
granted permission to plunder the hoard –
whichever warrior seemed worthy to Him.
    Then it was clear that, whoever devised it,
the evil scheme of hiding the hoard under the rock
had come to nothing; the guardian had killed
a brave and famous man; that feud
was violently avenged. The day that a warrior,
renowned for his courage, will reach the end
(as fate ordains) of his life on earth,
that hour when a man may feast in the hall
with his friends no longer, is always unpredictable.
It was thus with Beowulf when he tracked down
and attacked the barrow's guardian; he himself
was not aware how he would leave this world.

The glorious princes who first placed that gold there
had solemnly pronounced that until domesday
any man attempting to plunder the hoard
should be guilty of wickedness, confined,
tormented and tortured by the devil himself.
Never before had Beowulf been granted
such a wealth of gold by the gracious Lord.
    Wiglaf, the son of Weohstan, said:
'Many thanes must often suffer
because of the will of one, as we do now.
We could not dissuade the king we loved,
or in any way restrain the lord of our land
from not drawing his sword against the gold-warden,
from not letting him lie where he had long lain
and remain in his lair until the world's end;
but he fulfilled his high destiny. The hoard,
so grimly gained, is now easy of access;
our king was driven there by too harsh a fate.
I took the path under the earth-wall,
entered the hall and examined all
the treasures after the dragon deserted it;
I was hardly invited there. Hurriedly
I grasped as many treasures as I could,
a huge burden, and carried them here
to my king; he was still alive then,
conscious and aware of this world around him.
He found words for his thronging thoughts,
born of sorrow, he asked me to salute you,
said that as a monument to your lord's exploits
you should build a great and glorious barrow
over his pyre, for he of all men
was the most famous warrior on the wide earth
for as long as he lived, happy in his stronghold.
Now let us hurry once more together
and see the hoard of priceless stones,
that wonder under the wall; I will lead you
so that you will come sufficiently close
to the rings, the solid gold. After we
get back, let us quickly build the bier,
and then let us carry our king,
the man we loved, to where he must
long remain in the Lord's protection.'
    Then the brave warrior, Weohstan's son,
directed that orders be given to many men

(to all who owned houses, elders of the people)
to fetch wood from far to place beneath
their prince on the funeral pyre:
                                                                'Now flames,
the blazing fire, must devour the lord of warriors
who often endured the iron-tipped arrow-shower,
when the dark cloud loosed by bow strings
broke above the shield-wall, quivering;
when the eager shaft, with its feather garb,
discharged its duty to the barb.'
   I have heard that Weohstan's wise son
summoned from Beowulf's band his seven
best thanes, and went with those warriors
into the evil grotto; the man leading
the way grasped a brand. Then those retainers
were not hesitant about rifling the hoard
as soon as they set eyes on any part of it,
lying unguarded, gradually rusting,
in that rock cavern; no man was conscience-stricken
about carrying out those priceless treasures
as quickly as he could. Also, they pushed the dragon,
the serpent over the precipice; they let the waves take him,
the dark waters embrace the warden of the hoard.
Then the wagon was laden with twisted gold,
with treasures of every kind, and the king,
the old battle-warrior, was borne to Whaleness.
   Then, on the headland, the Geats prepared a mighty pyre
for Beowulf, hung round with helmets and shields
and shining mail, in accordance with his wishes;
and then the mourning warriors laid
their dear lord, the famous prince, upon it.
   And there on Whaleness, the heroes kindled
the most mighty of pyres; the dark wood-smoke
soared over the fire, the roaring flames
mingled with weeping – the winds' tumult subsided –
until the body became ash, consumed even
to its core. The heart's cup overflowed;
they mourned their loss, the death of their lord.
And, likewise, a maiden of the Geats,
with her tresses swept up, intoned
a dirge for Beowulf time after time,
declared she lived in dread of days to come
dark with carnage and keening, terror of the enemy,
humiliation and captivity.

                      Heaven swallowed the smoke.
Then the Geats built a barrow on the headland –
it was high and broad, visible from far
to all seafarers; in ten days they built the beacon
for that courageous man; and they constructed
as noble an enclosure as wise men
could devise, to enshrine the ashes.
They buried rings and brooches in the barrow,
all those adornments that brave men
had brought out from the hoard after Beowulf died.
They bequeathed the gleaming gold, treasure of men,
to the earth, and there it still remains
as useless to men as it was before.
   Then twelve brave warriors, sons of heroes,
rode round the barrow, sorrowing;
they mourned their king, chanted
an elegy, spoke about that great man:
they exalted his heroic life, lauded
his daring deeds; it is fitting for a man,
when his lord and friend must leave this life,
to mouth words in his praise
and to cherish his memory.
Thus the Geats, his hearth-companions,
grieved over the death of their lord;
they said that of all kings on earth
he was the kindest, the most gentle,
the most just to his people, the most eager for fame.

18. THE DEEDS OF CUCHULAIN

Although the ancient tales of Ireland were only written down from the twelfth century onwards, the language in which they are composed shows them to have much older origins, going back to at least the eighth century, and, in oral form, much further than that. These are stories on a Homeric scale, of epic warfare and mighty deeds, and the greatest of all the Irish heroes is Cuchulain. The main episode in which he appears is the rivalry of two neighbouring powers, as in Homer: for Greeks and Trojans, read the men of Ulster and the men of Connaught. Instead of an abducted princess, the quarrel is over more mundane matters, the primacy of the bull of Ulster, the Brown Bull of Cuailgne, over the bull of Connaught, Fionnbanach the White-Horned. But the action that ensues is as bitterly fought as any action beneath the walls of Troy.

The story of Cuchulain is rooted in Irish tradition, and some of its features may at first seem unfamiliar. In particular, the geasa *or taboos laid on the great heroes have no real parallel elsewhere. These are acts which are solemnly prohibited to a particular hero; if he breaks the* geasa, *disaster will inevitably follow. Cuchulain's death follows a series of episodes when he finds himself unable to avoid contravening these taboos, so that we follow events with an increasing sense of impending doom, until he meets his tragic end. Other figures, such as that of the Morrigan, are re-incarnations of the ancient deities of Ireland, and the tales belong firmly to a pre-Christian society of tribal loyalties and traditional warrior values. As to the style of the telling, two remarkable features are the boasting matches between the champions, a rhetorical hurling of insults before battle is joined; and the fascination with the origins of place-names which we have already noted in connection with the early Welsh stories.*

The version which follows is based on that of Lady Augusta Gregory, in her Cuchulain of Muirthemne; *I have used this since the best modern version of his story by Thomas Kinsella (*The Tain, *Oxford and Dublin 1970) only tells part of the story of Cuchulain.*

CONCHUBAR, king of Ulster, was making a feast one day at his palace of Emain Macha, for the marriage of his sister Dechtire with Sualtim, son of Roig. And at the feast Dechtire was thirsty, and they gave her a cup of wine, and as she was drinking it, a mayfly flew into the cup, and she drank it down with the wine. And presently she went into her sunny parlour, and her fifty girls along with her, and she fell into a deep sleep. And in her sleep, Lugh of the Long Hand appeared to her, and he said: 'It is I myself was the mayfly that came to you in the cup, and it is with me you must come away now, and your fifty girls along with you.' And he put on them the appearance of a flock of birds, and they went with

258

him southward till they came to Brugh na Boinne, the dwelling place of the Sidhe. And no one at Emain Macha could get tale or tidings of them, or know where they had gone, or what had happened to them.

It was about a year after that time, there was another feast in Emain, and Conchubar and his chief men were sitting at the feast. And suddenly they saw from the window a great flock of birds, that lit on the ground and began to eat up everything before them, so that not so much as a blade of grass was left.

The men of Ulster were vexed when they saw the birds destroying all before them, and they yoked nine of their chariots to follow after them. Conchubar was in his own chariot, and there were following with him Fergus, son of Rogh, and Laegaire Buadach, and Celthair, son of Uthecar, and many others, and Bricriu of the Bitter Tongue was along with them.

They followed after the birds across the whole country southward, across Slieve Fuad, by Ath Lethan, by Ath Garach and Magh Gossa, between Fir Rois and Fir Ardae; and the birds before them always. They were the most beautiful that had ever been seen; nine flocks of them there were, linked together two and two with a chain of silver, and at the head of every flock there were two birds of different colours, linked together with a chain of gold; and there were three birds that flew by themselves, and they all went before the chariots, to the far end of the country, until the fall of night, and then there was no more seen of them.

And when the dark night was coming on, Conchubar said to his people: 'It is best for us to unyoke the chariots now, and to look for some place where we can spend the night.'

Then Fergus went forward to look for some place, and what he came to was a very small poor-looking house. A man and a woman were in it, ...nd when they saw him they said: 'Bring your companions here along with you, and they will be welcome.'

Fergus went back to his companions and told them what he had seen. But Bricriu said: 'Where is the use of going into a house like that, with neither room nor provisions nor coverings in it; it is not worth our while to be going there.'

Then Bricriu went on himself to the place where the house was. But when he came to it, what he saw was a grand, new, well-lighted house; and at the door there was a young man wearing armour, very tall and handsome and shining. And he said: 'Come into the house, Bricriu; why are you looking about you?' And there was a young woman beside him, fine and noble, and with curled hair, and she said: 'Surely there is a welcome before you from me.' 'Why does she welcome me?' said Bricriu. 'It is on account of her that I myself welcome you,' said the young man. 'And is there no one missing from you at Emain?' he said. 'There is surely,' said Bricriu. 'We are missing fifty young girls for the length of a year.' 'Would you know them again if you saw them?' said the young man. 'If I would not know them,' said Bricriu, 'it is because a year might make a change in them, so that I would not be sure.' 'Try and know them again,' said the young man, 'for the fifty young girls are in this house, and this woman beside me is their mistress, Dechtire. It was they themselves, changed into birds, that went to Emain Macha to bring you here.'

Then Dechtire gave Bricriu a purple cloak with gold fringes, and he went back to find his companions. But while he was going he thought to himself: 'Conchubar would give great treasure to find these fifty young girls again, and his sister along with them. I will not tell him I have found them. I will only say I have found a house with beautiful women in it, and no more than that.'

When Conchubar saw Bricriu, he asked news of him. 'What news do you bring back with you, Bricriu?' he said. 'I came to a fine well-lighted house,' said Bricriu; 'I saw a queen, noble king, with royal looks, with curled hair; I saw a troop of women, beautiful, well-dressed; I saw the man of the house, tall and open-handed and shining.' 'Let us go there for the night,' said Conchubar.

So they brought their chariots and their horses and their arms; and they were hardly in the house when every sort of food and of drink, some they knew and some they did not know, was put before them, so that they never spent a better night. And when they had eaten and drunk and began to be satisfied, Conchubar said to the young man: 'Where is the mistress of the house that she does not come to bid us welcome?' 'You cannot see her tonight,' said he, 'for she is in the pains of childbirth.'

So they rested there that night, and in the morning Conchubar was the first to rise up; but he saw no more of the man of the house, and what he heard was the cry of a child. And he went to the room it came from, and there he saw Dechtire, and her girls about her, and a young child beside her. And she bade Conchubar welcome, and she told him all that had happened to her, and that she had called him there to bring herself and the child back to Emain Macha. And Conchubar said: 'It is well you have done by me, Dechtire; you gave shelter to me and to my chariots; you kept the cold from my horses; you gave food to me and my people, and now you have given us this good gift. And let our sister, Finchoem, bring up the child,' he said.

'No, it is not for her to bring him up, it is for me,' said Sencha son of Ailell, chief judge and chief poet of Ulster. 'For I am skilled; I am good in disputes; I am not forgetful; I speak before anyone at all in the presence of the king; I watch over what he says; I give judgment in the quarrels of kings; I am judge of the men of Ulster; no one has a right to dispute my claim, but only Conchubar.'

'If the child is given to me to bring up,' said Blai, the king's marshal, 'he will not suffer from want of care or from forgetfulness. It is my messages that do the will of Conchubar; I call up the fighting men from all Ireland; I am well able to provide for them for a week, or even for ten days; I settle their business and their disputes; I support their honour; I get satisfaction for their insults.'

'You think too much of yourself,' said Fergus. 'It is I that will bring up the child; I am strong; I have knowledge; I am the king's messenger; no one can stand up against me in honour or riches; I am hardened to war and battles; I am a good craftsman; I am worthy to bring up a child. I am the protector of all the unhappy; the strong are afraid of me; I am the helper of the weak.'

'If you will listen to me at last, now you are quiet,' said Amergin, 'I am able to bring up a child like a king. The people praise my honour, my bravery, my courage, my wisdom; they praise my good luck, my age, my speaking, my name, my courage, and my race. Though I am a fighter, I am a poet; I am worthy of the king's favour; I overcome all the men who fight from their chariots; I owe thanks to no one except Conchubar; I obey no one but the king.'

Then Sencha said: 'Let Finchoem keep the child until we come to Emain, and Morann, the judge, will settle the question when we are there.'

So the men of Ulster set out for Emain, Finchoem having the child with her. And when they came there Morann gave his judgment. 'It is for Conchubar', he said, 'To help the child to a good name, for he is next of kin to him; let Sencha teach him words and speaking; let Fergus hold him on his knees; let Amergin be his tutor.' And he said: 'This child will be praised by all, by chariot drivers and fighters, by kings and by wise men; he shall be loved by many men; he will avenge all your wrongs; he will defend your fords; he will fight all your battles.'

And so it was settled. And the child was left until he should come to sensible years, with his mother Dechtire and with her husband Sualtim. And they brought him up on the plain of Muirthemne, and the name he was known by was Setanta, son of Sualtim.

When Setanta was about seven, he heard of the fame of the court at Emain Macha, and despite his youth, insisted on setting out alone to join the young men in their games and hurling. When he arrived, he played so well that the others set upon him, but he defended himself stoutly, and attracted Conchubar's attention. When Conchubar learnt that he was his sister's son, he made him welcome.

There was a great smith in Ulster of the name of Culain, who made a feast at that time for Conchubar and for his people. When Conchubar was setting out to the feast, he passed by the lawn where the boy troop were at their games, and he watched them awhile, and he saw how the son of Dechtire was winning the goal from them all. 'That little lad will serve Ulster yet,' said Conchubar; and called him to the smith's feast. 'I cannot go with you now,' said Setanta when they had called to him, 'for these boys have not had enough of play yet.' 'It would be too long for me to wait for you,' said the king. 'There is no need for you to wait; I will follow the track of the chariots.'

So Conchubar went on to the smith's house, and there was a welcome before him, and fresh rushes were laid down, and there were poems and songs and recitals of laws, and the feast was brought in, and they began to be merry. And then Culain said to the king: 'Will there be anyone else of your people coming after you tonight?' 'There will not,' said Conchubar, for he forgot that he had told the little lad to follow him. 'But why do you ask me that?' he said. 'I have a great fierce hound,' said the smith, 'and when I take the chain off him, he lets no one come into the one district with himself, and he will obey no one but myself, and he has in him the strength of a hundred.' 'Let him out', said Conchubar, 'until he keeps a watch on the place.' So Culain loosed him out, and the dog made a course round the whole district, and then he came back to the place where he was used to lie and watch the house, and everyone was in dread of him, he was so fierce and cruel and savage.

Now, as to the boys at Emain, when they were done playing, every one went to his father's house or to whoever was in charge of him. But Setanta set out on the track of the chariots, and when he came to the lawn before the smith's house, the hound heard him coming, and began such a fierce yelling that he might have been heard through all Ulster, and he sprang at him as if he had a mind not to stop and tear him up at all, but to swallow him at the one mouthful. The little fellow had no weapon but his stick and his ball, but when he saw the hound coming at him, he struck the ball with such force that it went down his throat, and through his body. Then he seized him by the hind legs, and dashed him against a rock until there was no life left in him.

When the men feasting within heard the outcry of the hound, Conchubar started up and said: 'It is no good luck brought us on this journey, for that is surely my sister's son that was coming after me, and that has got his death by the hound.' On that all the men rushed out, not waiting to go through the door, but over walls and barriers as they could. But Fergus was the first to get to where the boy was, and he took him up and lifted him on his shoulder, and brought him in safe and sound to Conchubar, and there was great joy on them all.

But Culain the smith went out with them, and when he saw his great hound lying dead and broken, there was great grief in his heart, and he came in and said to Setanta: 'There is no good welcome for you here.' 'What have you against the little lad?' said Conchubar. 'It was no good luck that brought him here, or that made me prepare this feast for yourself, king,' he said; 'for from this out, my hound being gone, my substance will be wasted, and my way of living will be gone astray. And, little boy,' he said, 'That was a good member of my family you took from me, for he was the protector of my goods and my flocks and my herds and of all that I had.'

'Do not be vexed on account of that,' said the boy, 'and I myself will make up to you for what I have done.' 'How will you do that?' said Conchubar. 'This is how I will do it: if there is a whelp of the same breed to be had in Ireland, I will rear him and train him until he is as good a hound as the one killed; and until that time, Culain,' he said, 'I myself will be your watchdog, to guard your goods and your cattle and your house.'

'You have made me a fair offer,' said Culain. 'I could have given no better award myself,' said Cathbad the Druid. 'And from this out', he said, 'your name will be Cuchulain, the Hound of Culain.' 'I am better pleased with my own name of Setanta, son of Sualtim,' said the boy. 'Do not say that,' said Cathbad, 'for all the men in the whole world will some day have the name of Cuchulain in their mouths.' 'If that is so, I am content to keep it,' said the boy.

And that is how he came by his name.

Cuchulain heard Cathbad the Druid say one day that anyone who took up arms that day would have the greatest name in Ireland, but would not live long; so he went to Conchubar and demanded to have arms and weapons. Conchubar gave them to him, but was angry when he learnt of the prophecy. Cuchulain, however, said: 'If my life were to last one day and one night only, I would not care so long as my name would live after me.' He then tried eighteen chariots that were offered to him, and broke them all; only the king's chariot could hold him. He at once set out across the border of Ulster, and challenged and slew the sons of Nechtan. On the way back, he seized wild deer and swans and tied them to the chariot, and returned in triumph. Conchubar said: 'If his anger cannot be cooled, the young men at Emain Macha will be in danger from him.' So he sent three fifties of the women of Emain to meet him, and they naked as the day they were born. And Cuchulain was ashamed, and hid his face in the chariot, and his anger abated.

THE WOOING OF EMER

The men of Ulster took counsel about Cuchulain, because their wives and daughters all loved him greatly, and sent messengers throughout Ireland to find a wife for him. But none could be found worthy of him, until he himself set out to woo Emer, daughter of Forgall Manach the Wily.

He set out in his chariot, that all the chariots of Ulster could not follow by reason of its swiftness, and of the chariot chief who sat in it. And he found the young girl on the field where she played, with her companions about her – daughters of the landowners that lived near Forgall's dun [fortress mound], and they learning needlework and fine embroidery from Emer. And of all the young girls of Ireland, she was the one Cuchulain thought worth courting; for she had the six gifts – the gift of beauty, the gift of voice, the gift of sweet speech, the gift of needlework, the gift of wisdom, the gift of chastity. And Cuchulain had said that no woman should marry him but one that was his equal in age, in appearance, and in race, in skill and handiness; and one who was the best worker with her needle of the young girls of Ireland, for that would be the only one would be a fitting wife for him. And that is why it was Emer he went to ask above all others.

And it was in his rich clothes he went out that day, his crimson five-folded tunic, and his brooch of inlaid gold, and his white hooded shirt, that was embroidered with red gold. And as the young girls were sitting together on their bench on the lawn, they heard coming towards them the clatter of hooves, the creaking of a chariot, the cracking of straps, the grating of wheels, the rushing of horses, the clanking of arms.

'Let one of you see', said Emer, 'what is it that is coming towards us.' And Fiall, daughter of Forgall, went out and met him, and he came with her to the place where Emer and her companions were, and he wished a blessing to them. Then Emer lifted up her lovely face and saw Cuchulain, and she said, 'May the gods make smooth the path before you.' 'And you,' he said, 'may you be safe from every harm.' 'Where are you come from?' she asked him. And he answered her in riddles that her companions might not understand him. When she had asked him where he had come from, and how he had journeyed to her, she asked, 'And what account have you to give of yourself?' 'I am the nephew of the man that disappears in another in the wood of Badb,' said Cuchulain. 'And now, girl, what account have you to give of yourself?' 'That is not hard to tell,' said Emer, 'for what should a girl be but a watcher that sees no one, an eel hiding in the water, a rush out of reach. The daughter of a king should be a flame of hospitality, a road that cannot be entered. And I have champions that follow me,' she said, 'To keep me from whoever would bring me away against their will, and against the will and the knowledge of Forgall, the dark king.'

'Who are the champions that follow you, girl?' said Cuchulain. 'It is not hard to tell you that,' said Emer. 'Two of the name of Lui; two Luaths; Luath and Lath Goible, sons of Tethra; Triath and Trescath; Brion and Bolor; Bas, son of Omnach; the eight Condla, and Cond, son of Forgall. Every man of them has the strength of a hundred and the feats of nine. And it would be hard for me', she said, 'To tell of all the many powers

Forgall has himself. He is stronger than any labouring man, more learned than any druid, more quick of mind than any poet. You will have more than your games to do when you fight against Forgall, for many have told of his power and of the strength of his doings.'

'Why do you not count me as a strong man as good as those others?' said Cuchulain. 'Why would I not indeed, if your doings had been spoken of like theirs?' she said. 'I swear by the oath of my people,' said Cuchulain, 'I will make my doings spoken of among the great doings of heroes in their strength.' 'What is your strength, then?' said Emer. 'That is easily told; when my strength in fighting is weakest I defend twenty; a third part of my strength is enough for thirty; in my full strength I fight alone against forty; and a hundred are safe under my protection. For dread of me, fighting men avoid fords and battles; armies and armed men go backward from the fear of my face.'

'That is a good account for a young boy,' said Emer, 'but you have not reached yet to the strength of chariot chiefs.' 'But indeed,' said Cuchulain 'it is well I have been reared by Conchubar, my dear foster-father. It is not as a countryman strives to bring up his children between the flag-stones and the kneading trough, between the fire and the wall, on the floor of the one room, that Conchubar has brought me up; but it is among chariot chiefs and heroes, among jesters and druids, among poets and learned men, among landowners and farmers of Ulster I have been reared, so that I have all their manners and their gifts.'

'Who are these men, then, that have brought you up to do the things you are boasting of?' said Emer.

'That is easily told,' he said. 'Fair-speaking Sencha taught me wisdom and right judgement; Blai, lord of lands, my kinsman, took me to his house, so that I have entertained the men of Conchubar's province; Fergus brought me up to fights and to battles, so that I am able to use my strength. I stood by the knee of Amergin the poet, he was my tutor, so that I can stand up to any man, I can make praises for the doings of a king. Finchoem helped to rear me, so that Conall Cearnach is my foster-brother. Cathbad of the Gentle Face taught me, for the sake of Dechtire, so that I understand the arts of the druids, and I have learned all the goodness of knowledge. All the men of Ulster have had a hand in bringing me up, chariot-drivers and chiefs of chariots, kings and chief poets, so that I am the darling of the whole army, so that I fight for the honour of all alike. And as to yourself, Emer,' he said, 'how have you been reared in the Garden of Lugh?'

'It is easy to tell that,' said Emer. 'I was brought up', she said, 'in ancient virtues, in lawful behaviour, in the keeping of chastity, in stateli-ness of form, in the rank of a queen, in all noble ways among the women of Ireland.' 'These are good virtues indeed,' said Cuchulain. 'And why, then, would it not be right for us two to become one? For up to this time', he said, 'I have never found a young girl able to hold talk with me the way you have done.' 'Have you no wife already?' said Emer. 'I have not, indeed.' 'I may not marry before my sister is married,' she said then, 'for she is older than myself.' 'Truly, it is not with your sister, but with yourself, I have fallen in love,' said Cuchulain.

While they were talking like this, Cuchulain saw the breasts of the maiden over the bosom of her dress, and he said: 'Fair is this plain, the plain of the noble yoke.' And Emer said, 'No one comes to this plain who does not overcome as many as a hundred on each ford, from the fords at Ailbine to Banchuig Arcait.' 'Fair is the plain, the plain of the noble yoke,' said Cuchulain. 'No one comes to this plain', said she, 'who does not got out in safety from Samhain to Oilmell, and from Oilmell to Beltane, and again from Beltane to Bron Trogain.'*

'Everything you have commanded, so it will be done by me,' said Cuchulain.

'And the offer you have made me, it is accepted, it is taken, it is granted,' said Emer.

When Forgall came back to his dun, and his lords of land with him, their daughters were telling them of the young man that had come in a splendid chariot, and how himself and Emer had been talking together, and they could not understand their talk with one another. The lords of the land told this to Forgall, and this is what he said: 'You may be sure it is the mad boy from Emain Macha has been here, and he and the girl have fallen in love with one another. But they will gain nothing by that,' he said; 'for it is I will hinder them.'

With that Forgall went out to Emain, with the appearance of a foreigner on him, and he gave out that he was sent by the king of the Gauls, to speak with Conchubar, and to bring him a present of golden treasures, and wine of the Gauls, and many other things. And he brought some of his men with him, and there was a great welcome before them.

And on the third day, Cuchulain and Conall and other chariot chiefs of Ulster were praised before him, and he said it was right for them to be praised, and that they did wonderful feats, and Cuchulain above them all. But he said that if Cuchulain would go to Scathach, the woman warrior that lived in the east of Alban [Scotland], his skill would be more wonderful still, for he could not have perfect knowledge of the feats of a warrior without that.

But his reason for saying this was that he thought if Cuchulain set out, he would never come back again, through the dangers he would put around him on the journey, and through the wildness and the fierceness of the people about Scathach.

---

* From the end of summer to the beginning of spring, then to midsummer, and finally to the beginning of autumn. *Ed.*

So then Forgall went home, and Cuchulain rose up in the morning, and made ready to set out for Alban, and Laegaire Buadach the Battle-Winner, and Conall Cearnach said they would go with him. But first Cuchulain went across the plain of Bregia to visit Emer, and to talk with her before going in the ship. And she told him how it was that Forgall had gone to Emain, and had advised him to go and learn warriors' feats, so that they two might not meet again. Then each of them promised to be true to the other till they would meet again, unless death should come between them, and they said farewell to one another, and Cuchulain turned towards Alban.

When they came there, they stopped for a while at the forge of Donall, the smith, and then they set out to go to the east of Alban. But before they had gone far, a vision came before their eyes of Emain Macha, and Laegaire and Conall were not able to pass by it, and they turned back. It was Forgall raised that vision to draw them away from Cuchulain, that he might be in the more danger, being alone. Then Cuchulain went on by himself on a strange road, and he was sad and tired and downhearted for the loss of his comrades, but he held to his word that he would not go back to Emain without finding Scathach, even if he should die in the attempt.

Cuchulain encountered various adventures on the way; he met a lion, which he mounted and rode for four days, the beast going whichever way it chose. With the help of friendly strangers he crossed the plain of ill-luck, and avoided the monsters sent by Forgall to destroy him.

Then he came to the place where Scathach's scholars were, and among them he saw Ferdiad, son of Daman, and Naoise, Ainnle and Ardan, the three sons of Usnach, and when they knew that he was from Ireland they welcomed him with kisses, and asked for news of their own country. He asked them where Scathach was. 'In that island beyond,' they said. 'What way must I take to reach her?' he asked. 'By the bridge of the cliff,' they said, 'and no man can cross it till he has proved himself a champion, and many a king's son has got his death there.'

And this is the way the bridge was: the two ends of it were low, and the middle was high, and whenever anyone would leap on it, the first time it would narrow till it was as narrow as the hair of a man's head, and the second time it would shorten till it was as short as an inch, and the third time it would get slippery till it was as slippery as an eel of the river, and the fourth time it would rise up on high against you till it was as tall as the mast of a ship.

All the warriors and people on the lawn came down to see Cuchulain making his attempt to cross the bridge, and he tried three times to do it, and he could not, and the others were laughing at him, that he should think he could cross it, and he so young. Then his anger came on him, and the hero light shone round his head, and it was not the appearance of a man that was on him, but the appearance of a god. And he leaped upon the end of the bridge and made the hero's salmon leap, so that he landed on the middle of it, and he reached the other end of the bridge before it could raise itself fully up, and threw himself from it, and was on the ground of the island where Scathach's sunny house was; and it having seven great doors, and seven great windows between every two doors, and three times fifty couches between every two windows, and three times fifty young girls, with scarlet cloaks and beautiful blue clothing on them, waiting on Scathach.

And Scathach's daughter, Uacthach, was sitting by a window, and when she saw the young man, and he a stranger, and comeliest of the men of Ireland, making his attempt to cross the bridge, she loved him, and her face and her colour began to change continually, so that now she would be as white as a little flower, and then again she would grow crimson red. And in her needlework that she was doing, she would put the gold thread where the silver thread should be, and the silver thread in the place where the gold thread should be. And when Scathach saw that, she said: 'I think this young man has pleased you.' And Uacthach said: 'There would be great grief on me indeed, were he not to return alive to his own people, in whatever part of the world they may be, for I know there is surely someone to whom it would be great anguish to know the way he is now.'

Then, when Cuchulain had crossed the bridge, he went up to the house, and struck the door with the shaft of his spear, so that it went through it. And when Scathach was told that, she said, 'Truly this must be someone who has finished his training in some other place.' Then Uacthach opened the door for him, and he asked for Scathach, and Uacthach told him where she was, and what he had best do when he found her. So he went out to the place where she was teaching her two sons, Cuar and Cett, under the great yew-tree; and he took his sword and put its point between her breasts, and he threatened her with a dreadful death if she would not take him as her pupil, and if she would not teach him all her own skill in arms. So she promised him she would do that.

While Cuchulain was with Scathach, Lugaid, king of Munster, came to Forgall, and sought Emer's hand in marriage; but when Emer met Lugaid for the first time, she laid one of her hands on each side of his face, and said that it was Cuchulain whom she loved, and that no honourable man should force her to be his wife. And Lugaid did not dare to take her, for fear of Cuchulain.

After Cuchulain had been a good time with Scathach, a war began between herself and Aoife, queen of the tribes that were round about.

The armies were going out to fight, but Cuchulain was not with them, for Scathach had given him a sleeping-drink that would keep him safe and quiet till the fight would be over; for she was afraid some harm would come to him if he met Aoife, for she was the greatest woman-warrior in the world, and she understood enchantments and witchcraft. But after one hour, Cuchulain started up out of his sleep, for the sleeping-drink that would have held any other man for a day and a night held him for only that length of time. And he followed after the army, and he met with the two sons of Scathach, and they three went against the three sons of Ilsuanach, three of the best warriors of Aoife, and it was by Cuchulain they were killed, one after the other.

On the morning of the morrow the fight was begun again, and the two sons of Scathach were going up the Path of Feats to fight against three others of the best champions of Aoife, Cire, Bire and Blaicne, sons of Ess Enchenn. When Scathach saw them going up, she gave a sigh, for she was afraid for her two sons, but just then Cuchulain came up with them, and he leaped before them on to the Path of Feats, and met the three champions, and all three fell by him.

When Aoife saw that her best champions were after being killed, she challenged Scathach to fight against herself, but Cuchulain went out in her place. And before he went, he asked Scathach, 'What things does Aoife think most of in all the world?' 'Her two horses and her chariot and her chariot-driver,' said Scathach.

So then Cuchulain and Aoife attacked one another and began a fierce fight, and she broke Cuchulain's spear in pieces, and his sword she broke off at the hilt. Then Cuchulain called out, 'Look, the chariot and the horses and the driver of Aoife are fallen down into the valley and are loss!' At that Aoife looked about her, and Cuchulain took a sudden hold of her and lifted her on his shoulders, and brought her down to where the army was, and laid her on the ground, and held his sword to her breast, and she begged for her life, and he gave it to her. And after that she made peace with Scathach, and bound herself by sureties not to go against her again. And Aoife gave her love to Cuchulain; and out of that love great sorrow came afterwards.

After that, he stayed for another while with Scathach, until he had learned all the arts of war and all the feats of a champion; and then a message came to him to come back to his own country, and he bade her farewell. And Scathach told him what would happen to him in the time to come, for she had the druid gift; and she told him there were great dangers before him and that he would have to fight against great armies, and he alone; and that he would scatter his enemies, so that his name would come again to Alban; but that his life would not be long, for he would die in his full strength. Then Cuchulain went on board his ship to set out for Ireland, and in the same ship with him were Lugaid and Luan, the two sons of Loch, and Ferbaeth and Larin and Ferdiad, and Durst, son of Derb.

He made his way back to Emain Macha, and he told his whole story and all that had happened to him. And as soon as he had rested from the journey, he set out to look for Emer at her father's house. But Forgall and his sons had heard he was come home again, and they had made the place so strong, and they kept so good a watch round it, that for the whole length of a year he could not get so much as a sight of her. One day Cuchulain got his scythe chariot made ready, and he set out again for Forgall's dun. And when he got there, he leaped with his hero leap over the three walls, so that he was inside the court, and there he made three attacks, so that eight men fell from each attack, but one escaped in every troop of nine; that is, the three brothers of Emer, Seibur and Ibur and Catt. And Forgall made a leap from the wall of the court to escape Cuchulain, and he fell in the leap and got his death from the fall. And then Cuchulain went out again, and brought Emer with him, and her foster-sister and their two loads of gold and silver. And although Forgall's sister Scenmend and Forgall's men pursued them, they came safely to Emain Macha; and there Cuchulain took Emer for his wife after that long courting and all the hardships he had gone through.

THE HOUSE OF THE RED BRANCH

In the chief palace of Conchubar at Emain Macha there were three houses, the Royal House, the Speckled House and the House of the Red Branch, where the young men of whom Cuchulain had the headship dwelt. It was in the House of the Red Branch were kept the heads and the weapons of beaten enemies. It was the custom with the men of the Red Branch, if one of them heard a word of insult, to get satisfaction for it on the moment. He would get up in the feasting hall itself and make his attack; and it was to prevent that that the arms were kept together in the Speckled House. Conchubar's shield, the Ochain, that is the Moaning One, was hanging there; whenever Conchubar was in danger, it would moan and all the shields of Ulster would moan in answer to it.

And Cuchulain's shield was there, and the way he got it was this. There was a law made by the men of the Red Branch that the carved device on every shield should be different from every other. And the name of the man that used to make the shields was Mac Enge. Cuchulain went to him after coming back from Scathach and bade him make a shield, and put some new device on it. 'I cannot do that,' said Mac Enge, 'for all I can do I have done already on the shields of the men of Ulster.'

There was anger on Cuchulain then, and he threatened Mac Enge with death, despite his being under Conchubar's protection. And Mac Enge was greatly put out, and was thinking what was best for him to do, when he saw a stranger approaching. 'There is some trouble on you,' the man said. 'There is indeed,' said the shield maker, 'for I am in danger of death unless I make a shield for Cuchulain.' 'Clear out your workshop,' said the man, 'and spread ashes a foot deep on the floor.' And when this was done the man took a two-pronged fork and made a pattern in the ashes, to be cut on Cuchulain's shield. And when Cuchulain got it, it was called Dubhan, the Black One. And with the shield there hung Cuchulain's sword Cruaidin Cailidcheann, the Hard, Hard-Headed. And it had a hilt of gold with ornaments of silver, and if the point of the sword would be bent back to its hilt, it would come as straight as a rod back again. It would cut a hair on the water, or it would cut a man in two, and the one half of him would not miss the other for some time after.

And as for Cuchulain's terrible spear, the Gae Bolg, this is how he got it. There were two monsters fighting in the sea once, the Curruid and the Coinchenn their names were, and at the last the Coinchenn made for the strand to escape, but the other followed him and killed him there. Bolg, son of Buan, a champion from the east, found the bones of the Coin-chenn on the strand and he made a spear with them. It had to be made ready on a stream, and cast from the fork of the toes. It entered a man's body through a single wound, and then opened into thirty barbs. Only by cutting away the flesh could it be taken out again. And Bolg gave it to a great fighting man, and so it went from one champion to another, until it came to Aoife, the woman warrior, who gave it to Cuchulain. And with it he killed his son, and his friend Ferdiad afterwards.

And the twelve chief heroes of Conchubar's Red Branch were these: Fergus, son of Rogh; Conall Cearnach the Victorious; Laegaire Buadach the Battle-Winner; Cuchulain, son of Sualtim; Eoghan, son of Durthact, chief of Frenmaige; Celthair, son of Uthecar; Dubthach Doel Uladh, the Beetle of Ulster; Huinremar, son of Giergind; Cethern, son of Findtain; and Naoise, Ainnle and Ardan, the three sons of Usnach.

THE CHAMPION'S PORTION

Bricriu of the Bitter Tongue, whose delight it was to raise enmity and hatred, gave a great feast to Conchubar and the men of the Red Branch; and he took three of the heroes aside, Laegaire Buadach, Conall Cearnach and Cuchulain, and told each of them that it was he who deserved the Champion's Portion which he offered; and then he stirred up their wives, Fedlem of the Fresh Heart, Lendabair the Favourite and Emer of the Beautiful Hair, to a quarrel over who deserved the precedence. And Conchubar had much trouble to settle the argument; and in the end he sent the three heroes to Connaught, to the court of Ailell and Maeve, that Ailell and Maeve should judge between them. When they arrived at the court, Ailell was reluctant to judge them, but promised to do so in three days' time. Maeve sent them to her foster-father Ercol, who knew that they had been sent there to be tested. Cuchulain came off best in all the trials that Ercol devised, and Ailell and Maeve agreed that he should have the Champion's Portion; but to avoid the danger of offending the other champions, they gave them each a cup. Laegaire's was bronze, Conall's silver, and Cuchulain's gold; and they each promised not to reveal it until they returned to Conchubar's court. When Laegaire saw Cuchulain's cup, he accused him of bribing Ailell and Maeve, and buying the Champion's Portion for riches and treasures; 'but by my hand of valour, that judgement shall not stand'. Swords were drawn, but Conchubar made peace, and they were sent to Curoi, son of Daire, to be judged. Curoi was absent, but Blanad his wife made them welcome.

When bedtime came, Blanad told them they were each to take a night to watch the fort, till Curoi would come back. 'And it is what he said, that you should take your turn according to age.' Now in whatever part of the world Curoi was, he made a spell every night over the dun, so that it went round like a mill, and no entrance could be found in it after the setting of the sun.

The first night Laegaire Buadach took the watch, for he was the oldest of the three. As he was keeping watch, towards the end of the night he saw a great shadow coming towards him from the sea westward. Very huge and ugly and terrible he thought it, and it took the shape of a giant and reached up to the sky, and the shining of the sea could be seen between its legs. This is how it came, its hands full of what had the appearance of stripped oaks, and each of them enough for a load for six horses; and he hurled one of them at Laegaire, but it went past him. He did this two or three times, but the beam did not reach either the skin or the shield of Laegaire. Then Laegaire hurled a spear at him, and it did not hit him.

He stretched out his hand then to Laegaire, and the length of it reached across the three ridges that were between them while they were throwing at one another, and he gripped hold of him. Big and strong as Laegaire was, he fitted like a child of a year old into his hand. The giant turned him round between his two palms as a chessman is turned in a groove, and then he threw him half dead over the wall of the fort into a heap of mud. There was no opening there, and the people inside the dun thought he had leaped over from outside, as a challenge to the others to do the same.

At the fall of night, Conall went out to take the watch, as he was older than Cuchulain. Everything happened as it did to Laegaire the first night. And when the third night came, Cuchulain went into the seat of the watch. When midnight was come he heard a noise, and by the light of the cold moon he saw nine grey shapes coming towards him over the marsh.

'Stop,' said Cuchulain, 'who is there? If they are friends, let them not stir; if they are enemies, let them come on.'

Then they raised a great shout at him, and Cuchulain rushed at them and attacked them, so that the nine fell dead to the ground, and he cut their heads off and made a heap of them, and sat down again to keep the watch. Another nine, and then another, shouted at him, but he made an end of the three nines, and made one heap of their heads and arms.

While he was watching on through the night, tired and downhearted, he heard a sound rising from the lake, like the sound of a very heavy sea. However tired he was, his mind would not let him quiet, without going to see what was the cause of that great noise he heard. Then he saw a great worm coming up from the lake, and it raised itself into the air over him and made for the dun, and opened its mouth, and it seemed to him that one of the houses would fit into its gullet.

Then Cuchulain, with one leap, reached its head and put his arm round its neck, and stretched his hand across its gullet, and tore the monster's heart out, and threw it to the ground. Then the beast fell down, and Cuchulain hacked it with his sword, and made little bits of it, and brought the head along with him to the heap of skulls.

He was sitting there, towards the break of day, disconsolate and worn out, and he saw the great shadow shaped like a giant coming to him westward from the sea. 'This is a bad night,' he said. 'It will be worse for you yet,' said Cuchulain. Then he threw one of the beams at Cuchulain, but it passed him by, and he did that two or three times without reaching either his shield or his skin. Then he stretched out his hand to grip Cuchulain as he did the others, but Cuchulain leaped his salmon leap at the head of the monster, with his drawn sword, and brought him down. 'Life for life, Cuchulain,' he said, and with that he vanished and was no more seen.

Cuchulain returns to Curoi's dun by leaping over the wall, and landing in the middle, at the door of Curoi's house. Then he went through the door and gave a sigh. 'That is not the sigh of a beaten man, but a conqueror's sigh of triumph,' said Blanad, Curoi's wife. 'Now the Champion's Portion must go to Cuchulain.' But Laegaire and Conall still disputed this, saying his friends among the Sidhe had come to put them down and leave the field clear for Cuchulain. Blanad said that Curoi would bring his judgement to Emain Macha himself, and the three heroes were to return there and await him.

One evening, when Cuchulain and Conall were away from the court, as the men of Ulster were sitting in the House of the Red Branch, in came a great awkward ugly fellow: it seemed to them as if none of the men of Ulster could reach to half his height. He was frightful to look at; next to his skin he had an old cow's hide, and a grey cloak around him; and over him he had a great spreading branch the size of a winter shed under which thirty cattle could find shelter. Ravenous yellow eyes he had, and in his right hand an axe weighing fifty cauldrons of melted metal, its sharpness such that it would cut hairs, should the wind blow them against its edge. They asked his name, and what he wanted.

'Uath, the stranger, is my name, and the thing I want I cannot find, and I after going through the world of Ireland and the whole world looking for it, and that is a man that will keep his word and will hold to his agreement with me.'

'What agreement is that?' asked Fergus, son of Rogh.

'Here is this axe,' he said, 'and the man into whose hands it is put is to cut off my head today, I to cut off his head tomorrow. Let you find one among you that will hold to his word and keep to his bargain. Conchubar I put aside because of his kingship, and Fergus, son of Rogh, for the same reason. But outside these two, come, whichever of you will venture, he to cut off my head tonight, I to cut off his head tomorrow night.'

Laegaire leaped out on the floor of the hall. 'Stoop down, clown, that I may cut off your head tonight, you to cut off mine tomorrow night.'

Then Uath put spells on the edge of the axe, and laid his neck down on a block, and Laegaire struck a blow across it with an axe, till it went into the block underneath, and the head fell on the floor, and the house was filled with blood. But presently Uath rose up and gathered his head and his axe to his breast and went out from the hall, his neck streaming with blood, so that there was mortal terror on all the people in the house.

The next night the stranger returned, to have his agreement kept. But Laegaire's heart failed him, and he was nowhere to be found. Conall, however, had returned, and he said that he would make a new agreement; and all happened the same as the night before, but when Uath came again the next day, it was Conall who could not be found, his heart failing him when it came to the keeping of the bargain.

Cuchulain was there that night, and Uath came in and began to mock them all. 'Men of Ulster,' Uath said, 'all your courage and your daring is gone from you; you covet a great name, but you are not able to earn it. Where is that poor squinting fellow called Cuchulain, so that I can see if his word is any better than the word of the others?' 'I will keep my word without any agreement,' said Cuchulain. 'That may well be, you miserable fly, for it is in great fear of death you are.' Then Cuchulain made a leap towards him and gave him a blow with the axe, and hurled his head to the top rafter of the hall, so that the whole house shook.

On the morrow the men of Ulster were watching Cuchulain to see if he would break his word to the stranger, as the others had done. As Cuchulain sat there waiting for him they saw that he was very downhearted, and they were sure that his life was at an end, and that they might as well begin keening for him. And then Cuchulain said to Con- chubar, and there was hanging of his head on him, 'Do not go from this till my agreement is fulfilled, for death is coming to me, but I would sooner meet with death than break my word.'

They were there till the close of day, and then they saw Uath coming. 'Where is Cuchulain?' he said. 'Here I am,' he answered. 'It is dull your speech is tonight,' said the stranger; 'it is in great fear of death you are. But however great your fear, you have not failed me.'

Then Cuchulain went to him and laid his head on the block. 'Stretch out your head better,' said Uath. 'You are keeping me in torment,' said Cuchulain; 'put an end to me quickly. For last night, by my oath, I made no delay with you.' Then he stretched out his neck, and Uath raised his axe till it reached the rafters of the hall, and the creaking of the old hide that was about him, and the crashing of the axe through the rafters, was like the loud noise of a wood in a stormy night. But when the axe came down, it was with its blunt side, and it was the floor it struck, so that Cuchulain was not touched at all. And all the chief men of Ulster were standing around looking on, and they saw at that moment that it was no strange ugly fellow was in it, but Curoi, son of Daire, that had come to try the heroes through his enchantments.

'Rise up, Cuchulain,' he said. 'Of all the heroes of Ulster, whatever may be their daring, there is not one to compare with you in courage and in bravery and in truth. The Championship of the heroes of Ireland is yours from this out, and the Champion's Portion with it, and to your wife the first place among all the women of Ulster. And whoever tries to put himself before you after this,' he said, 'I swear by the oath my people swear by, his own life will be in danger.'

With that he left them. And this was the end of the quarrel among the heroes for the Championship of Ulster.

THE BROWN BULL OF CUAILGNE

One day Ailell, king of Connaught, quarrelled with his wife Maeve, saying that since he married her, she was much wealthier for it. So they reckoned up their belongings, those that were Ailell's on the one hand, those that were Maeve's on the other hand; and it was found that the two parts were alike, down to the last of their goods, and all the things belonging to their household, their flocks of sheep, their horses, their herds of swine out of the woods and valleys. But when it came to the counting of their cattle, they were found to be equal but for one thing only.

It happened a bull had been calved in Maeve's herd, and his name was Fionnbanach, the White-Horned. But he would not stay in Maeve's herds, for he did not think it fitting to be under the rule of a woman, and he had gone into Ailell's herds and stayed there; and now he was the best bull in the whole province of Connaught. And when Maeve saw him, and knew he was better than any bull of her own, there was great vexation on her, and it was as bad to her as if she did not own one head of cattle at all.

So she called Mac Roth the herald to her, and bade him to find out where there was a bull as good as the White-Horned to be got in any province of the provinces of Ireland. 'I myself know that well,' said Mac Roth, 'for there is a bull that is twice as good as himself at the house of Daire in the district of Cuailgne, and that is Donn Cuailgne, the Brown Bull of Cuailgne.' 'Then go to Daire without delay,' said Maeve, 'and ask the loan of that bull for a year, and I will return him at the end of the year, and fifty heifers along with him as fee for the loan; and if his people think ill of him for sending away that wonderful jewel, let Daire himself come with him, and I will give him the equal of his own lands on the smooth plain of Ai, and a chariot that is worth three times seven serving maids, and my own close friendship along with that.'

So Mac Roth went to Daire, and told him the whole story of the quarrel between Maeve and Ailell, and of the counting of their herds, and of the great rewards Maeve was offering for the loan of the Brown Bull of Cuailgne. And Daire was well pleased with his offer, and swore to send the bull, whether the men of Ulster liked it or not; and he gave a feast to Mac Roth and his company. But while they were sitting before the feast, one of Mac Roth's men boasted that if Daire had not given the loan of the bull of his own free will, then the strength of Ailell and Maeve would have brought it from him despite anything he could do. And when Daire's steward heard this boast, he told his master, and Daire answered: 'If they say that, I swear by the gods my people swear by, that they will not take him away till they take him by force.' The next day when Mac Roth asked to be shown where the bull was, Daire told him that he had heard of his men's boasting, and would not give him the bull; for all that Mac Roth said it was but the common talk of men after eating and drinking, Daire still refused to give the bull that time. And when Mac Roth came to Maeve and related what had happened, she said: 'Now we will take him from them by force.'

And this was the cause of the great war for the Brown Bull of Cuailgne.

And as the hosts set out, Maeve in her fine chariot, she saw a thing she wondered at, a woman sitting on the shaft of the chariot, facing her, a sword of white bronze in her hand, with seven rings of red gold on it, and she seemed to be weaving a web with it; and she was fair and sweet of voice, and she told Maeve that she was Fedelm of the Sidhe, and could see the future. And Maeve asked her: 'Tell me truly, what way do you see our hosts?' And Fedelm answered: 'I see crimson on them, I see red. And

I see a low-sized man doing many deeds of arms; there are many wounds on his smooth skin; there is a light about his head, there is victory on his forehead; he is young and beautiful, and modest towards women; but he is like a dragon in the battle. His appearance and his courage are like the appearance and courage of Cuchulain of Muirthemne; and who that Hound from Muirthemne may be I do not know; but I know this much well, that all this host will be reddened by him; he will make your dead lie thickly and the memory of the blood shed by him will be lasting.'

But the men of Ulster lay under a curse and a weakness put upon them because Conchubar had ill-treated the wife of a man named Crunden. Crunden had boasted that his wife could outrun the king's horses, and Conchubar had forced her to run against them, even though she was great with child; and when she won the race, the pains of childbirth came on her, and all the men of Ulster who heard her cry of anguish were cursed, save Cuchulain. And she said: 'From this out, at whatever time you most want your strength, at the time your enemies are closing on you, that is the time that the weakness of a woman in childbirth will come upon all the men of the province of Ulster.' And Cuchulain defended Ulster single-handed for many days, taunting Maeve and killing her dog, and the pine marten and pet bird that sat on her shoulders, with his slingshot; and he slew many of the best men of her army. And Maeve sent Mac Roth the herald to make him fair offers if he would stop killing her men and come over to her side; but he would not, and he made the same refusal to Fergus, who was in exile from Ulster and leading Maeve's army. But he agreed to fight one champion each day from among the men of Ireland, and Natchrantal was the first to go against him.

Natchrantal set out, but he would bring no arms with him but three times nine holly rods, and they having hardened points. Cuchulain was at that time following after a flock of wild birds, to bring some of them down for the evening's meal, and he took no notice of Natchrantal, but went on following the birds.

But Natchrantal thought that it was afraid of him he was, and he went back to Maeve's tent and said: 'That great Cuchulain there is so much talk about, is running away now after the challenge I gave him.' But Maeve did not believe him, and Fergus heard what was said; it vexed him that any man should say that Cuchulain had run before him. He sent Fiacha, son of Fiaba, to reproach him, but Cuchulain said: 'Tell me who I ran away from? Who makes this boast?' 'It is Natchrantal,' said Fiacha. 'What would Fergus have me do?' said Cuchulain; 'would he have me kill an unarmed man, bringing nothing with him but wooden rods. It is not my custom to wound unarmed men, but let him come armed to meet me on the morning of the morrow.'

So Fiacha went back to the camp, and the day seemed long to

Natchrantal till he could meet Cuchulain. But when he went out in the morning and came to the plain, he said to Cormac Conloingeas: 'Where is Cuchulain?'

'He is there before you,' said he.

'That is not the appearance that was on him yesterday,' said Natchrantal; for Cuchulain's anger had come on him so that the appearance he had was changed, and he was leaning against a pillar-stone, and in the strength of his anger, as he was throwing his cloak about him, he broke off the pillar-stone, and he never noticed it was wrapped between the cloak and himself; and Natchrantal threw his sword at him, and it broke to pieces against the pillar-stone, and then Cuchulain gave him a blow over the top of his shield that struck off his head.

As Cuchulain lay in his sleep one night a great cry from the north came to him, so that he started up and fell from his bed to the ground like a sack. He went out of his tent, and there he saw Laeg yoking the horses to the chariot. 'Why are you doing that?' he said. 'Because of a great cry I heard from the plain to the north-west,' said Laeg. 'Let us go there then,' said Cuchulain.

So they went on till they met with a chariot, and a red horse yoked to it, and a woman sitting in it, with red eyebrows and a red dress on her, and a long red cloak that fell onto the ground between the two wheels of the chariot, and on her back she had a grey spear. 'What is your name, and what is it you are wanting?' said Cuchulain. 'I am the daughter of king Buan,' she said, 'and what I have come for is to find you and offer you my love, for I have heard of all the great deeds you have done.' 'It is a bad time you have chosen for coming,' said Cuchulain, 'for I am wasted and worn out with the hardship of the war, and I have no mind to be speaking with women.' 'You will have my help in everything you do,' she said, 'and it is protecting you I was up to this, and I will protect you from this out.' 'It is not trusting to a woman's protection I am in this work I have in my hands,' said Cuchulain. 'Then if you will not take my help,' she said, 'I will turn it against you; and at the time when you will be fighting with some man as good as yourself, I will come against you in all shapes, by water and by land, till you are beaten.'

Then there was anger on Cuchulain and he took his sword and made a leap at the chariot. But on the moment chariot and horse and woman disappeared; all he saw was a black crow, and it sitting on a branch; and by that he knew that it was the Morrigan had been talking with him.

And not long after this Cuchulain killed a champion called Long; and the next day his brother Loch came to fight him, and he would not fight at the ford where his brother had been killed, but at a ford higher up the river. As they were fighting, the Morrigan came against Cuchulain with the appearance of a white, red-eared heifer, and fifty other heifers along with her, and a chain of white bronze between every two of them, and they made a rush into the ford. But Cuchulain made a cast at her, and wounded one of her eyes. Then she came down the stream in the shape of a black eel, and wound herself about Cuchulain's legs in the water, and while he was getting himself free of her, and bruising her against a green stone of the ford, Loch wounded his body. Then she took the appearance of a grey wolf, and took hold of his right arm, and while he was getting free of her, Loch wounded him again. Then great anger came on him, and he took the spear Aoife had given him, the Gae Bolg, and gave Loch a deadly wound.

But some days after, the Morrigan came to try to get healing of her wounds from him, for it was only by his own hand the wounds he gave could be healed. She took the appearance of an old woman on her, and she milking a cow with three teats. Cuchulain was passing by, and there was thirst on him, and he asked a drink, and she gave him the milk of one teat. 'May this be to the good of the giver,' he said, and with that her eye that was wounded was healed. Then she gave him milk from another teat, and he said the same words; then she gave him the milk from the third teat. 'The full blessing of the gods, and of the people of the plough, on you,' he said. And with that, all the wounds of the Great Queen were healed.

Maeve now broke her agreement to send only one man at a time against Cuchulain, though he still defeated all who challenged him, whether singly or together; but he was weary for lack of sleep. And Lugh of the Long Hand came to him from among the Sidhe, unseen by the men of Ireland, and said to him:

'Sleep now, Cuchulain, by the grave in the Lerga, and I myself will keep watch over you till the end of three days and three nights.' So Cuchulain fell asleep there and then by the grave that is in the Lerga, and no wonder in that, for he had been fighting since before the feast of Samhain without sleep, but all the while killing and attacking and destroying the men of Ireland – unless he might sleep a little while beside his spear in the middle of the day, his head on his hand, and his hand on his spear, and his spear on his knee. And while he was lying in his heavy sleep, the men of the Sidhe put druid herbs on his wounds, so that they were all healed.

While he slept, the boy troop of Ulster came from Emain Macha, and attacked Maeve's army; but though they killed three times their number, they were all killed in the end. And to revenge them, Cuchulain put on his armour, and took his spears, and his sword, and his shield that had a rim so sharp it would cut a hair against the stream, and his cloak that was made of the precious fleeces of the land of the Sidhe, that had been brought to him by Manannan from the king of Sorcha. He went out then against the men of Ireland, and attacked them, and his anger came on him, so that it was not his own appearance he had on him, but the appearance of a god. And after that he turned back and left them, and there was no wound on himself, or on the horses, or on his charioteer that day. And he made a round of the whole army, mowing men down on every side, in revenge for the boy troop of Emain.

But the next day he was standing on the hill, young, and comely, and shining, and the cloud of his anger gone from him. Then the women and the young girls in the camp, and the poets and the singers, came out to look at him; but Maeve hid her face behind a shelter of shields, thinking he might make a cast at her with his sling. And there was wonder on these women to see him so quiet and so gentle today, and he such a terror to the whole army yesterday; and they bade the men lift them up on their shields to the height of their shoulders, the way they could have a good sight of him.

Maeve sent other heroes against Cuchulain, and even forced Fergus to face him; but Cuchulain would not fight Fergus, and pretended to retreat before him. Calatin and his twenty-nine sons tried to overwhelm him by sheer numbers, but his fellow-countryman Fiacha, whom Fergus had sent to watch the fight, rescued him. At last Maeve decided to try to enlist Ferdiad, son of Daman.

For they had the same way of fighting, and it was with the same teachers they had learned the knowledge of arms, with Scathach and with Uathach and with Aoife; and neither of them had an advantage over the other, except that Cuchulain had the feat of the Gae Bolg. But Ferdiad had good armour to protect him against any man he would fight with.

So they sent messengers to bring Ferdiad, but he would not come to fight against his friend and fellow-pupil Cuchulain. Then Maeve sent the druids and the satirists to him, that they might make three hurtful satires and three hill-top satires on him, if he would not come, that would raise three blisters on his face, Shame and Blemish and Reproach, so that if he did not die on the moment, he would be dead before the end of nine days.

And Ferdiad came, for he thought it better to die by spears than by satires. Even so he would not fight, and praised Cuchulain as his friend, until Maeve taunted him with a lie: 'It is a true word that Cuchulain spoke, for he said it would be no great wonder if you would fall by him in the first trial of arms in this country.' 'He had no right to say that,' said Ferdiad, 'for it is not fear or want of skill he learned of me up to now. And I swear by my arms if it is true he said this thing, that I will be the first to fight with him tomorrow before the men of Ireland.'

Fergus went to warn Cuchulain of the coming encounter, saying that there was not the like of Ferdiad among any of the men who had fought him up to this. 'It is not easy to get the better of him,' said Fergus, 'for he is fierce in fighting, and he has the strength of a hundred.' 'There will be a sharp fight when myself and Ferdiad come to the ford,' said Cuchulain; 'it will not be without being told in stories.' 'O Cuchulain of the red sword,' said Fergus, 'it would be better to me than a great reward, you to carry proud Ferdiad's purple cloak eastward.' 'I give you my word and my oath,' said Cuchulain, 'it is I myself will get the victory over Ferdiad.'

And Cuchulain and Ferdiad fought: they met first in their chariots, and as Cuchulain leapt into his chariot, there shouted around him the Bocanachs and the Bacanachs, and the witches of the valley; for the Tuatha de Danaan would set up their shouts around him, the way the fear and the wonder would be great before him in every fight he would go into. And they welcomed each other at the first; but then they quarrelled, with bitter boasts and taunts, and each of them spoke sharp unfriendly words against the other, until Ferdiad said: 'It is too long we are delaying like this; what arms shall we use today, Cuchulain?' And Cuchulain gave him the choice of arms that day, until nightfall; and first they took their casting spears, but they were both so skilful in defence, that neither could harm the other. So they took their straight spears, and threw spears at each other from midday until the fall of evening; and each wounded the other in that time. And that night they shared their provisions and the healing herbs that were sent to them, and their horses were in one enclosure, and their chariot-drivers at the same fire.

The next day Cuchulain had the choice of arms; and he chose the great broad thrusting spears, 'for', he said, 'we shall be nearer to the end of our battle by the thrusting today than we were by the throwing yesterday.' And they wounded each other so that if it were the custom for birds in their fight to pass through the bodies of men, they could have passed through their bodies on that day, and they could have carried pieces of flesh and blood through their stabs and cuts, into the clouds and sky all around. And that night was as the previous night; they shared their provisions and the healing herbs that were sent to them, and their horses were in one enclosure, and their chariot-drivers at the same fire.

They rose up early on the morrow, and they came forward to the ford of battle. Cuchulain saw a sort of black look on Ferdiad that day. 'It is bad you are looking today, Ferdiad,' he said; 'There is a darkness on your face, and a heaviness on your eyes, and your own appearance is gone from you.' 'It is not from fear or dread of you I am like this today,' said Ferdiad; 'for there is not a champion in Ireland today I could not put down.'

And Cuchulain was fretted to see him that way, and it is what he said: 'O Ferdiad, if it is you yourself, I am sure you are a sorrowful man, to have come at the bidding of a woman to fight against your own companion.' But Ferdiad said: 'O Cuchulain, giver of wounds, true hero, every man must come in the end to the sod where his last grave should be. It was not you but Maeve that betrayed me; let you take the victory and the fame, for it is not on you that the blame is.' And Cuchulain said: 'My faithful heart is like a clot of blood; I have no strength for high deeds, fighting with you, Ferdiad.' 'Much as you are complaining over me now,' said Ferdiad, 'what arms shall we use today?' 'It is you have the choice today,' said Cuchulain, 'because it was I had it yesterday.' 'Let us then take to our swords, for we will be nearer the end of our battle by the hewing today, than we were by the thrusting yesterday.'

And then they put two long wide shields on them, and they took to their swords, and each of them continued to hack at the other, from the dawn of the early morning until the time of the fall of evening. And when they left off, it was the parting, mournful, sorrowful, downhearted, of two men that night. Their horses were not in the one enclosure that night, their chariot-drivers were not at the one fire.

And Ferdiad rose up early next morning, and went forward by himself to the ford. For he knew that day would decide the fight, and he knew one of them would fall on that day there, or they would both fall. He put on his battle suit, the shirt of striped silk, with its border of speckled gold, his coat of brown leather, his apron of purified iron, through dread of the Gae Bolg that day. He put his crested helmet of battle on his head, on which were forty carbuncles in each division, and it was studded with crystal and with shining rubies of the eastern world. And he took his spear and sword and shield, and began to show off many wonderful changing feats, that he had never learned with any other person, neither with Scathach nor with Uathach nor with Aoife, but that were made up that day by himself against Cuchulain.

Then came Cuchulain to the ford, and saw all that Ferdiad was doing. 'I see, my friend Laeg,' he said, 'all those feats will be tried on me one after another, and if because of that it is I that begin to yield today, reproach me with hard words, that my anger may grow on me. But if I have the upper hand, praise me, that my courage may be the greater.' And the choice of arms fell to Cuchulain that day; and he said 'Let us try the ford feat then.' And Ferdiad agreed with a heavy heart, for he knew that Cuchulain was used to put an end to every fighter that was against him in the feat of the ford.

It was great work, now, that was done on that day at the ford: the two champions of western Europe, the two gift-giving and wage-giving hands of the north-west of the world; the two pillars and the two keys of the courage of the Gael; to be brought from far off, to fight one against the other, through the stirring up and the meddling of Ailell and Maeve. Each of them began to throw his weapons at the other, from the dawn of early morning to the middle of midday. And when midday came, the anger of each grew hotter, and then it was that Cuchulain leaped on to the boss of Ferdiad's shield, to strike at his head over the rim of the shield. But Ferdiad gave the shield a blow of the left elbow, and threw Cuchulain from him like a bird on the brink of the ford. Laeg saw this and said, 'My grief indeed, the fighter that is against you, Cuchulain, casts you away as a light woman would cast her child, he throws you away as foam is thrown by the river, he grinds you as a mill would grind fresh malt, and from this out, you have no call nor claim to courage or a brave name to the end of life and time, you little fairy fighter.'

It is then that Cuchulain leaped up with the quickness of the wind, and with the readiness of the swallow, and with the fierceness of the lion, towards the troubled clouds of the air, until he lit on the boss of Ferdiad's shield, to strike at his head from above. But Ferdiad gave his shield a shake, and cast Cuchulain from him, the same as if he had never been cast off before at all.

And it is then Cuchulain's anger came on him, and the flames of the hero light began to shine about his head, like a red thorn bush in a gap, or like the sparks of a fire, and he lost the appearance of a man, and what was on him was the appearance of a god.

So close was the fight they made now, that their heads met above and their feet below, and their hands in the middle, over the rims and bosses of their shields. So close was the fight, that they broke and loosened their shields from the rim to the middle. So close was the fight, that they turned and bent and shattered their spears from the points to the hilts. So close was the fight, that the Bocanachs and Bacanachs and the witches of the valley screamed from the rims of their shields and from the hilts of their swords, and from the handles of their spears. So close was the fight, that they drove the river out of its bed and out of its course, so that it might have been a place for a king or a queen to rest in, so that there was not a drop of water in it, unless it dropped into it by the trampling and the hewing the two champions made in the middle of the ford.

So great was the fight, that the horses of the men of Ireland broke away in fright and shyness, with fury and madness, breaking their chains and their yokes, their ropes and their traces; and the women and the young lads and the children and the crazy and the followers of the men of Ireland broke out of the camp to the south-west.

They were using the edge of their swords through that time; and it was then Ferdiad found a time when Cuchulain was off his guard, and he gave him a stroke of the sword, and hid it in his body, and the ford was reddened with Cuchulain's blood, and Ferdiad kept on making great strokes at him. And Cuchulain could not bear with this, and he called to Laeg for the Gae Bolg, and it was sent down the stream to him, and he caught it with his foot. And when Ferdiad heard him call for the Gae Bolg, he made a stroke of his shield down to protect his body. But Cuchulain made a straight cast of the Gae Bolg, from the middle of his hand, and it passed through his armour and went out through his body, so that its sharp end could be seen.

Ferdiad gave a stroke of his shield up to protect the upper part of his body, but it was 'The relief after danger', as the saying is. 'That is enough,' said Ferdiad; 'I die by that. And I may say, indeed, you have left me sick after you, and it was not right that I should fall by your hand. O Hound of the Beautiful Feats, it was not right, you to kill me; the fault of my death is yours, it is on you my blood is. I am going away, my end is come. My ribs will not hold my heart, my heart is all turned to blood. I have not done well in the battle; you have killed me, Cuchulain.'

Cuchulain ran to him after that, and put his two arms about him, and lifted him across the ford northwards, so that his body should be by the ford on the north, and not on the west of the ford with the men of Ireland. He laid him down then, and a cloud and a weakness came over him as he stood over Ferdiad. Laeg saw that, and he saw that all the men of Ireland were rising up to come towards him.

'Good Cuchulain,' said Laeg, 'rise up now, for the men of Ireland are coming towards us, and it is not one man they will put to fight against us now that Ferdiad has fallen by you.' 'What use is it to me to rise up now, and he after falling by me?' said Cuchulain. But Laeg said: 'Rise up, O chained Hound of Emain; it is glad and shouting you have a right to be now, since Ferdiad of the hosts has fallen by you.' 'What are joy and shouting to me now?' said Cuchulain; 'it is to madness and to grief I am driven after the thing I have done, and the body I wounded so hard.' 'It is not right for you to be lamenting him,' said Laeg. 'It is making rejoicings over him you should be. It was at you he aimed his spears.' But Cuchulain said: 'Even if he had cut one arm and one leg from me, it is my grief Ferdiad not to be riding his horses through the long days of his lifetime.'

And Cuchulain began to keen and to lament for Ferdiad there, and it was he made the lament over Ferdiad, not any of the women of Ferdiad's race and house, for it was Scathach, his teacher who had bound them to friendship together. 'It is a sorrowful thing has happened to us the pupils of Scathach, he to have died, myself to be alive and strong; it is angry we were in the battle,' said Cuchulain. 'And, Laeg,' he said, 'Every other fight I ever made was as a game and a sport until Ferdiad came to the ford; we had the same ways, we used to do the same deeds; it was at the one time that Scathach gave a shield to me, and a shield to Ferdiad. Now this thing will hang over me for ever: yesterday Ferdiad was larger than a mountain; today there is nothing of him but a shadow.'

And then the men of Ulster awakened from the weakness and sleeping that had fallen on them because of the curse of the wife of Crunden upon the men of Ulster. And they set out in their strength, and came to the hill of Sleamhain, to fight against the men of Ireland.

Then the men of Ulster began to gather upon the plain in their full strength, and when Ailell heard it, he said: 'Let someone go up and watch them coming, and bring us a report of the appearance that is on them, and of the chief men that are leading them.' 'Let Mac Roth go,' said Fergus. So Mac Roth went out, and took a post on the plain from the early light of the morning till the fall of evening, and through all that time the men of Ulster were coming, so that the ground was not naked under them, every division under its own chief man, and every troop under its own lord, and each one of them apart from the others, and they came on till they had covered the hill of Sleamhain.

And when evening came, Mac Roth came back to Ailell and Maeve, and they questioned him and said: 'What sort were the men of Ulster as they came across the plain?' And Mac Roth said: 'The first troop I saw coming had three thousand men in it, and as soon as they got to the hill, they took the armour off, and they began to dig and to make a seat on the highest part of the hill for their leader to sit on until the rest of the army would come. He had the appearance of a tall, proud man, used to giving orders, and he had a yellow forked beard, and a red, pleasant face, and blue eyes you would be afraid to meet. A five-folded crimson cloak he had on him, and a gold pin over his breast, and a white shirt with threads of gold woven into it next his body.'

'Who was that man, Fergus?' said Ailell. 'He was Conchubar, son of Fachtna and of Ness, High King of Ulster.' 'There was a man stood beside him,' said Mac Roth, 'with scattered white hair and a purple cloak, and a shield with bosses of red brass, and a long iron sword of foreign make. And he looked up to the sky, and threw his hand upwards, and with that the clouds seemed like as if they were rushing at one another, and fire came from them towards the men of Ireland.' 'That was Cathbad the Druid,' said Fergus, 'and he trying by his enchantments to know how the battle would go tomorrow.'

'I saw another man with Conchubar,' said Mac Roth, 'and he having a smooth dark face and white eyes in his head; a long bronze rod in his hand, and a little bell beside him, and when he touched it with his rod, all the people near him began to laugh.' 'Who is that man?' said Ailell. 'It is easy to know that,' said Fergus, 'That is Rocmid, the king's fool. There was never trouble or tiredness on any man of Ulster that he would not forget if he saw Rocmid.'

'There came another troop then,' said Mac Roth, 'and it is what I thought, that the leader they had was the handsomest and the most comely of all the men of Ireland, tall and well formed. Deep red-yellow hair he had, his face wide at the top and narrow below; thin red lips and grey eyes that were laughing. A red and white cloak on him, that the wind stirred as he walked, a long dark green spear in his hand.' 'Who was that man, Fergus?' said Ailell. 'That man is himself half an army, Rochad, son of Fatheman, from Rachlainn, in the north', said Fergus.

'There was another troop came then,' said Mac Roth, 'and a quiet grey-haired man at the head of it. A dark-green, long-woolled cloak he had about him, and a white shirt, and a silver belt around his waist, and a bell branch at his shoulder. He sat before king Conchubar when he came to the hill, and his whole company sat about him. And the sound of his voice when he spoke before the king, and when he was advising him, was sweeter than a three-cornered harp in the player's hand.' 'Who was that man, Fergus?' said Ailell. 'That was Sencha the orator, the best-spoken of all the men of the whole world, and the peace-maker of the army of Ulster,' said Fergus; 'and the whole of the men of the world, from the rising to the setting of the sun, he would pacify with his three fair words. But by my word, it is no cowardly counsel that man will give his king today, but counsel of courage, and of strength, and of battle.'

'There came another troop,' said Mac Roth, 'and a man at the head of them, and it would not be easy to find a man with a better appearance, or with hair more like gold than what he has. There was a sword with an ivory hilt in his hand, and he throwing it up and catching it in his hand again, as it was coming on the heads of the people near him.' 'That is Aithirne, the poet and satirist,' said Fergus. It was said he was very covetous, and that he would ask the one-eyed man for his one eye, and that the rivers and the lakes went back before him when he made a satire on them, and rose when he praised them.

'I saw another troop coming,' said Mac Roth, 'wild-looking, and in the middle of it a young little lad, red and freckled. He had a silk shirt on him with a border of red gold, and a shield faced with gold, with a golden rim, and a little bright gold sword at his side.' 'Who is that, Fergus?' said Ailell. 'I do not remember leaving any such boy as that when I left Ulster,' said Fergus, 'but it is likely it may be Erc, son of Cairbre, that has come without leave of his father to help his grandfather, Conchubar, and the men of Teamhair with him. And if what I think is true, you will find that troop to be a drowning sea, and it is by that troop and by that little boy the battle will be won against you.'

'I saw another company coming,' said Mac Roth, 'and a great many in it; and they red with the fire of their anger, strong and eager and destroying. At their head an angry man, dreadful to look at, long-nosed, large-eared, with coarse grey hair; a striped cloak on him, an iron skewer in place of a brooch, a coarse striped shirt next his skin, a great spear in his hand.' 'I know that man,' said Fergus; 'Celthair, son of Uthecar; a head of battle in Ulster. And the spear in his hand is the great spear, the Luin, that was brought back from the East by the three sons of Tuireann.'

'I saw the troop that came last,' said Mac Roth, 'and it without a leader. There were thirty hundred in it, of proud clean ruddy men; long fair hair they had, and shining eyes, and long shining cloaks with good brooches, blue shining spears, good coverings on their heads, and shirts of striped silk. But they seemed to have some great trouble on them, and to be very downhearted.' 'What men are those, Fergus?' said Ailell. 'I know them well,' said Fergus. 'It is well for those on whose side they are, and it is a pity for those they are against; for they are able by themselves to fight the whole army of Ireland; for they are Cuchulain's men from Muirthemne.'

All this time Cuchulain was lying on his bed, with the dint of his wounds. But when he knew by the noise on the plain that the men of Ulster were gathering for the battle, he used all his strength and tried to rise up; and he gave a great shout, that all his own troop heard it, and all the whole army. But his people that were about him laid him down on the bed again by force, and put ropes and fastenings over him, the way he could not move from it to open his wounds again. And as he was lying there, two mocking women came from Ailell's camp, and stood beside his bed, and let on to be crying and lamenting; and it is what they told him, that the men of Ulster were beaten, and that Conchubar was killed and that Fergus was killed along with him. And in the night the Morrigan came like a lean, grey-haired hag, shrieking from the one army to the other, hopping over the points of their weapons, to stir up anger between them, and she called out that ravens would be picking men's necks on the morrow.

And with all this outcry, Cuchulain could not sleep, and when the day began to break, he said to Laeg: 'Look out now, and bring me word of everything that happens on this day.' So Laeg looked out, and he said: 'I see a little herd of cattle breaking out from the west of Ailell's camp, and there are lads following after them and trying to bring them back; and I see more lads coming out from the army of Ulster to attack them.' 'That little herd on the plain is the beginning of a great battle,' said Cuchulain, 'for it is the Brown Bull of Cuailgne and his heifers are in it, and now the young men of the east and of the west will come out against one another. And go now, Laeg,' he said, 'for I cannot go out myself, and call the men of Ulster, and stir them up to the battle.' So Laeg went out and called to them in Cuchulain's name to get themselves ready and to come out to the battle.

When the men of Ulster heard that message from Cuchulain, they rose up, and rushed out without stopping to put on their clothing, but only taking their weapons in their hands; and such of them as had the door of their tents facing eastwards did not wait to go through it, but broke out to the west.

But Conchubar was not in such haste to bring his own men out, but he said to Sencha: 'Keep them back till the right time will have come, when the sun will have lighted all the valleys and hills.'

Then Laeg went to look out again, and he saw the army of Ireland coming out to meet the men of Ulster, and there began a great fight between them, and it went on a good while without one side getting the better of the other. But when Maeve saw the battle going on, and neither side getting the victory, she called to Fergus, and she said: 'It is time for you, Fergus, to go out and avenge yourself on your enemy Conchubar; and besides that,' she said, 'it is right for you to go and fight for us now, after all the good treatment you got from us in Connaught.' 'I would go out willingly,' said Fergus, 'if I had my own sword again, the Caladcholg, the sword that Leite brought from the country of the Sidhe.' Then Ailell said to his chariot-driver, Ferloga: 'Go now and bring Fergus's sword that I bade you to hide away.'

So Ferloga brought the sword, and put it in Fergus's hand, and Fergus gave it a great welcome. 'Come now out into the battle, Fergus,' said Maeve, 'and spare no one today, unless it might be some very dear friend.'

Then Fergus and Maeve and Ailell went out into the battle, and three times they made the army of Ulster go back before them. And when Conchubar heard his people were being driven back, he called out to the household of the Red Branch: 'Let you hold the place I am in now, till I go to see who has turned back our men against us three times on the north side.' And the men of the Red Branch called back to him: 'We will do that, and unless the sky should fall on us, or the earth give way under us, we will not give up one inch of ground before the men of Ireland till you come to us again, or till we get our death.'

Then Conchubar went to see who it was that was driving back his army, and it was Fergus he found before him; and Fergus struck three great blows on Conchubar's shield, the Ochain, so that the shield screamed out loud, and all the shields of the army of Ulster screamed with it, and the three great waves of Ireland answered it.

Then Fergus said: 'Who is it is holding his shield against me?'

And Conchubar knew then who was before him, and he cried out: 'It is the man, Fergus, that is greater and more comely and younger and better than yourself, the man whose father and mother were better than your own; the man that put to death the three great candles of the valour of the Gael, the three prosperous sons of Usnach, in spite of your guarantee and your protection; the man that banished you out of your own country; the man that made your house a dwelling place for deer and foxes; the man that never left you so much as the breadth of your foot of land in Ulster; the man that drove you to the entertainment of a woman; and the man that will drive you back today in the presence of the men of Ireland, Conchubar, son of Fachtna Fathach, High King of Ulster, the High King of Ireland.'

When Fergus heard that, he took his sword, the Caladcholg, in his two hands, and he was swinging it over his head that it seemed to have the size and appearance of a rainbow, and he was about to give his three great strokes on the men of Ulster.

But Conchubar's son, Cormac Conloingeas, saw what he was doing, and he made a rush at Fergus, and put his arms about his knees, and he said: 'Do not put out your great strength, my master Fergus, to destroy the whole army of Ulster.' 'Let me go,' said Fergus, 'for I will not live through the day unless I strike my three blows on the men of Ulster.' But Cormac Conloingeas would not leave off from asking him, and then he said: 'Tell Conchubar to go back to his own place in the battle, and I will spare the army.' So Conchubar went back, and then Fergus struck his three blows on three little hills that were near him, and cut their tops off, and they are called 'The three bare hills of Meath' to this day.

But when Cuchulain heard the scream of Conchubar's shield the time Fergus struck it, he called out to Laeg: 'Who has dared to strike those three blows upon the Ochain, and I still living?' 'It is Fergus, son of Rogh, struck them', said Laeg. 'Where is the battle going on now?' said Cuchulain. 'The armies are come to Gairech,' said Laeg. 'By my hand of valour,' said Cuchulain, 'They will not have reached to Ilgairech before I will be with them.'

With that he put out all his strength, and he broke the ropes that were about him, and threw them off, and he scattered the grass that was on his wounds into the high air. And the two mocking women were there yet, and he dashed them one against the other, and left them there on the ground. And he looked for his arms, but he could see none of them; but only his chariot that was lying broken there. And he took hold of a shaft of it, and rushed, with all his wounds, straight into the battle, till he found Fergus, and he called to him to go back before him now, as he had promised he would do. But Fergus gave him no answer.

Then Cuchulain said: 'Go back, now, Fergus, or by the oath of my people, I will grind you to pieces as a mill grinds the malt.' Then Fergus said, 'Do not be giving out threats to me, for my army is well able to match the army of Ulster.' 'You gave me your promise, Fergus,' said Cuchulain, 'To go back before me when we would meet in the great battle, and when I would be covered in wounds. You bound yourself to that the time I went back before you, and you without your sword.'

Then Fergus, when he heard that, went back three steps, and then he turned, and his men with him, and gave way before Cuchulain. And all the men of Ireland turned when they saw that, and broke out of their ranks, and ran over the hill westward, and Cuchulain and the men of Ulster followed after them, making a great slaughter.

And Cuchulain came up with Maeve, and she called out: 'A gift to me, Cuchulain.' 'What is it you are asking of me?' he said. 'Take what is left of my army under your protection, and let it pass over the great ford westward.' So he agreed to do that, and what was left of the army of

Ireland went over the great ford of the Shannon at Athluain, and Maeve and Ailell and Fergus, and the Maines and the sons of Magach stayed to the last, and drew their shields of protection behind the men of Ireland, till they had got back to Cruachan in Connaught, the place they set out from. And as Fergus watched the men of Ireland escaping, he said: 'This army is swept away today; it is wandering and going astray, not knowing what path to take. And it is following the lead of a woman has brought it into this distress.' And so ended the battle, and so ended the war for the Brown Bull of Cuailgne.

But as the army returned to Connaught, the Brown Bull and the White-Horned met and fought. As soon as the bulls caught sight of one another, they pawed the earth so furiously that they sent the sods flying, and their eyes were like balls of fire in their heads; they locked their horns together, and they ploughed up the ground under them and trampled it, and they were trying to crush and to destroy one another through the whole length of the day.

Then when the night was coming on, Cormac Conloingeas took hold of a spear-shaft, and he laid three great strokes on the Brown Bull from head to tail, and he said: 'This is a great treasure to be boasting of, that cannot get the better of a calf of his own age.' When the Brown Bull heard that insult, great fury came on him, and he turned on the White-Horned again. And all through the night the men of Ireland were listening to the sound of their bellowing, and they going here and there, all through the country.

On the morrow, they saw the Brown Bull coming over Cruachan from the west, and he carrying what was left of the White-Horned on his horns. Then Maeve's sons rose up to make an attack on him on account of the Connaught bull he had destroyed. 'Where are those men going?' said Fergus. 'They are going to kill the Brown Bull of Cuailgne.' 'By the oath of my people,' said Fergus, 'if you do not let the Brown Bull go back to his own country in safety, all he has done to the White-Horned is little to what I will do now to you.'

Then the Brown Bull bellowed three times, and set out on his way. And when he came to the great ford of the Shannon, he stopped to drink, and the two loins of the White-Horned fell from his horns into the water. And that place is called Ath-luain, the ford of the loin, to this day. And its liver fell in the same way into a river of Meath, and it is called Ath-Truim, the ford of the liver, to this day.

Then he went on till he came to the top of Slieve Breagh, and when he looked from it he saw his own home, the hills of Cuailgne; and at the sight of his own country, a great spirit rose up in him, and madness and fury came on him, and he rushed on, killing everyone that came in his way.

And when he got to his own place, he turned his back to a hill and he gave out a loud bellowing of victory. And with that his heart broke in his body, and blood came bursting from his mouth, and he died.

CUCHULAIN'S SON

The time Cuchulain came back from Alban, after he had learned the use of arms under Scathach, he left Aoife, the queen he had overcome in battle, with child. And when he was leaving her, he told her what name to give the child, and he gave her a gold ring, and bade her keep it safe till the child grew to be a lad, and till his thumb would fill it; and he bade her to give it to him then, and to send him to Ireland, and he would know he was his son by that token. She promised to do so, and with that Cuchulain went back to Ireland.

It was not long after the child was born, word came to Aoife that Cuchulain had taken Emer to be his wife in Ireland. When she heard that, great jealousy was on her, and great anger, and her love for Cuchulain was turned to hatred; and she remembered her three champions that he had killed, and how he had overcome herself, and she determined in her mind that when her son would come to have the strength of a man, she would get her revenge through him. She told Conlaoch her son nothing of this, but brought him up like any king's son; and when he was come to sensible years, she put him under the teaching of Scathach, to be taught the use of arms and the art of war. He turned out as apt a scholar as his father, and it was not long before he had learnt all Scathach had to teach.

Then Aoife gave him the arms of a champion, and bade him go to Ireland, but first she laid three commands on him: the first never to give way to any living person, but to die sooner than be made to turn back; the second, not to refuse a challenge from the greatest champion alive, but to fight him at all risks, even if he was sure to lose his life; the third, not to tell his name on any account, though he might be threatened with death for hiding it. She put him under *geasa** not to do these things.

Then the young man, Conlaoch, set out, and it was not long before his ship brought him to Ireland, and the place he landed at was Baile's Strand, near Dundealgan. It chanced that Conchubar, the High King, was holding his court there at that time; when word was brought to him that there was a ship come to the strand, and a young lad in it armed as if for fighting, and armed men with him, he sent one of the chief men of

---

* *Geasa* is somewhere between a solemn bond and a magical spell. To break a *geasa* was to invite terrible consequences; the death of Cuchulain is attributed in some versions to his breaking a *geasa* against him. The *geasa* could be a kind of taboo against certain quite inconsequential acts as well as an injunction not to betray the highest form of trust. *Ed.*

his household to ask his name, and on what business he had come. The messenger's name was Cuinaire, and he went down to the strand, and when he saw the young man he said: 'A welcome to you, young hero from the east, with the merry face. It is likely, seeing you come armed as if for fighting, you are gone astray on your journey; but as you are come to Ireland, tell me your name and what your deeds have been, and what your victories in the eastern bounds of the world.'

'As to my name,' said Conlaoch, 'it is of no great account; but whatever it is, I am under *geasa* not to tell it to the stoutest man living.'

'It is best for you to tell it at the king's desire,' said Cuinaire, 'before you get your death through refusing it, as many a champion from Alban and from Britain has done before now.'

'If that is the order you put on us when we land here, it is I will break it,' said Conlaoch, 'and no one will obey it any longer from this out.'

So Cuinaire went back and told the king what the young lad had said. Then Conchubar said to his people: 'Who will go out into the field, and drag the name and the story out of this young man?' 'I will go,' said Conall, for his hand was never slow in fighting. And he went out, and found the lad angry and destroying, handling his arms, and they attacked one another with a great noise of swords and shouts, and they were gripped together, and fought for a while, and the praise that was on Conall, it was on the head of Conlaoch it was now.

Word was sent then to where Cuchulain was, in pleasant, bright-faced Dundealgan. And the messenger told him the whole story, and he said: 'Conall is lying humbled, and it is slow the help is in coming; it is a welcome there would be before the Hound.'

Cuchulain rose up then and went to where Conlaoch was, and he still handling his arms. And Cuchulain asked him his name and said: 'It would be well for you, young hero of unknown name, to loosen yourself from this knot, and not to bring down my hand upon you, for it will be hard for you to escape death.'

But Conlaoch said: 'If I put you down in the fight, the way I put down your comrade, there will be a great name on me; but if I draw back now, there will be mockery on me, and it will be said I was afraid of the fight. I will never give in to any man to tell the name, or to give an account of myself. But if I was not held to a *geasa*, there is no man in the world I would sooner give it to than to yourself, since I saw your face. But do not think, brave champion of Ireland, that I will let you take away the fame I have won for nothing.'

With that they fought together, and it is seldom such a battle was seen, and all wondered that the young lad could stand so well against Cuchulain. So they fought a long while, neither getting the better of the other, but at last Cuchulain was charged so hotly by the lad that he was forced to give way, and although he had fought so many good fights, and killed so many great champions, and understood the use of arms better than any man living, he was pressed very hard.

And he called for the Gae Bolg, and his anger came upon him, and the flames of hero-light began to shine about his head, and by that sign Conlaoch knew him to be Cuchulain, his father. And just at that time he was aiming his spear at him, and when he knew it was Cuchulain, he threw the spear crooked that it might pass beside him. But Cuchulain threw the Gae Bolg at him with all his might, and it struck the lad in the side and went into his body, so that he fell to the ground.

And Cuchulain said: 'Now, boy, tell your name and what you are, for it is short your life will be, for you will not live after that wound.'

And Conlaoch showed the ring that was on his hand, and he said: 'Come here where I am lying on the field, let my men from the east come round me. I am suffering for revenge. I am Conlaoch, son of the Hound, heir of dear Dundealgan; I was bound to this secret in Dun Scathach, the secret in which I have found my grief.'

And Cuchulain said: 'It is a pity your mother not to be here to see you brought down. She might have stretched out her hand to stop the Gae Bolg that wounded you.' And Conlaoch said, 'My curse be on my mother, for it was she put me under a *geasa*, it was she sent me here to try my strength against yours.' And Cuchulain said: 'My curse be on your mother, a woman full of treachery; it is through her harmful thoughts these tears have been brought on us.' And Conlaoch said: 'My name was never forced from my mouth until now; I never gave an account of myself to any man under the sun. But, O Cuchulain of the sharp sword, it was a pity you not to know me the time I threw the slanting spear behind you in the fight.'

And then the sorrow of death came upon Conlaoch, and Cuchulain took his sword and put it through him, sooner than leave him in the pain and punishment he was in. And then great trouble and anguish came on Cuchulain, and he made this lament: 'It is a pity it is, O son of Aoife, that ever you came into the province of Ulster, that you ever met with the Hound of Cuailgne. If I and my fair Conlaoch were doing feats of war on the one side, the men of Ireland from sea to sea would not be equal to us together. It is no wonder I to be under grief when I see the shield and the arms of Conlaoch. A pity it is there is no one at all, a pity there are not hundreds of men on whom I could get satisfaction for his death.

'It is a pity it was not one on the plains of Munster, or in Leinster of the sharp blades, or at Cruachan of the rough fighters, that struck down my comely Conlaoch.

'It is a pity it was not in the country of the Cruithne, of the fierce Fians, you fell in a heavy quarrel, or in the country of the Greeks, or in some other place of the world you died, and I could avenge you; there would not then be this death in my heart.

'It is very well for the men of Alban, it was not they destroyed your fame; and it is well for the men of the Gael.

'It is bad that it happened; it is on me is the misfortune, O Conlaoch of the Red Spear, I myself to have spilled your blood. I to be under defeat, without strength. It is a pity Aoife never taught you to know the power of my strength in the fight. It is no wonder I to be blinded after such a fight and such a defeat.

'It is no wonder I to be tired out, and without the sons of Usnach beside me. Without a son, without a brother, with none to come after me; without Conlaoch, without a name to keep my strength.

'I am the father that killed his son, the fine green branch; there is no hand or shelter to help me.

'I am a raven that has no home; I am a boat going from wave to wave; I am a ship that has lost its rudder; I am the apple left on the tree; it is little I thought of falling from it; grief and sorrow will be with me from this time.'

Then Cuchulain stood up and faced all the men of Ulster. 'There is trouble on Cuchulain,' said Conchubar; 'he is after killing his own son, and if I and all my men were to go against him, by the end of the day he would destroy every man of us. Go now,' he said to Cathbad the Druid, 'and bind him to go down to Baile's Strand, and to give three days fighting against the waves of the sea, rather than to kill us all.'

So Cathbad put an enchantment on him, and bound him to go down. And when he came to the strand, there was a great white stone before him, and he took his sword in his right hand, and he said: 'If I had the head of the woman that sent her son to his death, I would split it as I split this stone.' And he made four quarters of the stone.

Then he fought with the waves three days and three nights, till he fell from hunger and weakness, so that some men said he got his death there. But it was not there that he got his death, but on the plain of Muirthemne.

THE ENEMIES OF CUCHULAIN

Now after all the battles he had fought, and all the men he had killed, it is no wonder he had a good share of enemies watching to get the upper hand of him. And besides Maeve, those that had their minds most set against him were Erc, whose father Cairbre Niafer he had killed at Rosnaree, and Lugaid, whose father Curoi he had killed in his own house in Munster, and the three daughters of Calatin.

This, now, was the way it happened that Curoi got his death by him. He met with Blanad one time, a good while after Curoi had given him the Championship of Ulster, and it is what she told him that there was not a man on the face of the earth she loved more than himself. And she bade him come, near Samhain time, to Curoi's dun at Finglas, and his men with him, and to bring her away by force.

So when the time came, Cuchulain set out, and his men with him, and they came to a wood near the dun, that had a stream running through it, and he sent word to Blanad he was waiting there. And Blanad sent him back word to come and bring her away at whatever time he would see the stream in the wood turning white. And when what she thought to be a good time came, when all the men of the place were sent out looking for stones to build a great new dun, she milked the three white cows with red ears Curoi had brought away by force from her father Midhir, and she poured a great vessel of new milk into the stream where it ran by the dun. And when Cuchulain saw the stream turning white, he went up to the dun. But he found Curoi there before him, and they fought, and Curoi was killed, the son of Daire, lord of the southern sea, that had a great name and great praise on him before Blanad was his wife.

Then Cuchulain brought Blanad away with him to Ulster. But Curoi's poet Feirceirtne followed after them to avenge his master's death. And when they were come as far as the headland of Cian Beara, he saw Blanad standing on the edge of a high rock, and she alone. And he went up to her, and took her in his arms, and threw her, and himself along with her, over the rock, and they both got their death by the fall on the moment.

And as to the children of Calatin, this is the way it was with them. At the time Cuchulain made an end of Calatin at the ford, and of all his sons with him, Calatin's wife was with child. And when her time came, there were three daughters born at the one birth, and they deformed, and each of them having one eye.

Then Maeve came from Cruachan to visit them, and she brought away the children with her, and took the charge of them. And when they were come to sensible years, she came to see them, and she said: 'Do you know who it was killed your father?' 'We know well,' they said, 'it was Cuchulain, son of Sualtim, killed him.' 'That is so,' said Maeve, 'and let you make a journey now', she said, 'Through the whole world, to get knowledge of spells and enchantments from them that have it, the way you will be able to avenge your father when the time comes.'

When the three one-eyed daughters of Calatin heard that, they went out into Alban, and to every other country, from the rising to the setting of the sun, and they were learning every sort of enchantment and of witchcraft. And at the end they came back to Cruachan.

And as to Maeve, she went up one morning to her sunny parlour, and from there she saw the three daughters of Cruachan sitting on the grass outside. So she took her cloak, that had the beautiful embroidery on it, and put it about her, and went out and bade them welcome, and asked news of all they had done since they left Ireland. And they told her all they had learned. 'Do you remember it all?' said Maeve. 'We remember it well,' they said, 'and we can do many things, and we can make the appearance of terrible battles by secret words.'

And then Maeve sent word to Lugaid, and he came to Cruachan and himself and Maeve began to talk together. 'Do you remember', she said, 'who it was killed Curoi your father?' 'I remember it well,' he said, 'it was Cuchulain killed him.' Then Erc came to her, and she asked him the same question about his father Cairbre Niafer, and he made the same answer, for Cuchulain had slain him with his spear Dubach, the grim one, and had cut off his head and shaken it before the two armies, the time they fought at Rosnaree. 'What you say is true,' Maeve said then, 'and the children of Calatin are come back to me now, after going through the whole world, to fight against Cuchulain with their enchantments. And there is no king or chief man or fighting man in the four provinces of Ireland, but lost his friend or his comrade, his father or his brother, by him in the war for the Bull of Cuailgne, or at some other time. And now', said she, 'it is best for us to gather a great army of the men of Ireland to make an attack on him, for the men of Ulster have their weakness coming on them, and it is likely that they will not be able to help him.'

With that, Lugaid went away southward to the king of Munster, to bid him come and bring his men with him; and Erc went and called to the chief men of Leinster in the same way.

Then all the provinces gathered together to Cruachan, and they stopped there with feasting and merriment for three days and three nights. And at the end of that time they went out of Cruachan. But Maeve did not bring Fergus with them this time, for she was sure the men of Ireland would never be able to make an end of Cuchulain if Fergus was along with them.

And they went their way to the borders of Ulster; and Conchubar, king of Ulster got word that the borders of his province were being robbed and destroyed by the men of Munster and Leinster, and of Connaught. 'Where is Levarcham?', said Conchubar. 'I am here,' she said. 'Go out for me now,' said Conchubar, 'and bring Cuchulain here to Emain; for it is against him that this army is gathered. If he can put off this battle till I myself, and Conall, and all the men of Ulster, will be ready to go out with him, we will give them a great defeat, the way they will not come into my province again. For there are many bear him ill-will, on account of all he killed: Finn mac Ross, Fraoch mac Idath, and many of the best men of Ulster; and Cairbre Niafer at the battle of Rosnaree; and Curoi, son of Daire, High King of Munster, and many of the men of Munster besides him; and many more along with them.'

Levarcham found Cuchulain, between sea and land, on Baile's Strand, and he trying to bring down sea-birds with his sling; but with all the birds that were flying over him and past him, he could not bring one down, but they all escaped him. And there was heaviness on him, not to be able to hit them, for he knew it had some bad meaning. And indeed he had never been very happy in his mind since the death of the blossomed branch, Aoife's son, there on that strand.

Then he saw Levarcham coming, and he bade her welcome. 'I am glad of that welcome', said Levarcham, 'and it is with news from Conchubar I am come to you.' 'What is your news?' said Cuchulain. And then she told him all that Conchubar had said: 'And it is what all are asking of you,' she said: 'chief men and fighting men, poets and learned men, women and young girls, to keep aside from the men of Ireland that are coming here to Muirthemne, and not to go out alone against that great army.' 'I would sooner stop here and defend my own place,' said Cuchulain.

'It is best for you to go to Emain,' she said.

So after a while he gave in, and they went back to Dundealgan, and Emer came out to meet them, and they gave her the same advice, to go to Emain Macha where Conchubar and his chief men were gathered together. Then Emer got her chariot, and she sent her servants and the herds and the cattle to Slieve Cuillenn, and herself and Cuchulain set out for Emain. And that was the first time Dundealgan was emptied since Cuchulain had the sway over it.

And Conchubar bade Cathbad, and the learned men, and the women, to keep a good watch on Cuchulain, and to mind him well. 'For I leave the charge of him on you,' he said, 'To save him from the plans Maeve has made against him, and from the power of the children of Calatin. For if he should fall,' he said, 'it is certain the safety and the prosperity of Ulster will fall with him for ever.' 'That is true,' said Cathbad. 'Well,' said Geanann, Cathbad's son, 'I will go now and see him.' He went then to the place Cuchulain and Emer were, and the poets, and the women, and the learned men with them, and a feast laid out on the table, and all of them at drinking and pleasantness and games.

Now as to the men of Ireland, they came to the plain of Muirthemne, and they made their camp there, and they began to destroy and to take all they could find there, and in Macaire Conall; and when they knew Cuchulain had left Dundealgan, it is then the three daughters of Calatin went with the lightness and quickness of the wind to Emain Macha. And they sat down on the lawn outside the house where Cuchulain was, and they began to tear up the earth and the grass, and by means of their witchcraft they put the appearance of troops of men and of armies on stalks and coloured oak-leaves and the heads of dandelions; and the sounds of fighting and striking, and the shouting of a great army were heard on every side, as if there was an attack being made on the dun.

It was bright-faced Geanann, son of Cathbad, was keeping a watch on Cuchulain that day, and he saw him sit up and look out on the lawn, and redness and shame came on his face, when he saw, as he thought, two armies fighting one another, and he put out his hands as if to take his sword, but Geanann threw his two arms about him and hindered him, and told him there was nothing before him but witchcraft and enchantment, and the appearance of fighting made up by the children of Calatin to bring him out to his death. And Cathbad and all the learned men came then and told him the same thing. But after all that, it was hardly they were able to hold him back and to persuade him.

The next day Cathbad himself came to keep a watch on him with the rest, and after a while the noise of shouting began again, and for all they could do, Cuchulain went to see what it was. And the first thing he thought he saw was the army of Ireland standing there upon the plain. And then he thought he saw Gradh, son of Lir, standing there; and after that he thought he heard the harp of the son of Meardha playing the sweet music of the Sidhe; and he knew when he heard those sounds that his time was come, and that his courage and his strength would soon be made an end of. And then one of the daughters of Calatin took the appearance of a crow, and came flying over him and saying mocking words, and she bade him go out and save his own house and his lands from the enemies that were destroying them. And though Cuchulain knew well by this time it was witchcraft was being worked against him, he was as ready as before to rush out when he heard the sounds; and there came trouble and confusion on his mind with the noise of striking and of fighting, and with the sweet sounds of the harp of the Sidhe. But Cathbad did his best with him, and it is what he told him; that if he would but stop quiet for another three days in Emain, the power of the enchantments would be broken, and Conall Cearnach would have come to his help, and he could go out again, and the whole world would be full of his name and of his lasting victories.

And on the morning of the morrow, Conchubar called for Cathbad and bright-faced Geanann, and the rest of the druids. And Emer came along with them, and Celthair's daughter, Niamh, that Cuchulain loved, and the rest of the women of the House of the Red Branch. And Conchubar asked them in what way they could best keep a watch on Cuchulain through the day.

'We do not know that,' they said.

'I will tell you what is best to do,' said Conchubar then. 'Bring him away with you to Glean-na-Bodhar, the Deaf Valley. For if all the men of Ireland were letting out shouts and cries of war around it, no one that would be in that valley would hear any sound at all. Bring Cuchulain there, then,' he said, 'and keep him there with you till their enchantments will be spent, and till Conall Cearnach will come to his help out of the island of Leodus.'

'King,' said Niamh, 'we were asking him and persuading him all through yesterday to go to that valley, but he would not go there, for all

I myself or the rest of the women of Ireland could say. And let you yourself go to him now', she said, 'with Cathbad, and Geanann, and the poets, and with Emer, and let you bring him into that valley, and let there be music and pleasantness made about him there, the way he will not hear the shouts and the mocking words of the children of Calatin.' 'It is not I will go with him,' said Emer, 'but let Niamh go, and my blessing with her, for it will be hard for him to refuse her.'

Then Cathbad went out to Cuchulain, and said, 'Dear son, come with me today to use the feast I am making, and all the women and the poets will come with us. And there is a *geasa* on you not to refuse my feast.' 'My grief for that,' said Cuchulain. 'This is no fit time for me to be feasting and making merry, and the four provinces of Ireland burning and destroying Ulster, and the men of Ulster in their weakness, and Conall away, and the men of Ireland putting insults on me and reproaches, and saying I have run away before them. And but for yourself and Conchubar, I would fall on them and scatter them, that their dead would be more than their living.'

Then all the women persuaded him, and Emer spoke to him, and it is what she said: 'Little Hound, I never hindered you until this hour from any deed or any adventure you had a mind for. So now for my sake, my chosen heart, my first love and my first darling of the men of the world, go with Cathbad and with Geanann, with Niamh and with the poets, to share Cathbad's feast.'

Then Niamh went over to him and gave him three fond, loving kisses; and then they all rose up, and he along with them, heavy and sorrowful, and in that way he went in their company into Glean-na-Bodhar. And when they came into it, he said, 'My grief! that I should ever have come here; for now the men of Ireland will be saying it was to escape them I came here.' 'You gave me your word', said Niamh, 'That you would not go out to meet the men of Ireland without leave from me.' 'If I gave it,' said Cuchulain, 'it is right that I should hold to it.'

Their chariots were unyoked then, and the Grey of Macha and the Black Sainglain were let loose to graze in the valley, and they all went to the house Cathbad had made ready. And there was a great feast laid out, and Cuchulain was put in the chief place, and to his right hand were Cathbad and Geanann and the poets, and on the left was Niamh, daughter of Celthair, with the women. And then they all took to feasting and drinking and to game, and they made a great show of mirth and music and pleasantness before Cuchulain.

But as to the three deformed, one-eyed children of Calatin, they came quickly and lightly, the way they had come on the other days, to the lawn at Emain, to the place where they had got sight of Cuchulain in the house. And when they did not see him there, they searched through the whole of Emain, but when they did not find him with Conchubar, or with the men of the Red Branch, there was great wonder on them. And then they began to think it was Cathbad was hiding him from them, and they rose up high in the air, on a blast of moaning wind they made by their enchantments, and on it they went over the whole province, searching out every wood and every valley, every cave and secret path. But nothing they found, till at last they came above Glean-na-Bodhar, and there in the midst of the valley they saw the Grey of Macha, and the Black Sainglain, and Laeg, son of Riangabra, beside them.

They knew then that Cuchulain must be in the valley, and presently they heard the sounds of music and of laughter and of women's voices, where all the people in the feasting-house were trying their best to raise the cloud and the heaviness off Cuchulain's mind.

Then the children of Calatin came down into the valley, and the same way as before they took thistle-stalks and oak-leaves and the heads of dandelions and put on them the appearance of troops of armed men, so that there seemed to be no hill or no place outside the whole valley but was filled with battalions, coming hundred by hundred. And the air was all filled with sounds of battle and shouts, and of trumpets and dreadful laughter, and the cries of wounded men. And there seemed to be fires in the country about, and a noise of the crying of women. And great dread came on all that heard that outcry.

But when the women that were with Cuchulain heard those shouts, they shouted back again, and raised their voices, but with all they could do, they did not keep the outcry from reaching to Cuchulain. 'My grief!' he said, 'I hear the shout of the men of Ireland that are spoiling the whole of the province; my fame is at an end, my great name is gone from me, Ulster is put down for ever.' 'Let the noise pass by,' said Cathbad; 'it is only the noise made by the children of Calatin, that want to draw you out from where you are, to make an end of you. Stop here with us now, and put the trouble off your mind.'

Cuchulain stayed quiet then, but the children of Calatin went on a long time filling the air with battle noises. But they tired of it at last, for they saw that Cathbad and the women were too much for them. Then anger came on Badb, one of Calatin's daughters, and she said: 'Go on now, making sounds of fighting in the air, and I myself will go into the valley; for even if I get my death by it, I will speak with Cuchulain.'

With that, she went in the madness of anger to the very house where the feast was going on, and there she took the appearance of a woman of Niamh's household, and she beckoned Niamh out to speak with her. So Niamh came out, thinking she had news to give her, and a good many of the other women of Emain with her, and Badb bade them follow her. And she led them a long way down the valley, and then by her magic raised a thick mist, so that they could not find their way back, but were astray in the valley.

And she herself put on the appearance of Niamh, and went back to the feasting-house; and she came in to where Cuchulain was and called out: 'Rise up, Cuchulain; Dundealgan is burned, Muirthemne is destroyed, and Conaille Muirthemne. The whole province is trampled down by the men of Ireland. And it is on myself the blame will be laid,' she said, 'and all Ulster will say that I hindered you from going out to check the army, and to get satisfaction from the men of Ireland. And it is from Conchubar himself I will get my death on account of that.' For she knew that Cuchulain had given Niamh his promise that without leave from her, he would not go out to face the men of Ireland.

'It is hard to trust in women!' said Cuchulain then. 'For I thought that you would not have given me that leave for the whole riches of the world. But since you give me leave to go out and face the men of Ireland, I will do it.' And as he rose to go out, he threw his cloak about him, and his foot caught in the cloak, and the gold brooch that was in the cloak pierced his foot. 'Truly the brooch is a friend that gives me a warning,' said Cuchulain.

He went out then and bade Laeg yoke the horses and make ready the chariot. And Cathbad and Geanann and the women followed him out, and took hold of him, but they were not able to stop him. For the cries of battle were still in the air, and he thought he saw a great army standing on the lawn at Emain, and the whole plain crowded with troops and bands of men, with horses and arms and armour, and he thought that he saw all Conchubar's city burning, and all the hills round Emain full of booty, and he thought he saw Emer's sunny house thrown down, and the House of the Red Branch a tongue of fire, and all Emain ablaze under a pall of smoke.

And Cathbad tried to quiet him. 'Dear son, for this day only do not go out against the men of Ireland, and I will be able to save you from all the enchantments of the children of Calatin.' But Cuchulain said: 'Dear master, there is no reason for me to care for my life from this out, for my time is at an end, and Niamh has given me leave to go and face the men of Ireland.' And then Niamh herself came up and said, 'For grief, my little Hound, I would never have given you that leave for all the riches of the world; and it was not I that did that, but Badb, the daughter of Calatin, taking my shape upon her.' But Cuchulain would not believe her, but bade Laeg yoke the chariot, and put his armour in order. Laeg went to do that, but indeed that time above all others he had no mind for the work. And when he shook the bridles toward the horses as he was used to do, they went away from him; and the Grey of Macha would not let him come near him at all. So Laeg called out Cuchulain to speak to the Grey himself; and the horse turned his left side to his master three times. And Cuchulain reproached the horse: 'You were not used to behave like that to me,' he said. Then the Grey of

Macha came up to him and he let big round tears of blood fall on Cuchulain's feet.

Then the chariot was yoked; and it was the Morrigan had unyoked it and had broken it the night before, for she did not want Cuchulain to go out and get his death in battle. And Cuchulain set out and came to Emain, and to the house where Emer was, and she came out and bade him come down from the chariot. 'I will not,' he said, 'until I go first to Muirthemne to attack the four great provinces of Ireland, and to avenge all the hurts and insults they have put on me, and on Ulster, for I have seen their gatherings and their armies.' 'Those were made by enchantments,' said Emer. 'I tell you, woman,' he said, 'and I swear by my word, I will never come back here until I have made an attack upon them in their camp.'

Then he turned his chariot towards the south, by the road of Meadhon Luachair, and Levarcham cried out after him, and the three times fifty queens that were in Emain Macha, and that loved him, cried out upon him in their misery, and beat their hands together, for they knew that he would not come back to them again.

Cuchulain went on then to the house of his mother Dechtire to bid her farewell; and she brought out wine in a vessel to him, as her custom was when he passed that way. But when he took the vessel in his hand, it was red blood that was in it. 'For grief, Dechtire my mother, it is no wonder others forsake me when you yourself offer me a drink of blood.' And she filled the vessel a second and a third time, but each time when she gave it to him, there was nothing in it but blood. Then anger came on Cuchulain, and he broke the vessel against a rock, and said: 'The fault is not yours, mother, but my luck is turned against me, and my life is near its end; I shall not come back alive this time from facing the men of Ireland.' And she did all she could to turn him back and wait until Conall came to his aid. 'I will not wait, whatever you say, for I will not give up my great name and courage for all the riches of the world. From the day I first took arms to this day, I have never drawn back from a fight or a battle. And it is not now I will begin to draw back,' he said, 'for a great name outlasts life.'

Then he went on his way, and Cathbad caught up with him. And presently they came to a ford, and there they saw a young girl, thin and white, with yellow hair, washing and washing, and wringing out clothing that was stained crimson red, and she crying and keening all the time. 'Little Hound,' said Cathbad, 'do you see what it is that young girl is doing? It is your clothes that she is washing, and weeping as she does so, because she knows you are going to your death against Maeve's great army. And take the warning now and turn back again.'

'Dear master,' said Cuchulain, 'you have followed me far enough; for I will not turn back from my vengeance on the men of Ireland that are come to burn and to destroy my house and my country. And what is it to me, the woman of the Sidhe to be washing red clothing for me? It is not long till there will be clothing enough and armour and arms lying in pools of blood, by my own sword and my spear. If you are loath to let me go into the fight, I am glad to go into it, though I know as well as you that I must fall in it. Do not hinder me now; if I stay or if I go, death will meet me all the same. But go to Emain, to Conchubar and to Emer, and bring them life and health from me, for I will never go back to meet them again. And, Laeg, we are going away under trouble and under darkness from Emer now, when we often came back to her with gladness out of strange places and far countries.'

Then Cathbad left him, and he went on his way. And after a while he saw three hags, and they blind of the left eye, before him in the road, and they having a venomous hound they were cooking with charms on rods of the rowan-tree. And he was going by them, for he knew it was not for his good that they were there.

But one of the hags called to him: 'Stop a while with us, Cuchulain.' 'I will not stop with you,' said Cuchulain. 'That is because we have nothing better than a dog to give you,' said the hag. 'If we had a grand cooking-hearth, you would stop and visit us; but because it is only a little we have to offer you, you will not stop. But he that will not show respect for the small, though he is great, will get no respect himself.' Then he went over to her, and she gave him the shoulderblade of the dog out of her left hand, and he ate it out of his left hand. And he put it down on his left thigh, and the hand that took it was struck down, and the thigh he put it on was struck through and through, so that the strength that was in them before left them.

Then he went down to meet the army of the men of Ireland, and as he came towards them, Erc, son of Cairbre, saw him in his chariot, and his sword shining red in his hand, and the light of his courage plain upon him, and his hair spread out like threads of gold that change their colour on the anvil under the smith's hand, and the crow of battle in the air over his head.

'Cuchulain is coming at us,' said Erc to the men of Ireland, 'and let us be ready for him.'

So they made a fence of shields linked together, and Erc put a couple of the men that were strongest here and there, to pretend to be fighting one another, that they might call Cuchulain to them; and he put a druid with each pair, and he told the druid to ask Cuchulain's spears of him, for it would be hard for him to refuse a druid. For it was in the prophecy of the children of Calatin that a king would be killed by each one of those spears in that battle.

And he bid the men of Ireland to give out shouts, and Cuchulain came against them in his chariot, doing his three thunder feats, and he used his spear and his sword in such a way, that their heads and their hands and their feet and their bones were scattered over the plain of Muirthemne, like the sands on the shore, like the stars in the sky, like the dew in May, like snowflakes and hailstones, like leaves of the tree, like buttercups in a meadow, like grass under the feet of cattle on a fine summer day. It is red that plain was with the slaughter Cuchulain made when he came crashing over it.

Then he saw one of the men that was put to quarrel with the other, and the druid called to him to come and hinder them, and Cuchulain leaped towards them. 'Your spear to me,' cried the druid. 'I swear by the oath of my people', said Cuchulain, 'you are not so much in want of it as I am in want of it myself. The men of Ireland are upon me', he said, 'and I am upon them.' 'I will put a bad name on you if you refuse it to me,' said the druid. 'There was never a bad name put on me yet, on account of any refusal of mine,' said Cuchulain, and with that he threw the spear at him, and it went through his head, and it killed the men that were on the other side of him.

Then Cuchulain drove through the host, and Lugaid, son of Curoi, got the spear. 'Who is it will fall by this spear, children of Calatin?' said Lugaid. 'A king will fall by it,' said they.

Then Lugaid threw the spear at Cuchulain's chariot, and it went through and hit the driver, Laeg, son of Riangabra, and he fell back, and his bowels came out on the cushions of the chariot. 'It is hard I am wounded,' said Laeg. Then Cuchulain drew the spear out, and Laeg said his farewell to him. Cuchulain said: 'Today I will be a fighter and a chariot-driver as well.'

Then he saw the other two men that were put to quarrel with one another, and one of them called out that it would be a great shame for him not to give him his help. Then Cuchulain leaped towards them. 'Your spear to me, Cuchulain,' said the druid. 'I swear by the oath my people swear by', said he, 'you are not in such want of the spear as I am myself, for it is by my courage, and by my arms, that I have to drive out the four provinces of Ireland that are sweeping over Muirthemne today.' 'I will put a bad name upon you,' said the druid. 'I am not bound to give more than one gift in the day, and I have paid what is due to my name already,' said Cuchulain. Then the druid said: 'I will put a bad name on the province of Ulster, because of your refusal.' Cuchulain answered: 'Ulster was never dispraised yet for any refusal of mine, or for anything I did unworthily. Though little of my life should be left to me, Ulster will not be reproached for me today.' With that he threw his spear at him, and it went through his head, and through the heads of the nine men that were behind him, and Cuchulain went through the host as he did before.

Then Erc, son of Cairbre Niafer, took up his spear. 'Who will fall by this?' he asked the children of Calatin. 'A king will fall by it,' they said. 'I heard you say the same thing of the spear that Lugaid threw a while ago,' said Erc. 'That is true,' said they, 'and the king of the chariot-drivers of Ireland fell by it, Cuchulain's driver Laeg, son of Riangabra.' With that, Erc threw the spear, and it went through the Grey of Macha. Cuchulain drew the spear out, and they said farewell to one another. And the Grey went away from him, with half his harness hanging from his neck, and he went into Glas-Linn, the grey pool in Slieve Fuad.

Then Cuchulain drove through the host, and he saw the third couple disputing together, and he went between them as he did before. And the druid asked his spear of him, but he refused him. 'I will put a bad name on you,' said the druid. 'I have paid what is due to my name today,' said Cuchulain. 'I will put a bad name upon Ulster because of your refusal.' 'I have paid what is due for the honour of Ulster.' 'Then I will put a bad name on your kindred,' said the druid. 'The news that I have been given a bad name shall never go back to that place; I myself am never to return there, for it is little of my life that is left to me,' said Cuchulain. With that he threw the spear at him, and it went through him, and through the heads of the men that were alongside him.

'You do your kindness unkindly, Cuchulain,' said the druid as he fell. Then Cuchulain drove through the host for the last time, and Lugaid took the spear and he said: 'Who will fall by this spear, children of Calatin?' 'A king will fall by it,' they said. 'I heard you saying that a king would fall by the spear Erc threw a while ago.' 'It is true, for the Grey of Macha fell by it, that was king of the horses of Ireland.'

Then Lugaid threw the last spear, and the spear went through and through Cuchulain's body, and he knew that he had got his death-wound; and his bowels came out on the cushions of the chariot, and his only horse went away from him, the Black Sainglain, with half the harness hanging from his neck, leaving his master, king of the heroes of Ireland, to die upon the plain of Muirthemne.

Then Cuchulain said: 'There is great desire on me to go to that lake beyond, and to get a drink from it.' 'We will give you leave to do that', they said, 'if you will come back to us after.' 'I will bid you come for me if I am not able to come back myself,' said Cuchulain.

Then he gathered up his bowels into his body, and he went down to the lake. He drank his fill, and he washed himself, and he turned back again to his death, and he called to his enemies to come and meet him.

There was a stone pillar west of the lake, and his eye lit on it, and he went to the pillar and tied himself to it with his breast-belt, the way he would not meet his death lying down, but standing up. Then his enemies surrounded him, but they were in dread of going close to him, for they were not sure but he might still be alive.

Then the Grey of Macha came back to defend Cuchulain so long as there was life in him and the hero-light shining above him. And the Grey of Macha made three attacks against them, and he killed fifty men with his teeth, and thirty with each of his hoofs. And a bird came and settled on Cuchulain's shoulder. 'That is not a pillar on which birds were used to settle,' said Erc.

Then Lugaid came and lifted up Cuchulain's hair from his shoulders, and struck his head off, and the men of Ireland gave three great heavy shouts. The sword fell from Cuchulain's hand, and as it fell, it struck off Lugaid's right hand, which also fell to the ground. Then they cut off Cuchulain's hand, in satisfaction for it; and the light faded from about Cuchulain's head, leaving it as pale as the snow of a single night. Then all the men of Ireland said that as it was Maeve had gathered the army, it would be right for her to bring away the head to Cruachan. 'I will not bring it with me; it is for Lugaid that struck it off to bring it with him,' said Maeve. And so Lugaid and his men brought away Cuchulain's head and his right hand, and went southward.

At that time the army of Ulster was gathering to attack its enemies, and Conall was out before them, and he met the Grey of Macha, and his share of blood dripping from him. And then he knew that Cuchulain was dead, and himself and the Grey of Macha went looking for Cuchulain's body. And when they saw his body at the pillar-stone, the Grey of Macha went and laid his head in Cuchulain's breast. 'That body is a heavy care to the Grey of Macha,' said Conall.

Then Conall went after the army, thinking in his own mind what way he could get satisfaction for Cuchulain's death. For it was a promise between himself and Cuchulain that whichever of them would be killed the first, the other would get satisfaction for his death, within the same day, before the blood was cold on the ground. And he followed Lugaid down to the river Liffey.

Lugaid was going down to bathe in the water, but he said to his chariot-driver: 'Look out there over the plain, for fear that anyone comes at us unknown.' The chariot-driver looked around him and said: 'There is a man coming on us, and it is in great haste he is coming. All the ravens in Ireland are flying over his head, and there are flakes of snow speckling the ground before him.' 'It is not in friendship the man comes that is coming like that,' said Lugaid. 'It is Conall Cearnach it is, with Dub-dearg, and the birds that you see after him are the sods the horse has scattered from his hooves, and the flakes of snow are the froth that he scatters from the bit of his bridle. Look again, and see what way he is coming.' 'It is to the ford he is coming, where the army passed over,' said the chariot-driver. 'Let him pass by us,' said Lugaid, 'for I have no mind to fight with him.'

But when Conall came to the middle of the ford, he saw Lugaid and his chariot-driver, and he went over to them. 'Welcome is the sight of a debtor's face,' said Conall. 'The man you owe a debt to is asking payment of you now, and I myself am that man: you killed my comrade Cuchulain, and I am standing here now, to get that debt paid.' So they agreed to fight it out there, and in the fight Conall wounded Lugaid with his spear. 'I would like that you would give me fair play,' said Lugaid. 'What fair play?' said Conall Cearnach. 'That you and I should fight with one hand, for I have the use of but one hand.' 'I will do that,' said Conall. Then Conall's hand was bound to his side with a cord, and then they fought for a long time, and neither got the better of the other. And when Conall was not gaining on him, his horse Dub-dearg came up to Lugaid and took a bite out of his side.

'Misfortune on me,' said Lugaid, 'it is not right or fair that is, Conall!' 'It was for myself I promised to do what is right and fair,' said Conall. 'I made no promise for a beast that is without schooling and without sense.'

'It is well I know you will not leave me till you take my head, as I took Cuchulain's head from him,' said Lugaid. 'Take his head, then, along with my head. Put my kingdom with your kingdom, and my courage with your courage, for I would like that you would be the best champion in Ireland.'

Then Conall made an end of him, and he went back, bringing Cuchulain's head with him to the stone pillar where his body was. And by that time Emer had got word of all that had happened, and that her husband had got his death by the men of Ireland and the powers of the children of Calatin. For Levarcham had met Conall Cearnach on his way, who had bidden her bring the news to Emain Macha; and there she found Emer, and she sitting in her upper room, looking over the plain for some word from the battle. And Emer and her women went to the place where Cuchulain's body was, and they gathered round it there, and gave themselves over to keening and crying and weeping and burning tears.

And when Conall came back to that place, he laid the head with the body of Cuchulain, and he began to lament along with them, and it is what he said: 'It is Cuchulain had prosperity on him and a root of valour from the time he was but a soft child; there never fell a better hero than the hero that fell by Lugaid's hand. Until all the chief men of Ireland are fallen by me, it is not fitting that there should ever be peace. And it is grief to me, he to have gone into the battle without Conall being at his side; it was a pity for him to get here without my body beside his body. He was my foster-son, and now the ravens are drinking his blood; there will not be either laughter or mirth, since the Hound has gone astray from us.'

'Let us bury Cuchulain now,' said Emer.

'It is not right to do that until I have avenged him on the men of

Ireland.' And rage and madness came on Conall, and he went forward in his chariot to follow after the rest of the men of Ireland, the same way as he had followed after Lugaid.

And Emer took the head of Cuchulain in her hands, and she washed it clean, and she held it to her breast, and she began to cry with heaviness over it, and said: 'It is long that it was showed me in a vision of the night that Cuchulain would fall by the men of Ireland, and his shield split from lip to border, and his sword and his spears broken in the middle; and I saw Conall doing deeds of death before me, and myself and yourself in the one death. And oh! my love, we were often in one another's company, and it was happy for us; for if the world had been searched from the rising of the sun to sunset, the like would never have been found in one place, the Black Sainglain and the Grey of Macha, and Laeg the chariot-driver, and myself and Cuchulain. And it is breaking my heart is in my body, to be listening to the pity and the sorrowing of women and men, and the harsh crying of the young men of Ulster keening Cuchulain, and Ulster to be in its weakness and without strength to revenge itself upon the men of Ireland.'

And she brought Cuchulain's body to Dundealgan, and they keened and cried about him until the time that Conall Cearnach came back from making his red rout through the army of the men of Ireland. And when he returned with his men, they made no rejoicing, but brought the heads of the men of Ireland with him, and laid them out before the house; and the people gave three great shouts when they saw the heads. And Conall told Emer all he had done in vengeance for Cuchulain, and how among the heads were the heads of Erc, son of Cairbre, king of Meath; of yellow-haired Maine, son of Maeve, slain with all his people; of Laigaire and Clar Cuilt, who had wounded Cuchulain; of Lugaid himself, who had struck down the Hound, and of the daughters of Calatin, the enemies of the Hound, wise in enchantments, killed with their weapons in their hands.

And when Emer had seen the vengeance that Conall had wreaked on the men of Ireland for the sake of his foster-son Cuchulain, she said: 'O Conall, lift me now to my grave. Raise my stone over the grave of the Hound, for it is through grief for him that I go to my death; and lay my mouth to the mouth of Cuchulain. I am Emer of the Fair Form; there is no vengeance left that I may take; there is no man left that I love. It is sorrowful that my stay is after the Hound.'

And Emer bade Conall make a wide and very deep grave for Cuchulain; and she laid herself down beside her gentle comrade, and she put her mouth to his mouth, and she said: 'Love of my life, my friend, my sweetheart, my only choice of the men of this world, many are the women, wed or unwed, envied me, until today; and now I will not stay living after you.'

And her life went out from her, and she herself and Cuchulain were laid in the one grave by Conall, and the one stone over them; and he wrote their names there, and he himself and all the men of Ulster keened them.

But the three times fifty queens that loved Cuchulain saw him appear in his druid chariot, going through Emain Macha; and the song that he sang was the song of the Sidhe.

19. THE FOUR BRANCHES OF THE MABINOGI

The Welsh word mabinogi *originally meant 'youthful deeds', and gradually came to apply to the whole of a hero's exploits. The* Four Branches of the Mabinogi, *to give them their correct title, were written down in the fourteenth century, but probably date in their present form from the eleventh century. Originally, it has been argued, the common link was the career of Pryderi, whose birth takes place in the first story, and whose death occurs early in the last story. As the story has come down to us, he plays no part in the action of the second branch, but the third branch deals with his imprisonment in the otherworld. If the stories break off and characters disappear without apparent reason, this is in part due to the confused nature of what has reached us; but this suspension of ordinary laws of cause and effect, of deed and consequence, is also an inherent part of the tales. We are probably dealing with fragments of the ancient mythology of the Celts, as well as folklore, and the by now familiar tales designed as explanations of place-names. The identification of the individual characters with particular deities is a game best played by scholars; we have little to go on as to the names and nature of the Celtic pantheon.* Rhiannon *may be the Great Mother,* Modron; *Pryderi may be her son* Mabon *or* Maponos *in another guise: we cannot say for certain.*

But whatever hand chance has played in the construction of the final version, these are magical stories in every sense, with a sense not only for the marvellous but for the telling, everyday detail; the unknown author has a fine sense for drama and for character, and it is the people of the Mabinogi, Pryderi, Rhiannon, Manawyddan and the treacherous flower-woman Blodeuwedd, who remain in our memory once the last page is turned.

PWYLL, PRINCE OF DYFED

Pwyll, prince of Dyfed, was lord of the seven cantrefs* of Dyfed; and once upon a time he was at Arberth his chief palace, and he was minded to go and hunt, and the part of his dominions in which it pleased him to hunt was Glyn Cuch. So he set forth from Arberth that night, and went as far as Llwyn Diarwyn. And that night he tarried there, and early on the morrow he rose and came to Glyn Cuch, when he let loose the dogs in the wood, and sounded the horn, and began the chase. And as he followed the dogs, he lost his companions; and whilst he listened to the hounds, he heard the cry of other hounds, a cry different from his own, and coming in the opposite direction.

And he beheld a glade in the wood forming a level plain, and as his dogs came to the edge of the glade, he saw a stag before the other dogs. And lo, as it reached the middle of the glade, the dogs that followed the stag overtook it and brought it down. Then he looked at the colour of the dogs, without looking at the stag, and of all the hounds that he had seen in the world, he had never seen any that were like unto these. For their hair was of a brilliant shining white, and their ears were red; and as the whiteness of their bodies shone, so did the redness of their ears glisten. And he came towards the dogs, and drove away those that had brought down the stag, and set his own dogs upon it.

And as he was setting on his dogs he saw a horseman coming towards him upon a large light-grey steed, with a hunting horn round his neck, and clad in garments of grey woollen in the fashion of a hunting garb. And the horseman drew near and spoke to him thus.

'Chieftain,' said he, 'I know who thou art, and I greet thee not.' 'Perhaps', said Pwyll, 'Thou art of such dignity that thou shouldest not do so.' 'Truly,' answered he, 'it is not my dignity that prevents me.' 'What is it then, chieftain?' asked he. 'By heaven, it is because of your own ignorance and want of courtesy.' 'What discourtesy, chieftain, hast thou seen in me?' 'Greater discourtesy saw I never in man', said he, 'Than to drive away the dogs that were killing the stag and to set upon it your own. This was discourteous, and though I may not be revenged upon thee, yet I declare to heaven that I will do thee more dishonour than the value of an hundred stags.' 'O chieftain,' he replied, 'if I have done ill I will redeem thy friendship.' 'How wilt thou redeem it?' 'According as thy dignity may be, but I know not who thou art?' 'A crowned king am I in the land whence I come.' 'Lord,' said he, 'may the day prosper with thee, and from what land comest thou?' 'From Annwfn,' answered he; 'Arawn,

---

* Literally, 'a hundred towns', the equivalent of the medieval English 'hundred' as a division of a shire. *Ed*.

king of Annwfn, am I.' 'Lord,' said he, 'how may I gain thy friendship?' 'You may do so after this manner,' he said. 'There is a man whose dominions are opposite to mine, who is ever warring against me, and he is Hafgan, also king in Annwfn, and by ridding me of this oppression, which thou canst easily do, shalt thou gain my friendship.' 'Gladly will I do this,' said he. 'Show me how I may.' 'I will show thee; see, this is how you may do it. I will make firm friendship with thee; and this will I do. I will send thee to Annwfn in my stead, and I will give thee the fairest lady thou didst ever behold to be thy companion, and I will put my form and semblance upon thee, so that not a page of the chamber, nor an officer, nor any other man that has always followed me shall know that it is not I. And this shall be for the space of a year from tomorrow, and then we will meet in this place.' 'Yes,' said he; 'but when I shall have been there for the space of a year, by what means shall I discover him of whom thou speakest?' 'One year from this night', he answered, 'is the time fixed between him and me that we should meet at the ford; be thou there in my likeness, and with one stroke that thou givest him, he shall no longer live. And if he ask thee to give him another, give it not, how much soever he may entreat thee, for when I did so, he fought with me next day as well as ever before.' 'Truly,' said Pwyll, 'what shall I do concerning my kingdom?' Said Arawn, 'I will cause that no one in all thy dominions, neither man nor woman, shall know that I am not thou, and I will go there in thy stead.' 'Gladly then', said Pwyll, 'will I set forward.' 'Clear shall be thy path, and nothing shall detain thee, until thou come into my dominions, and I myself will be thy guide!'

So he conducted him until he came in sight of the palace and its dwellings. 'Behold', said he, 'The court and the kingdom in thy power. Enter the court, there is no one there who will know thee, and when thou seest what service is done there, thou wilt know the customs of the court.'

So he went forward to the court, and when he came there, he beheld sleeping-rooms, and halls, and chambers, and the most beautiful buildings ever seen. And he went into the hall to change out of his hunting clothes, and there came youths and pages and took his cloak, and all as they entered saluted him. And two knights came and drew his hunting-dress from about him, and clothed him in a vesture of silk and gold. And the hall was prepared, and he saw the household and the host enter in, and the host was the most comely and the best equipped that he had ever seen. And with them came in likewise the queen, who was the fairest woman that he had ever yet beheld. And she had on a yellow robe of shining satin; and they washed and went to the table, and sat, the queen upon one side of him, and one who seemed to be an earl on the other side.

And he began to speak with the queen, and he thought, from her speech, that she was the seemliest and most noble lady of converse and of cheer that ever was. And they partook of meat, and drink, with songs and with feasting; and of all the courts upon the earth, behold, this was the best supplied with food and drink, and vessels of gold and royal jewels.

And the time came for them to go to bed, and they went to their sleeping-quarters. As soon as they got into bed, he faced away from her, turning his back to her. And he spoke no word to her until morning. In the morning there was converse and good cheer between them. Whatever love was between them during the day, not a single night to the end of the year was any different from that first night.

And the year he spent in hunting, and minstrelsy, and feasting, and diversions, and discourse with his companions until the night that was fixed for the conflict. And when that night came, it was remembered even by those who lived in the furthest part of his dominions, and he went to the meeting, and the nobles of the kingdom with him. And when he came to the ford, a knight arose and spake thus. 'Lords,' said he, 'listen well. It is between two kings that this meeting is, and between them only. Each claims of the other his land and territory, and do all of you stand aside and leave the fight to be between them.'

Thereupon the two kings approached each other in the middle of the ford, and encountered, and at the first thrust, the man who was in the stead of Arawn struck Hafgan on the centre of the boss of his shield, so that it was cloven in twain, and his armour was broken, and Hafgan himself was borne to the ground an arm's and a spear's length over the crupper of his horse, and he received a deadly blow.

'Chieftain,' said Hafgan, 'what right hast thou to cause my death? I was not injuring thee in anything, and I know not wherefore thou wouldest slay me. But, for the love of heaven, since thou hast begun to slay me, complete thy work.' 'Ah, chieftain,' he replied, 'I may yet repent doing that unto thee; whoever gives thee another blow, I will not do so.' 'My trusty lords,' said Hafgan, 'bear me hence. My death has come. I shall be no more able to uphold you.' 'My nobles,' also said he who was in the semblance of Arawn, 'Take counsel and discover who ought to be my subjects.' 'Lord,' said the nobles, 'all should be, for there is no king over the whole of Annwfn but thee.' 'Yes,' he replied, 'it is right that he who comes humbly should be received graciously, but he that doth not come with obedience, shall be compelled by the force of swords.' And thereupon he received the homage of the men, and he began to conquer the country; and the next day by noon the two kingdoms were in his power. And thereupon he went to keep his tryst, and came to Glyn Cuch.

And when he came there, the king of Annwfn was there to meet him, and each of them was rejoiced to see the other. 'Truly,' said Arawn, 'may heaven reward thee for thy friendship towards me. I have heard of it. When thou comest thyself to thy dominions', said he, 'Thou wilt see that which I have done for thee.' 'Whatever thou hast done for me, may heaven repay it thee.'

Then Arawn gave to Pwyll, prince of Dyfed, his proper form and semblance, and he himself took his own; and Arawn set forth towards the court of Annwfn; and he was rejoiced when he beheld his hosts, and his household, whom he had not seen so long; but they had not known of his absence, and wondered no more at his coming than usual. And that day was spent in joy and merriment; and he sat and conversed with his wife and his nobles. And when it was time for them rather to sleep than to carouse, they went to rest.

And Arawn got into bed, and his wife followed him. The first thing he did was to talk to his wife, and take his loving pleasure with her. And she had not been accustomed to that for a year, and thought to herself, 'Ah God, what new thought has he had tonight after a whole year?' And she thought for a long while, and then he woke up, and spoke to her, not once but twice and three times; and she would not answer. 'Why', said he, 'do you not speak to me?' 'I tell thee', she said, 'for a whole year I have not said as much as this in this place.' 'Well then,' he said, 'now we have talked closely together.' 'Shame on me', she said, 'if for a year since last night, after we were beneath the bedclothes, there has been either speech or delight between us; you have not even turned your face towards me.' And he was silent, and lost in thought. Then he said, 'O Lord God, I found a true comrade indeed, who did not swerve from his fellowship with me.' And then he told her all his story. 'By my confession to God,' she said, 'you had a strong hold on a comrade, if he could keep such faith with thee and avoid the temptations of the flesh.' 'Lady, that was what I thought when I was silent just now.' 'Nor was it strange that you should think that,' she answered.

Pwyll, prince of Dyfed, came likewise to his country and dominions, and began to enquire of the nobles of the land, how his rule had been during the past year, compared with what it had been before. 'Lord,' said they, 'Thy wisdom was never so great, and thou wert never so kind or so free in bestowing thy gifts, and thy justice was never more worthily seen than in this year.' 'By heaven,' said he, 'for all the good you have enjoyed, you should thank him who hath been with you; for behold, thus hath this matter been.' And thereupon Pwyll related the whole unto them. 'Truly, lord,' said they, 'render thanks unto heaven that thou hast such a fellowship, and withhold not from us the rule which we have enjoyed for this year past.' 'I take heaven to witness that I will not withhold it,' answered Pwyll.

And thenceforth they made strong the friendship that was between them, and each sent unto the other horses and greyhounds, and hawks, and all such jewels as they thought would be pleasing to each other. And by reason of his having dwelt that year in Annwfn, and having ruled there so prosperously, and united the two kingdoms in one day by his valour and prowess, he lost the name of Pwyll, prince of Dyfed, and was called Pwyll, chief of Annwfn, from that time forward.

Once upon a time, Pwyll was at Arberth his chief palace, where a feast had been prepared for him, and with him was a great host of men. And after the first meal, Pwyll arose to walk, and he went to the top of a mound that was above the palace, and was called Gorsedd Arberth. 'Lord,' said one of the court, 'it is peculiar to the mound that whosoever sits upon it cannot go thence, without either receiving wounds or blows, or else seeing a wonder.'

Pwyll answered, 'I fear not to receive wounds and blows in the midst of such a host as this, but as to the wonder, gladly would I see it. I will go therefore and sit upon the mound.' And upon the mound he sat. And while he sat there, they saw a lady, on a pure white horse of large size, with a garment of shining gold around her, coming along the highway that led from the mound; and the horse seemed to move at a slow and even pace, and to be coming up towards the mound.

'My men,' said Pwyll, 'is there any among you who knows yonder lady?' 'There is not, lord,' said they. 'Go one of you and meet her, that we may know who she is.' And one of them arose, and as he came upon the road to meet her, she passed by, and he followed as fast as he could, being on foot; and the greater was his speed, the further was she from him. And when he saw that it profited him nothing to follow her, he returned to Pwyll, and said unto him, 'Lord, it is idle for anyone in the world to follow her on foot.' 'Truly,' said Pwyll, 'go unto the palace, and take the fleetest horse that thou seest, and go after her.'

And he took a horse and went forward. And he came to an open level plain, and put spurs to his horse; and the more he urged his horse, the further was she from him. Yet she held the same pace as at first. And his horse began to fail; and when his horse's feet failed him, he returned to the place where Pwyll was.

'Lord,' said he, 'it will avail nothing for anyone to follow yonder lady. I know of no horse in these realms swifter than this, and it availed me not to pursue her.' 'Of a truth,' said Pwyll, 'There must be some illusion here. Let us go towards the palace.'

So to the palace they went, and they spent that day. And the next day they arose, and that also they spent until it was time to go to meat. And after the first meal, 'Truly,' said Pwyll, 'we will go in the same company as yesterday to the top of the mound. And do thou', said he to one of his young men, 'Take the swiftest horse that thou knowest in the field.' And the young man did so. And they went towards the mound, taking the horse with them. And as they were sitting down they beheld the lady on the same horse, and in the same apparel, coming along the same road.

'Behold,' said Pwyll, 'here is the lady of yesterday. Make ready, youth, to learn who she is.' 'My lord,' said he, 'That will I gladly do.' And thereupon the lady came opposite to them.

So the youth mounted his horse; and before he had settled himself in his saddle, she passed by, and there was a clear space between them. But her speed was no greater than it had been the day before. Then he put his horse into an amble, and thought that notwithstanding the gentle pace at which his horse went, he should soon overtake her. But this availed him not; so he gave his horse the reins. And still he came no nearer to her than when he went at a foot's pace. And the more he urged his horse, the further was she from him. Yet she rode not faster than before. When he saw that it availed not to follow her, he returned to the place where Pwyll was.

'Lord,' said he, 'The horse can no more than thou hast seen.' 'I see indeed that it avails not that anyone should follow her. And by heaven,' said he, 'she must needs have an errand to someone in this plain, if her haste would allow her to declare it. Let us go back to the palace.' And to the palace they went, and they spent that night in songs and feasting, as it pleased them.

And the next day they amused themselves until it was time to go to meat. And when meat was ended, Pwyll said, 'Where are the hosts that went yesterday and the day before to the top of the mound?' 'Behold, lord, we are here,' said they. 'Let us go', said he, 'To the mound, to sit there. And do thou', said he to the page who tended his horse, 'saddle my horse well, and hasten with him to the road, and bring also my spurs with thee.' And the youth did thus. And they went and sat upon the mound; and ere they had been there but a short time, they beheld the lady coming by the same road, and in the same manner, and at the same pace. 'Young man,' said Pwyll, 'I see the lady coming; give me my horse.' And no sooner had he mounted his horse than she passed him. And he turned after her and followed her. And he let his horse go bounding playfully, and thought that at the second step or the third he should come up with her. But he came no nearer to her than at first. Then he urged his horse to his utmost speed, yet he found that it availed nothing to follow her. Then said Pwyll, 'O maiden, for the sake of him whom thou best lovest, stay for me.' 'I will stay gladly,' said she, 'and it were better for thy horse hadst thou asked it long since.'

So the maiden stopped, and she threw back that part of her headdress which covered her face. And she fixed her eyes upon him, and began to talk with him. 'Lady,' asked he, 'whence comest thou, and where cost thou journey?' 'I journey on mine own errand,' said she, 'and right glad am I to see thee.' 'My greeting be unto thee,' said he. Then he thought that the beauty of all the maidens, and all the ladies that he had ever seen, was as nothing compared to her beauty. 'Lady,' he said, 'wilt thou tell me aught concerning thy purpose?' 'I will tell thee,' said she. 'My chief quest was to seek thee.' 'Behold,' said Pwyll, 'This is to me the most pleasing quest on which thou couldst have come; and wilt thou tell me who thou art?' 'I will tell thee, lord,' said she. 'I am Rhiannon, the daughter of Hefeydd the Old, and they sought to give me to a husband against my will. But no husband would I have, and that because of my love for thee, neither will I yet have one unless thou reject me. And hither have I come to hear thy answer.' 'By heaven,' said Pwyll, 'behold this is my answer. If I might choose among all the ladies and damsels in the world, thee would I choose.' 'Truly,' said she, 'if thou art thus minded, make a pledge to meet me ere I am given to another.' 'The sooner I may do so, the more pleasing will it be unto me,' said Pwyll, 'and wheresoever thou wilt, there will I meet with thee.' 'I will that thou meet me this day twelvemonth at the palace of Hefeydd. And I will cause a feast to be prepared, so that it be ready against thou come.' 'Gladly', said he, 'will I keep this tryst.' 'Lord,' said she, 'remain in health, and be mindful that thou keep thy promise; and now I will go hence.'

So they parted, and he went back to his hosts and to them of his household. And whatever questions they asked him respecting the damsel, he always turned the discourse upon other matters. And when a year from that time was gone, he caused a hundred knights to equip themselves and to go with him to the palace of Hefeydd the Old. And he came to the palace, and there was great joy concerning him, with much concourse of people and great rejoicing, and vast preparations for his coming. And the whole court was placed under his orders.

And the hall was garnished and they went to meat, and thus did they sit; Hefeydd the Old was on one side of Pwyll, and Rhiannon on the other. And all the rest according to their rank. And they ate and feasted and talked one with another, and at the beginning of the carousel after the meat, there entered a tall auburn-haired youth, of royal bearing, clothed in a garment of satin. And when he came into the hall, he saluted Pwyll and his companions. 'The greeting of heaven be unto thee, my soul,' said Pwyll, 'come thou and sit down.' 'Nay,' said he, 'a suitor am I, and I will do mine errand.' 'Do so willingly,' said Pwyll. 'Lord,' said he, 'my errand is unto thee, and it is to crave a boon of thee that I come.' 'What boon soever thou mayest ask of me, as far as I am able, thou shalt have.' 'Ah,' said Rhiannon, 'wherefore didst thou give that answer?' 'Has he not given it before the presence of these nobles?' asked the youth. 'My soul,' said Pwyll, 'what is the boon thou askest?' 'The lady whom best I love is to be thy bride this night; I come to ask her of thee, with the feast and the banquet that are in this place.'

And Pwyll was silent because of the answer which he had given. 'Be silent as long as thou wilt,' said Rhiannon. 'Never did man make worse use of his wits than thou hast done.' 'Lady,' said he, 'I knew not who he was.' 'Behold this is the man to whom they would have given me against my will,' said she. 'And he is Gwawl, the son of Clud, a man of great power and wealth, and because of the word thou hast spoken, bestow me upon him lest shame befall thee.' 'Lady,' said he, 'I understand not thine answer. Never can I do as thou sayest.' 'Bestow me upon him', said she, 'and I will cause that I shall never be his.' 'By what means will that be?' asked Pwyll.

'In thy hand will I give thee a small bag,' said she. 'See that thou keep it well, and he will ask of thee the banquet, and the feast, and the preparations which are not in thy power. Unto the hosts and the household will I give the feast. And such will be thy answer respecting this. And as concerns myself, I will engage to become his bride this night twelvemonth. And at the end of the year be thou here,' said she, 'and bring this bag with thee, and let thy hundred knights be in the orchard up yonder. And when he is in the midst of joy and feasting, come thou in by thyself, clad in ragged garments, and holding thy bag in thy hand, and ask nothing but a bagful of food, and I will cause that if all the meat and liquor that are in these seven cantrefs were put into it, it would be no fuller than before. And after a great deal has been put therein, he will ask thee whether thy bag will ever be full. Say thou then that it never will, until a man of noble birth and of great wealth arise and press the food in the bag with both his feet, saying, "Enough has been put therein"; and I will cause him to go and tread down the food in the bag, and when he does so, turn thou the bag, so that he shall be up over his head in it, and then slip a knot upon the thongs of the bag. Let there be also a good bugle horn about thy neck, and as soon as thou hast bound him in the bag, wind thy horn, and let it be a signal between thee and thy knights. And when they hear the sound of the horn, let them come down upon the palace.'

'Lord,' said Gwawl, 'it is meet that I have an answer to my request.' 'As much of that thou hast asked as it is in my power to give, thou shalt have,' replied Pwyll. 'My soul,' said Rhiannon unto him, 'as for the feast and the banquet that are here, I have bestowed them upon the men of Dyfed, and the household, and the warriors that are with us. These can I not suffer to be given to any. In a year from tonight a banquet shall be prepared for thee in this palace, that I may become thy bride.'

So Gwawl went forth to his possessions, and Pwyll went also back to Dyfed. And they both spent that year until it was the time for the feast at the palace of Hefeydd the Old. Then Gwawl, the son of Clud, set out to the feast that was prepared for him, and he came to the palace, and was received there with rejoicing. Pwyll, also, the chief of Annwfn, came to the orchard with his hundred knights, as Rhiannon had commanded him, having the bag with him. And Pwyll was clad in coarse and ragged garments, and wore large clumsy old shoes upon his feet. And when he knew that the carousel after the meat had begun, he went towards the hall, and when he came into the hall, he saluted Gwawl, the son of Clud, and his company, both men and women.

'Heaven prosper thee,' said Gwawl, 'and the greeting of heaven be unto thee.' 'Lord,' said he, 'may heaven reward thee, I have an errand unto thee.' 'Welcome be thine errand, and if thou ask of me that which is just, thou shalt have it gladly.' 'It is fitting,' answered he. 'I crave but from want, and the boon that I ask is to have this small bag that thou seest filled with meat.' 'A request within reason is this,' said he, 'and gladly shalt thou have it. Bring him food.' A great number of attendants arose and began to fill the bag, but for all that they put into it, it was no fuller than at first. 'My soul,' said Gwawl, 'will thy bag be ever full?' 'It will not, I declare to heaven,' said he, 'for all that may be put into it, unless one possessed of lands, and domains, and treasure, shall arise and tread down with both his feet the food that is within the bag, and shall say, "Enough has been put therein".'

Then said Rhiannon unto Gwawl, the son of Clud, 'Rise up quickly.' 'I will willingly arise,' said he. So he rose up, and put his two feet into the bag. And Pwyll turned up the sides of the bag, so that Gwawl was over his head in it. And he shut it up quickly, and slipped a knot upon the thongs, and blew his horn. And thereupon his household came down upon the palace. And they seized all the host that had come with Gwawl, and cast them into his own prison. And Pwyll threw off his rags, and his old shoes, and his tattered array; and as they came in, every one of Pwyll's knights struck a blow upon the bag, and asked, 'What is here?' 'A badger,' said they. And in this manner they played, each of them striking the bag, either with his foot or with a staff. And thus played they with the bag. Everyone as he came in asked, 'What game are you playing at thus?' 'The game of Badger in the Bag,' said they. And then was the game of Badger in the Bag first played.

'Lord,' said the man in the bag, 'if thou wouldest but hear me, I merit not to be slain in a bag.' Said Hefeydd the Old, 'Lord, he speaks truth. It were fitting that thou listen to him, for he deserves not this.' 'Truly,' said Pwyll, 'I will do thy counsel concerning him.' 'Behold this is my counsel then,' said Rhiannon; 'Thou art now in a position in which it behoves thee to satisfy suitors and minstrels; let him give unto them in thy stead, and take a pledge from him that he will never seek to revenge that which has been done to him. And this will be punishment enough.' 'I will do this gladly,' said the man in the bag. 'And gladly will I accept it,' said Pwyll, 'since it is the counsel of Hefeydd and Rhiannon.' 'Such then is our counsel,' answered they. 'I accept it,' said Pwyll. 'Seek thyself sureties.' 'We will be for him', said Hefeydd, 'until his men be free to answer for him.' And upon this he was let out of the bag, and his liegemen were liberated.

'Demand now of Gwawl his sureties,' said Hefeydd, 'we know which should be taken for him.' And Hefeydd numbered the sureties. Said Gwawl, 'Do thou thyself draw up the covenant.' 'It will suffice me that it be as Rhiannon said,' answered Pwyll. So unto that covenant were the sureties pledged. 'Truly, Lord,' said Gwawl, 'I am greatly hurt, and I have many bruises. I have need to be anointed; with thy leave I will go forth. I will leave nobles in my stead, to answer for me in all that thou shalt require.' 'Willingly', said Pwyll, 'mayest thou do thus.' So Gwawl went towards his own possessions.

And the hall was set in order for Pwyll and the men of his host, and for them also of the palace, and they went to the tables and sat down. And as they had sat that time twelvemonth, so sat they that night. And they ate, and feasted, and spent the night in mirth and tranquillity. And the time came that they should sleep, and Pwyll and Rhiannon went to their chamber.

And next morning at the break of day, 'My lord,' said Rhiannon, 'arise and begin to give thy gifts unto the minstrels. Refuse no one today that may claim thy bounty.' 'Thus shall it be gladly,' said Pwyll, 'both today and every day while the feast shall last.' So Pwyll arose, and he caused silence to be proclaimed, and desired all the suitors and the minstrels to show and to point out what gifts were to their wish and desire. And this being done, the feast went on, and he denied no one while it lasted. And when the feast was ended, Pwyll said unto Hefeydd, 'My lord, with thy permission I will set out for Dyfed tomorrow.' 'Certainly,' said Hefeydd, 'may heaven prosper thee. Fix also a time when Rhiannon may follow thee.' 'By heaven,' said Pwyll, 'we will go hence together.' 'Willest thou this, lord?' said Hefeydd. 'Yes, by heaven,' answered Pwyll.

And the next day they set forward towards Dyfed, and journeyed to the palace of Arberth, where a feast was made ready for them. And there came to them great numbers of the chief men and the most noble ladies of the land, and of these there was none to whom Rhiannon did not give some rich gift, either a bracelet, or a ring, or a precious stone. And they ruled the land prosperously both that year and the next.

And in the third year the nobles of the land began to be sorrowful at seeing a man whom they loved so much, and who was moreover their lord and their foster-brother, without an heir. And they came to him. And the place where they met was Preseleu, in Dyfed. 'Lord,' said they, 'we know that thou art not so young as some of the men of this country, and we fear that thou mayest not have an heir of the wife whom thou hast taken. Take therefore another wife of whom thou mayest have heirs. Thou canst not always continue with us, and though thou desire to remain as thou art, we will not suffer thee.' 'Truly,' said Pwyll, 'we have not long been joined together, and many things may yet befall. Grant me a year from this time, and for the space of a year we will abide together, and after that I will do according to your wishes.'

So they granted it. And before the end of a year a son was born unto him. And in Arberth was he born; and on the night that he was born, women were brought to watch the mother and the boy. And the women slept, as did also Rhiannon, the mother of the boy. And the number of the women that were brought into the chamber was six. And they watched for a good portion of the night, and before midnight every one of them fell asleep, and towards break of day they awoke; and when they awoke, they looked where they had put the boy, and behold he was not there.

'Oh,' said one of the women, 'The boy is lost!' 'Yes,' said another, 'and it will be small vengeance if we are burnt or put to death because of the child.' Said one of the women, 'Is there any counsel for us in the world in this matter?' 'There is,' answered another, 'I offer you good counsel.' 'What is that?' asked they. 'There is here a stag-hound bitch, and she has a litter of whelps. Let us kill some of the cubs, and rub the blood on the face and hands of Rhiannon, and lay the bones before her, and assert that she herself hath devoured her son, and she alone will not be able to gainsay us six.'

And according to this counsel it was settled. And towards morning Rhiannon awoke, and she said, 'Women, where is my son?' 'Lady,' said they, 'ask us not concerning thy son, we have nought but the blows and the bruises we got by struggling with thee, and of a truth we never saw any woman so violent as thou, for it was of no avail to contend with thee. Hast thou not thyself devoured thy son? Claim him not therefore of us.' 'For pity's sake,' said Rhiannon; 'The Lord God knows all things. Charge me not falsely. If you tell me this from fear, I assert before heaven that I will defend you.' 'Truly,' said they, 'we would not bring evil on ourselves for anyone in the world.' 'For pity's sake,' said Rhiannon, 'you will receive no evil by telling the truth.' But for all her words, whether fair or harsh, she received but the same answer from the women.

And Pwyll, the chief of Annwfn, arose, and his household, and his hosts. And this occurrence could not be concealed, but the story went forth throughout the land, and all the nobles heard it. Then the nobles came to Pwyll, and besought him to put away his wife, because of the great crime which she had done. But Pwyll answered them, that they had no cause wherefore they might ask him to put away his wife, save for her having no children. 'But children has she now had, therefore will I not put her away; if she has done wrong, let her do penance for it.'

So Rhiannon sent for the teachers and the wise men, and as she preferred doing penance to contending with the women, she took upon her a penance. And the penance that was imposed upon her was, that she should remain in that palace of Arberth until the end of seven years, and that she should sit every day near unto a horse-block that was without the gate. And that she should relate the story to all who should come there, whom she might suppose not to know it already; and that she should offer the guests and strangers, if they would permit her, to carry them upon her back into the palace. But it rarely happened that any would permit. And thus did she spend part of the year.

Now at that time Teyrnon Twrf Liant was lord of Gwent Is Coed, and he was the best man in the world. And unto his house there belonged a mare, than which neither mare nor horse in the kingdom was more beautiful. And on the night of every first of May she foaled, and no one ever knew what became of the colt. And one night Teyrnon talked with his wife: 'Wife,' said he, 'it is very simple of us that our mare should foal every year, and that we should have none of her colts.' 'What can be done in the matter?' said she. 'This is the night of the first of May,' said he. 'The vengeance of heaven be upon me, if I learn not what it is that takes away the colts.'

So he caused the mare to be brought into a house, and he armed himself, and began to watch that night. And in the beginning of the night, the mare foaled a large and beautiful colt. And it was standing up in the place. And Teyrnon rose up and looked at the size of the colt, and as he did so he heard a great tumult, and after the tumult behold a claw came through the window into the house, and it seized the colt by the mane. Then Teyrnon drew his sword, and struck off the arm at the elbow, so that portion of the arm together with the colt was in the house with him. And then did he hear a tumult and wailing, both at once. And he opened the door, and rushed out in the direction of the noise, and he could not see the cause of the tumult because of the darkness of the night, but he rushed after it and followed it. Then he remembered that he had left the door open, and he returned. And at the door behold there was an infant boy in swaddling-clothes, wrapped around in a mantle of satin. And he took up the boy, and behold he was very strong for the age that he was.

Then he shut the door, and went into the chamber where his wife was. 'Lady,' said he, 'art thou sleeping?' 'No, lord,' said she, 'I was asleep, but as thou camest in I did awake.' 'Behold, here is a boy for thee if thou wilt,' said he, 'since thou hast never had one.' 'My lord,' said she, 'what adventure is this?' 'It was thus,' said Teyrnon; and he told her how it all befell. 'Truly, lord,' said she, 'what sort of garments are there upon the boy?' 'A mantle of satin,' said he. 'He is then a boy of gentle lineage,' she replied. 'My lord,' she said, 'if thou wilt, I shall have great diversion and mirth. I will call my women unto me, and tell them that I have been pregnant.' 'I will readily grant thee to do this,' he answered.

And thus did they, and they caused the boy to be baptised, and the ceremony was performed there; and the name which they gave unto him was Gwri Wallt Euryn, because what hair was upon his head was as yellow as gold. And they had the boy nursed in the court until he was a year old. And before the year was over he could walk stoutly. And he was larger than a boy of three years old, even one of great growth and size. And the boy was nursed the second year, and then he was as large as a child six years old. And before the end of the fourth year, he would bribe the grooms to allow him to take the horses to water. 'My lord,' said his wife unto Teyrnon, 'where is the colt which thou didst save on the night that thou didst find the boy?' 'I have commanded the grooms of the horses', said he, 'That they take care of him.' 'Would it not be well, lord,' said she, 'if thou wert to cause him to be broken in, and given to the boy, seeing that on the same night that thou didst find the boy, the colt was foaled and thou didst save him?' 'I will not oppose thee in this matter,' said Teyrnon. 'I will allow thee to give him the colt.' 'Lord,' said she, 'may heaven reward thee; I will give it him.' So the horse was given to the boy. Then she went to the grooms and those who tended the horses, and commanded them to be careful of the horse, so that he might be broken in by the time that the boy could ride him.

And while these things were going forward, they heard tidings of Rhiannon and her punishment. And Teyrnon Twrf Liant, by reason of the pity that he felt on hearing this story of Rhiannon and her punishment, enquired closely concerning it, until he had heard from many of those who came to his court. Then did Teyrnon, often lamenting the sad history, ponder within himself, and he looked steadfastly on the boy, and as he looked upon him, it seemed to him that he had never beheld so great a likeness between father and son, as between the boy and Pwyll, the chief of Annwfn.

Now the semblance of Pwyll was well known to him, for he had of yore been one of his followers. And thereupon he became grieved for the wrong that he did, in keeping with him a boy whom he knew to be the son of another man. And the first time that he was alone with his wife, he told her that it was not right that they should keep the boy with them, and suffer so excellent a lady as Rhiannon to be punished so greatly on his account, whereas the boy was the son of Pwyll, the chief of Annwfn. And Teyrnon's wife agreed with him, that they should send the boy to Pwyll. 'And three things, lord,' said she, 'shall we gain thereby. Thanks and gifts for releasing Rhiannon from her punishment; and thanks from Pwyll for nursing his son and restoring him unto him; and thirdly, if the boy is of gentle nature, he will be our foster-son, and he will do for us all the good in his power.' So it was settled according to this counsel.

And no later than the next day was Teyrnon equipped, and two other knights with him. And the boy, as a fourth in their company, went with them upon the horse which Teyrnon had given him. And they journeyed towards Arberth, and it was not long before they reached that place. And as they drew near to the palace, they beheld Rhiannon sitting beside the horse-block. And when they were opposite to her, 'Chieftain,' said she, 'go not further thus, I will bear every one of you into the palace, and this is my penance for slaying my own son and devouring him.' 'Oh, fair lady,' said Teyrnon, 'Think not that I will be one to be carried upon thy back.' 'Neither will I,' said the boy. 'Truly, my soul,' said Teyrnon, 'we will not go.' So they went forward to the palace, and there was great joy at their coming.

And at the palace a feast was prepared, because Pwyll was come back from the confines of Dyfed. And they went into the hall and washed, and Pwyll rejoiced to see Teyrnon. And in this order they sat. Teyrnon between Pwyll and Rhiannon, and Teyrnon's two companions on the other side of Pwyll, with the boy between them. And after meat they began to carouse and to discourse. And Teyrnon's discourse was concerning the adventure of the mare and the boy, and how he and his wife had nursed and reared the child as their own. 'And behold here is thy son, lady,' said Teyrnon. 'And whosoever told that lie concerning thee, has done wrong. And when I heard of thy sorrow, I was troubled and grieved. And I believe that there is none of this host who will not perceive that the boy is the son of Pwyll,' said Teyrnon. 'There is none', said they all, 'who is not certain thereof.' 'I declare to heaven', said Rhiannon, 'That if this be true, there is indeed an end to my trouble.' 'Lady,' said Pendaran Dyfed, 'well hast thou named thy son Pryderi, and well becomes him the name of Pryderi, son of Pwyll, chief of Annwfn.' 'Look you,' said Rhiannon, 'will not his own name become him better?' 'What name has he?' asked Pendaran Dyfed. 'Gwri of the Golden Hair is the name that we gave him.' 'Pryderi', said Pendaran, 'shall his name be.' 'It were more proper', said Pwyll, 'That the boy should take his name from the word his mother spoke when she received the joyful tidings of him.' And thus was it arranged.

'Teyrnon,' said Pwyll, 'heaven reward thee that thou hast reared the boy up to this time, and, being of gentle lineage, it were fitting that he repay thee for it.' 'My lord,' said Teyrnon, 'it was my wife who nursed him, and there is no one in the world so afflicted as she at parting with him. It were well that he should bear in mind what I and my wife have done for him.' 'I call heaven to witness', said Pwyll, 'That while I live I will support thee and thy possessions, as long as I am able to preserve my own. And when he shall have power, he will more fitly maintain them than I. And if this counsel be pleasing unto thee, and to my nobles, it shall be that, as thou hast reared him up to the present time, I will give him to be brought up by Pendaran Dyfed, from henceforth. And you shall be companions, and shall both be foster-fathers unto him.' 'This is good counsel,' said they all. So the boy was given to Pendaran Dyfed, and the nobles of the land were sent with him. And Teyrnon Twrf Liant and his companions set out for his country and his possessions with love and gladness. And he went not without being offered the fairest jewels and the fairest horses and the choicest dogs; but he would take none of them.

Thereupon they all remained in their own dominions. And Pryderi, the son of Pwyll, the chief of Annwfn, was brought up carefully as was fit, so that he became the fairest youth, and the most comely, and the best skilled in all good games, of any in the kingdom. And thus passed years and years, until the end of Pwyll, the chief of Annwfn's life came, and he died.

And Pryderi ruled the seven cantrefs of Dyfed prosperously, and he was beloved by his people, and by all around him. And at length he added unto them the three cantrefs of Ystrad Tywi, and the four cantrefs of Cardigan; and these were called the seven cantrefs of Seisyllwch. And when he made this addition, Pryderi, the son of Pwyll, the chief of Annwfn, desired to take a wife. And the wife he chose was Cigfa, the daughter of Gwyn Gohoyw, the son of Gloyw Wallt Lydan, the son of prince Casnar, one of the nobles of this island.

And thus ends this portion of the Mabinogi.

BRANWEN, THE DAUGHTER OF LLYR

Here is the second portion of the Mabinogi

Bendigeid Bran, the son of Llyr, was the crowned king of this island, and he was exalted from the crown of London. And one afternoon he was at Harlech in Ardudwy, at his court, and he sat upon the rock of Harlech, looking over the sea. And with him were his brother Manawyddan, the son of Llyr, and his brothers by the mother's side, Nissyen and Efnissyen, and many nobles likewise, as was fitting to see around a king. His two brothers by the mother's side were the sons of Eurosswydd, by his mother, Penardun, the daughter of Beli, son of Manogan. And one of these youths was a good youth and of gentle nature, and would make peace between his kindred, and cause his family to be friends when their wrath was at the highest; and this one was Nissyen; but the other would cause strife between his two brothers when they were most at peace.

And as they sat thus, they beheld thirteen ships coming from the south of Ireland, and making towards them, and they came with a swift motion, the wind being behind them, and they neared them rapidly. 'I see ships afar,' said the king, 'coming swiftly towards the land. Command the men of the court that they equip themselves, and go and learn their intent.'

So the men equipped themselves and went down towards them. And when they saw the ships near, certain were they that they had never seen ships better furnished. Beautiful flags of satin were upon them. And behold, one of the ships outstripped the others, and they saw a shield lifted up above the side of the ship, and the point of the shield was upwards, in token of peace. And the men drew near that they might hold converse. Then they put out boats and came towards the land. And they saluted the king. Now the king could hear them from the place where he was, upon the rock above their heads.

'Heaven prosper you,' said he, 'and be ye welcome. To whom do these ships belong, and who is the chief amongst you?' 'Lord,' said they, 'Matholwch, king of Ireland, is here, and these ships belong to him.' 'Wherefore comes he?' asked the king, 'and will he come to the land?' 'He is a suitor unto thee, lord,' said they, 'and he will not land unless he have his boon.' 'And what may that be?' enquired the king. 'He desires to ally himself with thee, lord,' said they, 'and he comes to ask Branwen, the daughter of Llyr, that, if it seem well to thee, the island of the Mighty may be leagued with Ireland, and both become more powerful.' 'Verily,' said he, 'let him come to land, and we will take counsel thereupon.' And this answer was brought to Matholwch. 'I will go willingly,' said he. So he landed, and they received him joyfully; and great was the throng in the palace that night, between his hosts and those of the court; and next day they took counsel, and they resolved to bestow Branwen upon Matholwch. Now she was one of the three chief ladies of this island, and she was the fairest damsel in the world.

And they fixed upon Aberffraw as the place where she should become his bride. And they went thence, and towards Aberffraw the hosts proceeded; Matholwch and his host in their ships, Bendigeid Bran and his host by land, until they came to Aberffraw. And at Aberffraw they began the feast and sat down. And thus sat they: the king of the island of the Mighty and Manawyddan, the son of Llyr, on one side, and Matholwch on the other side, and Branwen, the daughter of Llyr, beside him. And they were not within a house, but under tents. No house could ever contain Bendigeid Bran. And they began the banquet and caroused and discoursed. And when it was more pleasing to them to sleep than to carouse, they went to rest, and that night Branwen became Matholwch's bride.

And next day they arose, and all they of the court, and the officers began to equip and to range the horses and the attendants, and they ranged them in order as far as the sea. And behold one day, Efnissyen, the quarrelsome man of whom it is spoken above, came by chance into the place, where the horses of Matholwch were, and asked whose horses they might be. 'They are the horses of Matholwch, king of Ireland, who is married to Branwen, thy sister; his horses are they.' 'And is it thus they have done with a maiden such as she, and moreover my sister, bestowing her without my consent? They could have offered no greater insult to me than this,' said he. And thereupon he rushed under the horses and cut off their lips at the teeth, and their ears close to their heads, and their tails close to their backs, and wherever he could clutch their eyelids, he cut them to the very bone, and he disfigured the horses and rendered them useless.

And they came with these tidings unto Matholwch, saying that the horses were disfigured and injured so that not one of them could ever be of any use again. 'Verily, lord,' said one, 'it was an insult unto thee, and as such was it meant.' 'Of a truth, it is a marvel to me, that if they desire to insult me, they should have given me a maiden of such high rank and so much beloved of her kindred, as they have done.' 'Lord,' said another, 'Thou seest that thus it is, and there is nothing for thee to do but to go to thy ships.' And thereupon towards his ships he set out.

And tidings came to Bendigeid Bran that Matholwch was quitting the court without asking leave, and messengers were sent to enquire of him wherefore he did so. And the messengers that went were Iddic, the son of Anarawd, and Hefeydd Hir. And these overtook him and asked of him what he designed to do, and wherefore he went forth. 'Of a truth,' said he, 'if I had known I had not come hither. I have been altogether insulted, no one had ever worse treatment than I have had here. But one thing surprises me above all.' 'What is that?' asked they. 'That Branwen, the daughter of Llyr, one of the three chief ladies of this island, and the daughter of the king of the island of the Mighty, should have been given me as my bride, and that after that I should have been insulted; and I marvel that the insult was not done me before they had bestowed upon me a maiden so exalted as she.' 'Truly, lord, it was not the will of any that are of the court,' said they, 'nor of any that are of the council, that thou shouldest have received this insult; and as thou hast been insulted, the dishonour is greater unto Bendigeid Bran than unto thee.' 'Verily,' said he, 'I think so. Nevertheless he cannot recall the insult.'

These men returned with that answer to the place where Bendigeid Bran was, and they told him what reply Matholwch had given them. 'Truly,' said he, 'There are no means by which we may prevent his going away at enmity with us that we will not take.' 'Well, lord,' said they, 'send after him another embassy.' 'I will do so,' said he. 'Arise, Manawyddan, son of Llyr, and Hefeydd Hir, and Unic Glew Ysgwyd, and go after him, and tell him that he shall have a sound horse for every one that has been injured. And beside that, as an atonement for the insult, he shall have a staff of silver, as large and as tall as himself, and a plate of gold of the breadth of his face. And show unto him who it was that did this, and that it was done against my will; but that he who did it is my brother, by the mother's side, and therefore it would be hard for me to put him to death. And let him come and meet me,' said he, 'and we will make peace in any way he may desire.'

The embassy went after Matholwch, and told him all these sayings in a friendly manner, and he listened thereunto. 'Men,' said he, 'I will take counsel.' So to the council he went. And in the council they considered that if they should refuse this, they were likely to have more shame rather than to obtain so great an atonement. They resolved therefore to accept it, and they resumed to the court in peace.

Then the pavilions and the tents were set in order after the fashion of a hall; and they went to meat, and as they had sat at the beginning of the feast, so sat they there. And Matholwch and Bendigeid Bran began to discourse; and behold it seemed to Bendigeid Bran, while they talked, that Matholwch was not so cheerful as he had been before. And he thought that the chieftain might be sad, because of the smallness of the atonement which he had, for the wrong that had been done him. 'Oh, man,' said Bendigeid Vran, 'Thou dost not discourse tonight so cheerfully as thou west wont to do. And if it be because of the smallness of the atonement, thou shalt add hereunto whatsoever thou mayest choose, and tomorrow I will pay thee the horses.' 'Lord,' said he, 'heaven reward thee.' 'And I will enhance the atonement,' said Bendigeid Bran, 'for I will give unto thee a cauldron, the property of which is, that if one of thy men be slain today, and be cast therein, tomorrow he will be as well as ever he was at the best, except that he will not regain his speech.' And thereupon he gave him great thanks, and very joyful was he for that cause.

And the next morning they paid Matholwch the horses as long as the trained horses lasted. And then they journeyed into another commote, where they paid him with colts until the whole had been paid, and from thenceforth that commote was called Talebolion.

And a second night sat they together. 'My lord,' said Matholwch, 'whence hadst thou the cauldron which thou hast given me?' 'I had it of a man who had been in thy land,' said he, 'and I would not give it except to one from there.' 'Who was it?' he asked. 'Llaesar Llaesgyngwyd; he came here from Ireland with Kymideu Kymeinvoll, his wife, who escaped from the Iron House in Ireland, when it was made red hot around them, and fled hither. And it is a marvel to me that thou shouldst know nothing concerning the matter.'

'Something I do know,' said he, 'and as much as I know I will tell thee. One day I was hunting in Ireland, and I came to the mound at the head of the lake, which is called the Lake of the Cauldron. And I beheld a huge yellow-haired man coming from the lake with a cauldron upon his back. And he was a man of vast size, and of horrid aspect, and a woman followed after him. And if the man was tall, twice as large as he was the woman, and they came towards me and greeted me. "Verily," asked I, "wherefore are you journeying?" "Behold, this", said he to me, "is the cause that we journey. At the end of a month and a fortnight this woman will have a son; and the child that will be born at the end of the month and the fortnight will be a warrior fully armed." So I took them with me and maintained them.

'And they were with me for a year. And that year I had them with me not grudgingly. But thenceforth was there murmuring, because that they were with me. For, from the beginning of the fourth month they had begun to make themselves hated and to be disorderly in the land; committing outrages, and molesting and harassing the nobles and ladies; and thenceforward my people rose up and besought me to part with them, and they bade me to choose between them and my dominions.

'And I applied to the council of my country to know what should be done concerning them; for of their own free will they would not go, neither could they be compelled against their will, through fighting. And [the people of the country] being in this strait, they caused a chamber to be made all of iron. Now when the chamber was ready, there came there every smith that was in Ireland, and everyone who owned tongs and hammer. And they caused coals to be piled up as high as the top of the chamber. And they had the man, and the woman, and the children, served with plenty of meat and drink; but when it was known that they were drunk, they began to put fire to the coals about the chamber, and they blew it with bellows until the house was red hot all around them. Then was there a council held in the centre of the floor of the chamber. And the man tarried until the plates of iron were all of a white heat; and then, by reason of the great heat, the man dashed against the plates with his shoulder and struck them out, and his wife followed him; but except him and his wife none escaped thence. And then I suppose, lord,' said Matholwch unto Bendigeid Bran, 'That he came over unto thee.'

'Doubtless he came here,' said he, 'and gave unto me the cauldron.'

'In what manner didst thou receive them?'

'I dispersed them through every part of my dominions, and they have become numerous and are prospering everywhere, and they fortify the places where they are with men and arms, of the best that were ever seen.'

That night they continued to discourse as much as they would, and had minstrelsy and carousing, and when it was more pleasant to them to sleep than to sit longer, they went to rest. And thus was the banquet carried on with joyousness; and when it was finished, Matholwch journeyed towards Ireland, and Branwen with him, and they went from Aber Menei with thirteen ships, and came to Ireland. And in Ireland was there great joy because of their coming. And not one great man or noble lady visited Branwen unto whom she gave not either a clasp, or a ring, or a royal jewel to keep, such as it was honourable to be seen departing with.

And in these things she spent that year in much renown, and she passed her time pleasantly, enjoying honour and friendship. And in the meanwhile it chanced that she became pregnant, and in due time a son was born unto her, and the name that they gave him was Gwern, the son of Matholwch, and they put the boy out to be foster-nursed, in a place where were the best men of Ireland.

And behold in the second year a tumult arose in Ireland, on account of the insult which Matholwch had received in Cambria, and the payment made him for his horses. And his foster-brothers, and such as were nearest unto him, blamed him openly for that matter. And he might have no peace by reason of the tumult until they should revenge upon him this disgrace. And the vengeance which they took was to drive away Branwen from the same chamber with him, and to make her cook for the court; and they caused the butcher after he had cut up the meat to come to her and give her every day a blow on the ear, and such they made her punishment.

'Verily, lord,' said his men to Matholwch, 'forbid now the ships and the ferry boats and the coracles, that they go not into Cambria, and such as come over from Cambria hither, imprison them that they go not back for this thing to be known there.' And he did so; and it was thus for not less than three years.

And Branwen reared a starling in the cover of the kneading trough, and she taught it to speak, and she taught the bird what manner of man her brother was. And she wrote a letter of her woes, and the despite with which she was treated, and she bound the letter to the root of the bird's wing, and sent it towards Britain. And the bird came to this island, and one day it found Bendigeid Bran at Caer Seiont in Arfon, conferring there, and it alighted upon his shoulder and ruffled its feathers, so that the letter was seen, and they knew that the bird had been reared in a domestic manner.

Then Bendigeid Bran took the letter and looked upon it. And when he had read the letter he grieved exceedingly at the tidings of Branwen's woes. And immediately he began sending messengers to summon the island together. And he caused seven score and four countries to come unto him, and he complained to them himself of the grief that his sister endured. So they took counsel. And in the council they resolved to go to Ireland, and to leave seven men as princes here, and Caradawc, the son of Bran, as the chief of them, and their seven knights. In Edeyrnion were these men left. And for this reason were the seven knights placed in the town. Now the names of these seven men were Caradawc, the son of Bran, and Hefeydd Hir, and Unic Glew Ysgwyd, and Iddic, the son of Anaraw Gwalltgrwn, and Fodor, the son of Ervyll, and Gwlch Minascwrn, and Llassar, the son of Llaesar Llaesgyngwyd, and Pendaran Dyfed as a young page with them. And these abode as seven ministers to take charge of this island; and Caradawc, the son of Bran, was the chief amongst them.

Bendigeid Bran, with the host of which we spoke, sailed towards Ireland, and it was not far across the sea, and he came to shoal water. It was caused by two rivers; the Lli and the Archan were they called; and the nations covered the sea. Then he proceeded with what provisions he had on his own back, and approached the shore of Ireland.

Now the swineherds of Matholwch were upon the seashore, and they came to Matholwch. 'Lord,' said they 'greeting be unto thee.' 'Heaven protect you,' said he, 'have you any news?' 'Lord,' said they, 'we have marvellous news, a wood have we seen upon the sea, in a place where we never yet saw a single tree.' 'This is indeed a marvel,' said he; 'saw you aught else?' 'We saw, lord,' said they, 'a vast mountain beside the wood, which moved, and there was a lofty ridge on the top of the mountain, and a lake on each side of the ridge. And the wood, and the mountain, and all these things moved.' 'Verily,' said he, 'There is none who can know aught concerning this, unless it be Branwen.'

Messengers then went unto Branwen. 'Lady,' said they, 'what thinkest thou that this is?' 'The men of the island of the Mighty, who have come hither on hearing of my ill-treatment and my woes.' 'What is the forest that is seen upon the sea?' asked they. 'The yards and the masts of ships,' she answered. 'Alas,' said they, 'what is the mountain that is seen by the side of the ships?' 'Bendigeid Bran, my brother,' she replied, 'coming to shoal water; there is no ship that can contain him in it.' 'What is the lofty ridge with the lake on each side thereof?' 'On looking towards this island he is wroth, and his two eyes, one on each side of his nose, are the two lakes beside the ridge.'

The warriors and the chief men of Ireland were brought together in haste, and they took counsel. 'Lord,' said the nobles unto Matholwch, 'There is no other counsel than to retreat over the Linon (a river which is in Ireland), and to keep the river between thee and him, and to break down the bridge that is across the river, for there is a loadstone at the bottom of the river that neither ship nor vessel can pass over.' So they retreated across the river, and broke down the bridge.

Bendigeid Bran came to land, and the fleet with him by the bank of the river. 'Lord,' said his chieftains, 'knowest thou the nature of this river, that nothing can go across it, and there is no bridge over it? What', said they, 'is thy counsel concerning a bridge?' 'There is none,' said he, 'except that he who will be chief, let him be a bridge. I will be so,' said he. And then was that saying first uttered, and it is still used as a proverb. And when he had lain down across the river, hurdles were placed upon him, and the host passed over thereby.

And as he rose up, behold the messengers of Matholwch came to him, and saluted him, and gave him greeting in the name of Matholwch, his kinsman, and showed how that of his goodwill he had merited of him nothing but good. 'For Matholwch has given the kingdom of Ireland to Gwern, the son of Matholwch, thy nephew and thy sister's son. And this he places before thee, as a compensation for the wrong and despite that has been done unto Branwen. And Matholwch shall be maintained wheresoever thou wilt, either here or in the island of the Mighty.' Said Bendigeid Bran, 'Shall not I myself have the kingdom? Then peradventure I may take counsel concerning your message. From this time until then no other answer will you get from me.' 'Verily', said they, 'The best message that we receive for thee, we will convey it unto thee, and do thou await our message unto him.' 'I will wait,' answered he, 'and do you return quickly.'

The messengers set forth and came to Matholwch. 'Lord,' said they, 'prepare a better message for Bendigeid Bran. He would not listen at all to the message that we bore him.' 'My friends,' said Matholwch, 'what may be your counsel?' 'Lord,' said they, 'There is no other counsel than this alone. He was never known to be within a house, make therefore a house that will contain him and the men of the island of the Mighty on the one side, and thyself and thy host on the other; and give over thy kingdom to his will, and do him homage. So by reason of the honour thou doest him in making him a house, whereas he never before had a house to contain him, he will make peace with thee.' So the messengers went back to Bendigeid Bran, bearing him this message.

And he took counsel, and in the council it was resolved that he should accept this, and this was all done by the advice of Branwen, and lest the country should be destroyed. And this peace was made, and the house was built both vast and strong. But the Irish planned a crafty device, and the craft was that they should put brackets on each side of the hundred pillars that were in the house, and should place a leather bag on each bracket, and an armed man in every one of them. Then Efnissyen came in before the host of the island of the Mighty, and scanned the house with fierce and savage looks, and observed the leather bags which were around the pillars. 'What is in this bag?' asked he of one of the Irish. 'Meal, good soul,' said he. And Efnissyen felt about it until he came to the man's head, and he squeezed the head until he felt his fingers meet together in the brain through the bone. And he left that one and put his hand upon another, and asked what was therein. 'Meal,' said the Irishman. So he did the like unto every one of them, until he had not left alive, of all the two hundred men, save one only; and when he came to him, he asked what was there. 'Meal, good soul,' said the Irishman. And he felt about until he felt the head, and he squeezed that head as he had done the others. And, albeit he found that the head of this one was armed, he left him not until he had killed him. And then he sang an englyn:

> There is in this bag a different sort of meal,
> The ready combatant, when the assault is made
> By his fellow-warriors, prepared for battle.

Thereupon came the hosts unto the house. The men of the island of Ireland entered the house on the one side, and the men of the island of the Mighty on the other. And as soon as they had sat down there was concord between them; and the sovereignty was conferred upon the boy. When the peace was concluded, Bendigeid Bran called the boy unto him, and from Bendigeid Bran the boy went unto Manawyddan, and he was beloved by all that beheld him. And from Manawyddan the boy was called by Nissyen, the son of Eurosswydd, and the boy went unto him lovingly. 'Wherefore', said Efnissyen, 'comes not my nephew, the son of my sister, unto me? Though he were not king of Ireland, yet willingly would I fondle the boy.' 'Cheerfully let him go to thee,' said Bendigeid Bran, and the boy went unto him cheerfully. 'By my confession to heaven,' said Efnissyen in his heart, 'unthought of by the household is the slaughter that I will this instant commit.'

Then he arose and took up the boy by the feet, and before anyone in the house could seize hold of him, he thrust the boy headlong into the blazing fire. And when Branwen saw her son burning in the fire, she strove to leap into the fire also, from the place where she sat between her two brothers. But Bendigeid Bran grasped her with one hand, and his shield with the other. Then they all hurried about the house, and never was there made so great a tumult by any host in one house as was made by them, as each man armed himself. Then said Morddwydtyllyon, 'The gadflies of Morddwydtyllyon's Cow!' And while they all sought their arms, Bendigeid Bran supported Branwen between his shield and his shoulder.

Then the Irish kindled a fire under the cauldron of renovation, and they cast the dead bodies into the cauldron until it was full, and the next day they came forth fighting-men as good as before, except that they were not able to speak. Then when Efnissyen saw the dead bodies of the men of the island of the Mighty nowhere resuscitated, he said in his heart, 'Alas! woe is me, that I should have been the cause of bringing the men of the island of the Mighty into so great a strait. Evil betide me if I find not a deliverance therefrom.' And he cast himself among the dead bodies of the Irish, and two unshod Irishmen came to him, and, taking him to be one of the Irish, flung him into the cauldron. And he stretched himself out in the cauldron, so that he rent the cauldron into four pieces, and burst his own heart also.

In consequence of that the men of the island of the Mighty obtained such success as they had; but they were not victorious, for only seven men of them all escaped, and Bendigeid Bran himself was wounded in the foot with a poisoned dart. Now the seven men that escaped were Pryderi, Manawyddan, Gluneu Eil Taran, Taliesin, Ynawc, Grudyen the son of Muryel, and Heilyn the son of Gwynn Hen.

And Bendigeid Bran commanded them that they should cut off his head. 'And take you my head,' said he, 'and bear it even unto the White Mount, in London, and bury it there, with the face towards France. And a long time will you be upon the road. In Harlech you will be feasting seven years, the birds of Rhiannon singing unto you the while. And all that time the head will be to you as pleasant company as it ever was when on my body. And at Gwales in Penfro you will be four score years, and you may remain there, and the head with you uncorrupted, until you open the door that looks towards Aber Henfelen, and towards Cornwall. And after you have opened that door, there you may no longer tarry, set forth then to London to bury the head, and go straight forward.'

So they cut off his head, and these seven went forward therewith. And Branwen was the eighth with them, and they came to land at Aber Alaw, in Talebolion, and they sat down to rest. And Branwen looked towards Ireland and towards the island of the Mighty, to see if she could make them out. 'Alas,' said she, 'woe is me that I was ever born; two islands have been destroyed because of me!' Then she uttered a loud groan, and there broke her heart. And they made her a four-sided grave, and buried her upon the banks of the Alaw.

Then the seven men journeyed forward towards Harlech, bearing the head with them; and as they went, behold there met them a multitude of men and of women. 'Have you any tidings?' asked Manawyddan. 'We have none', said they, 'save that Caswallawn, the son of Beli, has conquered the island of the Mighty, and is crowned king in London.' 'What has become', said they, 'of Caradawc, the son of Bran, and the seven men who were left with him in this island?' 'Caswallawn came upon them, and slew six of the men, and Caradawc's heart broke for grief thereof; for he could see the sword that slew the men, but knew not who it was that wielded it. Caswallawn had flung upon him the Veil of Illusion, so that no one could see him slay the men, but the sword only could they see. And it liked him not to slay Caradawc, because he was his nephew, the son of his cousin. And now he was the third whose heart had broke through grief. Pendaran Dyfed, who had remained as a young page with these men, escaped into the wood,' they said.

Then they went on to Harlech, and there stopped to rest, and they provided meat and liquor, and sat down to eat and to drink. And there came three birds, and began singing unto them a certain song, and all the songs they had ever heard were unpleasant compared thereto; and the birds seemed to them to be at a great distance from them over the sea, yet they appeared as distinct as if they were close by, and at this repast they continued seven years.

And at the close of the seventh year they went forth to Gwales in Penfro. And there they found a fair and regal spot overlooking the ocean; and a spacious hall was therein. And they went into the hall, and two of its doors were open, but the third door was closed, that which looked towards Cornwall. 'See, yonder,' said Manawyddan, 'is the door that we may not open.' And that night they regaled themselves and were joyful. And of all they had seen of food laid before them, and of all they had heard of, they remembered nothing; neither of that, nor of any sorrow whatsoever. And there they remained four-score years, unconscious of having ever spent a time more joyous and mirthful. And they were not more weary than when first they came, neither did they, any of them, know the time they had been there. And it was not more irksome to them having the head with them, than if Bendigeid Bran had been with them himself. And because of these four-score years, it was called 'The Entertaining of the noble Head.' The entertaining of Branwen and Matholwch was in the time that they went to Ireland.

One day said Heilyn the son of Gwynn, 'Evil betide me, if I do not open the door to know if that is true which is said concerning it.' So he opened the door and looked towards Cornwall and Aber Henfelen. And when they had looked, they were as conscious of all the evils they had ever sustained, and of all the friends and companions they had lost, and of all the misery that had befallen them, as if all had happened in that very spot; and especially of the fate of their lord. And because of their perturbation they could not rest, but journeyed forth with the head towards London. And they buried the head in the White Mount, and when it was buried, this was the third goodly concealment; and it was the third ill-fated disclosure when it was disinterred, inasmuch as no invasion from across the sea came to this island while the head was in that concealment.

And thus is the story related of those who journeyed over from Ireland.

In Ireland none were left alive, except five pregnant women in a cave in the Irish wilderness; and to these five women in the same night were born five sons, whom they nursed until they became grown-up youths. And they thought about wives, and they at the same time desired to possess them, and each took a wife of the mothers of their companions, and they governed the country and peopled it.

And these five divided it amongst them, and because of this partition are the five divisions of Ireland still so termed. And they examined the land where the battles had taken place, and they found gold and silver until they became wealthy.

And thus ends this portion of the Mabinogi, concerning the blow given to Branwen, which was the third unhappy blow of this island; and concerning the entertainment of Bran, when the hosts of seven-score countries and ten went over to Ireland to revenge the blow given to Branwen; and concerning the seven years' banquet in Harlech, and the singing of the birds of Rhiannon, and the sojourning of the head for the space of four-score years.

MANAWYDDAN, THE SON OF LLYR

Here is the third portion of the Mabinogi

When the seven men of whom we spoke above had buried the head of
Bendigeid Bran, in the White Mount in London, with its face towards
France, Manawyddan gazed upon the town of London, and upon his
companions, and heaved a great sigh; and much grief and heaviness came
upon him. 'Alas, almighty heaven, woe is me,' he exclaimed, 'There is
none save myself without a resting-place this night.' 'Lord,' said Pryderi,
'be not so sorrowful. Thy cousin is king of the island of the Mighty, and
though he should do thee wrong, thou hast never been a claimant of land
or possessions. Thou art the third disinherited prince.' 'Yes,' answered he,
'but although this man is my cousin, it grieveth me to see anyone in the
place of my brother Bendigeid Bran; neither can I be happy in the same
dwelling with him.' 'Wilt thou follow the counsel of another?' said
Pryderi. 'I stand in need of counsel,' he answered, 'and what may that
counsel be?' 'Seven cantrefs remain unto me,' said Pryderi, 'wherein
Rhiannon my mother dwells. I will bestow her upon thee and the seven
cantrefs with her, and though thou hadst no possessions but those
cantrefs only, thou couldst not have seven cantrefs fairer than they. Cigfa,
the daughter of Gwynn Gloyw, is my wife, and since the inheritance of
the cantrefs belongs to me, do thou and Rhiannon enjoy them, and if
thou ever desire any possessions thou wilt take these.' 'I do not, chieftain,'
said he; 'heaven reward thee for thy friendship.' 'I would show thee the
best friendship in the world if thou wouldst let me.' 'I will, my friend,'
said he, 'and heaven reward thee. I will go with thee, to seek Rhiannon
and to look at thy possessions.' 'Thou wilt do well,' he answered; 'and I
believe that thou didst never hear a lady discourse better than she, and
when she was in her prime none was ever fairer. Even now her aspect is
not uncomely.'

They set forth, and, however long the journey, they came at length
to Dyfed, and a feast was prepared for them against their coming to
Arberth, which Rhiannon and Cigfa had provided. Then began
Manawyddan and Rhiannon to sit and to talk together, and from their
discourse his mind and his thoughts became warmed towards her, and he
thought in his heart he had never beheld any lady more fulfilled of grace
and beauty than she. 'Pryderi,' said he, 'I will that it be as thou didst say.'
'What saying was that?' asked Rhiannon. 'Lady,' said Pryderi, 'I did offer
thee as a wife to Manawyddan the son of Llyr.' 'By that will I gladly
abide,' said Rhiannon. 'Right glad am I also,' said Manawyddan; 'may
heaven reward him who hath shown unto me friendship so perfect as
this.'

And before the feast was over she became his bride. Said Pryderi,

'Tarry ye here the rest of the feast, and I will go into Lloegyr to tender my homage unto Caswallawn, the son of Beli.' 'Lord,' said Rhiannon, 'Caswallawn is in Kent, thou mayest therefore tarry at the feast, and wait until he shall be nearer.' 'We will wait,' he answered. So they finished the feast. And they began to make the circuit of Dyfed, and to hunt, and to take their pleasure. And as they went through the country, they had never seen lands more pleasant to live in, nor better hunting grounds, nor greater plenty of honey and fish. And such was the friendship between those four, that they would not be parted from each other by night nor by day.

And in the midst of all this he went to Caswallawn at Oxford, and tendered his homage; and honourable was his reception there, and highly was he praised for offering his homage.

And after his return, Pryderi and Manawyddan feasted and took their ease and pleasure. And they began a feast at Arberth, for it was the chief palace; and there originated all honour. And when they had ended the first meal that night, while those who served them ate, they arose and went forth, and proceeded all four to the Gorsedd of Arberth, and their retinue with them. And as they sat thus, behold, a peal of thunder, and with the violence of the thunderstorm, lo there came a fall of mist, so thick that not one of them could see the other. And after the mist it became light all around. And when they looked towards the place where they were wont to see cattle, and herds and dwellings, they saw nothing now, neither house, nor beast, nor smoke, nor fire, nor man, nor dwelling; but the houses of the court empty, and desert, and uninhabited, without either man or beast within them. And truly all their companions were lost to them, without their knowing aught of what had befallen them, save those four only.

'In the name of heaven,' cried Manawyddan, 'where are they of the court, and all my host beside these? Let us go and see.' So they came into the hall, and there was no man; and they went on to the castle, and to the sleeping-place, and they saw none; and in the mead-cellar and in the kitchen there was nought but desolation. So they four feasted, and hunted, and took their pleasure. Then they began to go through the land and all the possessions that they had, and they visited the houses and dwellings, and found nothing but wild beasts. And when they had consumed their feast and all their provisions, they fed upon the prey they killed in hunting, and the honey of the wild swarms. And thus they passed the first year pleasantly, and the second; but at the last they began to be weary.

'Verily,' said Manawyddan, 'we must not bide thus. Let us go into Lloegyr [England], and seek some craft whereby we may gain our support.' So they went into Lloegyr, and came as far as Hereford. And they took to making saddles. And Manawyddan began to make housings, and he gilded and coloured them with blue enamel, in the manner that he had seen it done by Llaesar Llaesgyngwyd. And he made the blue enamel as it was made by the other man. And therefore is it still called Calch Lasar [blue enamel], because Llaesar Llaesgyngwyd had wrought it. And as long as that workmanship could be had of Manawyddan, neither saddle nor housing was bought of a saddler throughout all Hereford; till at length every one of the saddlers perceived that they were losing much of their gain, and that no man bought of them, but him who could not get what he sought from Manawyddan. Then they assembled together, and agreed to slay him and his companions.

Now they received warning of this, and took counsel whether they should leave the city. 'By heaven,' said Pryderi, 'it is not my counsel that we should quit the town, but that we should slay these boors.' 'Not so,' said Manawyddan, 'for if we fight with them, we shall have evil fame, and shall be put in prison. It were better for us to go to another town to maintain ourselves.' So they four went to another city.

'What craft shall we take?' said Pryderi. 'We will make shields,' said Manawyddan. 'Do we know anything about that craft?' said Pryderi. 'We will try,' answered he. There they began to make shields, and fashioned them after the shape of the good shields they had seen; and they enamelled them, as they had done the saddles. And they prospered in that place, so that not a shield was asked for in the whole town, but such as was had of them. Rapid therefore was their work, and numberless were the shields they made. But at last they were marked by the craftsmen, who came together in haste, and their fellow-townsmen with them, and agreed that they should seek to slay them. But they received warning, and heard how the men had resolved on their destruction. 'Pryderi,' said Manawyddan, 'These men desire to slay us.' 'Let us not endure this from these boors, but let us rather fall upon them and slay them.' 'Not so,' he answered; 'Caswallawn and his men will hear of it, and we shall be undone. Let us go to another town.' So to another town they went.

'What craft shall we take?' said Manawyddan. 'Whatsoever thou wilt that we know,' said Pryderi. 'Not so,' he replied, 'but let us take to making shoes, for there is not courage enough among cordwainers either to fight with us or to molest us.' 'I know nothing thereof,' said Pryderi. 'But I know,' answered Manawyddan; 'and I will teach thee to stitch. We will not attempt to dress the leather, but we will buy it ready dressed and will make the shoes from it.'

So he began by buying the best cordwal that could be had in the town, and none other would he buy except the leather for the soles; and he associated himself with the best goldsmith in the town, and caused him to make clasps for the shoes, and to gild the clasps, and he marked how it was done until he learnt the method. And therefore was he called one of the three makers of gold shoes; and, when they could be had from him, not a shoe nor hose was bought of any of the cordwainers in the town. But when the cordwainers perceived that their gains were failing (for as Manawyddan shaped the work, so Pryderi stitched it), they came together and took counsel, and agreed that they would slay them.

'Pryderi,' said Manawyddan, 'These men are minded to slay us.' 'Wherefore should we bear this from the boorish thieves?' said Pryderi. 'Rather let us slay them all.' 'Not so,' said Manawyddan, 'we will not slay them, neither will we remain in Lloegyr any longer. Let us set forth to Dyfed and go to see it.'

So they journeyed along until they came to Dyfed, and they went forward to Arberth. And there they kindled fire and supported themselves by hunting. And thus they spent a month. And they gathered their dogs around them, and tarried there one year. And one morning Pryderi and Manawyddan rose up to hunt, and they ranged their dogs and went forth from the palace. And some of the dogs ran before them and came to a small bush which was near at hand; but as soon as they were come to the bush, they hastily drew back and returned to the men, their hair bristling up greatly. 'Let us go near to the bush,' said Pryderi, 'and see what is in it.' And as they came near, behold, a wild boar of a pure white colour rose up from the bush. Then the dogs, being set on by the men, rushed towards him; but he left the bush and fell back a little way from the men, and made a stand against the dogs without retreating from them, until the men had come near. And when the men came up, he fell back a second time, and betook him to flight. Then they pursued the boar until they beheld a vast and lofty castle, all newly built, in a place where they had never before seen either stone or building. And the boar ran swiftly into the castle and the dogs after him. Now when the boar and the dogs had gone into the castle, they began to wonder at finding a castle in a place where they had never before seen any building whatsoever. And from the top of the Gorsedd they looked and listened for the dogs. But so long as they were there they heard not one of the dogs nor aught concerning them.

'Lord,' said Pryderi, 'I will go into the castle to get tidings of the dogs.' 'Truly,' he replied, 'Thou wouldst be unwise to go into this castle, which thou hast never seen till now. If thou wouldst follow my counsel, thou wouldst not enter therein. Whosoever has cast a spell over this land has caused this castle to be here.' 'Of a truth,' answered Pryderi, 'I cannot thus give up my dogs.' And for all the counsel that Manawyddan gave him, yet to the castle he went.

When he came within the castle, neither man nor beast, nor boar nor dogs, nor house nor dwelling saw he within it. But in the centre of the castle floor he beheld a fountain with marble work around it, and on the margin of the fountain a golden bowl upon a marble slab, and chains hanging from the air, to which he saw no end.

And he was greatly pleased with the beauty of the gold, and with the rich workmanship of the bowl, and he went up to the bowl and laid hold of it. And when he had taken hold of it his hands stuck to the bowl, and his feet to the slab on which the bowl was placed, and all his joyousness forsook him, so that he could not utter a word. And thus he stood. And Manawyddan waited for him till near the close of the day. And late in the evening, being certain that he should have no tidings of Pryderi or of the dogs, he went back to the palace. And as he entered, Rhiannon looked at him. 'Where', said she, 'are thy companion and thy dogs?' 'Behold', he answered, 'The adventure that has befallen me.' And he related it all unto her.

'An evil companion hast thou been,' said Rhiannon, 'and a good companion hast thou lost.' And with that word she went out, and proceeded towards the castle according to the direction which he gave her. The gate of the castle she found open. She was nothing daunted, and she went in. And as she went in, she perceived Pryderi laying hold of the bowl, and she went towards him. 'Oh, my lord,' said she, 'what dost thou do here?' And she took hold of the bowl with him; and as she did so her hands became fast to the bowl, and her feet to the slab, and she was not able to utter a word. And with that, as it became night, lo, there came thunder upon them, and a fall of mist, and thereupon the castle vanished, and they with it.

When Cigfa, the daughter of Gwynn Gloyw, saw that there was no one in the palace but herself and Manawyddan, she sorrowed so that she cared not whether she lived or died. And Manawyddan saw this. 'Thou art in the wrong', said he, 'if through fear of me thou grievest thus. I call heaven to witness that thou hast never seen friendship more pure than that which I will bear thee, as long as heaven will that thou shouldst be thus. I declare to thee that were I in the dawn of youth I would keep my faith unto Pryderi, and unto thee also will I keep it. Be there no fear upon thee, therefore,' said he, 'for heaven is my witness that thou shalt meet with all the friendship thou canst wish, and that it is in my power to show thee, as long as it shall please heaven to continue us in this grief and woe.' 'Heaven reward thee,' she said, 'and that is what I deemed of thee.' And the damsel thereupon took courage and was glad.

'Truly, lady,' said Manawyddan, 'it is not fitting for us to stay here, we have lost our dogs, and we cannot get food. Let us go into Lloegyr; it is easiest for us to find support there.' 'Gladly, lord,' said she, 'we will do so.' And they set forth together to Lloegyr.

'Lord,' said she, 'what craft wilt thou follow? Take up one that is seemly.' 'None other will I take', answered he, 'save that of making shoes, as I did formerly.' 'Lord,' said she, 'such a craft becomes not a man so nobly born as thou.' 'By that however will I abide,' said he.

So he began his craft, and he made all his work of the finest leather he could get in the town, and, as he had done at the other place, he caused gilded clasps to be made for the shoes. And except himself all the cordwainers in the town were idle, and without work. For as long as they could be had from him, neither shoes nor hose were bought elsewhere. And thus they tarried there a year, until the cordwainers became envious, and took counsel concerning him. And he had warning thereof, and it was told him how the cordwainers had agreed together to slay him.

'Lord,' said Cigfa, 'wherefore should this be borne from these boors?' 'Nay,' said he, 'we will go back unto Dyfed.' So towards Dyfed they set forth.

Now Manawyddan, when he set out to return to Dyfed, took with him a burden of wheat. And he proceeded towards Arberth, and there he dwelt. And never was he better pleased than when he saw Arberth again, and the lands where he had been wont to hunt with Pryderi and with Rhiannon. And he accustomed himself to fish, and to hunt the deer in their covert. And then he began to prepare some ground, and he sowed a croft, and a second, and a third. And no wheat in the world ever sprung up better. And the three crofts prospered with perfect growth, and no man ever saw fairer wheat than it.

And thus passed the seasons of the year until the harvest came. And he went to look at one of his crofts, and behold it was ripe. 'I will reap this tomorrow,' said he. And that night he went back to Arberth, and on the morrow in the grey dawn he went to reap the croft, and when he came there he found nothing but the bare straw. Every one of the ears of the wheat was cut from off the stalk, and all the ears carried entirely away, and nothing but the straw left. And at this he marvelled greatly.

Then he went to look at another croft, and behold that also was ripe. 'Verily,' said he, 'This will I reap tomorrow.' And on the morrow he came with the intent to reap it, and when he came there he found nothing but the bare straw. 'Oh, gracious heaven,' he exclaimed, 'I know that whosoever has begun my ruin is completing it, and has also destroyed the country with me.'

Then he went to look at the third croft, and when he came there, finer wheat had there never been seen, and this also was ripe. 'Evil betide me,' said he, 'if I watch not here tonight. Whoever carried off the other corn will come in like manner to take this. And I will know who it is.' So he took his arms, and began to watch the croft. And he told Cigfa all that had befallen. 'Verily,' said she, 'what thinkest thou to do?' 'I will watch the croft tonight,' said he.

And he went to watch the croft. And at midnight, lo, there arose the loudest tumult in the world. And he looked, and behold the mightiest host of mice in the world, which could neither be numbered nor measured. And he knew not what it was until the mice had made their way into the croft, and each of them climbing up the straw and bending it down with its weight, had cut off one of the ears of wheat, and had carried it away, leaving there the stalk, and he saw not a single stalk there that had not a mouse to it. And they all took their way, carrying the ears with them.

In wrath and anger did he rush upon the mice, but he could no more come up with them than if they had been gnats, or birds in the air, except one only, which though it was but sluggish, went so fast that a man on foot could scarce overtake it. And after this one he went, and he caught it and put it in his glove, and tied up the opening of the glove with a string, and kept it with him, and returned to the palace.

Then he came to the hall where Cigfa was, and he lighted a fire, and hung the glove by the string upon a peg. 'What hast thou there, lord?' said Cigfa. 'A thief', said he, 'That I found robbing me.' 'What kind of thief may it be, lord, that thou couldst put into thy glove?' said she. 'Come and see, and I will tell thee,' he answered. Then he showed her how his fields had been wasted and destroyed, and how the mice came to the last of the fields in his sight. 'And one of them was less nimble than the rest, and is now in my glove; tomorrow I will hang it, and before heaven, if I had them, I would hang them all.' 'My lord,' said she, 'This is marvellous; but yet it would be unseemly for a man of dignity like thee to be hanging such a reptile as this. And if thou doest right, thou wilt not meddle with the creature, but wilt let it go.' 'Woe betide me', said he, 'if I would not hang them all could I catch them, and such as I have I will hang.' 'Verily, lord,' said she, 'There is no reason that I should succour this reptile, except to prevent discredit unto thee. Do therefore, lord, as thou wilt.' 'If I knew of any cause in the world wherefore thou shouldst succour it, I would take thy counsel concerning it,' said Manawyddan, 'but as I know of none, lady, I am minded to destroy it.' 'Do so willingly thee,' said she.

And then he went to the Gorsedd of Arberth, taking the mouse with him. And he set up two forks on the highest part of the Gorsedd. And while he was doing this, behold he saw a scholar coming towards him, in old and poor and tattered garments. And it was now seven years since he had seen in that place either man or beast, except those four persons who had remained together until two of them were lost.

'My lord,' said the scholar, 'good day to thee.' 'Heaven prosper thee, and my greeting be unto thee. And whence dost thou come, scholar?' asked he. 'I come, lord, from singing in Lloegyr; and wherefore dost thou enquire?' 'Because for the last seven years', answered he, 'I have seen no man here save four secluded persons, and thyself this moment.' 'Truly, lord,' said he, 'I go through this land unto mine own.' 'And what work art thou upon, lord?' 'I am hanging a thief that I caught robbing me,' said he. 'What manner of thief is that?' asked the scholar. 'I see a creature in thy hand like unto a mouse, and ill does it become a man of

rank equal to thine to touch a reptile such as this. Let it go forth free.' 'I
will not let it go free, by heaven,' said he; 'I caught it robbing me, and
the doom of a thief will I inflict upon it, and I will hang it.' 'Lord,' said
he, 'rather than see a man of rank equal to shine at such a work as this, I
would give thee a pound which I have received as alms, to let the reptile
go forth free.' 'I will not let it go free,' said he, 'by heaven, neither will I
sell it.' 'As thou wilt, lord,' he answered; 'except that I would not see a
man of rank equal to shine touching such a reptile, I care nought.' And
the scholar went his way.

And as he was placing the crossbeam upon the two forks, behold a
priest came towards him upon a horse covered with trappings. 'Good day
to thee, lord,' said he. 'Heaven prosper thee,' said Manawyddan; 'Thy
blessing.' 'The blessing of heaven be upon thee. And what, lord, art thou
doing?' 'I am hanging a thief that I caught robbing me,' said he. 'What
manner of thief, lord?' asked he. 'A creature', he answered, 'in form of a
mouse. It has been robbing me, and I am inflicting upon it the doom of a
thief.' 'Lord,' said he, 'rather than see thee touch this reptile, I would
purchase its freedom.' 'By my confession to heaven, neither will I sell it
nor set it free.' 'It is true, lord, that it is worth nothing to buy; but rather
than see thee defile thyself by touching such a reptile as this, I will give
thee three pounds to let it go.' 'I will not, by heaven,' said he, 'Take any
price for it. As it ought, so shall it be hanged.' 'Willingly, lord, do thy
good pleasure.' And the priest went his way.

Then he noosed the string around the mouse's neck, and as he was
about to draw it up, behold, he saw a bishop's retinue with his sumpter-
horses, and his attendants. And the bishop himself came towards him.
And he stayed his work. 'Lord bishop,' said he, 'Thy blessing.' 'Heaven's
blessing be unto thee,' said he; 'what work art thou upon?' 'Hanging a
thief that I caught robbing me,' said he. 'Is not that a mouse that I see in
thy hand?' 'Yes,' answered he. 'And she has robbed me.' 'Aye,' said he,
'since I have come at the doom of this reptile, I will ransom it of thee. I
will give thee seven pounds for it, and that rather than see a man of rank
equal to thine destroying so vile a reptile as this. Let it loose and thou
shalt have the money.' 'I declare to heaven that I will not set it loose.' 'If
thou wilt not loose it for this, I will give thee four-and-twenty pounds of
ready money to set it free.' 'I will not set it free, by heaven, for as much
again,' said he. 'If thou wilt not set it free for this, I will give thee all the
horses that thou seest in this plain, and the seven loads of baggage, and
the seven horses that they are upon.' 'By Heaven, I will not,' he replied.
'Since for this thou wilt not, do so at what price soever thou wilt.' 'I will
do so,' said he. 'I will that Rhiannon and Pryderi be free,' said he. 'That
thou shalt have,' he answered. 'Not yet will I loose the mouse, by
heaven.' 'What then wouldst thou?' 'That the charm and the illusion be
removed from the seven cantrefs of Dyfed.' 'This shalt thou have also; set

therefore the mouse free.' 'I will not set it free, by heaven,' said he. 'I will know who the mouse may be.' 'She is my wife.' 'Even though she be, I will not set her free. Wherefore came she to me?'

'To despoil thee,' he answered. 'I am Llwyd the son of Kilcoed, and I cast the charm over the seven cantrefs of Dyfed. And it was to avenge Gwawl, the son of Clud, from the friendship I had towards him, that I cast the charm. And upon Pryderi did I revenge Gwawl, the son of Clud, for the game of Badger in the Bag, that Pwyll chief of Annwfn played upon him, which he did unadvisedly in the court of Hefeydd Hen. And when it was known that thou wert come to dwell in the land, my household came and besought me to transform them to mice, that they might destroy thy corn. And it was my own household that went the first night. And the second night also they went, and they destroyed thy two crofts. And the third night came unto me my wife and the ladies of the court, and besought me to transform them. And I transformed them. Now she is pregnant. And had she not been pregnant thou wouldst not have been able to overtake her; but since this has taken place, and she has been caught, I will restore thee Pryderi and Rhiannon; and I will take the charm and illusion from off Dyfed. I have now told thee who she is. Set her therefore free.'

'I will not set her free, by heaven,' said he. 'What wilt thou more?' he asked. 'I will that there be no more charm upon the seven cantrefs of Dyfed, and that none shall be put upon it henceforth.' 'This thou shalt have,' said he. 'Now set her free.' 'I will not, by my faith,' he answered. 'What wilt thou furthermore?' asked he. 'Behold,' said he, 'This will I have; that vengeance be never taken for this, either upon Pryderi or Rhiannon, or upon me.' 'All this shalt thou have. And truly thou hast done wisely in asking this. Upon thy head would have lighted all this trouble.' 'Yes,' said he, 'for fear thereof was it, that I required this.' 'Set now my wife at liberty.' 'I will not, by heaven,' said he, 'until I see Pryderi and Rhiannon with me free.' 'Behold, here they come,' he answered.

And thereupon behold Pryderi and Rhiannon. And he rose up to meet them, and greeted them, and sat down beside them. 'Ah, chieftain, set now my wife at liberty,' said the bishop. 'Hast thou not received all thou didst ask?' 'I will release her gladly,' said he. And thereupon he set her free. Then Llwyd struck her with a magic wand, and she was changed back into a young woman, the fairest ever seen.

'Look around upon thy land,' said he, 'and then thou wilt see it all tilled and peopled, as it was in its best state.' And he rose up and looked forth. And when he looked he saw all the lands tilled, and full of herds and dwellings. 'What bondage', he enquired, 'has there been upon Pryderi and Rhiannon?' 'Pryderi has had the knockers of the gate of my palace about his neck, and Rhiannon has had the collars of the asses, after they have been carrying hay, about her neck.' And such had been their bondage. And by reason of this bondage is this story called the Mabinogi of Mynnweir and Mynord.

And thus ends this portion of the Mabinogi.

MATH, THE SON OF MATHONWY

Here is the fourth portion of the Mabinogi

Math, the son of Mathonwy, was lord over Gwynedd; and Pryderi, the son of Pwyll, was lord over the one-and-twenty cantrefs of the south; and these were the seven cantrefs of Dyfed, and the seven cantrefs of Morganwc, the four cantrefs of Ceredigiawn, and the three of Ystrad Tywi.

At that time, Math, the son of Mathonwy, could not exist unless his feet were in the lap of a maiden, except only when he was prevented by the tumult of war. Now the maiden who was with him was Goewin, the daughter of Pebin of Dol Pebin, in Arfon, and she was the fairest maiden of her time who was known there.

And Math dwelt always at Caer Dathyl, in Arfon and was not able to go the circuit of the land, but Gilfaethwy, the son of Don, and Eneyd, the son of Don, his nephews, the sons of his sisters, with his household, went the circuit of the land in his stead.

Now the maiden was with Math continually, and Gilfaethwy, the son of Don, set his affections upon her, and loved her so that he knew not what he should do because of her; and for this reason his hue, and his aspect and his spirits changed for love of her, so that it was not easy to know him. One day his brother Gwydion gazed steadfastly upon him. 'Youth,' said he, 'what aileth thee?' 'Why,' replied he, 'what seest thou in me?' 'I see', said he, 'That thou hast lost thy aspect and thy hue; what therefore aileth thee?' 'My lord brother,' he answered, 'That which aileth me, it will not profit me that I should own to any.' 'What may it be, my soul?' said he. 'Thou knowest', he said, 'That Math, the son of Mathonwy, has this property, that if men whisper together, in a tone however low, if the wind meet it, it becomes known unto him.' 'Yes,' said Gwydion, 'hold now thy peace, I know thy intent, thou lovest Goewin.' When he found that his brother knew his intent, he gave the heaviest sigh in the world. 'Be silent, my soul, and sigh not,' he said. 'It is not thereby that thou wilt succeed. I will cause', said he, 'if it cannot be otherwise, the rising of Gwynedd, and Powys, and Deheubarth, to seek the maiden. Be thou of glad cheer therefore, and I will compass it.'

So they went unto Math, the son of Mathonwy. 'Lord,' said Gwydion, 'I have heard that there have come to the south some beasts, such as were never known in this island before. What are they called?' he asked. 'Pigs, lord.' 'And what kind of animals are they?' 'They are small animals, and their flesh is better than the flesh of oxen.' 'They are small then?' 'And they change their names. Swine are they now called.' 'Who owneth them?' 'Pryderi the son of Pwyll; they were sent him from Annwfn, by Arawn, the king of Annwfn, and still they keep that name, half hog, half pig.' 'Verily,' asked he, 'and by what means may they be obtained from him?' 'I will go, lord, as one of twelve, in the guise of bards, to seek the swine.' 'But it may be that he will refuse you,' said he. 'My journey will not be evil, lord,' said he. 'I will not come back without the swine.' 'Gladly,' said he, 'go thou forward.'

So he and Gilfaethwy went, and ten other men with them. And they came into Ceredigiawn, to the place that is now called Rhuddlan Teifi, where the palace of Pryderi was. In the guise of bards they came in, and they were received joyfully, and Gwydion was placed beside Pryderi that night. 'Of a truth', said Pryderi, 'gladly would I have a tale from some of your men yonder.' 'Lord,' said Gwydion, 'we have a custom that the first night that we come to the court of a great man, the chief of song recites. Gladly will I relate a tale.' Now Gwydion was the best teller of tales in the world, and he diverted all the court that night with pleasant discourse and with tales, so that he charmed every one in the court, and it pleased Pryderi to talk with him.

And after this, 'Lord,' said he unto Pryderi, 'were it more pleasing to thee, that another should discharge my errand unto thee, than that I should tell thee myself what it is?' 'No,' he answered, 'ample speech hast thou.' 'Behold then, lord,' said he, 'my errand. It is to crave from thee the animals that were sent thee from Annwfn.' 'Verily,' he replied, 'That were the easiest thing in the world to grant, were there not a covenant between me and my land concerning them. And the covenant is that they shall not go from me, until they have produced double their number in the land.' 'Lord,' said he, 'I can set thee free from those words, and this is the way I can do so; give me not the swine tonight, neither refuse them unto me, and tomorrow I will show thee an exchange for them.'

And that night he and his fellows went unto their lodging, and they took counsel. 'Ah, my men,' said he, 'we shall not have the swine for the asking.' 'Well,' said they, 'how may they be obtained?' 'I will cause them to be obtained,' said Gwydion.

Then he betook himself to his arts, and began to work a charm. And he caused twelve chargers to appear, and twelve black greyhounds, each of them white-breasted, and having upon them twelve collars and twelve leashes, such as no one that saw them could know to be other than gold. And upon the horses twelve saddles, and every part which should have been of iron was entirely of gold, and the bridles were of the same workmanship. And with the horses and the dogs he came to Pryderi.

'Good-day unto thee, lord,' said he. 'Heaven prosper thee,' said the other, 'and greetings be unto thee.' 'Lord,' said he, 'behold here is a release for thee from the word which thou spakest last evening concerning the swine; that thou wouldst neither give nor sell them. Thou mayest exchange them for that which is better. And I will give these twelve horses, all caparisoned as they are, with their saddles and their bridles, and these twelve greyhounds, with their collars and their leashes as thou seest, and the twelve gilded shields that thou beholdest yonder.' Now these he had formed of fungus. 'Well,' said he, 'we will take counsel.' And they consulted together, and determined to give the swine to Gwydion, and to take his horses and his dogs and his shields.

Then Gwydion and his men took their leave, and began to journey forth with the pigs. 'Ah, my comrades,' said Gwydion, 'it is needful that we journey with speed. The illusion will not last but from the one hour to the same tomorrow.'

And that night they journeyed as far as the upper part of Ceredigiawn, to the place which, from that cause, is called Mochdref still. And the next day they took their course through Melenydd, and came that night to the town which is likewise for that reason called Mochdref between Keri and Arwystli. And thence they journeyed forward; and that night they came as far as that commote in Powys, which also upon account thereof is called Mochnant, and there they tarried that night. And they journeyed thence to the cantref of Rhos, and the place where they were that night is still called Mochdref.

'My men,' said Gwydion, 'we must push forward to the fastnesses of Gwynedd with these animals, for there is a gathering of hosts in pursuit of us.' So they journeyed on to the highest town of Arllechwedd, and there they made a sty for the swine, and therefore was the name of Creuwyryon given to that town. And after they had made the sty for the swine, they proceeded to Math, the son of Mathonwy, at Caer Dathyl. And when they came there, the country was rising. 'What news is there here?' asked Gwydion. 'Pryderi is assembling one-and-twenty cantrefs to pursue after you,' answered they. 'It is marvellous that you should have journeyed so slowly.' 'Where are the animals whereof you went in quest?' said Math. 'They have had a sty made for them in the other cantref below,' said Gwydion.

Thereupon, lo, they heard the trumpets and the host in the land, and they arrayed themselves and set forward and came to Penardd in Anon. And at night Gwydion, the son of Don, and Gilfaethwy his brother, returned to Caer Dathyl; and Gilfaethwy took Math, the son of Mathonwy's couch with Goewin, daughter of Pebin. And he turned out the other damsels from the room discourteously, and lay with Goewin against her will.

And when they saw the day on the morrow, they went back unto the place where Math, the son of Mathonwy, was with his host; and when they came there, the warriors were taking counsel in what district they should await the coming of Pryderi and the men of the south. So they went in to the council. And it was resolved to wait in the strongholds of Gwynedd, in Arvon. So within the two Maenors they took their stand, Maenor Penardd and Maenor Coed Alun. And there Pryderi attacked them, and there the combat took place. And great was the slaughter on both sides; but the men of the south were forced to flee. And they fled unto the place which is still called Nantcall. And thither did they follow them, and they made a vast slaughter of them there, so that they fled again as far as the place called Dol Pen Maen, and there they halted and sought to make peace.

And that he might have peace, Pryderi gave hostages; he gave Gwrgi Gwastra and three-and-twenty others, sons of nobles. And after this they journeyed in peace even unto Traeth Mawr; but as they went on together towards Melenryd, the men on foot could not be restrained from shooting. Pryderi despatched unto Math an embassy to pray him to forbid his people, and to leave it between him and Gwydion, the son of Don, for that he had caused all this. And the messengers came to Math. 'Of a truth,' said Math, 'I call heaven to witness, if it be pleasing unto Gwydion, the son of Don, I will so leave it gladly. Never will I compel any to go to fight, but that we ourselves should do our utmost.'

'Verily,' said the messengers, 'Pryderi saith that it were more fair that the man who did him this wrong should oppose his own body to his, and let his people remain unscathed.' 'I declare to heaven, I will not ask the men of Gwynedd to fight because of me. If I am allowed to fight Pryderi myself, gladly will I oppose my body to his.' And this answer they took back to Pryderi. 'Truly,' said Pryderi, 'I shall require no one to demand my rights but myself.'

Then these two came forth and armed themselves, and they fought. And by force of strength, and fierceness, and by the magic and charms of Gwydion, Pryderi was slain. And at Maen Tyriawc, above Melenryd, was he buried, and there is his grave.

And the men of the south set forth in sorrow towards their own land; nor is it a marvel that they should grieve, seeing that they had lost their lord, and many of their best warriors, and for the most part their horses and their arms.

The men of Gwynedd went back joyful and in triumph. 'Lord,' said Gwydion unto Math, 'would it not be right for us to release the hostages of the men of the south, which they pledged unto us for peace? For we ought not to put them in prison.' 'Let them then be set free,' saith Math. So that youth, and the other hostages that were with him, were set free to follow the men of the south.

Math himself went forward to Caer Dathyl. Gilfaethwy, the son of Don, and they of the household that were with him, went to make the circuit of Gwynedd as they were wont, without coming to the court. Math went into his chamber, and caused a place to be prepared for him whereon to recline, so that he might put his feet in the maiden's lap. 'Lord,' said Goewin, 'seek now another to hold thy feet, for I am no longer a maiden.' 'What meaneth this?' said he. 'An attack, lord, was made unawares upon me; but I held not my peace, and there was no one in the court who knew not of it. Now the attack was made by thy nephews, lord, the sons of thy sister, Gwydion, the son of Don, and Gilfaethwy, the son of Don; unto me they did rape and wrong, and unto thee dishonour, for I was lain with in thy chamber and thy bed.' 'Verily,' he exclaimed, 'I will do to the utmost of my power concerning this matter. But first I will cause thee to have compensation, and then will I have amends made unto myself. As for thee I will take thee to be my wife, and the possession of my dominions will I give unto thy hands.'

And Gwydion and Gilfaethwy came not near the court, but stayed in the confines of the land until it was forbidden to give them meat and drink. At first they came not near unto Math, but at the last they came. 'Lord,' said they, 'good-day to thee.' 'Well,' said he, 'is it to make me compensation that ye are come?' 'Lord,' they said, 'we are at thy will.' 'By my will I would not have lost my warriors, and so many arms as I have done. You cannot compensate me my shame, setting aside the death of Pryderi. But since ye come hither to be at my will, I shall begin your punishment forthwith.'

Then he took his magic wand, and struck Gilfaethwy, so that he became a deer, and he seized upon the other hastily lest he should escape from him. And he struck him with the same magic wand, and he became a deer also. 'Since now ye are in bonds, I will that ye go forth together and be coupled, and possess the nature of the animals whose form ye bear, and there will be offspring from this union. And this day twelvemonth come hither unto me.'

At the end of a year from that day, lo, there was a loud noise under the chamber wall, and the barking of the dogs of the palace together with the noise. 'Look', said he, 'what is without.' 'Lord,' said one, 'I have looked; there are there two deer, and a fawn with them.' Then he arose and went out. And when he came he beheld the three animals. And he lifted up his wand. 'As ye were deer last year, be ye wild hogs each and either of you, for the year that is to come.' And thereupon he struck them with the magic wand. 'The young one will I take and cause to be baptised.' Now the name that he gave him was Hydwn. 'Go ye and be wild swine, each and either of you, and be ye of the nature of wild swine. And this day twelvemonth be ye here under the wall with your young.'

At the end of the year the barking of dogs was heard under the wall of the chamber. And the court assembled, and thereupon he arose and went forth, and when he came forth he beheld three beasts. Now these were the beasts that he saw; two wild hogs of the woods, and a well-grown young one with them. And he was very large for his age. 'Truly,' said Math, 'This one will I take and cause to be baptised.' And he struck him with his magic wand, and he become a fine fair auburn-haired youth, and the name that he gave him was Hychdwn. 'Now as for you, as ye were wild hogs last year, be ye wolves each and either of you for the year that is to come.' Thereupon he struck them with his magic wand, and they became wolves. 'And be ye of like nature with the animals whose semblance ye bear, and return here this day twelvemonth beneath this wall with your cub.'

And at the same day at the end of the year, he heard a clamour and a barking of dogs under the wall of the chamber. And he rose and went forth. And when he came, behold, he saw two wolves, and a strong cub with them. 'This one will I take', said Math, 'and I will cause him to be baptised; there is a name prepared for him, and that is Bleiddwn. Now these three, such are they:

> The three sons of Gilfaethwy the false,
> The three faithful combatants,
> Bleiddwn, Hydwn, and Hychdwn the Tall.'

Then he struck the two with his magic wand, and they resumed their own nature. 'Oh men,' said he, 'for the wrong that ye did unto me sufficient has been your punishment and your dishonour. Prepare now precious ointment for these men, and wash their heads, and equip them.' And this was done.

And after they were equipped, they came unto him. 'Oh men,' said he, 'you have obtained peace, and you shall likewise have friendship. Give your counsel unto me, what maiden I shall seek.' 'Lord,' said Gwydion, the son of Don, 'it is easy to give thee counsel; seek Arianrod, the daughter of Don, thy niece, thy sister's daughter.'

And they brought her unto him, and the maiden came in. 'Ha, damsel,' said he, 'art thou a maiden?' 'I know not, lord, other than that I am.' Then he took up his magic wand, and bent it. 'Step over this,' said he, 'and I shall know if thou art a maiden.' Then stepped she over the magic wand, and there appeared from her a fine chubby yellow-haired boy. And at the crying out of the boy, she went towards the door. And thereupon some small form was seen; but before anyone could get a second glimpse of it, Gwydion had taken it, and had flung a scarf of velvet around it and hidden it. Now the place where he hid it was the bottom of a chest at the foot of his bed.

'Verily,' said Math, the son of Mathonwy, concerning the fine yellow-haired boy, 'I will cause this one to be baptised, and Dylan is the name I will give him.'

So they had the boy baptised, and as they baptised him he plunged into the sea. And immediately when he was in the sea, he took its nature, and swam as well as the best fish that was therein. And for that reason was he called Dylan, the son of the Wave. Beneath him no wave ever broke. And the blow whereby he came to his death was struck by his uncle Gofannon. The third fatal blow was it called.

As Gwydion lay one morning on his bed awake, he heard a cry in the chest at his feet; and though it was not loud, it was such that he could hear it. Then he arose in haste, and opened the chest: and when he opened it, he beheld an infant boy stretching out his arms from the folds of the scarf, and casting it aside. And he took up the boy in his arms, and carried him to a place where he knew there was a woman that could nurse him. And he agreed with the woman that she should take charge of the boy. And that year he was nursed.

And at the end of the year he seemed by his size as though he were two years old. And the second year he was a big child, and able to go to the court by himself. And when he came to the court, Gwydion noticed him, and the boy became familiar with him, and loved him better than anyone else. Then was the boy reared at the court until he was four years old, when he was as big as though he had been eight.

And one day Gwydion walked forth, and the boy followed him, and he went to the castle of Arianrod, having the boy with him; and when he came into the court, Arianrod arose to meet him, and greeted him and bade him welcome. 'Heaven prosper thee,' said he. 'Who is the boy that followeth thee?' she asked. 'This youth, he is thy son,' he answered. 'Alas,' said she, 'what has come unto thee that thou shouldst shame me thus? Wherefore cost thou seek my dishonour, and retain it so long as this?' 'Unless thou suffer dishonour greater than that of my bringing up such a boy as this, small will be thy disgrace.' 'What is the name of the boy?' said she. 'Verily,' he replied, 'he has not yet a name.' 'Well,' she said, 'I lay this destiny upon him, that he shall never have a name until he receives one from me.' 'Heaven bears me witness', answered he, 'That thou art a wicked woman. But the boy shall have a name how displeasing soever it may be unto thee. As for thee, that which afflicts thee is that thou art no longer called a damsel.' And thereupon he went forth in wrath, and returned to Caer Dathyl, and there he tarried that night.

And the next day he arose and took the boy with him, and went to walk on the seashore between that place and Aber Menei. And there he saw some sedges and seaweed, and he turned them into a boat. And out of dry sticks and sedges he made some Cordovan leather, and a great deal thereof, and he coloured it in such a manner that no one ever saw leather more beautiful. Then he made a sail to the boat, and he and the boy went in it to the port of the castle of Arianrod. And he began forming shoes and stitching them, until he was observed from the castle. And when he knew that they of the castle were observing him, he disguised his aspect, and put another semblance upon himself, and upon the boy, so that they might not be known. 'What men are those in yonder boat?' said Arianrod. 'They are cordwainers,' they answered. 'Go and see what kind of leather they have, and what kind of work they can do.'

So they came unto them. And when they came he was colouring some

Cordovan leather, and gilding it. And the messengers came and told her this. 'Well,' said she, 'Take the measure of my foot, and desire the cord-wainer to make shoes for me.' So he made the shoes for her, yet not according to the measure, but larger. The shoes then were brought unto her, and behold they were too large. 'These are too large,' said she, 'but he shall receive their value. Let him also make some that are smaller than they.' Then he made her others that were much smaller than her foot, and sent them unto her. 'Tell him that these will not go on my feet,' said she. And they told him this. 'Verily,' said he, 'I will not make her any shoes, unless I see her foot.' And this was told unto her. 'Truly,' she answered, 'I will go unto him.'

So she went down to the boat, and when she came there, he was shaping shoes and the boy stitching them. 'Ah, lady,' said he, 'good-day to thee.' 'Heaven prosper thee,' said she. 'I marvel that thou canst not manage to make shoes according to a measure.' 'I could not,' he replied, 'but now I shall be able.'

Thereupon behold a wren stood upon the deck of the boat, and the boy shot at it, and hit it in the leg between the sinew and the bone. Then she smiled. 'Verily,' said she, 'with a steady hand did the fair one aim at it.' 'Heaven reward thee not, but now has he got a name. And a good enough name it is. Llew Llaw Gyffes be he called henceforth.'

Then the work disappeared in seaweed and sedges, and he went on with it no further. And for that reason was he called the third gold-shoemaker. 'Of a truth,' said she, 'Thou wilt not thrive the better for doing evil unto me.' 'I have done thee no evil yet,' said he. Then he restored the boy to his own form. 'Well,' said she, 'I will lay a destiny upon this boy, that he shall never have arms and armour until I invest him with them.' 'By heaven,' said he, 'let thy malice be what it may, he shall have arms.'

Then they went towards Dinas Dinllef, and there he brought up Llew Llaw Gyffes, until he could manage any horse, and he was perfect in features, and strength, and stature. And then Gwydion saw that he languished through the want of horses and arms. And he called him unto him. 'Ah, youth,' said he, 'we will go tomorrow on an errand together. Be therefore more cheerful than thou art.' 'That I will,' said the youth. Next morning, at the dawn of day, they arose. And they took way along the sea-coast, up towards Bryn Aryen. And at the top of Cefn Clydno they equipped themselves with horses, and went towards the castle of Arianrod. And they changed their form and pricked towards the gate in the semblance of two youths, but the aspect of Gwydion was more staid than that of the other. 'Porter,' said he, 'go thou in and say that there are here bards from Glamorgan.' And the porter went in. 'The welcome of heaven be unto them, let them in,' said Arianrod.

With great joy were they greeted. And the hall was arranged, and they went to meat. When meat was ended, Arianrod discoursed with Gwydion of tales and stories. Now Gwydion was an excellent teller of tales. And when it was time to leave off feasting, a chamber was prepared for them, and they went to rest.

In the early twilight Gwydion arose, and he called unto him his magic and his power. And by the time that the day dawned, there resounded through the land uproar, and trumpets and shouts. When it was now day, they heard a knocking at the door of the chamber, and therewith Arianrod asking that it might be opened. Up rose the youth and opened unto her, and she entered and a maiden with her. 'Ah, good men,' she said, 'in evil plight are we.' 'Yes, truly,' said Gwydion, 'we have heard trumpets and shouts; what thinkest thou that they may mean?' 'Verily,' said she, 'we cannot see the colour of the ocean by reason of all the ships, side by side. And they are making for the land with all the speed they can. And what can we do?' said she. 'Lady,' said Gwydion, 'There is none other counsel than to close the castle upon us, and to defend it as best we may.' 'Truly,' said she, 'may heaven reward you. And do you defend it. And here may you have plenty of arms.'

And thereupon went she forth for the arms, and behold she returned, and two maidens, and suits of armour for two men, with her. 'Lady,' said he, 'do you accoutre this stripling, and I will arm myself with the help of thy maidens. Lo, I hear the tumult of the men approaching.' 'I will do so, gladly.' So she armed him fully, and that right cheerfully. 'Hast thou finished arming the youth?' said he. 'I have finished,' she answered. 'I likewise have finished,' said Gwydion. 'Let us now take off our arms, we have no need of them.' 'Wherefore?' said she. 'Here is the army around the house.' 'Oh, lady, there is here no army.' 'Oh,' cried she, 'whence then was this tumult?' 'The tumult was but to break thy prophecy and to obtain arms for thy son. And now has he got arms without any thanks unto thee.' 'By heaven,' said Arianrod, 'Thou art a wicked man. Many a youth might have lost his life through the uproar thou hast caused in this cantref today. Now will I lay a destiny upon this youth,' she said, 'That he shall never have a wife of the race that now inhabits this earth.' 'Verily,' said he, 'Thou wert ever a malicious woman, and no one ought to support thee. A wife shall he have notwithstanding.'

They went thereupon unto Math, the son of Mathonwy, and complained unto him most bitterly of Arianrod. Gwydion showed him also how he had procured arms for the youth. 'Well,' said Math, 'we will seek, I and thou, by charms and illusion, to form a wife for him out of flowers. He has now come to man's stature, and he is the comeliest youth that was ever beheld.' So they took the blossoms of the oak, and the blossoms of the broom, and the blossoms of the meadowsweet, and produced from them a maiden, the fairest and most graceful that man ever saw. And they baptised her and gave her the name of Blodeuwedd.

After she had become his bride, and they had feasted, said Gwydion: 'It is not easy for a man to maintain himself without possessions.' 'Of a truth,' said Math, 'I will give the young man the best cantref to hold.' 'Lord,' said he, 'what cantref is that?' 'The cantref of Dinodig,' he answered. Now it is called at this day Eifionydd and Ardudwy. And the place in the cantref where he dwelt, was a palace of his in a spot called Mur y Castell, on the confines of Ardudwy. There dwelt he and reigned, and both he and his sway were beloved by all.

One day he went forth to Caer Dathyl, to visit Math, the son of Mathonwy. And on the day that he set out for Caer Dathyl, Blodeuwedd walked in the court. And she heard the sound of a horn. And after the sound of the horn, behold a tired stag went by, with dogs and huntsmen following it. And after the dogs and the huntsmen there came a crowd of men on foot. 'Send a youth', said she, 'To ask who yonder host may be.' So a youth went, and enquired who they were. 'Gronw Pebyr is this, the lord of Penllyn,' said they. And thus the youth told her.

Gronw Pebyr pursued the stag, and by the river Cynfael he overtook the stag and killed it. And what with flaying the stag and baiting his dogs, he was there until the night began to close in upon him. And as the day departed and the night drew near, he came to the gate of the court. 'Verily,' said Blodeuwedd, 'The chieftain will speak ill of us if we let him at this hour depart to another land without inviting him in.' 'Yes, truly, lady,' said they, 'it will be most fitting to invite him.'

Then went messengers to meet him and bid him in. And he accepted her bidding gladly, and came to the court, and Blodeuwedd went to meet him, and greeted him, and bade him welcome. 'Lady,' said he, 'heaven repay thee thy kindness.'

When they had disaccoutred themselves, they went to sit down. And Blodeuwedd looked upon him, and from the moment that she looked on him she became filled with his love. And he gazed on her, and the same thought came unto him as unto her, so that he could not conceal from her that he loved her, but he declared unto her that he did so. Thereupon she was very joyful. And all their discourse that night was concerning the affection and love which they felt one for the other, and which in no longer space than one evening had arisen. And that evening they slept together. The next day he sought to depart. But she said, 'I pray thee go not from me today.' And that night he tarried also. And that night they consulted by what means they might always be together. 'There is none other counsel', said he, 'but that thou strive to learn from Llew Llaw Gyffes in what manner he will meet his death. And this must thou do under the semblance of solicitude concerning him.'

The next day Gronw sought to depart. 'Verily,' said she, 'I will counsel thee not to go from me today.' 'At thy instance will I not go,' said he, 'albeit, I must say, there is danger that the chief who owns the palace may return home.' 'Tomorrow', answered she, 'will I indeed permit thee to go forth.'

The next day he sought to go, and she hindered him not. 'Be mindful', said Gronw, 'of what I have said unto thee, and converse with him fully, and that under the guise of the dalliance of love, and find out by what means he may come to his death.'

That night Llew Llaw Gyffes returned to his home. And the day they spent in discourse, and minstrelsy, and feasting. And at night they went to rest, and he spoke to Blodeuwedd once, and he spoke to her a second time. But, for all this, he could not get from her one word. 'What aileth thee?' said he, 'art thou well?' 'I was thinking', said she, 'of that which thou didst never think of concerning me; for I was sorrowful as to thy death, lest thou shouldst go sooner than I.' 'Heaven reward thy care for me,' said he, 'but until heaven take me I shall not easily be slain.' 'For the sake of heaven, and for mine, show me how thou mightest be slain. My memory in guarding is better than shine.' 'I will tell thee gladly,' said he; 'not easily can I be slain, except by a wound. And the spear wherewith I am struck must be a year in the forming. And nothing must be done towards it except during the time of Mass on Sundays.' 'Is this certain?' asked she. 'It is in truth,' he answered. 'And I cannot be slain within a house, nor without. I cannot be slain on horseback nor on foot.' 'Verily,' said she, 'in what manner then canst thou be slain?' 'I will tell thee,' said he; 'by making a bath for me by the side of a river, and by putting a roof over the cauldron, and thatching it well and tightly, and bringing a buck, and putting it beside the cauldron. Then if I place one foot on the buck's back, and the other on the edge of the cauldron, whosoever strikes me thus will cause my death.' 'Well,' said she, 'I thank heaven that it will be easy to avoid this.'

No sooner had she held this discourse than she sent to Gronw Pebyr. Gronw toiled at making the spear, and that day twelvemonth it was ready. And that very day he caused her to be informed thereof.

'Lord,' said Blodeuwedd unto Llew, 'I have been thinking how it is possible that what thou didst tell me formerly can be true; wilt thou show me in what manner thou couldst stand at once upon the edge of a cauldron and upon a buck, if I prepare the bath for thee?' 'I will show thee,' said he.

Then she sent unto Gronw, and bade him be in ambush on the hill which is now called Bryn Kyfergyr, on the bank of the river Cynfael. She caused also to be collected all the goats that were in the cantref, and had them brought to the other side of the river, opposite Bryn Kyfergyr. And the next day she spoke thus. 'Lord,' said she, 'I have caused the roof and the bath to be prepared, and lo! they are ready.' 'Well,' said Llew, 'we will go gladly to look at them.'

The day after they came and looked at the bath. 'Wilt thou go into the bath, lord?' said she. 'Willingly will I go in,' he answered. So into the bath he went, and he anointed himself. 'Lord,' said she, 'behold the animals which thou didst speak of as being called bucks.' 'Well,' said he, 'cause one of them to be caught and brought here.' And the buck was brought. Then Llew rose out of the bath, and put on his trousers, and he placed one foot on the edge of the bath and the other on the buck's back.

Thereupon Gronw rose up from the hill which is called Bryn Kyfergyr, and he rested on one knee, and flung the poisoned dart and struck him on the side, so that the shaft started out, but the head of the dart remained in. Then Llew flew up in the form of an eagle and gave a fearful scream. And thenceforth was he no more seen. As soon as he departed, Gronw and Blodeuwedd went together unto the palace that night. And the next day Gronw arose and took possession of Ardudwy. And after he had overcome the land, he ruled over it, so that Ardudwy and Penllyn were both under his sway.

Then these tidings reached Math, the son of Mathonwy. And heaviness and grief came upon Math, and much more upon Gwydion than upon him. 'Lord,' said Gwydion, 'I shall never rest until I have tidings of my nephew.' 'Verily,' said Math, 'may heaven be thy strength.' Then Gwydion set forth and began to go forward. And he went through Gwynedd and Powys to the confines. And when he had done so, he went into Arfon, and came to the house of a vassal, in Maenor Penardd. And he alighted at the house, and stayed there that night. The man of the house and his household came in, and last of all came there the swineherd. Said the man of the house to the swineherd, 'Well, youth, hath thy sow come in tonight?' 'She hath,' said he, 'and is this instant returned to the pigs.' 'Where doth this sow go to?' said Gwydion. 'Every day, when the sty is opened, she goeth forth and none can catch sight of her, neither is it known whither she goeth more than if she sank into the earth.' 'Wilt thou grant unto me', said Gwydion, 'not to open the sty until I am beside the sty with thee?' 'This will I do, right gladly,' he answered.

That night they went to rest; and as soon as the swineherd saw the light of day, he awoke Gwydion. And Gwydion arose and dressed himself, and went with the swineherd, and stood beside the sty. Then the swineherd opened the sty. And as soon as he opened it, behold she leaped forth, and set off with great speed. And Gwydion followed her, and she went against the course of a river, and made for a brook, which is now called Nant y Llew. And there she halted and began feeding. And Gwydion came under the tree, and looked what it might be that the sow was feeding on. And he saw that she was eating putrid flesh and vermin. Then looked he up to the top of the tree, and as he looked he beheld on the top of the tree an eagle, and when the eagle shook itself, there fell vermin and putrid flesh from off it, and these the sow devoured. And it seemed to him that the eagle was Llew. And he sang an englyn:

> Oak that grows between the two banks;
> Darkened is the sky and hill!
> Shall I not tell him by his wounds
> That this is Llew?

Upon this the eagle came down until he reached the centre of the tree. And Gwydion sang another englyn:

> Oak that grows in upland ground
> Is it not wetted by the rain? Has it not been drenched
> By nine-score tempests?
> It bears in its branches Llew Llaw Gyffes.

Then the eagle came down until he was on the lowest branch of the tree, and thereupon Gwydion sang this englyn:

> Oak that grows beneath the steep;
> Stately and majestic is its aspect
> Shall I not speak it? That Llew will come to my lap?

And the eagle came down upon Gwydion's knee. And Gwydion struck him with his magic wand, so that he returned to his own form. No one ever saw a more piteous sight, for he was nothing but skin and bone.

Then he went unto Caer Dathyl, and there were brought unto him good physicians that were in Gwynedd, and before the end of the year he was quite healed.

'Lord,' said he unto Math, the son of Mathonwy, 'it is full time now that I have retribution of him by whom I have suffered all this woe.' 'Truly,' said Math, 'he will never be able to maintain himself in the possession of that which is thy right.' 'Well,' said Llew, 'The sooner I have my right, the better shall I be pleased.'

Then they called together the whole of Gwynedd, and set forth to Ardudwy. And Gwydion went on before and proceeded to Mur y Castell. And when Blodeuwedd heard that he was coming, she took her maidens with her and fled to the mountain. And they passed through the river Cynfael, and went towards a court that there was upon the mountain, and through fear they could not proceed except with their faces looking backwards, so that unawares they fell into the lake. And they were all drowned except Blodeuwedd herself, and her Gwydion overtook. And he said unto her, 'I will not slay thee, but I will do unto thee worse than that. For I will turn thee into a bird; and because of the shame thou hast done unto Llew Llaw Gyffes, thou shalt never show thy face in the light of day henceforth; and that through fear of all the other birds. For it shall be their nature to attack thee and to chase thee from wheresoever they may find thee. And thou shalt not lose thy name, but shalt be always called Blodeuwedd.' Now Blodeuwedd is an owl in the language of this present time, and for this reason is the owl hateful unto all birds. And even now the owl is called Blodeuwedd.

Then Gronw Pebyr withdrew unto Penllyn, and he despatched thence an embassy. And the messengers he sent asked Llew Llaw Gyffes if he would take land, or domain, or gold, or silver, for the injury he had received. 'I will not, by my confession to heaven,' said he. 'Behold this is the least that I will accept from him; that he come to the spot where I was when he wounded me with the dart, and that I stand where he did, and that with a dart I take my aim at him. And this is the very least that I will accept.'

And this was told unto Gronw Pebyr. 'Verily,' said he, 'is it needful for me to do thus? My faithful warriors, and my household, and my foster-brothers, is there not one among you who will stand the blow in my stead?' 'There is not, verily,' answered they. And because of their refusal to suffer one stroke for their lord, they are called the third disloyal tribe even unto this day. 'Well,' said he, 'I will meet it.'

Then they two went forth to the banks of the river Cynvael, and Gronw stood in the place where Llew Llaw Gyffes was when he struck him, and Llew in the place where Gronw was. Then said Gronw Pebyr unto Llew, 'Since it was through the wiles of a woman that I did unto thee as I have done, I adjure thee by heaven to let me place between me and the blow, the slab thou seest yonder on the river's bank.' 'Verily,' said Llew, 'I will not refuse thee this.' 'Ah,' said he, 'may heaven reward thee.' So Gronw took the slab and placed it between him and the blow. Then Llew flung the dart at him, and it pierced the slab and went through Gronw likewise, so that it pierced through his back. And thus was Gronw Pebyr slain. And there is still the slab on the bank of the river Cynfael, in Ardudwy, having the hole through it. And therefore is it even now called Llech Gronw.

A second time did Llew Llaw Gyffes take possession of the land, and prosperously did he govern it. And, as the story relates, he was lord after this over Gwynedd.

And thus ends this portion of the Mabinogi.

20. THE VOYAGE OF ST BRENDAN

The historical Saint Brendan was born about 484, and was a descendant of the Irish royal family who ruled Munster. He is known to have sailed to the Orkneys and Shetlands in order to convert the inhabitants, and may have ventured as far as the Faeroes. He also seems to have visited Brittany, and he was for a time abbot of a monastery in South Wales. In an age when any journey was fraught with difficulties, he was a notable traveller, and it was for this that he was remembered. In the course of time, other stories about Irish seafarers were attached to his name, in particular the adventures of Mael Duin, and the definitive account of his wanderings was written in Latin in Germany, near Trier, at the beginning of the tenth century. His adventures are an immram, *an Irish word for voyage which came to mean a voyage into the unknown in which the pilgrim surrenders himself to God's will. It is a theme which occurs both in Ireland and at the other end of the Eurasian land-mass, in the stories of Buddhist monks in Japan. The following version of Saint Brendan's story is based on a fifteenth century English retelling, which in turn derives from a translation into Anglo-Norman French made for king Henry I in the first quarter of the twelfth century. In recent years, Tim Severin has shown that it is possible to sail a curragh such as Saint Brendan might have used as far as Newfoundland, making Brendan a possible precursor of the Viking settlers there.*

HERE begins the life of saint Brendan. Saint Brendan, the holy man, was a monk; he was born in Ireland, and there he was abbot of a house in which were a thousand monks. He led a strict and holy life, in great penance and abstinence, and he governed his monks most virtuously. There came to him a holy abbot called Beryne to visit hym, and each was very glad to see the other; and then saint Brendan began to tell abbot Beryne of the many wonders that he had seen in different lands. And when Beryne heard what saint Brendan said, he began to sigh, and started to weep. And saint Brendan comforted him as best he could, saying, 'You came here to rejoice with me, so for the love of God cease your weeping, tell me what marvels you have seen in the great sea and in the ocean which encircles the world, and from which flow all the other streams in every corner of the earth.' Then Beryne began to tell saint Brendan and his monks the marvels that he had seen, weeping all the time, and said, 'I have a son, his name is Meruoc, and he was a monk of great fame, who had a great desire to set sail from different countries to find a solitary place where he might dwell secretly, away from the busyness of the world, so that he could serve God quietly with greater devotion; and I advised him to sail to an island a long way out to sea, near the Mountains of Stones, which is very well known. So he made his preparations and sailed there with his monks. And when he came there, he liked that place very well, and he and his monks served our Lord most devoutly.' And then Beryne saw in a vision that this monk Meruoc had sailed very far out to sea to eastward, more than three days' voyage, and it seemed that a dark cloud suddenly came up and covered them, so that for most of the day they saw no light; and at our Lord's pleasure, the cloud passed away, and they saw a very fair island, for which they steered. In that island there was joy and mirt, and all the earth there shone as bright as the sun, and there were the fairest trees and herbs that anyone ever saw, and there were many precious stones shining bright, and every leaf there was full of figures, and every tree full of fruit; so that it was a glorious sight, and it was like heaven to stay there. And then a fair young man came and welcomed them very courteously, calling every monk by his name; he said that they should praise the name of our Lord Jesu, who of his grace had shown them that glorious place, where it is ever day, and never night, and this place is called the earthly paradise. By this island there is another island where no-one can land. And this young man said to them 'You have been here for half a year, and you have had nothing to eat or drink, nor have you slept.' And they thought that they had been there less than half an hour, because they were so merry and joyful. The young man told them that this is the place where Adam and Eve first lived, and should have lived there always if they had not broken the commandment of God. Then the young man brought them back to their ship, and said that they could no longer stay there; and when they were all on board, this young man suddenly vanished out of their sight. Soon after this, by the guidance of our Lord Jesu, they came to the abbey where saint Brendan lived; he and his brethren received them well, and asked where they had been so long; they said, 'We have been in the land of promise, in front of the gates of Paradise, where it is ever day, and never night.' And they all said that the place is very delightful, and their clothes smelled of the sweet and joyful place.

Then saint Brendan decided soon after to seek that place with God's help, and began to provision a good strong ship, and victualled it for a voyage of seven years. Then he took his leave of all his brethren, and took twelve monks with him. Before they entered the ship they fasted for forty days, and lived devoutly, and each of them received the sacrament. And when saint Brendan and his twelve monks had entered the ship, two more of his monks came to him, and begged him to allow them to go with him. He replied, 'You can sail with me, but one of you shall go to hell before you return.' But this did not deter them, and they went with him.

Then saint Brendan ordered the sailors to hoist the sail, and they sailed out in God's name. The next day they were out of sight of land; for forty days and forty nights after that they sailed due east. Then they saw an island in the far distance, and they sailed towards it as fast as they could; they saw a great rock of stone appear above the sea, which they sailed round for three days before they could find a place to land. But at last, by the providence of God, they found a little harbour and they all went ashore. A fine hound suddenly appeared and fell down at the feet of saint Brendan, and welcomed him as best he could. Then Brendan said to his brethren, 'Be of good cheer, for our Lord has sent to us His messenger, to lead us to some good place.' And the hound brought them into a fine hall, where they found the tables spread ready, full of good meat and drink. Saint Brendan said grace, and then he and his brethren sat down and ate and drank of whatever they found; and there were beds ready for them, in which they took their rest after their long labours. The next day they returned to their ship and sailed for a long time across the sea before they could find any land, until at last, by God's providence, they saw far away, a very beautiful island, full of green fields, in which there were the whitest and biggest sheep that they had ever seen; for each sheep was as large as an ox.

And soon after this a handsome old man came to them and welcomed them warmly, and said, 'This is the Island of Sheep; there is never cold weather here, but it is always summer, and that is why the sheep are so big and white; they eat the best grass and herbs that is to be found anywhere.' He took his leave of them, and told them to sail due east, and if God favoured them they would come within a short time to a place like paradise, where they should celebrate Easter. So they sailed on, and came soon after to that land; but they had difficulty in landing because in some places it was shallow, and elsewhere there were great rocks. At last they managed to land on a nearby island, thinking that they would be safe there; they lit a fire to cook their dinner, but saint Brendan stayed in the ship. When the fire was really hot, and the meat almost cooked, the island began to move. This terrified the monks, and they fled in haste to the ship, leaving the fire and meat behind, They marvelled greatly that the island had moved; saint Brendan reassured them, and told them that it was a great fish named Jascony, which tries night and day to put its tail in its mouth, but it is too large to do so. After this they sailed westwards for three days and three nights before they saw land, which made them very anxious.

But soon after, as God ordained, they saw a fair island, full of flowers, herbs, and trees; and they thanked God for his good grace before they landed there. When they had gone a long way inland, they found a clear well, near which stood a tree with many branches, and on every bough sat a fair bird, and they sat so thick on the tree that hardly a leaf of the tree could be seen. There were so many of them, and they sang so merrily that it was a heavenly noise to hear. Saint Brendan knelt and wept for joy, and prayed devoutly to our Lord God to know what these birds meant. And one of the birds flew from the tree to saint Brendan, and fluttered his wings, which made music like that of a fiddle; and Brendan thought he had never heard such a joyful melody. He commanded the bird to tell him why they sat so thick on the tree, and sang so merrily. Then the bird said, 'We were once angels in heaven, but when our master Lucifer fell down to hell for his mighty pride, we fell with him for our offences, some higher, and some lower, according to the degree to which they had sinned; and because our sins are only little, our Lord has set us here, free of all pain, in great joy and mirth, as it has please him to do; we serve him here on this tree in the best manner that we can. Sunday is a day of rest from all worldly occupations, and so on that day we are all made as white as snow, to praise our Lord in the best way we can.'

Then the bird said to saint Brendan, 'It is twelve months since you left your abbey, and in seven years' time you will see the place that you wish to find; but every year for seven years you shall celebrate Easter here with us. At the end of seven years you shall come into the Land of Promise.' And it was on Easter day that the bird told saint Brendan this. Then the bird flew back to his fellows on the tree. Then all the birds began to sing evensong so merrily, that it was a heavenly noise to here; and after supper saint Brendan and his companions went to bed, and slept well, and on the next day they got up early. Then those birds began matins, prime, and all the services that Christians were accustomed to sing. And saint Brendan and his companions stayed there for eight weeks, until Trinity Sunday was past; and then they sailed back to the Island of Sheep, and took on supplies, and took their leave of the old man, and returned to their ship. Then the bird from the singing tree came again to saint Brendan, and said, 'I have come to tell you that you shall sail from here to an island, where there is an abbey of 24 monks, which is a long way off. There you shall hold Christmas, and your Easter with us, as I said before.' And the bird flew back to his fellows. Saint Brendan and his company sailed out into the ocean; and soon after a great tempest overwhelmed them; they were greatly troubled for a long time, and hard put to it to keep afloat. They saw, by God's providence, an island in the far distance, and prayed fervently to our Lord that He would send them there safely; but it was forty days before they reached it, and all the monks were so weary from their troubles that they did not expect to survive, and cried out to our Lord all the time to have mercy on them and bring them safely to that island. In the end they came into a little harbour, but it was so narrow that the ship could scarcely get in. They anchored, and the monks landed, and walked about for a long time, until at last they found two wells; one had fair and clear water, while the other was rather disturbed and murky. They wanted to drink from the clear well, but saint Brendan ordered them to take nothing without asking, 'for if we abstain for a while, our Lord will provide the best for us.' At this a fair old man with white hair appeared, and welcomed them humbly, and kissed saint Brendan. He led them past many clear wells until they came to a fine abbey, where they were received with great honour, and a solemn procession, with twenty four monks all in royal copes of cloth of gold, and a royal cross carried before them. Then the abbot welcomed saint Brendan and his companions, and kissed them with all respect, and took saint Brendan by the hand, and led him and his monks into a fair hall, and made them sit down on the bench in a row; and the abbot of the place washed their feet with fair water from the well that they saw before, and after led them into the frater, and made them sit down among his monks. And then as God had provided, a man came and served them with excellent meat and drink. For every monk had set before him a good white loaf and white roots and herbs, which were very delicious, but they did not know what kind of roots they were; and they drank the water of the fair clear well that they had seen when they first landed, and which saint Brendan forbad them to take.

Then the abbot came and spoke cheerfully to saint Brendan and his monks, and begged them to eat and drink their fill, 'for every day our Lord sends a goodly old man who lays this table, and puts out our meat and drink; but we do not know how it comes. We never arrange for meat and drink for ourselves, and yet we have been here for seventy years, and our Lord (praise to His name!) always feeds us. We are twenty-four in all, and every weekday he sends us twelve loaves; and every Sunday and feast day, twenty-four loaves, and the bread that we leave at dinner we eat at supper. And now that you have come, our Lord has sent us forty-eight loaves, so that we can eat together with you as brethren. And twelve of us always go to dinner, while twelve others keep the choir; and we have done this for seventy years, for as long as we have been here. We came here out of St Patrick's abbey in Ireland; and as you see, our Lord has provided for us, but none of us knows how it comes save God alone, to whom be given honour and praise, world without end. The weather is always fair here, and none of us has ever been sick since we came. When we go to Mass, or to any other service of our Lord in the church, seven tapers of wax are set in the choir, and are lit each time without human help; they burn day and night at every hour when there is a service, and they have never grown any less in all the seventy years we have been here.'

Then saint Brendan went to the church with the abbot of the place, and they said evensong together very devoutly. Saint Brendan looked upwards at the crucifix, and saw our Lord hanging on the cross, which was made of fine crystal and skilfully made; and in the choir there were twenty-four seats for the twenty-four monks, and the seven tapers burning, and the abbot's seat was in the middle of the choir. Saint

Brendan asked the abbot how long they had kept silence, for none of them spoke to each other.' And he said: 'These twenty-four years we have not spoken a word to each other.' Then saint Brendan wept with joy at the holiness of their conversation.

Saint Brendan asked the abbot if he and his monks could stay there with him. But the abbot said, 'Sir, that you cannot do under any circumstances, for our Lord has showed you how you shall journey until the seven years are past, and after that you and your monks shall return to Ireland, except for the two monks who joined you as the last moment. One of them shall stay in the Island of Hermits, and the other shall go to hell while he is still alive. As saint Brendan kneeled in the church, he saw a bright shining angel come in at the window, and he lighted all the lights in the church, and flew out of the window back to heaven; and saint Brendan marvelled at how the candles burned so well and yet did not go down. The abbot said that it is written in scripture that Moses saw a bush all on fire, and yet it burned not, 'and so do not marvel at this, for the power of our Lord is now as great as ever it was.' When saint Brendan had stayed there from Christmas until after Twelfth Night, he took his leave of the abbot and convent, and went aboard his ship with his monks. He sailed from there towards the abbey of saint Hilary, but they encountered great storms at sea from then until Palm Sunday. Then they came to the Island of Sheep, and the old man met them and brought them to a fine hall and served them with food. And on Maundy Thursday after supper he washed their feet and kissed them, as our Lord did to his disciples, and they stayed there until the evening of Easter Saturday. Then they departed and sailed to the place where the great fish lay; they saw their cauldron on the fish's back which they had left there twelve months before, and they celebrated the service of the Resurrection on the fish's back. The same morning they sailed to the island where the tree of birds was. The same bird welcomed saint Brendan and all his companions, and went back to the tree and sang very cheerfully. He and his monks lived there from Easter till Trinity Sunday, as they did the year before, in great joy and happiness; and every day they heard the cheerful service sung by the birds sitting on the tree.

Then the bird told saint Brendan that he was to return at Christmas to the abbey of monks, and at Easter he was to come back to the tree of birds; for the rest of the year he must labour in the ocean and endure great danger; and this would be his life from year to year until seven years had passed. 'Then you shall come to the joyful place of Paradise, and stay there for forty days in great joy and mirth; after this you shall return home to your own abbey in safety, and there end your life and come to the bliss of heaven, which our Lord bought for you with his precious blood.' Then the angel of our Lord supplied everything that saint Brendan and his monks wanted, food and water and all other things that were necessary. They thanked our Lord for his great goodness, which He had often showed them when they were most in need of it. When they set sail, they voyaged into the great sea or ocean, waiting for the mercy of our Lord in the great trouble and tempests which they endured. Not long after this there came to them a horrible fish, which followed the ship for a long time, spurting such fountains of water out of his mouth that they expected to be drowned. So they prayed devoutly to God to deliver them from that great danger. At this another fish, larger than the first, appeared out of the west, and fought with him, and in the end he tore him into three pieces, and vanished. They thanked our Lord for delivering them from this great peril; but they were very depressed, because their supplies were nearly finished.

But our Lord sent a bird which brought them a great branch from a vine, full of red grapes, on which they lived for fourteen days. They came to a little island, where there were many vines full of grapes, and they landed there, gave thanks to God, and gathered enough grapes to live on for the next forty days, as they sailed on through storms and tempests. As they sailed, a great griffin suddenly flew towards them, and attacked them; they thought it would destroy them, and they prayed for the help and aid of our Lord Jesu Christ. Then the bird from the tree on the island where they had spent Easter appeared and fought the griffin; it pecked out both its eyes and then killed him, for they thanked our Lord.

They sailed without touching land until saint Peter's day, when they sang a solemn service in honour of the saint's feast day. The water was so clear that they could see thousand of fishes all round them; at which they were very afraid, and the monks advised saint Brendan to stop singing for all the fishes lay as if they were asleep. And saint Brendan said, 'Do not be afraid, for you have kept the Feast of the Resurrection upon the great fish's back, so do not be frightened by these little fishes.' Saint Brendan prepared himself and went to say Mass, and told his monks to sing as best they could. And all the fishes awoke and crowded so closely round the ship that they could scarcely see the water for them. And when the mass was ended, all the fishes departed, and not a single one could be seen.

For seven days they sailed in clear water. Then a south wind came and drove the ship northwards, where they saw a dark island, full of stench and smoke; and there they heard great blowing and blasting of bellows, but they could see nothing; all they heard was great thundering, which made them very frightened, so that they crossed themselves again and again. A man came rushing out, burning and all on fire, and stared in ghastly fashion at them with great staring eyes; the monks were aghast, and when he went away again, he made the most horrible cry that they had ever heard. Next there came a huge number of fiends and attacked them with hooks and red-hot nails; they ran over the water and pursued their ship so that it seemed that the whole sea was like oil on fire; but by the will of God they had no power to hurt or annoy them or their ship. So the fiends began to roar and cry, and threw their hooks and hammers at them. They were very afraid, and prayed to God for comfort and help; for they saw the fiends all round the ship, and it seemed to them that the whole island and the sea were on fire. And with a sorrowful cry all the fiends departed from them and returned to the place that they came from. Saint Brendan told them that this was part of hell, and he warned them to be steadfast in the faith, for they would see many more dreadful places before they returned home.

Then the south wind came and drove them farther north, where they saw a hill on fire, and foul smoke and stench coming from it, and the fire was on one side of the hill like a burning wall. One of his monks began to cry and weep bitterly, and said that his end had come, and that he could no longer stay in the ship, and with that he jumped out of the ship into the sea, where he cried and roared pitifully, cursing the time that he was born, and also his father and mother, because they did not punish him in his youth, 'for now I must go to perpetual pain.' So the saying of saint Brendan came true; he had told the monk when he came on board the ship. It is good for a man to do penance and forsake sin, for the hour of death is uncertain.

After that the wind turned into the north, and drove the ship southwards for seven days on end; and they came to a great rock standing in the sea, on which there sat a naked man; and the waves of the sea had so beaten his body that all the flesh had gone, and nothing was left but sinews and bare bones. And when the waves were gone, there was a canvas that hung over his head which beat his body harshly when the wind blew. There were also two ox-tongues and a great stone that he sat on, which made him more comfortable. Saint Brendan ordered him to tell him who he was. He answered, 'My name is Judas, who sold our Lord Jesu Christ for thirty pieces of silver. I sit here in a wretched state, but I deserved the greatest torment that can be imagined. Yet our Lord is so merciful that he has rewarded me better than I have deserved, for by rights my place is in the flames of hell; but I am here only at certain times of the year, that is, from Christmas to Twelfth Night, and from Easter till after Whitsuntide, and every festival day of Our Lady, and every Saturday at noon till after evensong on Sunday. At all other times I am continually in hell in the ever-burning fire with Pilate, Herod, and Caiaphas; a curse on the time that ever I knew them.' Then Judas begged saint Brendan to stay there all that night, because then the fiends would not be able to take him back to hell. And Brendan said, 'With God's help you shall stay here tonight.' Then he asked Judas what cloth it was that hung over his head. And he said it was a cloth that he gave to a leper, which was bought with the money that he stole from our Lord when he kept his purse; 'which is why it does me such harm and beats my face when the wind blows. And these two ox-tongues that hang above me, I once gave to two priests to pray for me. I bought them with my own money, and so they help me, because the fishes of the sea gnaw them rather than me. And this stone that I sit on once lay in a desolate place where it did no-one any good. I took it and put it on a muddy path, where it was a help to passers-by; so now it helps me and eases my pain; for every good deed shall be rewarded, and every evil deed shall be punished.'

And on the Sunday, as it grew dark, there came a great multitude of fiends, blasting and roaring, and told saint Brendan to go away so that they could fetch their servant Judas, 'for we dare not show our faces before our master, unless we take him to hell with us.' And saint Brendan said, 'I will not let you do as your master says; but by the power of our Lord Jesu Christ I order you to leave him here for the night, until tomorrow dawns.' 'How dare you help the man who sold his master for thirty pieces of silver to the Jews, and caused him to die the most shameful death upon the cross?' Saint Brendan ordered the fiends, by the Passion of Our Lord, not to trouble him that night. The fiends went on their way, roaring and crying, towards hell and their master, the great devil. Then Judas thanked saint Brendan so penitently that it was piteous to watch; and on the next day the fiends came making a horrible noise, saying that they had been severely punished that that night because they failed to bring Judas, and threatened that he would suffer twice as badly for the next six days. And they took Judas with them, trembling with fear.

Saint Brendan sailed southwards for three days and three nights, and on the Friday they saw an island. He began to sigh and said, 'I see the island where saint Paul the hermit lives; he has been there for forty years, and has never touched meat or drink that any man has prepared.' And when they landed, saint Paul came and welcomed them humbly. He was old and bent and covered in hair so that no-one could see his body. Saint Brendan wept and said, 'Now I see a man that lives more like an angel than a man; wretches like us should be ashamed that we do not lead better lives.' Saint Paul said to saint Brendan, 'You are better than I; for our Lord has shown you more of his secrets than he has done for me, so you deserve more praise than I do.' Saint Brendan answered, 'We are monks and must labour for our food, but God has provided for you such food as satisfies you, so you are much better than I.' Saint Paul said, 'Once I was a monk of St Patrick's abbey in Ireland, and kept the gate by which men enter saint Patrick's purgatory. One day there came a man to me, and I asked him who he was. He said, 'I am your abbot Patrick, and I order you to leave here early tomorrow and go down to the sea shore; and thee you will see what God has arranged for you, Whose will you must accomplish. And so the next day I got up and went down and found a ship; I went on board, and by God's providence I was brought to this island seven days later, and then I left the ship and went on shore. I walked up and down for a good while, when an otter appeared, walking on his hind feet, with a flint with which to strike fire in his two fore-claws, and many fish hung round his neck, which he threw down at my feet and disappeared. I made a fire of sticks and lit it with the flint, and boiled the fish; I lived on them for three days. Then the otter came again, and brought me fish for the next three days; and he has done this, as God has willed, for fifty-one years. And there was a great stone, from which our Lord caused a spring of clear water to flow, sweet and clean, which I drink from each day. I have lived like this for fifty-one years; I was sixty when I arrived, and am now a hundred and eleven years old, and I will stay here until it pleases the Lord to send for me. If it so pleased Him, I would gladly be quit of this wretched life.'

Then he told saint Brendan to take water from the well to his ship, 'for it is time for you to set out, as you have a great journey to do; for you will sail to an island which is forty days' voyage from here, where you will celebrate Easter as you have done before, where the tree of birds is. From there you shall sail to the Land of Promise, and shall stay there for forty days, before returning home safely.' Then these holy men took leave of each other, and they wept greatly and kissed each other. Saint Brendan went into his ship, and sailed for forty days, always to the south, amid great storms. And on Easter even they came to the man who had provided for them before, and he welcomed them as on the previous occasions. From there they came to the great fish, where they said matins and Mass on Easter day. Once the mass was done, the fish began to move, and swam off swiftly into the sea, which greatly astonished the monks who were standing on him, for it was a great marvel to see such a fish, as large as a whole country, swimming so fast through the water; but by the will of our Lord God this fish set all the monks on land in the Paradise of Birds, and all of them were whole and well. And the fish returned to the place that he came from. Then saint Brendan and his monks thanked our Lord God for their escape from the great fish, and kept Eastertide until Trinity Sunday just as they had done before.

They went back on board ship and sailed east for forty days, and at the end of forty days it began to hail very hard, and then a dense fog came down, which lasted a long while, and frightened saint Brendan and his monks, who prayed to our Lord to keep and help them. Then the man who had provided for them on the island appeared and told Saint Brendan to be cheerful, because they had come to the Land of Promise.

And soon after that mist cleared, and they saw to the east the fairest country that anyone ever saw. It was so clear and bright that it was a heavenly sight to behold; and all the trees were full of ripe fruit and bushes full of flowers. Here they walked for forty days, but could not see the end of that land; and it was always day and never night, and the land was temperate, neither too hot nor too cold. At last they came to a river, but they did not dare to go over. A fair young man came and welcomed them courteously, and called each of them by his name, and treated saint Brendan with great reverence. He said to them, 'Rejoice now, for this is the land that you have sought; but our Lord wills that you leave here quickly, and He will show to you more of his secrets when you set out to sea; and our Lord wills that you load your ship with the fruit of this land, and go away from here, because you cannot stay here any longer. But you shall sail back to your own country, and soon after you come home, you will die. And this stretch of water that you see here divides the world in two; for no man can cross to the other side of the water while he is still alive. And the fruit that you see is always as ripe as this whatever the time of the year, and it is always as light here as you see it now; and he who keeps the Lord's commands at all times shall see this land before he passes out of this world.'

Then saint Brendan and his monks took as much as they wanted of that fruit, and also a great quantity of precious stones. Then they took their leave and went to their ship, weeping bitterly because they could no longer stay there. Then they went on board their ship and came home to Ireland in safety, where their brethren received them with great joy, giving thanks to our Lord, who had kept them all those seven years from many a peril, and brought them home in safety; to whom be given honour and glory, world without end: Amen. And soon afterwards, this holy man saint Brendan grew weak and sick, and found little joy in the things of this world, but his joy and his thoughts were on the joys of heaven. So he, being full of virtues, departed this life into everlasting life, and was worshipfully buried in a fair abbey, whiche he himself had founded; in that place our Lord shows many great miracles for the sake of this holy saint. So let us pray devoutly to this holy saint and entreat him to pray for us to our Lord, that He have mercy on us; to whom be given praise, honour, and empire, world without end. Amen

The Celtic Church did not fully acknowledge the supremacy of Rome until the twelfth century, although the old native practices began to give way to the Roman rituals and practices from the eighth century onwards. One aspect of the life of the church in Wales and Ireland was the existence of local, native saints, neither formally canonised nor recognised in any way by Rome. The stories told about them were more concerned with the super-natural, with miracles of a peculiarly Celtic nature, than with demon-strations of sanctity in the usual sense. The saint's power over secular rulers is the truest indication of his holiness, and the greater the ruler who is forced to abase himself before the saint, the greater the saint's prestige. When the stories came to be recorded, there was a further motive: after the Norman invasion of Wales, there was a new insistence on written records and deeds as evidence for the ownership of property, replacing the old Welsh system which relied much more on memory and oral evidence. So many stories of the Welsh saints are in fact designed to show that particu-lar monasteries had title to lands which had been given to the saint, or which they had received in his honour. The old Welsh tales designed to explain place-names reappear here in a new guise, justifying the monas-tery's possession of a place through a story about the saint.

The Life of Saint Cadog was written down in the mid-twelfth century, but as usual contains much older, traditional material, includ-ing the obligatory appearance of Arthur. Since Arthur is a king, he appears in a distinctly unflattering light, so that the saint's reputation can be enhanced by his little victories over even the greatest of Welsh kings.

KING Gwynllyw, ruler of Dyfed, fell in love with the beautiful daughter of a neighbouring king, Brychan. Her name was Gladys, and she was of most noble lineage, of elegant appearance, and clad in silk raiment. He sent very many messengers to the girl's father, demanding she might be given to him as wife; but the father of the girl was indignant, and refused to bestow his daughter on him, dismissing the messengers without honour. When the king heard what had happened, he was furious, and armed with all possible speed three hundred of his young men to take the girl by force. They set out at once, and reaching Brychan's court at Talgarth, they found the girl and her sisters sitting and talking outside their rooms. They seized her and beat a hasty retreat. Brychan, mourning the loss of his beloved daughter, summoned his friends and his subjects to recover her, and followed hot on the heels of the men of Dyfed. Gwynllyw, when he saw that they were giving chase, ordered that the girl should be brought to him, and he made her ride with him and went on in front. Brychan attacked his men, and killed two hundred of them; but

Gwynllyw and the girl reached the borders of his own land safely.

As they passed, three vigorous champions, Arthur with his two knights Kai and Bedwyr, were sitting on the top of the aforesaid hill playing with dice. Seeing the king and the girl approaching them, Arthur was immediately very inflamed with lust for the girl and said to his companions, 'I am full of desire for the girl whom that soldier is carrying off on horseback.'

But they said, 'It would be a crime to seize her, especially as we usually help those in need and distress. Instead, we ought to hurry to them and make an end of the battle.'

He replied, 'Since you both prefer to help the man than to seize the girl from him for me by force, go and ask them which is the owner of this land.' They went and asked as the king instructed them. Gwynllyw answered that he was the owner of this land. When Arthur heard this, he and his companions armed themselves and routed the enemies of Gwynllyw, and Gwynllyw reached his own court in triumph through Arthur's assistance, with the girl.

Gwynllyw married Gladys, the daughter of Brychan, and she conceived: every night from the hour of her conception four lights were seen shining with fiery splendour in the four corners of the house in which she stayed, until she brought forth her first-born son. One night some of Gwynllyw's brigands arrived to loot a certain town, where an Irish hermit called Meuthi lived; he served God very devotedly. He possessed no worldly goods except one cow in calf, which supplied enough milk for the hermit and his twelve attendants; which cow the aforesaid thieves vilely stole. That same night, Gladys gave birth to her son; and her husband heard a voice in his sleep saying, 'By God's will a certain holy hermit will come to you tomorrow at dawn; beg him to baptise your son, who is to be called Cadfael.' And that night an angel of the Lord also appeared to the hermit, saying to him, 'Get up, your cow has been taken away by thieves; you will find her at the court of king Gwynllyw. But you are to go there to baptise the son of that king, by whom your cow is detained. When the child is seven years old, instruct him in the writings of the Holy Scriptures.'

The following day the hermit started out early in the morning with his disciples to get his cow back; he went to the king's chamber, but was prevented from entering by the savage doorkeepers. But when the king heard of this, he was at once allowed to enter, his cow was restored to him, and he was warmly welcomed. For the king knew at once that he was the servant of God, who had been revealed to him by divine oracle, and asked him to baptise his son.

At the saint's birth, the cellars were found filled with milk and honey, as if prepared to supply a banquet, for during the three previous days they had been entirely emptied at the royal expense. On which wonder there followed a greater wonder, for the more that the cellars were emptied, the more they filled with abundance of goods.

When Cadfael was seven, he was sent to Meuthi for instruction, and given a new name, Cadog.

One day, when the fire was out, the hermit sent Cadog to fetch fire to cook the food. He went at once to the threshing-floor where he found one of his master's servants drying oats, and asked for fire for his master. But the man rudely refused to give it to him unless he would carry the burning coals in his cloak. He, trusting in the Lord and taking the coals of fire in his garment, brought them to the hermit with his clothes unharmed. As he went, Cadog prayed that the man and the threshing-floor should be consumed by fire as a sign of God's power. And when he looked back, both the man and the threshing-floor were burnt to ashes, and in that place there appeared a horrible black bog instead.

Cadog now left his master, and disciples gathered round him, so he set out to find a site for his first monastery; a local lord granted him land for that purpose.

In the valley which Cadog had been granted there was no dry ground, but a festering marsh, producing nothing besides a thicket of reeds full of all sorts of reptiles and snakes. There was just one bush, under which a large white boar had made its den, and in the middle of the same bush a swan nested every year.

Cadog prayed that he might be shown where he could build in this wilderness, and as soon as he had finished, an angel of the Lord appeared to him in a dream, saying, 'Your prayer has been heard by the Lord. Rise at first light and you will find a place for building an oratory, levelled and cleared. When you walk on it, a white boar, bristly and of great age, will come out of its den; there you shall lay the foundation of your church, in the name of the Holy Trinity. Where the boar next stops, you are to build a dormitory, and at his last halt, build your refectory.'

All this happened as the angel had foretold, and Cadog marked the three places which the boar had shown him with twigs. At the first he built a notable little monastery of timber, at the second a refectory, and at the third a dormitory.

There was a certain chief, named Sawyl, living not far from his monastery, who arrived with his accomplices at his abode, and seized food and drink from the monks, which he and his followers devoured. The clergy fled into the church, dismayed at such shameful behaviour. Cadog was absent at the time, and when he returned he enquired why they were so sorrowful. When he had learnt what had happened, he said, 'Be patient, for they will fall into a heavy sleep after their debauchery. When they are asleep, shave off half their beards and their hair, and cut off the lips and ears of their horses to shame them.' The monks did as he told them, and the brigands, still stupefied with drink, rode off as soon as they awoke.

Cadog, however, said, 'We must go out to meet them, for they will return to kill us when they discover how we have mocked them.' And they went up a nearby hill to meet the fearful tyrant with chants and hymns and psalms. As they watched Sawyl and his men approach, the earth opened its mouth, and swallowed them all because of their wickedness. The ditch into which they disappeared is there to this day, nor is anyone allowed to fill it in.

About the same time a brave leader of the British called Ligessauc Longhand killed three soldiers of Arthur, king of Britain. Arthur pursued him everywhere, and he could find nowhere to take refuge, until he came to Cadog and asked for sanctuary. Cadog, not in the least afraid of Arthur, received Ligessauc kindly, and he remained there in safety for seven years. But then he was betrayed to Arthur, who arrived with a great army to argue his cause, since he did not dare to use force against the man of God. They encamped on the river Usk and Cadog sent messengers to ask the king if he would submit the dispute to the verdict of skilful judges. This was agreed, and both sides presented their case; and after long arguments, the more learned of the judges decreed that Arthur should receive three of the finest oxen for each man slain. But other judges ordered that he should be given a hundred cows as compensation for the death of the three men, as this was the traditional price among the Britons.

Arthur accepted this verdict, but tauntingly refused cows of one colour: he would only take cows which were red in the forepart and white behind. Ligessauc, not knowing where he might find such beasts, turned to Cadog for help. The man of God ordered young men of the council to drive to him one hundred heifers, whatever colour they might be. When the animals were brought to him, he prayed that they should be changed into the colours perversely demanded by Arthur, which immediately happened. Cadog then asked the judges what he should do with the cattle, and was told that he should drive them into the middle of the ford over the river Usk, where Arthur, Kai and Bedwyr met them. Kai and Bedwyr eagerly drew them by the horns to the other bank, but as soon as they touched them they were turned into bundles of fern. Arthur, much abashed by this miracle, begged the saint's pardon, and granted him a charter giving him rights of sanctuary at his monastery for all who might seek refuge there.

Some years later, King Maelgwn sent his son Rhun to ravage the south of Britain, but ordered him in the strictest terms not to inflict any injury on Cadog, with whom he had sworn an oath of spiritual friendship. Rhun's men came to the borders of Cadog's lands, and found

Cadog's men going about their business without fear of attack, because they knew of the bond between Maelgwn and their master. But twelve squires went to water their horses in a nearby river; they could not drink the water themselves, and decided to go to Cadog's barn and demand some milk from the steward. He refused them, because they threatened him, and in a fury they tried to set fire to the barn, which only smouldered.

As the smoke drifted over Rhun's camp, he was playing at dice, and suddenly found that the smoke had made him blind. He pretended that nothing had happened, and ordered his servants to continue to play, but they admitted that they could see nothing. Rhun said that someone must have harmed Cadog's lands, and as soon as he discovered who it was, he summoned Cadog, and admitted that his men had been at fault. Cadog cured his blindness by praying, and they exchanged gifts. The king gave him his own best stallion with its trappings, and three chief weapons, to wit, shield, sword, and spear, and also everything which he had brought with him, except the food he needed for the journey. Cadog gave the sword to Gwrgran Brych, king of Glamorgan, in exchange for a half share of the fish of the river Usk, so that he would always have food for Lent at Llancarfan. And he gave the horse to the same king for a half share of the fish of the river Neath, so that he might have fish at his monastery, either boiled or roast. And he possessed as well two wooden horses so inestimably swift that no animal could be compared with them in speed, on which his servants brought every necessary from all parts. It was a day's journey for the wooden horses from Llancarfan to Neath and Brycheiniog in going and returning.

Cadog went to Scotland after he had made three pilgrimages to Jerusalem, to pray at the church of Saint Andrew, and prepared to build a monastery there.

One day, when St Cadog was digging the ground for the building, he found a collarbone of some ancient hero, monstrous and enormous, of incredible bulk, through which a knight on horseback could ride easily. St Cadog swore to abstain from food and drink and devote himself to prayer until the mystery of this strange discovery was revealed. He dreamt that the giant to whom it had belonged would be revived the next day, and while he was still telling everyone about his dream, there appeared a living giant of huge stature, horrible and immense. At this sight everybody in the town, terrified, exclaimed, 'It is a spectre in the shape of a man which has come to carry us all off.'

But the monstrous hero immediately fell at the feet of the man of God, begging Cadog to release his soul from the torments of hell. Cadog asked him who he was, and he replied: 'I once reigned beyond mount Bannog for very many years. I and my band of marauders once landed on this coast to pillage and lay waste the country; but the king of this region pursued us with his army, and killed me and my host in battle. From that day to this we have been tormented in the flames of hell, but my punishment exceeded all the torments of the rest in the enormity of my pains.'

Cadog asked him his name and he said that he had been called Caw of Prydein. 'Caw', said Cadog, 'you have cause for rejoicing, for God has granted me that you shall live again in this world, and if you heed my teaching, you will in the end attain everlasting glory.'

From that day until the day of his death, Caw worked for Cadog, digging the foundations and other works for his monastery; and as the fame of this miracle spread throughout Scotland, the kings of the Scottish folk presented him with twenty-four homesteads.

On the death of his father Gwynllyw, Cadog returned to Wales.

At another time Cadog one day sailed with his two disciples Barruc and Gualehes from the island of Holm to Barry. When he had landed, he asked his disciples for his handbook; but they confessed that they had left it behind on the island. At this he ordered them to return, saying in a fury, 'Go, and never come back.' They at once took ship, landed on the island and fetched the book. But as Cadog watched them return, the boat was suddenly overturned; they were both drowned and the book was lost. That evening, Cadog ordered his disciples to fetch fish for his supper. As they set out to sea, they found on the sand a huge salmon; they took it back and gutted it, and found the missing book in its entrails, unharmed by the water. The man of the Lord quickly took it up, and declared that nothing was impossible to God.

Another extraordinary miracle happened when Cadog's sheep were feeding on the island of Echni. Two wolves swam across to the mainland, and savaged several of the sheep. But when they attempted to swim back across the channel to Wales, once they were in mid-channel, they were transformed into stones, which are called in the British speech Cunbleid, that is, wolflike stones, because the wolves had provoked the servant of God and torn his sheep.

One day an official of St Cadog, whom at that time they used to call the sexton of Llancarfan, went on business to the court of a certain local lord, carrying with him the gospel of Gildas. There was in that court the same day an action against a certain peasant, who had stolen an ox, but denied the crime with all his might. Then the sexton came up to him, and in jest bared his large knife and brandishing it at him, said, 'You fool, this is the knife of St Cadog. If you commit perjury, you will die at once, because it will stab you in the stomach.'

The terrified peasant threw himself at the feet of the sexton and admitted his guilt; at which the king delivered the thief in perpetual servitude to the monastery of St Cadog.

In the monastery which Cadog built in Scotland, three of his disciples are buried in marble sepulchres. No one dares to look inside the tombs except a bachelor, virgin or priest. But there is an opening outside in the wall of the porch, through which kings and lords of that country, if a great dispute has to be resolved, will put in their hands and swear a solemn oath. If anyone breaks that oath, he will die before the end of that year. One year, as the feast day of St Cadog was being celebrated, a stupid peasant, wishing to show off, asked if he could look through the opening; the priests said, 'If you do so, may St Cadog put a mark on you in revenge.'

So he rashly ran to the opening, and covered one eye with his hand; he pressed the other to the opening, and looked in. At once his eye burst from its socket and hung down his face; he rushed in agony through the crowd, who praised St Cadog for his power. For years afterwards, he would show his torn eye, which he kept covered, for a small reward.

At the end of his life, Cadog was translated to Benevento in a cloud, like Elijah; at Benevento he became abbot under the name of Sophias, where he was martyred when the monastery was pillaged by a local tyrant. Miracles continued to be associated with him after his death.

After Cadog's death, an English sheriff came with a large army to plunder Glamorgan, and the monks of Llancarfan fled with their relics to the monastery of Mammelliat, where they hid themselves. But a mob of plunderers, Danes and English, attacked the place, and tried to seize the shrine of St Cadog, which was the principal relic. But a hundred of them were unable to move it from the spot, at which one of them struck it with a cudgel. When it was struck, it gave a loud bellow like a bull, and terrified the whole army: this was at once followed by a great earthquake. In the end, when the shrine had been abandoned by them, one wretch greedily broke off its gilded wing with an axe. But when he hid it in its cloak, it immediately burnt him like fire; in agonising pain, he quickly put it back where it had come from, and it at once stuck fast, as if welded with gold. And the man who had violated the shrine melted away in the sight of the whole army, like wax in front of the fire. At this they all fled in terror; and afterwards they showed no inclination to plunder the monasteries of St Cadog.

Maredudd, king of Rheinwg, came to Glamorgan with a strong army, intending to conquer it. When he arrived he gave orders to gather loot and to drive oxen to the camp for food. So they brought up a hundred oxen, among which was a very fat one which had been snatched from the blessed Cadog's townsmen. This was killed and roasted for the hungry king and his companions, but its flesh could not be roasted on the coals or boiled in water. When the king learnt of this, he ordered all the oxen to be returned to their owners. And when they were all brought together, the slaughtered ox appeared among the rest alive and unhurt.

At one time a king of Reinmuc called Cynan Carwyn invaded Glamorgan with a large army, intending to loot it and conquer it for himself. The army encamped on the river Neath, and the king of Glamorgan, fearing that he would be defeated, begged the monks of Llancarfan to go to meet the king of Reinmuc bearing the coffin and relics of St Cadog, and to beg that he would leave them in peace. As they went to the riverbank, one of them climbed a tree, so that he could shout across to the king, because the river was in flood and they could not cross. While he was addressing the king, the tree bent down to the ground, and formed a bridge across the river, so that he could speak to the king face to face. Seeing this miracle, the king of Reinmuc returned home in peace, without invading Glamorgan.

Maelgwn was the high king of the Britons, who ruled the whole of Wales; he was paid annually a hundred cows and a hundred calves from each district, though this tribute was not paid willingly but collected by force. When the tax-gatherers of king Maelgwn came to collect tribute in Gwynlliog, they seized a very handsome girl, Abalcem by name, daughter of Guiragon, an official of the monastery of St Cadog, and bore her away with them. The girl's family at once rode angrily in pursuit, blowing their horns; and all the warriors of the district heard this and joined in the chase. They slew three hundred men; only one escaped and told the king what had happened. The king was furious and led a great army to seek revenge. St Cadog with all the inhabitants of Gwynlliog went to meet the king, and he and all who were with him fasted as they went. Maelgwn sent his messenger to the saint, ordering him to pay a fine for the death of the men at Riucarn; but the saint replied that he would only pay the fine if the case was tried by the justice of God and of men. But the king refused to submit the case to judgment, and led his troops forward to slaughter the people of the district. As soon as he did so, he was blinded, and did not know which way to go. So he sent messengers to St Cadog, to tell him what had happened to him, and begged that he would come to him and restore his lost sight. But the man of God refused to do so until the king came to confession. So the king came to him and granted whatever Cadog wished; and these gifts of Maelgwn, of privileges and of exemptions, were the foundation of the wealth of the monastery at Llancarfan, and were solemnly ratified and recorded by both parties.

22. ST JOSEPH OF ARIMATHEA AND GLASTONBURY

When the monks at Glastonbury 'discovered' the tomb of king Arthur in 1191, they began the now famous connection between Glastonbury and the Arthurian legend, which was elaborated as the centuries passed, until the Reformation swept away the monuments they had created. The link between Joseph of Arimathea and Glastonbury is, like the presence of Arthur's body, unknown to William of Malmesbury, the earliest and most reliable historian of the abbey; and it is only in the thirteenth century that we begin to hear stories about him. What follows comes from the history compiled in the fourteenth century by one of the monks, John of Glastonbury, which gives the legend as it was generally known in the middle ages.

The connection between Joseph of Arimathea and the Grail is first found in the romance written to explain the history of the holy vessel before it arrived at Arthur's court; but this was dangerous ground in religious terms, and the monks never claimed that it was at Glastonbury. All they said was that Joseph had brought two 'cruets' containing the blood and sweat of Christ, which were buried with him; but they never pointed out his tomb, though a certain John Blome was given royal permission to dig for it in 1345, provided that the abbot and convent agreed. It was never found, and the only evidence of St Joseph was a chapel in the crypt of the Lady Chapel, which, by the end of the middle ages, was a much-visited shrine. If the monks did not make the connection with the Grail, popular imagination did; the name of 'Chalice Well', and the cup known as the Nanteos Grail, which is reputed to have come from Glastonbury, are witnesses to the popular enthusiasm for the idea that Joseph brought the Grail to England. The last and most famous development of the legend was the story that Christ himself visited Glastonbury to dedicate the 'Old Church', which was to inspire William Blake's famous lines:

> And did those feet in ancient time
> Walk upon England's mountains green?

Here begins the treatise of St Joseph of Arimathea, taken from a book which the emperor Theodosius found in Pilate's council-chamber in Jerusalem

Matters which admit doubt often deceive the reader; in order to dispel doubts regarding the antiquity of the church of Glastonbury, therefore, we have added some undisputed facts, gathered from the ancient sayings of historians.

When the Lord had been crucified and everything had been fulfilled which had been prophesied of him, Joseph of Arimathea, that noble decurion, came to Pilate as the Gospel story explains, asked for the body of Jesus, wrapped it when he had received it in linen, and placed it in a monument in which no one had yet been laid. But the Jews, hearing that Joseph had buried the body of Jesus, sought to arrest him, along with Nicodemus and the others who had defended him before Pilate. When they had all hidden themselves, these two – that is Joseph and Nicodemus – revealed themselves and asked the Jews, 'Why are you grieved against us because we have buried the body of Jesus? You have not done well against a righteous man, nor have you considered what benefits he bestowed upon us; instead you have crucified him and wounded him with a lance.'

When the Jews heard these words, Annas and Caiaphas seized Joseph, shut him up in a cell where there was no window, sealed the door over the key, and posted guards to watch over him. But Nicodemus they sent away free, since Joseph alone had requested Jesus' body and had been the principal instigator in his burial. Later, when everyone had assembled, along with the priests and Levites, all through the Sabbath they considered how they should kill Joseph. After the assembly had gathered, the chief officials ordered Annas and Caiaphas to present Joseph; but when they opened the seals on the door they did not find him. Scouts were sent out everywhere, and so Joseph was found in his own city, Arimathea. Hearing this, the chief priests and all the people of the Jews rejoiced and glorified the God of Israel because Joseph had been found, whom they had shut up in a cell. They then made a great assembly, at which the chief priests said, 'How can we bring Joseph to us and speak with him?'

They took up a piece of parchment and wrote to Joseph, saying, 'Peace be with you and yours. We see that we have sinned against God and against you. Deign therefore to come to your fathers and your sons, for we have marvelled greatly over your assumption. Indeed, we know that we have plotted evil counsel against you, and the Lord has freed you from our evil counsel. Peace to you, lord Joseph, honourable among all the people.'

And they chose seven men who were friends of Joseph and said to them, 'When you reach Joseph, greet him in peace and give him this letter.'

When the men had reached him, they greeted him peaceably and gave him the letter. Joseph read the letter and said, 'Blessed are You, O Lord my God, who have liberated Israel, that he should not shed my blood. Blessed are You, O my God, who have protected me under Your wings.'

And Joseph kissed the men who had come to him and took them into his house. The next day he climbed upon his ass and went with them until they came to Jerusalem, and when all the Jews heard of it they ran to meet him, saying, 'Peace at your coming in, father.' Joseph responded to them, saying, 'Peace be with you all.' And they all kissed him, and Nicodemus received him into his house and made a banquet for him.

The next day the Jews all came together, and Annas and Caiaphas said to Joseph, 'Make confession to the God of Israel, and reveal to us all that you are asked. We quarrelled with you because you buried the body of Jesus and shut you up in a cell on account of the Sabbath; on the following day we sought you but did not find you. Therefore we were greatly astonished, and fear has held us even up until now, when we have received you. Now that you are present, tell us before God what happened to you.'

Joseph answered them, saying, 'When you shut me up at evening on the day of preparation, while I stood at my Sabbath prayers, the house in which I was held was taken up in the middle of the night by four angels, and I saw Jesus like a flash of light. I fell for fear onto the ground, but, holding my hand, he lifted me up from the ground and covered me with the scent of roses. As he wiped my face he kissed me and said to me, "Do not fear, Joseph; look upon me and see who I am." I looked at him and said, "Rabbi Elijah." And he said to me, "I am not Elijah, but Jesus, whose body you buried." Then I said to him, "Show me the monument where I laid you." And taking my hand, he led me to the place where I buried him and showed me the linen shroud and the facecloth in which I had wrapped his head. Then I recognised that he was Jesus, and I adored him, saying, "Blessed is he who comes in the name of the Lord." Then, holding my hand, he led me into my house in Arimathea and said to me, "Peace be with you. Do not go out of your house until the fortieth day. I shall go to my disciples." And when he had said these things he disappeared.'

After all this, the noble Joseph of Arimathea, animated by an ardent faith, became the disciple of blessed Philip the apostle, and, filled to overflowing with his saving doctrine, was baptised by him along with his son Josephes. Later he was appointed guardian of the blessed ever-virgin Mary by blessed John the apostle, while John himself laboured at preaching to the Ephesians: Joseph was present at the Assumption of the same glorious Virgin, along with blessed Philip and his other disciples, and he preached incessantly through many lands the things which he had heard and seen of the Lord Jesus Christ and his mother Mary; finally, converting and baptising many, in the fifteenth year after the Blessed Virgin's Assumption he came to St Philip the apostle in Gaul, along with his son Josephes, whom the Lord Jesus had earlier consecrated bishop in the city of Sarras.

For when the disciples dispersed throughout the various parts of the world after the Lord's Ascension – as Freculph bears witness in his second book, fourth chapter – Philip came to the kingdom of the Franks to preach, and he converted and baptised many into the faith of Christ.

Since, then, the holy apostle wished to spread the Word of God, he sent twelve of his disciples to Britain to proclaim the good news of the Word of Life; over these he set his dear friend, the aforesaid Joseph who buried the Lord, along with his son Josephes. More than six hundred came with them – as is read in the book called 'The Holy Grail' – men as well as women, all of whom vowed that they would abstain from their own spouses until they had come into the land appointed to them. They all made a sham of their oath, however, except for a hundred and fifty, who at the Lord's command crossed the sea upon Josephes's shirt on Easter Eve and landed in the morning. The others repented, and, through Josephes's prayers on their behalf, a ship was sent by the Lord which king Solomon had artfully constructed in his time and which endured all the way to the time of Christ.

That same day, they and a duke of the Persians named Nasciens reached their companions: Joseph had earlier baptised Nasciens in the city of Sarras, along with the king of the city, whose name was Mordrain. The Lord later appeared to Mordrain in a vision and showed him his pierced hands and feet and his side wounded by the lance. Taking great pity upon him, the king said, 'O Lord my God, who has dared to do such a thing to You?' And the Lord answered, 'The faithless king of North Wales has done these things to Me, he who has bound in prison my servant Joseph and his companions, who were preaching My name in his territories, and who has inhumanly denied them necessary sustenance. You, then, do not delay but hasten to those parts, girded with your sword, to avenge My servant upon the tyrant and free them from their chains.'

The king, then, awoke and rejoiced in the Lord because of the vision revealed to him, made disposition of his house and kingdom, began his journey with his army and, coming to the place by God's guidance, commanded the aforesaid king to permit God's servants to depart freely. But the Welsh king, altogether refusing the command, indignantly ordered him to leave his land without delay. When king Mordrain had heard this, he and the aforesaid duke Nasciens came against him with their army, and Nasciens killed the Welsh king in a battle of just vengeance. Then king Mordrain went to the prison where the wicked king held Joseph and his companions under arrest, led him thence in great joy, and told him the vision which the Lord had revealed to him in order to free them. Then all were filled with great joy and thanked the Lord mightily.

After this, St Joseph and his son Josephes and their ten companions travelled through Britain, where king Arviragus then reigned, in the sixty-third year from the Lord's Incarnation, and they trustworthily preached the faith of Christ. But the barbarian king and his nation, when they heard doctrines so new and unusual, did not wish to exchange their ancestral traditions for better ways and refused consent to their preaching. Since, however, they had come from afar, and because of their evident modesty of life, Arviragus gave them for a dwelling an island at the edge of his kingdom, surrounded with forests, thickets and swamps, which was called by the inhabitants Ynswytryn – that is 'the glass island'. Of this a poet has said, 'The twelvefold band of men entered Avalon: Joseph, flower of Arimathea, is their chief. Josephes, Joseph's son, accompanies his father. The right to Glastonbury is held by these and the other ten.'

When these saints, then, had lived in that desert for a short time, the archangel Gabriel admonished them in a vision to build a church in honour of the holy Mother of God, the ever-virgin Mary, in the place which heaven would show them. Obeying the divine admonitions, they finished a chapel, the circuit of whose walls they completed with wattles, in the thirty-first year after the Lord's Passion, the fifteenth, as was noted, after the Assumption of the glorious Virgin, and the same year, in fact, in which they had come to St Philip the apostle in Gaul and had been sent by him to Britain. Though it was of unsightly construction, it was adorned with the manifold power of God; and since it was the first church in this land, the Son of God distinguished it by a fuller dignity, dedicating it in his own presence in honour of his Mother.

And so these twelve saints offered there devout service to God and the blessed Virgin, freeing themselves up for fasting and prayers; and in their necessities they were revived by the assistance of the Virgin Mother of God. When the holiness of their lives was discovered, two other kings, though pagans – Marius, the son of king Arviragus, and Coel, son of Marius – granted them each a hide of land and at the same time confirmed the gift. Thus, to this day the twelve hides take their names from them. When a few years had passed, these saints were led forth from the workhouse of the body. Among their number Joseph also was buried and laid on a divided line next to the aforesaid oratory. The spot which had previously been a dwelling of saints then became a den of wild beasts, until it pleased the blessed Virgin to restore her oratory to the memory of the faithful.

This passage is found among the deeds of the glorious king Arthur

The book of the deeds of the glorious king Arthur bears witness that the noble decurion Joseph of Arimathea came to Great Britain, which is now called England, along with his son Josephes and many others, and that there they ended their lives. This is found in the portion of the book dealing with the search carried out by the companions of the Round Table for an illustrious knight called Lancelot du Lac – that is, in the part of the book where a hermit explains to Gawain the mystery of a fountain which keeps changing taste and colour: in the same place it is also written that that miracle will not end until a great lion comes whose neck is bound in heavy chains. It is also reported practically at the beginning of the quest for the vessel which is there called the Holy Grail, where the White Knight explains to Galahad, son of Lancelot, the mystery of a miraculous shield which he enjoins him to carry and which no one else can bear, even for a day, without grave loss.

This passage is found in the Book of Melkin who preceded Merlin

'The isle of Avalon, eager for the death of pagans, at the burial of them all will be decorated beyond the others in the world with the soothsaying spheres of prophecy, and in the future will be adorned with those who praise the Most High. Abbadare, powerful in Saphat, most noble of the pagans, took his sleep there with a hundred and four thousand men. Among these Joseph of Arimathea received eternal slumber in a marble tomb, and he lies on a divided line next to the oratory's southern corner where the wickerwork is constructed above the mighty and venerable Maiden and where the aforesaid thirteen spheres rest. Joseph has with him in the sarcophagus two white and silver vessels, full of the blood and sweat of the prophet Jesus. Once his sarcophagus is discovered, it will be visible, whole and undecayed, and open to the whole world. From then on those who dwell in that noble island will lack neither water nor the dew of heaven. For a long time before the day of Judgment in Josaphat these things will be openly declared to the living.' Thus far Melkin.

Verses on St Joseph from the Aurora or versified Bible

'When late in time, Joseph was made a wealthy decurion, the just and honourable citizen of Ramatha was at hand. Secretly was he a servant of Christ; he therefore requested the body of Jesus from the magistrate, and the latter ordered it to be given him. Nicodemus offered him assistance, who had come to Jesus in the nighttime, confessing the faith in his heart. These two wrapped the pure body in pure linen and buried in rock him who was our rock.'

This passage bears witness that king Arthur descended
from the stock of Joseph

'Helains, Joseph's nephew, begat Josue. Josue begat Aminadab. Aminadab begat Castellors. Castellors begat Manael. Manael begat Lambord and Urlard. Lambord begat a son who begat Igerna, of whom king Uther Pendragon begat the noble and famous king Arthur – by which it is evident that king Arthur descended from the stock of Joseph.'

   Again on the same subject: 'Peter, cousin of Joseph of Arimathea and king of Organia, begat Erlan. Erlan begat Melian. Melian begat Arguth. Arguth begat Edor. Edor begat Loth, who took to wife king Arthur's sister, of whom he begat four sons, namely Gawain, Agravains, Guerrehes, and Gaheriet.'

23. ST GEORGE

St George has no real connection with Britain. He seems to have been a Christian martyr from eastern Turkey, where churches were dedicated to him in the fourth century: he was also known as Nestor, which may have been his real name. He is identified with the story told by Eusebius, bishop of Caesarea, about a soldier who tore down a copy of the edict proclaimed by Diocletian, under which the Christian religion was proscribed. But his existence is so uncertain that he belongs to that distinguished band of saints disowned in recent years by the Vatican as insufficiently historical. Certainly the part of his exploits by which he is usually remembered belongs to the world of myth; he has adopted the guise of the dragon-slaying divine hero who appears in a number of Near Eastern religions, and whose deeds have very little of the Christian about them.

St George was one of a number of military saints who, in the tenth and eleventh centuries, became the object of popular cults in western Christendom. The Normans were particularly attached to St Michael, leader of the hosts of heaven, whose shrines they built on hilltops, as at Mont St Michel and Monte Gargano in southern Italy. St George first figures largely in western annals when the soldiers of the First Crusade, fighting for their lives before the Syrian city of Antioch, saw a vision of a mighty host led by St George and St Demetrius, coming to their aid. Richard I's men invoked St George a century later in similar circumstances, and his popularity grew during the thirteenth century. It was Edward III who is said to have joined the name of St George to that of Edward the Confessor as the English battlecry, the cry immortalised in Shakespeare's **Henry V.** *The ancient link between St George and the crusaders is still visible whenever the English flag is flown, for the red cross is that worn by the crusaders.*

ST GEORGE was a knight and born in Cappadocia. Once he came into the province of Libya, to a city which is called Silene. And by this city was a pond like a sea, wherein was a dragon which envenomed all the country. And the people assembled in order to slay him, but when they saw him they fled. And when he came near the city he venomed the people with his breath, and therefore the people of the city gave to him every day two sheep for to feed him, so that he should do no harm to the people, and when there were not enough sheep, a man and a sheep were taken. Then a law was made in the town that the children and young people of the town should be taken by lot, and each one, were he gentle or poor, should be delivered when the lot fell on him or her. So it happened that many of the townspeople were delivered to the dragon; and in the end the lot fell upon the king's daughter; the king was sorrowful at this and said to the people: 'For the love of the gods take gold and silver and all that I have, and let me have my daughter.'

They said: 'Sir! you have made and ordained the law, and our children are now dead, and you would do the contrary. Your daughter shall be given, or else we shall burn you and your house.' When the king saw he might do no more, he began to weep, and said to his daughter: 'Now I shall never see you married.'

Then he went back to the people and asked for eight days' respite, and they granted it to him. And when the eight days were passed they came to him and said: 'You can see that all in the city will perish from the dragon's venom.' Then the king had his daughter dressed as if for her wedding, and embraced her, kissed her and gave her his blessing. Then he led her to the place where the dragon was.

When she was there St George passed by, and when he saw the lady, he asked her what she was doing there, and she said: 'Go your way, fair young man, or you will perish too.' Then he said: 'Tell me what troubles you and why you are weeping, and have no fear.' When she saw that he wanted to know, she told him how she was delivered to the dragon. Then said St George: 'Fair daughter, have no fear of this, for I shall help thee in the name of Jesus Christ.' She said: 'For God's sake, good knight, go your way, and do not stay with me, for you cannot free me.'

As they were speaking, the dragon appeared and came running to them. St George, who was on horseback, drew out his sword and made the sign of the cross. He rode boldly against the dragon which came towards him, and smote him with his spear and hurt him sore and threw him to the ground. Then he said to the girl: 'Give me your girdle, and bind it about the neck of the dragon and do not be afraid.' When she had done so the dragon followed her like a meek and gentle beast. Then she led him into the city, and the people fled to the mountains and valleys, and said: 'Alas! alas! we shall be all dead.'

Then St George said to them: 'Fear nothing, but believe in God, Jesu Christ, and be baptised and I shall slay the dragon.'

Then the king was baptised and all his people. And St George slew the dragon and smote off his head, and commanded that he should be thrown in the fields, and they took four carts with oxen that drew him out of the city. Then were there well fifteen thousand men baptised, not counting the women and children, and the king built a church dedicated to our Lady and St George, in which a fountain of living water still runs, which heals sick people that drink from it.

After this the king offered to St George as much money as there was in the city, but he refused all and commanded that it should be given to poor people for God's sake; and he ordered the king to do four things: that he should pay for the churches, and that he should honour the priests and hear their service diligently, and that he should have pity on the poor people. And he kissed the king and departed.

Now it happened that in the time of the emperors Diocletian and Maximian, that there was such a great persecution of Christians that twenty thousand were martyred within a month, and the Christians were so terrified that some forsook God and did sacrifice to the idols. When St George saw this, he abandoned the habit of a knight and sold all that he had, and gave it to the poor, and took the habit of a Christian, and went into the middle of the pagans and began to cry: 'All the gods of the pagans and gentiles are devils; my God made the heavens and is very God.'

Then said the provost to him: 'Why are you so presumptuous as to say that our gods are devils? Tell us who you are and what is your name.'

He answered: 'I am named George, I am a gentleman, a knight of Cappadocia, and have left all to serve the God of heaven.'

Then the provost tried to convert him to his own by fair words, and when he could not bring him over, he raised up a gibbet and hung him on it; and he had him beaten with great staves and rods of iron, that his body was broken in pieces. And then he took red-hot iron and pressed it against his side, until his bowels came out, which he then rubbed with salt, and sent him to prison. But our Lord appeared to him the same night with great light and comforted him sweetly. And by this great consolation he took such good heart that he feared no torment that they might make him suffer.

Then, when Dacian the provost saw that he might not overcome him, he called his enchanter and said to him: 'I see that these Christian people do not fear our torments.'

The enchanter swore that his head could be cut off if he did not overcome the Christian's resistance. He took strong venom and mixed it with wine, and invoked the names of his false gods, and gave it to St George to drink. St George took it and made the sign of the cross on it, and drank it without it causing him any harm. Then the enchanter made it with more venom than before and gave it him to drink, and it still did not harm him. When the enchanter saw that, he kneeled down at the feet of St George and begged him that he would make him Christian. And when Dacian knew that he had become a Christian he had his head cut off.

The next morning, he had St George to be set between two wheels, which were full of swords, sharp and cutting on both sides, but the wheels broke and St George escaped without hurt. And then Dacian commanded that they should put him in a cauldron full of molten lead, and when St George got into it, by the virtue of our Lord it seemed that he was in a bath well at ease. Then Dacian seeing this began to temper his wrath, and to flatter him by fair words, and said to him: 'George, our gods are too patient with you for your blasphemy; fair son, I pray you to return to our law and make sacrifice to the idols, and leave your foolishness, and I will advance you to great honour.'

Then St George began to smile, and said to him: 'Why did you not say this at the beginning? I will do as you say.'

Dacian was glad and proclaimed throughout the town that all the people should assemble to see St George make sacrifice, because he had resisted so fiercely. The city was hung with flags, and a festival was proclaimed, and all came to the temple to see him.

When St George was on his knees, and they expected him to worship the idols, he prayed our Lord God of heaven that he would destroy the temple and the idol in the honour of his name, to make the people to be converted. At once fire descended from heaven and burnt the temple, and the idols, and their priests; and the earth opened and swallowed all the cinders and ashes that were left.

Then Dacian had him brought before him, and said to him: 'What evil deeds you have done, and what lies you have told!' St George said to him: 'Do not believe what you have been told, but come and see me sacrifice.' Dacian replied: 'I see through your trickery; you will make the earth swallow me, just as you have done to the temple and my gods.' St George said: 'Wretched man, tell me how your gods can help you when they cannot help themselves!'

Then Dacian was so angry that he said to his wife: 'I shall die of anger if I cannot get the better of this man.' But she said to him: 'Cruel and wicked tyrant! Can you not see the great virtue of the Christian people? I said to you that you should not do them any harm, for their God fights for them. I tell you, I shall become a Christian.'

Dacian was much abashed and said to her: 'So you will become a Christian?' He took her by the hair, and beat her cruelly. Then she asked St George: 'What will become of me? I am not christened.'

The blessed George answered: 'Do not fear, fair daughter, for you shall be baptised in your blood.' And she began to worship our Lord Jesu Christ, and so she died and went to heaven. The next day Dacian pronounced sentence, that St George should be dragged through all the city, and his head should be smitten off. And before he was executed he prayed that anyone who asked for what they desired might get it of our Lord God in his name, and a voice came from heaven which said that his prayer was granted. After he had prayed, his head was smitten off, about the year of our Lord two hundred and eighty-seven. As Dacian went home from the place where he was beheaded towards his palace, fire fell down from heaven upon him and burnt him and all his servants.

Gregory of Tours tells us that there were some men carrying certain relics of St George, and came into a certain oratory in a hospital, and on the morning when they wanted to leave, they could not move the door till they had left there part of their relics. The history of Antioch also relates that when the Christians went overseas to conquer Jerusalem, that a handsome young man appeared to a priest of the army and advised him that he should carry with him some of the relics of St George, for he was leader of battles, and he managed to obtain the relics. When they besieged Jerusalem and dared not scale the walls because of the Saracen crossbowmen, they plainly saw St George, bearing a shield with a red cross, going up before them on the walls, and they followed him, and thus Jerusalem was taken by his help. And between Jerusalem and the port of Jaffa, by a town called Ramleh, there is a chapel of St George which is now desolate and uncovered. Christian Greeks live there, and in the chapel lies the body of St George, but not the head. And there lie his father and mother and his uncle, not in the chapel but under the wall of the chapel; and the keepers will not let pilgrims to come in, unless they pay two ducats; so few go inside, but make their offerings at an altar outside the chapel. The body of St George lies in the middle of the choir of the said chapel, and in his tomb is an hole that a man may put his hand in. If a Saracen who has been struck by madness is brought there, and puts his head in the hole, he is at once cured, and restored to his wits.

This blessed and holy martyr St George is patron of this realm of England and the cry of men of war. In honour of him the noble order of the Garter and a noble college in the castle of Windsor were founded by kings of England, in which college is the heart of St George, which Sigismund, the emperor of Germany, brought and gave to king Harry the fifth as a great and precious relic: Sigismund was a brother of the order of the Garter. There is a piece of his head, and the college is endowed to the honour and worship of Almighty God and his blessed martyr St George.

Let us pray to him that he be the special protector and defender of this realm.

24. HELENA AND THE TRUE CROSS

Through a confusion over her place of birth, Helena, the mother of Constantine, was believed by Geoffrey of Monmouth to be British; in fact, she was born at Drepanum in Bithynia. In Geoffrey's version, she is the daughter of Coel (the 'old King Cole' of the nursery rhyme). As to her story, he evidently knew the tale of Maxen Wledig; but he reverses it, for Maxentius is the tyrant at Rome whom Constantine and Helena's kinsmen oust; so it would seem that he imagined the empress Helena and Helen of the Hosts to be one and the same. The story of the finding of the True Cross is told in the Anglo-Saxon poem Elene *by Cynewulf, and belongs to the history of the pilgrimage to Palestine, which was beginning to develop at the time that Helena journeyed there, and which was considerably increased by her discovery.*

The version which follows is from the Acts of Saint Cyriacus, *which was probably one of Cynewulf's sources. The anti-Jewish prejudice is, unfortunately, typical of the texts of this period, but serves within this story to point up Judas's virtue in converting to Christianity.*

IN the two hundred and thirty-third year after the Passion of our Lord Jesus Christ, in the sixth year of the reign of Constantine (a great man and reverent worshipper of God), a large barbarian host gathered beyond the Danube, prepared to wage war against the Roman empire. When this was announced to king Constantine, he too mustered a great army and set out against the enemy. He found they had laid claim to and had occupied parts of Roman territory on the Danube. Seeing their countless numbers, he was sad and mortally afraid.

During the night a man surrounded by radiance came and woke him and said, 'Constantine, do not be frightened, but look up to heaven and see.' When he cast his eyes towards heaven, he saw the sign of Christ's Cross fashioned out of pure light; over it was written in letters the title: *Conquer through this.* Having beheld the sign, king Constantine made a replica of the Cross he had seen in the heavens; and marching off, he attacked the barbarians with the sign of the Cross before him. He and his army came upon the barbarians, and directly it was dawn, he began to massacre them. The barbarians were terrified and fled along the banks of the Danube: not a few of them died. On that day God gave victory to king Constantine through the power of the Holy Cross.

When king Constantine returned to his city, he called together all the priests of every god and idol and asked them to whom this sign of the Cross belonged or what it meant. They could not tell him. But certain of them replied, 'This is the sign of the God of heaven.' When the few Christians who were present at the time heard this, they came to the king and preached the mystery of the Trinity and the Advent of God's Son – how He was born, crucified and rose again on the third day.

King Constantine sent to Eusebius, the bishop of the city of Rome, and ordered him to come to him. Eusebius instructed Constantine in the Christian faith and all its rites. He baptised him in the name of our Lord Jesus Christ, and confirmed him in Christ's faith. Constantine ordered churches to be built everywhere, but the idols' temples to be destroyed. Blessed Constantine, perfect in his faith and fervent with the Holy Spirit, studied Christ's Holy Gospels.

When he learnt from them where the Lord had been crucified, he sent Helena, his mother, to seek the holy wood of the Lord's Cross and to build a church in the same place. The grace of the Holy Spirit reposed in the emperor Constantine's most blessed mother, Helena. She studied all the scriptures, had exceeding love for our Lord Jesus Christ and afterwards sought for the life-giving wood of the Holy Cross. When she had read attentively about the coming of our [Lord] Jesus Christ, the Saviour of mankind, His crucifixion on the Cross, and resurrection from the dead, she lost no time till she found the wood of Christ's victory, upon which the Lord's Holy Body had been nailed. This is how she found it.

On the twenty-eighth day of the second month, Helena entered the holy city of Jerusalem with a mighty army and gathered there a large assembly of the wicked Jewish race. She ordered not only those present in the city to be assembled, but also those from the surrounding area who lived in castles, estates and towns. However, Jerusalem was deserted at the time, so scarcely three thousand Jews in all could be found.

Helena proceeded into Jerusalem and diligently asked the natives about the place where the holy body of our Lord and Saviour, Jesus Christ, had hung, fixed to the Cross. It was difficult to find for this reason. Long ago during the reign of the emperor Hadrian, a persecutor of Christians, a statue of Venus had been erected in that place, so that any Christian who wished to worship Christ there would appear to be worshipping Venus. Consequently, the place had been nearly forgotten. But when someone remembered the temple, which had been entirely demolished, and also the idol, the faithful queen discovered ancient ruins under the mounds of rubbish. Using a crowd of soldiers and peasants, she had the whole place emptied of everything brought there by the envious Jews since the time of the Lord's Passion.

After this she gathered a great assembly of the wicked Jewish race, and, summoning them, blessed Helena said, 'I have learnt from the prophets' holy books that you were God's chosen ones. Rejecting all wisdom, however, you cursed Him who wanted to redeem you from the curse; you wronged Him who with His spit brought light to your eyes, spitting filthily instead on Him; you betrayed into death the man who brought life to your dead; you assumed the light was darkness and the truth a lie; accordingly, the curse which is written in your law has come upon you. Now from among yourselves choose men who know your law well, so they can answer the questions I shall ask them.'

When they had departed full of fear and had argued much among themselves, they found a thousand doctors of the law whom they led to Helena. They vouched that these doctors had great knowledge of the law. Helena said to them, 'Listen to my words; give an ear to my speech. For neither you nor your fathers have understood how the prophets' sayings foretold Christ's coming. It was prophesied before, "A child will be born and his mother will not know men." And Isaiah told you, "I have begotten and raised children, but they have spurned me. The ox knew his owner and the ass his master's stable, but Israel did not know me nor my people understand me". All Scripture has spoken about Him. You, who knew the law, have erred. Now from among yourselves choose those who have earnestly acquired a knowledge of the law, so they may reply to my questions.' And she ordered the soldiers to guard them with great care.

When the council had assembled, they chose from among themselves fifty of the best doctors of the law, who came and stood before Helena. She said, 'Who are these men?' They said to her, 'They are the men who know the law best.' She said to them again, 'According to the Scriptures, you are the sons of Israel; yet how stupid you are! You have followed your fathers' blindness in saying that Jesus is not God's Son; you have read the law and the prophets and not understood them.'

But they said, 'We have read the Scriptures and we do understand them. Lady, explain why you are saying this to us, so we too may know and reply to what you ask.' Once more she said to them, 'Go away again and choose better doctors of the law.'

As they departed, they said among themselves, 'Why do you think the queen puts us to this trouble?'

One of them called Judas said, 'I know. She wants to question us about the wood on which our fathers hanged Christ. Therefore, see that no one confesses to her. For truly our ancestral traditions will be destroyed and the law reduced to nothing. Zachaeus, my grandfather, warned my father, and my father, as he was dying, informed me. He said, "Son, when someone asks about the wood on which our fathers hanged Christ, tell them about it before you are tortured. For then the Hebrew race will reign no more; but they who worship the Crucified Christ will reign, and He will reign for ever and ever." I said to him, "Father, if our ancestors knew that this man was the Christ, why did they lay their hands on Him?" He said, "Listen to me, son, and know by His ineffable Name that I never gave them advice or agreed with them, but I contradicted them many times. Yet because Christ challenged our elders and high priests, they condemned Him to be crucified – thinking to bring death to Him who is deathless. They took Him down from the Cross and buried Him. But the third day after He was buried, He rose again and showed Himself to His disciples. For these reasons, Stephen, your brother, believed in Him and began to teach in His name. When the Pharisees and Sadducees had assembled in council, they condemned Stephen to be stoned, and the multitude took him away and stoned him. As he was giving up his soul, blessed Stephen spread his hands towards heaven and prayed, 'Lord, do not hold this sin against them.' Listen, son, and I will teach you about Christ and His mercy. Paul, who sat in front of the temple carrying out his job as a scribe, had persecuted those who believed in Christ. He incited the people against your brother, Stephen; and the Lord, taking pity on Stephen, made him one of His saints. On this account my parents and I believed in Him, that He is truly the Son of God. Now, son, neither blaspheme Him nor those who believe in Him, and you will have eternal life." Simon, my father, bore me witness of these things. Lo, you have heard all. If she questions us about the wood of the Cross, what do you wish to do?'

The others said, 'We have never heard such things as you have told us today. So if there is an inquiry about this, make sure you reveal nothing. Since you tell us this, you obviously know the place.' After they had said this, lo, soldiers came to them and said, 'Come, the queen calls you.'

When they arrived, they were interrogated by her; but they did not wish to answer her questions truthfully. Then blessed Helena ordered them all to be cast into the fire. Because they were afraid, they delivered Judas to her and said, 'Here is the son of a just man and a prophet; he knows the law and its statutes. Lady, he will carefully show you all your heart desires.' After everyone had vouched for him, she dismissed them and kept only Judas. Then she called him and said, 'Life and death are set before you. Choose which you want: life or death.'

Judas said, 'When someone in solitary confinement has loaves set before him, will he eat stones?' Blessed Helena said, 'If you want to live in heaven and on earth, tell me where the wood of the precious Cross is hidden.' Judas said, 'How can I attest to something which happened two hundred years ago, more or less? Since we are much younger than that, how can we know this?' Blessed Helena said, 'History records that many generations ago there was a war in Ilium and in the Troad and yet all who died there are now remembered; history also records their localities and monuments.' Judas said, 'True, lady, but it is because those happenings were written down. However, we do not have these events preserved in writing.'

Blessed Helena said, 'Why did you yourself acknowledge a little while ago that something happened?' Judas said, 'I spoke in doubt.' Blessed Helena said, 'I have the blessed voice of the Gospels to tell me where the Lord was crucified. Just show me the place called Calvary and I will have it purified. Perhaps I shall find there my heart's desire.' Judas said, 'I do not know the place since I was not there at the time.' Blessed Helena said, 'By Him who was crucified, I will kill you with hunger, unless you tell me the truth.' When she had said this, she ordered him to be cast into a dry pit, and guarded by gaolers for seven days. After seven days had elapsed, Judas cried out from the pit, 'I implore you, take me out and I will show you Christ's Cross.'

When Judas had come out of the pit, he hurried to the place, not knowing for certain where Christ's Cross lay buried. Speaking in Hebrew, he raised his voice to the Lord and said, 'God, God, you who made heaven and earth; you who measured heaven with the palm of your hand and earth with your fist; you who sit upon the chariot of the cherubim – cherubim fly through the courses of the air in endless light where human nature cannot go, and you made them for your ministry. There are six creatures with six wings: four of these flying beings are called cherubim and are your ministrants; they cry with unceasing voice, "Holy, Holy, Holy." Two of them you have put in paradise to guard the Tree of Life, and they are called Seraphim – you have dominion over all things, for we are of your making. You cast the unbelieving angels into deep Tartarus and they dwell in the bottom of the abyss, tortured by the dragon's stench, unable to contradict your command. Now, Lord, if it is your will that Mary's Son, who was sent by you, shall reign – unless He came from you, He would not have performed such great miracles; unless He was your Son, you would not have raised Him from the dead – give us a sign, Lord. Just as you listened to your servant, Moses, and showed him the bones of our father, Joseph, so now, if it is your will, show us the hidden treasure. Make a smoke full of the fragrant sweetness of spices rise from the place, and I also will believe that Christ Crucified is the king of Israel, both now and for ever.'

When Judas had prayed thus, immediately the place was in turmoil and a smoke dense with the sweet aroma of spices rose so that Judas clapped both his hands in wonder and said, 'In truth, Christ, you are the world's Saviour. Thank you, Lord. Although I am unworthy, you have not deprived me of the gift of your grace. I beseech you, Lord Jesus Christ, remember me and wipe away my sins; number me with my brother, Stephen, who has been written about in the Acts of your twelve apostles.'

After he had said this, he took a spade, girded himself manfully and began to dig. When he had dug twenty paces, he found three hidden crosses which he lifted out and carried into the city. Blessed Helena asked which was Christ's Cross – for we know that the other two were the thieves' crosses who were crucified with Him. They laid them down in the middle of the city and waited for the glory of Christ. Around the ninth hour a dead boy was carried in on a litter.

Full of joy, Judas said, 'Lady, now you will recognise the beloved Tree and its power.' Judas took hold of the litter and ordered the dead man to be set down. He put the crosses on him one by one and he did not rise. But when he had put the third, the Lord's Cross, on him, the young man, who was dead, rose at once. All those present glorified the Lord.

However, the devil, always envious of everything good, shouted furiously into the air, 'Who is this who once again will not allow me to receive my own souls? Jesus, Nazarene, you have drawn all men to you; lo, you have uncovered your Cross in order to harm me. Judas, why did you do this? Wasn't it through a Judas that I first effected Jesus' betrayal and incited the people to act wickedly? Lo, now it is through a Judas that I am cast out of here. I will see what I can do against you. I will raise up another king who will forsake Christ Crucified and follow my counsels; he will inflict grievous torments on you. When you have been tortured, you will deny Christ Crucified.'

But Judas, crying aloud with the Holy Spirit, said, 'May Christ who raised the dead damn you to the abyss of everlasting fire.'

Hearing this, blessed Helena marvelled at Judas's faith. And when she had placed the precious Cross among gold and precious stones with great care, she made a silver coffer and put Christ's Cross in it. She also built a church on Calvary. Judas received the baptism of incorruptibility in Christ Jesus; for his previous actions attested to his faith. Helena commended him to the bishop who was still in Jerusalem at the time, and he baptised him in Christ. While blessed Helena lingered in Jerusalem, it happened that the blessed bishop fell asleep in Christ. Blessed Helena summoned Eusebius, bishop of the city of Rome, and he consecrated Judas bishop of Christ's church in Jerusalem. Judas changed his name and was called Cyriacus.

Blessed Helena was filled with God's faith and understood the Scriptures, both the Old and New Testaments. Instructed and filled by the Holy Spirit, she began again to enquire zealously for the nails which had been fixed in the Cross and with which the wicked Jews had crucified the Saviour. When she had summoned Judas, surnamed Cyriacus, she said to him, 'My wish concerning the Cross has been granted, but I am very sad about the nails which were fixed in it. I shall not rest in this matter until the Lord grants my desire. Come here and pray to the Lord about it.'

Holy bishop Cyriacus came to Calvary with the many brothers who believed in Jesus Christ because of the discovery of the Holy Cross and the miracle wrought upon the dead man. Raising his eyes to heaven and striking his breast with his hands at the same time, he cried to the Lord with his whole heart, and, confessing his former ignorance, blessed all those who believed in Christ or who would believe in the future. For a long time he prayed that some sign be shown him and that God would do for the nails what He had done for the Cross. When he said 'Amen' at the end of his prayer, such a sign did occur, which we all saw who were present. A great radiance shone from the place where the Holy Cross had been found, brighter than the sun's light. And at once appeared the nails which had been fixed in the Lord's body, blazing like gold in the earth. As a result, everyone believed without any doubt and said, 'Now we know in whom we believe.' With great fear Cyriacus received the nails and took them to blessed Helena, who knelt down, bowed her head and worshipped them.

Full of wisdom and much knowledge, Helena wondered what to do with the nails. When she had been able to examine in herself every way to the truth, the grace of the Holy Spirit inspired her to do something which would remind future generations of what the prophets had foretold many ages before. She summoned a man, faithful and learned, whom many people vouched for, and said to him, 'Keep the king's commands; carry out the royal pledge. Take these nails and make them into bits for the bridle of what will be the king's horse. They will be invincible arms against all his adversaries. Victory and peace from war will be the king's, so that the words of the prophet Zacharias may be fulfilled, "On that day what is in the horse's bridle will be called sacred to the Lord." '

After blessed Helena had encouraged all those in Jerusalem who had the faith of Jesus Christ and had completed all her work, she persecuted the Jews, because they had not believed, and frightened them out of Judaea. Such grace attended Saint Cyriacus, the bishop, that he cast out demons through his prayers and healed all the infirmities of men. When blessed Helena had left many gifts with the holy bishop Cyriacus to minister to the poor, she died in peace on the fifteenth of April; and charged everyone who loved Christ, both men and women, to commemorate the day when the Holy Cross had been discovered, that is the third of May.

Whoever remembers the Holy Cross, may he join with God's mother, Holy Mary, and with our Lord Jesus Christ, who with the Father and the Holy Spirit lives and reigns forever, world without end.

HISTORY AND ROMANCE

25. THE LIFE OF KING HAROLD

Rumours of the survival of famous men after their supposed death are a familiar theme; from Charlemagne to Hitler, the disappearance of a dominating figure has been met with disbelief, and the 'real' version of what happened has soon circulated. A similar tale to The Life of King Harold *was told of Edward II, who was reputed to have survived in an Italian monastery, and there are other medieval examples.*

But this is a different kind of survival story to that of Arthur or of Frederick Barbarossa, who are supposed to return to lead their people to victory. Here the contrast is between the royal state kept by Harold before his defeat, and his humble – indeed anonymous – existence after Hastings. The object of the narrator, who claims to have known Harold's servant personally, is to emphasise the miraculous power of the Holy Cross at Waltham, the abbey founded by Harold, in first healing the king physically and then converting him from the ways of the world to those of religion. The story is splendidly taken up by Rudyard Kipling in Puck of Pook's Hill, *but is otherwise relatively little known.*

TO review the actions of the most illustrious and rightfully appointed king HAROLD, at this time duly and lawfully crowned, is nothing else than to display to pious minds a brilliant reflection of a divine serenity and meekness. Godwin, a most powerful earl, was his father; his mother was sister to Canute, king of the English and the Danes, and Harold was therefore brother of the queen whom the king and most holy confessor Edward had married. And although she was married to him, the match was not consummated, since both wished to preserve their virginity; nonetheless, she was a cause of much preferment to her father's family. It is plain, however, that her father, or some of the other members of her family, had been heavily branded with the mark of treason and other crimes.

Godwin, indeed, first entangled himself in these misdeeds, because he found himself threatened with imminent destruction; but he later continued his deceits, when he saw his prosperity declining. For when Canute, king of Denmark, had usurped the diadem of England, and he saw that Godwin, who was as bold as he was cunning, was gradually rising to a high position, he began to fear the spirit of this young native. And although he had found his industry very useful to him on many occasions, he decided to destroy him by trickery, since he could not do so openly without seeming spiteful and malicious. So he sent Godwin into Denmark, as if on important business concerning both kingdoms.

Now on the voyage, the young man began to be troubled by suspicions, despite the lavish preparations that had been made for him. He had been given letters sealed with the king's signet, one for each of the chief men of that country, but knew nothing of the contents; so he carefully broke one of the seals, and discovered that he would be put to death as soon as he landed if he delivered the letters as he had been commanded.

So he decided to escape the trick by another trick. This is what he did: he broke open each letter, and substituted a fresh letter written by the clever hand of a clerk, the substance of which was that Godwin was to receive in marriage the king's sister, and that he was to be obeyed in matters concerning the king as if he were the king himself in person. The king, on his return, had to accept what had been done for fear of betraying himself, and made Godwin a royal official, finding him a watchful and prudent minister.

But Godwin quarrelled with many of his own family, and destroyed some members of the royal family by treachery, among them the brother of the holy Edward. All this has been used to discredit his son Harold; but although the latter was not entirely free of his father's vices, it is much more to his credit that he overcame any tendency towards them, as we shall see. Thus a thorn brings forth bright red roses, and produces, so to speak, snow-white lilies, from whose natural functions the meaner property of the thorn subtracts not, but rather adds to it, from the combination, an increase of beauty.

Harold excelled in strength of body, and became famous for shrewdness of mind and vigour in arms: this was proved by the way he subdued Wales. These victories gained him a high position even during the lifetime of the holy Edward; and as a result of them the kingdom was at peace. But at the height of his fame, God afflicted his flesh with a grievous stroke, in order that he might obtain by his present and future wounds a remedy for his soul. Harold, suddenly attacked and paralysed by this, became the occasion of an extraordinary sorrow, for everyone grieved for him, especially the king. It tends, indeed, to Harold's honour at this period, that such a saintly man should love him, foreseeing that Harold would be an everlasting co-heir with him in heaven, rather than his temporary successor on earth. The king's own special physicians gathered round the sick man, and tried everything that their skill suggested, but the power of man cannot put aside the hand of the Almighty. The sad news reached the ears of the German emperor, who, out of friendship for the king, sent a certain physician named Ailard, well practiced in the healing arts, and a devout man to whom God showed much favour in effecting the cure of the sick. On being led to the sick man Ailard carefully examined the nature of the illness, and devoted every attention to him; but every labour is of no avail when a heavenly worker operates in opposition to the art of man.

About this time a stone figure of Christ Crucified had recently been revealed and brought by God's desire to Waltham, where it had become famous for its miraculous virtues. Ailard, concluding that to attempt a cure was impossible when it contradicted God's wishes, persuaded Harold to put his hope in Him who is the salvation of them who trust faithfully in Him, and to seek a cure at the place where the miraculous Cross displayed its mighty gifts. Here he prayed earnestly he might obtain pardon for his sins and alleviation of his sufferings; in a word, health for both the inner and outer man. Nor was the mercy of the Saviour long wanting; for soon the pain and weakness of his body grew less. And as he became stronger his love and devotion for the observances of the Holy Cross increased; he proved by acts of generosity how indebted he was to the medicine by which he had regained his health. He came to the Holy Cross of Waltham, and offered costly presents, gave rich gifts to the attendants, and said that he intended to endow it with still more exalted honour. The whole court rejoiced, not only because Harold had recovered his health, but because it was from heaven he had recovered it.

But this excellent man, eager to exalt the abbey at Waltham, proposed to build there a new temple, to increase the number of attendants, and to augment their revenues; and he caused, by a prudent arrangement, schools to be founded there, under the direction of Master Ailard, the preserver of his health. Foundations of a large church were rapidly laid; the walls rose; lofty columns at equal distances united the walls with interlacing arcades or vaults; a roof of leaden plates kept out the wind and the inclemencies of the weather. The number of clergy was increased from a shameful two to the mystic twelve of the company of the apostles. He also endowed them with estates and possessions, that they might have sufficient for their necessities; and he obtained a confirmation of these gifts by the king's authority.

But afterwards – through jealousy of Harold – William, the first Norman king of England, carried off to Normandy from Waltham seven shrines, of which three were gold and four silver-gilt, full of relics and precious gems; four books of Holy Writ, ornamented with gold, silver and gems in their bindings; four large gold and silver censers; six candelabra, of which two were gold and the rest silver; three large pitchers of Greek work, silver and gilt; four crosses worked in gold and silver and precious stones; one cross that was cast from fifty gold marks; and many other precious items, which were known to have been offered to the Holy Cross by Harold in his piety, and taken away by William through hatred. The latter, however, seems to have palliated the heinousness of the robbery by an easy kind of compensation by disseminating a clear account of the progress of events by which the Cross was discovered and conveyed to Waltham.

Who knows how the bones of a man are framed in the womb of her who is with child? And who has learnt, or who can learn, what is best for a man in his lifetime? One man generally rules another to his hurt. Sometimes a man is subdued and subjected by one man to another for his good. Harold, to return to our subject, sometime after the events we have recounted, was suddenly raised, as it were, on the wind, and was in a moment violently thrown down. He was raised to be king by the acclamation of the kingdom; he returned victorious from the battle in triumph, having slain the barbarians who had attacked him. He was not afraid on hearing that his late enemy [i.e. William] had come to attack him, but mocked his efforts, hastening to attack his destroyer, as though he would at one blow overthrow him. He joined battle, but in that battle he fell; he attacked, and was cut down, but was it to his destruction?

The hand of the crucified King permitted the enemy's spear to pierce his body and to grievously wound him, but only so that he should increase in his devotion to our Lord. But it was generally related that Harold had succeeded to the earthly kingdom of the most blessed Edward, and had triumphed over the Norwegians; and that he had bravely – some said impulsively and unprepared – gone against the Normans who were attacking him. It was further related that when his comrades were slain, he fell on the enemy single-handed, and was also slain. But I, God helping me, will write our account of what happened to him after these events, the facts of which have escaped the notice of most chroniclers.

Some of these things I heard from a certain hermit of venerable life, Sebricht by name, who, while he lived, was servant for many years to Harold; and others from equally trustworthy authorities. Sebricht became a hermit at a town called Stanton in Oxfordshire, where he lived until his death. Here I, when still of a tender age, and young in the profession of religion, had visited him sometimes in my own person, and was at last admitted to the inmost sanctities of a familiar friendship. At length, when I was older, I advanced so far that he would scarcely hide any of his secrets from me which seemed useful for my instruction as I talked with him on the state of the inner man. And he, though he was country-bred, and ignorant of any language but English, could express his thoughts cleverly in his own language: he used to tell me: 'Let me say what I think – I believe that the sum total of my salvation consists in patience and hope.' He would add how many things the Lord had shown him in the shape of many and great tribulations, and how mercifully he had, by converting him, given him new life, and how powerfully he had led him from the depths of earth. Of such things he would speak with much feeling, without complaining about the hardship of his sufferings, but remembering that consolation and spiritual grace which he had found to be the alleviation of his trials.

Speaking of Harold, he would call him his master, rejoicing that he had in heaven an advocate whom, when on earth, he had as a preceptor. And it was this man who told us of the things which followed, as well as others who knew Harold after he had become a man of religion. Some of the latter were ignorant that Harold was once, when he lived, a crowned king; but they knew well in what places he lived from the time when he spent his life in solitude in England. For when Harold resolved to live in his own country, he took a new name, and changed his dwelling-place from time to time lest by some chance it should be betrayed to anyone. This, then, is what we learnt from Sebricht and the others.

When the English army was beaten at the first attack of the Normans, king Harold, pierced with numerous blows, was thrown to the ground among the dead. As the enemy's host departed from the scene of the slaughter, he was found stunned and scarcely breathing by some women whom pity, and a desire to bind up the wounds of the maimed, had drawn thither. They bound up his wounds, and carried him to a neighbouring hut. From thence, he was borne by two common men, freemen or serfs, unrecognised and cunningly hidden, to the city of Winchester. Here, he hid in a certain cellar, and succeeded in keeping the secret of his hiding-place for two years, during which time he was cured by a certain woman, a Saracen, very skilled in the art of surgery. On regaining his strength thus, he thought he would prove by great deeds the courage of his royal spirit which his soul had not lost in the overthrow of his body. The nobles of his kingdom, as well as the people, had already bowed their necks to the yoke of the conqueror; and his chief lords had nearly all either perished or been driven from the country, leaving their ancestral honours to be divided and possessed by strangers.

Harold, therefore, resolved that he would perish with his people or procure assistance for them. He crossed over to Germany, the home of his race, with the intention of proceeding to Saxony; but was grieved to find that already the miserable overthrow of his nation was common talk in all quarters. He begged his kinsfolk to help one of their own race, and argued that it was the very bravery of the Saxons which had caused the disaster, because their recent victory had led them to oppose such a multitude of the enemy with too small a force of soldiers.

'For,' said he, 'accustomed as I am to victory, and unacquainted with defeat, I should have thought myself beaten if I had been but a little more tardy in gaining a fresh victory over the enemy. For when, by divine grace, the Norwegians and their king, who had overrun our territory from the north, were slain by us, and our armies and generals had been dismissed to their own homes, suddenly the Normans came upon us from the south. And I, meeting them hastily with a small force, inferior in numbers, but not in courage or spirit, at length fell; but though I was conquered, I did not yield. Accident, and not bravery, made them our superiors, and we shall easily defeat them with your help.'

But despite Harold's arguments, he was unable to enlist any help. For he who was now king of the English as well as duke of the Normans, in his foresight for his own security, had been prudent enough to anticipate Harold by hastening to ally himself with the Danish king, as well as with the rulers of the neighbouring countries, and to obtain their favour.

Harold, coming at length to himself, and returning, as it were, from his fantastic dream, completely changed his heart. He belatedly realised that it was God who was opposing him in the way in which he was so fruitlessly walking, and that it was His angel's sword which had been borne against him and his obstinate efforts. Putting on one side, then, his vain desire of a temporal kingdom, and casting off the fatal purposes of earthly strife, he changed both his outward appearance and his inward disposition. The hand which he was wont to arm, he supported with a spear shortened into a staff. Instead of a shield, a wallet hung from his neck. His head, which he was accustomed to equip with a helmet, and adorn with a diadem, was protected by a hat. His feet and legs, in the place of sandals and leg-armour, were either bare, or encased in stockings.

Fearful of discovery, and instructed by such divine orders as these from the Holy Spirit, he left all his friends who had seemed to support him up to that time: he deserted his kinsfolk: he withdrew secretly from all who had known him: he approached people hitherto unknown to him. He departed then to a far-distant country to visit sacred places, to honour the relics of the saints in their own homes and shrines; to obtain more fully and perfectly by their intercession the kingdom of God which he already held within his breast, intending after that to return to his own country.

He had visited the resting-places of Christ's most exalted apostles in the past, before he succeeded to the throne of the English, for the most devout reasons, but also with the object of bringing holy relics from their city to his own, rather than worshipping them in theirs. For he had had a very fervent desire to collect sacred relics, especially from the time he began to build and found the church of the Holy Cross at Waltham. Having obtained numerous pledges of the saints, he appears also, by payment of vows and prayers and money, to have carried off from Rome on his return to his own country the blessed bones of the martyrs Chrysanthus and Daria. But the Romans, realising that they were being robbed of a great treasure, followed the pious plunderer just as he departed and stopped his progress. For a whole host of the natives were not inclined to allow a few pilgrims to resist them by force or break away in flight. Harold was stopped, bound, and overwhelmed with insults;

hardest of all, he was compelled to give up those pearls of priceless value which he had lawfully obtained from their former possessors, as they indeed confessed. But despite this he managed to obtain some very precious relics at Rome, and brought them home to be reverently preserved in the church which has so often been mentioned.

We are unable to accompany Harold to every place and on every single day as he wanders through many countries of Christendom and spends his time so beneficially; but if we cannot relate every single thing he did or suffered on his long pilgrimage, let us at all events go and meet him as he returns to us with all speed. First, however, we must speak of the sins of which he was accused, and which made God's favour to him all the more remarkable. With what calmness and favour didst Thou take hold of this man, and, as some think, on account of his wickedness; yet didst Thou not hurl him into eternity, but, taking hold of him and correcting him, brought him forth from his very iniquity to be more careful for himself, more devoted to Thee.

Since many historians say much about Harold's sin, we ought to bring forward for impartial consideration what those, who have a desire to exaggerate or detract from it, think on the matter. For the majority accuse him of having committed a sin of no common kind; but of such heinousness, indeed, that they are of opinion the downfall of English liberty must be imputed to its enormity. For it is asserted that he took the name of the Lord God in vain, and feared not to pollute it with a false oath; and they also add that this act of sin was marked out by a wonderful miracle from heaven.

For the oak under which Harold made the oath to the duke of the Normans, which was once a tree of great height and beauty, as is proved by those who behold it today, as soon as Harold usurped the kingdom which he had sworn to preserve for William, and thus broke his oath, is said to have shed its bark, and to have lost its greenness and its foliage. The lasting nature of the withered tree, an indestructible oak, increases the miracle of the blight falling upon it, and this we have frequently, in common with many more, wondered at.

Who, indeed, would not be amazed that this oak, of such vast magnitude, not weakened by small branches but everywhere unbroken, stripped of every covering of bark, had not already yielded to the course of time, and, wasted by decay or wind and rain, had not grown rotten? But when we saw the ill-fated tree, one hundred and forty years after this event, it still stood at a short distance from Rouen, overhanging a pleasant glade, which is not far from the bridge over the Seine leading towards the hermitage of Grandmont.

On the other hand, some people try to justify the non-fulfilment of the oath, and hold that Harold was quite right in assuming the kingly power. For judging from what happened after, if what he had sworn had been observed, it would have been beyond a doubt a disastrous thing to the nation, as it was against his own wish and disadvantageous to the safety of his people. For he made the oath in fear of death or everlasting imprisonment, neither of which he was prepared to embrace. Nor was there any other way out of the difficulty, confined as he was in a foreign country and in such powerful hands. So, yielding to the dictates of human frailty, which never gives up life willingly, and to the advice of some friends who were with him at the time, he took the oath thus presented to him.

As to whether it was right to extort such an oath, others may argue as they wish. But it was lawful for him not to fulfil an oath thus forced from him, if – and no one denies it – the oath itself were illegal; and that was how (there was no other way) he escaped from the Normans who were keeping him prisoner. And when at length he was restored to his own people, he told everyone openly what he had suffered and what he had done. Those who heard him were of one mind in angrily rejecting an agreement sworn under compulsion and declared vehemently that it should not be observed: 'Heaven forbid that we should serve the Normans! Heaven forbid that the liberty of our city and of our English nobility should ever be subservient to the barbarian yoke of Norman pride!'

Since everyone regarded the oath as worthless, Harold was in due course unanimously acclaimed as king. But it soon appeared that this was not in accordance with the divine will. When the Norwegian king sailed to England with a numerous fleet, and attacked the province of York with fire and sword, and had begun to lay waste everything that came in his way, the newly-elected king hastened to meet him with an army he had collected, but was suddenly seized with a violent pain in his leg.

In agony for the peril of his subjects rather than at his own pain, he passed nearly the whole night in prayer, without sleep, and begged for the familiar assistance of the Holy Cross. That very night there appeared to Elfin, the abbot of Ramsey, the late king Edward, the holy and watchful defender of his people, who told the abbot of Harold's predicament and prayers, and said to him, 'Rise, go and tell your king from me that, at my intercession, God has granted him the victory. This news will cure him, and your vision will be an assurance of his coming triumph.'

Encouraged by this heavenly message, Harold attacked the enemy with confidence, and easily conquered them, showing that he obtained the kingdom by the connivance of his most holy predecessor and the ordaining of God.

So his legal assumption of the kingly power was proved by these events and signs. And another miracle confirmed God's favour towards him as king, and defended his honour against the reproaches of defamers. As he was returning from the slaughter of his enemies, this most valiant king, despite his haste to meet some new adversaries who had attacked him, refused to pass by his beloved church, but turned aside to visit it. He entered and prostrated himself before the Holy Cross, offering thanks for the victory he had just gained, and humbly praying that he might obtain another victory. As he finished his prayers and devotions, he bowed before the Holy Cross, as is the custom; and in response the head of the crucified image itself bowed down.

This wonderful and auspicious action of the Saviour gladdened while it terrified some of those who stood by. For what could be conceived more auspicious than that the immortal King of Eternity should be seen to answer the salute of a king of miserable mortals! A man, destined soon to be a king no longer, prays, and the neck of stone which a human craftsman could never bend suddenly bends of its own accord, yet is not broken. And we can still behold the effect of this miracle today, for the stone did not crack, nor did the silver plate break or wrinkle, though it was stretched as the neck was bent. Yet there was a considerable change, for the chin of the image used to stand straight out, and now it hangs down on the breast.

Although this marvel seemed at the time a happy and auspicious omen, yet some people afterwards said that it foretold an unlucky and disastrous event. For when, a short time after, the king was beaten with his army, many thought that the bending of the image signified the subjugation of the English and the downfall of the kingdom. But if we consider the order in which the events happened, our first interpretation of this divine action seems more probable.

But the eternal and unchanging God offers His worshippers for their labours not transitory and perishable things, but rather stable, good and eternal things. Therefore He took away a shadowy kingdom from him for whom He preserved a true and everlasting one, that the former might not be even a slight hindrance to his passing to the latter.

But let it suffice that we have touched upon both sides of these matters which some say happened in favour of king Harold, and others in opposition to him, leaving the settlement of the question to the final decision of the reader, or rather of the immortal God who knoweth all things.

It remains for us now to go and meet the erstwhile king on his return from his long journey, and to follow him to the best of our power with the service of our trusty pen, as he returns home first to the home of the Angles and then of the Angels.

After spending many years in the holy labour of a religious pilgrimage, Harold decided to practise a new method of life, worn out as he was with long toils and old age. He had learnt, indeed, the countless virtues and most holy lives of the saints whom he had visited, and he now resolved to make an end of his wanderings. But lest this bodily repose should bring laziness or torpor upon his mind, he chose to stay in that land where he could gain a greater exercise and a more effective proof of his patience and goodness, namely the land which contained as many of his persecutors as there were dwellers therein. But he did not commit himself to such a danger without due consideration; for he was well aware of the strength of Him who dwelt in him.

Led, then, at length to his former kingdom – which he had possessed, indeed, with great danger, but lost to his great gain – ready to fight manfully with those weapons with which he was armed for a new and incomparably better kingdom, he entered the camp equipped with all his armour. For, retiring into a cavern hard by Dover, he first composed his mind, then, rising up out of himself, he beheld the land far above him, whose King sometimes his eyes could see in all His glory. Here, fulfilling all the commandments, he spent ten years of solitary life: like a soldier who begins as a recruit and at length becomes a veteran, he strove, by leading a godly life, to exceed even rather than fulfil the vital precepts of the divine law.

Now this place, where he had thus determined to spend his life, was not far distant from the spot where he had formerly lost his earthly kingdom by nearly meeting his death. But he wished to intensify the danger in which he lived, so, bidding farewell to Kent, he proceeded to Wales, and stayed there in various places for a long time. He lived with the Welsh and prayed for them, although they continually made unprovoked attacks on him, despite the fact that he had concealed both his features and his name, wearing always in public a veil before his face. If his name were asked, he would say that men called him Christian. For he was afraid that he might be betrayed by these indications. For it was very probable, if his secrets were known, that he might be troubled by what was worse than torture or imprisonment, namely, praise and applause. For who would not show all the reverence and honour he could to such a man, when he saw how lowly-minded and mild he was; and how, by his own free will, he had become an object of contempt to lovers of the world, when in former times he had held a conspicuous position in the world, and had been rich and powerful? In truth he suffered from these treacherous, savage and despicable men only what he looked for and expected, for he was often violently beaten at the hands of robbers, from whom also he suffered every possible injury. They pilfered his provisions, and robbed him of his clothes; and tortured him for his money, of which he had none.

But the man of God bore it all with a tranquil mind, a cheerful countenance, a gentle voice, and a generous hand. Nor did his pious habits cease, for he gave food and drink to his enemies, as the apostle tells us to do. He softened the hearts of his despoilers by kindnesses, so that they began to worship and honour him whom they had been accustomed to mock and scourge. For the sweet fragrance of his holy reputation, gliding into their senses, drove away that devil's breath of rage from the hearts of these brutes.

But this man of God, this lover of quietness, decided that he must fly from those whom he had first sought out to persecute him, but who now were inclined to worship him. The virtue of his bodily strength, which would not yield to labours, but was become broken with years, began to give way in him. Now the decrepit old man was to experience that 'old age brings everything'. He begged that God with His wonted kindness would grant him a resting-place, where he might pass the remainder of his life in the quiet of a much desired repose, and there end his days by a happy death.

He caused himself to be mounted on a poor beast, and, content with his usual attendant, started on the journey, deliberately ignorant of his journey's end. Led by angelic guidance, he reached at length the city of Chester, where, as the day was declining towards evening, he arrived in the midst of the city.

His attendant asked where they were to stay, when an unseen voice spoke. 'Go,' it said, 'good man, to the church of St John; there you shall find a resting-place prepared for you.' The attendant, astonished at what he heard, sought for the owner of the voice, but no one was visible. It was clear that it was the Lord's holy angel who, accompanying them on their journey, and ordering everything for their benefit, had told the man of God that a place was prepared for him. He was wearing his customary veil which covered nearly the whole of his face, both in case he frightened those who met him by the remarkable appearance of his wounds; and equally to avoid being recognised.

The bystanders soon pointed out the church which the divine oracle had indicated. Here Harold was heartily welcomed as a guest sent by heaven. For the fact was that a venerable hermit of that place had recently departed this life, thus leaving his little dwelling vacant for a successor, who was thus divinely provided. And while he lived there, he was frequently asked by those who came to visit him whether he was present at the battle in which king Harold was said to have been killed. He would reply, 'I was certainly there.' But to some who suspected that perhaps he might be Harold himself, and who questioned him more closely than was right, he would sometimes thus speak of himself: 'When the battle of Hastings was fought, there was no one more dear to Harold than myself.' With these ambiguous words, he did not so much confirm the truth of the facts, as refuse to strengthen doubtful conjectures. But how the truth eventually became known, we will tell in the words of a venerable man who succeeded Harold in his habitation at the same hermitage.

The general belief that Harold had died at Hastings is indeed mistaken, but it can be explained by what took place at Waltham after the battle, events which were famous throughout the land. For, in truth, the terrible news had reached the ears of the private domestic canons of the king at Waltham. The clerks, mindful of the devotion due to their most generous patron, sent a certain woman of a shrewd intelligence, Edith by name, to the district where the battle had been fought, that she might carry away the limbs of their dead lord, to be buried reverently in their church. She seemed a suitable person to make the attempt, because the weaker sex would be considered less an object of suspicion to the cruel officers in authority, and more an object of compassion. But this woman seemed more fitted than all others to carry out this affair, because she could more easily discover among the thousands of corpses him she sought, and would handle his remains more tenderly, because she loved him exceedingly, and knew him well, since she had been frequently present in the secret places of his chamber. But when she reached the ill-omened spot, she heard from many Normans that the king of the Angles was ignominiously beaten, with his cross broken in halves, and that he was lying on the battlefield, amongst the slain.

But the truth is that they who had carried off the king half dead had put about this report, foreseeing that it would be dangerous if the enemy should hear that he was alive. The mistake of the woman sent to find his body is therefore not surprising; unable to discern the features of the body – hacked about as it was, covered with blood, already becoming black and decomposed – carried off with her another man's mangled corpse, since she could not find one which she could be certain was the king's, to satisfy those who had sent her. And this was the body which was received in all reverence by the canons of Waltham, without questioning the truth of the matter, and was handed over for burial in the church of the Holy Cross.

In the days of king Henry II, a brother of Harold named Gurth, who at the time of the battle had been little more than a boy, but in wisdom and uprightness of mind almost a man, was brought before both the king and his nobles. But he was then of a great age, and, as we heard from many who saw him at that time, still handsome and very tall. The abbot of the regular canons at Waltham, the Lord Walter, of pious memory, was the first to see him; and was very eager to ask him, as well as his brothers, who were about the king's court at Woodstock, whether in real truth the ashes of his brother were preserved in their monastery, as was generally believed. He replied in English, 'You may have some country-man, but you have not Harold.' Yet he came to the place himself to worship the Holy Cross, and when his brother's coffin was shown to him, looking askance at it, said: 'Man knoweth not' (these were his words) 'Harold lies not here.' Michael, chamberlain of the church at Waltham, firmly asserts that he heard these words from the man's own mouth, and many of the bystanders are still alive.

But here my own book comes to an end, and the narrative of the hermit follows.

It is written that tribulation worketh patience, patience experience, experience hope. For the experience of patience and confirmation of a pious hope, God sometimes permits His people to have tribulation in this life that He may free them from an eternal tribulation, wherefore He also allowed the venerable Harold, once king of the Angles, to have tribulation, and to be overcome by his enemies and expelled from his kingdom lest he might grow proud because he had gained a victory; and lest, having been raised to kingly power, he might put on one side the love of God because of his prosperity, but having been placed in poverty that he might live a more holy and blessed life, while he had his mind altogether free from earthly occupations.

Therefore, after the loss of his kingdom, and the cure of the wounds he had received at the hands of the Normans, he made a [journey] in the guise of a pilgrim to holy places through many lands, working for God on his holy pilgrimage. But after a time, being stiff with old age and shattered by his long journey, he became desirous to inflict on his weary body another form of religious practice. And because to live on one's native soil is always pleasant, he made all haste to England, where he had formerly been king, that he might spend there the remainder of his days, poor, despised and meanly clad, where once he had flourished as a king, wealthy, exalted and clad in costly garments; and in order that his merit might increase in the sight of God (in proportion as he might possess a more benevolent spirit) because he would be able every day to look upon his adversaries and be happy in the kingdom he had lost, and also to obey the Lord's command in praying faithfully to God for them.

On arriving at the shores of his native country, he chose the solitary life of a hermit, and, living there in many places, unknown to all, till he made his last farewell to earthly things, he ministered to God by faith. Nor did he change his place of abode by any caprice, but he sought where he might serve God with most tranquillity. Now this same noble man had formerly an attendant named Moses, who attended me also for two years, when I, the present writer, was confined in the same place at Chester where the lord Harold, the hermit and friend of God, died. And I will tell you briefly and faithfully, though I must omit much, the events which follow according to the account of Moses and other faithful men.

At length the man of God came to Shropshire, to a place called Cheswardine (Ceswrthin), where, for seven years leading the life of a hermit, with this Moses for his attendant, he was very much disturbed by Welsh robbers, and was frequently and violently afflicted at their hands by their robberies and assaults. All this he bore with patience, in all things giving thanks to God with humility. But after a time, lest outward tribulation should cast him down from his position of control over his inward self, he left that place, and followed by the above-mentioned attendant, set out for Chester: and there, in the chapel of St James, which is situated on the river Dee, outside the walls of the city in the cemetery of St John Baptist, he spent a hermit's life with great strictness for seven years, until his death.

He wore for a long time a corslet next to his skin, till it was all rotten, and quite worn away. But the cuttings and loose pieces he bade his servant throw secretly into the river, that it might appear to no man that he had worn it. In his body, indeed, he was most chaste and continent: in heart, lowly and prudent. Of what station of life he was he always kept a secret, that he might not by chance be held in too great veneration by men, whereby, his mind being elated, he might slip from the path of uprightness, and the merit of his humility might be diminished in the sight of God. He rarely quitted the chapel, but was constant in continual prayer, doing what God has said: that men ought always to pray and not to faint. In front of his eyes he hung at all times a cloth, which covered nearly the whole of his face, so that when he wished to walk at all far he required the hand of a guide. Why he did this, his attendant did not know; but perhaps he did it to hide the appearance of the wounds upon his gashed face, or lest, if a free outlet for his eyes existed, an opening for secular vanities might be made for his soul, or else it was that he might not be recognised and venerated by any who had seen him in former times.

Now as the day of the death of the venerable Harold drew near, and as that last moment of extreme necessity arrived when the holy man demanded the consolation of the Holy Sacrament, a priest, whom I knew well, named Andrew, came and visited the sick man and administered to him all that the Christian rite requires. But as he was listening to his last confession, he asked him of what station of life he was?

He replied: 'If you will promise me, on the Word of the Lord, that, as long as I live, you will not divulge what I tell you, I will satisfy the motive of your question.' The priest answered: 'On peril of my soul, I declare to you that anything you shall tell me shall be preserved a secret from everyone till you have drawn your last breath.' Then he replied: 'It is true that I was formerly the king of England, Harold by name, but now am I a poor man, lying in ashes; and, that I might conceal my name, I caused myself to be called Christian.'

Not long after this he gave up the ghost, and now, conqueror over all his enemies, he departed to the Lord. But the priest at once told them all that the man of God had confessed to him, in his last words, that he was indeed king Harold.

26. HEREWARD THE WAKE

Hereward the Wake is a historical character, and much of The Deeds of Hereward the Saxon *can be confirmed in outline by reputable historical records, including* The Anglo-Saxon Chronicle *and* Domesday Book. *The Peterborough version of the Chronicle records his sack of Peterborough in 1070, and his landholdings are recorded in* Domesday Book. *Many of his exploits centre on Ely, where he is known to have defied William the Conqueror for a year or so, and the monks at Ely seem to have written down something of what they knew about him; so we are looking at stories which are on, if not over, the borderline with history. There are some intriguing details, such as Hereward's insistence that only priests can make true knights, and his strategy at the siege of Ely, which seem to ring true, while other episodes, for instance the witch brought to cast spells on the English by Ivo Taillebois, seem pure invention. Hereward's exile in Flanders, and his exploits in Ireland, seem to be imported from romance. Another version of his story, written down in Lincolnshire about fifty years after his death, describes how he was murdered by a jealous group of Norman knights while on campaign with William the Conqueror in France, after he had made his peace with the king*

Hereward became a legendary figure because he represented the last surge of Anglo-Saxon resistance in the south of England; though he was a practical leader, and he never seems to have considered attempting to restore the English dynasty. Instead, he was fighting for a just settlement for the Saxon landowners like himself within the framework of Norman rule, which was why his reconciliation with the Conqueror was possible. But this side of his character was forgotten, and the image of the 'last of the Englishmen' has remained with him to this day.

*

The author begins by describing how his patron had found a brief account of Hereward's exploits, and had sent it to him. He had searched for more material, but had only found a few leaves of an account of his early deeds in English, written by Leofric of Bourne, which he had difficulty in deciphering. So he talked to men who had known him, particularly his knights Siward, now a monk at Bury St Edmunds, and Leofric the Black. The author says that the little history which follows is based on what they told him, as well as the fragments of written record.

MANY of the mightiest men are recorded from among the English people, and the outlaw Hereward is reckoned the most distinguished of all – a notable warrior among the most notable. Of very noble descent from both parents, his father was Leofric of Bourne, nephew of earl Ralph the Staller, and his mother was Eadgyth, the great-great-niece of duke Oslac. From his childhood he exhibited grace and vigour of body; and, from practice when a youth, the quality of his courage proved him a perfect man.

Although tough in work and rough in play, readily provoking fights among those of his own age and often stirring up strife among his elders in town and village, he had no equal in acts of daring and bravery. He spared nobody whom he thought to be in any way a rival in courage or in fighting. In consequence he often caused strife among the populace and commotion among the common people. As a result of this he made his parents hostile towards him; for because of his deeds of courage and boldness, they found themselves quarrelling with their friends and neighbours every day, and almost daily having to protect their son with drawn swords and weapons when he returned from sport or from fighting. Unable to stand this, his father eventually drove him out of his sight. He didn't keep quiet even then: when his father went visiting his estates, Hereward and his gang often got there first, distributing his father's goods among his own friends and supporters. And on some of his father's properties he even appointed stewards and servants of his own to see to provisions for his men. So his father ensured that he was banished from king Edward and his homeland. This being done, he at once acquired the name of 'outlaw', being driven away from his father and his native land when he was eighteen years old.

Hereward went to his godfather, Gisebert of Ghent, in Northumberland, with just one servant.

At Easter, Whitsun and Christmas that wealthy man had the custom of testing the strength and spirit of those young men who were hoping for the belt and arms of knighthood by letting wild beasts out of cages. Hereward asked to be allowed to take on one of the beasts – in point of fact, a very large bear which was there. This was the offspring of a famous Norwegian bear, which had the head and feet of a man, and human intelligence; which understood the speech of men and was cunning in battle. Its father was said to have raped a girl in the woods and through her to have engendered Beorn, king of Norway.

Hereward couldn't get permission, for though the lord perceived the bravery of the young man, he feared for his youthfulness. The next day, however, the animal broke its chains and burst out of the bars of the cage, tearing to pieces and killing every living thing it could reach. When the lord heard about this, he immediately ordered the knights to get ready to attack it with spears. Meanwhile, alerted by the screams of the terrified people, Hereward encountered the blood-stained beast as it was on its way to the lord's chamber, where his wife and daughters had fled in fright. At once it tried to rush at him, but he forestalled it, driving his sword through its head down to the shoulder-blades. Leaving the blade there, he lifted up the animal in his arms and held it out to those who followed, at which sight they were much amazed.

His lord and lady gave him no little thanks, but the knights and pages of the household displayed deep envy and hatred. Through this deed he gained the rank of a knight, though he put off being made a knight, saying that he ought to find a better test of his courage and spirit. The women and girls sang about him as they danced, much to the annoyance of his enemies, who looked for a chance to kill him.

One day when their lord was away hunting in the woods, the knights of the household tried to despatch him by getting one of his most familiar friends to throw a javelin at him; this was a man whom Hereward had rescued from the enemy and saved from death only three days earlier. A servant warned Hereward of the plot, however, and he transfixed his attacker in the act of throwing the javelin. He told his lady about this, and said that he must depart at once: she begged him to stay until his lord returned, but he would not listen and set off.

He next joined the court of the prince of Cornwall, whose name was Alef. At the court was a proud and evil man called Ulcus Ferreus, who had long hoped to win the prince's beautiful daughter through his remarkable courage: he was reckoned to be the strongest warrior among both the Scots and the Picts. He was very boastful, and once, disparaging the English, claimed to have killed three of them with one blow. Hereward answered: 'Since your imagination created these men, it is right that your mouth should kill them all at once!' This amused the prince's daughter so much that she burst out laughing; but Ulcus said, 'If it wasn't for the presence of my lord, you would have joined them in death!' Hereward replied, 'If you are as tough as you pretend to be, and fight fair, I shall be ready for you.'

A few days later, Hereward, who was unarmed, met him in a neighbouring wood, and Ulcus said, 'Now I shall take my revenge, and the princess will either laugh or weep when I give her your scalp.' Hereward said, 'There is no glory in killing an unarmed man; give me an hour to confess and give my goods to the poor, and I will return at once.' When Hereward swore to do so, Ulcus released him; but Hereward returned fully armed, and wounded Ulcus through the thighs at the first blow, and though Ulcus was much stronger, he managed to evade him until he saw his chance and drove his sword under the mailcoat into Ulcus's groin.

When the prince's household heard the noise of the struggle and realised what was happening, they told the prince, who sent armed knights to separate them and save Hereward; but when they arrived, they did not find what they expected, for Ulcus was dead. Hereward was seized and led before the prince, and the prince's followers demanded that he should be put to death. But the prince kept him in prison for his own safety, while his daughter tended Hereward's wounds, delighted to be free of her hated betrothed. In the end she contrived his escape, sending him to the son of the king of Ireland with a letter describing how he had killed her enemy.

When he arrived in Ireland, he was received with great honour, and invited to stay; but he found there his cousins, Siward the Blond and Siward the Red, who told him that his father was dead, and his mother was alone on the estate, which was now his. But before he could leave to go to her, the king of Ireland set out to make war on the king of Munster, and begged Hereward to go with him. Hereward and six other men were assigned to attack the king of Munster in his camp, and forced their way to his tent: they ordered him to surrender and come with them, but he refused, so Hereward killed him and his two chief councillors before retreating with his men. The king of Ireland attacked the camp, and the men of Munster fled in terror when they learnt that their king was dead. Hereward's bravery led many nobles to seek him out to learn the skill of arms, and within a year he had defeated all the king of Ireland's enemies.

But while they were far from court, a messenger came to them from the Cornish princess saying that despite the fact that she had been betrothed to the king of Ireland's son, whom she loved, she was being forced to marry another man. The king's son at once set out to rescue her, and sent messengers to the king of Cornwall reminding him of their agreement. Hereward and three companions went secretly by another road; when they arrived they found that the messengers had been imprisoned, and that the wedding was due to take place the next day.

Hereward had dyed his blond hair black, and his beard red, to disguise himself, and got himself invited to the wedding feast as a distinguished stranger who happened to be passing. He attracted attention to himself by his rude behaviour, and the princess eventually recognised him. The jester taunted him for his manners, but Hereward replied that he could play his harp better than its owner. The jester gave it to him, thinking he would fail to make good his boast, but he played so well that the princess gave him a fine cloak, and the bridegroom offered him anything he wanted, save his wife and his lands. Hereward asked for the Irish messengers to be set free, but one of the courtiers saw through his motives, and suggested that he should be ambushed, and the messengers should be blinded before they were released. The king's daughter warned Hereward of what was planned, and he was able to free them unharmed so that with their help he succeeded in carrying off the bride and bringing her to the son of the king of Ireland; after a forced march of three days, he found him at midnight encamped on the road to Cornwall, and the two lovers were married at once.

As a reward, the Irish king gave Hereward two fully equipped ships, though he delayed for a long while in the hope that Hereward could be persuaded to remain in Ireland, and marry one of his nieces or the daughter of a nobleman. But Hereward insisted on returning home before he would think of settling in Ireland. His journey was ill-fated; he was driven to the Orkneys, where one of his ships was lost, and then by another fierce storm to Flanders, where he was shipwrecked. The count, Manasar the Old, had him and his men arrested on suspicion of being the advance guard of an invading army, because they were so splendidly equipped. Hereward told his story, but refused to reveal his name, and the count ordered that he and his men should remain with him for the time being, in honourable detention.

Manasar was at war with the count of Guines, and their men fought in single combat outside the castles which were being besieged. Hereward begged to be allowed to fight for Manasar, and distinguished himself in the encounter. However, he was soon recognised by a man who had met him in Ireland, and he admitted his identity to the count. Soon after this he defeated the most famous champion in the count of Guines's army, his nephew Hoibrict, and took him captive. These and other exploits earned him the love of a beautiful girl who lived in St Omer, named Turfrida, who was both well-educated and skilled in handicrafts. But she had another suitor, the nephew of a powerful lord in St Valery, and the latter learnt of her affection for Hereward. One day, as they were both going to a tournament, Hereward saw that his rival was wearing a favour which Turfrida had given him; he at once charged him and unseated him, seizing both his horse and the girl's favour.

However, the presence of his enemies meant that Hereward had great difficulty in seeing Turfrida, and he determined to make his way to her home in secret. When he arrived, he pretended to be Siward the Blond, his cousin, but Turfrida soon recognised him and fell into his arms. When they parted, Hereward went to stay at an inn, where a follower of his rival recognised him; as Hereward slept, he tried to attack him with an axe, but Hereward woke just in time, and turned away to avoid the blow. After this episode, he never slept unguarded.

The count of Flanders appointed Hereward as one of the commanders for an invasion of Frisia, where he succeeded in defeating the Frisian army by means of a feigned retreat, and secured their offer of submission.

Meanwhile it was reported to Hereward that there was a remarkable brood herd of particularly swift horses on a certain island nearby, so he went there with a few fellow-soldiers and some men who knew the difficult roads. There he bought a mare of exceptional speed, and an especially handsome colt. The mother he named Swallow, and her colt Lightfoot. As he was returning from the place, however, he fell among a band of robbers in a certain secluded spot among the valleys, hills and woods. For two days he resisted their ambush vigorously, but by the third day he was weak from hunger and confused by the violent blows of the brigands. However, by the sixth day, they managed to hasten to rejoin their army; the next day was that appointed for the submission of the Frisians.

The Frisians duly submitted, but when the army returned to Flanders, they found that the count had died and another man had been elected in his place who refused to reward them for their achievement. So Hereward suggested that the soldiers should share out the rich booty they had brought from Frisia among themselves, before returning to England, which was now under Norman rule.

Hereward wished to visit his father's house and his homeland, now subject to the rule of foreigners and almost ruined by the exactions of many men: he wanted to help any of his friends and neighbours who had survived. He returned from foreign parts with his personal attendant Martin Lightfoot as his sole companion, leaving his nephews, Siward the Blond and Siward the Red with his newly-wedded wife, Turfrida. He arrived back at his father's manor at Bourne one evening, and was entertained on the outskirts of the village by Osred, one of his father's soldiers. He found him and his neighbours very gloomy, full of grief and in great fear because they were now ruled by foreigners. Even worse, they were bewailing the fact that they were subject to the men who the day before had killed the innocent younger son of their lord.

Hereward, who pretended to be a stranger, at once asked who was responsible for the death of the son of their erstwhile lord, and why it had happened. They replied: 'Although we do not wish to impose our grief on you, you seem to be a man of great reputation who might be able to help us, so we will tell you. Our previous lord had a younger son, whom, as he lay dying, he commended to us, saying that he should be our lord, with his mother, if his brother Hereward did not return. Hereward was a very bold and brave man, but his father had driven him out because of his wild ways while he was still a youth. Three days ago, with the king's agreement, certain men seized his inheritance and took it into their own hands. And they killed our lord's younger son, because he defended his widowed mother when they abused her and demanded his father's money and goods from her, and had killed two of the Normans. As a warning to others, they cut off his head and set it up over the gate of the house, and it is still there. If only his brother Hereward were here, he would soon kill the lot of them!'

Hereward kept his thoughts to himself, but grieved inwardly, and soon retired to his bed. But he heard in the distance people singing, music and merriment. He called a boy, who told him that it was the Normans celebrating the acquisition of their new inheritance and the killing of the lord's son. After a little while Hereward called his servant, and put on a mailcoat and helmet; his servant put on light armour. They went to the place where the party was being held; but before he went in, he saw his brother's head over the gate. He took it down, kissed it and hid it in a cloth. Then he went in, to find the Normans lying by the fire, drunk, with some English girls whom they had seized. A jester was mocking the English with his antics, copying their dances in a ludicrous fashion; and he demanded part of the dead man's inheritance as payment. At this, one of the girls, unable to restrain herself, said: 'Hereward, the brother of the man you killed, is still alive; if he was here, none of you would survive until dawn!' The new lord was angry at this and answered: 'I know that scoundrel well; he stole the gifts which were sent to the count of Flanders by the Frisians when they surrendered, and then ran away for fear of ending on the gallows!' The jester took up this theme, and started to sing a mocking song; Hereward, unable to bear it any longer, struck him dead with a single blow, and then turned to the other guests, killing fourteen of them, including their lord, with the help of his companion. He cut off their heads, and put them over the gate in place of that of his brother.

The next morning, the men of the district were amazed by what had happened. And almost all the Normans in the area were terrified; they abandoned their lands and fled, lest they should meet the same fate. The English, however, hastened to congratulate him on his return and his regaining his father's inheritance. But they warned him to beware of the king's anger; so he armed forty-nine of the bravest men from his father's estate and from among his kinfolk, equipping them with full armour. He intended to complete his task by taking vengeance on those of his enemies who still occupied his manors.

Hereward now realised that he was the leader and lord of such men, and day by day his force grew larger with fugitives, condemned men and those who had been disinherited. He remembered that he had never been girded with the belt and sword of knighthood according to the tradition of his race. So he and two of his most eminent men, Winter and Genoch, went to the abbot of Peterborough, whose name was Brand, a man of the noblest birth, so that he could be given the sword and belt of knighthood in the English manner, lest, when he was leader of so many men, he should be reproached for not being a knight. He received the accolade of knighthood from the abbot on the Feast of the Nativity of the Apostles Peter and Paul. And in his honour a monk of Ely called Wulfwine, who was the prior and had been a friend of Hereward's father, made his comrades knights.

Hereward wanted himself and his men to be knighted this way because he had heard that the Normans had decreed that if anyone were to be knighted by a monk or priest it should not be regarded as a real knighting, because it was invalid and old-fashioned. In order to defy this ruling, Hereward wanted almost everyone who served under him to be knighted by monks, and anyone who wished to join him had to be knighted in this way, by a monk if not by a priest. Hereward used to say that in his experience anyone who received his sword from a servant of God – 'a knight of the kingdom of heaven' – would be unstinting in his courage and devotion to knighthood. This was the origin of the custom at Ely that if anyone there wished to be made a knight, he always offered his naked sword on the altar at high Mass, and received it again after the gospel had been read from the monk who was singing Mass; the sword was placed on his bare neck with a blessing. (Later Hereward was to go to the isle of Ely and defend it and its inhabitants against king William, who by then was lord of almost the entire country.)

Hereward forestalled an attempt by Frederick of Warenne, brother of the earl of Surrey, to ambush him and kill him in revenge for his slaughter of the Normans, by ambushing him in turn and killing him as he travelled through Norfolk with the intention of seeking out Hereward. He then went to Flanders, partly to avoid retaliation by the Normans, and partly to see his wife and his nephews. Here he was again invited to join a military campaign, a private war between a knight called Baldwin and his enemies. He fought so bravely that, when he was isolated and at the enemy's mercy, the enemy leaders called off their men, saying that there would be no honour in killing such a brave man when he was completely outnumbered. When he returned to Baldwin's camp, he reported the enemy's generosity, and as a result the two sides were reconciled.

Hereward had promised his men that he would return to England, and he now did so with his nephews and with his wife Turfrida, who had proved herself capable of dealing with any difficulty that might befall her husband. He also brought his chaplain, Hugo the Breton, as distinguished in arms as in piety, and his brother Wivhard, a courageous knight. When he reached England, he sent some of his followers to see what had happened to his estates and to his father's house, and to seek out his supporters, who had scattered throughout England. They found his estates untouched, and his supporters soon rallied to him again. He also gained a number of distinguished new recruits to his cause.

When they had gathered, Hereward saw that they were all eminent men, none of whom had achieved knightly rank without first achieving notable deeds. There was Wulfric the Black, so called because he had once daubed his face with charcoal and gone unrecognised into a Norman garrison, laying low ten soldiers with a single spear. There was his friend Wulfric the Heron, who got his name because he once happened to be at Wroxham bridge when four brothers who he knew to be innocent were brought there for execution. The hangmen mocked him and called him 'heron' but he terrified them into releasing the innocent men, and killed a number of their enemies. And there was Leofwine the Sickle, who was called this because when he happened to be alone in a meadow cutting grass, he was set upon by a score of local peasants with iron pitchforks and spears; at which he charged them by himself, wounding many and killing some with his sickle, like a reaper, and put them all to flight. Besides these there were many other distinguished knights.

When the men of the isle of Ely, who had begun to hold out against king William, heard that Hereward had returned to England, they sent messengers to him and negotiated for him to join them with all his men. The leader in this was abbot Thurstan, who with his monks had the lordship of the isle, and had put it in a state of defence against the king, because William intended to set a foreign monk over them, one of a group whom he was bringing over to replace the English clergy. However, a knight called Brunman, who was also a sailor, got wind of this, and because he knew the coasts well, he intercepted them, ducked them in the sea in a large sack which he had tied to the prow of his ship, and sent them back, thus freeing the English monasteries from foreign domination for the time being.

Hereward was delighted to receive the abbot's envoy, and prepared for the journey, embarking at Bardney. But William de Warenne, earl of Surrey, whose brother Hereward had recently slain, got word of this, and prepared a number of ambushes for him. Warenne's men came across some stragglers from Hereward's force, whom they attacked; but Hereward came up and turned the tables. When he had captured his enemies, he learnt that William de Warenne had tried to set the ambush, and that he was coming to Earith the next day.

So Hereward gathered his men there, hiding them near the river bank. He himself went to the bank opposite the place where the earl had just landed, and one of the earl's men approached them, asking if they were from the company of that scoundrel Hereward, because of whom he and his fellows were forced to live in the detestable swamps near Ely. 'If only someone would betray Hereward,' he continued, 'because he will die soon in any case, because the king is on his way with an army to besiege him and destroy all the inhabitants of Ely.' One of Hereward's men answered: 'Don't ask us to betray our lord, but run off and tell your leader that the man he is looking for is here!' The earl came up and urged his men to take their revenge on Hereward, but they refused, suspecting a trap. Hereward shot at the earl, and although the arrow did not pierce his mail, it stunned the earl, and he fell from his horse. His men at once retreated, carrying the earl with them.

The same day Hereward and his men entered Ely, where they were welcomed by the abbot and monks, and by three Saxon noblemen, once earls – Edwin of Leicester, Morcar of Warwick and Tostig of Northumbria

– all of whom had fled to Ely to join those who had been wronged by the new king. This infuriated the king, who determined to storm the isle. He moved his whole army to Aldreth, where the surrounding water and swamp was narrower, the breadth being only four hundred yards. The king had tools and timber and stone brought, and a causeway was built through the swamp, though it was too narrow to be of any use. They also assembled in the same place great tree trunks joined with beams, underneath which they tied whole sheepskins, sewn up and fully inflated, so as to support the weight of those who used it to cross over. Rumour had it that there were great hoards of gold and silver stored on the isle of Ely, and when this structure was ready, so many men rushed onto it at once that those in front were drowned when it went under, destroying the causeway as well. Those in the middle fell into the swamp, which swallowed them up, and only a few at the rear escaped with difficulty.

One man, a knight called Deda, succeeded in getting across to the isle, where he was captured, and led before Hereward and the abbot. They asked him why he had come when it was clear that the main attack would fail; and he replied that the king had said that the first man to reach the isle could ask for any property there, and he would have it when the place was conquered. They praised his boldness and courage, and made him stay with them for a few days so that he could experience their determination at first hand, and realise what a secure and strongly fortified position they held, manned by distinguished soldiers. For the Saxons had the reputation of being less skilled in matters of arms than other nations; but before he left, Deda acknowledged that they were masters of military affairs. He was given permission to leave on condition that he only reported exactly what he had seen and heard, and he was made to swear that he would do this.

When he returned to William's court, he was questioned before everyone, and told them how he had managed to enter the isle unharmed. He then related how Hereward had treated him well, and described the skill with which the arrangements for the defence of the isle had been made, naming the leaders of the Saxons, the three earls Edwin, Morcar and Tostig, and the noblemen Ordgar and Thurcytel. He praised Hereward and his knights as being superior to any soldiers he had even seen, whether in France, Germany or even Byzantium. Some men, he said, might be Hereward's equal in courage, but no one could surpass him.

At this, William de Warenne, whose brother Hereward had recently killed, exclaimed that Deda had been taken in by Hereward, and was trying to persuade the king to show mercy to the greatest scoundrel alive. Deda answered that he had neither been bribed nor cajoled, but had simply sworn to tell the simple truth, which he had done to the best of his ability. To do otherwise would have offended the king, and broken his oath. When he was asked what might persuade the rebels to end their resistance, he said that there was just one thing, and that was the king's insistence that foreign monks should be appointed deans and priors in the churches in England. For this reason the monks had put the isle of Ely into a state of defence, and given the richness of its natural resources, and the arms they had gathered there, combined with the excellent garrison – for even the monks themselves were skilled in arms – there was no reason why they should ever surrender. He concluded: 'All the same, I hope that my lord king will not desist from attacking them, for then he will find that I have told nothing but the truth, and will realise that it will be better to make peace than to wage endless war on them without achieving anything.'

As he finished, one of the soldiers who had been manning the blockade came in and described how the previous day a group of seven men, five of whom were obviously monks, had made a sortie and set fire to the village of Burwell; when a Norman patrol attacked them, they killed them all except for one; Hereward called his men off, saying that it was shameful for two or three to fight one man. A larger Norman force came up and rescued the one survivor, which was how they had learnt of Hereward's generosity; they had taken one of Hereward's men captive, who confirmed that five of the men were indeed monks.

The king decided on the strength of this that it would be best to make peace, but when he summoned his magnates to tell them of his decision, they quickly dissuaded him, saying that the islanders had seized their property, and if they were allowed to get away with this and were pardoned, 'everyone will laugh at your supremacy and no one will be afraid to imitate them throughout the kingdom'. The king angrily replied that he could not take the isle, or any place like it, because it was provided with such natural fortifications by the will of God. One of his magnates, Ivo de Taillebois, indignantly answered: 'For a long time I've known of a certain old woman who, by her art alone, if she were here, could crush all their courage and defence, and drive them all out of the isle in terror.' He said that he was willing to send for her, and all those present urged the king to do so, in order to overcome his enemies. The king gave orders for her to be found, but it was to be done secretly, not publicly; and in the meanwhile he ordered his army to encircle the isle again, and impose a very strict blockade.

This new blockade disheartened the men on the isle, because they did not know what it meant, or what form the new attack might take. So they decided that someone should go and reconnoitre; and as no one suitable could be found, it seemed best to Hereward to go out himself, though the others strongly objected. He took his mare Swallow, who, though she always seemed to move awkwardly and with difficulty, was both very swift and could endure for long distances. As Hereward left, he changed his clothes, cut his hair, and put on an old greasy cloak. He met a potter, whose jars he seized, and made his way to the king's court at Brandon. Here he happened to lodge in the same house as the witch whom the king had summoned, and heard them discussing in French how they would destroy the isle; they assumed that Hereward was a peasant who could not understand their language. During the night he saw them go out to a nearby spring, where they appeared to question the unseen guardian of the spring, and await his replies. They spent so long outside that Hereward was unable to kill them on their return as he would have wished.

The next day he went to the king's court, ostensibly to sell his pots, and went into the kitchen, where one of the bailiffs of the town happened to come in, and exclaimed that he had never seen anyone who looked so like Hereward. Others came to see this man who looked like Hereward, and in the end he was led in front of the knights and squires in the hall. Some of them declared that if Hereward was no taller than the man before them, they could not understand his reputation for courage and great deeds. Others asked if he had ever seen Hereward, and he pretended that he had been robbed of his cattle by him, and was eager to get his revenge on him. So he went back to the kitchen; but after dinner the cooks and potboys got drunk, and started to make fun of him, trying to shave his head and pluck his beard, and making him break his pots. Hereward refused to submit to their buffoonery, and one of them hit him for his obstinacy. At this Hereward knocked him unconscious, and the rest attacked him with forks. Hereward defended himself with a piece of wood, killed one of them, and wounded the rest. As a result he was seized and made prisoner; but the next day, while the king was hunting, a guard came into his cell, with a sword in one hand and iron shackles in the other, which he intended to use to chain up Hereward.

Before he could do so, Hereward seized his sword and killed him and several others. He escaped into the lower courtyard, found his horse, and outdistanced all his pursuers; travelling at night, by moonlight, he came safely to the isle of Ely. On the way only one man encountered him, a man from the king's retinue who had been sent in search of him: when Hereward saw him, he asked him who he was, and the man explained, adding, 'If you've seen Hereward or heard anything of him, for God's sake be kind, and tell me!' Hereward answered, 'Since you ask me to be kind for God's sake, I'll tell you that I am the man you are looking for. Go back to the king and tell him that you have spoken to me; but leave me your sword and spear as a token of good faith, and promise to tell nothing but the truth!' When the king heard this, he was amazed and declared that Hereward was a generous and most remarkable knight.

The king now attacked the isle of Ely from his base at Aldreth, and summoned the local fishermen to bring wood and stone for the construction of ramparts there. Hereward disguised himself as a fisherman, and went with them. He ferried wood all day, and as he left set fire to the woodpile, which was entirely destroyed, killing several Normans. Hereward had shaved his beard and head so that the enemy would not recognise him, preferring to go around bald and beardless in order to attack his enemies with impunity. The king, although angry that Hereward had once more fooled him, ordered that Hereward was to be taken alive and brought to him, and was on no account to be harmed; and he set a guard on the camp by day and night.

At the end of a week, the king's men had succeeded in building a mound and had set up four wooden bases for siege engines. But the men of the isle built counterworks to oppose them. On the eighth day the Normans massed all their forces for an attack on the isle, placing the witch whom Ivo de Taillebois had found in the midst of their ranks on a high platform. She harangued the inhabitants of the isle for a long time, and cast spells against them, denouncing them as saboteurs; and when she had finished her incantations and rantings, she bared her arse at them three times. At this, Hereward's men, who had been concealed in the reeds and brambles of the marshland, set fire to part of it so that the smoke and flames roared up in the direction of the king's camp; the crackling of twigs in the brushwood and willows made a terrible noise. The king's men were stupefied by this, and fled in fear, each for himself, but in the marshes many of them lost their way and were drowned, while others died at the hands of the Saxon archers. The witch fell headlong from her platform and broke her neck.

Among the few who escaped – few indeed in comparison with those who fell – the king himself returned to his camp with an arrow stuck fast in his shield. His men feared that he was wounded, but he reassured them, saying that he was not wounded, but was deeply pained that he had not adopted a sounder plan for the start. 'Almost all our men have fallen, deceived by the cunning of an abominable woman and encouraged by our ignorance of her detestable art – we should have been damned just for listening to her. We deserve what has happened to us.'

There was now a split in the Saxon ranks, because Ralph Guader assembled a large army, and the earls and other nobles, thinking that he was going to make a bid for the throne, went to join him, leaving Hereward alone. William changed his tactics, giving the abbey's lands outside the isle of Ely to his followers in return for their maintaining a blockade, but abandoning the attempt to take the place by force. In order to get back their lands, the monks now agreed terms with the king, and arranged that the royal forces should enter Ely when Hereward was out foraging, so that there should be no bloodshed. Hereward was absent when this secret agreement was made.

But one of the monks, Eadwine son of Ordgar, went to tell Hereward that the monks had already been received by the king, and had struck a bargain with him. He met Hereward already en route to set fire to the church and town, because he had learnt of the monks' treachery. Eadwine persuaded him to abandon his plan, and to look to his own safety, because the king was only a mile or two away with his whole army. So Hereward put his boats to guard the waters round the isle and protect his retreat, and withdrew to a nearby mere, which had many channels and an easy escape route. He had some difficulty regrouping his men, since they had been despatched to ravage a nearby village; some mistook his messengers for the enemy, while two others, fearing for their lives, decided they would have a better chance if they were monks, and gave each other crude tonsures with their swords.

Hereward was now so hard-pressed in the marshes that in despair he killed his splendid horse with his own hands, so that no one should boast that they owned Hereward's horse. But in the end he got out of the Fens safely, and retreated to the forests of Northamptonshire, where he and his men continued to raid the lands held by the Normans. He was continually on the move, and had his horses' shoes put on back to front, so that they could not be tracked. Because the enemy were closing in on him on all sides – he was now in the forests near Peterborough – he decided to attack them before they were ready for battle. The Normans had a large number of footsoldiers and knights, led by Turold, abbot of Peterborough, and Ivo de Taillebois.

Hereward positioned his archers and slingsmen in the trees, and then advanced into a clearing to charge the enemy, while the archers provided covering fire. When they had charged, they returned to the woodland to recover before launching another attack. Eventually the Normans moved off, and abandoned their attempts to besiege his camp, at which Hereward attacked their rear, capturing the abbot of Peterborough and other distinguished prisoners. Hereward later released the abbot for a ransom of thirty thousand pounds, while his nephew and others were released as a mark of respect. But the abbot continued to wage war on them, distributing the abbey's lands to knights on condition that they helped him to fight against Hereward. Hereward, on hearing this, set fire to the town, plundered the abbey of its treasures, and chased the abbot, though he evaded them by hiding.

The next night, however, Hereward dreamt that he saw an awesome stranger standing before him and threatening him with a great key, saying that if he did not return the church's goods he would die a miserable death the next day. In terror at this vision of St Peter, he at once returned everything, and then moved on with his men. However, they lost their way in the forests, and were only saved by a miracle, for a huge wolf appeared, and led them down the right path, while lights like will-

o'-the-wisps gathered on the soldiers' lances, which could not be put out
or thrown off. At daybreak they found that they were once more on the
right road, beyond Stamford; the wolf vanished and the lights went out.

But Hereward had received messengers from the widow of earl
Dolfin, who was both very rich and beautiful, saying that if he would
abandon Turfrida and marry her, she would obtain his pardon from the
king, and indeed that the king had already agreed to this. So he sent messengers to the king accepting the countess's offer. Turfrida went to
Crowland, where she became a nun; but Hereward did not prosper as he
had done in the past, and many things happened to him in later years
which would not have come about if she had been there, because she was
very wise and good with advice in an emergency.

Hereward made his way to court with three companions, Gaerwig,
Wennoth and Maethelgar. On the way they encountered a Saxon soldier
called Letold, who was tall in stature and very brave, famous at home and
abroad for his valour in war. Hereward greeted him courteously, and
asked who he was, what his rank might be, and from what family he
came. Letold disdained to answer him, calling him a simpleton and a
peasant: they quarrelled, and soon came to blows, their companions
joining in the fray. Hereward's men soon despatched their opponents,
even though they were outnumbered five to three, but Letold continued
to fight with Hereward. Hereward's men wanted to help him, but he
forbade them to do so, because it was shameful to fight two against one.
So the fight went on, when suddenly Hereward's sword broke, and he
fell over a helmet: Letold was so surprised that he stood thunderstruck.
Gaerwig reminded his lord that he had a second sword, because
Hereward had evidently forgotten this, and Hereward renewed the
attack; he feinted at Letold's head, and struck him in the thigh instead,
bringing Letold to his knees. Letold continued to fight from this
position, declaring that he would never surrender, but Hereward, full of
admiration, withdrew from the fight, and left him, saying that he had
never met an enemy whom he had such difficulty in defeating.

As Hereward approached the royal court, he thought to himself that to
arrive with only three companions would not be a fitting entrance; so he
turned back, and found forty others, all tall and splendidly equipped, and
came into the king's presence. The king welcomed them, but would not let
Hereward's men stay at court, lest a disturbance should break out between
them and the courtiers; he gave orders for them to be entertained in the
next town, where he visited them the following day and admired their
impressive appearance. However, Hereward let them all return home,
keeping only five men with him. When he had paid homage to the king,
he waited to receive his father's estate as it had been left to him.

But some of the king's men at court were angry that an enemy of
theirs and of the king should suddenly come into favour, and tried to lay

an ambush for him. So they incited one of their best fighters, a man named Ogga, to challenge Hereward to single combat in provocative terms, pretending that Hereward had insulted him and knowing that Hereward could not contain himself in such circumstances. The encounter was to be fought in secret in case the king got to hear of it and prevented it. So it was arranged that they should meet in a wood a little way from the court, each with three companions who were under oath not to assist them, but simply to see fair play. Hereward tried to dissuade Ogga from fighting, even after they had started, but the latter thought that he was acting out of weakness, and became even more confident of victory. In the end, however, he was forced to beg for mercy, even though Hereward was badly wounded in the right arm.

This episode came to the ears of his other enemies, who used it and many other invented slanders to persuade the king that he should not allow such a man to be near him. The king did not take much notice of them, but in order to prevent further trouble, he ordered that Hereward should be taken into custody, and gave him to a well-respected man, Robert de Horepol, to guard at Bedford. Here he stayed for a whole year, bound only with fetters. But William de Warenne and Robert Malet dissuaded the king from releasing him, saying that it was only because he was in captivity that the land was at peace.

When Hereward's men heard that he was confined, they went their various ways, but remained in touch with him through a clerk of his called Leofric the Deacon, a clever man who could pretend to be stupid when the occasion demanded it. Utlah the cook, a cautious man who could be very witty at the expense of the Normans, also went with him to see Hereward; and they were both with him one day when Robert de Horepol told them that through the machinations of Ivo de Taillebois, Hereward was to be imprisoned in Rockingham castle. 'If only the men he had once rewarded and honoured, or who had fought with him on the isle, could intercept him on the way, they could set Hereward free!' he said.

Hereward's men returned home and sought out his followers, and described what had happened. So they laid an ambush, and surprised the guards who were escorting Hereward before they could arm themselves properly. But there were so many soldiers – almost all the local garrisons, in fact – and they fought so bravely, that it was only after a long struggle that they were able to free Hereward. Hereward insisted that Robert de Horepol should not be harmed; when it was clear that Hereward's men had the upper hand, Robert asked for a truce, and begged to be allowed to go with his men. Hereward not only granted this, but thanked him repeatedly for treating him with courtesy and honour while he had been his captive. He also asked Robert to intercede with the king on his behalf.

Robert de Horepol at once went to the king, and told him the whole story of the ambush in front of the court, ending with the way in which Hereward had released him. He asked that Hereward might benefit from the king's mercy, since he had been unjustly put into custody while he was under the king's protection and safe-conduct. He added that Hereward realised that his imprisonment had been brought about by his enemies, and that he would serve the king loyally if he was received back into favour. The king thought for a little while, and then declared that Hereward had not been justly treated; at which Robert, realising that the king had taken his remarks favourably, added more stories in support of Hereward, showing how he had always been faithful and trustworthy to his friends. Finally, he said that if the rebellion was renewed, Hereward would go back to his old ways unless the king treated him favourably rather than unjustly, and that he should be given his father's estates as a mark of the king's esteem. The king at once agreed that this should be done, and had a writ made out to Hereward and the men of the district saying that he was to receive his father's lands and was to enjoy quiet possession of them, so long as he pursued peace rather than his former foolish ways, which he would have to do if he was to retain the king's friendship.

Thus the famous knight Hereward was received into the king's favour, and lived as the king's loyal servant on his father's estates for many years. At the last he rested in peace; may God have mercy on his soul.

27. RICHARD COEUR DE LION

Richard I is the most heroic figure among the historical kings of England, outshining Edward III and even Henry V in the popular imagination. This reputation dates from his lifetime; Philip Augustus, the French king, was said to have quarrelled with him during their joint crusade because he was jealous of Richard's fame as a warrior. Legendary stories about him began to accumulate very soon after he died; at first, surprisingly enough, these were tales of how he had made a truly Christian ending, forgiving the crossbowman who mortally wounded him at the siege of a small castle in central France in 1199. His reward was a mere thirty-three years in purgatory, and in 1232 the bishop of Rochester had a vision in which he learned that Richard had ascended into heaven.

About thirty years later, a French poet from Reims recorded the most romantic episode of Richard's career, that in which the faithful minstrel Blondel finds his master, who is being held captive anonymously, by singing to him a song which they had composed jointly, and which only he and Richard know. As the poet in question was himself a minstrel, he had an excellent motive for making much of the story, which has its basis in Richard's historically recorded interest in troubadour poetry. In fact, Richard's whereabouts during his captivity were reported to the government in England very soon after he fell into the hands of the duke of Austria; and curiously the story was little known in the middle ages, coming into its own only in the late eighteenth century.

The story of Blondel does not figure in the medieval English romance about Richard the Lionheart, which probably dates from the mid-fourteenth century, but is a translation of a lost, earlier, French romance. This supplies us with the episode which supposedly gave Richard his name 'Lionheart', a neat piece of invention to account for an epithet which was current as early as 1199, the year of his death. It also gives an account of the most celebrated mythical episode of his career as far as a medieval audience was concerned, his famous single combat with Saladin. This was pictured in the Antioch chamber at Henry III's palace at Clarendon in Oxfordshire, and on pavement tiles found in Westminster palace, as well as in marginal illuminations in that masterpiece of medieval art, the Luttrell Psalter, and elsewhere.

NOW we will tell about king Richard, whom the duke of Austria kept in prison; no one had news of him, and only the duke and his council knew where he was. It so happened that the king had a minstrel called Blondel, whom he had brought up from childhood. The latter thought that he would seek him throughout the world, until he had news of him. He set out, and travelled in foreign countries for a year and a half; but he could not get any news of the king.

He wandered so far that he came to Austria, and, as chance would have it, went straight to the castle where the king was imprisoned. And he found lodgings with a widow, whom he asked about the castle, which was a fine strong fortress, well placed. His hostess said that it belonged to the duke of Austria. 'Fair hostess,' said Blondel, 'is there a prisoner in the castle?' 'Yes,' said the good woman, 'certainly; just one, who has been there for four years. But we cannot discover who he is; and I can assure you that he is guarded well and carefully, so we believe him to be a nobleman and a great lord.'

When Blondel heard this, he was overjoyed, for he felt in his heart that he had found what he was looking for; but he did not say a word to his hostess. He was well at ease that night, and slept until it was daylight; and when he heard the watch blow their horns to signal daybreak, he got up and went to the minster to pray to God for His help. And he went to the castle, and introduced himself to the lord of the castle, saying that he was a minstrel, and would be very pleased to stay there if he could. The lord of the castle was a young and handsome knight, who said that he would be glad to have him as his retainer.

Blondel was pleased, and went to fetch his viol and his instruments; and he served the lord of the castle so well that he earned his goodwill, and was in favour with all his followers. Blondel stayed there for the whole winter; but he could not discover who the prisoner was, and one day at Eastertide he went alone into a garden at the foot of the tower, and began to look around, to see if he could discover where the prison was. As he stood in thought, the king looked out of an arrow-slit and saw Blondel. He wondered how to make himself known to him, and then remembered a song which they had composed together, and which no one else knew.

So he began to sing the first words, in a high clear voice, because he was a good singer; and when Blondel heard him, he knew that it was his lord. And he was more joyful than he had been for a very long time. He left the garden and went to his chamber, and fetched his viol; and he began to play, and as he played he expressed his delight at having found his lord. Blondel stayed there until Whitsuntide, and he concealed matters so cleverly that no one there realised his business.

Then Blondel went to the lord of the castle and said, 'Lord, if it be your pleasure, I would like to go to my own country, because it is a long time since I was there.' 'Blondel, my brother, you will not do that if you listen to me; stay here and I will make you a rich man.' 'Lord,' said Blondel, 'I shall not stay here.' When the lord of the castle realised that he could not hold him back, he gave him leave to go, and a new robe and a horse to ride as well.

Blondel left the lord of the castle, and travelled day after day until he reached England, and told the king's friends and the barons that he had found the king, and where he was. When they heard the news, they were very happy, for the king was the best knight that ever put spur to a horse. And they conferred together, and decided to send word to the duke of Austria to ransom the king; and they chose two bold and very wise knights to go there.

And they travelled until they came to Austria and found the duke at one of his castles, and greeted him on behalf of the barons of England, and said: 'Lord, we are sent here by the barons of England, and we have learnt that you are keeping king Richard in your prison. They require and request that you set a ransom for him, and they will give you whatever you ask.' The duke replied that he would speak with his councillors, and when the council had been held, he said, 'Fair lords, if you wish to have him, you must ransom him for two hundred thousand marks in sterling. And say no more to me, for it would be a waste of your time.'

So the messengers took their leave, and said that they would report this to the barons, and take their counsel. And they returned to England, and told the barons what the duke had said to them. And they said that he would not have to wait for the ransom, which they gathered and sent to the duke. And the duke released the king, but not until he had taken surety that the king would never do him harm.

The romance version of king Richard's life may also date from the late thirteenth century. Much of it is almost historical, but the incident of his imprisonment in Austria is placed before, rather than after, his exploits in Palestine. As the king returns from pilgrimage, he travels through Austria: at one inn, he refuses to give money to a female minstrel, who denounces him to the duke, who imprisons him and his companions as spies. Richard protests his innocence, but is thrust into prison.

The porter took Richard by the hand, and both his companions as well, and put them in prison. The next day, the king's son came to see them, and their troubles began. He was called Wardrew, and was a very famous knight; he was tall, strong and fierce, and no one in that country could rival him. He asked the porter if he could see the prisoners, and, when Richard was brought before him, he said: 'Are you Richard, the strong man, whom everyone talks about? Do you dare to receive a blow from me, if I give you leave to return it on the next day?' King Richard agreed to this, and the king's son struck him on the ear so that fire seemed to come out of his eyes. Richard swore to repay him the next day. The king's son ordered that the three Englishmen should be well fed, so that no one could say that Richard had been too weak to return the blow properly, and Richard was given his bed in which to sleep. The next day Richard got up and coated his hands with clear wax, until there was the thickness of a straw all over it. The king's son came in and ordered him to smite him as hard as he could; Richard hit him on the cheek, and those who saw it said that he carried away flesh and bone, broke his cheekbone, and felled him dead to the floor.

For this, the sorrowing king condemns Richard to death, but his daughter Margery has fallen in love with him.

She and three of her attendants went to the prison at midday, and demanded to be let in. The gaoler brought Richard, who asked her what she wanted of him. 'Richard, save for God above, I love you most of all,' she said. Richard replied, 'I am a prisoner, falsely accused and starving; what good can my love do you?'

When she learnt that he had not eaten or drunk for three days, she ordered food and drink to be brought, and told the gaoler to unlock his fetters. That evening he was to be disguised as a squire, and brought to her chamber. This went on for seven nights, until one of the knights of the household saw him and told the king.

The king was furious, and summoned his council; when, a fortnight later, all his lords and barons had gathered, he told them how he had imprisoned Richard, and how Richard had killed his son and seduced his daughter. 'I would gladly put him to death, but no one has the right to execute a king.' The barons argued for three days, but could not come to a decision. Then a knight suggested that the king's lion should be starved for three days, and put into Richard's prison: it would certainly kill Richard, but the king would not be to blame.

But Margery heard the plot, and warned Richard, suggesting that they should seize the king's treasure and flee together. Richard disdained this suggestion, and said that he had no fear of the lion, but would give her the lion's heart, if she would provide him with forty white silk kerchiefs. Margery spent the night with Richard in his prison, and wanted to stay with him, but Richard ordered her to leave. He wound the kerchiefs round his arm, and prepared a trick to kill the lion. He faced the beast dressed only in a gown. When the gaoler opened the door to let it in, the lion beat his tail and roared, opening his mouth wide. Richard at once thrust his arm down the lion's throat, and ripped out its lungs and liver, and everything he found there. The lion fell dead on the ground, and Richard was quite unharmed; he knelt and thanked our Lord for having delivered him. Taking the lion's heart he carried it before the king and nobles, who were at dinner. Putting salt on it, he ate it raw in front of them all. The king exclaimed: 'This is a devil, not a man – he has killed my lion and plucked out its heart, and now he eats it as if it were a delicacy. Men may well call him Richard the Lionheart!'

The king saw that there was nothing for it but to ransom Richard, and this was agreed; the ransom was paid, and the king ordered his daughter to leave his lands at once. But the queen prevented him, saying that she should stay there until Richard sent for her to be his wife.

*Richard returned to England, but almost at once set out on crusade. He assem-
bled a vast army, and before he started the crusade proper, he returned to
Austria, to retrieve the ransom which the king had unfairly extorted from him,
and to claim Margery's hand. He was successful in both these aims, and the
king not only swore an oath of friendship, but joined him on crusade.*

*The story now follows, broadly speaking, the history of Richard's crusade,
with assorted embellishments and flourishes. Many of these emphasise Richard's
unremitting hatred of the Saracens, and his extreme cruelty, telling us more
about the attitude of the writer than about the historical king. One episode has
him dying of a fever which can only be cured by eating pork; as the Saracens
abhor pork as unclean, there is none to be had, so 'an old knight' has a Saracen
roasted and served to the king instead, who takes it for excellent pork and at
once recovers. In another episode, the boiled heads of Saracen captives, labelled
with their names, are served to a Saracen embassy at Richard's table, and
Richard eats them with relish. He later orders sixty thousand captives to be
killed; the executioners lead them to the place where they are to be slain, and
hear 'angels of heaven crying in French, "Lords, kill, kill!"'*

*Somewhat less gruesome and grisly is the account of Richard's famous single
combat with Saladin. Richard has driven Saladin back to his city of Babylon,
but is deserted by his fellow-crusader king Philip of France, and is therefore
unable to continue the blockade. Saladin sends him a challenge the next day.*

The messengers came from Saladin and greeted Richard as follows: 'Sir, you are strong in flesh and bone, and our lord the Sultan is a doughty man. He complains that you are doing him great harm, destroying his land and his men, for no good cause, and trying to seize his territory, to which you have no right. You boast that your god is a mighty god; he asks if you will grant him a single combat in open field, in full armour, on fine steeds, to settle which is the more powerful, Jesus or Jupiter? And he offers you one of his horses, the like of which you have never seen; Favel of Cyprus or the precious Lyard, your best horses, are nothing compared to him. If you agree, we will bring it to you today to try.'

Richard replied, 'I would gladly have such a horse to ride, because mine are weary and out of condition. I shall shed the Sultan's blood for the love of my Lord, who rules in heaven above. If he will do as he has promised, I will meet him in the open field, by my soul. Tell him to send that horse to me, and I will test its mettle; if it is good, I will ride no other horse into battle.'

The messengers returned, and told Saladin that Richard had accepted his challenge. Saladin summoned a noble cleric, a master of magic, who, using the powers of hell, conjured two powerful fiends of the air into the shape of two horses, both the same colour; one a mare and the other a colt. Wherever the colt was, no knight, however strong, could hold him back if the mare neighed; he would at once gallop up to her, kneel down and suckle her. Saladin hoped to have his revenge on Richard when he sent him the colt; but at midnight an angel appeared to Richard, who told him that the horse was a fiend in disguise, and how Saladin intended to trick him. If Richard rode him in God's name, he would do no harm, provided Richard put a bridle on him. Richard was also to put a forty-foot beam across his neck, and the horse would then fell anyone who came within reach of the beam, while if the king took a steel spearhead, he would easily pierce Saladin's armour.

The next day Richard did as the angel had commanded, and took a strong saddle with iron saddle-peaks from which he hooked a chain around the horse. He stopped the colt's ears with wax, so that it could not hear its mother neighing. Then he commanded the horse in the name of the twelve apostles and of our Saviour and the Trinity, to serve him as he wished: it shook its head, as if to agree, and stood quite still.

When the two armies were drawn up outside the city, Richard's men brought the great beam and fastened it to the saddle with the hooks and chain. Richard was in his finest armour, with a helm which had as crest the Holy Ghost in the form of a dove above a scene of the crucifixion. He was armed with an axe and a spear with a steel tip, with God's high name engraved on it. It was agreed that if Richard slew Saladin, he should have Babylon and all Macedonia, while if Saladin was victor, the Christians were to leave the country for ever. Saladin appeared on his mare, which was hung with bells, a great dagger in his hand, intending to stab Richard when his horse kneeled down by the mare. When the mare neighed, Richard was not frightened, but charged Saladin, and killed his horse. He pierced Saladin's armour with his spear and drove it through his shoulder, bearing him to the earth. Then he spurred his horse and charged the heathen host, sweeping a path on either side of him for the length of the beam.

In the ensuing battle, the Saracens were defeated, and Saladin fled, with Richard in pursuit. But Saladin plunged into the nearby forest, and Richard, whose horse still had the beam across its crupper, was unable to follow him through the trees.

Richard's further exploits are largely historical, though described in suitably exaggerated terms. The romance ends with his victory at Jaffa, when he defeats a besieging army and slays nearly two hundred thousand Saracens, before – on angelic instructions – concluding a truce with Saladin and returning to England.

28. KING HORN

King Horn is an Anglo-Norman romance of the late twelfth century, which was translated into English some fifty years later. It is a work of pure imagination, deriving possibly from a folktale; no one has claimed to detect any kind of historical originals in it, and the geography is equally invented. It is a traditional adventure of exile and return, with a good measure of suspense thrown in; it has the repetitions of folktale, and often uses formulas to describe the same situations. But it is a good story, with the strength of a saga and the tenderness of a romance, and some splendidly unexpected turns of phrase. It was directed at an aristocratic but not necessarily very sophisticated audience, and was clearly a success in these circles. There is little of the courtly manners and elaborate psychological analysis of the contemporary French romances; we are in a simple and robust world, where the hero is heroic and the villain villainous, with no subtle shading in between.

LET everyone who hears my story be cheerful! The story tells of Murry, a king in the west. His queen, the loveliest of ladies, was Godhild, and his son was Horn. Rain could not fall nor sun shine on a more handsome boy; at fifteen he was bright as glass. He had twelve companions, rich men's sons and noble youths, and of them he loved two the most, Athulf the good, and Fikenhild the bad.

One summer's day Murry, riding along the seashore as was his custom, found fifteen ships there, crewed by fierce Saracens. When he asked what they were seeking, or what they were bringing to the land, a pagan replied: 'We have come to kill the people here and all who believe in Christ, and you will be the first of all!'

The king dismounted from his horse, as did the two knights who were his only companions. Gripping their swords they struck together beneath the shields so that the enemy felt it. But the king and his men were all too few against so many evil opponents, and the pagans easily killed all the three. They entered the country and seized it; they conquered the people and destroyed the churches. No one was left alive unless they forsook their own faith and followed that of the heathen. Of all women Godhild was the most to be pitied; she wept bitterly for Murry and still more for Horn. Leaving her hall and her servants, she lived under a stony rock in solitude, and the pagans never knew that she served God there, in defiance of their ban. She prayed unceasingly that Christ would be merciful to Horn.

Now Horn and all his companions were in the hands of the heathen. If he had not been so handsome, they would have killed him and all the children; there were some who would have flayed him alive. So one of the emirs spoke bluntly to him: 'It is easy to see that you are brave, Horn, and you are already strong and handsome. In seven years' time you will be even stronger, and you may well, if you and your comrades escape alive, kill us all to avenge your father's death. We will put you in a ship, and let you drown in the depths of the sea, and little shall we care.'

At this the children, who were in despair, were brought down to the beach and put aboard the ship. Horn had been sad before, but never so much as then. The tide took them and Horn began to row, but the sea drove the ship so fast the children were afraid. All that day and all that night they expected to die, until dawn sprang up and Horn saw land, and men passing to and fro. 'Young friends,' he cried, 'I have good news. I can hear birdsong and I can see green grass. We are lucky to be alive – our ship has reached the shore.'

As they left the boat and stepped on the ground, Horn said: 'Ship, may you have good days on the sea flood, and may the water never over- whelm you! If you come to Suddenne, greet my family and especially my mother, Godhild, the good queen, and tell the pagan king, that enemy of Christ, that I have reached this land safely; tell him also that he shall meet his death at my hands.'

The children went across country until they found Ailmar, king of Westernesse. He asked Horn kindly: 'Where do you come from, noble youths? By God who made me, I have never seen thirteen such hand- some lads anywhere in the west. Tell me what you seek.'

Horn answered: 'We are from Suddenne, of noble kindred and of Christian blood. Pagans came and killed our people. So Christ help me, we were put into a galley and for two days, without sail or rudder, we were at the mercy of the sea. Our ship came of its own accord to this land, and we are yours to kill or take prisoner, but we beg you to be merciful and help us.'

The good king, who would never have done evil to strangers, answered: 'Tell me, child, what is your name? You shall have nothing but joy now.'

'I am called Horn,' said the boy, 'and I come from the ship. May God reward you for your kindness, lord.'

'You shall live up to your name, Horn,' answered the king, 'for the sound of your fame shall echo from hill and dale; your name will go from king to king, and your glory and the strength of your hand shall be known in this and every other land. You are a fine lad, Horn; I cannot let you go.'

Then king Ailmar rode home with his foundling and all those com- panions who were dear to him. When the king reached his hall, he called to him among his knights, Athelbrus, the steward of his house.

'Steward,' he said, 'take this lad whom I have found, and teach him all you know. Teach him the lore of the wood and of the river, how to hunt and fish; teach him music, how to play the harp with his nails sharply pointed; teach him the ways of the court so that he can carve before me, and serve me with drink from the cup. Teach him all you like of everything you know, and train his fellows in other ways of service. But teach Horn to play the harp and to sing.'

Then Athelbrus began to teach Horn and his fellows, and Horn remembered everything that he learnt. All men loved him, in and out of the court, and Rymenhild, the king's own daughter, came to love him most of all. She thought constantly of him, and soon she grew almost mad with the longing in her heart. She could not speak to him at table, nor in the hall among the knights, nor in any other place, for fear of what people would say. Her pining never ceased until, at last, she sent a message to Athelbrus that he should come to her chamber and bring Horn with him. The message said she lay sick and sad. At that the steward was very anxious, and did not know what to do: it seemed extraordinary that Rymenhild wanted Horn brought to her, and he did not think any good would come of it. So he took another with him, Athulf, the brother of Horn.

'Athulf,' he said, 'you must come with me now to speak in private with Rymenhild and find out what she wants. You must pretend to be Horn, because if he himself goes, I am very afraid that she will lead him to harm.'

Then Athelbrus led Athulf into the chamber, and Rymenhild, believing it was Horn, grew wild with love. She made him sit on the couch, and threw her arms around him. 'Horn,' she said, 'I have loved you greatly, for a long time. Now take my hand and promise to take me as your wife, as I shall take you for my lord.'

Then Athulf whispered softly in her ear: 'Say no more of this, I beg you, for Horn is not here, nor are we alike. Horn is more handsome and greater than any man that ever lived. Even if he lay buried in the earth or was a thousand miles away, I would deceive neither him nor you.'

Rymenhild turned round and bitterly accused Athelbrus. 'Get out, you wretched thief; I will never trust you again. Leave my chamber; I will see that you come to a shameful end on the gallows!'

Athelbrus fell on his knees. 'My own lady,' he cried, 'listen to me for a moment, and I will tell you why I was afraid to bring Horn. He is handsome and noble, and Ailmar, your good father, gave him into my care. If he were here and you made love to him, the king would make us sorry. Yet forgive me, Rymenhild, and I will bring Horn, despite everything.'

'Go quickly,' she said, and laughed: 'and in the afternoon, when the king goes to ride in the woods, send Horn to me, dressed as a squire. There will be no one to betray him.'

Athelbrus left her and found Horn in the hall, serving red wine at the king's table. 'Horn,' he said, 'go now to the women's chambers to speak to Rymenhild. Be bold and brave, Horn, be true to me, and you will not regret it.'

Horn took note of what Athelbrus said, and shortly he went to the beautiful Rymenhild. He knelt before her and greeted her with sweet words. He was so handsome that the chamber seemed the brighter for his presence. He spoke in courteous fashion; no man needed to teach him that. 'It is a fair sight to see you, Rymenhild, the king's daughter, sitting with your six maidens. The king's steward sent me to your chamber to speak to you. Say what you have to say, and I shall hear what you wish.'

Rymenhild took him by the hand, and led him to where she was sitting; she offered him wine to drink, and then she put her arms about his neck and kissed him as often as she wished. 'Horn,' she said, 'have pity on me and promise to be mine. I will be your wife, and no one shall oppose my wish.'

Horn thought quickly how he should answer her. 'Christ guard you and give you joy of your husband wherever he may be; I am too lowly for a lady such as you. I come from a family of servants, and I am your father's foundling; it would be against Nature for us to marry. A wedding between a servant and a king's daughter would not be a good or suitable match.'

Rymenhild did not like Horn's answer and, sighing bitterly, she released him, and fell in a faint. Horn was full of grief, and took her in his arms, kissing her often and saying: 'O my beloved, govern your heart. Help me to be dubbed by my lord the king, and when as a knight I am no longer a servant, I will be great and do as you wish, my darling.'

At this Rymenhild came to her senses. 'You shall be dubbed a knight, Horn, before the week is out. Take this cup and ring to Athelbrus, and see that he keeps his word. Tell him that I beg him to ask the king to knight you. He will be well rewarded with silver and gold; may Christ help him to do as you wish.'

At this Horn left Rymenhild, for it was nearly evening, and he went in search of Athelbrus and gave him her gifts; he soon told what had happened, and what was now needed, and what Athelbrus's reward should be. Athelbrus went cheerfully into the hall. 'Lord king,' he said, 'tomorrow is a feast day, when you will wear your crown in state; it would be a good day to dub Horn knight, for he will serve you bravely!'

'That is well said,' answered the king. 'Horn has found favour with me, and I will dub him, and he shall be my special knight. He himself shall knight his twelve comrades.'

It seemed a long wait until dawn for both Ailmar and Horn. At daybreak Horn and his fellows stood before him, and giving a little blow, the king dubbed him knight and told him to be brave, and gave him a sword; he put boots and shining spurs on his feet and set him on a white horse. At this Athulf knelt before the king.

'Noble king,' he cried, 'give me a boon. Horn of Suddenne is lord of our land and of us, and now that he is a knight with your arms and shield, let him dub us too, for that is his right.'

When Ailmar had answered, 'Do as you will,' Horn dismounted and made them all knights. It was a cheerful feast, and there was good company there, but Rymenhild was not there, and it seemed to her that the feast lasted for seven years. At last she sent for Horn and he went to her chamber, but not alone, for he insisted on taking Athulf with him. Rymenhild stood waiting, glad to see Horn again.

'Welcome, sir Horn,' she cried, 'and Athulf, a knight as well. Now is the time to keep your word, Horn. If you are true, take me as your wife. You have what you desired; now release me from my pain.'

'Enough of that, Rymenhild,' he answered, 'I will do as you wish. But first I must ride out, spear in hand, and give proof of my knighthood. We are only young knights, knights of a day, and we must follow knightly ways and fight for our lady before we take a wife. I am all the more eager to set out for that reason; and indeed this very day, if Christ help me, I will do brave deeds on the battlefield for the sake of your love for me. If I come back alive, then I will marry you.'

'True knight,' she said, 'I believe you. Take this golden ring; it is richly set with jewels, and on it is engraved, "Rymenhild the Young"; no one has ever seen its like. Wear it for my love's sake. The stones have such power that you need never fear wounds, nor death by treachery, if you look on it and think of your love. Your brother, Sir Athulf, shall have one like it. I place you in God's keeping, Horn; may Christ bring thee back.'

When she had blessed him, the knight kissed her and took his leave. He went through the hall, where all the knights were gathered, to the stable. There he took his coal-black steed, and all the courtyard rang as the horse leapt and shook Horn's coat of mail. He sang merrily as he rode on for a mile or more, until he came to a shipload of pagans. He asked them what they sought or brought to land, and one of them answered fiercely that they would conquer the land and kill its people. Then Horn gripped his sword and wiped it on his arm. His blood grew hot as he struck at the heathen, and at each blow a head fell. But the dogs gathered round him, for he was alone, until he thought of Rymenhild. Then he killed at least a hundred, and of those who were left alive, none ever recovered from their wounds. Horn took their master's head on his swordpoint, and went back to the hall.

'Lord king,' he cried, 'it is right for you and your knights to sit here. But I rode out after my dubbing, to seek adventures, and I found a ship rowed by Saracens, strangers to these shores, who had come to conquer you and your lands. They attacked me, but my sword did not fail me. In a short time I struck them all to the ground, and I have brought you their leader's head. Now have I repaid you, lord king, for making me a knight.'

It was on the day after this that, early in the morning, the king rode out to hunt. Fikenhild, the worst man alive, rode by the king's side. But Horn was not thinking of him, and went to Rymenhild's tower. There he found Rymenhild sitting in the sunlight, looking distraught, with tears on her cheeks. Horn exclaimed: 'Dear, why are you so sad and full of tears?'

'I am not weeping now,' she answered, 'but I shall weep before I sleep. In a dream I thought I cast a net in the sea but it would not stay whole. A great fish broke the net, and I think now that I shall lose the fish that I want to keep.'

'May Christ and St Stephen change your dream!' said Horn, 'I shall never deceive nor anger you. I will make you my own, in front of all the world, and I give your my solemn promise.' But both of them were full of sorrow as he said this; Rymenhild wept, and Horn's own tears fell in secret.

'My darling, listen,' he said, 'either your dream is wrong, or someone will bring us harm. We shall soon find out what it means.'

Now while Horn was with Rymenhild, Fikenhild, who was mad with jealousy at Horn's success, said to the king, as he rode by the river Stour: 'Ailmar, I warn you that Horn is plotting against you. I heard him swear to kill you and take Rymenhild for his wife. At this very moment he is lying in her arms in her chamber, as he often does. You will find him there if you go there at once.'

Ailmar, full of grief and mourning his fate, went quickly to the women's quarters. He found Horn lying in Rymenhild's arms. 'Get out, you vile thief!' he cried, 'I will never be your friend again! Leave my hall or I will strike you with my sword; leave my land or you will come to harm.'

Horn saddled his steed, put on his arms, laced up his armour, and took up his sword; he did not hesitate for a moment. He went quickly to Rymenhild, his wife. 'My darling love,' he said, 'your dream has proved all too true; the fish that tore your net has parted me from you. The king is angry and has banished me. Farewell, Rymenhild, I cannot stay any longer. I shall stay in a foreign land, seeking new adventures, for seven years. If by then I have neither come back nor sent word to you, marry a new husband, and do not wait for me. Now take me in your arms and give me a long kiss.'

Rymenhild kissed him and fainted. Horn took his leave, because he could not stay any longer. He embraced Athulf, his brother, and said: 'True knight, guard my love well; do not forsake me, but guard and care for Rymenhild.' With that he mounted his horse and rode to the harbour, where he hired a good ship to take him out of the western land. Athulf and all who saw him wept.

Now the wind rose and drove Horn to Ireland, where he landed. By the wayside he found the two sons of the king; one was called Harild and the other Berild. They asked Horn to tell them his name and purpose.

'My name is Cutberd,' he answered, 'and I have just landed from that ship. I come from the far west, and I am seeking to make my fortune.'

Berild rode up to him and took his bridle, saying, 'It is good to have found you, knight; now stay with me for a while, for you must serve the king. You are the noblest knight that I ever saw.'

Leading Cutberd to the king's hall, Berild knelt before the king and greeted him. 'Lord king,' he said, 'you must provide for this man. Let him defend your kingdom and no one shall harm it. He is the best of all the knights who have ever come here.'

The king welcomed Berild and told him to see that Horn was well cared for. 'But when if you go wooing, Berild,' he said, 'beware of Cutberd; he will drive you away from your beloved because he is so handsome, and you will never win her hand.'

When it came to Christmastide, the king made a feast with his best knights. As they were feasting, a giant suddenly appeared. 'Sit still, lord king, and hear what I have to say. Pagans have landed in your country, and one of them will fight against three of your knights. If the three kill our man, the land shall be yours; but if our man overcomes your three, it shall be ours. The fight shall be tomorrow, at dawn.'

'Cutberd shall be one, Berild another, and the third his brother Harild,' replied king Thurston, 'for they are the strongest and the best in arms. But I fear death will come to us.'

Then Cutberd, who was sitting at table, spoke. 'Lord king, there is no justice in the fight of one against three, three Christian men against one hound. Lord, I will fight alone, and will easily kill that one man with my sword.'

The next day the king got up full of sorrow; Cutberd left his bed and put on his armour, and went to the king.

'Let us go to the field, lord king,' he cried, 'there you will watch the fight.' They rode out at nine in the morning, and found the giant in a grassy clearing, his comrades beside him, awaiting their fate. Cutberd began the battle, and gave his enemy plenty of blows. The giant fell unconscious, and his comrades retreated from the field. He cried out: 'Knight, let us both rest for a time. I have never felt such heavy blows from any man's hand except from Murry, Horn's father, whom I killed in Suddenne.'

Horn was mad with anger and his blood rose as he saw before him the man who had driven him from his land and murdered his father. Drawing his sword, he looked on his ring, thought of Rymenhild, and drove the blade through the giant's heart. The pagans, who had been so bold up to now, took to their heels, but Horn and his company quickly pursued them and killed them all before they reached their ships; they paid a high price for his father's death! Few of the king's knights were slain, but among them were the king's two sons. He wept bitterly as his men laid them on their bier and brought them to burial. When he was at home in his hall, he said: 'Cutberd, I wish you to obey me. Both my sons are dead, and you are a knight of great fame and strength, handsome and tall. You shall rule my kingdom and marry my daughter Reynild.'

'Lord king,' answered Cutberd, 'it would be wrong for me to marry your daughter, as you have ordered me to do, or to reign over your kingdom. I will serve you for much longer before death takes you. Your sorrow will pass within seven years: when it is gone, then give me my reward. When I ask for your daughter in marriage, do not refuse her.'

Horn lived there, calling himself Cutberd, for more than six years; he sent no word to Rymenhild nor did he go to her himself. Meanwhile she was sorrowful in Westernesse, for a king came there who wished to marry her, and he and Ailmar agreed that she should marry him. It was not long until the wedding day, and Rymenhild dared not delay. She devised a message which Athulf wrote for her, and she sent her messenger to seek Horn in every land. But Horn heard nothing until one day, as he went to hunt with his bow in the forest, he met Rymenhild's page, and asked him: 'My dear friend, what are you seeking here?'

'That can be told quickly, since you ask, sir knight,' answered the boy. 'I come seeking Horn, a knight of Westernesse, and I am sent by a girl called Rymenhild, who sorrows for him night and day. King Modi of Reynes, an enemy of Horn's, will marry her. I have travelled far, on many shores, but I can get no word to him nor can I find him, more is the pity, for Rymenhild will be betrayed.'

Horn hearkened and spoke through bitter tears. 'Fortune has favoured you, lad; Horn stands by your side. Go back to Rymenhild and tell her not to mourn. I will be there by Sunday morning, and will be in good time.'

The boy hurried off joyfully, but he fell into the sea just below Rymenhild's tower, and drowned, to her great grief. When she unbolted her door, and looked to see if there was any sign of Horn, she found the drowned boy, and was in despair.

Meanwhile Horn went to king Thurston and told him the news: how he had been found, how Rymenhild was his, how he was son of the king of Suddenne, and how he had slain his father's murderer. 'Lord king,' he cried, 'repay my service now, help me to win Rymenhild, and I will see that your daughter is married well. She shall have Athulf, my loyal companion, for husband, one of the best and noblest of men.'

The king said that he would do everything he wanted, and sent writs through Ireland to summon Irish knights, who are quick and skilful fighters. Many men came to help Horn and he set out in a well-equipped galley. The wind and sea took him to Westernesse, where he lowered his sail and mast, and anchored the boat. It was Sunday and Mass had been sung for Rymenhild and king Modi while Horn was still at sea; he had arrived just in time! He left his ship, and, going on the land, hid his men in the wood. He was all by himself, and walked on until he met a pilgrim, whom he greeted fairly and asked what news he had.

'I come from a wedding,' said the pilgrim, 'the wedding of Rymenhild, who could not keep back her tears. She said she had a husband, though he was away. I was at the gate inside the castle wall, but they would not let me in, and I came away, for I could not bear such grief. It is a pity when a bride weeps as sadly as she did.'

'Christ help me, we will exchange clothes,' said Horn; 'take mine and give me your pilgrim's cloak. I shall drink there today, and will make some of them repent it.'

The pilgrim did not hesitate, but took off his robe and put on Horn's, and Horn took the pilgrim's staff and scrip. He twisted his lips and made a foul face and blackened his neck, making himself ugly, which he had never been. He came to the gate-keeper who answered him roughly, though Horn politely asked him again and again to open the gate. In the end Horn kicked open the side-gate; the porter paid well for his delay, for Horn threw him over the bridge and broke his ribs. The knight entered at once, and sat in a humble corner among the beggars. Disguised by his black face he looked round and saw Rymenhild sitting as if she were out of her mind, weeping and weeping: no one could stop her. Horn looked in every corner, but he could not see his friend Athulf anywhere, for this reason: he was standing on one of the towers watching to see if a ship would bring Horn.

'Horn, you are taking a long time,' he was saying to himself; 'you gave me Rymenhild to care for, and I have always guarded her, but you never came. Be quick, or never come at all, for I cannot guard her any longer.'

In the hall after the feast, Rymenhild rose from her seat to pour out the wine. As was the custom, she carried a horn in her hand, and all the knights and squires drank. Horn alone, sitting on the ground, lost in thought, did not take part. 'Gracious queen,' he said at last, 'turn towards me; we should be served first, for beggars are very thirsty.'

She laid down the horn and filled him a gallon bowl, for she thought he was a glutton. 'Have this cup and drink it,' she said, 'you are the boldest beggar I ever saw.'

Horn gave it to his companions, saying: 'Dear queen, I will only drink wine from a silver cup. You think I am a beggar, but I am a fisherman come from the west to fish at thy feast. My net has lain here for seven years, and I have come to see if it has caught any fish. Drink to me, drink to Horn from the horn, for I have come a long way.'

As Rymenhild looked on him her heart grew cold. She did not understood what he meant by fishing, nor did she recognise him; and it was a mystery why he should tell her to drink to Horn. She filled her horn and drank to the pilgrim. 'Drink as much as you want,' she said, 'and tell me if you have seen Horn?'

For a moment Horn drank, and he threw his ring into the horn. 'Queen,' he answered, 'look in your cup.'

The queen withdrew with her four attendants to her chamber and there she found the gold engraved ring which she had given Horn. Seeing the ring, she was terrified that Horn was dead; she sent a girl to fetch the pilgrim. 'Honest pilgrim,' she said, 'tell me where you got the ring you threw in the cup, and why you have come here.'

'By St Giles,' he answered, 'I went many miles to the west, seeking my fortune, when I found Horn embarking for Westernesse. I sailed on the ship with Horn, but he sickened and died on the voyage. But first he said to me "Take this ring to Rymenhild", kissing it often. May God rest his soul!'

Then Rymenhild said: 'Break now, my heart, for you will never have Horn, for whom you have longed all these years.' She fell on her bed, where she had hidden a knife, with which to kill the hateful king and herself on her wedding night. She put the knife to her heart, but Horn prevented her. Wiping away the black from his neck, he cried: 'Do you not recognise me, my sweet darling? I am your own Horn, Horn of Westernesse. Take me in your arms and kiss me.' I know for certain that they kissed then, and great happiness was theirs.

But after a little while Horn said: 'I have knights at the end of the wood, Rymenhild, and I must go. My Irish knights are armed beneath their cloaks and all ready to fight. They will anger the king and his guests who come to this feast.'

Horn threw off his pilgrim's robe and ran out of the hall. The queen went to her chamber and found Athulf there. 'Athulf, share my joy,' she said, 'and go quickly to join Horn, who is in the forest; he has many knights with him.' At this news Athulf hurried after Horn as fast as his horse would take him, and when he caught up with him, they were overjoyed to see each other again.

Shortly after, armed from head to foot, Horn returned; the gates were undone, and he put to death all who were at the feast except Ailmar and his own twelve comrades. Horn did not take vengeance for Fikenhild's false tongue, and each one there took oath he would not betray Horn, even if he lay at death's door. With bells ringing, Horn led Rymenhild to her father's palace. A sweet wedding it was; men ate there richly, and the joy was beyond all speech.

When Horn was seated, he asked them all to listen. 'Lord king,' he said, 'you always loved a story. I say my name is Horn, and I have no reason to be ashamed of it. You made me a knight, and I think I have proved myself a worthy knight. Men say I betrayed you, king, and you exiled me from your land. You thought I had slept with Rymenhild; but I have never done so, and do not mean to until I have won Suddenne. Now keep her while I go to win back my inheritance and avenge my father. I shall be king of a city then and wear a crown, and Rymenhild shall share a king's bed.'

With his Irish companions and his brother Athulf, Horn went down to his ship, and the wind blew fiercely, so that in five days, at midnight, they landed in Suddenne. Taking Athulf with him, Horn went ashore and on the roadside, asleep beneath his shield on which was drawn Christ's cross, they found a knight. Horn seized him and said: 'Awake, knight, and tell us what you are guarding and why you are sleeping here. The shining cross on your shield tells me you are a Christian. But speak, or I will kill you.'

'I have served the pagans against my will,' answered the terrified knight. 'I was a Christian before the hateful Saracens came to this country. They made me forsake God and sent me here to guard this shore against Horn, a noble knight in the west who has now come of age. They killed, together with many hundred others, Murry, Horn's father and the gracious king of this land. They sent Horn away with twelve comrades. Among them was my own child, Athulf. I wish that the wind would drive the two of them here; if I could only see them, I should die of joy.'

'Then now is the time for joy,' said Horn, 'for Horn and Athulf, his friend, are here.' Then they were all glad.

'My children, how have you done?' asked the old knight. 'Will you conquer this country and kill the people here? Horn, your mother Godhild is still living, and she would be the happiest of women if she knew that you were alive.'

'Then I bless the time I came to Suddenne,' cried Horn. 'My Irishmen will teach the pagans to talk our language, and will kill them all.' With that he blew his horn; his men heard it and came from the ship. All night until daybreak they fought and killed; they went throughout the country and put all the Saracens to death. Horn had chapels and churches built, and bells were rung and masses sung. He found his mother in her hermitage on the rock, and they kissed and embraced each other. Horn made a cheerful feast there when he wore his crown for the first time.

But while Horn was away, Rymenhild paid dearly for his absence. Proud-hearted Fikenhild began to woo her and the king did not dare to forbid him. Fikenhild gave great gifts to young and old to buy their loyalty, and he built a strong stone castle, surrounded by the sea. Only a bird in flight could land there, but men could come when the tide went out. On the day set for the wedding, Fikenhild went to king Ailmar to fetch the beautiful Rymenhild, who suffered so much that she wept tears of blood. At night he married her and led her to his castle in the darkness; before the sun rose he began the wedding feast.

Now one night Horn dreamed a terrible dream, that his lady had been taken on board a ship which started to overturn. She tried to swim to land, but Fikenhild thrust her back with his swordhilt. Horn awoke from his sleep and hurried to prepare himself. 'Athulf,' he cried, 'we must sail at once! Fikenhild has deceived me and has harmed Rymenhild in some way. May Christ bring us there quickly!'

Almost before Horn knew it and before the sun was up, his ship lay beneath the tower where Rymenhild was. She had no idea that Horn was there, and, as the castle was so new, he did not know she was there either; but when the sand was dry, he made his way across and there he found Arnoldin, Athulf's cousin, waiting for him. 'Horn, king's son,' he said, 'you have made a good landfall. Today Fikenhild has married your sweet lady, Rymenhild; that is the truth. He has fooled you twice, and he has built this tower for her sake, which no one can ever enter against his will. May Christ guide you, or you will lose her!'

Now Horn was as crafty as any man alive, so he took a harp and a few of his fellow-knights, whom he dressed in skins, with swords beneath their shirts. They sang cheerfully and made music, so that Fikenhild might hear, and went across the sands to the castle. When Fikenhild asked who they were, they said they were harpers, jongleurs and fiddlers, and he let them in. Then Horn sat down on a bench near the hall door, and, stringing his harp, he sang a song in praise of Rymenhild. No one laughed when she fell in a faint, and Horn's heart was near to bursting. He looked on his ring, thought of her, and went up to the high table, drawing his sword. Fikenhild's crown and head were struck off together, and the men around him were killed. When they were all dead, Horn made Arnoldin lord there after king Ailmar, and knights and barons paid him tribute. Taking Rymenhild by the hand, Horn led her down to the shore; he took with him also Athelbrus, the steward of her father's house. The tide rose and they sailed to the kingdom ruled by Modi, whom Horn killed. He made Athelbrus ruler there, because he had taught him so well. Then Horn went to Ireland, where he gave Reynild in marriage to Athulf; and at last he went to Suddenne, to his own people, and made Rymenhild his queen. In faithful love they lived, and cherished the law of God.

The tale of Horn, strong and handsome, is ended. Let us rejoice, and may Jesus, the King of Heaven, give us all His blessing.

29. HAVELOK THE DANE

Havelok has some pretensions to a historical background, and in places carries clear traces of the Danelaw, the lands in the east of England which were under Danish rule for many years in the tenth and eleventh century. It seems to have been written in Lincolnshire; an early version of it appears in a history of the English people written for a Lincolnshire lady in the first part of the twelfth century, and there is a brief Anglo-Norman poem about Havelok. The English romance was written towards the end of the twelfth century. The marriage of Havelok, prince of Denmark, and Goldborough, heiress to England, recalls the union of the two countries under the Danish king Canute, but here history ends, and the romance begins: it is in a very similar vein to King Horn, *with which it shares a number of themes, particularly that of exile and return. But there is an interesting, over-arching concern with good government: it is partly the story of Havelok's spiritual growth until he is fit to play his role as king, and partly a warning against the tyrants who deprive him and Goldborough of their rightful inheritance, and rule cruelly and unjustly. Behind the adventures, there is a moral tract for the times, when good governance by the king was of very real importance to his subjects.*

LISTEN, good people, wives, girls and men, and I will tell you the story of Havelok, the mightiest man that ever rode a horse. But fill my cup with good ale before the story begins.

In the old days there lived a king who made good laws, and was loved by old and young alike. He protected holy Church and righteous men but he hated robbers, and all the outlaws whom he could find he hung high on the gallows. In his time a man with bright gold in his bag was not troubled by anyone; merchants could travel throughout England and openly buy and sell, and anyone who harmed them was quickly brought to grief. The land was at peace and everyone praised the king. He took pity on the fatherless; he imprisoned any knight, however great, who wronged widows; and he destroyed anyone who committed rape. He was strong and fearless and honourable, and the bread on his table was there to feed any passing traveller, even the poor who went on foot.

This king's name was Aethelwold, and he had no heir save a pretty little girl, too young to walk or speak. When he fell ill and knew that he was dying, he summoned all his lords, from Roxburgh to Dover, to come to him at Winchester where, no longer able to sleep or eat, he lay on his hard bed. There, full of grief and tears, they greeted him, but he told them to be quiet. 'Tears do not help,' he said. 'I am at death's door. I need your advice: who will take charge of the girl who will be your queen?'

When they replied that it should be earl Godrich of Cornwall, who was

453

wise and greatly feared, the king was pleased. He ordered a cloth to be brought on which was the Mass book, the chalice, the paten, the corporal – all that was necessary for the Mass. On these he made Godrich swear to guard the girl till she was twenty years old, and had learnt courtly ways, and the ways of love. Then he was to give her to the handsomest and strongest man alive. When this oath was sworn, the king gave England and his daughter to the earl, and began his prayers to God. When he had said, 'Into thy hands, O Lord,' he died in the presence of them all.

When the king was buried, earl Godrich took the whole of England and treated it as his own. He put knights whom he could trust into the castles. He made the people swear loyalty to him, sent justices through the land and appointed magistrates, and serjeants of the peace with long swords to keep the forests from evil-doers. Everything was done according to his own will, and soon England stood in fear of him.

Meanwhile, Goldborough, the king's daughter, came to be the loveliest of women, wise and virtuous. Many people pitied her, but when earl Godrich heard that they said she was beautiful and good, and the rightful heir, he said to himself: 'Why should she be queen and rule over me? Why should I give this land to a mere girl whom I have treated too gently?' So, in complete disregard of his oath, like a wicked Judas, he took her from Winchester to Dover. There, in a castle by the sea, he fed and clothed her poorly and let no one come near her who might avenge her wrongs. She mourned her fate, but we will leave her in her prison and speak of other things.

In Denmark in those days there was a rich and powerful king named Birkabeyn, who had a son and two beautiful daughters whom he loved as his own life. But death, which does not distinguish between rich and poor, took him. Then earl Godard, his friend, who was chosen by his knights to care for the children, took Havelok, the heir, and his sisters, Swanborough and Helfled, and shut them up in a castle, where they wept bitterly for hunger and cold. Once he had got the whole country into his power, he plotted great treachery against them. He went to their tower, where Havelok spoke out boldly. 'We are hungry,' he said. 'We have nothing to eat, and no knights or servants to attend us. Is there no corn here to make bread? We are very nearly dead!'

But Godard took no notice, and, as if to amuse himself, took the girls, who were pale and sick with hunger, and cut their throats. As they lay by the wall in their own blood, Havelok, terrified, saw the knife at his own heart. Even though he was only very young, he kneeled down before the treacherous earl and said:

'Have pity on me! I will renounce my claim to Denmark if you will let me live. I will swear on the Bible never to bear shield or spear to harm you, and I will leave Denmark this very day, never to return.'

When this devil heard Havelok's words, he began to relent. He drew back the knife, still warm with the children's blood, and it was a miracle that he left the boy alive. But though he would not kill the boy himself, he grieved that Havelok was not dead. In a frenzy he tried to decide what to do next, and then he sent for a fisherman, whom he knew would do his will.

'Grim, you are my servant,' he said, 'you know that you must do whatever I say. Tomorrow I will make you a free man and give you a rich reward if, as soon as the moon rises tonight, you will take a child and throw him in the sea. I will take responsibility for the sin as if I had done it myself.'

So Grim took the child, and bound him securely; he wrapped him in an old cloth, gagged him with foul rags, so that he could not speak or breathe, and put him in a black sack. He lifted him on his back, and carried him to his cottage, and gave him to Leve, his wife. When he told her what his lord had ordered him to do, she jumped up and threw the boy down so hard that his head cracked against a great stone.

The child lay like this until midnight, when Grim told Leve to bring a light so that he could put on his clothes. As she did so, she saw a very clear bright light shining round the child. From his mouth there came a ray like a sunbeam, and it was as light as though wax candles were burning in the house.

'Jesus Christ!' said Leve: 'what is this light in the house? Get up, Grim, and see what it means.'

Both of them hurried to the boy and untied him, and when they took off his shirt, they found on his right shoulder a bright mark which showed that he was a king.

'God knows, this is the heir to the throne of Denmark,' cried Grim; and he knelt before Havelok, for he was very troubled by this discovery. 'O Lord, have pity on me and on Leve here! Both of us are your servants and slaves. We will feed you well until you can ride and bear helmet and shield and spear, and Godard, that wicked traitor, will never know! I will not claim my freedom unless it is granted by you.'

Then Havelok was very happy, and sat up and asked hungrily for bread. Leve said: 'It is just as well that you are still able to eat. I will fetch you bread and cheese, butter and milk, pasties and meat. As the saying goes, "Where God will help, nothing shall harm."'

Then Havelok ate ravenously, and when he had been fed, Grim made a comfortable bed, undressed him and put him in it. 'Sleep well,' he said, 'and do not be afraid at night, for your sorrow has turned to joy.'

As soon as it was daybreak, Grim went to Godard, that wicked regent of Denmark, and told him the boy was dead, asking for his reward and freedom.

Godard looked at him grimly. 'So you would like to be an earl now, would you?' he said. 'Go away, you vile creature, and stay a serf, just as you were before. Any more requests like that and I will hang you on the gallows.'

At last Grim realised that he would have to escape from that traitor. 'What shall I do?' he asked himself. 'If Godard gets to know that Havelok is alive, he will hang us both. It will be better for us to flee the land and save our lives.'

Then Grim sold all his corn and his sheep, his cow, horse, swine and goat, the geese and the hens in the farmyard; he sold everything that he could and turned it into money. He tarred his ship, and put in a mast, strong ropes, good oars, and a sail. When everything was made ready, he took young Havelok, himself and his wife, his three sons, and his two pretty daughters, and set out on the high seas. When he was about a mile from land the north wind sprang up and drove them to England, which would later belong to Havelok.

Grim landed in the north of Lincolnshire, in the Humber, and, drawing up his ship on the sand, he built a little house there out of clay. Because he owned it, the place was called Grimsby after him.

Grim was a skilful fisherman: with net and hook he caught many good fish, sturgeon, whale, turbot, salmon, seal and cod, porpoise, herring, mackerel, flounder, plaice and thornback. He made baskets for himself and his three sons to carry the fish they sold inland. He went to the towns and farms, and never came home empty handed. He often went to Lincoln, and would go from end to end of the city till he had sold everything. When he came home he brought with him cakes, and his bags were full of corn and meat. He brought hemp as well, and strong ropes for the nets he cast in the sea.

Grim lived like this for twelve years or more, and he fed his family well. But then Havelok realised that while he was at home, Grim was working hard to get them food, and he thought: 'I am no longer a child, but a growing youth, and I can easily eat more than Grim can ever get. I will go and learn to work for my meat. It is not shameful to do that: I will be happy to carry the baskets, however heavy they are.'

The next day, as soon as it was light, Havelok jumped out of bed and shouldered a basket stacked high with fish; he carried as much as four men all by himself. He sold every bit and brought home all the money, keeping back not a farthing. He never lay abed after that, but went out each day to learn his trade.

But a great dearth of bread and corn happened soon after this, and Grim did not know how to feed his family. He was very concerned because Havelok was so strong and could eat so heartily. So he said to him: 'Havelok, I think we will soon die of hunger, for our meat is long since gone, and the famine is continuing. I am not worried about myself, but it would be better that you left us before it is too late. You know the way to Lincoln, and there are many good men there in whose service you can earn your bread. But you cannot go naked; I will make you a coat from my sail, so you will not catch cold.'

Taking down the shears from the peg, Grim made the coat, and Havelok put it on. Dressed only in this coat, and barefoot, he went to Lincoln. He had no friend there and did not know what to do. For two days he went without food, but on the third he heard a man calling: 'Porters, porters, come here!' At once all the poor men rushed forward, and Havelok was in their midst. He was first to reach the earl's cook, who was buying meat at the bridge. He carried the food to the castle and for this he got a farthing cake. On another day when the cook called the porters, Havelok knocked down sixteen good lads who stood in his way, and ran with his fish basket and began snatching up the fish. He lifted up a whole cartload of cuttlefish, of salmon and plaice, great lampreys and eels, and he did not rest until he came to the castle and men took the burden from his head. The cook looked at him and, thinking he was a strong fellow, asked: 'Will you be my servant? I will be happy to feed you.'

'That is all that I ask for, sir. Give me enough to eat and I will make the fire burn clear, break sticks for eel-skinning, and wash your dishes until they shine.'

When the cook had said, 'That is good enough for me,' and told him to sit down, Havelok was still as a stone till he had eaten enough. Then he went to the well and, filling a great tub, bore it alone to the kitchen. He would let no one fetch water, nor bear meat from the bridge; he carried the peat, the rushes and the wood, and drew all the water that was needed, all by himself. He took no more rest than a beast, and he was the humblest of men. He was always laughing and cheerful, for he was good at hiding his sorrows. Havelok would play with the children, however little, and both young and old, knights and children, gentle and bold, all who saw him, loved him. His fame spread, and men said that he was meek and strong and handsome, but had nothing to wear save one unwieldy wretched coat. Then the cook took pity on him and bought him brand new clothes, stockings and shoes, and he put them on quickly. When he had proper clothes, no one seemed more handsome or indeed more fit to be king. When all the earl's men were together at the Lincoln games, Havelok stood like a mast, head and shoulders above them. He threw everyone at wrestling, and yet for all his strength he was gentle, and even if a man did him harm, he never attacked him and took his revenge.

It so happened that earl Godrich summoned the barons and earls and all the men of England to Lincoln to a parliament. With them came many champions, and some nine or ten began to compete in different games, while grooms and ploughmen gathered to watch. They used a bar as a marker, and the strong young men began to throw a stone. Anyone who could lift it knee-high was a strong man, and anyone who could throw it an inch was reckoned to be a champion. As the crowd stood and stared, cheering the best throw, Havelok watched. He had never seen this sport before, and knew nothing about it. His master told him to see what he could do: half afraid, he took up the heavy stone, and at his first attempt hurled it twelve feet beyond all other throws. The champions that saw it nudged each other and laughed. 'We've stayed here too long,' they said, and would not continue with the game.

This feat could not be hidden, and soon the story of Havelok's prowess in hurling the stone was known the length and breadth of England. In castles and halls, the knights talked of it and of how strong and handsome he was, strong and fair, until Godrich, hearing them, thought to himself: 'Through this low-born fellow, my son and I will win England. King Aethelwold made me swear by the holy Mass that I would give his daughter to the tallest, strongest, handsomest man alive. Even if I searched as far as India, where could I find one so suitable as Havelok? It is he who shall have Goldborough.'

This was his plot, for he believed that Havelok was the son of a serf. Godric sent quickly for Goldborough and told her, though she vowed she would wed no one save a king or a king's son, that the next day she would wed his cook's servant. When the day came, Godric summoned Havelok and asked him if he would marry.

'No, on my life!' said Havelok. 'What should I do with a wife? I could not feed or clothe her, and where would I shelter a woman? I have neither cattle nor house, not even a stick or a blade of grass, no food or clothes, except for one old white coat. The clothes I am wearing are the cook's, and I am his servant.'

Godrich leapt up and struck him: 'Unless you take the woman who I am going to give you as your wife, I will hang you or blind you.' Then Havelok was afraid and agreed to do as he demanded; and Goldborough too, though she did not like it at all, did not dare to oppose the marriage. She thought it was the will of God who makes the growing corn and who had made her a woman. So they were married, according to the proper ritual, and Mass was said for them. The clergyman who married them was the Archbishop of York.

When the marriage was over, Havelok did not know what to do, where to stay, nor where to go, for he saw that Godrich hated both him and his wife. Havelok knew that shame would come to his wife if he stayed, so he decided that they should escape and go to Grim and his three sons, since they might hope to be fed and clothed there. They had no choice but to go on foot, and followed the road until they came to Grimsby. They found that Grim had died, but his five children were still alive and they welcomed Havelok joyfully. They knelt before him and

said: 'Welcome, dear lord, and welcome to your fair companion; blessed
be the day when you wed her. It is good to see you alive. We have goods
and horses, nets and ships in the sea, gold, silver, and many things which
our father Grim ordered us to give to you. Stay here, and everything we
have is yours. You will be our lord and we will serve both of you. Our
sisters will wash and wring her clothes, and bring water for her hands,
and they will make your bed.'

Full of joy, they broke sticks and made a blazing fire. They killed geese
and hens and ducks until there was plenty of meat for all, and fetched
wine and ale. But even so, Goldborough wept as she lay down at nightfall, thinking how she had been married to a man unworthy of a king's
daughter. Suddenly a light, bright as a flame, filled the room, and she
saw that it came from the mouth of him who slept beside her. 'He is
dead,' she thought, 'or else most nobly born.' Then she saw on his
shoulder a red gold cross, and the voice of an angel said: 'Goldborough,
do not weep. That cross shows that he who has wedded you is a king's
son, and that you shall be queen of Denmark and of England; he shall
rule those lands.'

When she had heard these words of the heavenly angel, she was too
happy to hide her joy, and she kissed Havelok as he slept unaware. He
woke suddenly from his sleep and said: 'Lady, I have had a marvellous
dream. I thought I was in Denmark, standing on a hill so high that I
could see the whole world. I sat there, and my arms were so long that I
could hold all Denmark. But when I wanted to withdraw my arms,
everything there was clung to them, and the keys of strong castles fell at
my feet. And I dreamed another dream; that I flew over the salt sea to
England. I closed my hand over it and, Goldborough, I gave it to you.'

'May Christ turn your dreams to joy,' she answered. 'I believe that
within a year you will wear England's crown, and be king of Denmark
too. But do not delay your departure; take Grim's sons with you, for
they are eager and love you with all their hearts.'

When day came, Havelok rose and went first of all to the church,
where he knelt and called on Christ and the cross: 'O you who rule the
wind and water, the wood and field, of your mercy pity me, Lord. Give
me vengeance on the foe who killed my sisters and bade Grim drown me
in the sea. With wicked wrong he holds my land and has made me a
beggar, though I never did him harm. Let me pass safely across the sea,
O Lord, and bring me to that land which Godard holds.'

Laying his offering on the altar, Havelok returned home and found
Grim's sons going out fishing. He called Robert the Red, the eldest
brother, and William Wendut and Hugh Raven, and told his story. 'And
now', he said, 'I am of age and am able to wield weapons, and I shall
never be glad until I see Denmark. I ask you to come with me, and I will
make you all rich men.'

So Grim's sons sailed with Goldborough and Havelok to Denmark, where they came to earl Ubbe. The earl was a justice, and Havelok offered him a golden ring in return for leave to sell his wares through one town and another. Ubbe saw that Havelok was strong, broad in the chest, and tall, more suited to carrying shield and spear than merchant's goods: he said that Havelok should have what he asked if the next day he would come to dine and bring his wife with him.

Now Havelok, though he feared that shame might come to Goldborough, led her to Ubbe's hall. Robert the Red was at her side, who would have died before any evil came to her, and on the other hand was William Wendut. At the sight of them, when they came to the court, Ubbe and his knights and men all leapt to their feet. Havelok towered over them all. Ubbe found Havelok handsome and courteous, and when it was time to eat, he brought in his own wife and said jestingly: 'Lady, you and Havelok shall eat together, and Goldborough with me.'

The blessing was said and before them was put the best food that ever king or emperor ate. Crane, swan, venison, salmon, lamprey, sturgeon, were set before them, together with spiced wine, and white wine and red, of which no page was too little to taste. When the time came for their departure, Ubbe thought: 'If I let them go alone, there will be trouble because of this woman. For her sake men will kill her lord.' So he called forth ten knights and sixty men with their bows and lances and sent them all to Bernard Brown, the magistrate of the town, and told him to guard Havelok and Goldborough as his own life.

Bernard was a generous man, and he prepared a rich feast for Havelok's entertainment. But just as they were about to dine, a man in a doublet, and sixty others with drawn swords and long knives and spears in hand, demanded entrance to the house. Bernard leapt up, seized an axe, and ran to the door. 'Do you think we are afraid?' said one of the men. 'We will get in at this door in spite of you.'

He seized a rock and hurled it at the door, breaking it down. Havelok saw that, and drawing back the great bar, he opened the door wide. 'Come quickly,' he cried, 'and a curse on anyone who runs away.' Then one of the men drew his sword and with two other robbers tried to wound Havelok, but he lifted up the bar and at one blow killed all three. Five more lay dead before the others agreed on a plan, and divided into two parties to rush on him, like dogs on a baited bear. They were strong and quick, and soon they had wounded him in more than twenty places. Seeing the blood running from his sides like water from a well, Havelok was in a fury; he mowed them down with the bar. Then they all shouted, and retreated, because they did not dare approach him, any more than they would have approached a boar or a lion; and from a distance they hurled stones and spears at him.

Now Hugh Raven heard the noise and feared that his lord had come to some harm. He seized an oar and a long knife, he hurried there and saw the men standing around Havelok, beating him as a smith does his anvil. 'Alas,' he cried, 'that I was born to see this grief! Robert! William! where are you? Get bars and flay these dogs till our lord is avenged. Come quick and follow me. I have an oar.'

'Yes, yes,' answered Robert, grasping a beam strong enough to carry a net, and William Wendut took a bar bigger than his own thigh, and Bernard had his axe. They hurled themselves into the fight like madmen. Bodies were broken, brown heads and black, until none of the thieves were left alive. The next day the robbers lay on one another, torn like dogs; some were slung into ditches, some were dragged by the hair into the ploughed fields and left there.

News of this soon came to Ubbe; and he leaped on a horse and rode with his knights to the town. He called Bernard out of his house; he came all tattered and torn; his clothes were almost gone.

'O lord,' he cried, 'when the moon came up last night, more than sixty robbers with wide sleeves and hoods close on their heads came here to rob and kill me. They soon broke down the door and would have bound me, if Havelok had not jumped up and, seizing a bar, and then a stone, driven them out like dogs from a mill house. He is worth a thousand men by himself! If it was not for him I should be dead. But he is badly injured, for they gave him such wounds that the smallest would bring down a horse, and I am very much afraid that he will die. He is wounded in the side, in the arm, in the thigh, in more than twenty places; though when he first felt the pain no boar fought like him. As a hound follows a hare, he followed the thieves and did not spare any of those accursed men until they all lay still.'

'Is this the truth, Bernard?' asked Ubbe; and all the burgesses who stood about said that he spoke truly. 'The thieves would have taken all his goods', they said, 'if this man from a far-off land had not killed them, who could stand alone in the night against so many stalwart men. They were led by Griffin Gall.'

'Fetch Havelok quickly', answered Ubbe, 'that I may see his wounds. If he can be healed, I myself will dub him knight. If those vile men were still alive, I would have hanged them all.'

Now Havelok was brought to Ubbe, who was very grieved by his wounds until a doctor looked at them and said they could be healed. Then Ubbe was reassured: 'Come with me,' he said, 'you and Goldborough and your three servants. I will guarantee your safety. No friend of the men you have killed shall lie in wait to slay you, for I will lend you a room in my high tower. Nothing shall be between us except a panelled pine wall; whether you speak loudly or softly, you will hear and see me whenever you wish. And no knight or clerk of mine shall harm your wife any more than they would harm mine.'

Ubbe soon brought Havelok and his wife and his three men joyfully to his city. It was about midnight on the first night they were there, that Ubbe saw a light like daylight in that tower, and he wondered what it might be, for at that hour he did not think that anyone was awake except for revellers and thieves. He went and peered in through a crack, and saw the five lying fast asleep. From Havelok's mouth there came a light as bright as the sun; Ubbe called a hundred of his knights and men to witness it. The brightness was as if a hundred and seven candles burned there. Havelok lay on his left side with his bride in his arms, the fairest pair the knights had ever seen. On Havelok's naked shoulder they were aware of a cross, clear and brighter than gold in the light. It shone like a ruby, giving enough light to see the king's head on a coin. Everyone recognised it as a mark of royal birth, and knew that they gazed on Birkabeyn's own son. 'He is Birkabeyn's heir,' they said, 'for no brother was so like brother in Denmark as this man is like the king.'

They all knelt before him, with tears in their eyes, for they were as glad as if they had drawn him from the grave; they kissed his feet so that he woke. At first he was angry, for he thought they intended to kill him.

But Ubbe said: 'Lord, be not afraid. I am overjoyed to see you, dear son, and I offer you my homage, for it is my duty to swear fealty to you. You are Birkabeyn's son, and you shall be king of Denmark; tomorrow you shall take homage of earl, baron, warrior and thane. We will make you a knight, and celebrate the occasion.'

This made Havelok very happy, and he thanked God with all his heart. When dawn came and the shadows of night vanished, Ubbe summoned all his lords to come before him, as they loved their own lives and their wives and children. No one failed to appear to learn what the Justice wished; he said to them: 'You all know well that when Birkabeyn was on his deathbed, this land was his. By your advice he gave his three children, Havelok and his two daughters, and all his possessions, into Godard's charge. The earl swore to care for them by the Bible and by the holy Mass, but he broke his oath! He killed the girls, and would have done the same to the boy had not God saved him. But Grim saw how handsome Havelok was and knew that he was the true heir. He fled from Denmark into England, where for many winters Havelok has been fed and fostered. Now he is here: there is no one to equal him in all this world. Be glad that he is with us, and come to do homage to your lord. I myself will do it first.'

So Ubbe knelt, and everyone saw how he became Havelok's man. Every baron in the town followed him, and then the warriors, thanes, knights and common men, swore fealty to their lord; at the end of the day everyone had done fealty to Havelok. When all were sworn, Ubbe dubbed Havelok a knight with a fine sword, and made him king in noble fashion. There was much rejoicing, and the sports began: there were spear fights and buckler play, wrestlings, stone-puttings, harping and piping, gambling, readings of romances and the singing of old tales, and players striking on the tabor. Bulls and boars were baited with lively dogs. Gifts of clothes were made, and there was great plenty of food. The king knighted Robert and William Wendut and Hugh Raven and made all three barons, and gave them lands, so that each one had twenty knights day and night in his retinue.

When the feast was done, the king kept a thousand knights and five thousand men. I will not lengthen the story, but when he had all the land in his power, he vowed, and his men with him, that they would never cease fighting until they had revenge on Godard. They did not delay in setting out to attack him, and Robert, who was master of the army, was the first to encounter Godard. Robert declared loudly that Godard should come with him to the king. But Godard struck him a mighty blow with his fist before Robert seized his long knife and wounded him in the arm. When Godard's men saw that, they began to flee, but he cried: 'Knights, what are you doing? I have fed you, and will do so in future if you will help me in this need. Shame on you, if you let Havelok do as he wants.'

Then his men rallied and killed one of the king's knights and a common man and wounded ten others. But the king's men killed them all except for Godard, whom they tied securely, though he roared like a bull trapped in a corner and baited by dogs. They threw him on a wretched mare with his face to the tail, and in this fashion he was brought to Havelok. Now he paid for the evil he had done long ago. The king called Ubbe and all his lords and thanes together and told them to give their judgment on Godard. This was their sentence.

'We decree', they said, 'that Godard be flayed alive, drawn to the gallows at the tail of this wretched horse, and hanged. And over him it shall be written: "This is that wicked man who thought to take from the king his land, and who killed the king's sisters." The sentence is decreed, we say no more.'

With this judgment given, Godard was shriven by the priest, then quickly a lad came with a knife of ground steel and from top to toe he flayed Godard, who shrieked vainly for mercy. The old horse was brought, and with a sail-rope Godard was bound to her tail and drawn to the gallows, not by the road, but over the fallow fields.

Now after Godard was dead the king took all his land, houses and goods, and gave it to Ubbe. Then Havelok swore that because of the good Grim had done him while he was poor, he would found a priory of black monks at Grimsby to serve Christ till doomsday. But when Godrich of Cornwall heard that Havelok was king of Denmark and had come to England, and that Goldborough, the rightful heiress, was at Grimsby, he was deeply sorrowful. At once he summoned every man who could ride a horse or bear a weapon, whether axe, scythe, spike, spear, dagger or long knife, and ordered them to come to Lincoln on the seventeenth of March. If anyone rebelled and would not come, he swore by Christ and St John to make him and his children serfs. Because the English feared him as a horse fears the spur, they all came on the appointed day.

'Listen,' he said, 'at Grimsby strangers have come and taken the priory; Havelok burns the churches, binds the priests, and strangles both monks and nuns. What is your advice? If Havelok rules like this for long, he will be master of us all, to kill or enslave us. Let us set out at once and kill these dogs. I shall never be happy, nor will I take the Host, or be absolved of my sins, until he is driven from the land. Follow me, for I will be the first to strike with drawn sword. Curses on anyone who does not stand fast beside me.'

'Yes, yes,' cried earl Gunther, and 'Yes' repeated earl Reyner of Chester, and so did all who were gathered there. They all pulled on their mailcoats and helmets, and in no time they were setting out towards Grimsby.

Now Havelok had learned of their departure, and came with all his army to resist them. He struck off the head of the first knight he met and Robert killed another, and William Wendut cut off the arm of a third. Ubbe encountered Godrich and they fought grimly until both fell to the ground. Then they drew their swords and drenched in sweat, they fought so furiously that at each blow a flint would have shattered. The fight lasted from morning until sunset, when Godrich gave Ubbe such a cruel wound in the side that he would have fallen had not Hugh Raven borne him away. Before he was rescued a thousand knights had been killed on each side, and such a slaughter had been made of the common soldiers that all the pools on the field overflowed with blood that ran down the hillside. Godrich rushed like lightning on the Danes, who fell like grass before the scythe.

When Havelok saw how his people died, he urged on his horse. 'Godrich,' he cried, 'why do you do this? You know that Aethelwold made you swear by the Mass that you would give England to his daughter when she came of age. If you surrender it now without fighting, I will forgive you everything, for I see how great your strength and valour are.'

'I will never do that!' answered Godrich, and he gripped his sword and struck Havelok so hard that he split Havelok's shield in two. When he was put to shame like this in front of his army, Havelok felled Godrich to the earth. But Godrich did not lie at his feet for long; he jumped up and struck Havelok, so that he gashed his coat of mail, and the blood streamed down to his feet. Havelok lashed out at his enemy, swinging his sword high above his head, and struck off Godrich's hand. Then he bound the traitor in chains of steel and sent him to the queen who had good cause to hate him. But, since Godrich was a knight, Havelok commanded that no one should beat him, or do him shame, until the knights had pronounced a just sentence on him.

Now the English, when they learnt that Goldborough was England's rightful heir and that Havelok had wedded her, all begged for his mercy and offered him homage. But Havelok would take nothing from them until the queen was brought. Six earls accompanied her, that peerless, gracious lady. The English fell weeping on their knees before her.

'By Christ's mercy and yours,' they cried, 'we have done you great wrong by breaking faith with you. For England ought to be yours and we should be your men. All of us, young and old, know that Aethelwold was king here and you are his heir.'

'Since you know it now,' said Havelok, 'I order you to sit down and judge Godrich rightfully according to his deeds; and judge him justly, for judgment spares neither clerk nor knight. Then, if you wish and advise it, according to the law of the land, I will take your homage.'

So they sat down, for none dared to prevent judgment. And they condemned Godrich to be tied to a worthless ass, with his head to the tail, and in wretched clothes: he was to be led through Lincoln to a green (which is, I think, still there), there to be bound to a stake with a great fire, until he was burned to dust. To warn other traitors, they also judged that, for his misdeeds, his children should forfeit his inheritance for ever. This judgment was soon carried out; Goldborough rejoiced and gave thanks to God, and Havelok then took homage of all the English and made them swear to bear good faith to him.

Then he summoned the earl of Chester, a young unmarried knight, and said: 'Earl, if you will take my advice, I will give you the fairest woman alive as your wife; Gunnild of Grimsby, daughter of Grim who fled with me from Denmark to save me from death. I advise you to marry her for she is beautiful and noble, and I will show you how dear she is to me, for as long as I live, you shall be dear to me as well, for her sake.'

The earl could not refuse the king, and on that same day he wedded her. When Gunnild was brought to Chester, Havelok did not forget Bertram, the earl's cook.

'Friend, you shall have a rich reward', he cried, 'for the good deeds you did me when I was in need. For when I wore just a coat, and had no bread, nor food, nor anything of my own, you fed and clothed me well. In return, you shall have the earldom of Cornwall and all Godrich's lands; moreover, I wish you to marry Grim's daughter, Levive the gracious. She is courteous, and lovely as a flower; her cheek is like the new rose on the bush when it lies open in the warm bright sun.'

Then Havelok girded Bertram with the sword of the earldom, and made him knight with his own hand. He was soon married to that sweet girl. Then Havelok gave a great feast for his Danes and gave them rich lands and goods. Soon afterwards he went to London with his army for his crowning, and both the English and Danes there saw how proudly he bore it. His coronation feast lasted for forty days or more; then, because he saw the Danes were ready to return to Denmark, he gave them leave to go. He commanded that Ubbe, his justice, should so rule Denmark that no complaint should come to him.

When they were gone, Havelok remained in England, and for sixty years he was king there with Goldborough for his queen. So great was their love that all the world spoke of them. Neither was happy away from the other, and they were never angry, for their love was always new. They had fifteen sons and daughters, all of whom, by God's will, became kings or queens.

Now you have heard the whole story of Havelok and Goldborough, how they were born, how they were wronged in their youth, and how they were avenged. I have told you everything. In return I beg each one of you who had heard it to say an 'Our Father' for him who has made the rhyme and who, for its sake, has waked many a night. May Christ at the end bring his soul to glory.

30. GUY OF WARWICK

Just as the king and his court were glad to listen to stories of the exploits of rulers of ancient days, so baronial households liked to hear the adventures of their forebears, and Guy of Warwick *is one of these 'ancestral' romances, perhaps written in honour of the earl of Warwick and his family by a canon of Osney Abbey, a house of which the earl was a patron.*

There is a strong, and unexpected, religious theme, and Guy's sudden departure on pilgrimage and final retreat to a hermitage smack more of a pious example than something which really belongs with the spirit of the rest of the story, though it holds our attention because we do not anticipate it. The hermitage to which Guy retired was shown to the curious in the fifteenth century, at Guy's Cliff near Warwick, and in the fifteenth century a manual of religious instruction was entitled The Mirror of Guy of Warwick.

The other interesting feature is that Guy is noble by character rather than by birth; he is certainly not the social equal of the earl's daughter whom he marries, and this is unexpected in a work designed to glorify his family. But the poet certainly achieved his aim of providing the family with a famous ancestor; relics of Guy can still be seen at Warwick Castle, and the story itself was popular throughout Europe down to the seventeenth century.

MANY adventures have taken place since Christ's birth, and not all of them have been told. The story I am going to tell is about an earl, his honest steward, and the steward's son – a handsome squire, who loved the earl's sweet daughter. The earl was an Englishman, and held Warwick: he was rich and powerful, and no one dared oppose him. His name was Rohold and he was also lord of Oxford and Buckingham. The earl's daughter, Felice la Belle, was as accomplished as she was beautiful, and dukes and earls had sought her hand in marriage in vain. The earl's steward, named Seward, was a worthy man and of good family; he held Wallingford in his own right, and served his lord faithfully, keeping such strict order in his lands that a man could openly carry gold without fear of robbers. His son was handsome and courteous, and everyone loved him: he was the earl's cupbearer and one of his knights of the chamber. He was called Guy of Warwick, and all men spoke well of him. He had been taught knightly skills by a noble knight called sir Harold of Arderne.

One Whitsuntide, the earl held a splendid gathering of knights, earls and barons from many places. The knights ate in the great hall, the ladies in the private chamber. The earl sent Guy to wait on his daughter, and Guy went into the chamber. Felice asked him who he was, and he told her that his father was the earl's steward. Guy served Felice and the thirty maidens who sat at table with her all that day, and bore himself so well that all thirty of them fell in love with him; but Guy thought only of Felice, whom he loved above all others. As evening fell, he took his leave of her and made his solitary way home.

For Guy was sad at heart, by day and night, and did not know what to do: he lay awake when all around were asleep and thought of his sorrow, for he was deeply wounded by love, and could see no hope for his cause. He was sick for a fortnight, and everyone pitied him and missed his presence at the earl's table. When the great festival drew to an end, Guy returned to the earl's court, where he went in search of Felice. When he found her, he threw himself at her feet and declared his love. But she merely called him foolhardy, and threatened to tell her father if he did not get out of her sight at once. This reception hardly improved Guy's state of mind, and his sickness returned, worse than before. The earl was deeply concerned and sent various doctors to him, but Guy did not tell them the truth about his sickness, and they were unable to cure him. One day, when he had fainted merely because he had looked at the tower where Felice lived, he decided to try his luck once more, whatever the consequences. He found her in the garden, and began by admitting that he was at fault for coming despite her orders, but pleaded that his suffering was too great: he wanted to die for her sake. As he finished, he fainted again, but Felice's companion revived him and brought him to her mistress, who once again rebuked him and told him that he spoke like a fool.

But Felice's companion said: 'Even if my father was a king or emperor, and Guy was a poor man, if he loved me like this, I could not deny him my love.'

Felice promised to help him to win any lady he wished, but Guy declared that there was only one whom he loved, namely herself. Again he fainted, and this time Felice took him in her arms: she said: 'Dukes and earls have sought my hand; how would it look if I married a young and untried squire? When you have proved yourself in battle and have been knighted, then you shall have my love.'

At this, Guy's weakness overcame him again, and he fainted once more, this time for joy; Felice comforted him.

Two days later he was quite recovered, and went to the earl, asking to be knighted. The earl promised to do so, and Guy chose twenty companions to share the ceremony with him. They held vigil the night before, and were knighted according to the ancient ritual: the knighting was followed by a great festival. Guy went to Felice and said: 'Now that I am a knight, beloved, keep your promise.' But she said, 'You have acted too quickly; you still need to earn your knighthood and to prove your valour, before I give myself to you.'

Guy went to the earl, and begged leave to depart in search of deeds of arms in foreign lands, which the earl readily granted him. His father was more reluctant to let him go, saying that he was too young, and not skilful enough in arms, but in the end gave him much gold and three knights, Harold, Torold and Urry, as his companions. They set sail for Normandy and came to a city, where they learnt that there was to be a tournament in honour of the German emperor's daughter. The prizes for the winner were to be a falcon, a greyhound, a snow-white steed and the hand of the emperor's daughter.

Guy determined to enter the lists at the tournament, and duly did so. His first opponent proved to be the emperor's son, whom he unhorsed; and he wreaked havoc on the other knights in the field, including the dreaded duke Otho of Pavia, and two other dukes. His companions did equally well, and on the third day Guy was declared the victor. A squire brought the falcon, steed and greyhound to Guy's lodgings; Guy sent them to earl Rohold, with a message telling of his success. The earl and Guy's mother and father were delighted with the news; meanwhile, Guy and his companions went in search of tournaments in Normandy, France, Germany and Lombardy, and travelled as far as Rome. Here his companions declared that they wished to return to England, and Guy agreed that they should leave the next morning. In due course they reached Warwick, and found earl Rohold, who was delighted to see them back, as were Guy's mother and father.

Guy sought out Felice and reminded her of her promise; he said that he had fulfilled all that she had required, and asked her once more to marry him. But she replied that she would not give him her love until such time as he was deemed to be the bravest knight in the world, the strongest and the best jouster in the lists. Guy was in despair, but swore that he would set out once again to prove that he was the best knight in Christendom. He took his leave of the earl and his parents, who tried to dissuade him from going, saying that he should rest from deeds of arms, and pass his time hunting and hawking. But he would not listen, and left once more for Normandy. This time his search for deeds of chivalry led him into Brittany, Spain, Germany and Lombardy.

One day he was wounded at a tournament at Benevento in Italy; and duke Otho of Pavia, who had hated him ever since their first encounter in the lists, sent his men to lay an ambush for him. When Guy approached, he was riding on a mule because of his wounds, but he heard horses neighing and saw the flash of helmets. Suspecting treachery, he hastily armed himself and mounted a war-horse, and he and his companions prepared to fight. Harold told him to leave them, and get to a safe place, but he refused. In the fight that followed, the duke's cousin and the emperor's son were slain, but Guy lost all three of his companions. In the end, only Guy and one of Otho's men were left alive, and Guy, despite his own injuries, wounded him severely, so that he fled for his life and told Otho of the failure of his plot. Guy mourned the loss of his companions, telling himself that they had died because of Felice, and regretting that he had not taken the earl's advice and stayed at home. He found a hermitage, and had Torold and Urry buried there, while Harold was taken for burial at a nearby abbey. Guy left in search of a hermit who had cured his wounds once before; but after he had gone, a monk who was skilled in medicine looked at Harold, and, seeing that his wounds did not seem mortal, he succeeded in bringing him back to life.

Guy was in due time cured of his injuries, and travelled to the courts of Apulia, Saxony and Burgundy, where he was made welcome. His generosity made him popular with everyone, and many ladies fell in love with him: but all in vain, for he loved only Felice. While he was in Burgundy, he went hunting, and on the way met a pilgrim, who told him that he had lost his lord through the treachery of Otho of Pavia. When Guy asked him the lord's name, he said: 'Guy of Warwick, for I am Harold of Arderne, his companion.' Guy was overjoyed at this, and asked him if he did not recognise him. They told each other their adventures, and Guy took Harold back to the court, where they resolved to travel back to England.

But just as they were about to embark, they heard of a quarrel between the duke of Louvain and the emperor; the latter's son had taunted the duke at a tournament, and had been killed by the duke. Although the duke had been provoked, the emperor was seeking revenge by seizing his lands, and, as the duke was besieged in Louvain, Guy and Harold decided to go to his aid. They defeated an army led by the emperor's steward, but the emperor, urged on by Otho of Pavia, renewed the attack with an even larger force. Otho led the first attack, but was beaten off; he himself was twice nearly killed by Guy, and was severely wounded, and the Germans suffered heavy losses. When the emperor heard this, he himself led the next attack, in which his son was taken prisoner. On successive days the attack was renewed, but Louvain was well defended. After a time, the emperor decided to spend a day hunting in a nearby forest: a spy told the duke of this, and Guy offered to take a hundred men and invite the emperor to dine with the duke in Louvain. His mission succeeded, and the emperor agreed to come. After the feast, the duke begged for pardon on bended knee, saying that he had killed the emperor's son in self-defence. All, except the traitor Otho of Pavia, took the duke's part, and he was forgiven, much to Otho's displeasure. Guy challenged him to a duel, but the emperor forbade them to fight.

Guy and Harold took their leave of the duke of Louvain, and went to the emperor's court. One day Greek merchants came to court, and Guy learnt from them that Constantinople was being besieged by the sultan. He asked Harold what he should do, and Harold advised him to go to the aid of the Greek emperor. Guy set out with a hundred knights and when he reached Constantinople he was welcomed by the emperor, who offered him his daughter's hand in marriage. Guy's first sally was against the sultan's cousin, whose head he cut off and sent back to the city. A fierce fight ensued, with heavy losses on both sides, but in the end the Saracens fled. Guy pursued them, and wounded their leader, Astadart, who escaped on a swift horse.

When he returned to Constantinople, the emperor once more offered him his daughter's hand, and said that he would like him to be his successor on the imperial throne. This aroused the envy of the emperor's steward, who began to plot against Guy. Before the sultan's next attempt on the city, he first accused Guy, who had been playing chess with the princess while her father went hunting, of trying to rape her; and when the emperor refused to believe the steward, the latter told Guy that the emperor was plotting to kill him. Guy, in a fury, decided to go over to the sultan, but as they were leaving, he and his men happened to meet the emperor, who persuaded them that he had no ill intentions. Guy was put in charge of the defence of the city against the sultan's next assault, which took place on the following day. His strategy was so successful that ten thousand Saracens were killed in the first attack, including the king of Tyre; and although the Greeks had to abandon their position before the next charge, Guy and his men turned the tables on them after a fierce struggle, and the Christians were victorious. When the sultan was told of this, he went to the shrine containing his idols, reproached them for ingratitude, and threw them out.

Morgadour, the emperor's steward, was still attempting to plot Guy's downfall, and now persuaded the emperor to send a messenger to the sultan to challenge him or one of his men to a single combat which would decide the victory. Various knights, including Harold, offered to go, but in the end Guy declared himself ready to undertake the mission, and set out alone. He found the sultan in a splendid tent, marked by a golden eagle, and delivered his challenge; but when the sultan asked his name, he did not conceal it. The sultan, discovering that this was the man who had killed his cousin, ordered him to be seized and thrown into a pit: Guy responded by striking off the sultan's head and galloping away with it. The Saracens pursued him, and had almost captured him when Harold, who had been uneasy about Guy, met them with his followers, and slew a great many of the enemy. The sultan's head was set on a marble pillar inside a brass head, as a warning to the emperor's enemies.

Guy stayed at the emperor's court, and one day he and the emperor went hunting. As they rode through the countryside, a lion appeared, pursued by a hideous dragon. Guy attacked the dragon with his spear, and soon killed it by a thrust under its wing. When he went back to the hunting party, the lion followed him, like a hound, gambolling round him as he rode; and after this he went everywhere with Guy, sleeping in his chamber.

Soon after this, the emperor summoned Guy, and said to him: 'You have done everything that you said you would do for me, and tomorrow you shall marry my daughter.'

In the morning, Guy put on his finest clothes, and went to church in a cheerful mood; he and his company were a fine sight. At the church, kings, dukes and barons awaited his coming, as did the bishops who were to marry the couple. The emperor told them all that he was giving Guy his daughter's hand, and that he was to be emperor after his death. The bishop then approached, bearing the wedding rings; but when Guy saw these, he was reminded of Felice, and suddenly his love for her overcame him; he fainted, and when he regained consciousness he asked the emperor to delay the marriage until he had recovered. The emperor's daughter was disconsolate, for she loved Guy with all her heart. Guy took to his bed, where the lion guarded him and refused to eat for three days because his master was ill.

At length Guy told Harold what troubled him, and asked his advice. At first Harold advised him to forget Felice and to marry the emperor's daughter, but Guy was adamant that he could not do this. 'If that is the case', said Harold, 'do not forsake Felice.'

Guy rose from his bed and went to court, where he was made much of. This aroused Morgadour's envy again, and, finding the lion alone in the garden, he wounded it with a spear thrust: but he had been seen by a girl sitting in an arbour. The lion ran home and died at Guy's feet, much to his sorrow. Guy vowed vengeance, and eventually learned the truth from the girl: he went in search of Morgadour, and found him playing chess. He accused him of killing the lion, and cut off his head. Guy now used this as an excuse for leaving the court, saying that he could not stay in a place where a stranger was exposed to such harm and villainy in return for his good service. The emperor tried to calm him, but Guy went on to declare that if he married the princess, there would be other Greek lords who would be jealous of him. Refusing all the emperor's offers of wealth, Guy left the Greek court with Harold, and made his way back to Germany, and thence to Lorraine.

As they rode through a wood in early May, Guy sent his men on to find lodgings for him in the next town, while he rode at ease in the beautiful landscape. But as he rode, he heard a loud moaning, and found a knight under a hawthorn bush, badly wounded. He asked his name, and who had wounded him, but the knight refused to answer unless Guy would promise to assist him with all his power.

This aroused Guy's curiosity, and he said he would do so. The knight explained that he was Tirry, a duke's son, who had been in the service of the duke of Lorraine, and had fallen in love with Ozelle, the duke's daughter. Like Guy, after he had been knighted, he had gone in search of adventures in order to prove himself worthy of her love, but when he was at Rome, he heard that Ozelle was to be married to Otho of Pavia unless he came to her rescue. He had arrived just in time to carry her off from the church door, but while he rested with her in a forest after their escape, he was wounded by robbers, who took Ozelle with them, as well as his horse. Guy quickly caught up with the robbers and regained Ozelle, but when he went back to the spot where he had met Tirry, the latter had vanished. This time Guy found several knights carrying off the wounded man, led by Otho's steward, and he soon overcame them; but when he went to find Ozelle, she had disappeared again. He went back to the town where his men had found lodgings, and discovered that they had searched for him, and found Ozelle. She and Tirry were reunited, and Tirry was cured of his wounds.

Otho, having failed to avenge himself on Tirry, had turned instead on Tirry's father Aubrey, with the help of the duke of Lorraine. When Tirry and Guy learnt of this, they went to Aubrey's aid. Aubrey, complaining that because of his age he was now 'unmighty and unbold' made Guy commander-in-chief of his men, and they soon engaged in a fierce battle with the duke of Lorraine's troops, whom they defeated, capturing the duke's constable. The next day the duke himself led his army against them, with Otho at his side. Once again, Guy and his men were victorious, and his companion Harold pursued the fleeing Otho; they fought a vicious duel, but Harold was captured. Guy rescued him, and nearly killed Otho, who managed nonetheless to reach his camp.

Realising that he could not defeat Aubrey in the field, Otho now turned to treachery. He persuaded the duke of Lorraine to send messengers to Tirry saying that he was willing to let him marry his daughter if he came to the duke's city. Once they were on the way an ambush would be set: Tirry and his company would be killed, and Ozelle returned to her father to be married to Otho. At first the duke would have none of it, but Otho then said that it would be enough to capture and ransom them, and the duke agreed to the plan. A bishop was sent as messenger, and persuaded Tirry of the duke's honest intentions, despite some misgivings on Guy's part; and they all went to meet the duke in the country between the two cities, except Aubrey, who returned home. Once they had met, after a long ride, they halted to rest; and as soon as they had dismounted, Otho commanded his men to seize Tirry, Harold and Guy as traitors. Guy, despite being unarmed, fought his way out and rode off, pursued by Otho's men. He seized a pole from a passing peasant, and killed the first knight to come up with him; he gave the knight's horse to the peasant in return for the loan of the pole. Guy finally escaped by fording a great river, and his pursuers turned back to face the wrath of Otho. Harold was imprisoned by the duke of Lorraine, who let Otho take Tirry with him to Pavia, but warned him to treat his prisoner honourably. Otho now wanted to wed Ozelle at once, but she persuaded him to allow her a delay of forty days, determining to kill herself before the day came.

Guy, desperate at the loss of his companions, found shelter in a castle at nightfall: this proved to be the home of Amys, a knight who had once been his squire. Amys immediately offered to assemble five hundred knights to help him, but Guy declared that there was no time to be lost and set out alone. He disguised himself and presented Otho with a fine steed; then, having made the duke's acquaintance, he claimed that Tirry had slain his brother, and he was seeking revenge. The duke made him Tirry's jailer, and Guy was able to smuggle food to him. One of Otho's men discovered this, but Guy killed him, and told the duke that his man had been trying to betray him by helping Tirry. When he managed to tell Ozelle who he was, she fainted for joy, as the wedding was set for the next day. Guy promised that he would rescue her, and he set Tirry free, sending him to Amys, who made him welcome. Otho, meanwhile, had made great preparations for the wedding, and on the appointed day rode to church with Ozelle. Guy rode after him and overtook him: he revealed who he was and accused him of all kinds of treason towards himself and Tirry. Drawing his sword, he killed him on the spot, and carried off Ozelle. One of Otho's men, Barraud, pursued them and challenged Guy to single combat. Guy unhorsed him, at which Barraud slew his own steed in a fury; but Guy refused to renew the fight on foot and made his way with Ozelle to Amys's castle, where she and Tirry were joyfully reunited.

They all journeyed to Tirry's home, and when the duke of Lorraine heard of their arrival, he sent Harold to them with a message, saying that he regretted his involvement in Otho's treachery and wanted to be reconciled with them. When Harold approached they were out in the open fields, and at first suspected a surprise attack; but as soon as they realised who it was, their suspicion turned to delight. Once at the court of Lorraine, the reconciliation took place; the duke gave Tirry Ozelle's hand in marriage, and bestowed the greater part of his duchy on him.

Guy now determined to return to England, much to Tirry's sorrow: Tirry offered him rich rewards, even his own earldom, if he would stay, but Guy longed to see his beloved, and insisted on departing. When he landed in England, accompanied by Harold, he came to Winchester, where the king received him nobly. While Guy was at court, news came one day – as he was playing chess with the king – that a dragon was laying waste the countryside. Guy at once undertook to slay the monster, but insisted on setting out alone. When he found the dragon, he attacked it with his spear, but the spear broke on the dragon's scaly hide; his sword made no impression either, and the dragon wrapped its tail round him, breaking two of his ribs. But Guy succeeded in cutting off the tail and the dragon roared in anguish. He realised that no weapon, even of the best steel, could harm the dragon's body or head, but at last succeeded in driving his sword in between the dragon's wings and giving it a mortal wound. The beast was sixty feet long, and Guy cut off its head, sending it to the king at York.

After all his wanderings, Guy at last reached his home, to find that his father had died long ago, and that he was now lord of Wallingford. He gave his lands to Harold, and rewarded his other companions, before making his way to Warwick. Here the earl welcomed him with open arms, and he at last saw Felice again. He told her how he had refused the emperor's daughter for her sake, 'for on you was all my thought'; she in turn said that she had been wooed by kings and dukes, but had refused them all, because Guy had taken her love with him. A few days later, the earl told his daughter that it was time she married; and Felice, having asked for three days' grace to think the matter over, finally told her father that she would wed no one but Guy. Her father warmly approved her choice and offered Guy her hand. The wedding was soon arranged, and the festivities lasted for a fortnight.

But the couple's hard-won happiness was destined to be very brief. A little more than a month after their wedding, Guy returned from a successful day's hunting, and in the evening climbed one of the towers to admire the beauty of the landscape. As night fell, he watched the stars in the clear sky, and thought how God had made him a great man, famous for his deeds. Yet all his efforts had been for Felice, and not for God, his Creator, who was the source of all his good fortune. He at once resolved to spend the rest of his life in His service. Felice, searching for him, found him deep in thought. He told her how, in order to win her, he had slain men, stormed cities and given much wealth to his followers; but he had done nothing for God's sake, and for this reason he was determined to live in penance. Felice at first suspected that he had another mistress and wished to be rid of her, but Guy assured her that she was the only one he loved. She tried to persuade him to build an abbey, where holy men might pray for them, rather than go into exile; but Guy was inexorable, promising only to return once he had completed his penance, and telling her to entrust the child she was expecting to the care of his companion Harold when he came of age. When they parted, Felice gave Guy a ring, fainting as she did so, and after he had gone, it was only the thought of her child that prevented her from killing herself. As soon as the earl heard of Guy's departure, he sent men in search of him to persuade him to return, but he was nowhere to be found. Harold set out in pilgrim's garb to seek him, but after travelling through Normandy, France, Germany and Saxony, he returned without having heard any news of Guy.

Guy had made his way to Jerusalem and thence to Antioch, and on the road between the two cities he fell in with a poor pilgrim, who told him that he was an earl, but that he and his fifteen sons had been captured by the Saracen king Triamour and had been imprisoned for twelve years. A little while before, Triamour's son and the son of the sultan of Egypt, Triamour's ally, had been playing chess: they had quarrelled, and Triamour's son had killed the sultan's son. The sultan had declared that he would only pardon Triamour if he or his champion would fight a gigantic warrior from the sultan's army. Neither Triamour nor his men were prepared to meet this Goliath in the field, and in despair he had summoned Jonas and had asked him if he knew of a Christian champion who might take up the challenge. If he could find someone, he would be released and richly rewarded. Jonas had named Guy of Warwick and his companion Harold, and had journeyed to Warwick to find him, only to discover that Guy's whereabouts was unknown, and Harold was in search of Guy.

Guy, without revealing his identity, offered to undertake the combat. Jonas was doubtful, as the stranger, though tall and well-built, seemed very thin and ill-kempt. Guy assured him that, feeble as he might look, God would strengthen him and give him the victory. When they came before the king, the king was also doubtful, particularly as Guy still did not reveal his true name. In the end, the king asked Guy to undertake the combat, and offered him rich clothes and money; but Guy would have neither, merely saying that as long as he had his fill of meat and drink, that would be sufficient.

At length the day of the combat, which had been fixed for thirteen months after the original challenge, came; and Guy was armed as richly as possible. His helmet was the one that Alexander had won from Porus; he had Hector's own sword, and a shield that nothing could damage. His opponent, the giant Ameraunt, had a sword which belonged to Hercules; more important, he was huge and powerful, and Guy thought he was the devil incarnate. The fight began, and Ameraunt killed Guy's horse, throwing Guy to the ground. Guy, praying to God that he might not be shamed that day, quickly recovered, and slew the giant's horse in turn. The fight was long and fierce, and both men were knocked down in turn. As the heat of the day rose, the giant grew very thirsty, and asked Guy to be allowed a moment's truce so that he could drink from a nearby river, promising that he would let Guy do the same if he wished. Guy granted this, but when he held the giant to his word a little later, the giant refused to allow it, because he had wounded Guy and thought that he had the advantage. He called on Guy to surrender, saying that he wanted to destroy Triamour, and would spare Guy's life if he did so. But Guy said that it was not the custom of his country to surrender, and fought on. The giant then offered to allow Guy to drink if he would tell him his true name; but when Guy did so, the giant once more went back on his word, saying that he hated him above all other men because he had slain his kinsmen. Guy went into the river all the same, and managed to secure a drink as they fought. It was now nearing evening, and the battle had lasted all day: at last Guy managed to strike a decisive blow, and cut off the giant's right arm, followed by his left arm, and finally his head. Triamour was thus cleared of guilt, and Jonas and his sons were set free. Guy, refusing all the wealth and honours offered him, first by Triamour and then by Jonas, visited all the saints' shrines in the country around, and then made his way to Constantinople.

Meanwhile, Felice had devoted herself to charitable works: since Guy's departure she had never been seen to smile. When her son was born, she named him Reynbrun, and as soon as he was old enough, entrusted him to Harold to be educated. While Reynbrun was with Harold, some Russian merchants came to Wallingford one day, and gave Harold presents to gain his favour. They saw Reynbrun playing in the hall and were struck by his beauty: they decided to kidnap him, and, with the porter's help, succeeded in doing so. They left for London, and took ship for Russia, but a violent tempest struck their ship near the Russian coast and carried them to Africa. Here they gave Reynbrun to the king, to gain his favour, and the king's daughter begged that he should be brought up in her chamber. Meanwhile Harold searched everywhere in vain for Reynbrun, and was in despair when he could not find him. At the same time, other troubles befell him: he was one of king Athelstan's most trusted advisers, even though he was only a knight and not a great lord, and at a council meeting duke Merof accused him of selling Reynbrun to the Russian merchants. Both Harold and his steward Edgar challenged Merof to single combat, but the king would not permit them to fight. When Harold returned home, he entrusted his estates to Edgar, and went overseas in such of Reynbrun. He travelled almost as far as Constantinople, but a tempest drove him to the African coast, where he was captured by the Saracens and thrown into prison. Merof, hearing of Harold's departure, attacked his estates, but was driven off with heavy losses by Edgar.

Guy had been in Constantinople, and now determined to return to England. As he travelled through Germany, he met a pilgrim in a sorry state, almost starving, who had obviously seen better days. After some talk, the pilgrim revealed himself as Tirry, though he failed to recognise Guy. Otho's cousin Barraud had used his influence to imprison Tirry for having caused Otho's death, and his friends had only been able to obtain his release on condition that he found Guy, who was to fight for him to prove his innocence. But he was unable to find either Guy or Harold, and had only one day left before he had to appear at court again.

Guy fainted at this news, but Tirry thought it was merely the falling sickness (which we would call an epileptic fit). Still maintaining his disguise, he agreed to go with Tirry to the emperor's court at Speyer to see what he could do. On the way, Tirry felt weary and went to sleep, and as he slept, Guy saw a creature like a white ermine come out of his mouth and disappear into a nearby hill; it soon returned, and Tirry awoke, saying that he had dreamed that he had found a dead dragon with a great treasure heaped around it and a bright sword in the nearby hill, and also that he had slept in Guy's arms. Guy took it as a good omen, and insisted on going to look in the hillside. They found the treasure and the sword just as Tirry had dreamt; Guy took the sword, and left the treasure to Tirry.

That night they reached Speyer, and the following day they went to the emperor's court, where Guy succeeded in picking a quarrel with Barraud, who challenged him to fight for Tirry in the supposed absence of his champion. Guy accepted the challenge and asked the emperor for armour, which he was given. On the following day, the emperor's daughter herself armed him, and he took the dragon's sword: everyone asked whether this was really the poor pilgrim they had seen yesterday. Tirry was the only man in the city who did not go to see the combat; a priest found him praying in a church and thought that he must be a holy man. The battle lasted until nightfall, when the combatants were parted. Barraud was to be guarded by four barons, while the emperor himself cared for the pilgrim. But Barraud sent four of his cousins to seize Guy, whom they found fast asleep. They carried him, still on his bed, to the seashore, and threw him into the sea. Guy thought he was about to drown, and mourned his failure to rescue Tirry, when a fisherman in a small boat found him. Guy told him his story, but said he did not know how he came to be in the sea. The following morning, the pilgrim was of course nowhere to be found; and the emperor accused Barraud of having had him killed. He said that unless he produced the pilgrim, he would hang him; Barraud replied that he would gather an army in Lombardy and attack the emperor. But at that moment the fisherman came to court and told everyone how he had found the pilgrim. The emperor sent for the latter, and the battle started again. Barraud wounded Guy in the face and broke his shield, forcing him to the ground; but Guy leapt up and attacked him fiercely, cutting off his right arm and then wounding him in the body, so that he soon died of his injuries. Guy was sorry that such a stalwart knight should have been so treacherous, and the onlookers said that Barraud must have been descended from a Saracen.

Tirry was now acquitted of all blame, but he was not present at the fight, and Guy at length found him in a church and said that the emperor wanted to see him. At first he thought that the pilgrim had betrayed him, but Guy soon explained that the emperor's intentions were friendly, and that Barraud was dead. The emperor said he would make him his steward in Barraud's place, and Tirry and the pilgrim returned to seek Ozelle, who had hidden herself for fear of Barraud. They all returned to Tirry's castle, and Tirry had the dragon's treasure fetched, which he offered to the pilgrim. Guy, however, refused it all, and soon took his leave of Tirry to return to England. Tirry accompanied him for a short distance, and when they were quite alone, Guy revealed his identity. Tirry was sorry that he had failed to recognise him, and tried to persuade him to return with him, but Guy refused. He commended his son to Tirry and asked Tirry to help him if he could ever do so; then the two friends parted, never to meet again.

Guy at last returned to England, where he found that the Danish king had sent a champion to challenge king Athelstan, saying that either Athelstan had to do homage to him or find a knight who would fight the Danish warrior, a giant called Collebrand. Athelstan held a council to discuss the danger, but could not find anyone to take up the challenge. When Guy, whom no one had recognised, heard this, he asked where Harold was, as he was the man to take up the challenge. He was told that he had gone in search of Guy's son Reynbrun, who had been kidnapped by foreign merchants, and that his mother Felice spent her time in doing good works, feeding the poor, founding abbeys and 'making bridges and causeways', but praying every day that she might see Guy once more. Guy made his way to Winchester, where he was met by the king: the king had dreamt the previous night that an angel had told him to go to the north gate, where he would find a pilgrim who would undertake the combat for him. He begged him to stay with him and to fight for him, and Guy readily promised to do so. Messengers were sent to the Danish king to accept the challenge, and Guy made ready for the appointed day. But no armour large enough for him could be found, until he said that he had heard that there used to be a knight at Warwick called Guy, who was very tall: perhaps his armour might do. A request was sent to Felice for the loan of the armour, which she readily granted; she had kept it carefully, and it was as good as new.

Thus equipped, Guy appeared at the appointed place and time: when he arrived, he knelt and prayed for God's help, while the kings swore an oath to observe the conditions of the duel: if Guy won, the Danes would never return to England in the lifetime of their king, but if Collebrand won, Athelstan would owe homage to the Danish king. Collebrand appeared: he was so tall that no horse could bear his weight, and he always fought on foot. For the first time in his life Guy was afraid, but he opened the attack by throwing three javelins at Collebrand; the third broke his helm. Collebrand's first assault killed Guy's horse, and Guy was thrown to the ground; he leapt up and fought so fiercely that sparks flew from Collebrand's armour. He wounded the giant in the shoulder, but after a further exchange of blows, his sword broke. Collebrand called on Guy to surrender, but he refused, saying that the giant should lend him a weapon. Collebrand said that he would do no such thing, but before he could stop Guy, the latter seized one of his great axes. Collebrand tried to strike him, but the blow was badly aimed, and he dropped his sword, at which Guy cut off his right arm. The giant, unable to fight with his left hand, soon fell victim to his own axe.

Athelstan and the English nobles were overjoyed, and led Guy into the city in solemn procession. Athelstan offered him great rewards, but Guy refused everything, and would not tell anyone his name. At length he agreed to reveal his identity to the king, provided that Athelstan would come with him a mile or two outside the city, with no other company. The king agreed, and Guy told him who he was, but swore him to absolute secrecy. Athelstan was astonished by this, and once more offered him wealth and power: Guy would have none of it, asking only that if Harold returned from his travels, Athelstan would treat him with honour. The king went back to Winchester, and, although his companions questioned him about the pilgrim, he steadfastly refused to tell them the secret.

Guy now made his way back to Warwick, but he was so changed in appearance that even here he went unrecognised. He lived among the poor men of the town, to whom Felice gave meat and drink every day, and one day was among those summoned to the castle. His appearance attracted attention, and he was invited to return each day, and to speak with the countess after dinner. But Guy instead left the town at once, and found a nearby hermitage, whose occupant had recently died, at a place called Gibcliff. When Felice asked after the stranger, she was told that he had disappeared.

Guy's life as a hermit was as holy as it was brief; for soon afterwards he fell ill, and the archangel Michael appeared to him in a dream, telling him that he would die in a week's time, and Felice forty days later. Guy resigned himself into God's hands, and sent his page to Warwick with the ring that Felice had given him long ago, when they had parted. The page came into the castle hall and knelt before the countess, saying that he had come from the pilgrim who had been there a little while ago, and that he was living in a hermitage in the forest. His lord had told him to bring her a ring, which he presented to her. She recognised it at once, and asked to be taken to Guy immediately. She set off on her palfrey, with a great company following her, and found Guy at the point of death. He opened his eyes, and raised his hands to her, and kissed her, but was unable to speak. They embraced each other, but Guy's spirit departed at that moment; St Michael took it, like a white dove, to God in heaven, where they sang 'Gloria in excelsis'.

Felice the beautiful mourned Guy, and wanted to bury him at Warwick; Guy's body gave out a sweet savour, which healed the sick, and which God granted in honour of his great deeds and holiness. But despite the efforts of thirty knights, the body could not be moved from the hermitage, and he was buried there. Felice refused to leave the spot, and died there forty days later; she was interred at her lord's side.

But the tale does not end there; for we have not yet learnt of the fate of Harold and of Reynbrun, son of Guy and Felice. The lord who had captured Harold was attacked by a powerful king, and, learning of Harold's reputation for prowess, released him on condition that he fought for him in his war. This he did with such success that he regained all the land that his captor had lost, and carried the war into the enemy's territory. He almost captured the king himself, but was prevented by a young knight, with whom he fought a fierce duel. Harold demanded to know his name, but the young knight refused: a little later, however, the latter, who had never met such a strong adversary, agreed to tell him, on condition that he was told the other's name in return. The youth proved to be Reynbrun, who had been knighted by the Saracen king, and they went together to Harold's lord and asked permission to return home.

On the way home, they came to a castle in a lonely stretch of land, which proved to be that of Guy's old companion Amys, who had been exiled by Barraud's intrigues because of his friendship for Guy, and was now living in what his wife called 'a land full of elves'. Amys had fallen out with an elvish knight, and had been captured by him, and his wife despaired of seeing him again. Reynbrun at once offered to rescue him, and set out to the hill where Amys had disappeared. He rode in through a wide gate which shut behind him, leaving him in darkness; but soon he saw a bright light, and found himself in a landscape with a jewel-clad palace beyond a river. He crossed himself and rode his horse into the river; his steed swam across with him and he entered the palace, which was deserted. After a long search, he found Amys, and rode off with him, seizing an elvish sword as he went. The lord of the palace soon appeared in pursuit of them, and after a fierce duel, Reynbrun had him at his mercy and was about to kill him, but the elvish knight offered to give him all his wealth and to release all his prisoners if he would spare him. Reynbrun refused his riches, but accepted the release of the prisoners, and they all escaped with Reynbrun and Amys. On their return to Amys's castle, they heard news of Barraud's death at the hands of the unknown pilgrim: the emperor had restored Amys to his former estates, and he was free to return home.

Harold and Reynbrun next came to Burgundy, which they found wasted by civil war. They learnt that the most redoubtable warrior in the conflict was to be found defending a mountain pass, where he challenged all comers, providing them with armour if they had none, and taking the goods of merchants who came that way. Reynbrun determined to challenge him, and a violent battle ensued; Reynbrun admitted that he had met his match, and asked the knight his name. If he would surrender, they would be friends for ever. To this the knight replied that he was sure of killing him, and would kill his companion as well, whom he took to be

Reynbrun's father. The fight was continued, until Harold intervened and advised the stranger to surrender, lest they should both be slain. When Harold addressed the stranger, the latter began to quake like a leaf and demanded to know who he was. Harold said that he must first reveal his own name; and he proved to be Aslak, Harold's own son, who had been searching for him ever since he disappeared in quest of Reynbrun. With this reunion, the quests and adventures were at an end: the three knights returned to England, where Harold took up his lands at Wallingford again and Reynbrun received the homage of his vassals as earl of Warwick.

31. BEVIS OF HAMPTON

Our next 'ancestral romance' probably also started as a compliment to a noble family, in this case William de Albini, the earl of Sussex, who had recently been granted the honour of Arundel. It lacks the religious element of Guy of Warwick; like King Horn, it hardly touches on the real world, and was all the more popular for it: it is mentioned in Provençal songs of the mid-twelfth century, though the first surviving version is an Anglo-Norman text of the end of that century; what follows is based on the later English translation. Versions of the story were almost as widespread as those about Arthur, and it turns up as far afield as Norway, Russia and Italy. The poet reflects the prejudices of his audience: Bevis slaughters the citizens of London, of whom the barons were deeply suspicious because they stood outside the feudal hierarchy and made their money through trade. And he echoes their enthusiasms: Bevis's horse Arondel is an important figure throughout the poem, and his delightful final injunction to pray for Arondel when the horse dies, 'if a man may pray for a horse', was clearly a popular line. The catalogue of slain enemies is less appealing, but Bevis's occupation is to be a warrior, and this is, in the poet's view, the best measure of his success.

LISTEN, lords, and I will tell you a story, more cheerful than a nightingale's song, of a knight called Bevis and of his father, sir Guy of Hampton. Sir Guy lived too long without marrying, and he was an old man when he took as his wife the beautiful daughter of the king of Scotland. But before her marriage, this proud and strong-willed girl had loved the emperor of Germany, who had often sent messengers to her father and had gone himself, asking for her hand. But the king gave her to sir Guy, and in time they had the boy, Bevis, a brave and handsome child; he was only seven years old when his father was killed.

For the lady had grown weary of her lord and laid an evil plan to bring him to his death by treachery. She sent for her messenger, and promised him gold and knighthood if he would not betray her. When he vowed to do her will, the lady was very glad. 'Go quickly to Germany', she said, 'and greet the emperor. Tell him to be ready with his company on the first of May, for love of me, in the forest beside the sea. I will send my lord there so that he can kill him; when he has done so, he shall have my love.'

The messenger sailed for Germany, and the wind that took him there was all too good. He found a man who told him where the emperor was; he went to him, and knelt before him, as custom required, and gave him his message. The emperor was delighted by the news, and gave the messenger a horse laden with gold. The messenger returned to

Southampton, and told the lady how the emperor was ready for the meeting in the forest.

The lady was happy; on the first of May, she lay in bed and told her lord that she was so ill that she thought she would die. Sorrowfully the earl asked if anything could help her; she said, treacherously, that the flesh of a wild boar that lived in the forest by the sea would cure her of her fever. The earl vowed that he would capture the boar. Mounting his horse, he hung his shield by his side, put on his sword and with three companions started on his way. When he reached the forest the emperor was waiting for him. He rode out boastfully and cried: 'Yield, you old fool! I will hang you by the neck and your son as well, and I shall have your wife for my lover.'

Sir Guy spurred his horse; he had been a powerful fighter in his time, and he struck the emperor with his spear and threw him to the ground. 'Traitor!' he cried; 'do you think because I am old I am afraid?' He drew his sword and would have killed the emperor, if a great number of knights had not come and killed both Sir Guy and the three who were with him. Then the emperor sent word to the lady, and she told him to come to her chamber.

Bevis was overcome with grief, and he wept bitterly. 'Mother, you may be beautiful, but if wild horses dragged you to pieces, I would cheer them on,' he cried. 'You have killed my father and it is not the time to play the wanton now. One thing I swear: if ever I bear arms and come of age, I will kill all those who killed my father.'

His mother struck him on the side of the head and the child fell down. His tutor, Saber, a knight from his own family, loyal and strong, took Bevis and carried him to his own house. When the mother sent word that Bevis should die, Saber had a pig killed, and sprinkled the child's fine clothes with the blood as if he had been cut to pieces. Saber meant to show these to the lady. Out of fear of what might happen to the boy, he clothed him in rags, and sent him to look after his sheep until the feasting was ended. He promised that in a fortnight Bevis should be sent to a wealthy earl in the south who would teach him courtesy and guide him till he came of age.

While Bevis was a shepherd boy on the downs, he looked toward the town and the tower that should have been his. Hearing the trumpets and drums and the noise of rejoicing, he angrily seized his stick and started forth. At the tower he begged the porter to let him in. 'Go home, you son of a wanton, you truant,' said the porter, 'or you'll regret it.'

'Before God,' said Bevis, 'a wanton's son I may be, but I am not a truant.' He lifted his mace in a fury, and struck the porter to the ground. Then he went into the hall and looked round him. 'What are you doing here, with that lady in your arms?' he cried boldly to the emperor. 'It is my mother whom you are embracing – take her, but get out of here.'

When the emperor said, 'Be silent, fool,' Bevis was almost mad with rage. In spite of everyone there, he struck the emperor three times on the head, so that he fell unconscious. His mother cried, 'Seize the traitor,' but the knights sympathised with the child, and let him go; Bevis went as fast as he could to find Saber, and told him what he had done. Then his mother came to Saber's house, and though he swore Bevis was dead, she said the knight would suffer if she was not taken to the boy. Bevis heard his master threatened, and cried: 'Do not harm him for my sake. Here I am!'

His mother took him by the ear – she would have been happier if he had been dead – and summoned four knights. 'Go down to the harbour,' she said. 'If you can find a pagan ship, sell this brat to them. I do not care how much or how little you get, but sell him into heathendom.'

The child's heart grew cold, when the knights took him and sold him to Saracen merchants, but he had no choice but to go with them. They travelled to the land of king Ermin, whose wife Morage was dead, but who had a young daughter, Josian. Who could describe that girl? No one had ever seen such a beautiful, gentle being; she was learned too, though she was ignorant of the Christian faith. The merchants went to king Ermin and presented Bevis to him as a gift to secure his favour; the king was very pleased with him and thanked them many times. 'I never saw a boy more handsome,' he said. 'Where were you born, boy, and what is your name?'

Then Bevis told his name and how his father died and how he would avenge him; and the king said: 'I have no heir other than my beautiful daughter Josian. If you will forsake your God and worship the lord Apollo, I will give you her in marriage, and you shall succeed me on the throne.'

But Bevis answered: 'For all the silver or gold that is under heaven, nor for your beautiful daughter, I would not ever forsake Jesus, who so dearly bought me.'

The king loved him the more for that, because Bevis stood in fear of no man. 'While you are a boy,' he said, 'you shall be my chamberlain, and when you are dubbed a knight, you shall be my standard-bearer in every battle.' Bevis agreed to this, and the king loved him as a brother, as did Josian. By the time he was fifteen years old, there was no knight or squire so bold as to dare to ride against him.

The first battle Bevis fought was on Christmas Day. He was riding on his horse Arondel, with fifteen Saracens beside him, when one of them asked what day it was. 'I have no idea,' said Bevis, 'for I was only seven when I was sold out of Christendom.'

The Saracen laughed. 'I know this day well enough; it is the first day of Christmas, when your God was born. For that Christian men make more joy than men here in heathen lands.'

'I still remember something of Christendom,' said Bevis. 'On this day I have seen many a noble knight armed for the tournament, and if I was as strong as my father Guy was, I would for my Lord's love fight with each one of you.'

The Saracens cried out: 'Brothers, listen to the young Christian hound boasting that he would overthrow us all. Shall we kill the traitor?' They pressed hard around him and wounded him badly. When he felt his injuries, Bevis plucked up heart, and, wrenching a sword from a Saracen's hand, he struck some of them so that their heads flew into the river and some fell beneath their horses' feet. He killed them all, and their horses galloped riderless home. Bevis himself rode back, his wounds bleeding on each side. He stabled his horse and, going to his chamber, fell unconscious on the ground, just as news was brought to Ermin that Bevis had harmed his men. The king swore he should be killed, but Josian begged that Bevis should be fetched to tell his own tale.

Now Josian called to her two knights and sent them to ask Bevis to come to her. But in his chamber he lifted up his head and looked at them so frightfully with his glittering eyes and gloomy brows that they were beside themselves with fear. 'If you weren't messengers', he cried, 'I would kill you. I will not stir from here to speak with a heathen dog. She is one, and so are you. Get out!'

The knights hurried out, glad to escape, and told Josian: 'We would not want to see him again, not if you gave us the whole kingdom.' But she said she would see that they were safe, and went back with them. 'For God's love,' she cried to Bevis, 'speak to me,' and she kissed and comforted him, so that his sorrow vanished, and they went together to her father. Bevis told him how the quarrel began and showed his forty grisly wounds. Then the old king said: 'I would not have you dead, Bevis, for all the lands I possess. Daughter, try to heal, as best you can, this brave man's wounds.' Then the girl took Bevis to her chamber, and had baths made which were so effective that in a little while he was restored to health, and was as fresh as a falcon for a fight.

It was at this time there was a wild boar in the district, which everyone feared, for he was totally unafraid of the knights who hunted him. Five tusks grew out of his mouth, each five inches round; his flanks were hard and strong and his bristles were huge. One night, as Bevis lay in bed, he decided to try his strength alone against the creature; and in the morning he had his horse saddled, put on his sword, took up his spear, hung his shield by his side, and started for the wood; Josian watched him go, filled with love. When he came to the wood he tied his horse to a tall thorn-tree and blew three notes on his horn. In front of the boar's den he saw the bones of dead men. 'Come out, you fiend,' he said, 'and fight me.'

The boar saw him, and, with his bristles on end, he stared at Bevis with hollow eyes. Bevis's spear broke on him, for the boar's hide was as hard as flint; then he drew his sword and they fought until evensong. By the grace of God, Bevis struck off two tusks and part of his snout. At that the boar roared so loudly that men heard it as far as king Ermin's castle; but soon Bevis cut off its head, and, sticking it on his spear handle, blew a flourish on his horn, for sheer joy at his success in the hunt.

Now there was a steward in king Ermin's service, who was very jealous of Bevis: he armed twenty-four knights and ten foresters, and took them into the wood. Bevis knew nothing of this, and was riding on his way in peace when the steward cried: 'Attack him and kill him.' Then Bevis would have drawn his sword, but he had left it where he killed the boar. In desperation, he pulled the boar's head off his spear and fought with the head. Presently he won a mighty sword called Morgelay, and with it he cut the king's steward in two and killed the others. All this was seen by Josian as she stood alone in her tower. 'O Lord Mahomet,' she cried, 'how strong Bevis is! If I had the whole world, I would give it away if he would marry me. O sweet Mahomet, counsel me, for I am in love with him, and Bevis does not know it. But unless he loves me, I shall die.'

As she said this, Bevis left the wood and went home with the boar's head, which he gave to Ermin. The king was glad for that, and thanked him many times, but that was before he learnt that his steward was dead.

It was a year after this battle with the boar that there came to Ermonye a king named Brademond, who hoped to win Josian as his wife. If she were not given to him, he boasted, he would kill Ermin and, after taking the girl for his own, give her to a carter. Ermin took counsel with his knights, and at the plea of Josian, who said, 'If Bevis were a knight, he would defend you,' the king dubbed Bevis, and gave him a shield with three azure eagles and a ground of gold with five bright tassels of silver. He girded Bevis with the sword Morgelay, and Josian brought him a fine banner. When he had put on his quilted jacket, she brought him his hauberk which was so well fashioned that no blade could pierce it; and after that she gave him the swift horse Arondel.

Bevis leaped into the saddle, and his army, thirty thousand and fifteen, with bright banners and shields, followed him. Brademond came out against them, his banner borne by king Redefoun. Bevis spurred Arondel on with his golden spurs and struck Redefoun through both sides, so that he fell dead. 'You would have done better to stay at home,' said Bevis, and shouted to his army to attack. By sunset, he and his men had killed sixty thousand of the enemy. Brademond fled along the coast, till he came on two of Bevis's knights, whom he would have held and ransomed for a great sum. But Bevis rode after them and dealt Brademond a blow on the helm so that he fell to the ground. The king begged for mercy, and offered Bevis sixty walled cities with their citadels if he was allowed to escape.

'No, by St Martin,' Bevis answered, 'I have sworn to serve king Ermin,' and he made Brademond swear never to make war on the king, but to pay him tribute each year. When Brademond had done this, Bevis let him go, though he was to regret it later. Then he rode home to tell the king. Ermin was overjoyed, and he told Josian to take off Bevis's armour and to give him food. The girl did not hesitate, but led him to her chamber; she herself gave him water in which to wash his hands. When he had eaten, and was sitting there on her couch, she told him all that was in her heart. But Bevis went away angry and ashamed, because she called him churlish when he would not listen to her declaration of love.

Bevis vowed never to see her again, and the girl was in despair; she felt as if the tower was falling on her. She sent Boniface, her chamberlain, to tell Bevis she would make up for anything she had said. But when he came, Bevis said: 'Tell her that you had no success here, but for bringing the message, here is a white cloak, bordered with Toulouse silk and laced with red gold.'

Then Boniface returned and told the girl that she had not done well by insulting so noble a knight. When she learned who had given the mantle, she said: 'No one who was not generous at heart would give a messenger such a gift. Since he will not come, I will go to his chamber myself.'

Bevis heard the girl come and pretended to be asleep. But when she cried, 'Have pity on me, my love! Men say a woman's bolt is soon shot. Forgive me and I will forsake my false gods, and for love of you become a Christian.' He answered, 'I will have pity on you indeed, sweet lady,' and kissed her.

But for this he almost died, for the two knights he had rescued from Brademond went and told king Ermin that Bevis was sleeping with Josian. Ermin thirsted for revenge on Bevis, so the traitors said he should make Bevis ride to Brademond's city, making sure that he had neither Morgelay nor Arondel with him, and carrying a letter to the king which would cause his own death. Everything went according to plan, and Bevis arrived in Damascus. It was about midday, and seeing a great multitude of Saracens come from a temple, he rushed in and killed their priest and threw their gods in the fen. Then he rode to the castle gate, and going into the hall he gave the letter to Brademond himself.

Brademond was terrified, but he opened the letter and read it. Then, traitor that he was, he summoned twenty kings to welcome Bevis, and, while he held the knight's hand, he called: 'As you love me, throw this man to the ground.' They crowded round him like a swarm of bees, and in a moment Bevis was brought down. Brademond gave orders that he should be bound to a great stone and cast into a prison a hundred and twenty feet deep, where he was to be given only a quarter of a loaf of bread each day. In the prison there were a mass of snakes and newts and toads, which were always trying to kill the knight with their poison. But he killed them all with a spear handle he found at the prison door. He also used it to kill a flying adder – it was coal-black with age, and it fell. As it did so it bit him on the forehead and he almost died of the wound.

For seven years Bevis lay in chains suffering these torments, with little to drink and less to eat. One day, when he was faint and in deep distress, he made a desperate prayer to Jesus and his mother Mary. The gaolers heard him; and one of them lowered a lamp and, taking his sword, went down on a rope and struck Bevis so that he fell to the ground. 'Alas!' cried the knight, 'if I had had my good horse Arondel, and Morgelay, my sword, when first I came here, I would have taken on the whole of Damascus. Now the meanest wretch of all can knock me down. But I swear by my salvation that I will be avenged.'

Bevis broke the gaoler's neck with his fist, and when his fellow called down from above, Bevis disguised his voice and said, 'Come and help kill the thief,' and then he cut the rope off as high as he could reach. The gaoler came down, and, when he came to the end of the rope, Bevis thrust the sword through his body. For three days Bevis lay in his chains neither eating nor drinking, for the dead gaolers were the men who had brought his food. But at last Christ granted his prayers, and his chains broke and the great stone fell from his waist. Climbing up the rope, he went to the castle and found no one awake. In a room under a watch tower he saw lighted torches, and going there found the door unfastened and twelve knights asleep who were meant to be guarding the castle. He quietly went in and armed himself in the best armour he could find, took a good sword and spear, hung a shield around his neck and hurried out to the stable, where he surprised and killed the men who kept the horses. Then he chose the best horse he could find, saddled it and rode off, calling loudly to the porter: 'Wake up, man; you ought to be hanged and drawn. The gates are open, Bevis has escaped from prison, and I have been sent to catch the traitor, if I can.' The porter opened the gates at once; Bevis rode out and headed towards Ermonye.

But he had only ridden seven miles when he was overcome with sleep. He tied his horse by the reins to a chestnut-tree and fell asleep; he dreamed that Brademond and seven kings were standing over him with drawn swords. Terrified, he leaped on his horse and in his confusion rode toward Damascus. There he was seen by king Grander, whom Brademond had ordered to recapture Bevis. Grander rode on Trinchefis, a very valuable horse, and there were seven knights with him. He called to Bevis: 'Surrender, you fox, or I will kill you with my own hands.'

'God help me,' answered Bevis, 'it would win you no honour if you killed me. I have not eaten or drunk for four days, but if I must, I will do my best to defend myself.'

They rode at each other and fought so fast that sparks flew from their armour. Finally Bevis cut off king Grander's head, and killed the seven heathen knights. Then he mounted Trinchefis and rode off; but Brademond pursued him with all his host. They drove Bevis to the edge of a cliff, where he either had to leap into the raging sea or fight all the hosts of heathendom.

But he was saved by a miracle. Bevis prayed to Christ and set spurs to his horse Trinchefis, who leaped into the deep sea and in a day and night crossed to the other shore. When the horse came out and shook himself, Bevis fell to the ground for hunger. He rested for a little while before he remounted and rode till he came to a castle. Here he begged the lady of the castle for food.

The lady answered: 'Leave this place, or you will get the worst kind of dinner. My lord is a giant who believes in Mahomet and Termagant. He hates Christians like dogs, and kills them.' 'By God,' said Bevis, 'I swear that, whether he is friend or foe, I will eat if there is anything to be had.'

At this the lady was angry and went to tell her lord. The giant, who was thirty feet tall, took an iron bar in his hand; when he saw Bevis, he looked hard at him, because he recognised his horse. 'Where did you steal Trinchefis?' he shouted, 'he belonged to my brother Grander: you must have killed him. I will not let you go before I have avenged him.' He aimed a great blow at Bevis, but it struck Trinchefis on the head, and the horse fell dead.

'That was an evil blow,' said Bevis, 'to spare me and kill my horse.' He drew his sword and they gave each other more blows than I can count. The giant at last shot an arrow through Bevis's shoulder, and the blood ran down to his feet. When Bevis saw his own blood, he was almost mad with rage: he ran to seize the giant and broke his neck. Then he went into the castle and ordered the terrified lady to give him food. He made her taste every dish and drink the wine first, in case she should try to poison him. When he had eaten enough, he bound up his wound with a piece of cloth and ordered her to saddle a horse for him. She was glad to do this to get rid of him; and Bevis leaped into the saddle, without touching the stirrups.

Bevis rode on until he came to Jerusalem. There he told his whole story to the Patriarch, who enjoined him not to take a wife unless she was a virgin. Bevis promised: early the next morning, he rode away, intending to go to his lady Josian and to the land of Ermonye where he had met with so much sorrow. As he went on his way he met a knight whom he had known in the old days in Ermonye, and they embraced and asked each other how they were. When Bevis asked about Josian, the knight said: 'Josian has been married against her will: it is seven years or more since the rich king Ivor became her husband. He has got the sword Morgelay and the good horse Arondel. But I have never seen such entertainment as on the day Ivor tried to ride to Mombrant on Arondel. The horse was in a furious temper; he ran away with the king and threw him on a moor, almost killing him. He was later captured and tied up, but he has never left the stable since then, and no one has dared to ride him.'

Bevis was delighted by this news about Arondel. 'If Josian had been as true as my horse,' he thought, 'I might yet overcome my sorrow.' He asked for directions to Mombrant, and turned and rode northward until he came to that rich Saracen city: there is no other like it. Outside the town he met a pilgrim, whom he greeted, and asked him if he knew where the king and queen were. 'She is in her chamber', the pilgrim answered, 'and he is hunting with fifteen kings.'

'Pilgrim, be my friend,' said Bevis, 'and give me your dress in exchange for mine and for my horse.'

The pilgrim said, 'That seems a good exchange to me!' Bevis dressed the pilgrim as a knight, and for his staff and cloak, he gave him his horse. Disguised as the poorest of men, Bevis went to the castle gate, where he found pilgrims of many kinds. He asked them what they were doing. They told him that every day of the year at noon, the queen gave alms to all whom she found there; it was in memory of a knight, Bevis of Hampton, that she was so kind to pilgrims.

But it was still early, so Bevis wandered about inside the castle walls; and as he walked, he heard weeping and crying. It was Josian, who for seven years had mourned his departure every day. When she went to the gate where the crowd of pilgrims was, Bevis waited so that he was last among them. Josian saw him but did not recognise him. 'You look like an honourable man, with courteous manners,' she said: 'you shall sit at the head of the table today.'

They were served with food and spiced wine, and when they had finished the queen said to each of them: 'Did you ever hear on your travels anyone who spoke of a knight called Bevis of Hampton?'

Everyone said that they had not heard of him until she asked the pilgrim who had just arrived, 'What about you?'

'I knew that knight well,' said Bevis: 'at home I am an earl, and so is he. When we were in Rome, he told me about a horse called Arondel, and I have spent much money in seeking it. I am told that it is here. If you ever loved that knight, let me see the horse.'

So Josian, with Boniface her chamberlain, led Bevis to the stable door, and when the horse heard the voice of his lord, he broke his chains and came into the courtyard, where he neighed proudly and joyfully.

Josian was alarmed and said, 'Many men will be killed today before that horse is caught again.' Then Bevis laughed and said: 'I can catch it all right, if you will let me, and no one will be hurt.' 'Catch it,' she said, 'and lead it into the stable and tie it where it stood, and you shall be well rewarded.'

Bevis went to the horse, which did not move from the spot, and threw himself into the saddle. Then the girl recognised him. 'O Bevis, my dearest love,' she cried, 'let me ride home to your own country with you. Remember how you took me as your wife when I forsook my false gods. You have your horse, and I will fetch your sword.'

But Bevis said: 'I have suffered much because of you, and have been imprisoned for seven years: should I love you for that? And the Patriarch made me vow only to wed a virgin, and you have been a queen beside your husband for seven years.' 'Noble lord,' she said, 'take me home with you, and if you do not find me a virgin, you can send me back to my foes naked but for my shift.' For Josian had worn a ring for all those years, for love of Bevis, which prevented anyone from making love to her.

Bevis agreed to this, and Boniface advised him what to do next. He went to the gate and stood among the throng of beggars in his pilgrim's cloak, with his staff and scrip by his side. His beard was yellow and long, but everyone said they had never seen such a handsome pilgrim. When Ivor returned from hunting, his nobles were full of admiration for Bevis and the king called to him. 'You have travelled far, pilgrim. Tell me news of wars and of peace, but tell me the truth.'

Bevis answered: 'Lord, I am come from Jerusalem, from Nazareth and Bethlehem; I have been in Sinai, India, Europe, Asia, Egypt, Greece, Sicily, Saxony, Friesland, Sidon and Tyre, Africa and many an empire, but everywhere there is peace except in the land of Dabilent, where there is war with all its sorrows. The lord of the land is being attacked by three kings and five dukes who have defeated his army, destroyed his people, taken his cities and burnt his towns. They have driven him to a castle on a cliff by the sea, and are besieging him there.'

Ivor was deeply dismayed. 'It is my brother who is shut up in that castle. We must take up arms and set out quickly to help him.' Ivor and his fifteen kings armed themselves, and went to the city of Dabilent. At home Ivor left an old king, the knight Garcy, to guard Josian, his queen.

Bevis wanted to leave at once, but Boniface said: 'Beware of this old king Garcy; he is skilled in magic, and can see everything you do in his gold ring. I will send for a wild herb that grows in the wood which I know, and put it in some Rhenish wine. Whoever drinks it will sleep afterwards for a day and night.'

Sir Boniface did this, and at dawn they took as much silver and gold and other treasures as they needed, and went on their way. When Garcy woke, he was amazed to find that he had slept for so long. He looked into his ring, and saw there the queen escaping with the pilgrim. He and his knights armed quickly and set out in pursuit. Then Bevis said to Boniface: 'Guard Josian well, and I will stand and fight them. I have rested for many days; now I will fight for as long as I can, and defeat them all, if God will help me.'

But Boniface persuaded him to go into a nearby cave, where Garcy would not be able to find them. The king and his army returned home empty-handed, but Josian and Bevis stayed in the cave without food or drink for two more days. They were very hungry and Josian told sir Bevis to go out in the forest and hunt deer to provide them with food.

Bevis left the lady in Boniface's care, and went off into the forest. But as soon as he had gone, two raging lions came, and though sir Boniface armed himself and fought them in battle, he was not strong enough; one lion killed his horse, the other killed Boniface himself. Josian fled into the cave and the lions gnashed at her angrily, but they could do her no harm, for it is in their nature that they cannot harm a king's virgin daughter. Soon Bevis came back from his hunting with three deer, and he found the horse gnawed to the bone and Josian gone. He nearly fainted for sorrow, and searched for her from cave to cave till at last he saw her sitting terrified between the two lions. She cried to him for help, and said she would hold one while he killed the other. But Bevis told her to let it go. 'I would not want anyone to say that I killed one lion while a woman held the other. You would only reproach me with it when we came to my country.'

Then she released the lion and Bevis attacked them both. It was the greatest of all the battles I have heard described in romances. Before Bevis realised it, the lioness had torn his hands and the lion had broken his armour and given him a great wound in the thigh. So fierce and strong were the beasts that Bevis had difficulty in defending himself; but in the end he killed them both. He rejoiced and thanked God for his victory, though he mourned the loss of Boniface. Then he mounted Josian on a mule and they rode on for a little while, till they met Ascopard, a ugly-looking giant, who was thirty feet tall. He had a great beard, and his brow was a foot wide; his club was the trunk of a small oak-tree.

Bevis was astonished by this sight, and asked his name and if men of his country were as tall as he was. 'My name is Ascopard,' he answered: 'Garcy sent me here to bring back this lady. I am Garcy's champion and was driven from my home because I was so small. There everyone used to hit me and call me a dwarf, because I was so little and delicate. But here in this land I am the tallest of all. And now, Bevis, I shall kill you if I can.'

Bevis spurred on Arondel and gave Ascopard a blow on the shoulder, and the giant, in striking back, slipped and fell. Then Bevis dismounted and was about to cut off Ascopard's head, but Josian pleaded for him, saying she would see that he did not betray them. So Ascopard did homage to Bevis and became his page, and the three of them journeyed on together till they came to the seashore. They found there a large ship filled with Saracens, who wanted to go into their own land, but they had no pilot. They thought Ascopard would guide them, for he was a good pilot if he had to be; but as soon as he was aboard, he drove them all out. He carried Arondel to the ship on his arm, and then Josian and the mule. They set sail, and made a good voyage to Cologne.

Now when Bevis came into Cologne, he found the bishop there was his uncle, Saber Florentine. The bishop welcomed him and asked who his companions, the beautiful lady and the broad-browed giant, might be; and Bevis told him and asked that they be christened. Then the bishop on the day after that christened Josian and had a large cask made for Ascopard. But when the bishop tried to put him in it, he leaped on the bench and cried: 'Priest, are you trying to drown me? The devil curse you, I am too big to be baptised.'

It was after Josian's christening that Bevis fought with a dragon, a battle greater than any other except for those of sir Lancelot du Lac, who fought with a fire-breathing dragon, and sir Guy of Warwick, who killed a dragon in Northumberland. This dragon at Cologne lived under a cliff; eight tusks stood out of his mouth, the least seventeen inches in circumference; he had a mane like a horse, and his body was like a wine cask, twenty-four feet from shoulder to tail, and the tail itself was sixteen feet long. In the sunlight his wings shone like glass, and his sides were brazen, and his breast hard as stone. He was the most horrifying creature on earth.

Bevis awoke one night and heard someone weeping piteously. 'The venom has touched me', the voice said, 'and I lie here and my flesh rots from the bone.' Bevis asked who it was that cried out; he was told that a knight, a valiant fighter, had encountered this vile dragon, which had thrown venom over him. 'Lord Christ,' said Bevis, 'can anyone kill the dragon?' Everyone said that it was impossible, but Bevis said: 'Ascopard, where are you? Shall we go and kill the dragon?'

'I will go happily,' he answered. So Bevis put on good armour, and rode out of the gate with Ascopard at his side. They talked of many strange things until the dragon, lying in his den, saw them and made a noise like thunder. This terrified Ascopard, who did not want to go any further. 'I am tired,' he said. 'I must have a rest.' 'It would be a shame to turn back now,' said Bevis and spurred on his horse. The dragon opened his jaws as if to swallow him; at the sight of this, Bevis wished that he could have hidden in the ground. He struck the dragon on the side with his spear, but it shattered into five pieces, like hail on a rock. He drew his sword, and they fought till dark night. Then Bevis had such a thirst he thought his heart would break. He saw water near him, and though the dragon attacked him so fiercely that he broke his shield in two, Bevis leaped into the well.

Now this was a magic well: a virgin who lived in that country had bathed in it, and the water was so holy that the dragon did not dare to come within forty feet of it. Bevis was very glad when he saw this, and he took off his helmet and cooled himself. Then he left the well and the dragon attacked him, spitting venom on him so that he became like a foul leper; his skin rankled and swelled. His arms began to crack, his vizor broke, and his hauberk fell into a thousand pieces. The dragon smashed the knight's helmet with his tail; twice Bevis fell and twice he got up again; the third time he went into the water, where he lay upright, not knowing whether it was day or night. The water healed his injuries and he prayed aloud: 'Help me, you Son of God, for unless I kill the dragon before I leave this place, no man alive in Christendom will ever kill it.'

Now the dragon heard that and flew away as if he were mad. Bevis ran after him and struck the dragon so hard, that he cut its head. It took a hundred blows to sever the head from the body; then the knight cut out the dragon's tongue and put it on the truncheon of his spear. He rode back to Cologne, where he heard bells and clergy and priests singing: someone told him that it was a dirge for sir Bevis.

'I think not, by St Martin,' said Bevis, and he went to find bishop Florentine. When the bishop saw him, he and all the people thanked Jesus and accompanied Bevis into the town in triumph.

One day sir Bevis said to his uncle: 'What shall I do about the emperor of Germany, who has my lands at Hampton?' The bishop replied, 'Nephew, your uncle Saber is in the isle of Wight, and every year for your sake he attacks the emperor of Germany, because he thinks you are dead. I will give you a hundred good men, and you will go to Saber and give him my greetings. And if you are in trouble, send word to me and I will help you fight against the emperor with all my men.'

Bevis went to his lady Josian. 'Sweetheart,' he said, 'it is time for me to get my revenge on my enemies, and, somehow, win back my inheritance. My uncle, the bishop Florentine, and Ascopard, my good page, will look after you.' 'If Ascopard is guarding me', she said, ' I shall not be afraid of anyone. But come back to me as soon as you can.'

Now Bevis and the men the bishop gave him set out and travelled until they came within a mile of Hampton. 'Lords,' Bevis said, 'are any of you bold enough to go to Hampton and find the emperor, and say: "There are a hundred knights newly arrived from France who will fight for you with spear and lance." Always speak French, whether in jest or earnest, and say that I am called Gerard, and that I am sure of victory if he will hire me.'

A man who spoke French came forward, and he went to the castle and said everything just as Bevis had instructed him; that night the emperor and Bevis sat together at supper.

'Gerard,' said the emperor, 'before I married my lady, she had an earl as her husband, and they had a son – a proud, rude fellow. His father was from a bad family, and this boy, as soon as he was of age, sold me his inheritance and spent his money in shameful ways. Since then he has left England. Now his uncle Saber, who is a powerful man, has come from the isle of Wight, claiming the inheritance and doing me much harm. If you can kill him, I will be happy to pay you.'

'Lord,' replied Bevis, 'I have good knights here, but they are unarmed. If you will arm my knights and give them good horses, and send a hundred of your own men yourself, and prepare ships for me as well, I promise that I will attack Saber in such a way that you will soon hear of a strange success.'

The emperor did as he was asked, and the knights set sail. Bevis put his knights and the emperor's men in alternate places; as soon as they were in midstream, each of Bevis's knights threw his neighbour overboard, so that not one of the emperor's knights was left alive.

Meanwhile Saber watched them come from his castle, and, seeing a mass of banners, was afraid that the emperor had come with an army. Bevis guessed this, and he raised a streamer on the topmast with his father's escutcheon, which Saber had often borne into battle. Saber recognised it and understood that Bevis had come to England. He and his knights went down to the landing-place and made them all very welcome; and Bevis told him how he had tricked the emperor. Then he asked for someone bold enough to go to Hampton, and a brave fellow offered. He crossed over in a boat and greeted the emperor as he sat at supper.

'Lord emperor,' he said, 'this is my news. That knight who had supper with you last night sends his greetings; his name is not Gerard, but Bevis, and he claims the lordship of Hampton. He has come to avenge his father's death and to kill you in the fashion you deserve, without honour.'

When the emperor heard this, he wanted to kill that messenger. He threw his knife at him, but his aim was bad and it struck his own son who was standing in front of the table. 'That was an evil present,' cried the messenger, 'but a worse fate awaits you!' He set spurs to his horse and galloped out of the hall. When he returned to the isle of Wight, he told Bevis how the boy had been killed, and Bevis was glad.

Meanwhile Josian had been staying at Cologne with Bevis's uncle. Here an earl named Miles fell in love with her, and tried to win her with fair words. But Josian would not hear, and when his wooing turned to threats she said: 'While I have Ascopard with me, I am not in the least afraid of your boasting, however angry you are.'

So earl Miles laid a trap: he had a letter written, apparently from Bevis, ordering Ascopard to meet his master at a castle on an island three miles across the river. So Ascopard hurried there, but when he was on the other side of the river and inside the castle gate, they tied him securely with ropes. Then earl Miles said to Josian: 'Now that there is no one to prevent me, I will marry you tomorrow against your will.' And he kissed her and sent for his barons and knights to come and join in the feasting.

Now Josian sent a messenger to Bevis telling him what was happening, but the night passed and day came and the wedding took place. At nightfall the next day, supper was prepared, and a splendid meal it was. Then the earl ordered Josian to be led to her chamber, and she was sitting on her bed when he came to her with a great company of knights, with spiced wines and and ready to make merry. But Josian did not want this, and said: 'Lord, grant me one thing: let no man or woman come in here, but lock them out if you love me.'

The earl agreed, and drove out the knights and squires, the ladies and the girls, and locked the door, little suspecting what was in store for him. He turned to Josian, saying: 'Lady, I have done as you asked, and now I shall have to take off my own shoes, which I have never done before.' Now there was a curtain on a rail round the bed, so that no one could see the bed. Josian thought quickly and making a noose with a towel, she threw it about his neck. She pulled it up over the rail and left him to hang there all night as she lay in her bed, though she was terrified at what she had done. At daybreak the barons rose, and some of them went hunting, while other men went to church or to work. As midday drew near, the earl's men were astonished that the earl stayed so long in bed, and at noon, one of the boldest knocked on the door so hard that it came open.

'Wake up, sir Miles,' he called, 'you have slept so long that your head must be aching. Lady, you should make him some medicine.' Josian said, 'I have dealt with him so his head will never ache again. Yesterday he wedded me wrongfully; tonight I have hanged him for it. Do what you like with me; he will never harm another woman.'

There was much mourning in the city, and that very day Josian was sentenced to be burned in a great barrel. A stake was set up outside the walls and the fuel made ready. Ascopard watched the people from the other side of the river, and, astonished to see his mistress at the stake, he broke down the castle wall and plunged into the water. He swam towards the boat of a fisherman, who thought he was a fiend and jumped out for fear. Ascopard rowed to land, where he met Bevis, whom he told of Miles's treachery, and together they ran to where Josian was. Blessed be the priest who heard Josian's confession, because he kept her long enough for them to arrive! She was standing by the fire almost naked when Bevis and Ascopard came in haste. They killed all the guards, and Bevis snatched up Josian onto his horse and rode away. They embarked and sailed to the isle of Wight, where Saber met them, and rejoiced to see them.

Bevis and Saber now sent out a summons to many countries to gather a huge army; the emperor, hearing of it, was terrified. His wife comforted him, saying he should send for his army from Germany and ask her father in Scotland for help. Messengers took his letters, and in May the king of Scotland came, and thirty thousand knights as well. The emperor told them how Saber had long troubled him, how Bevis was threatening to win the land and that the giant Ascopard was with him. 'But, lords,' he cried, 'let us arm ourselves and besiege them. Ascopard is powerful, but many hands make light work.'

They quickly set out, and positioned their camp and siege-engines around Saber's castle. When the emperor heard the blowing of Saber's horn, he and the king of Scotland led out their armies to battle. Saber rode out of the castle followed by three hundred bold knights. Sir Morice of Mounclere rode against him and Saber cut him down. Then Bevis charged into the fray on Arondel, and meeting his stepfather the emperor, he unseated him. Bevis would have beheaded him with his sword Morgelay but the emperor's men came strongly to his rescue. Bevis grew angry, and he summoned Ascopard, who crushed both men and horses as he came to his master. 'The emperor is riding on a white horse,' said Bevis. 'If you can bring him to me in the castle, I will reward you richly.'

The giant laid about him in such a fashion that no armour could withstand his blows. He struck the king of Scotland so that horse and man fell dead, and he went to the emperor and caught his horse's mane, and led him against his will to the castle. Saber and Bevis put the rest of the enemy to flight, and they returned to the castle with great joy and gladness. Bevis had a cauldron filled with pitch and brimstone and hot lead, and when it was all boiling, put the emperor in it. His soul went elsewhere!

From the castle window Bevis's mother saw her husband in the cauldron, and was overcome with sorrow: she fell and broke her neck. Bevis was as glad of that as of his stepfather's death; but he was most joyful of all when all the lords of Hamptonshire did fealty and homage to him. He summoned his uncle from Cologne, and the bishop came and wedded Bevis and Josian. It was a royal feast, with all manner of food and drink, served with great ceremony.

Now that he had recovered his lands, Bevis went to king Edgar in London, and was made a marshal, as his father had been before him. About Whitsun, a great race was held: the distance was seven miles. Bevis raced on Arondel, and although two knights had started before the rest without anyone noticing, he beat them all and won the prize, a thousand pounds in gold. With this money and other revenues, Bevis built the castle of Arondel: everyone praised his horse because it had run so well. Edgar's son asked Bevis to give it him, and when the knight would not, he planned to steal the horse. Now it is the custom for all kings to go crowned into the hall at dinner, and for every marshal to go before them, his staff in hand. It was while Bevis was doing this that the king's son went to Bevis's stable. But he went too close to Arondel and the horse kicked out with his hoof and dashed out the prince's brains. There was much mourning at this, and the king wanted to have Bevis hung and drawn by wild horses, but his lords would not allow it. Bevis had served him, they said, and all they could do was to hang the horse.

Bevis vowed to leave England rather than lose his horse; he went straight to Hampton, and took Terri, Saber's son, end Josian and Ascopard with him into exile. But when Ascopard learned what was happening, he hurried to Mombrant to betray Bevis. When a man falls into poverty, as Bevis had done, he has few friends. Ascopard told king Ivor that all the time he had been away he had been seeking for the queen, and had undergone many hardships. 'Now, however, I will bring her to you, if you give me forty strong knights. Bevis is a powerful fighter in any battle and I need help to attack him.' Ivor agreed to this, letting Ascopard choose the knights and arm them before they set out.

Bevis, meanwhile, was riding through France and Normandy: as they passed through a wood, Josian went into labour. Bevis and Terri made a lodge and carried her into the shelter, since this was all they could do. 'For the love of God, dear lord,' she said, 'go with Terri and leave me with Our Lady.'

The knights went out and left her so that they did not hear her pain, but they went too far. She had just given birth to two boys when Ascopard came with his Saracens, and despite her sorrow and suffering they made her go with them. They mocked her, and beat her with their naked swords. Josian, full of sorrow, remembered the knowledge of physic and surgery that she had learned from the great masters at Cologne and Toledo; she picked a herb that was growing by the wayside which made anyone who ate it seem like a foul leper. They had not gone five miles before her appearance changed, and when she was brought before king Ivor he ordered Ascopard to take her away to a castle in desert country. There for half a year the giant fulfilled her needs and was her warden.

Bevis, when he returned to the shelter, found nothing except two fine children. He fainted for grief, and Terri, bitterly cursing Ascopard's treason, comforted him. They cut their cloaks of ermine, wrapped the children in them, and then mounted their horses and rode away. In the wood they met a forester, to whom Bevis gave one child, telling him to call him Guy and to keep him for seven years. Bevis gave the other to a fisherman, and named him Miles. He and Terri rode on till they came to a great city and stopped at a great inn. When Bevis looked out of the window, he was amazed to see the street full of horses and armour: he learned that a great tournament had been proclaimed. Whoever was declared the best knight would have the king's daughter and the whole land of Aumbeforce. 'Shall we take part in the tourney?' asked Bevis, and Terri cried, 'By St Thomas of India, when did we lag behind?'

The knights were up with the lark the next morning, and equipped themselves well. They bore royal arms, with the three bright azure eagles and the golden field flowered with red roses. As they rode through the city famous noblemen marvelled at their arms, for they had never seen such shields before in that country.

The trumpets blew and the knights rode into the lists. They set about each other furiously with spear and truncheon, and no one recognised another. Knights were hurled from their saddles and horses were won and lost. The son of the king of Asia thought he would win the prize, but Bevis brought him down and he was carried home upon his shield. Bevis defeated a noble duke, Balim of Nubia, and seven earls as well and Terri won many a good horse as well. After the fighting was over, the lady of the land wanted to take Bevis for her husband: when he refused, she said that for seven years he should be her husband in name, and then if his wife returned, she would marry Terri.

Meanwhile in Hampton, Saber dreamt that Bevis was wounded, and his wife interpreted the dream as meaning that Bevis had lost his lady or child. Saber dressed twelve knights in pilgrim's dress; their staffs were made of long steel pikes. They crossed the sea of Greece, helped by fair wind and weather, and came to the land where, men said, Ascopard held the queen. They found the castle in the wilderness, where they attacked the giant and cut him in pieces; and they released Josian from prison. She soon made her skin clear again with an ointment; Saber dressed her in a pilgrim's habit and they set out together to search for Bevis.

But Saber fell gravely ill in Greece, and for half a year he could not rise from his bed. Josian, who had learned the art of the minstrel in Ermonye, bought a fiddle for forty pence and wandered about the city every day to win her sustenance. When Saber recovered, they set out again, and came at last to where Bevis had lived since the tournament. At the gate Saber saw his son Terri and asked him for a gift.

'Pilgrim, I will give you a feast', said Terri, 'for love of my father, for you are very like him.' 'That was what your mother said,' answered Saber, and then Terri took him in his arms and they were both joyful. Josian was dressed in fine clothes and brought to sir Bevis, the dearest message he ever received. He sent for their children and everyone rejoiced: Terri married the lady of the land soon afterwards, as had been agreed when Bevis won the tournament.

Then Bevis went to Ermonye where Ivor was besieging Ermin in his city. Bevis forgave the old king his misdeed, and he fought with and captured Ivor. Ivor had to send to Tabefor, his chamberlain, for a great ransom – sixty pounds of red gold, four hundred cups of pure gold and as many of brass – before he was released from Ermin's prison. After this

Ermin fell sick, and before he left this world he crowned sir Guy, Bevis's son, and gave him his kingdom. Together, after Ermin died, Bevis and Guy made Ermonye a Christian land.

Ivor, swearing to make Bevis atone for the ransom he had won from him, stole Arondel, but Saber cunningly won back the horse. Then Ivor came with a great army to besiege Bevis. He called to him: 'Sir Bevis, you have a great many men in there, and I have as many brave knights out here. There will be great slaughter if we allow a battle to begin. Will you agree to fighting me in single combat? If you kill me, I will bequeath all my lands to you.'

They held up their gloves as a sign of agreement, and, putting on their armour, they crossed over to an island near that city. Bevis prayed for help to Mary and her Son, and king Ivor to Mahomet and Termagant; then they rode together angrily and their spears went through their shields. Their girths broke and both fell to ground. They grappled with each other and used their daggers, fighting from nine in the morning until sunset. About midday Ivor cut off the gold circlet from Bevis's helmet, and the sword slipped down and shaved off half his beard, but did not harm his flesh. The Saracens cried, 'Bevis the Tall will soon be brought low!' but in fury the Christian knight struck Ivor on the shoulder with Morgelay, so that it pierced his armour. Ivor fell to his knees, then, jumping up, gave Bevis such a blow that more than a quarter of his shield flew into the river. But before he could draw back his hand, Bevis cut through his shield and cut off Ivor's left hand. Then, though Ivor fought madly, Bevis cut off his right arm and shoulder. 'Have mercy, Termagant, Mahomet, Jove and Jupiter!' cried Ivor: 'save me now or I shall die.'

'Do not call to them', said Bevis, 'but to God and Mary, and be christened before you die. Otherwise you will go the worse way and live for ever in the torments of hell.'

But Ivor answered: 'I shall never be a Christian: my faith is better.'

When Bevis heard that, he knocked Ivor to the ground, unlaced his helmet, struck off his head and put it on his spear. All the Christians who saw that sight thanked God heartily, but the Saracens were terrified. They tried to get back to Mombrant, but Saber made them turn and, with Bevis and his sons, cut them down, so that no one, whether great or small, escaped.

Bevis was crowned king of Ivor's land and the fair and beautiful Josian was queen there for the second time. But one day as they rode by the river, a messenger brought news that king Edgar had taken Saber's lands and disinherited Robert, his son. Bevis at once vowed that he would go with Saber to England: he crossed the sea with sixty thousand knights and arrived at Southampton. Leaving the queen at Putney, he and six knights went across the Thames to Westminster, where he found the king and demanded his inheritance. The king would have made peace, if his steward had not denounced Bevis as a banished man and dangerous.

When Bevis heard that, he was furious and, leaping on his horse, rode away with his knights to Tower Street in London. There he went to dinner while the steward, his foe, with sixty knights, raised a hue and cry in Cheapside and ordered everyone, in the king's name, to capture Bevis.

The people armed hurriedly. They took their staves, barred the gates, and some went up onto the wall with bows and crossbows. Great chains were fastened across every lane and street. Bevis saw the crowd and the innkeeper warned him of the danger. So Bevis armed his six knights and himself and he rode out on Arondel. In the street the steward called to him to yield, but Bevis struck him on the right side and he fell dead on the pavement. 'That will teach greedy men to slander honest lords,' said Bevis.

Then the people attacked Bevis and his six knights on every side, but they defended themselves with all their might and killed five hundred men. With the crowd following, Bevis rode to Cheapside: he would have escaped through Goose Lane, but he was too hemmed in by men on foot with great clubs. His knights were cut to pieces. In that narrow lane Arondel could not turn, and Bevis, praying that the blow would succeed, struck the chain across it and broke it: he rode off with the people following and shouting: 'Yield, Bevis! Yield!'

'I will yield to God in heaven, but not to man while I have my weapons,' answered Bevis. Then he began his great battle against the city. New, fresh companies of men came up to him, but ever Arondel fought fast and loyally, so that he trampled people to the ground for forty feet around. Bevis had soon killed five thousand men there.

News came to Josian in Putney that Bevis was slain. Half-fainting, she sent for Guy and Miles – who gently comforted her – and asked them to avenge their father's death. They knelt and asked her blessing, and then rode in haste to London. At the gate they found men armed to the teeth, but they made short work of them and set the gate on fire. Then they rode on, and just as an evil Lombard hit Bevis with a huge club on his helmet, so that he collapsed on his saddle for pain, Guy drew his sword and struck the fellow down. His brother Miles joined them, and Bevis thanked the Lord that help had come. He attacked the people eagerly, and so many were killed there that the Thames ran blood-red. When night fell they went to London Hall, and Josian was brought there with a great escort. For fourteen nights a feast was held for all who wished to come.

King Edgar was told how Bevis had killed his men, and he mourned them greatly. 'I have lived for a long time without fighting, and now that I am old I can no longer wield my weapons,' he said. 'Since Bevis has two sons, it seems best to let Miles take my daughter and so make peace.'

All this was arranged, and Miles and the girl were married in the town of Nottingham, with a royal feast as befitted such a marriage and a coronation; for it was agreed that Miles should have all England after Edgar died. Then Bevis took his leave, giving his earldom to his uncle Saber. He left his son Guy in Ermonye with good lords to help him rule, and installed Terri at Aumbeforce; he himself went to Mombrant, where he was king.

Now Bevis lived there, with no more griefs or cares, with queen Josian for twenty years, until she fell so ill that it was clear that she was not long for this world. She sent for Guy and Terri to be at her deathbed, and when they were all there, Bevis went to his stable. There he found Arondel dead, and, going sadly back to the queen's chamber, he saw that Josian was at death's door. He wrapped his arms about her body before it grew cold, and they died there together. Guy would not have them buried in the earth, but built a fine marble chapel dedicated to St Lawrence, with golden corners, and laid them both in it; and he founded a house of religious men to sing for them. May God have pity on their souls, and on Arondel's too, if men may pray for a horse!

32. ROBIN HOOD

*The search for the real Robin Hood, like the search for the real Arthur, is
something which will occupy both scholars and amateurs alike for many
years to come; part of the attraction is the insolubility of the historical
mysteries which they pose. Robin Hood has a literary predecessor in* The
Tale of Gamelyn, *which also has an outlaw hero who robs the avaricious
clergy, outwits a wicked sheriff; and is pardoned by the king in the end.
But we know so little of Robin Hood in the middle ages that it is possible
that* Gamelyn *derives from Robin's own tale, rather than the other way
round. In William Langland's* Piers Plowman, *a priest who confesses
that he does not really know the Mass boasts that he knows 'rymes of Robin
Hood'. The outlaw hero, defying the norms of society, is a not uncommon
topic in the medieval period, and by the time the earliest surviving account
of Robin's exploits was set down in the fifteenth century, there were a
number of such stories current.*

*What we know of Robin Hood comes, appropriately for a popular hero,
largely from ballads, most of them written down in the sixteenth and
seventeenth century, and printed in abbreviated form in broadsheets.
Within the last few years, a new seventeenth-century manuscript containing fuller versions of many of the well-known ballads, as well as two
hitherto unknown ballads, has come to light.*

The most famous version of his exploits is A Little Gest of Robin
Hood, *which exists in fragmentary printed versions from the early sixteenth century. It is this which is presented below; the modernisation is my
own, but it has been put into rhyme with great aplomb by Sue Bradbury.*

I

Be still and listen, gentlemen,
That are of free-born blood;
I'll tell you of a good yeoman
Whose name was Robin Hood.

He was as proud an outlaw
As walked upon the ground;
And none so courteous before
Or since was ever found.

He stood one day in Barnsdale,
Leaning against a tree;
And by his side was Little John,
A valiant yeoman he.

504

There also too was Will Scathlock
And Much, the miller's son –
And every inch of his body
Was worth another man.

Then up spake valiant Little John
And said to Robin Hood,
'Master, it's time you went to dine,
For it would do you good.'

But thus brave Robin answered him:
'To dine I've no desire
Till I have met a bold baron,
Or else perhaps some squire,

'And him by deed persuaded
To furnish of the best –
Some bold baron, or knight, or squire
That dwells here in the west.'

Wherever Robin found himself
He had a custom fine –
Three Masses he would always hear
Before he went to dine.

The first was for the Father,
Next, for the Holy Ghost,
The last for Our dear Lady –
For her he loved the most.

His love for Our dear Lady
Kept him from deadly sin.
He'd never harm a company
That any woman was in.

Then Little John said, 'Master,
If we our board would spread,
We need to know what we must do
To earn our daily bread.

'Whither to go, what life to lead,
And what to leave behind,
Where we shall we rob, and where attack,
And where our pleasures find?'

'We shall do well,' said Robin,
'If we together stand;
Though look you harm no farmer
That tills with plough the land.

'Nor shall you harm a yeoman
That through the greenwood goes;
Nor shall you harm nor knight nor squire
If they are good fellows.

'The bishops and archbishops –
Them shall you beat and bind:
Let the high sheriff of Nottingham
Be foremost in your mind.'

'We'll keep your word,' said Little John,
'And learn our lesson straight.
God send us soon a ready guest
For it's already late.'

'Take your good bow in hand,' said he,
'And Much shall lead the way,
Will Scathlock too shall go with you
And I alone will stay.

'Go you up to Sayles,' he said,
'And on to Watling Street,
And wait there for any unknown guest
Whom you may chance to meet.

'Be he earl, or be he baron,
Be he abbot, or a knight,
Insist he come and stay with me
And dine with me this night.'

So up they went to Sayles,
Those valiant yeomen three,
They looked to the east and to the west
But no man could they see.

But then they looked down Barnsdale,
Along a hidden way,
They saw a knight come riding
And met without delay.

He wore a dreary countenance,
And little was his pride:
One foot was in its stirrup,
The other dangled wide.

His hood hung over brow and eyes,
Full simple his array,
A sorrier man there never rode
All on a summer's day.

John greeted him full courteously,
Kneeling upon his knee;
'Welcome you are, most gentle knight,
Welcome you are to me,

'And welcome to the greenwood.
My master will you greet,
For he has fasted full three hours
And now, sir, he will eat.'

'Who is your master?' asked the knight,
John answered: 'Robin Hood.'
'He's a fine yeomen,' said the knight,
'Of him I've heard much good.

'So I'll go in your company,
My brothers, on your way;
Although in Blyth or Doncaster
I'd thought to dine today.'

Forth with them went the gentle knight,
His face was full of woe,
The tears ran coursing down his cheeks
And through his beard did flow.

They brought him to the lodge's door
Where Robin did appear;
Full courteously he doffed his hood
And knelt before him there.

'Welcome sir knight,' said Robin,
'Welcome you are to me,
For I have waited without food,
Good sir, these hours three.'

Then answered him the gentle knight
In words both fair and free;
'God keep you safe, good Robin,
And all your company.'

Then they did wash and dry their hands,
And sat down to their meat:
Of bread and wine they had their fill,
And of the deer did eat.

Both swan and pheasant graced their board,
And fowls from the river's edge,
Down to the smallest birds of all
That breed in briar and sedge.

'Eat gladly, sir,' said Robin,
And he replied, 'I will,
And thank you, sir, it is three weeks
Since last I dined my fill;

'And Robin, should I come again
Into this country,
I'll make as good a feast for you
As you have made for me.'

'I thank you, sir,' said Robin,
'For this my future meat,
And God be praised, no greed have I
Nor care I when I eat;

'But pay before you go,' said he,
'That surely must be right.
By God, it's not the custom
That yeoman pay for knight.'

'There's nothing in my coffer,'
The knight said, 'to my shame.'
Then Robin commanded Little John
To verify the same.

'Tell me the truth,' said Robin,
'So God be part of you.'
'Ten shillings have I,' said the knight,
'And God knows that is true.'

'If that is all you have, sir,
Not a penny will I take.
And if you need more,' said Robin,
'A loan to you I'll make.

'Go forth,' he said to Little John,
'And tell me what you see.
If ten shillings is all he has
Not a penny comes to me.'

Then Little John spread out his cloak
Fairly upon the ground,
And in that good knight's coffer
Ten shillings was all he found.

There on the ground he left it,
And close to Robin drew.
'Well, and what tidings?' Robin asked.
He said: 'The knight speaks true.'

'Pour the best wine,' said Robin,
'Sir knight, you will begin.
I had thought it something wondrous
Your apparel was so thin.

'Tell me one thing,' said Robin,
'And then we'll let it be.
Either you are a knight by force
Or else of yeomanry.

'Or maybe your estate's destroyed –
By enmity and strife,
By debt or lechery,' he said,
'You have misspent your life.'

'Nay, none of those,' the knight replied,
'My ancestors have been
Knights for a hundred winters past,
As God himself has seen.

'But oft it happens, Robin,
That a good man's estate
May fall into disgrace, by God,
And suffer a cruel fate.

'Two years ago, good Robin,
As my neighbours will attest,
I could four hundred pounds have spent
Of coin of the best.

'Now I have nothing', said the knight,
'But my children and my wife.
As God alone has shaped my fate,
So He must shape my life.'

'But how have you lost all your wealth?'
Asked Robin. He replied:
'Through folly and through kindness, sir,
That would not be denied.

'I have a son, good Robin,
That should have been my heir.
At twenty winters in the field
He would joust full fair.

'He slew a knight of Lancaster;
Slew too his squire bold.
To save his honour and his life
All of my goods are sold.

'My lands are pledged in bond, Robin,
For a certain day,' said he,
'To a rich abbot dwells nearby
In St Mary's Abbey.'

'What do you owe?' said Robin.
'Come, tell me but the truth.'
'Sir,' said he, 'four hundred pounds,
The abbot said in sooth.'

Said Robin, 'What will come of you
Should you then fail to pay?'
The knight said, 'Over the salt seas
I'll swiftly sail away

'To see the land where Our Lord lived
And died on Calvary.
And so I'll say farewell, good friend,
For what must be must be.'

Tears then fell from both his eyes;
He would have gone his way:
'There is no other path for me,
So farewell and good-day.'

'Where are your friends?' asked Robin.
'Sir, they now disown
The very man who, in his wealth,
They boasted to have known.

'Like a herd of lowly beasts
My presence now they shun,
And as if they knew me not,
Away from me they run.'

For sorrow then wept Little John
And Much let fall a tear,
Till Robin said, 'Give him good wine,
For that is simple cheer.

'Have you some friend,' asked Robin,
'That might your warrant be?'
He said, 'No friend have I save Him
That died upon the tree.'

'Jest not with me,' quoth Robin,
'For fain such jesting is:
Nor God's, nor Peter's, Paul's nor John's
Warrant need I in this.

'No, by the God that made me,
And shaped both moon and sun,
A better warrant for such a loan
I need, so find me one.'

'In truth I have no other,'
Said the knight, 'lest it be
Our Lady, who until this day
Has never failed me.'

'By God,' said noble Robin,
'If I sought England through,
I could find no better warrant
For the deed that I now do.

'So Little John, come forward;
Go to my treasury;
There count out four hundred pounds
And bring it here to me.'

Out of the lodge went Little John,
Will Scathlock went before,
They counted out four hundred pounds
By eight and twenty score.

Asked Much: 'Think you this is well done?'
John said: 'What else should we
Do for to help a gentle knight
That's come to poverty?

'Master,' then said Little John,
'His garments are full thin.
Pray give the knight a livery
To clothe his body in.

'You have cloth of green and scarlet,
Master, in rich array.
No man in merry England
Has cloth so rich and gay.'

'Three yards of every colour,'
Said Robin, 'grant him so;
And measure it well.' Then Little John
Took measure with his bow.

For every handful that he pulled
He added three feet more.
'You must be the devil's draper,'
Cried Much, 'of that I'm sure.'

Will Scathlock stood by laughing,
He said, 'By God's own might,
To give the knight good measure
Costs Little John but light.'

'Now gentle master,' Little John
To Robin Hood did say,
'You must give the knight a horse
To bear his goods away.'

'A grey courser shall he have,'
Said Robin, 'with saddle new.
He is Our Lady's messenger;
God grant that he be true.'

'And a good palfrey,' added Much,
'Equip him as is right.'
'And a pair of boots,' said Scathlock,
'For he's a gentle knight.'

'What would you grant him, Little John?'
Asked Robin. 'Sir, bestow
Some fine gilt spurs on him, and pray
To bring him out of woe.'

'When may I requite you, sir?'
The knight said: 'Set a day.'
'A year from now, under this tree,
Your debt you must repay.

'And as it would be shame,' quoth he,
'For gentle knight to ride
Without a yeoman, squire or page
To journey at his side,

'I'll lend you my man, Little John,
To serve you in your quest.
In yeoman's place he will attend
And serve you as is best.'

II

Now rode that noble knight away,
His spirits full and good;
And when he looked on Barnsdale
Then blessed he Robin Hood.

And when he thought on Barnsdale,
On Scathlock, Much and John,
He blessed the noblest company
That he had come upon.

Anon up spoke the noble knight,
To Little John said he:
'Tomorrow I must go to York,
Unto St Mary's Abbey

'And to the abbot of that place,
So it be understood,
Four hundred pounds I needs must pay
Or my land is lost for good.'

Now the abbot addressed his convent:
'Twelve months ago', quoth he,
'A knight borrowed four hundred pounds
From this our company.

'This loan he took against his lands:
Unless he comes', said he,
'To pay it on this very day
Forfeit his lands shall be.'

'It is still early,' said the prior,
'The day is not yet sped.
A hundred pounds I'd rather pay
To go straight to my bed.

'This knight is far beyond the sea –
In England is his right –
Hunger and cold are his portion,
And many a sorry plight.

'It would be shame,' the prior said,
'Thus promptly to fulfil
The debt, unless your conscience says
You do the knight no ill.'

'By God and good St Richard,
'You're always in my hair,'
The abbot swore; just then came in
The fat old cellarer.

'He's dead or hanged, you may be sure,
By God who bought me dear,'
He said with glee, 'and we shall have
Four hundred pounds a year.'

So the abbot and high cellarer
Boldly pursued their aim,
And laid before the justice
Of England their whole claim.

The chief justice and many more
Had interests in the debt,
And every penny now they sought
To wrong him even yet.

The abbot and his men spoke up
And charged the knight full ill.
'If he comes not this very day,'
They said, 'we'll take our fill.'

'He will not come,' the justice said,
'That I can plainly state.'
But at that moment, woe to them,
The knight came to the gate,

And there addressed his company,
Putting them at their ease:
'Dress yourselves in the simple clothes
That you wore overseas.'

So thus arrayed in simple clothes
They came to the gates anon,
And met there from the porter
A welcome every one.

'Welcome, sir knight,' the porter said,
'My lord is at his meat,
And so is many a gentleman
That gently you would greet.'

Then the porter swore an oath,
'God's truth indeed,' said he,
'Here are the finest horses
That ever I did see.

'Lead them into the stables;
Let them be eased and fed.'
But the knight refused: 'Till I'm assured
They'll stay outside,' he said.

'Be of good cheer, sir abbot,'
He cried, 'I have kept my day.'
The first words that the abbot spoke
Were, 'Have you come to pay?'

'Not a penny piece,' the knight said,
'By God that created me.'
'A wise debtor,' the abbot said,
'Sir justice, drink to me.

'Why come you?' asked the abbot,
'If your debt you cannot pay?'
The knight said: 'Before God and you,
To beg a longer stay.'

'Your time's up,' said the justice,
'Your land in forfeit goes.'
'Now good sir justice, be my friend,
Defend me from my foes.'

'I'm on the abbot's side,' said he,
'I took his gifts and fee.'
'Now good sir sheriff, be my friend.'
'Nay, before God,' said he.

'Now good sir abbot, be my friend,
And in all courtesy
Till I have settled all my debt
Hold you my land in fee,

'And I will serve you,' said the knight,
'And gladly honour you
Till you have from me four hundred pounds
Of money good and true.'

'By God', then swore the abbot,
'That hung upon the tree,
Wherever else you get your land,
You will get none of me.'

'By the dear God that made me,
And all this world has wrought,
Give me my land, or else', he said,
'It shall be dearly bought.

'God, that was of a maiden born,
Now grant that we succeed.
Full fair it is to find a friend
When a fair friend you need.'

The look the abbot cast was black,
And 'villain' did him call.
'Go,' he said, 'you knight so false;
I charge you leave my hall.'

Then said the gentle knight, 'You lie,
Sir abbot, in your hall,
For villain false I never was,
By God that made us all.'

Then up he got, that gentle knight,
And to the company
He said, 'To make me kneel so long
Is less than courtesy.

'In jousting and in tourney
I have travelled far and wide,
And put myself as far in fight
As any that I spied.'

The justice said, 'What will you give
If the knight should make release?
Or else that land, I dare well swear,
You'll never own in peace.'

'A hundred pounds,' the abbot said.
Said the justice, 'Give him two.'
'By God,' the knight said, 'There's no way
My land shall come to you.

'Though you should give a thousand more
You'll not get your desire,
For my heir there shall never be
Justice, abbot nor friar.'

And going to the table,
Towards that table round,
Out of his bag right there and then
He shook four hundred pound.

'Take back the gold, sir abbot,
That you lent me before.
Had you but shown me courtesy
I'd have repaid you more.'

The abbot ceased his feasting,
He ignored his royal fare;
His head cast on his shoulder,
At the justice he did stare:

'Give me that gold again,' he said,
'The gold I gave so free.'
'Not a penny,' said the justice,
'By God that died on tree.'

'Sir abbot, and you men of law,'
Said the knight, 'I kept my day.
Now shall I have my land again
For ought that you can say.'

Out he went, out through the gate,
He cast off all his care
And put his richest garments on:
The others he left there.

He went his way with merry song,
Or so men tell the tale:
His lady met him at his gate
At home in Verysdale.

'Welcome, my lord,' his lady said,
'Is your land lost for good?'
'Be merry, dame,' the knight replied,
'And pray for Robin Hood.

'His soul should ever be in bliss,
He helped me out of woe.
Had he not shown me kindness
To beggary we'd go.

'Now I have settled everything;
The abbot's had his pay.
That gentle yeoman lent it me
As I came by the way.'

The gentle knight dwelled fair at home
Until, the truth to say,
He'd garnered the four hundred pounds
All ready to repay.

He bought himself a hundred bows,
The strings were fair and tight,
And a hundred sheaves of arrows good –
Their heads were burnished bright.

Each arrow was an ell in length,
With peacock feather flight,
And furnished with white silver –
It was a goodly sight.

He hired himself a hundred men,
Armed and equipped aright,
And he himself rode at their head
Arrayed in red and white.

A lance he carried in his hand,
A page to guide his horse,
And they with many a cheerful song
To Barnsdale took their course.

A wrestling match upon a bridge
He stopped awhile to see;
And there were all the best yeomen
That dwelled in the west country.

A fine white bull would be the prize
For the winner of the fight,
And a great courser, too, with golden
Harness burnished bright.

A pair of gloves, a red-gold ring,
A pipe of wine also:
Whoever should perform the best,
To him the prize would go.

There was a yeoman in that place
Whose worthiness was plain;
Yet far from friends and home was he,
And might well have been slain.

On him the knight had pity,
And seeing how things stood,
He vowed the man would take no harm
For love of Robin Hood.

He made his way into the crowd,
His men they followed free,
With bows drawn back and arrows sharp
To shame that company.

The crowd thrust back and gave him space
To hear what he would say.
The knight then raised his hand on high
And gave that man the play.

Five marks he paid him for the wine,
And broached it on the ground,
He offered there and then a drink
To every man around.

And thus he stayed, that gentle knight,
Until the games were done,
Though Robin waited for his meat
Until mid-afternoon.

III

Be still now, listen, gentlemen,
All who are gathered here,
I'll tell you the tale of Little John
And good mirth you shall hear.

The young men went out shooting
Upon a merry day,
And Little John he took his bow
To challenge them in play.

Three times he loosed his trusty bow,
Three times he split the wood,
So that the sheriff of Nottingham,
Who proud by the target stood,

Right there and then he swore an oath,
Saying, 'By Him who died,
That archer is the greatest man
That I have ever spied.

'Tell me,' he said, 'you brave young man,
What name to you they give,
And in what country were you born,
And where do you now live?'

'Sir, I was born in Holderness,
My mother gave me care;
Men call me Reynold Greenleaf
Who know me from up there.'

'Tell me, Reynold Greenleaf,
Would you come live with me?
Each year I'll pay you twenty marks
And that shall be your fee.'

'I have a master,' then said John,
'A courteous knight is he;
If you can get full leave of him,
Then better it would be.'

The knight relinquished Little John
For twelve months to the day,
The sheriff then a brave good horse
He gave him right away.

So Little John, full craftily,
Became the sheriff's man,
And thus for all the sheriff's tricks
To pay him back began.

'So God me help,' said Little John,
'Now by my faith,' he swore,
'I'll be the vilest servant
That ever sheriff saw.'

The sheriff then went hunting
Upon a fine Wednesday,
But Little John he stayed behind
Alone, his tricks to play.

He lay in bed till afternoon,
No food had he to eat:
'Good steward,' he cried, 'I beg of you
To give me now my meat!

'It's far too long for Greenleaf
Thus fasting to remain;
Therefore I beg you, steward,
My dinner for my pain!'

The steward said, 'No meat or drink
Till my lord comes to town.'
'By God,' said Little John, 'I vow
I'd rather crack your crown.'

Insolently the butler stared
As he stood on the floor,
Then straightway to the buttery
He ran, and shut the door.

But John, he gave him such a tap
He nearly broke his back,
And though he lived a hundred years
He'd not forget that crack.

Then with his foot he kicked the door
Till it burst open wide,
And helped himself to the ale and wine
That he did find inside.

'Since you will not dine,' said he,
'I'll give you so much drink,
That should you live a hundred years
Of me you'll always think.'

Then Little John he ate and drank
Until he'd had his fill;
But in the sheriff's kitchen
Was a cook with a strong will.

'I vow to God,' the bold cook said,
'You are a brazen knave,
Thus to live in your master's house
And all his meat to crave.'

And with these words on Little John
Three lusty strokes he laid.
'You please me well,' cried Little John,
'Such strokes shall be repaid.

'You are both bold and hardy,
To that I can attest.
Before I leave this place, I vow
I'll put you to the test.'

Right there and then he drew his sword;
The cook took his in hand.
Neither thought to turn and flee,
But boldly took their stand;

And there they fought together,
Covering two miles of ground,
But though they fought for nigh an hour
Neither received a wound.

Said Little John, 'In truth and faith,
To God I make my vow,
A better man with sword in hand
Never I saw till now.

'If you could draw a bow as well,
Then should you come with me
To Robin and the greenwood,
And from him take your fee.

'He'll give you twenty marks a year,
And clothe you in green,' said he.
'Put up your sword,' the cook replied,
'And we will fellows be.'

Then the best meat of a doe
To Little John he fed,
And there the two men ate and drank
Their fill of wine and bread.

And when they had both drunk their fill
They pledged right solemnly
That on the very selfsame night
With Robin they would be.

They went into the treasure house
As soon as they were done,
And all the locks of full good steel
Were broken every one.

They took away the silver plate
And all that they could find.
When they had gone, no plate, nor cup,
Nor spoon was left behind.

More than three hundred pounds they took
Of coin there beside;
Then straightway to the greenwood
And Robin they did ride.

'God save you, my dear master,
And Christ you save and see!'
And Robin said to Little John,
'Right welcome you shall be,

'And welcome to the yeoman
That you have brought with you.
What tidings now from Nottingham?
Tell me, what is to do?'

'The proud sheriff greets you well,
And sends you here with me
His cook, and all his silver plate,
Three hundred pounds and three.'

'I vow to God,' said Robin Hood,
'And to the Trinity,
It never was with his goodwill
That these goods came to me.'

Then Little John bethought himself
A crafty trick to play:
Five miles through the wood he ran
Until he found his prey.

There was the proud sheriff
Hunting with horn and hound,
And there before him courteously
John knelt upon the ground.

'God save you, my dear master,
And Christ you save, I vow.'
'Reynold Greenleaf,' the sheriff said,
'Where have you been till now?'

He answered, 'In this forest
A fair sight have I seen;
Indeed, perhaps the fairest sight
That there has ever been.

'Yonder I saw a fine young hart,
And green he was all over;
Round him a herd of seven-score deer
To give the hart good cover;

'And sixty of them had such horns,
As sharp as sharp can be;
Master, I dared not shoot at them
For fear they would gore me.'

'I vow to God', the sheriff said,
'That sight I'd gladly see.'
'Then come with me, dear master,
At once, and follow me.'

The sheriff rode, and Little John
On foot was quick and smart,
And when they came to Robin, cried:
'Lo, sir, here is the hart!'

Then the sheriff stood stock still,
A proud man, and afraid.
'I curse you, Reynold Greenleaf,
For me you have betrayed.'

'You are to blame,' said Little John,
'Master, you did decline
When I was in your service
To let me drink or dine.'

Soon they sat down to supper,
On silver it was served;
But the sheriff was filled with sorrow
When he that plate observed.

'Be of good cheer,' said Robin,
'Sheriff, do not despair,
For the love of Little John
Your life I'll gladly spare.'

When they all had supped their fill
The day was almost sped;
Then Robin commanded Little John
His garments there to shed –

His hose, his shoes, his kirtle,
His coat all furred and fine –
And gave him a green mantle
To wrap his body in.

Then all Robin's brave young men
Under the greenwood tree,
Lay wrapped in green, as he had said,
That the sheriff might them see.

And the proud sheriff only
His shirt and breeches wore;
He lay beneath the greenwood tree
Till his bones ached full sore.

'Be of good cheer,' said Robin,
'Sheriff, in charity;
To lie so is our custom
Under the greenwood tree.'

'It is a harder way of life
Than any monk's, I fear.
For all the gold in England
I would not long live here.'

'For twelve long months', said Robin,
'You shall remain with me.
And, sheriff, I shall teach you
An outlaw for to be.'

'I would not stay another night,'
The sheriff said. 'Instead,
I would forgive you, Robin,
If you cut off my head.

'I beg you, let me go,' said he,
'For holy charity,
And then for ever and a day
I your best friend will be.'

'Swear me an oath,' said Robin,
'Upon my sword's bright blade,
That neither on water nor on land
Shall any trap be laid;

'And should you find a man of mine,
Either by night or day,
Upon that same oath you must swear
To help him if you may.'

Now has the sheriff sworn his oath,
And home at last is gone.
He was as green as is young wood,
Hard as a heap of stone.

IV

The sheriff dwelled in Nottingham,
And, glad that he was gone,
Robin and his merry men
Returned to the woods anon.

'Now let us dine,' said Little John,
But Robin Hood said, 'Nay,
Our Lady must be wroth with me:
She has not sent my pay.'

'Master, doubt not,' said Little John,
'The sun is not yet set.
The knight is true, and I dare swear
He will repay you yet.'

Said Robin, 'Take your bow in hand,
And Much, for company;
Take William Scathlock too; let none
Of you abide with me.

'Go you up under the Sayles
And so to Watling Street;
And wait there for whatever guest
That you may chance to meet.

'Whether he be a messenger,
Or quick with joke and jest,
Or just a poor man, of my goods
I'll give him all the best.'

So on his way went Little John
Full anxious for the knight;
Under his mantle girded was
A full good sword and bright.

And up they went onto the Sayles,
Robin's yeomen three;
They looked to the east and to the west
But no man could they see.

Then, as they looked towards Barnsdale,
Along the road they see
A pair of monks, all dressed in black,
Each on a good palfrey.

Then up spoke brave Little John
And to his friends did say:
'I'll pledge my life that these two monks
Are bringing us our pay;

'So make good cheer,' said Little John,
'And loose your bows of yew.
Look that your hearts be sober,
And your strings sure and true.

'That monk has two-and-fifty men
And seven horses strong:
So royally no bishop rides
In all this land along.

'We are but three', said Little John,
'Who wait here in this place.
But if we bring them not to dine
Robin we dare not face.

'So bend your bows,' said Little John,
'And make their mob to stand.
The man in front – his life and death
I hold here in my hand.

'Now monk or churl,' said Little John,
'No further shall you ride:
Your life, by God, is in my hand,
And here you shall abide.

'Bad luck be on your head,' said John,
'And under your hat no good.
Our master's angry that you keep
Him so long from his food.'

'Who is your master?' asked the monk.
John answered, 'Robin Hood.'
The monk said, 'Of that lusty thief
I never heard much good.'

'Why then you lie,' said Little John,
'And that you will regret:
That yeoman asks you now to dine
And he awaits you yet.'

Much had prepared already
An arrow of the best,
And that the monk should tumble down
He pushed him in the chest.

Of the two-and-fifty yeomen,
There now abode not one,
Except a little page and groom
To lead the horses on.

They brought the monk to Robin's door
Though he was loath to go;
For he should speak with Robin Hood
Whether he willed or no.

Good Robin then threw back his hood
And showed the monk his face.
The monk was not so courteous:
His hood he left in place.

'Master, he's nothing but a churl,
By God,' said Little John.
'What care I for a man like that
Who courtesy knows none?'

'How many men', asked Robin,
'Were with him, Little John?'
'Two-and-fifty when we met,
But most of them are gone.'

'Now blow your horn,' said Robin Hood,
'And call our fellows here.'
Full seven score of yeomen brave
Then marching did appear.

Their scarlet and striped mantles
Bravely they did display;
They came before good Robin Hood
To hear what he would say,

And sit with him at dinner.
Then Robin and Little John
They bade the monk to wash and dry,
And served him food anon.

'Eat well, sir monk,' said Robin.
'I thank you, sir,' said he.
'Where do you make your vows?' they asked,
'And which is your abbey?'

'St Mary's Abbey,' said the monk,
'Though I be humble here.'
'What is your office?' Robin asked.
'Sir, the high cellarer.'

'You are more welcome then, sir monk,
So may we thrive,' said he,
'Give him the best of all our wines
That he may drink to me.

'And yet I marvel,' Robin said,
'Through all this livelong day;
I fear my Lady's anger
That she sends not my pay.'

'Master, fear not,' said Little John,
'You have no need to fear.
The monk is from her abbey; surely
He has brought it here.'

'She was the warrant,' Robin said,
'Between the knight and me,
Of the money that I lent him
Under the greenwood tree.

'So if you come with silver,
I pray you, let me see;
And I shall help you any time
That you have need of me.'

The monk then swore a full great oath
And said, with sorry face,
'Good sir, of such a warranty
I never heard a trace.'

Said Robin, 'Sir, you are to blame,
I vow to God it's so.
For God is held a righteous man,
His Mother is also,

'And you, sir, are their servant,
You cannot tell me nay;
With your own tongue you told me
You serve her every day,

'So you must be her messenger,
And should my money pay;
Therefore I thank you all the more
That you have come today.

'Now, what is in your coffers,'
Said Robin, 'tell me true.'
'Sir, twenty marks; I cannot lie,
Lord strike me if I do.'

'If that is all you have, sir monk,
I'll not one penny take;
Indeed, if you have need of more,
I'll lend it for your sake;

'But if I find that you have more
Then forfeit it shall be.
But of your spending money, monk,
I'll not touch one penny.

'Little John, I bid you go
And tell the truth to me.
If there be more than twenty marks,
The rest shall come to me.'

So John he spread his mantle
As he had done before,
And counted out of the monk's bag
Eight hundred pounds or more.

Then Little John he left it there
And to his master went.
'The monk is true enough,' said he,
'There's double what you lent.'

'I vow to God,' said Robin,
'What did I say to you?
Of all the women in the world
Our Lady is most true.

'By dear and worthy God,' he said,
'If I searched England through,
I'd never find to pay me back
A warrant half so true.

'Now fill his glass and make him drink
To Our Lady's health: indeed,
A friend she'll find in Robin Hood
Should ever she have need.

'And should she need more silver,
Then let her come to me,
And for this token that she sends
I will repay her three.'

The monk was bound for London,
To a great assembly there:
He hoped to trample underfoot
The knight that rode so fair.

'Where lies your way?' asked Robin.
'Sir, there are manors near
Where the reeves have done great wrong,
And that we must repair.'

'Come you forth now, Little John,
And hearken unto me:
To search through a monk's coffers
There's no better man than he.

'What carries he on yonder horse?
The truth we now must find.'
'By Our good Lady,' said the monk,
'That would be less than kind –

'To bid a man to dinner
And him to beat and bind.'
Said Robin, 'It is our custom
Little to leave behind.'

The monk he spurred his horse away,
Longer he would not bide.
Said Robin, 'Have one drink at least
Before you further ride.'

'Nay,' said the monk, 'I'm sorry
That ever I came so near.
More cheaply I'd have dined at Blyth
Or Doncaster than here.'

'Greet well your abbot and your prior,'
Said Robin, 'and, I pray,
Bid him send me such a monk
To dine here every day.'

Now let us leave the monk alone
And speak we of our knight,
Who truly came to keep his day
While it was still daylight.

Straightway he went to Barnsdale
Under the greenwood tree,
And there he found good Robin,
With all his company.

The knight from his fine palfrey
Dismounted then with ease.
He courteously put back his hood
And knelt down on his knees.

'God save you now, bold Robin,
And all your merry men.'
'Right welcome to you, gentle knight,'
Said noble Robin then.

Thus Robin Hood addressed himself
Unto the knight so free:
'What drives you to the greenwood,
I pray you, sir, tell me.

'Though you have tarried overlong,
You're welcome, gentle knight.'
'The abbot and high justice, sir,
Brought lawyers to the fight.'

'But have you your land again, good sir?'
Asked Robin, 'Tell me true.'
'Yes, and for that', replied the knight,
'I thank both God and you.

'I was delayed along the way.
It happened in this wise:
At a wrestling match they tried to rob
The winner of his prize.

'I helped him – take it not amiss.'
'No, sir, by God,' said he,
'A knight that helps a yeoman
My friend shall always be.'

'Here then is four hundred pounds,
The coin you lent to me,
And twenty marks as well, to thank
You for your courtesy.'

Said Robin, 'You shall keep it all.
It is your own. Indeed,
Our Lady sent her cellarer
Who gave us all we need.

'If I should take it twice, sir knight,
Then shame it were to me;
And truly I may say that you
Most welcome are to me.'

When Robin told him all the tale,
He laughed and made good cheer.
'Yet, by my oath,' the knight then said,
'Your money is all here.'

'Then use it well,' said Robin,
'You gentle knight so free;
I hope you find your welcome good
Under my meeting tree.

'But what are those bows,' asked Robin,
'Those feathered arrows too?'
'A poor present,' the good knight said,
'That I would give to you.'

'Come forth, now, Little John,' said he,
'And to my coffers go –
Bring me back four hundred pounds,
The monk would wish it so.

'And now here is four hundred pounds,
You noble knight and true,
To buy a horse and harness fine
And gild your spurs anew.

'And should you lack for money,
Remember Robin Hood,
For by my truth you'll never need
While I can do you good.

'Use well the money, gentle knight,
And heed you my advice:
Dress not so meanly, gentle knight,
Now that you have the price.'

This then is how good Robin
Succoured the gentle knight;
And God who sits in heaven
Grant that we too do right.

V

The knight his leave has taken,
Bravely he rode away.
But Robin and his merry men
Dwelled there for many a day.

So soft, and listen, gentlemen,
And hear what I proclaim:
The proud sheriff of Nottingham
Announced a fine good game.

He bade the archers of the north
Assemble on one day,
And he who shot the best of all
Should bear the prize away.

A pair of goodly butts were set
Up by the greenwood there,
And he that shot the best of all –
The furthest, low and fair –

A right good arrow should he win,
With shaft of silver white,
And rich red-golden feathers –
It was a noble sight.

Robin he heard about the game
Under his meeting tree.
'Make you ready, bold young men,
That contest we shall see.

'Hurry now, my merry men,
And I will go with you.
Together we'll test that sheriff's oath
To see if he is true.'

They took their feathered arrows,
And each man notched his bow:
For seven score of bold young men
With Robin Hood would go;

And when they came to Nottingham
The butts were fair and long,
And there were many archers
That shot with bows full strong.

'Only six shall shoot with me,
You others, guard my head.
Stand with your bows full ready,
Lest I be betrayed,' he said.

The fourth outlaw bent his bow
And that was Robin Hood:
The proud sheriff noted it
As by the butts he stood.

Three times good Robin drew his bow,
Three times he split the wand,
As did the good knight Gilbert,
The one they call White Hand.

Little John and Scathlock
Were archers good and free,
And Much and Reynold not the worst
Among that company;

But when they all had shot in turn,
Those archers fair and good,
There was one better than the rest
And he was Robin Hood.

The prize of the fine arrow
On him they did bestow,
Right courteously he took the gift,
But when he turned to go

They cried out loud upon him,
The horns began to blow:
'Woe on you! Treason!' Robin cried,
'Your evil now you show!

'Now woe to you, proud sheriff,
For treating thus your guest.
Is this the faith you promised me
In yonder wild forest?

'If you were in the greenwood
Under my meeting tree,
I'd have shown you better faith
Than you have shown to me.'

Then many an arrow there was loosed,
And many a bow was bent,
And many a man was wounded there,
And many a mantle rent.

But the outlaws won the day,
The sheriff was outfaced:
He and his men, full cowardly,
They fled away in haste.

When Robin saw the ambush fail,
At home he longed to be,
For many an arrow had been shot
Among that company.

Poor Little John was sorely hurt
With an arrow in the knee,
And he could neither walk nor ride –
'Twas pitiful to see.

'Master,' then said Little John,
'If ever you loved me,
Then for the love of that same Lord
Who died upon the tree,

'Reward me for my service,
And any sin forgive:
Don't let the sheriff find me
And take me while I live.

'Better to take your noble sword
And smite clean off my head:
Give me wounds both deep and wide –
But make sure I am dead.'

'Nay, Little John,' said Robin,
'I will not see you slain.
Though all the gold in England
Were paid me for my pain.'

'Nay, God forbid,' said little Much,
'That died upon a tree.
If I can stop it, you shall never
Leave our company.'

He took him up upon his back
And carried him away,
Though many a time he stopped and shot
To keep his foes at bay.

There was a noble castle
That lay within that wood:
With double ditches all around
Within fair walls it stood;

And in it dwelled the gentle knight,
Sir Richard of the Lee,
To whom Robin had lent his wealth
Under the greenwood tree.

He ushered in good Robin
And all his company:
'Welcome you are, bold Robin Hood,
Welcome you are to me.

'I thank you for your kindness
And all your courtesy;
For the comfort that you gave me
Under the greenwood tree.

'I love no man as much as you:
That love I now shall pay.
Despite the sheriff of Nottingham
Right here you all shall stay.

'Shut the gates and raise the bridge
And let no man come in.
Now arm you well, and man the walls,
And let the siege begin.

'Swear by St Quentin, Robin,
To this you will resign –
To live with me for forty days
And eat and sup and dine.'

Quickly were the tables laid,
The cloths were quickly spread,
And Robin and his merry men
To dinner soon were sped.

VI

Be still and listen, gentlemen,
And hearken to my song:
The proud sheriff of Nottingham
Took men in armour strong,

And canvassed the high sheriff
To raise the country round,
To lay siege to the castle
That stood so walled around.

Then the proud sheriff loudly cried
And said, 'You traitor knight,
You harbour the king's enemies
Against both law and right.'

'Sir, I admit that I have done
The deed that you indite:
I swear it on my lances,
As I am a true knight.

'Go now, sirs, be on your way
And leave me safe until
You have consulted with the king
And know full well his will.'

The sheriff had his answer,
And it was straight and true.
He went to London and the king
Without more ado:

There he told him of the knight
And about Robin Hood
And all his many archers,
So noble and so good.

'And he admits what he has done
To add strength to his hand:
He would be lord and master
Of all the northern land.'

'To Nottingham within two weeks
I'll go,' then vowed the king,
'And justice to bold Robin
And that knight I'll surely bring.

'Go home now, sheriff: look you do
As I command,' said he,
'And order archers good enough
From all the wide country.'

The sheriff took his leave at once,
And rode upon his way,
While Robin to the greenwood went
Upon a certain day.

Now Little John had healed well
Of the arrow in his knee,
And went straightway to Robin Hood
Under the greenwood tree.

So Robin strode the forest
Under the leaves so green;
But, woe unto the sheriff,
Nowhere could he be seen.

The sheriff failed to find him,
And, thwarted of his prey,
He lay in wait for the gentle knight
Instead, by night and day.

He waited for that gentle knight,
Sir Richard of the Lee,
As all along the river banks
He flew his hawks so free;

And there he took him prisoner:
Binding him foot and hand,
He led that knight to Nottingham
Guarded by his own band.

The sheriff swore a goodly oath
By Him that died on the rood,
Rather than have a hundred pounds
He'd capture Robin Hood.

The knight's wife overheard these words
And she was fair and free.
She rode straightway to Robin
Upon her fine palfrey.

When she came to the forest,
Under the greenwood tree,
There she found brave Robin Hood
And all his company.

'God save you now, good Robin,
And all your band, I say,
And for Our dearest Lady's sake
Grant me a boon, I pray.

'My wedded lord a prisoner
To Nottingham is taken,
And, lest he shamefully be slain,
Don't let him be forsaken.'

Then Robin answered her at once,
That lady fair and free:
'Who is the man has taken him?'
'The sheriff proud,' said she.

'That sheriff proud, he has him fast,
This is the truth, I say.
He cannot yet have travelled more
Than three miles on his way.'

Then up sprang noble Robin,
As though he were possessed:
'Hasten now, my merry men,
And put you to the test;

'And he that shall reject this trial,
By Him that died on tree,
Here in the greenwood shall that man
No longer dwell with me.'

Soon were many good bows bent,
And more than seven-score men
Took hedge and ditches in their stride
To prove their worth again.

'I vow to God,' said Robin,
'Or else it were my shame,
That sheriff I must overthrow
And finish off this game.'

Soon they arrived in Nottingham,
And, walking down the street,
With the proud sheriff of that town
They finally did meet.

'Abide, proud sheriff,' Robin said,
'For, without more ado,
Some tidings of our noble king
I fain would hear from you.

'In seven years, by God,' said he,
'I never moved so fast.
Proud sheriff, you will rue this day
Before this day is past.'

Then Robin bent a good full bow,
And arrow drew at will;
He hit him so that on the ground
The sheriff lay full still,

And then, before he could arise,
Before he could stand upright,
He struck the sheriff's head clean off
With his sword blade so bright.

'Now lie you there, proud sheriff,
Your evil in the dust;
For while you lived no other man
In your false word could trust.'

Then his band drew out their swords
So sharp and keen and bright;
They fought the sheriff's men and drove
Them off with all their might.

Then Robin went and put a bow
Into the good knight's hand;
He cut the prisoner's hood in two
And bade him by him stand.

'Leave now your horse behind you,
And teach yourself to run;
Come with me to the greenwood
Through mire and moss and fen;

'Come with me to the greenwood,
And there within that place
Remain until our comely king
Shall grant us both his grace.'

VII

The king came up to Nottingham,
With many knights and good,
To capture both the gentle knight
And Robin if he could.

He asked after bold Robin
Throughout the country wide,
And also after that stout knight
That stood at Robin's side.

The king he listened to their tale,
And hearing what they said
He ordered that the good knight's lands
To him were forfeited.

And right across to Lancashire
He journeyed far and near,
Until in Plumpton Park he found
That he'd lost many deer.

King Edward there was wont to find
Full many a herd of deer,
And yet scarce a single beast
With good horns did appear.

The king was very angry;
He swore by the Trinity:
'I wish I had bold Robin Hood
Before my eyes,' said he.

'He who will rid me of the knight
And bring me now his head,
Then all the lands sir Richard owns
I'd grant to him,' he said.

'I'd give it with my charter,
And seal it with my hand,
To have and hold for evermore
In this, our merry land.'

Then up spoke a fair good knight,
Faithful and true: 'I pray,
My liege lord, listen to me now
And heed what I shall say.

'No man in this fair country
Shall have that good knight's land
While Robin Hood can ride and walk
And bear a bow in hand –

'For he would lose his head for sure,
The best ball in his hood,
Give that land to no man, sire,
To whom you wish some good.'

In Nottingham our comely king
Then lingered half a year;
But where brave Robin Hood might be
He not a word could hear.

Meanwhile good Robin went his ways
By hiding place and hill,
And where he found the good king's deer
He slew them with a will.

Then up spoke a proud forester
Who with our king did stay;
'If you would see good Robin
You must do as I say.

'Choose from those within your court
Five knights of the best;
Then go you to the abbey
And there as monks be dressed.

'As guide and spy, to Nottingham
I then will lead you down;
And, I will bet my life on it,
Before we come to town

'There shall you meet bold Robin
If he's alive and free.
Before we get to Nottingham
With your own eyes you'll see.'

The king in haste made ready,
And the five knights also.
They dressed themselves in monks' habits
And made good haste to go.

Our king looked solemn in his cowl,
With broad hat on his crown.
He truly looked the abbot's part
As they rode into town.

He wore stiff boots, so I've heard tell,
And truly now do say:
And singing to the woods he rode;
His men were clothed in grey.

His packhorse and his sumpters
Followed him close behind,
Until a mile within the trees
The greenwood they did find.

And there they met bold Robin
Standing to bar their way,
With many a goodly archer –
Truly as I do say.

Swiftly he laid hold of the horse
That our bold king did ride,
Saying: 'Sir abbot, by your leave
A while you must abide.

'We are yeomen of the forest;
We range the greenwood here,
And so that we shall never starve
We feed off the king's deer.

'You have your churches and your rents
And gold in great plenty.
Now give us some of your riches,
For holy charity.'

To Robin then our comely king
Quickly replied – said he:
'I brought no more than forty pounds
To the greenwood with me.

'For I have lain at Nottingham
This fortnight with our king,
And much of my wealth I there have spent
On many a great lording.

'To me remain but forty pounds,
And that is all my due;
But if I had a hundred pounds
I'd give it all to you.'

Robin then took the forty pounds,
Divided it in two,
And half he gave to his merry men
To enjoy as was their due.

Full courteously then Robin said,
'Take this for your spending.
Sir, we shall meet another day.'
'I thank you,' said our king,

'For good king Edward greets you well,
And sends his seal by me:
He bids you come to Nottingham
To feast right merrily.'

The royal seal he then displayed
For Robin Hood to see;
And Robin knew how to behave –
He knelt down on his knee.

'I love no man in all the world
As well as my lord king.
Welcome are you, both seal and monk
That does the seal bring.

'Sir abbot, for your tidings
You now shall dine with me,
All for the love of my lord king,
Under my meeting tree.'

Then Robin took him by the hand
And led him to a seat,
And many a deer was swiftly slain
And cooked, that they might eat.

Robin took his full great horn
And loud began to blow,
Till seven score of brave young men
Stood ready in a row.

They bent their knees to Robin,
And when king Edward saw
How they did kneel before him,
By St Austin he swore:

'By God's pain, it is seemly
To see a sight so fine:
His men are more at his bidding
Than my men are at mine.'

Quickly was their dinner served
And to their meat they fell:
And Little John and Robin Hood
They served our king full well.

Before our king they set a plate
Of venison full fine,
With good brown ale and good white bread
And also good red wine.

'Now make good cheer,' said Robin,
'Abbot, for charity;
And for the news that you have brought
Blessed may you be.

'But you shall see the life we lead
Before you go away;
And you can then inform our king
When next you with him stay.'

Then up the outlaws leaped in haste
And bent their bows again:
Our comely king was sore aghast
He thought he would be slain.

Instead they set a pair of wands
And went towards them straight.
'By fifty paces', said our king,
'The distance is too great.'

On each side hung rose garlands,
While from behind the line
Shot each in turn: 'Should any miss,
His bow shall be his fine,'

Said Robin. 'He shall give it
To his master without fail.
Mark you, no man shall I spare,
As I drink wine and ale.

'A buffet on that man's bare head
Shall be his lot also.'
And all who missed the rose garland
Received a mighty blow.

But Robin shot twice in his turn
And twice he split the wand.
The only man who matched him there
Was Gilbert the White Hand.

Though Little John and good Scathlock
Did what they could and more,
When they both missed the garland
Robin struck them full sore.

But then on Robin's final shot
He evened up the score
Missing the garland mark himself
By three fingers or more.

Then bravely spoke good Gilbert –
To Robin he did say:
'Master, your bow is forfeit.
Now stand and take your pay.'

'Since I deserve no better,'
Said Robin, 'it must be so.
Sir abbot, take my arrows too,
And, pray you, strike the blow.'

'My order', said our noble king,
'Forbids me raise my arm.
For if I struck a yeoman
I might well do him harm.'

'Nay, boldly strike,' cried Robin,
'I freely give you leave.'
No sooner said than done; our king
Then folded up his sleeve

And such a blow he gave, he nearly
Felled him to the ground.
'By God, you are a stalwart friar,'
Cried Robin, 'I'll be bound

'There's such strength in your arm that you
Could draw a bow apace.'
And thus at last did Robin
And our king meet face to face.

Robin looked our comely king
Intently in the face:
So did sir Richard of the Lee –
They knelt down in that place.

And seeing Robin Hood kneel down
His outlaws did likewise.
'My lord the king of England –
Now I you recognise!'

'I cry you mercy,' said our king,
'Under your meeting tree,
Of all your goodness and your grace
Both to my men and me.

'Yes, before God,' the king went on,
'Pardoned you both shall be.
But you must leave the greenwood,
With all your company,

'And come home, Robin, to my court,
With me there to reside.'
'I vow to God,' said Robin Hood,
'And by that vow abide:

'I'll willingly come to your court
Your service for to see;
And I'll bring with me of my men
Full seven score and three.

'But, unless I like it well,
I swear I'll come back here
To shoot as I was wont to do
My monarch's quick brown deer.'

VIII

'Have you green cloth', asked our king,
'That you can sell to me?'
'Yes, before God,' said Robin Hood,
'Some thirty yards and three.'

'Then, Robin,' said our comely king,
'In your generosity,
Sell me some of that good cloth
To clothe my men and me.'

'Yes, before God, or else I'd be
A fool,' said Robin Hood.
'Come Christmas you'll be clothing me,
I think, and for my good.'

The king threw off his cowl right then
And dressed himself in green;
And every knight there did the same –
A great sight to be seen.

When all were clothed in Lincoln green
They threw away their grey.
'Now we shall go to Nottingham,
Just as our king did say.'

Outlaws and knights together
To Nottingham they went;
They drew their bows and shot full well
Until their shafts were spent.

Our king, he rode with Robin,
As I have heard men say:
The two men shot 'pluck-buffet'
As they went on their way.

From Robin Hood the king received
Some goodly blows that day,
For Robin would not spare him –
Each time he made him pay.

The king said, 'God me help, this game
Cannot be learned, I fear:
I would not win a shot from you
Though I shot all this year.'

All the folk from Nottingham
Could only stand and stare:
Nothing they saw but mantles green
Filling the fields there;

And to each other they did say
'Our king is dead, I fear:
If Robin comes to town he'll leave
No townsman living here.'

So, yeoman and knave, they quickly turned
And fled, for safety's sake:
Old wives with sticks who could scarce walk
Went hopping in their wake.

Our comely king laughed long and loud
And ordered their return:
And when they saw our comely king
Their hearts with joy did burn.

They ate and drank and made good cheer,
And sang both high and free:
Then up spoke our comely king
To Richard of the Lee.

He gave the knight his land again
And good he bade him be.
Then Robin thanked our comely king
And kneeled down on his knee.

Robin, for three months and a year,
Within the court did stay:
He spent above a hundred pounds
And all his yeomen's pay.

For every place that Robin went
His money he laid down,
For to do good to knights and squires
And win himself renown.

And when the year had run its course
To him remained two men:
Little John and good Scathlock
Did not desert him then.

And when he saw the young men shoot
Gaily upon a day:
'Alas,' then said good Robin Hood
'My wealth has slipped away;

'Yet once I was a bold archer,
The stoutest of my band,
The strongest archer, and the best
In all this merry land.

'Alas!' then said good Robin,
'My woe has no relief.
If I dwell longer with the king
I shall be slain with grief.'

Forth then went good Robin
And came unto the king:
'My lord the king of England,
Grant me my asking.

'For I have built in Barnsdale
A chapel fine to see.
It is for Mary Magdalene
And there I wish to be.

'During these past seven nights
I have not slept a wink,
Nor, during these past seven days,
Have I had food or drink.

'I long to be in Barnsdale,
I can no longer stay.
Barefoot, and dressed in coarse wool cloth,
I must go on my way.'

'If it is so,' then said our king,
'And may no better be,
Then seven nights I give you leave
To stay away from me.'

Kneeling down upon his knee,
'Thank you,' said Robin Hood,
And taking leave most courteously
He went to the greenwood.

And coming to the greenwood
One merry bright morning,
He heard again the clear high notes
Of the merry birds that sing.

'It is too long', said Robin,
'Since I have tarried here.
I long to stay a little while
To shoot the quick brown deer.'

Then Robin slew a full great hart,
And loud his horn he blew,
And all the outlaws in the wood
Full well that horn they knew.

They gathered all together
And to the tree did go,
Till seven score of brave young men
Stood ready in a row.

There they all put off their hoods,
And there they bent the knee:
'Welcome,' they said, 'our master,
Under this greenwood tree.'

Robin, for two and twenty years,
Dwelt in the greenwood then.
For dread of good king Edward
He'd not go back again.

Yet in the end he was beguiled,
And by a woman's sin –
The prioress of Kirkesley
That was his kith and kin.

She loved a knight of Doncaster,
Sir Roger was his name,
Who hated Robin above all men
And vowed to bring him shame.

Counsel they took together
To see how they might slay
Bold Robin, and to pick the men
To kill him if they may.

Then up spoke good Robin
Under the greenwood tree:
'I fear I must go to be bled
Tomorrow in Kirkesley.'

There sir Roger of Doncaster
Made love to his prioress,
And there was Robin Hood betrayed
Through his and her falseness.

Now Christ that died have mercy
On the soul of Robin Hood!
For he was a good outlaw
And did poor men much good.

33. MACBETH

Macbeth is a respectable historical figure, king of Scotland from 1040 to 1057. He was a sub-king and commander of the royal forces for king Duncan, but rebelled against his master, whom he killed in battle at Dunsinane, and usurped the throne. We know little of the events of his reign, except for his pilgrimage to Rome in 1050. He was in turn defeated by Siward, the Anglo-Saxon earl of Northumbria, in 1054; Siward, who had made an abortive invasion of Scotland in 1045–6, now established his nephew Malcolm, king Duncan's son, as ruler of Cumbria and southern Scotland. Three years later, Malcolm killed Macbeth at Lumphanan in Mar, and regained his kingdom. Macbeth seems to have drawn his support from the north and west, against the lords of southern Scotland with their growing ties with England. The version of his story in Holinshed's **Chronicle of Scotland** *was used by Shakespeare as the basis for his play; it is this, in modernised form, that is the basis for the account below.*

MALCOLM was succeeded by his grandson Duncan, the son of his daughter Beatrice. His other daughter, Doada, married Sinell, the thane of Glamis, by whom she had a son named Macbeth, a valiant man, who, if he had not been somewhat cruel by nature, might have been considered worthy to govern the kingdom. Duncan had so soft and gentle a nature that the people wished the inclinations and manners of these two cousins had been divided more equally between them, the one being too clement and the other too cruel.

The beginning of Duncan's reign was very quiet and peaceful, without any notable trouble; but once it was realised how negligent he was in punishing offenders, evil-doers seized the occasion to trouble the quiet state of the commonwealth. These seditious commotions started in this fashion. Banquo, the thane of Lochaber, gathered the finances due to the king and inflicted sharp penalties on any offenders: for this he was attacked by a number of rebels living in that district and robbed of the money he had collected, as well as other possessions, and was so badly wounded that he barely escaped with his life. When he had somewhat recovered and was able to ride, he went to the king's court where he laid a serious complaint before the king, who ordered that a sergeant-at-arms should be sent to arrest the offenders and bring them to answer the charges. But they added to the mischief they had caused by taunting the messenger and finally killing him. Fearing that the king would now invade them with all his men, Macdowald, one of the ringleaders, formed a confederacy of his friends and kinsmen, and appointed himself captain of the rebels. He proclaimed Duncan to be a faint-hearted milk-sop, more suited to the cloister than the throne.

He was persuasive and subtle enough to gather a mighty power of men: out of the Western Isles men flocked to over their assistance in his rebellion, while from Ireland many fighting men called gallowglasses were glad to offer him their service. With this powerful force under his command, Macdowald attacked those of the king's men who were sent into Lochaber to pursue him. He defeated them in a pitched battle, took their captain Malcolm prisoner, and at the end of the battle smote off his head. The king, hearing of this defeat, was extraordinarily frightened, since he lacked skill in warlike affairs. He summoned his council and asked their best advice as to how to subdue Macdowald and the other rebels.

After various opinions had been put forward, Macbeth addressed the king, reproaching him for his softness and slackness in punishing offenders, as a result of which they had been able to gather a large force. But he nonetheless promised that, if he and Banquo were given the command, he would vanquish the rebels and entirely suppress them. And this he did: when he appeared with a new army in Lochaber, the rumour of his arrival caused a large number of rebels to steal secretly away from Macdowald; Macbeth then forced the latter to meet him in pitched battle and defeated him. Macdowald fled for refuge to his castle where his wife and children were, but found that he could not hold it against Macbeth. He therefore killed his wife and children and then himself, because he knew that if he was captured he would be severely tortured. Macbeth, however, found Macdowald's body among the slain and cruelly cut off the head, which he sent to the king: the torso was hung on a high pair of gallows. Justice and law was thus restored through Macbeth's diligence.

No sooner had he conquered Macdowald when word came that Sweyn, king of Norway, had arrived in Fife with a powerful army in order to subdue the whole realm of Scotland. The army raised to resist Sweyn was divided into three battalions; the van and rear were assigned to Macbeth and Banquo respectively, while Duncan commanded the main body. The Scots won a notable victory, and after they had gathered and divided the spoils, they caused solemn processions to be made in all places of the realm and thanks to be given to almighty God that had sent them so fair a day over their enemies. But even as these processions were taking place, word was brought that a new fleet of Danes had arrived, sent by Canute, king of England, to exact revenge for the defeat of his brother Sweyn. Macbeth and Banquo were sent with the king's authority to confront them, and their army was sufficiently powerful to defeat the enemy, killing some and pursuing the rest to their ships. Those that escaped sent messengers to Macbeth offering a great sum of gold to bury their dead at Inchcolm in the Firth of Forth, to which he agreed.

Shortly after this, there happened a strange and uncouth wonder, which afterwards was the cause of much trouble in the realm of Scotland, as you shall after hear. It fortuned as Macbeth and Banquo journeyed towards Forres, where the king then lay, they went sporting by the way together without other company, save only themselves, passing through the woods and fields, when suddenly, in the midst of a clearing, they met three women in strange and wild apparel, resembling creatures of the other world. As they watched them, wondering much at the sight, the first woman spoke and said: 'All hail, Macbeth, thane of Glamis!' (for he had lately entered into that dignity and office by the death of his father Sinell).

The second of them said: 'Hail, Macbeth, thane of Cawdor!'

But the third said: 'All hail, Macbeth, that hereafter shalt be king of Scotland!'

Then Banquo said: 'What manner of women are you that seem so little favourable to me, promising me nothing at all, whereas to my fellow here, besides high offices, you assign also the kingdom?'

'Yes,' said the first of them, 'we promise greater benefits to you than to him for he shall reign indeed, but with an unlucky end: neither shall he leave any issue behind him to succeed in his place, whereas, on the contrary, though you shall not reign at all, of you shall be born those who shall govern the Scottish kingdom by long order of continual descent.' With this the women vanished immediately out of their sight.

At first this was reputed by Macbeth and Banquo, to be nothing but a vain, fantastical illusion, insomuch as Banquo would call Macbeth in jest king of Scotland; and Macbeth, again in sport, would call him the father of many kings. But afterwards the common opinion was that these women were either the weird sisters, that is to say the goddesses of destiny, or else some nymphs or fairies imbued with knowledge of prophecy by their necromantical science, because everything came to pass as they had spoken. For shortly afterwards the thane of Cawdor was condemned at Forres of treason committed against the king, and his lands, livings and offices, of the king's liberality, were given to Macbeth. The same night, at supper, Banquo jested with him and said: 'Now, Macbeth, you have obtained those things which the two former sisters prophesied; it remains only for you to purchase that which the third said should come to pass.' Whereupon Macbeth, revolving the thing in his mind began even then to devise how he might attain to the kingdom: though as yet he thought he would have to wait for the opportunity which would advance him to it, as it had come to pass in his former preferment.

But shortly after it chanced that king Duncan made his elder son Malcolm prince of Cumberland, as if to appoint him his successor in the kingdom immediately after his decease. Macbeth was sorely troubled by this, because he saw that it would diminish his hopes (for by the old laws of the realm, the ordinance was that if he that should succeed were not of age to take the charge upon himself, he that was next of blood to him should be advanced). He began to take counsel how he might usurp the kingdom by force, feeling that he had just cause, since Duncan did all he could to defraud him of those titles and claims by which he might, in time to come, aspire to the crown.

The words of the three weird sisters greatly encouraged him; but his wife especially urged him to attempt the thing, as she was very ambitious – burning with unquenchable desire to bear the name of a queen. At length therefore, after communicating his purposed intent to his trusty friends, amongst whom Banquo was the chiefest, and having confidence in their promised aid, Macbeth slew the king at Inverness in the sixth year of his reign. Then gathering around him the company he had made privy to his enterprise, he caused himself to be proclamed king, and forthwith went to Scone, where (by common consent) he received the investiture of the kingdom according to the accustomed manner.

The details of the murder of Duncan are not given in Holinshed, but Shake-speare borrowed his description of Donwald's murder of Duff at his castle at Forres to provide the dramatic scenes surrounding the king's killing. Holinshed describes Macbeth's subsequent reign as follows:

Macbeth, after the departure of Duncan's sons, used great liberality towards the nobles of the realm in order to win their favour; and when he saw that no man was disposed to trouble him, he directed his whole intention towards maintaining justice, and to punishing all the enormities and abuse which had been occasioned by the feeble and slothful admini-stration of Duncan . . . Thus Macbeth, showing himself a most diligent punisher of all injuries and wrongs attempted by any disordered person within his realm, was accounted the sure defence and buckler of innocent people . . . To be brief, such were the worthy doings and princely acts of this Macbeth in the administration of the realm, that if he had attained to the throne by rightful means, and continued as he began in uprightness of justice till the end of his reign, he might well have been numbered amongst the most noble princes that had reigned anywhere.

But this zeal for equity was counterfeit, demonstrated only to purchase the favour of the people, and going somewhat against his natural inclina-tion. Shortly after he began to show what he really was, practising cruelty instead of fairness. For the prick of conscience caused him ever to fear, lest he should be served with the same cup as he had administered to his predecessor. And he could not put the words of the three weird sisters out of his mind, for though they had promised him the kingdom, so likewise they had promised it Banquo's descendants. He willed therefore that the same Banquo, with his son Fleance, should come to a supper that he had prepared for them; where he had devised death for them, at the hands of certain murderers, hired to execute that deed. They were appointed to accost the same Banquo and his son outside the palace as they returned to their lodgings, and there to slay them. In that way Macbeth's house would not be slandered, and in time to come he could clear himself if anything were laid to his charge upon any suspicion that might arise.

The night was dark, and though the father was slain, the son, with the help of almighty God who reserved him to better fortune, escaped that danger; and afterwards, having some inkling from some friends at the court that his father was slain not by chance (as Macbeth would have had it to appear) but by a premeditated plot, and that his life was sought no less than his father's, fled into Wales to avoid further peril.

After he had contrived the slaughter of Banquo nothing prospered with Macbeth: every man began to fear for his own life and hardly any dared to appear in the king's presence. And even as there were many that stood in fear of him, so likewise stood he in fear of many, and on one pretext or another he began to do away with those whom he thought most able to work him any displeasure. At length he found such sweetness in putting his nobles to death that his earnest thirst after blood could in no wise be satisfied. For you must consider that he won double profit hereby: first, those whom he feared were rid out of the way, and then again, his coffers were enriched by their goods which were forfeited to his use, and that way he could better maintain a yard of armed men about him to defend his person from injury by any man of whom he was suspicious.

Further, in order that he might the more cruelly oppress his subjects with all tyrantlike wrongs, he built a strong castle on the top of a high hill called Dunsinane, situated in Gowrie, ten miles from Perth, on such a proud height that standing there aloft a man might behold well nigh all the countries of Angus, Fife, Stormont and Strathern. This castle, being founded on the top of that high hill, put the realm to great expense before it was finished, for all the stuff necessary to the building could not be brought up without much toil and business. But Macbeth, being once determined to have the work go forward, caused the thanes of each shire in the realm to come and help towards that building. At last it was the turn of Macduff, thane of Fife, to do his part; but he sent workmen with all needful provision and commanded them to show such diligence that no occasion might be given for the king to find fault with him for not coming himself as others had done. He refused to do so for fear that the king, bearing him no great goodwill, would lay violent hands upon him as he had done upon various others. Shortly after, Macbeth came to behold how the work went forward and found that Macduff was not there. At this he was sore offended and said: 'I perceive this man will never obey my commandments till he be ridden with a snaffle; but I shall provide well enough for him.'

He would surely have put Macduff to death for this, but that a certain witch in whom he had great trust had told him that he should never be slain by man born of any woman, nor vanquished till the wood of Birnam came to the castle of Dunsinane. Because of this prophecy Macbeth put all fear out of his heart, supposing he might do what he would without any fear of punishment, for by the one prophecy he believed it were impossible for any man to vanquish him, and by the other that it was impossible to slay him. This vain belief caused him to do many outrageous things, to the grievous oppression of his subjects. At length Macduff, in peril of his life, decided to go into England and get Malcolm Canmore to claim the crown of Scotland; but he did not do it so secretly that Macbeth had no knowledge of it – for kings have sharp sight like the lynx and long ears like Midas. In every nobleman's house Macbeth had one sly fellow or other in fee to him to reveal all that was said or done there.

As soon as he was advised where Macduff was going, he came with a great force into Fife and besieged the castle where Macduff dwelled, expecting to find him there. They that kept the house opened the gates without any resistance and suffered him to enter, mistrusting none evil. But Macbeth most cruelly caused the wife and children of Macduff to be slain, along with all the others he found in that castle. Also he confiscated the goods of Macduff, proclaimed him traitor and confined him out of all the parts of his realm; but Macduff had already escaped out of danger and had reached Malcolm Canmore in England hoping that with his support he could revenge the slaughter so cruelly executed on his wife, his children and other friends.

When he came before Malcolm, he declared into what great misery the estate of Scotland was brought by the detestable cruelties exercised by the tyrant Macbeth: he had committed many horrible slaughters and murders both of the nobles and of the common people, for which he was hated right mortally by all his liege people, who desired nothing more than to be delivered of that intolerable and most heavy yoke of thraldom which they sustained at such a caitiff's hands. Malcolm, hearing Macduff's words, lamentations, bewailing the miserable state of his country, for mere compassion and very ruth piercing his sorrowful heart, fetched a deep sigh; and Macduff, perceiving it, most earnestly advanced with him the enterprise of delivering the Scottish people out of the hands of the kind of cruel and bloody tyrant that Macbeth, by too many plain experiments, had shown himself to be. This was an easy matter for him to bring to pass, considering not only the good title Malcolm had, but also the earnest desire of the people to have the chance of being revenged of those notable injuries which they daily sustained as a result of the outrageous cruelty of Macbeth's misgovernance.

Malcolm, to test Macduff's loyalty and determination, pretended that his own vices – lust, avarice and deceit – were as bad as those of Macbeth; Macduff at first sought to pretend that he could pander to Malcolm's desires, but finally burst out in despair, bewailing Scotland's fate with a tyrant on the throne and a claimant who was equally evil. Malcolm admitted his pretence, and the two plotted to invade Scotland.

Soon after, Macduff, repairing to the borders of Scotland, addressed his letters with secret despatch to the nobles of the realm. He declared that Malcolm was his ally and would shortly come into Scotland to claim the crown, and therefore he required them, since Malcolm was the rightful heir, to assist him with their powers to recover the same out of the hands of the wrongful usurper. In the meantime Malcolm purchased such favour at king Edward's hands that old Siward, earl of Northumberland, was appointed with ten thousand men to go with him into Scotland to support him in this enterprise for recovery of his right.

After this news was spread abroad in Scotland, the nobles split into two separate factions, the one taking part with Macbeth and the other with Malcolm. Sundry bickerings and divers light skirmishes ensued; for those that were of Malcolm's side would not hazard to join with their enemies in a pitched battle till he came out of England to their support. After that, Macbeth perceived his enemy's power increase by the aid that came out of England with his adversary Malcolm, and recoiled back into Fife, there purposing to abide in camp fortified at the castle of Dunsinane, there to fight with his enemies if they meant to pursue him. But some of his friends advised that it should be best for him either to make some agreement with Malcolm or else to flee with all speed into the Isles and to take his treasure with him. There he might pay wages to sundry great princes of the realm to take his part, and receive strangers in whom he might better trust than in his own subjects, who were deserting him daily: but he had such confidence in his prophecies that he believed he should never be vanquished till Birnam wood were brought to Dunsinane, nor yet be slain by any man that should be, or was, born of any woman.

Malcolm, following hastily after Macbeth, came the night before the battle to Birnam wood; and, when his army had rested a while there to refresh themselves, he commanded every man to get a bough of some tree or other in his hand, as big as he might bear, and to march forth in such wise, that on the next morning they might come close to their enemies without being sighted. On the morrow, when Macbeth beheld them approaching like that, he first marvelled what the matter meant, but in the end realised that the prophecy which he had heard long before that time, of the coming of Birnam wood to Dunsinane castle, was likely now to be fulfilled. Nevertheless, he brought his men in order of battle and exhorted them to do valiantly. His enemies had scarcely cast their boughs away, however, when Macbeth, perceiving their numbers, betook him straight to flight, Macduff pursuing him with great hatred even until he came to a nearby town. Here Macbeth, perceiving that Macduff was hard at his back, leapt off his horse, saying: 'You traitor, what do you mean by following me in vain? I am not destined to be killed by any creature born of woman! Come on, and receive the reward you deserve!' and therewithal he lifted up his sword, thinking to have slain him. But Macduff, quickly dismounting from his horse before he came at him, answered (with his naked sword in his hand): 'It is true, Macbeth; now your insatiable cruelty comes to an end, for I am the man your wizards told you of: I was never born of my mother, but torn from her womb before my time.' With this he goes up to him and kills him on the spot. Then cutting his head from his shoulders, he set it upon a pole and brought it to Malcolm. This was the end of Macbeth, after he had reigned seventeen years over the Scottishmen.

34. LADY GODIVA

Godiva, or (to give her her Saxon name) Godgifu, was in real life the wife of earl Leofric of Chester, and founded a number of religious houses. Other sources ascribe to her a devotion to the Virgin Mary, and she was certainly the moving force behind the foundation of the monastery at Coventry, one of the richest in the land, 'resplendent with gold and gems to a degree un-equalled in England at that date'. The legend of her ride through Coventry is first recorded in the early thirteenth century, two hundred years after it is supposed to have taken place, and it is this which is given here, from Roger of Wendover's Flowers of History. *The other character involved in the story, 'Peeping Tom', whose nickname has passed into common use, does not appear – surprisingly – until the mid-eighteenth century. He was the only man in the room to have looked at Godiva as she rode; he is said to have been a tailor, and to have been punished for his curiosity by blindness.*

EARL Leofric was lord of Coventry; his wife was Godiva, renowned for her beauty. The townsmen of Coventry were heavily taxed and bound to their lord as serfs, and Godiva often begged her husband, in the name of the Holy Trinity and the Blessed Virgin, that this burden might be eased. But the earl called her request foolish, as it would be very harmful to him, and constantly forbade her to raise the subject again. But she, with womanly persistence, continued to request it, until her husband was driven to anger, and finally answered as follows: 'Mount your horse naked,' he said, 'and ride through the market of the town from one end to the other while everyone is there, and you shall have what you ask when you return.'

The countess replied, 'And if I wish to do this, do I have your permission?'

'I will give it,' answered the earl.

Then the countess Godiva on a certain day mounted her horse naked, and loosed her hair which covered her body except for her beautiful white legs; she completed the journey unseen by anyone, and returned to her husband, who took this as a miracle. And indeed the aforesaid earl Leofric lifted the burden of taxation from the townsmen, as his charter, furnished with his seal, confirmed.

EPILOGUE:

Song, from King Edward the Third *by William Blake*

O Sons of Trojan Brutus, cloath'd in war,
Whose voices are the thunder of the field,
Rolling dark clouds o'er France, muffling the sun
In sickly darkness like a dim eclipse,
Threatening as the red brow of storms, as fire
Burning up nations in your wrath and fury!

Your ancestors came from the fires of Troy,
(Like lions rouz'd by light'ning from their dens,
Whose eyes do glare against the stormy fires)
Heated with war, fill'd with the blood of Greeks,
With helmets hewn, and shields covered with gore,
In navies black, broken with wind and tide!

They landed in firm array upon the rocks
Of Albion; they kiss'd the rocky shore;
'Be you our mother, and our nurse,' they said;
'Our children's mother, and thou shalt be our grave;
The sepulchre of ancient Troy, from whence
Shall rise cities, and thrones, and arms, and awful pow'rs.'

Our fathers swarm from the ships. Giant voices
Are heard from the hills, the enormous sons
Of Ocean run from rocks and caves: wild men,
Naked and roaring like lions, hurling rocks,
And wielding knotty clubs, like oaks entangled
Thick as a forest, ready for the axe.

Our fathers move in firm array to battle;
The savage monsters rush like roaring fire;
Like as a forest roars, with crackling flames,
When the red lightning, borne by furious storms,
Lights on some woody shore; the parched heavens
Rain fire into the molten raging sea.

The smoaking trees are strewn upon the shore,
Spoil'd of their verdure! O how oft have they
Defy'd the storm that howled o'er their heads!
Our fathers, sweating, lean on their spears, and view
The mighty dead; giant bodies streaming blood,
Dread visages frowning in silent death!

Then Brutus spoke, inspir'd; our fathers sit
Attentive on the melancholy shore:
Hear ye the voice of Brutus – 'The flowing waves
Of time come rolling o'er my breast', he said;
'And my heart labours with futurity:
Our sons shall rule the empire of the sea.

'Their mighty wings shall stretch from east to west,
Their nest is in the sea; but they shall roam
Like eagles for the prey; nor shall the young
Crave or be heard; for plenty shall bring forth,
Cities shall sing, and vales in rich array
Shall laugh, whose fruitful laps bend down with fulness.

'Our sons shall rise from thrones in joy,
Each one buckling on his armour; Morning
Shall be prevented by their swords gleaming,
And Evening hear their song of victory!
Their towers shall be built upon the rocks,
Their daughters shall sing, surrounded with shining spears!

'Liberty shall stand upon the cliffs of Albion,
Casting her blue eyes over the green ocean;
Or, tow'ring, stand upon the roaring waves,
Stretching her mighty spear o'er distant lands;
While, with her eagle wings, she covereth
Fair Albion's shore, and all her families.'

INDEX OF PERSONS

This index is selective and does not include names which merely appear in lists. However, it does include named animals and weapons. References are to chapter numbers, not pages.

INDEX OF PLACES

This index is selective and does not include names which merely appear in lists.
Italics indicate a fictional or unidentified place. References are to chapter numbers
not pages.